Handbook of Bioethics and Religion

Handbook of
Bioethics
and Religion

EDITED BY DAVID E. GUINN

OXFORD
UNIVERSITY PRESS

2006

OXFORD
UNIVERSITY PRESS

Oxford University Press, Inc., publishes works that further
Oxford University's objective of excellence
in research, scholarship, and education.

Oxford   New York
Auckland   Cape Town   Dar es Salaam   Hong Kong   Karachi
Kuala Lumpur   Madrid   Melbourne   Mexico City   Nairobi
New Delhi   Shanghai   Taipei   Toronto

With offices in
Argentina   Austria   Brazil   Chile   Czech Republic   France   Greece
Guatemala   Hungary   Italy   Japan   Poland   Portugal   Singapore
South Korea   Switzerland   Thailand   Turkey   Ukraine   Vietnam

Published by Oxford University Press, Inc.
198 Madison Avenue, New York, New York 10016

www.oup.com

Oxford is a registered trademark of Oxford University Press

Library of Congress Cataloging-in-Publication Data
Handbook of bioethics and religion / edited by David E. Guinn.
    p. cm.
Includes bibliographical references and index.
ISBN-13 978-0-19-517873-9
ISBN 0-19-517873-4
1. Medical ethics—Religious aspects.   2. Bioethics—Religious aspects.
3. Religion and ethics.   I. Guinn, David E.
[DNLM: 1. Bioethics.   2. Religion and Medicine. WB 60 H2356 2006]
R725.55.H36 2006
174'.957—dc22   2005021704

9 8 7 6 5 4 3 2 1

Printed in the United States of America
on acid-free paper

To my parents, Earl and Wanda, whose faith is an inspiration and a mystery to me and who have supported me even when they had no idea why I did what I did

Contents

Contributors

Lisa Sowle Cahill, Ph.D., J. Donald Monan Professor in the Department of Theology at Boston College. Professor Cahill has taught at Boston College since 1976 and been a visiting professor at Georgetown and Yale Universities. She is past president of the Catholic Theological Society of America and the Society of Christian Ethics and is currently a fellow of the American Academy of Arts and Sciences. Among her many publications are *Sex, Gender, and Christian Ethics* and *Genetics, Theology, Ethics: An Interdisciplinary Conversation*.

Nigel M. de S. Cameron, J.D., Institute on Biotechnology and the Human Future, Illinois Institute of Technology, Research Professor of Bioethics, Chicago-Kent College of Law. Professor Cameron is the former provost and distinguished professor at Trinity International University in Deerfield, Illinois. He has published widely in his academic fields of theology and bioethics. He was founding editor of the international journal *Ethics and Medicine*, and he has authored and edited books on bioethics, including *Death without Dignity: Euthanasia in Perspective* and *The New Medicine: Life and Death after Hippocrates*. His research focuses on the relationship between ethics and public policy.

Tod Chambers, Ph.D., Associate Professor of Bioethics and Medical Humanities and of Medicine at Northwestern University's Feinberg School of Medicine. Professor Chamber's areas of research include the rhetoric of bioethics and cross-cultural issues in clinical medicine. He is the author of the book *The Fiction of Bioethics* and coeditor of *Prozac as a Way of Life*. He is presently working on a second monograph on the rhetoric of bioethics.

Clarke E. Cochran, Ph.D., Professor of Political Science and Adjunct Professor, Health Organization Management, Texas Tech University. Professor Cochran specializes in religion and politics and in health care policy. He held the position of Research Fellow in the Erasmus Institute at the University of Notre Dame and the Shannon Chair in Catholic Studies at Nazareth College. He is author of numerous articles and several books, including (coauthored with David Carroll Cochran) *Catholics, Politics, and Public Policy: Beyond Left and Right*. Professor Cochran serves on the Board of Directors of Covenant Health System, Lubbock, Texas, and is a Member of Hope Ministries, Philadelphia, a cosponsor of Catholic Health East.

Cynthia B. Cohen, Ph.D., J.D., Senior Research Fellow, Kennedy Institute of Ethics, Georgetown University. In addition to her duties as a Senior Research Fellow at the Kennedy Institute of Ethics at Georgetown University in Washington, D.C., Dr. Cohen is a member of the Canadian Stem Cell Oversight Committee and a Fellow of the Hastings Center in Garrison, New York. Her publications include eight books that she has authored or edited and numerous articles. She is currently writing a book, *Renewing the Stuff of Life: Ethics and Stem Cell Research*, to be published by Oxford University Press.

Elliot N. Dorff, Ph.D., Director and Distinguished Professor of Philosophy, University of Judaism in Los Angeles and Vice Chair of the Conservative Movement's Committee on Jewish Law and Standards. Rabbi Dorff's papers have formulated the validated stance of the Conservative Movement on infertility treatments and on end-of-life issues, and his rabbinic letters on human sexuality and on poverty have become the voice of the Conservative Movement on those topics. He has served on President Clinton's Health Care Task Force; the surgeon general's commission to draft a Call to Action for Responsible Sexual Behavior; the National Human Resources Protections Advisory Commission; and the American Association for the Advancement of Science's Dialogue on Science, Ethics, and Religion Advisory Committee.

H. Tristram Engelhardt Jr., Ph.D., M.D., Professor of Philosophy, Rice University. Dr. Engelhardt is professor emeritus, Department of Medicine, Baylor College of Medicine, Houston, Texas. His most recent book-length publication is *The Foundations of Christian Bioethics*. Engelhardt serves as editor of the *Journal of Medicine and Philosophy* and the *Philosophy and Medicine* book series. In addition, he is senior editor of the book series *Philosophical Studies in Contemporary Culture* and the journal *Christian Bioethics*.

John H. Evans, Ph.D., Associate Professor, Department of Sociology, University of California, San Diego. Professor Evans is the author of *Playing God? Human Genetic Engineering and the Rationalization of Public Bioethical Debate* and coeditor (with Robert Wuthnow) of *The Quiet Hand of God: Faith-Based Activism and the Public Role of Mainline Protestantism*. He has also published a number of articles on opinion polarization in the United States over abortion, homosexuality, and related issues. His research focuses on the sociology of religion, culture, knowledge, science, and, in particular, bioethics.

Allen Glicksman, Ph.D., Director of Research and Evaluation, Philadelphia Corporation for Aging. Dr. Glicksman's gerontological interests can be divided into three categories. The first focuses on issues of health, gender, ethnicity, and class. The second is the evaluation of programs and services designed to enhance the lives of older Philadelphians. Finally, Dr. Glicksman has an ongoing research agenda focused on the lives of older refugees, ranging from work on access and barriers to social and health services to examining the experience of refugees who are also trauma survivors in long-term care settings.

Gail Gaisin Glicksman, Ph.D., Dean of Students and Assistant Professor of the Social Sciences, Reconstructionist Rabbinical College. Rabbi Glicksman has taught at the University of Pennsylvania, Temple University, and Gratz College, was rabbi of Adath Shalom Congregation in Philadelphia, and served as a chaplain at several nursing homes. She was director of the Judaism and Health Care Ethics Initiative at the Park Ridge Center for the Study of Health, Faith, and Ethics in Chicago. She was involved in the Shleimut Institute and is a partner of the Kalsman Institute on Judaism and Health of the Hebrew Union College–Jewish Institute of Religion in Los Angeles.

Michele Goodwin, J.D., LL.M., J.S.D., Associate Professor of Law and Wicklander Fellow, Director of the Health Law Institute, and Director of the Center for the Study of Race and Bioethics, DePaul University College of Law. Professor Goodwin is a leading bioethics and biotechnology scholar. Her publications address property and tort issues regarding the human body. She offers a unique perspective on race to discussions about law and medicine. She has written numerous law review articles and is completing a forthcoming book with Cambridge University Press on the trade in human body parts. She is the former secretary general of the International Academy of Law and Mental Health.

David E. Guinn, J.D., Ph.D., Senior Research Fellow, International Human Rights Law Institute, DePaul University College of Law. Dr. Guinn is a moral, political, and legal philosopher and lawyer with a diverse range of scholarship. He has written extensively on issues of national and international religious freedom, pluralism, and law, including the books *Faith on Trial: Communities of Faith, the First Amendment, and the Theory of Deep Diversity* and *Religion and Law in the Global Village*. He was previously a research associate at the Park Ridge Center for the Study of Health, Faith, and Ethics.

Albert R. Jonsen, Ph.D., Emeritus Professor of Ethics in Medicine, School of Medicine, University of Washington. Professor Jonsen is a member of the Institute of Medicine, National Academy of Sciences and served on the National Commission for Protection of Human Subjects of Biomedical and Behavioral Research and the President's Commission for the Study of Ethical

Problems in Medicine. He is now co-director of the Program in Medicine and Human Values, California Pacific Medical Center, San Francisco.

M. Cathleen Kaveny, J.D., Ph.D., John P. Murphy Foundation Professor of Law and Professor of Theology, University of Notre Dame Law School. Professor Kaveny has published more than forty articles and essays in journals and books specializing in law, ethics, and medical ethics. She has served on a number of editorial boards, including those of the *American Journal of Jurisprudence*, the *Journal of Religious Ethics*, the *Journal of Law and Religion*, and the *Journal of the Society of Christian Ethics*. She has been a Senior Fellow at the Martin Marty Center at the University of Chicago (2002–2003) and the Royden B. Davis Visiting Professor of Interdisciplinary Studies at Georgetown University (1998).

Edward W. Keyserlingk, LL.M, Ph.D., Emeritus Professor, Medical Ethics Unit, Faculty of Medicine, McGill University. Professor Keyserlingk is currently the Government of Canada Public Service Integrity Officer. His research interests are in the areas of critical care (informed consent, end-of-life decision making, euthanasia, sanctity of life/quality of life, advance directives); medical judgment (standards of care, negligence, physicians as moral agents); research ethics (dementia research, research codes); cross-cultural law and ethics (international research ethics codes, HIV/AIDS research in Africa); environmental ethics and law; and the interaction of law and ethics in biomedicine.

Karen Lebacqz, Ph.D., Robert Gordon Sproul Professor of Theological Ethics, Emerita, Pacific School of Religion/Graduate Theological Union. The Rev. Lebacqz is the author of more than eight books and numerous articles. She is best known for her work in theories of justice, professional ethics, and bioethics. She has taught at McGill University and at Yale University, and she is ordained in the United Church of Christ.

M. Therese Lysaught, Ph.D., Associate Professor of Religious Studies, University of Dayton. Prior to coming to the University of Dayton, Professor Lysaught conducted research on the relationship between theology and bioethics at an institute in Chicago and spent a year as an NIH/ELSI fellow at the University of Iowa, working in a genetics lab. She has been a member of the Recombinant DNA Advisory Committee of the National Institutes of Health, and currently works in a number of capacities with the Catholic Health Association.

Wendy Morton obtained a B.A. (Hons) in 1982 from Bishop's University, LL.B. from Queen's University in 1986, and LL.M. (bioethics) from McGill University in 1989. She has practiced law in Ontario and Alberta, was affiliated with the Center for Law, Medicine, and Ethics at McGill, and is currently employed with Merck Frosst Canada.

Ronald Y. Nakasone, Ph.D., Professor in Residence, Graduate Theological Union; Stanford Medical School Buddhist cleric. Ronald Y. Nakasone is Professor in Residence at the Center for Art, Religion, and Education, an affiliate of the Graduate Theological Union, core faculty at the Stanford University

Geriatric Education Center, and fellow at the Open Research Center at Ryukoku University in Kyoto, Japan. His current reflections on interfaith and intercultural issues, bioethics, and other topics explore an individual's porously laminated multilayered experiences within a complex nexus of relationships and events.

Maura A. Ryan, Ph.D., Associate Professor of Christian Ethics at the University of Notre Dame. She served as Associate Provost at Notre Dame from 2001 to 2004. Professor Ryan's primary interests are in the areas of bioethics and health policy, feminist ethics, and fundamental moral theology. She coedited a book on global stewardship with Todd David Whitmore in 1997 and is the author of *Ethics and Economics of Assisted Reproduction: The Cost of Longing*. She has served on the Board of Directors for the Society of Christian Ethics and the editorial boards of the *Religious Studies Review* and *Ethics and Behavior*. She has served on the St. Joseph County Healthcare Advisory Consortium and the ethics committee for Hospice of St. Joseph County.

Abdulaziz Sachedina, Ph.D., Francis Ball Professor of Religious Studies, University of Virginia. Dr. Sachedina, who has studied in India, Iraq, Iran, and Canada, has conducted research and has written in the field of Islamic law, ethics, and theology for more than two decades. In the last ten years he has concentrated on social and political ethics, including interfaith and intrafaith relations and Islamic biomedical ethics. Dr. Sachedina's publications include *Islamic Messianism, Human Rights and the Conflicts of Culture* (coauthored), *The Just Ruler in Shi'ite Islam* (Oxford University Press, 1988), *The Prolegomena to the Qur'an* (Oxford University Press, 1998), and *The Islamic Roots of Democratic Pluralism* (Oxford University Press, 2002), and numerous articles in academic journals. He is presently completing a book on Islamic biomedical ethics. He is an American citizen born in Tanzania.

Handbook of Bioethics and Religion

Introduction: Laying Some of the Groundwork

The religious must not retreat before the evangelizing armies of the secular. We should neither settle for reducing our faith to the "God of the gaps" . . . nor accept the bizarre proposition that religion is wholly private, thus not entitled to a place at the democratic dinner table where we squabble over serious matters.

—Stephen Carter

The happy, Jeffersonian, compromise that the Enlightenment reached with religions . . . consists in privatizing religion—keeping it out of what [is called] "the public square," making it seem bad taste to bring religion into discussions of public policy.

—Richard Rorty

In a liberal, religiously pluralistic country like the United States, what role should religion play in the formation and development of public policies and practices regarding health care? As illustrated by the quotes above—one from a supporter of, what might be referred to as "public religion" (a faith active in the public sphere), one from a critic—the very idea provokes strong reactions. Indeed, the broad question of the appropriate role for religion in law and public policy has generated significant litigation[1] and an enormous body of literature.[2] It has also emerged as a topic of debate in regard to the specific issue of religion and public policies relating to bioethics.[3]

Unfortunately, the discussion to date, at least with respect to public bioethics, has often generated more heat than light. Indeed, the topic is so vituperative that of the nearly one dozen scholars critical of religious engagement in the formation of public bioethical policy approached to contribute to this volume, none were willing to do so in light of the volume's premise that religion is, has been, and always will be an active concern within public bioethics.

The absence of these critics might be considered a weakness of the present volume. It is true that their voices will be missed. Nonetheless, while I will attempt to highlight the broad contours of their objections to religion participating in public bioethics, in many ways one does not need the opinions of these, public religion's most adamant critics. As suggested by Stephen Carter, hostility toward religion in the public square, where public policy is formed, is so pervasive that it has become the norm against which people of faith must present arguments.[4] That is to say, the presumption that religion is something that is merely a private and personal concern with no place in public debate has become so pervasive that people of faith feel compelled to explain why they believe religions should have a place on the public stage or, worse, to defer to this idea without reflection or demure.

Perhaps more important, focusing upon the debate as to whether religion should participate in public bioethics simply misses the point. As will be amply demonstrated in many of the pieces that follow, religion cannot be excluded from public bioethics. It is an inevitable presence—a force to be reckoned with. The more interesting and important question is *how* religion plays a role and normatively what *should be* its role in public bioethics. That is the goal of this book. While the pieces that follow, for the most part, start with a positive appreciation of religion and how it can inform public bioethics, that does not mean that they are univocal on how it should take its place in public debate or the ways in which it informs public discourse. For example, while Tristram Engelhardt (chap. 8) is skeptical of the existence of a viable secular ethical discourse and its capacity to successfully engage a particularist religious (i.e., Christian) ethical discourse, Elliot Dorff (chap. 7) draws upon talmudic resources in order to elaborate a broader model of bioethical discourse tolerant of religious diversity.

Approaching the issue from a non-absolutist position (i.e., that religion should or should not participate in public bioethics) also allows for a more nuanced consideration of the normative values and effects of religious participation. For example, as the question is posed in the piece by Therese Lysaught (chap. 5): To what extent does religious participation in politics of public bioethics represent a risk or potential harm to religion itself? More critically, what happens when religion is treated as a health care resource, an instrument of the medical profession? And, as Michele Goodwin (chap. 17) asks, Can religion undermine health?

In this introduction, I want to lay some of the groundwork for our discussion of religion and public bioethics. I will try to raise the questions commonly cited by the critics of public religion and provide a preliminary response that will be built on and elaborated by many of our contributors.

The Problem

As previously noted, the basic question that concerns us here is this: In a liberal, religiously pluralistic country like the United States, what role should religion play in the formation and development of public policies and practices regarding health care? Can the government or one of its instrumentalities (i.e., special commissions, administrative agencies, etc.) consider religious positions in developing and justifying its policy recommendations, or does the First Amendment protections of freedom of religion preclude any consideration of religious belief in public policy development? The issue came to the fore with particular force during the National Bioethics Advisory Commission's discussions and deliberations over the issue of cloning in 1997.

The National Bioethics Advisory Commission (NBAC)[5] was mandated to examine "bioethical issues" and develop "broad principles" for use in guiding the development of public policy on these issues.[6] Though these terms are not defined in the presidential order creating the commission or in the NBAC charter,[7] in practice the commission interpreted its mandate to mean developing policy recommendations in accord with the moral norms of our society at large. In particular, the commission sought testimony from a wide range of experts and scholars familiar with the issues under discussion and the values that should be considered in their regulation.[8]

Religious faith, commonly recognized as a source of moral norms, is a powerful social fact in the United States. More than 90 percent of Americans express a belief in God,[9] approximately 67 percent identifying themselves as members of the traditional trilogy (as defined by the pollsters): Christianity, Catholicism, and Judaism.[10] For many people in the United States, religion and morality are inseparable. In one survey, more than 90 percent of the members of Congress said they consulted their religious beliefs before voting on important matters.[11] More than 60 percent of Americans believe that having strong values begins with believing in God and answering to a higher power, with more than 80 percent taking guidance in living their own lives from the Bible.[12]

In light of this, any legitimate effort to identify the moral norms of the American people must consider what religion has to say. Thus, in its work on cloning research, NBAC made a particular effort to solicit the testimony of religious scholars and representatives.[13] The commission was severely criticized both for soliciting religious testimony[14] and for using the religious testimony in the way that it did.[15]

Much of the criticism against soliciting religious opinion reflected misperceptions and ignorance of religious argument and thought. As Courtney Campbell put it, "Otherwise very intelligent people can say some very stupid things about religion."[16]

Nonetheless, serious questions were raised that do deserve attention—especially questions relating to religious freedom. Specifically, many people were concerned that engaging people of faith in the NBAC process violates our long history of church-state separation (a misnomer for religious freedom and non-establishment). They, in line with numerous theorists, question the constitutionality and legitimacy of a government commission using religious arguments to justify state action.[17]

The Constitutional Question

The First Amendment to the Constitution states: "Congress shall make no law respecting an establishment of religion [the establishment clause] or prohibiting the free exercise thereof [the free exercise clause]." Discerning the meaning of these deceptively simple provisions of the Constitution as interpreted by the Supreme Court is notoriously difficult. Interpretations range from two extremes. Some argue that the Constitution requires that the government maintain strict separation between religion and the state—where religion is to be a private matter totally separated from public concern or attention.[18] Others argue that the protection of religious freedom demands a more generous policy of religious accommodation if not outright encouragement.[19] The one point that both sides agree on is that the Court's interpretation of the First Amendment's demands is generally "irrational" and "intellectually incoherent."[20] In the absence of a clear decision by the Court upon the specific facts in question, one is left to speculate as to the Court's intentions based upon the best arguments on hand.

In attempting to answer the question of the constitutionality of religious participation in policy formation by NBAC, three questions must be answered. First, what principle should be used to set the standard for constitutional behavior? Second, how does the principle apply to the rights of the individual under the free exercise clause? And third, does the proposed practice violate the prohibition against the establishment of religion?

The Principle of Government Neutrality

Many people confuse First Amendment protections for religious freedom with the unfortunate metaphor "a wall of separation between Church and State," penned by Thomas Jefferson in a letter to the Danbury Baptists ten years after the drafting and ratification of the First Amendment.[21] Though the Supreme Court has used this metaphor in a number of its opinions,[22] the metaphor is misleading. It suggests a much more rigorous separation between religion and the state than the courts have ever held necessary—or even possible.[23] As acknowledged by Justice Brennan, "The fact is that the line which separates the secular from the sectarian in American life is elusive."[24]

Though the Court has adopted metaphors like the "wall of separation" and "the line between" religion and the state, it generally (though not always consistently) applies a neutrality standard: the state cannot discriminate between particular religions or between religion and non-religion.[25] The state may not act in any way that would favor or disfavor religion as opposed to non-religion.[26]

In applying a neutrality standard, there are four areas of concern under the free exercise and establishment clauses of the Constitution. First, how does this standard apply to the individual as a participant in policy making? Second, how does it apply to the state in taking into consideration religious arguments and justifications? Third, to what extent does the adoption of policies that rest (at least in part) on religious justifications affect the individual's right to free exercise of religious belief when the policy applies to them? Finally, to what extent may the government acknowledge religious values as justification for its policies?

Individual Participation

It is generally acknowledged that the government cannot discriminate against the individual in the exercise of his or her political rights. The state cannot treat religious identity or affiliation as a disability to participation in the public arena. As Justice William Brennan wrote: "Religionists no less than members of any other group enjoy the full measure of protection afforded speech, association, and political activity generally. The establishment clause . . . may not be used as a sword to justify repression of religion or its adherents from any aspect of public life."[27] People of faith have the same right to express their opinions and participate in public benefits as their nonreligious counterparts.[28]

State Action and Religious Justification

There is, of course, a distinction between what a citizen can do and what the state may do. Obviously, an individual can act on or advocate a public position based upon his or her particular beliefs, whether they are religiously grounded or not. However, the state cannot adopt a specific religious view or use it as the basis for government action. But does that mean that it cannot rely upon or justify its actions on religious grounds at all?

On first reading, it would appear that the state cannot. The Supreme Court has repeatedly stated that state action must be justified by a secular legislative intent or purpose.[29] In order to support this position, the Court has gone so far as to discover secular intent for actions clearly motivated by religious interests (such as Sunday blue laws[30] and the display of religious symbols on public property[31]) and discovering religious intent for laws for which the affected legislature offered secular rationales.[32]

On a second reading, the Court's interpretation does not make sense. In adopting the secular justification standard, the Court presupposes that the secular is a religiously neutral concept. As articulated by its intellectual supporters,[33] secular reason (which John Rawls refers to as "public reason") is interpreted as providing a neutral ground for political engagement. Arguments and justifications for state actions using secular reason are, they claim, accessible to any reasonable person and do not rely upon religious traditions or beliefs. It is a forum and form of dialogue equally accessible to the religious and nonreligious person.

Critics, on the other hand, argue that favoring secular reason is inherently discriminatory to religion. As Michael McConnell puts it, "In the marketplace of ideas, secular viewpoints and ideologies are in competition with religious viewpoints and ideologies. It is no more neutral to favor the secular over the religious than it is to favor the religious over the secular."[34]

The problem is that the terms "religion" and "the secular" are not well defined. Whereas the Court generally treats religion and the secular as dichotomous, almost unrelated categories, critics like McConnell recognize the two as closely related. Moreover, the Court itself in certain tough cases is forced to recognize the difficulty in distinguishing between the two.[35]

The Supreme Court has generally avoided defining exactly what it means when it uses the term "religion." In many ways, as in the comparison suggested by Richard McBrien, the Court has looked at religion much as it looks at pornography: "It's very difficult to define, but you're supposed to know it when you see it"[36]

William James argued that the attempt to define religion is futile. "The word 'religion' cannot stand for any single principle or essence, but is rather a collective name."[37] Indeed, some argue that the attempt to define religion potentially infringes religious freedom—placing a limitation upon those "religions" that do not conform to that definition.[38] When the lower courts have alluded to the meaning of religion or, at least in one case at the appellate level attempted to define religion,[39] one finds that the description used largely conforms to a description of Judeo-Christian traditions.

When forced to define religion so as to avoid discriminating against standards of equal protection for all citizens, the Supreme Court adopted a broad definition that essentially identifies religion as any worldview that serves the function of religion for the person of faith.[40] Justice Black, in his famous dicta, recognized atheism and secular humanism as forms of religious association.[41] This broad understanding also conforms to the practices of the Internal Revenue Service, which recognizes the religious tax-exempt status of groups such as Scientology, Atheism, and the Ethical Culture society.[42]

This definition has merit in that it highlights the often unappreciated commonality between religion and other worldviews that we use to make moral and legal judgments.[43] Ultimately, all worldviews rest upon certain unprovable assumptions.[44] For religious worldviews these foundational assumptions may be identified with beliefs about the transcendent or the ultimate reality. Philosophically or empirically based worldviews rest upon certain assumptions about the nature of the world (e.g., that happiness is an absolute good [utilitarianism]; that the world is a closed reality in which cause and effect can be determined by observation [empiricism]). Each worldview is ultimately unprovable. What distinguishes these worldviews is that most people view religious worldviews as resting upon belief, whereas other worldviews are commonly viewed as resting upon truth or fact.[45] They are, of course, wrong.

Clearly to avoid favoring religion generally or one religion over another, the state (as represented by NBAC) cannot justify its decision by relying solely upon one religious tradition—or by relying solely upon traditional religions as a group. At the same time, this broader understanding similarly argues against relying solely upon isolated secular justifications not shared by religious traditions. To do so would violate the neutrality standard.

The Individual and the State Regulation of Morality

The First Amendment protection of religious freedom is embodied in two clauses. The first precludes the establishment of religion (i.e., the state favoring or advancing religion). The second protects the right of the individual to live according to the tenets of his or her faith (the free exercise clause). Does acknowledging the "religious" character of both secular and traditional religious beliefs mean that application of a policy justified by these worldviews infringes upon the individual's free exercise right?

As a practical matter, the answer is clearly "no." The courts have long acknowledged the right of states to regulate behavior—even when that prohibition has its roots in traditional religion.[46] Prohibiting murder does not violate the establishment clause simply because it is included in the Ten Commandments. Moreover, the right of free exercise is not an absolute right. It does not privilege behavior that violates a legitimate state interest.[47]

In order to avoid conflict between moral/religious belief and public policy, some people attempt to define moral behavior as a strictly private concern, not involving a state interest. There are liberal theorists who appear to argue that all moral judgments are fundamentally private. So long as the proposed action does not harm another person, deciding whether or not to act should be left up to the individual.[48] This has never been widely accepted. The law regularly intervenes to regulate behavior based upon moral concerns.[49] Moreover, drawing the line between the public and the private is difficult and issue specific. For example, in the abortion debates, pro-choice activists argue that abortion is a private moral decision to be made by the woman. Pro-life activist stress that it is a public concern affecting the rights of the unborn. The Supreme Court holds that it is both—with the unfortunate consequence of provoking an ongoing war of legislation and litigation. While asserting that the decision to have an abortion is fundamentally a private, nonpolitical issue, the Court has simultaneously recognized that the state has a legitimate interest in regulating certain ill-defined aspects of pregnancy termination.[50]

Trying to redefine the abortion controversy as a religious dispute doesn't help. It is not sectarian in the sense of being limited to a conflict among particular types of religious worldviews. While the right-to-life movement is commonly identified with the Religious Right and Roman Catholicism, it also includes people who are not affiliated with traditional religions. Moreover, many people of faith support choice. The issue is disputed on a variety of grounds, only some of which are traditionally religious.

Justifying Policy Decisions

Once the state has determined that an issue is of public or political concern and therefore subject to state regulation, it has to offer reasons to justify its decision to act in a certain way in regulating that issue. Laws are routinely reviewed to determine whether they represent the widely accepted norms of society or are attempts to advance the interests of special groups.[51] This is particularly true when the law restricts individual freedom.[52]

Where religion is involved, the Court has traditionally relied upon the requirement of secular justification for the law. The assumption has been that secular justification is a neutral term with respect to religion. However, as suggested above, this term favors worldviews that are indistinguishable from religious worldviews. Though the goal of secular justification attempts to avoid favoring sectarian interests, the tactic does not succeed.

Instead, the state needs to broaden its perspective.[53] In the words of John Rawls, the state must seek to identify the appropriate norms of society based upon an "over-lapping consensus" within society at large.[54] In arguing about physician-assisted suicide, for example, a Marxist might argue that it should be prohibited because in a capitalist society it will inevitably be used against the proletariat, and the life in question will be weighed against the cost to society. A feminist might argue that it discriminates against women, who are most likely to feel compelled to save their families the cost of expensive health care. A Catholic, in turn, may cite the sanctity of life and the doctrine that committing suicide is a mortal sin. All of these critics of physician-assisted suicide may agree that it should be prohibited, yet they justify their decision on different grounds.

Advocates of secular rationale or public reason assume that these divergent justifications can be translated into a neutral language. That common principles can be abstracted from these arguments and expressed in secular language acceptable by all involved.[55] Religious critics deny this. They point out that this process of translation favors those worldviews that find secular justifications persuasive and discriminates against people of faith. Those people of faith feel discriminated against in the same way that many feminists feel discriminated against by the grammatical rule that masculine pronouns are neutral and represent any person. Though the rule states that the masculine is to be understood as being inclusive, its use discriminates against women by hiding them; readers often perceive sentences using masculine pronouns as being about men. Hiding the religious justification for a policy has a similar effect. It conveys the message that religious justification is not legitimate. It is not something that the state can acknowledge and, as such, it is not an important justification for acting in the public realm.

Clearly, the state should not adopt an exclusively religious justification for its actions. That would be a sectarian preference that would discriminate against other worldviews and would simply reverse the pattern of discrimination currently practiced under the secular rationale. Instead, the state should offer the widest possible range of justifications for its decision, including both religious and nonreligious arguments, explaining, where possible, how they interrelate. Ronald Dworkin provides an example of this in his book *Life's Dominion*.[56] He attempts to address the controversy over abortion by drawing

attention to the commonality between religious and nonreligious understandings of the sacredness of life. He first acknowledges that each understanding
is grounded in different sources and then advances an argument based upon
how the two overlap. (Whether he succeeds in his argument is less important
for my purposes here than the fact that he illustrates how such an argument
can be constructed in a way that is respectful to all involved.)

The Morality of Religious Participation

To say that the state cannot preclude people of faith advancing their religious
beliefs within the process of public policy formation does not address the wisdom or morality of doing so. The bulk of this book will address these types of
moral/prudential arguments raised by critics of religious participation.

As suggested above, the common distinctions between religion, the secular, and the public or private are inadequate to justify restricting religious
participation in the formulation of public policy. Insofar as people of faith can
participate in developing policy, the state should be able to use the reasons
offered by people of faith in the same way that it uses the reasons offered by
traditional secularists. While the state could not adopt the justifications offered
by a single tradition (whether traditionally religious or secular) because that
would be sectarian, favoring one religion (broadly defined) over all others, it
can and should justify its actions based upon the norms found common among
all worldviews.

While admitting the constitutionality of religious participation in the public square, many critics nonetheless argue that the unique characteristics of
traditional religion justify the state in refraining from adopting religious justifications. They argue that, unlike other worldviews or ideologies, religion is
uniquely dangerous, threatening the stability and function of the public realm.
Robert Audi, for example, acknowledges that his arguments against religious
participation in public discussion is directed with particular force against traditional theistic-oriented religion and may not be equally applicable to other,
nontheistic religions.[57] For Audi, excluding theistic religion from the public
domain is an act of political morality. Many of these suspicions have been
adopted by the courts.[58]

Many of the contributors will address one or more of these arguments.
The goal here is simply to provide a brief overview of the most common arguments on political morality. While I provide some of the counterarguments,
many of those arguments will be fleshed out in far greater detail in the principal
papers in the book.

Violence

First, many secularists argue that the purpose of church/state separation was
to avoid the violence of religiously inspired conflict. They cite the historic re-

ligious wars and their current manifestations in areas such as Afghanistan, the Middle East, Bosnia, and Northern Ireland. In this country, they cite the violence surrounding abortion and the radical right-to-life movement.

This analogy is flawed in two ways. First, while it is true that religion has been a source of enormous conflict and bloodshed, it is not always clear that religion is the primary motivation for that conflict. While religion is often used to justify violence and is frequently associated with the adversaries in that conflict, that doesn't mean it is the source of the violence.[59] The conflicts in Northern Ireland and Bosnia are more accurately described as civil wars grounded in history, nationalism, and ethnic conflict in which the antagonists are identified with particular religious traditions rather than as wars over religious belief. As one commentator put it, the "conflict in Northern Ireland is not about transubstantiation."[60]

Second, the allegation that religion presents a greater threat of violence than secular ideology ignores modern history. The Stalinist purges of the 1930s, the Cultural Revolution in China, and the killing fields of Cambodia were not motivated by religion—they were motivated by secular ideologies. Even the Nazi Holocaust, though drawing upon the appalling tradition of Christian anti-Semitism, was framed as an effort toward racial purity and was also applied to gypsies, people with mental or physical disabilities, homosexuals, and Slavs.

If we turn to this country, the violence associated with abortion may be an example of religious violence. However, there are many examples of secularly inspired violence that can be cited as well: the Students for a Democratic Society, the Black Panthers, and the FALN (Fuerzas Armadas de Liberacion Nacional Puertorriquena) were all sources of ideologically inspired violence in the recent past. Again, religion is not unique as a source of violence.

While fear of violence is among the more frequently raised arguments against public religion, few thinkers take the argument seriously within the domestic arena.

Authoritarianism

One of the critics of the NBAC engagement with religious representatives complained that the sole task of religion is "theological hermeneutics—the interpretation of sacred texts. . . . [Religion] abolish[es] the hard ethical questions" because the answers are to be found in the texts of revelation.[61] This statement reflects a profound ignorance about how religious ethicists do their work. While it is true that they may use religious texts as a primary (if not exclusive) source for their reflection (and not all religions have clearly codified texts), these texts rarely provide simple authoritative answers. People of faith are forced to struggle to discern how the values in the text apply to a given situation. How they achieve this is no different from how secular ethicists use philosophical ethics, narrative ethics, or other techniques to interpret general values they deem normative to see how they apply in a particular situation (see, e.g., chaps. 2, 11, 12, 13, and 14).

What is different is how the starting point is viewed. Because many people of faith derive their values from received authority, those values are perceived as resting solely upon unsupported belief. Yet how is that different from the fundamental values of secular ethics? In attempting to explain the source of the value supporting the pro-choice movement, Ronald Dworkin suggests that it derives from a *secular* belief in the "sacredness" of life. Whether grounded in philosophy or intuition, this secular sacredness has power simply by virtue of its acceptance by many individuals as grounds upon which to act and understand their life.

Accessibility

Related to the issue of authority, many critics argue that religious arguments are not accessible to nonbelievers. That is to say, they do not provide information sufficient for the nonreligious person to evaluate and understand the arguments being made by the person of faith. Insofar as government action should rest upon arguments that are acceptable and understandable by those subject to them, then a justification based upon religious faith would not satisfy this requirement.

This critique rests upon three errors. First, it mistakes disbelief in the grounding authority of a value for a person's not being able to understand it. One may understand the grounding authority without believing in it. This applies to both people of faith and people of nonfaith. Neither may believe in the authority relied upon by the other—but that doesn't mean that they cannot understand how the other uses it as grounding for their ethical judgments.

Second, this critique ignores the difference between a person's grounding belief (e.g., belief in God, belief in dialectic materialism, etc.) and the principle or symbol used to express it at a high level of generality. For example, a person of faith may address the issue of cloning by drawing upon the biblical vision of humanity being created "in the image of God."[62] A nonbeliever does not have to believe in divine creation or worship in order to recognize that this symbol demands a profound respect for each human being.

Finally, it mistakes consensus on basic authority for consensus on practical application. The real question is whether people can understand how the policy was developed drawing upon the variety of perspectives brought to bear on it. The grounding authorities will be different, but the process of reaching consensus will be open and explained in a variety of ways.

Again, this argument is not unique to religion. For people of faith, the grounding beliefs of people of nonfaith may be comparably inaccessible.

Religious Argument Prevents Public Discussion

A more serious version of the accessibility critique is that the use of religious argument precludes public discussion and prevents political consensus. Michael Perry adopts a version of this argument when he argues that people of faith should be prepared to offer secular reasons for their judgments without imposing a similar requirement on people of nonfaith.[63] He argues that because people of non-faith do not believe, they cannot be expected to offer religious reasons for their positions.[64] Not only is Perry's argument unfair to people of faith (by treating religious and secular worldviews differently), it also precludes public participation by those individuals unable or unwilling to "translate" their religious insights into secular terms.

The overall argument that religion prevents public discussion fails for two reasons. First, this critique fails to appreciate the nature of public religious argument and the possibility that people of faith and nonfaith can engage in meaningful dialogue. While it is true that some people of faith simply leap from grounding belief to conclusion (e.g., "God said this, therefore cloning is wrong"), the same could be said for some people of nonfaith (e.g., for some ideological pro-choice activists: "I'm a woman, therefore I have a right to decide about having an abortion"). The better forms of religious argument not only assert a grounding belief, they develop their arguments to explain how that belief results in their judgment in a particular situation. A person of nonfaith does not need to accept the grounding belief in order to enter into the argument of the believer. The same rules of logic, coherence, and consistency apply to religious and nonreligious argument. Often, the person of faith will draw upon illustrative examples and intermediary arguments justifying an argument that a secularly oriented person can equally use based upon his or her own worldview beliefs.

Second, this critique assumes that in order to resolve the policy dispute, people of faith and people of secular beliefs need to reach consensus upon a single justification for that policy. However, it is unlikely that anyone will alter his or her fundamental worldview in order to reach a political policy judgment. Flexibility and compromise rest not at the level of fundamental belief but at the level of judgment about how those beliefs find expression in a particular situation. Therefore, the formation of public policy can result from a collection of overlapping but discrete public conversations addressed to particular audiences within the whole. The objective is consensus on a particular policy that may rest upon a pluralistically acceptable range of justifications.

Religion Is Not Shared

One of the rationales supporting the demand for secular justification is that it is assumed that secular reasoning is neutral—that it is shared by all members of society. Religion, on the other hand, is distinctly idiosyncratic, unique to each separate believer and/or a tradition. However, as pointed out above, secular reason is not neutral. It reflects, to a large extent, the worldview of a particular group of people (of varying religious-based and nonreligious-based traditions). Consequently, the objective in policy formation should not be the identification of shared worldviews or justifications, but the identification of shared practices based upon a variety of worldviews.

Religion Is Divisive

Many people believe that religion is uniquely divisive. It evokes passions and emotion as well as reason and judgment.[65] As acknowledged by Michael McConnell, "in the current political climate, many of the most heated political controversies involve a clash between largely religious forces of cultural traditionalism and largely secular forces of cultural deconstruction. It would be difficult to say which side in these conflicts was more strident, more intolerant, or more absolutist."[66]

Passionate disagreement is part of American history and the political process. From the Revolutionary War and the conflict between Loyalists and the revolutionaries, through the abolitionist movement, the Civil War, the early labor movement, the Civil Rights movement and the antiwar movement, it has been a feature of American governance. Though religion was present in some of these conflicts, it was not in others. Restricting religious participation will not end the reality that people of conviction bring their passion to the political arena.

Moreover, the effort to secularize the public sphere has alienated many people of faith, creating a backlash feeding the emergence of the Religious Right.[67] As argued by Stephen Carter,[68] this perceived antagonism toward religion and the resulting alienation has energized the so-called Religious Right. "Nothing creates political energy quite so well as insults, and nothing makes [members of the Religious Right] harder to slow than the ignorance of their critics."[69]

Faction

The founders of the American Republic feared political faction as one of the great threats to stable government. A "zeal for different opinions concerning religion" was Madison's first example in Federalist No. 10 of the causes of this type of faction.[70] However, religion was not the only example. Madison recognized that religion was not unique, simply that it was one of many sources of political faction.

The faction argument is, essentially, the political extension of the decisiveness argument. Religion is not only a potential source of passionate conflict, but also a unifying force giving that conflict political power. It is not just that religion has the power to divide individuals; it may lead to political conflict between religious groups.

The response of the secularists has been to attempt to repress religion, to find a single common (i.e., secular) belief system that all citizens can share. As evident from the reactions of the Religious Right, this effort is doomed to failure. Madison recognized this and rejected this as "impractical" if not impossible.[71] Instead, he argued, stability is better served by seeking to control the effects of faction. As argued by Michael McConnell, "His solution was not to keep any such factions 'out of politics,' but to extend the sphere of the Union to ensure that there would be such a multiplicity of sects and facts that none would be able to suppress the others."[72]

Moving Forward

The arguments and discussion of the moral place of religion in public bioethics will proceed as follows. We consider in part I the history of bioethics and the role that religion has played within that history. In part II we consider the place of religion in the public square: how it grounds moral decision making, how it can participate in public discourse and what it might offer as a resource or model for public debate. In part III we turn to the nature of religious public discourse, its sources of authority, and the nature of the conversations promoted by it. We then consider, in part IV, how official sources draw upon religious or moral values in justifying state policies. In part V, we explore the nature and contributions that religion offers in the actual process of ethical decision making. In part VI, we explore the increasing trend to treat religion as an instrument of health care and research. Finally, in part VII we consider the implications of institutional religion on public health and public health policy.

NOTES

1. See, e.g., *Everson v. Board of Education*, 330 U.S. 1 (1947); *Lemon v. Kurtzman*, 403 U.S. 602 (1971); *McGowan v. Maryland*, 366 U.S. 420 (1961); *Agostini v. Felton*, 521 U.S. 203 (1997).

2. See, e.g., Robert Audi, *Religious Commitment and Secular Reason* (New York: Oxford University Press, 2000); Stephen Carter, *The Culture of Disbelief* (New York: Basic Books, 1993); Kent Greenawalt, *Private Consciences and Public Reasons* (New York: Oxford University Press 1995); Isaac Kramnick and R. Laurence Moore, *The Godless Constitution* (New York: W.W. Norton, 1996); Richard P. McBrien, *Caesar's Coin: Religion and Politics in America* (New York: Macmillan, 1987); John Courtney Murray, *We Hold These Truths: Catholic Reflections on the American Proposition* (New York: Sheed & Ward, 1960); Richard John Neuhaus, *The Naked Public Square: Religion and Democracy in America* (Grand Rapids, Mich.: William B. Eerdmans, 1984); Michael Perry, *Love and Power* (New York: Oxford University Press, 1991).

3. Critical of religious involvement: R. C. Lewontin, "The Confusion over Cloning" *New York Review of Books*, Oct. 23, 1997, 22–23; Gregory Pense, *Who's Afraid of Cloning?* (Lanham, Md.: Rowman & Littlefield, 1998), 35; Daniel Wikler, "Remarks on Religion and Bioethics," first meeting of the American Society for Bioethics and Humanities, November 1998. Supportive of religious engagement: Courtney Campbell, "Bearing Witness: Religious Practices and Meaning" in *Notes from a Narrow Ridge: Religion and Bioethics*, ed. Dena S. Davis and Laurie Zoloth (Hagerstown, Md.: University Publishing Group, 1999), 40–44; Courtney Campbell, "In Whose Image," *Second Opinion*, September 1999, 40.

4. Carter, *Culture of Disbelief*; see also Stephen Carter, *Dissent of the Governed* (Cambridge, Mass.: Harvard University Press, 1995) and *God's Name in Vain* (New York: Basic Books, 2000).

5. The mandate of NBAC expired Oct. 3, 2001. It has been replaced by the President's Council on Bioethics, which largely serves the same purpose. See webpage at http://bioethics.gov (accessed March 13, 2005).

6. Executive Order 12977, as amended, 60 F.R 52063–52065.

7. See the NBC webpage at bioethics.gov.

8. See, e.g., the NBAC reports "Cloning Human Beings" (1997), and "Research Involving Persons with Mental Disabilities" (1998), at bioethics.gov.

9. CNN/Gallup Dec. 1999 News Poll, see http://www.gallup.com/poll/releases/pr991224.asp (accessed March 13, 2001).

10. First Amendment Center, *State of the First Amendment 2000* (Washington, D.C.: First Amendment Center, 2000).

11. Carter, *Culture of Disbelief,* 111.

12. Oxygen/Markel, *Pulse Study: Values and Politics* (accessed at www.pulse.org, Aug. 10, 2000).

13. NBAC, "Cloning" (1997), esp. Vol. 2.

14. Lewontin, "The Confusion over Cloning," 22–23; Pense, *Who's Afraid of Cloning?* 35; Wikler, "Remarks on Religion and Bioethics."

15. Campbell, "Bearing Witness, 40–44.

16. Campbell, "In Whose Image," 40.

17. See, e.g., Greenawalt, *Private Consciences,* esp. chap. 14.

18. See, e.g., Audi, *Religious Commitment;* Kramnick and Moore, *Godless Constitution.*

19. See, e.g., Stephen V. Monsma and J. Christopher Soper, eds., *Equal Treatment of Religion in a Pluralistic Society* (Grand Rapids, Mich.: Eerdmans, 1998).

20. See, e.g., Mary Ann Glendon, "Law, Communities, and the Religious Freedom Language of the Constitution," *George Washington Law Review* 60 (1992): 672; Lawrence Tribe, *American Constitutional Law,* 2nd ed. (Mineola, N.Y.: Foundation Press, 1988); Michael McConnell, "The Religion Clauses and the First Amendment: Where Is the Supreme Court Heading?" *Catholic Law Review* 32, (1989): 187.

21. Thomas Jefferson, "Letter of January 1, 1802," in *Writings of Thomas Jefferson,* ed. Albert E. Bergh. 20 vols. (Washington, D.C.: 1904–1905), 16:281–282.

22. See, e.g., *Reynolds v. United States,* 98 U.S. 145, 164 (1879); *Everson v. Board of Education.*

23. *Walz v. Tax Commissioner of New York City,* 397 U.S. 644, 669–70 (1970); *Lemon v. Kurzman; Roemer v. Board of Public Works of Maryland,* 426 U.S. 736, 745 (1976).

24. *Abington School District v. Schempp,* 374 U.S. 203, 231 (1963).

25. *Everson* at 15–16.

26. *Rosenberger v. Rector of the University of Virginia.* 515 U.S. 753 (1995),

27. *McDaniel v. Platty,* 435 U.S. 618, 641 (1978).

28. See, e.g., *Widmer v. Vincent,* 454 U.S. 263 (1981); *Rosenberger v. Rector of the University of Virginia.*

29. *Abington; Board of Education v. Allen,* 392 US 236, 243 (1968); *Lemon* at 612.

30. *McGowan v. Maryland,* 366 U.S. 420 (1961).

31. *County of Allegheny v. American Civil Liberties Union, Greater Pittsburgh Chapter,* 492 U.S. 573 (1989); and *Lynch v. Donnelly,* 465 U.S. 668 (1984).

32. See, e.g., *Stone v. Graham,* 449 U.S. 39 (1980); *Epperson v. Arkansas,* 393 U.S. 97 (1968).

33. See, Audi, *Religious Commitment,* chap. 4; John Rawls, *Political Liberalism,* Lecture VI (New York: Columbia University Press, 1993).

34. Michael McConnell, "Equal Treatment and Religious Discrimination," in *Equal Treatment of Religion in a Pluralistic Society*, ed. Stephen V. Monsma and J. Christopher Soper (Grand Rapids, Mich.: Eerdmans, 1998), 33.

35. See, e.g., *United States v. Seeger*, 380 U.S. 163 (1965); *Torcaso v. Watkins*, 367 U.S. 488, 495 n.11 (1961).

36. McBrien, *Caesar's Coin*, 8.

37. William James, *The Varieties of Religious Experience* (New York: NAL, 1958), 39.

38. Jonathan Weiss, "Privilege, Posture, and Protection: 'Religion' in the Law," *Yale Law Journal* 73 (1964): 594; Timothy L. Hall, "Religion, Equality, and Difference," *Temple Law Review* 65 (1992): 1.

39. *Africa v. Commonwealth of Pennsylvania*, 662 F.2d 1025 (3d Cir. 1981).

40. See, e.g., *Seeger*.

41. *Torcaso v. Watkins*, 376 U.S. 495 n. 11 (1961)

42. See, e.g., *Hernandez v. Commissioner*, 490 U.S. 680 (1989).

43. Franklin I. Gamwell, "The Compound Conception of Justice: Politics and Religious Pluralism," in *Religion and Law in the Global Village*, ed. David E. Guinn, Chris Barrigar, and Katherine K. Young (Atlanta: Scholars Press, 1999).

44. Richard Rorty, "The Priority of Democracy to Philosophy," in *Prospects for a Common Morality*, ed. Gene Outka and John P. Reeder Jr. (Princeton, N.J.: Princeton University Press, 1993).

45. See, e.g., *Edwards v. Aguillard*, 482 U.S. 578 (1987); Frederick Mark Gedicks, *The Rhetoric of Church and State* (Durham, N.C.: Duke University Press, 1995), 32–37.

46. See, e.g., *McGowan v. Maryland*.

47. See, e.g., *Reynolds v. United States*; *Employment Division, Department of Human Resources of Oregon v. Smith*, 494 U.S. 872 (1990).

48. See, e.g., John Stuart Mill, *On Liberty* (Indianapolis, Ind.: Bobbs-Merrill, 1976), 13.

49. See, e.g., Harry M. Clor, *Public Morality and Liberal Society: Essays on Decency, Law, and Pornography* (Notre Dame, Ind.: University of Notre Dame Press, 1996); Robert P. George, *Making Men Moral: Civil Liberties and Public Morality* (Oxford: Oxford University Press, 1993).

50. See, e.g., *Roe v. Wade*, 410 U.S. 113 (1973).

51. See, e.g., *Epperson v. Arkansas*; *McGowan v. Maryland*.

52. See, e.g., *Griswold v. Connecticut*, 381 U.S. 479 (1965).

53. See David E. Guinn, *Faith on Trial: Communities of Faith, the First Amendment, and the Theory of Deep Diversity* (Lanham, Md.: Lexington, 2002).

54. Rawls, *Political Liberalism*, 133ff.

55. See, e.g., Audi, *Religious Commitment*; Rawls, *Political Liberalism*.

56. Ronald Dworkin, *Life's Dominion: An Argument About Abortion, Euthanasia, and Individual Freedom* (New York: Vintage, 1994).

57. Audi, *Religious Commitment*, 34

58. See, e.g., *Everson*.

59. See, e.g., Liz Fawcett, *Religion, Ethnicity and Social Change* (New York: St. Martin's Press, 2000), esp. the introduction and 16–20; R. Scott Appleby, *The Ambivalence of the Sacred* (Lanham, Md.: Rowman & Littlefield, 2000).

60. Private communication with the author by Eric Treene of the Becket Fund for Religious Freedom.

61. Lewontin, "The Confusion over Cloning," 7.

62. See NBAC, "Cloning."

63. See Michael Perry, *Love and Power* (New York: Oxford University Press, 1991).

64. Personal conversation with the author, April 1998.

65. See, e.g., *Lemon*, 402 US at 622.

66. Michael McConnell, "Five Reasons to Reject the Claim That Religious Arguments Should be Excluded from Democratic Deliberation," *Utah Law Review* 49 (1999): 649.

67. Neuhaus, *Naked Public Square*; Carter, *Culture of Disbelief*.

68. See Carter, *Dissent of the Governed* and *God's Name in Vain*.

69. Carter, *God's Name In Vain*, 57.

70. Alexander Hamilton, James Madison, and John Jay, *The Federalist Papers*, ed. Clinton Rossiter (New York: NAL, 1961), 79.

71. Ibid., 78.

72. McConnell, "Five Reasons": 645.

PART I

Historical Perspectives

Debates about religious participation in public political discourse often present a picture of the world that views religion as an interloper intruding into spheres of life that were previously secular. This is historically inaccurate as a general proposition and, more specifically, in relation to what I have referred to as public bioethics in naming this book. As noted by Albert Jonsen in the following essay, "Bioethics began in religion," though he promptly adds that it has now become a commonplace opinion that "religion has faded from bioethics."

Attending to the history of religion in bioethics does more than simply rebut this historically inaccurate argument. It highlights the ongoing and ever present struggle with the question of how religion can and should participate in the public forum of bioethics. The struggle between the sacred and the secular is not new. The various methods adopted to address the struggle may offer insights for normative judgments.

One may start with the observation that bioethics is a relatively new discipline, emerging in the early '70s, according to Jonsen, or perhaps the late '60s, as described by Lisa Sowle Cahill. Issues relating to medical care and ethics predated the emergence of the discipline of bioethics. Religion, as a critical resource for ethical reflection and morals, was a preeminent participant in conversations about those issues. What makes the emergence of bioethics significant is that it makes questions of medical ethics a public act rather than a penitential one between a patient or doctor and his spiritual advisor. Moreover, the discipline specifically came to public attention and acquired its primary disciplinary tools (i.e., principalism[1]) through the deliberations of the National Commission for the Protection of Human Subjects of Biomedical and Behavioral Research in its *Belmont Report: Ethical Principles and Guidelines for the Protection of Human Subjects of Research.*[2] The field shifted from what might be considered simply a private concern (that of the patient or doctor and his or her personal morality) to a public concern over the proper policy of the government in regulating the field of medicine and health care research.

The emergence of the discipline immediately raised the question of how people of faith should participate in formation of bioethical policy. As Cahill's essay demonstrates, the possible options for participation vary significantly, from that of adopting neutral, secular language to total rejection of secular language in favor of a strictly religious perspective. However, what is particularly telling about the field of bioethics is that in spite of the presence on the commission of some of the leading religious thinkers of the time—including Albert Jonsen, James Childress, and Karen Lebacqz—the commission adopted in its first major disciplinary expression, the *Belmont Report,* a set of strictly secular, philosophic principles as the standards by which to analyze research standards. The decision to adopt strictly secular norms and language may be justified on pragmatic grounds as necessary for a new field to acquire legitimacy or authority (see, e.g., Tod Chambers's essay in chap. 4) or on normative grounds that reflect a judgment that public discourse should always be given in secular terms. Nonetheless, one may wonder whether this decision ultimately created the current controversy by delegitimating religious discourse at the outset of the public conversation.

NOTES

1. See, e.g., Tom Beauchamp and James F. Childress, *Principles of Biomedical Ethics,* 1st ed. (New York: Oxford University Press, 1979); Edwin R. DuBose, Ron Hamel, and Laurence J. O'Connell, eds., *A Matter of Principle* (Valley Forge, Pa.: Trinity Press, 1994).

2. DHEW Publication No. (OS) 78–0012 (1978).

I

A History of Religion and Bioethics

Albert R. Jonsen

In 1582, an Italian Jesuit, Matteo Ricci, crossed a frontier. He entered the Forbidden Empire of China. He had petitioned the governor of Guangdong Province to come, not as a missionary or merchant or military man but as a humble scholar desiring to learn the culture of China. He was the first Westerner of modern times to dwell in China. He adopted the dress and culture of a Confucian scholar, introduced Euclidean geometry, Western geography, chronology, cosmology, and astronomy, interpreted Confucius to the West and wrote admired Chinese poetry. Almost thirty years later, he died at Beijing, honored with the epithet "Wise Man of the West," and honored by the emperor with burial near the Forbidden City. He had not made many converts to Christianity but had opened a conversation between two previously isolated cultures.[1]

Four hundred years later, many theological scholars crossed the frontier from denominational ethics to bioethics. Like Ricci, they doffed the intellectual garb of religious ethics and donned, if not the white coats of doctors, the distinctly secular mentality of modern medicine.

"Bioethics began in religion, but religion has faded from bioethics." This opinion is a commonplace among many who have opinions about bioethics. The purpose of this chapter is to examine this commonplace. I write more of a memoir than a history. I was present at the beginnings of bioethics in the United States. I was one of those early bioethicists identified with a religious tradition, Roman Catholicism. I knew most of the early bioethicists. So unlike a historian who must critically evaluate sources, I will tell this history out of personal recollections. I hope these recollections correspond to the facts, such as they are. I do not do theorize about how religious doctrine, tradition, and belief have, or have not, affected the field we call bioethics, nor do I attempt to explain how and why bioethics became secularized. Other essays in this volume will assume these tasks.

I designate the beginnings of bioethics in the several years around 1970.[2] Walter Mondale, then a U.S. senator, held Senate hearings on Health, Science, and Society in 1968. The Hastings Center opened in 1969, the Kennedy Institute in 1971. Van Rensselaer Potter published his article *Bioethics, the Science of Survival* in 1970, and his book *Bioethics: Bridge to the Future* in 1971.[3] Paul Ramsey's *Patient as Person* (in my opinion the first genuine example of bioethics), a book of lectures given in 1969, appeared in 1970.[4] Unquestionably, dating the birth of any intellectual or social movement is perilous. Certainly, many other events and ideas precede the chosen date and prepare for it. Many other observers will have their own preferences for the birthday. Even the idea of a birthday may be silly: bioethics is not a baby but a set of ideas and attitudes, a collection of writings and a covey of courses. Nevertheless, I believe that in the several years around 1970, many of these disparate elements flowed together to form a discernable stream that could be given a name. In 1973, Dan Callahan wrote a seminal essay, "Bioethics as a Discipline."[5] The title of this essay is the first entry of the word "bioethics" in the catalogue of the National Library of Congress.[6]

In 1973, I crossed the frontier from the country of Roman Catholic moral theology into the world of medical ethics. I was appointed associate professor of bioethics at the School of Medicine, University of California, San Francisco (UCSF). I was, at that time, a Roman Catholic priest, a member of the Jesuit order. I had been trained in Roman Catholic moral theology in the pre–Vatican II era, teaching in a Catholic College. When I moved to UCSF, I entered the very secular world of a state medical school with a clearly known religious identity. I did not, however, wear the distinctive garb of a Catholic priest. By changing from clerical collar to sport jacket and tie, I imitated Father Ricci, who shed his Roman cassock for a mandarin's silk gown. Like him, I had also crossed a frontier into a strange land. I had to learn a new language, filled with the words of anatomy, physiology, pathophysiology, and pharmacology. I had to learn the culture of medicine and of hospitals. I had to converse with men and women who did not share my faith or even my interests. No one knew what a bioethicist, much less an ethicist, was (I was once introduced as an "anesthetist"). Above all, I had to learn the values that prevail in the world of medicine so that I could even ask "ethical" questions or dare to teach ethics. Most problematic: What "ethics" would I teach? The person most responsible for my arrival in the medical school, a world-distinguished surgeon, had been educated by Jesuits and simply assumed that the ethics he learned from them could be imported into medicine. I was much more skeptical.

Traditional Catholic moral theology did contain a large treatise on ethical questions arising in medical practice. That treatise, developed over the centuries since the Middle Ages, dealt with abortion, amputation, contraception, euthanasia (topics still relevant) and some antiquated question such as recourse to magic remedies. During the papacy of Pius XII (1939–1958), this traditional treatise had been modernized because of the pope's interest in moral theology. He had, for example, clarified the discussion of euthanasia by amplifying the concepts of "ordinary" and "extraordinary" care, specified the conditions for ethical experimentation on humans and revised the treatise on amputation to accommodate new developments in organ transplantation. So, being trained in moral theology, I felt that I had something to say about some current issues in medicine.

However, Catholic moral theology is not simply a catalogue of issues. It is a methological approach to those issues. The method is the Catholic interpretation of natural law ethics. This doctrine, adopted from Cicero and the Roman jurisprudents, and refined by Aquinas's interpretation of Aristotle, had come under critical scrutiny during the decades after World War II. Catholic philosophers, such as Jacques Maritain and Yves Simon, had attempted to construct a way of thinking about morality that, in their view, would appeal to any rational person. They saw natural law ethics was not only an ethics for Catholics but for all persons, in all cultures and times. It was a universal ethic.

My Jesuit training provided me with another method, namely, casuistry. While an integral part of Catholic moral theology, casuistry was a Jesuit method par excellence. It insisted that moral issues had to be embedded in real cases: the circumstances of specific cases would affect the justification and judgment to be made about the case. Casuistry allows the ethicist to work with ethical problems in relative isolation from the foundations of ethics in theory and in doctrine. It is also very congenial to the medical mind, accustomed to thinking about the case of this patient with this condition. So it was possible to address many troublesome ethical cases without reference to religious doctrine. The ongoing debate in bioethics between casuistry and principlism has shown that the independence of casuistry from foundations is illusory but, even then, casuistry as a practical exercise often serves the ethicist well. When I was appointed to the National Commission on the Protection of Human Subjects of Biomedical and Behavioral Research in 1974, I met philosopher Stephen Toulmin, who was also intrigued by casuistry. Together we wrote *The Abuse of Casuistry*, in which we attempted to resuscitate this antiquated and often ridiculed form of moral reasoning.[7] So, in my work at UCSF and other settings such as the National Commission, I had gradually shed the priestly robes and clothed myself as a nondenominational bioethicist. In my personal life, I resigned from the Jesuits, thus becoming a naturalized citizen of the secular world.

Another Jesuit also crossed the frontier into bioethics. Richard McCormick (1923–2000) was professor of moral theology at a Jesuit seminary and editor of "Notes on Moral Theology" in the most prestigious journal of Catholic theology, *Theological Studies*. He was held in high respect among Catholics as a conscientiously orthodox but carefully reforming scholar. His moderately liberal stance caught the attention of leading Protestant thinkers, and he was often invited to participate in ecumenical debates as the "Catholic representative." As issues concerning human experimentation and care of the dying moved into public discussion, McCormick made measured contributions. In 1974, Dr.

Andre Hellegers, founder of the Kennedy Institute for Bioethics, brought him to Georgetown University. McCormick became a full-time bioethicist.

His passage across the frontier was not as definitive as mine. He did not move into the setting of secular medical education. He had long been familiar with the medical world and often spoke to medical audiences (his father had been president of the American Medical Association). He worked within a Catholic institution. He always maintained public identity as a Jesuit priest and was always the Catholic participant in the dialogue. Still, the dialogue was now consistently with persons outside his tradition and outside his discipline. He published not only in *Theological Studies* but also in the *Journal of the American Medical Association*. He was appointed to governmental and professional committees where he had to deliberate public policy suited to a multifaith, democratic, and secular society.

In all this work, McCormick exploited the natural law theory that formed his thinking. He found it a subtle and supple way to formulate arguments and believed that these arguments could appeal to all rational persons. He knew the theoretical shortcomings of natural law theory and attempted to remedy them, but he remained, in essence, a natural law ethicist. Just as I had been able to move into the secular world with an ethical method that was not denominational or "faith-based" in its language or arguments, McCormick also, Catholic though he clearly was, could do the same and did it exceptionally well.[8] Unquestionably, his arguments often showed their Christian foundations. In a fine article about life support, he defended allowing patients to die under certain circumstances. He used and refined the natural law reasoning about ordinary and extraordinary means of care but argued that, in the final analysis, preservation of life cannot be obligatory if it renders impossible the "the higher, more important good . . . the love of God and neighbor which is the meaning, substance and consummation of life from a Judeo-Christian perspective." But even before this theological coda, McCormick had made a convincing ethical argument that sustaining a meaningless life was irrational.[9]

Another element of Roman Catholic moral theology was less amenable to the secular world. From the seventeenth century onward, papal authority inserted itself more and more into moral teaching. In prior centuries, Catholic moral teaching evolved from episcopal teaching throughout the worldwide Church, as interpreted by theologians. Very few moral teachings issued directly from papal authority, except when rare cases of widespread dissension, as over the issue of usury, required settlement of the dispute at the highest level of authority. From the seventeenth century onward, particularly from the latter part of the eighteenth, the Vatican more frequently issued authoritative statements about moral matters. Abortion and contraception were among these moral matters. Natural law theologians, accustomed to justifying their positions by convincing logical reasoning, were summoned to obey these authoritative statements.

Still, authoritative statements on moral matters were not divorced from natural law reasoning. The Vatican would assert that its teaching was itself based on natural law, of which it was making a definitive interpretation. Usually, moral theologians would accept. However, in 1968, Pope Paul VI issued the encyclical *Humanae Vitae*, in which he declared that contraceptive acts, whatever the intention or modality, were mortally sinful. Many theologians worldwide found the reasoning behind this decision faulty. A *crise de conscience* erupted among Catholic moral theologians. McCormick struggled to develop a reasonable interpretation; many others, like myself, felt that we could not remain Catholic theologians. This crisis had its repercussions in bioethics. Catholic bioethicists (many of whom also disagreed with the church's authoritative teaching that human life begins at fertilization) were no longer able to propose themselves as proponents of a universal ethics. If natural law reasoning could be authoritatively reinterpreted in ways that appeared to many as irrational, natural law lost its highest and best attraction as an appeal to reason.

The particular features of Roman Catholic moral theology, especially natural law theory and casuistry, had allowed Roman Catholics to move across the frontiers from denominational ethics to bioethics with relative ease. They had a kind of ethical lingua franca. They could talk about ethics in a language that the non-Catholic and the non-Christian could understand. Some (like McCormick) chose to speak that language and to also retain an ecclesiastical accent, making reference to church teachings and authoritative statements; others, like myself, tried to stay with the lingua franca and embellish it with language from secular moral philosophy.

Protestant theological ethics did not have the same fluency in two vernaculars. From the time of the Reformation, ethical doctrine had developed as a many-branched tree. For the most part, Protestant thinkers repudiated natural law theory and casuistry. The Scriptures were mined for the moral messages of the prophets, the apostles and, above all, of Jesus. The language of moral exhortation was emphatically evangelical. Although some theologians sought rational foundations in secular moral philosophers (Kant was particularly appealing to Lutherans and Calvinists), little reliance was placed on the suspect arguments from natural reason. Anglicans alone retained some attachment to natural law and to casuistry and it was from the Anglican tradition, in its American Episcopal form, that one of the first bioethicists emerged.

Joseph Fletcher (1905–1991) was professor of pastoral theology and Christian ethics at Episcopal Theological School in Cambridge, Massachusetts. He was an unusual moral theologian. He had the heart not of scholar but of a social activist. His goal was to convert the church to its Jesus-given mission of serving the poor and oppressed. He was often arrested and beaten in strike sympathy marches and protests. Yet he was a wonderfully benevolent, gentle, and charming person, with a persuasive eloquence. In 1949, Harvard University invited Dr. Fletcher to give the Lowell Lectures. The donor of those lectures provided that they be given by someone who believed in the divine revelation of the Old and New Testaments. Dr. Fletcher confessed that, at least in this, he "could claim fitness for the venture."

The venture was an exciting one. He wished to explore "the problems of conscience, certain ethical issues, which arise in the course of medical care." This was an unusual topic, for apart from Catholic treatises on medical morality, very little had been written by American Protestant theologians, and certainly nothing had been written in the fashion that Fletcher approached his subject. He proposed the thesis that every patient had the right to choose euthanasia, sterilization, contraception, and artificial insemination. This proposal repudiated not only the tenets of most Christian denominations at that time but also the moral beliefs of many physicians. Several years later, the lectures appeared as *Morals and Medicine*.[10] It is not, in my view, the first book of the new bioethics but the last book of the old medical ethics. Its topics were, for the most part, the topics of conventional medical ethics. However, Fletcher placed in the midst of these topics a revolutionary idea, the moral principle of autonomy, thereby turning what had been a structure of deontological rules into a set of arguments in favor of personal independence, supported by the skills of medicine.

There is very little theology in *Morals and Medicine*. References to biblical and church teaching occasionally support an argument, but he usually introduces them as obfuscating rather than clarifying the issue. Fletcher does invoke the biblical concept of *agape*, or other-regarding love, as the central ethical imperative of Christianity but makes no systematic argument explaining how it supports his claims. Rather, he believes that, in practical terms, *agape* translates into utilitarian beneficence. Familiar with the Anglican tradition of moral theology, which admits a modest version of natural law and of casuistry, he is willing to employ both but, essentially, his ethics is a mix of utilitarianism and pragmatism. In 1966, he published his most famous book, *Situation Ethics*, in which he explicitly identified himself as an act utilitarian, doing little more than varnishing that secular doctrine with Christian love as its motive.[11]

Joseph Fletcher became a popular spokesman for a new medical ethics. Although *Morals and Medicine* dealt with conventional medicine, he later turned his attention to cutting-edge medical science, especially genetics and reproductive science. Here also, he saw all innovations as liberation of humans from the constraints of suffering and the limits of the human condition. In particular, all the techniques of reproductive science, from in vitro fertilization to cloning, seemed to him victories over the "reproductive roulette" to which humans are bound by sexual reproduction.[12] In the early 1980s, Joseph Fletcher crossed another frontier. Already in his seventies, he left the ministry and the church and joined the faculty of the School of Medicine of the University of Virginia, where he continued to preach, not the gospel, but a message of liberation and social justice in the world of biological science. He won many admirers.

Paul Ramsey was not among those admirers. A professor of religion at Princeton University, he was among the Protestant scholars engaged in revitalization of what had become a rather flaccid Christian ethics. With theologians James Gustafson, Paul Lehmann, Roger Shinn, and a few others, he endeavored to locate the moral teaching of Protestant tradition on a solid doctrinal and biblical basis. Influenced by H. Richard Niebuhr and Karl Barth, he centered his theology on the idea of covenant, in which God's steadfast love endows human life and freedom with sanctity and expects faithful response of obedience. The basic outline of Christian morality could be drawn from that fundamental idea.[13] He was an insightful, logical thinker and a powerful preacher in the Methodist manner that flowed into his teaching and lectures. During the 1960s, he encountered the fascinating progress of biological science, particularly genetics, and engaged in debates with leaders in that field (he argued against cloning with geneticist Joshua Lederberg, who was a close friend of Joseph Fletcher's!). He also entered the abortion debate, siding generally but not totally with the Catholic side.

Ramsey also was attracted to the Catholic doctrine of natural law. He found it not only in Catholic thinkers but also in many other secular moralists and believed that it could be used in Christian ethics.[14] He appreciated the casuistical analysis he found in Catholic moral theologians. So although an explicitly theological Christian moralist, he understood that moral reasoning could be framed in ways that spoke to reasonable people beyond the pale of the church. When invited to deliver the Beecher Lectures at Yale Divinity School in 1969, he delved into the issue of contemporary medical science and care. After preparing himself by six months of immersion in the life of Georgetown Medical Center, he chose to speak on human experimentation involving children, decisions to forgo life support, determination of death, organ transplantation, and allocation of scarce medical resources. These topics represented medicine at the frontier and, unlike Joseph Fletcher's *Morals and Medicine* of some twenty years earlier, which had criticized the morals of conventional medicine, Ramsey's book represented a genuine ethical encounter with the new medicine. His lectures appeared as *The Patient as Person. Explorations in Medical Ethics*, the first major contribution to bioethics as a discipline.[15]

In this pioneering book and for the rest of his career, devoted largely to bioethical issues, he expounded a soundly conservative doctrine on almost all bioethical matters: genetic manipulation was perilous; reproduction must be protected within the sanctity of marriage; life must be protected and preserved; the search for scientific knowledge must never override the consent of patients. Though he proposed a reasonable approach to forgoing life support, he fiercely opposed assistance in dying (with but a small exception). He was highly suspicious of appeals to quality of life, seeing them as a cover for disrespect for the sanctity of life. He repudiated any form of utilitarian ethics, thus placing him in ineluctable opposition to Joseph Fletcher. Indeed, he rejected Fletcher's liberal approach to almost every bioethical issue.

Despite his persistent theological perspective, his arguments on most questions moved on the plane of natural law reasoning and casuistry. *Patient as Person* opens with the italicized assertion, "*Just as man is a sacredness in the social and political order, so he is a sacredness in the natural, biological order.*" The book, he explains, is written "to find the actions and abstentions that come from adherence to *covenant*, to ask the meaning of the *sanctity* of life, to articulate the requirements of steadfast *faithfulness* to a fellow man." Three pages later, he states, "Medical ethics today must, indeed, be 'casuistry,'" and "an ethicist is only an ordinary man and a moral theologian is only a religious man endeavoring to push out as far as he can the frontier meaning of the practice of a rational or a charitable justice."[16] After posing the religious premises of his argument, he delves into the casuistry with but an occasional glance back at them. He supposes that his readers, being ordinary men, will understand his arguments. And, although his arguments are often arcane and convoluted, they are intelligible to readers who might not share or care about his theological premises. His ideas penetrated deeply into early bioethics, but largely because they are reasonably persuasive rather than theologically grounded.

I have presented to you my three friends, Richard McCormick, Joseph Fletcher, and Paul Ramsey. Much more can be said about each of them.[17] They were the theological giants of early bioethics. Each crossed frontiers from the culture of denominational theology into the culture of secular medicine, science, and public policy. Each was, to some extent, like the Jesuit Ricci. They learned the language and values of that world and appreciated its mode of argument. They became respected immigrants. But they differed significantly. Matteo Ricci was accused by other Catholic missionaries, particularly the Franciscans, of being an "accommodationist," of not only appearing like his hosts but of disguising, even abandoning, the Christian message he had come to preach. Fletcher's foes, particularly Ramsey, accused him of the same strategy. They said he completely accepted the values of science and medicine and merely blessed them with his version of an ethical benediction. Ramsey chose to be Franciscan. He wanted to have a voice in the world of science and medicine but always a critical voice, stirring the conscience of decent people so dedicated to their work that they failed to grasp its implications. Yet even when he did that, he used the rhetoric of reason rather than faith. Faith colored his rhetoric less by doctrine than by (sometimes grandiloquent) enthusiasm. McCormick used that same rhetoric, shaping it into an Aristotelian mean between the extremes of acceptance and condemnation, occasionally pointing to the authoritative teaching of his church as a wise, if perhaps incomprehensible, caution.

It is important to recall that during the decade of bioethics' birth, Catholic and Protestant theologians were engaged in a broader endeavor. Within the major denominations, intense scholarly effort was directed toward the theoretical foundations of Christian ethics. As mentioned above, Ramsey was one of a group of Protestant theologians who were revising Christian ethics, moving it from what had become more an appeal to the heart toward a soundly based doctrinal, scriptural, and even philosophical discipline. Among Catholic theologians, a similar introspection was propelling a somewhat stale rationalistic moral theology into a more vital challenge to Christian life. These movements were to some extent ecumenical (the leading Catholic moral theologian Bernard Häring spent a year as a visiting professor at very Protestant Yale during my student days there). The common ecumenical question was "What makes Christian ethics different from secular or philosophical ethics?" However, the movement ran in different directions for Catholics and Protestants: the former sought to restore to moral theology the message of Scripture that had long been at the heart of Protestant ethics; the latter sought a place for natural reasoning and natural justice that had traditionally guided Catholic theologians. The theologians who crossed the frontier into bioethics came with these innovative ideas about ethics in their minds, ready to test them against the challenging moral problems of biomedical science and practice.

The place of religion in early bioethics was much larger than these three major figures. Return to Yale in the late 1960s. There Professor James Gustafson, who had himself reflected on the ethical and theological dimensions of the new sciences, particularly brain science, was training, unintentionally, the first cadre of bioethicists.[18] I was his student; in the same class were James Childress, LeRoy Walters, and Stanley Hauerwas. Childress remained a professor of Christian ethics but devoted his intellectual skills to bioethics. His scholarly work in bioethics is, with few exceptions, not marked by religious or theological perspectives. Walters became a bioethicist at the Kennedy Institute and contributed greatly to the ethics of genetics. It would be difficult to discern his theological ancestry. Hauerwas alone remained theologically faithful. He began to explore bioethics but found it too restrictive for his capacious mind and too secular for his Christian dedication. Catholic priests like Charles Curran, David Thomasma, Warren Reich, Thomas Shannon, Daniel Maguire, and George Kanoti entered the field. Curran, though remaining a Catholic priest and a theologian, was censured by the church for his liberalism. Reich, Thomasma, Shannon, Maguire, and Kanoti resigned from the priesthood, as did I, and crossed the frontiers into bioethics. It is possible to hear the accent of natural law in their contributions, but each spoke in their own voice. Episcopal ministers Harmon Smith and John Fletcher were early contributors. Smith's *Ethics and the New Medicine*[19] had the bad luck of being published in the same year as Ramsey's blockbuster, *Patient as Person*. Otherwise, Smith would have been the pioneer author. Although he was professor of religious ethics at Duke University, his analysis of the "new ethics" bears little mark of theology. He did not continue to contribute to bioethics. John Fletcher, also a moral theologian, made the full border crossing from seminary president to the assistant for bioethics to the director of the NIH Clinical Center. As he became a prominent bioethicist, his frequent publications and lectures were unmarked by theological argument or concepts. He resigned from the Episcopal ministry in the early 1990s.

Robert Veatch had a youthful ambition to become a Methodist medical missionary, but he followed a Riccian path. Shifting out of theological education into a Harvard doctoral path of his own design, he received, in 1971, the first Ph.D. in medical ethics. He was the first associate for ethics at the Hastings Center and later director of the Kennedy Institute for Bioethics. His contribution to bioethics has been enormous, yet, despite his interest in religion, his contribution has been from the beginning thoroughly secular. Danner Clouser, one of the most effective (and entertaining) early bioethicists was trained at a Lutheran seminary, but, apart from an early article explaining the meaning of "sanctity of life," he wrote no theological bioethics. Karen Lebacqz, a Harvard graduate in religious ethics, almost alone among the many early bioethicists in being theologically trained, has consistently woven theological concepts into her writings about bioethics.

Kenneth Vaux, a minister at the Institute of Religion at Texas Medical

Center, produced one of the earliest conferences on the topic of bioethics, Who Shall Live? With Fletcher and Ramsey and the prominent German Lutheran theologian Helmut Thielicke, who had been Vaux's teacher, it sounded a distinct theological note. Thielicke's keynote address saw the ethical problems of bioethics as "a manifestation of the half-light between creation and fall, between mankind as he was intended to be and as he presently is, standing in sinful contradiction to his intended destiny. . . . [T]here is an ambiguity about man's creativity." Despite this Lutheran eloquence, the theological contradiction between Creation and Fall was easily translated into a secular insight, rooted in psychoanalysis, cultural anthropology, and Enlightenment philosophy, about moral ambiguity.[20]

The Society for Health and Human Values reveals the ambiguous place of religion in bioethics. In 1965, the Committee on Medical Education and Theology was formed by a collaboration of the Methodist and Presbyterian churches to explore the religious ministry in medical education. Its goal was to counter the "depersonalization" of medical students and the "mechanistic way" in which medicine was being taught. This committee evolved into the Committee on Health and Human Values and, in 1969, into a "society" that consisted of ministers and medical educators. Several years later, it welcomed membership by subscription. Its enlarged membership brought an enlarged mission: how to incorporate humanities into medical education. The Institute on Human Values in Medicine became its educational arm. As the Society for Health and Human Values reached out, its earlier religious emphasis faded into the colors of medical humanities and ethics. This society became the principal place where bioethicists met, and it eventually assumed the function of their professional organization. It merged with several other groups in 1998 and changed its name to American Society for Bioethics and the Humanities. Beginning as a collectivity of ministers and theologians, it had evolved into a community of nondenominational, largely non-religiously affiliated bioethicists.

This history has been, up to this point, a Christian story. Judaism, like Roman Catholicism, has long had a body of scholarly reflection on matters of medicine and human life. The reflection follows the rabbinic style of moral analysis, which involves intricate analysis of biblical texts and commentary. Almost totally unknown to non-Jewish scholars until Immanuel Jacobovits published *Jewish Medical Ethics* in 1959, and almost impenetrable to those unfamiliar with the style, Jewish thought contains many insights relevant to bioethics.[21] Also, Jewish law exists for Jews, not for non-Jews, and though Jewish law has a version of "natural law," its teachings are not intended for the wider world. Yet the problems posed by contemporary medical technology and biomedical science are common to all who are patients and physicians, regardless of their faith. Several rabbis, J. David Bleich, Moshe Tendler, and David Feldman, with the collaboration of a physician, Fred Rosner, began to explore their tradition in light of the new problems.[22]

Two philosophers deeply immersed in the rabbinic tradition crossed the frontier into bioethics. Baruch Brody and David Freedman recognized the light that ancient tradition could shed on many questions. They drew from it selectively in order to engage in the larger bioethical conversations. They disengaged traditional arguments somewhat from their literary sources and elucidated their relevance for contemporary discussion. They converted the language of Jewish law into terms comprehensible to a general audience. In so doing, these scholars made their most significant contributions to bioethics by writing in a predominately secular mode.[23]

No Muslim or Buddhist or Hindu scholars crossed the frontiers into bioethics during its first decade. Indeed, in Islamic and Buddhist cultures, certain questions central to bioethics, such as extension of life by life-support technology and transplantation of organs, were beginning to appear. In Islam, a body of law relative to health and medicine has grown over the centuries, and Islamic scholars did issue opinions on some contemporary questions. There is not a similarly extensive tradition in Buddhism and Hinduism. Yet during the 1980s, bioethical discussions emerged in countries with Islamic, Buddhist, and Hindu cultures. Communication between American and European bioethicists and these cultures increased. Certain problems, such as an international commerce in organ transplantation and biomedical experimentation in developing nations, encouraged serious conversation. Transnational associations of bioethicists came into being. Islam, Buddhism, and Hinduism are present in modern bioethics, yet their translation across frontiers, religious and cultural, remains as yet unclear.

During the first two decades of bioethics, many scholars from outside the theological disciplines entered the conversation. Philosophers such as Hans Jonas, Samuel Gorovitz, Sissela Bok, and Dan Callahan, physicians such as Edmund Pellegrino, Willard Gaylin, Eric Cassel, lawyers such as Jay Katz, George Annas, and Alex Capron collaborated to create a field of questions and arguments that merited the name bioethics. The initial theologians moved easily into this collaboration and, as they did, lost their distinctive mode of discourse. Bioethics was not, and has never been, a unitary discipline. It is an amalgam of many modes of discovery and discourse.

This memoir about religion in bioethics concludes with several reflections. First, the maxim "Bioethics began in religion, but religion has faded from bioethics" requires some qualifications. Bioethics began with many persons of faith coming to the discussion of the questions. This does not mean that bioethics began in religion. Individuals from quite different denominational backgrounds with very different training addressed the issues. Almost all these participants employed ethical methods that allowed them to analyze moral problems in terms and with concepts that were not explicitly theological or denominational. Almost all of them did so largely because of the audiences that they addressed. Many of them might begin with a reminder of some theological doctrine that had shaped their thinking or that they felt might be powerfully impressive even to a secular audience, but those theological doctrine were almost never carried through the sustained argument for their position. The explicit natural law theories of the Catholic participants and the implicit use of natural law by some of the Protestant participants made this possible.

The taste for casuistry, which allowed foundational issues to be suspended, also contributed.

A second reflection bears on the apparent revival of interest in religion. As I said at the beginning of this essay, the other authors in this book will explore whether and why such a revival is taking place. It is not my task to do so. Yet I may, at least, wonder about the whether and the why. If there is such a revival, it may be in response to the border crossing of the early decades. Early religious bioethicists followed the Riccian method: they dispensed with their outward religious appearance in order to make themselves welcome and comprehensible to the secular world.

Certainly, within the first decade of its existence, bioethics looked very much as Ricci did after his first few years in China. It had taken off its ministerial robes. As he had donned the garb of the Confucian scholar, ready to engage in informed, reasonable discussion with any willing conversationalist, so they put on the intellectual style of secular conversation. A common style of speech aids this conversation. Questions are defined in similar terms by most participants; arguments and counterarguments run along familiar lines. This has the advantage of gathering many conversationalists. It allows arcane issues to be debated by a wide audience and for policies to be formulated for wide communities. This Riccian tactic may be necessary for any successful crossing of frontiers. It has, in my eyes, been remarkably successful in bioethics. A wide world of discourse has been opened; comprehensible language, spoken with many accents, makes debate possible.

Ricci, however, wondered at the end of his own career whether he had acted rightly. He realized that, despite his preeminence, he had converted few Mandarins to Catholicism. When chided on this, he answered, "We are not in China to reap or even sow, but simply to clear the forest." It may be that the early border-crossing bioethicists did the same: they cleared the forest for a conversation between science and society that might not otherwise have taken place. However, the conversation was intended to be about ethics; just as Ricci intended his conversation to be covertly about the gospel. As the conversation went on, some bioethicists might realize that secular ethics stands on weak foundations. Casuistry is good as far as it goes, but it does not go to deep foundations. The assumed deep foundations of natural law are hard to find amid the pluralistic assumptions of postmodern thought. So in the search for an end to an argument, a terminus to discussion, a vision of the solidity of religion may summon. As I read the publication of President Bush's Council on Bioethics, *Monitoring Stem Cell Research*, with its balanced display of arguments pro and con for each major point, I see a sample of secular bioethics. No argument can be driven to a resounding conclusion. But I also glimpse a desire to come to such a conclusion, hindered by the secular (and, for public policy, a constitutional) prohibition against invoking a religiously based premise. Chapter 3 of that book, "Ethical and Policy Developments," concludes: "As we have seen, strong and powerfully argued views have been presented on various sides of each of these questions. For now, neither side to the debate seems close to fully persuading the other of the truth it thinks it sees."[24]

Unquestionably, a religiously based presentation of the same questions could close the debate, although it might not be able to "fully persuade the other." *The Declaration on the Production and the Scientific and Therapeutic Use of Human Embryonic Stem Cells,*" issued by the Vatican Academy of Life Sciences, does not display pro-and-con arguments. It goes straight to the point: an unequivocal condemnation of stem cell research.[25] Might not many a bioethicist, frustrated by the shifting sands of casuistic argumentation and polite conversation about pro and con, rejoice to find such certitude? It may be time for a prophet to appear and disrupt the conversation. Perhaps that prophet will talk the strange tongues of faith, tongues that could, in the biblical story of Pentecost, be understood by persons from every nation.

NOTES

1. Jonathan Spence, *The Memory Palace of Matteo Ricci* (New York: Viking Press, 1984).

2. Albert R. Jonsen, *The Birth of Bioethics* (New York: Oxford University Press, 1998).

3. Van Rensselaer Potter, "Bioethics: The Science of Survival," *Perspectives in Biology and Medicine* 14 (1970): 127–153; *Bioethics: Bridge to the Future* (Englewood Cliffs, N.J.: Prentice-Hall, 1971).

4. Paul Ramsey, *The Patient as Person* (New Haven, Conn.: Yale University Press, 1970).

5. Daniel Callahan, "Bioethics as a Discipline," *Hastings Center Studies* 1 (1973): 66–73.

6. Warren T. Reich, "The Word 'Bioethics': Its Birth and the Legacies of Those Who Shaped Its Meaning," *Kennedy Institute of Ethics Journal* 4 (1994): 319–336.

7. Albert R. Jonsen and Stephen E. Toulmin, *The Abuse of Casuistry: A History of Moral Reasoning* (Berkeley: University of California Press, 1987).

8. Richard A. McCormick, *How Brave a New World? Dilemmas in Bioethics* (Garden City, N.Y.: Doubleday, 1981).

9. Richard A. McCormick, "To Save or Let Die," *Journal of the American Medical Association* 229 (1974): 172–177.

10. Joseph Fletcher, *Morals and Medicine. The Moral Problems of: the Patient's Right to Know the Truth, Contraception, Artificial Insemination, Sterilization and Euthanasia* (Princeton, N.J.: Princeton University Press, 1954).

11. Joseph Fletcher, *Situation Ethics: The New Morality* (Philadelphia: Westminster Press, 1966).

12. Joseph Fletcher, *The Ethics of Genetic Control: Ending Reproductive Roulette* (Garden City, N.Y.: Doubleday, 1974).

13. Paul Ramsey, *Basic Christian Ethics* (New York: Charles Scribner's Sons, 1950).

14. Paul Ramsey, *Nine Modern Moralists* (New York: Prentice-Hall, 1962).

15. Ramsey, *Patient as Person.*

16. Ibid., xlvi, 1.

17. Allan Verhay and Stephen Lammers, eds., *Theological Voices in Medical Ethics* (Grand Rapids, Mich.: Eerdmans, 1993).

18. James Gustafson, *The Contributions of Theology to Medical Ethics* (Milwaukee: Marquette University Press, 1975).

19. Harmon Smith, *Ethics and the New Medicine* (Nashville: Abington Press, 1970).

20. Kenneth Vaux, ed., *Who Shall Live? Medicine, Technology, and Ethics* (Philadelphia: Fortress Press, 1970).

21. Immanuel Jakobovits, *Jewish Medical Ethics: A Comparative and Historical Study of the Jewish Religious Attitude to Medicine and Its Practice* (New York: Bloch, 1959).

22. J. David Bleich and Fred Rosner, *Jewish Bioethics* (New York: Yeshiva University Press, 1979).

23. Baruch Brody, *Abortion and the Sanctity of Life* (Cambridge: MIT Press, 1975).

24. *Monitoring Stem Cell Research. A Report of the President's Council on Bioethics.* (Washington, D.C., 2004), p. 97.

25. Pontifical Academy for Life Sciences, *The Declaration on the Production and the Scientific and Therapeutic Use of Human Embryonic Stem Cells* (Vatican City, 2000).

2

Theology's Role in Public Bioethics

Lisa Sowle Cahill

Theology and the Public Sphere: A Paradigm Shift

For at least two decades, the role of theology in public matters has been governed by what might be termed a "liberal consensus." This consensus, shared by policymakers, theologians, philosophers, and the public, has two parts. First, the preeminent criteria of law and public policy are individual liberties and rights. Second, the only appropriate "public" language in which to justify, qualify, and reconcile liberties and rights is neutral, secular, and rational. By and large, theologians have not responded to this consensus by challenging it, but by arguing about how to define their own role in relation to it. Many theologians have tried to adopt the terms of the public language when arguing about public matters, for example abortion, infertility therapies, euthanasia, or health care reform. A significant number of others urge fellow theologians to stay away from "secular bioethics" for two reasons. The first is that persons of faith would never be able to advocate for their values and have an impact in the secular public realm. The second is that the very attempt to do so dilutes distinctly religious values and identities, so that they are disabled from producing religiously authentic behavior on biomedical issues, even with faith communities.

The thesis of this chapter is that such a framing of the issues is outmoded. To begin with, the "secular" sphere is not neutral, since all participants inevitably come from communities of identity, and continually participate in many such communities. Therefore, it is appropriate to use religious narratives and language, or those of any moral tradition (which includes liberalism), as long as they are not propounded dogmatically or in a way that undermines democratic process and participatory politics. Moreover, the public sphere typically has been envisioned by both joiners and resisters as a sphere of "discourse," where the emphasis is on "language," "arguments," and "rationality." This is a false or at least insufficient depiction of what really goes on in the process of shaping and renegotiating the norms, practices, and institutions through which persons and groups interact with one another in any society, even a pluralistic and democratic one.

Language always is embedded in and reflects the practices in which the participants engage; and ultimately, the "language" of public discourse aims to replace, change, or initiate practices. Therefore, people engage one another in the public sphere not only with words but with action, especially collective action. That which is contested and negotiated in the public sphere is not primarily speech but the social arrangements represented by speech. "Public debate" is not at bottom about theories, but about patterns of interaction through which power is distributed and goods accessed. Language and speech address these patterns in multiple ways, not only by the force of argument. Equally if not more important to social debate are the emotions, dispositions, and imaginative construals of the world that public language evokes, and by means of which audiences are persuaded to enact different practices, and to ratify and normalize them by means of laws, policies, and regulations.

Election 2004: A Case in Point

The 2004 U.S. presidential election brought home the fact that "the liberal consensus" had missed the boat. "Liberals," arguing publicly and in the national media about matters of national importance, failed to elect their candidate, U.S. Sen. John Kerry, a Democrat from Massachusetts. This was despite the fact that polls before and after elections showed that most Americans agreed with the Kerry on the need for more international cooperation on the war in Iraq, on the need for health care reform, and on the need for a progressive tax policy that favored the rich less and was fairer to the middle class. Incumbent President George W. Bush, a Republican, was against such policies, even though they would have benefited the majority of voters. In an election postmortem, Fordham sociologist James Kelly remarked, "Given the large agreements with domestic issues of a concern for poverty, and the great preference expressed for cooperation with international organizations to maintain peace, the Kerry loss, at the very least, is a statistical bafflement."[1]

A key part of the solution to the puzzle is the way the Bush team exploited religious identity and participation in favor of its political goals. Bush had widespread religious support, and spoke in unabashedly religious terms about his values: freedom, free enterprise (including the for-profit health-care industry), a strong military, the sanctity of the nuclear family, rejection of gay marriage, and opposition to abortion and stem cell research. An important part of his campaign, masterminded by Karl Rove, was to solicit grassroots support through churches and religious organizations throughout the country. Bush strategists built a coalition of social conservatives among evangelicals, Catholics, Jews, Hispanics, and African Americans, all of whom felt that liberals and popular culture had disparaged and trivialized their religious faith. In each of these groups, Bush had a better showing than he had enjoyed four years previously.[2]

Bush's opponent, John Kerry, advocated domestic policies that would have benefited more voters. He proposed international policies that more people endorsed, especially people of faith. Yet Kerry expressed his own faith reluctantly and awkwardly. While his campaign team tried to get poor and minority voters to the polls, they did relatively little campaigning at the grassroots level in the churches, synagogues, and mosques. For instance, Kerry invoked Catholic social justice teaching in a speech or two reported in the national media, but did little to counteract at the local level the way the Catholic bishops were catering to pro-life, antigay demands by circulating in parishes and through diocesan mailings materials favoring the Republican candidate, and by threatening to excommunicate Kerry. Unlike Bush, Kerry did not take his case to "the people," using community outreach to religious groups throughout the United States.

Moreover, following a long-standing trend in liberal and progressive politics, Kerry campaigners were reticent about speaking in language that referenced transcendent values or invoked an ultimate worldview. Instead, they posed their goals in "reasonable" terms that supposedly all voters could understand and endorse. In so doing they cut off the higher horizon that truly persuades and motivates people. Stephen Hart criticizes liberal and progressive political actors for using "constrained" discourse. They tend to shy away from the "life-affirming values found in religious communities," which most community organizers, for instance, understand to be "the heart of the process."[3] It is sacredness, transcendence, and passion—the elements of "expansive" discourse—that engage people even when they are interacting in the public, political sphere.[4]

Speaking in terms of bioethics, the 2004 election result resulted in an administration that opposed stem cell research and universal health coverage but favored business interests that resulted ultimately in the promotion of stem cell research for profit. These same interests militate against adequate health care for the poor and much of the middle class. The poor and middle class also will not be able to afford stem cell therapies, should the extravagant promises about their potential ever come to fruition. Obviously, these consequences are not the only possible outcome of "religious" values, nor would they be identified by all believers as an acceptable representation of their faith. As Kelly notes, all religious traditions have an important commitment to the welfare of the poor, and the limitation of the prerogatives of the rich. At least half of U.S. voters believe government should do more to fight hunger and poverty, even if it means raising taxes on the affluent.[5]

Theological Bioethics in Public—A Contested Role

When the modern field of bioethics first emerged in the 1960s, several important theologians shaped the new discipline and brought it public recognition and influence. James Gustafson, Paul Ramsey, Richard McCormick, John Fletcher, Karen Lebacqz, David Bleich, and Fred Rosner may be named, among others. Religiously grounded thinkers were active in the formation of bioethics institutes and publications, like the Institute for Society, Ethics, and the Life Sciences, and its journal, *The Hastings Center Report*. Their views were welcome in scientific venues, such as medical journals and medical schools. Theologians even served on the National Commission for the Protection of Human Subjects, established by Congress in 1974. These theologians seemed to use different kinds of arguments for different audiences, but they were not reticent in making their theological premises evident and in displaying them publicly for the appeal they might have to others of similar or compatible convictions. For instance, Gustafson wrote that an attitude of self-criticism because of human sinfulness and finitude was a "contribution of theology to medical ethics";[6] Ramsey construed obligations to patients in terms of covenant fidelity and love, even though he wanted to address "the widest possible audience";[7] and Richard McCormick published an article on care for newborns in the *Journal of the American Medical Association*, alluding to a "higher, more important good" than life, and citing Pope Pius XII.[8]

Critics of theological participation in public debates have been numerous in more recent years. Some believe that public debate ought to occur on "neutral" ground, and reject theological interventions as attempts to impose religious dogma on those of differing convictions. Addressing the issue of stem cell research, political philosopher William Galston outlines differences between Catholics and Jews. Galston worries that "theological problems" may "spill over into politics": "Conflicting views on divisive issues of law and policy can rest on religious differences, rooted in what differing faiths regard as authoritative 'revealed truth' that reason cannot adjudicate."[9] Such fears can be allayed if theologians are willing to agree that even positions inspired by religious commitment have to be "translated" into moral terms that can be accepted by all in order to have public viability. In other words, they have to sink or swim on the basis of their appeal to secular thinkers and philosophers. In Galston's own view, in order "to justify coercive public law across the boundary of diverse faith communities, only arguments that do not rely, explicitly or tacitly, on disputed theological propositions count as valid reasons for public law to forbid a practice."[10]

But some theologians do not believe that the best insights of religious traditions can be captured in language designed to appeal to the lowest common moral denominator, nor, indeed, that such translations can result in any significant influence for theology in the public realm. Instead, they assert, theologians ought to stick to their own convictions and remain unabashedly theological in orientation and expression. Perhaps they need to accept the fact that although they can shape bioethics in their own faith communities, their chance of gaining a voice in an essentially hostile secular environment is next to nil. Stephen Lammers describes this perspective, which he admits has some appeal, in the following terms:

> The claim here would be that it is a piece of foolishness for the churches to ask to be included in conversations in which their message will inevitably be distorted. Better to stand on the edges and witness to what they know to be true than to try to influence the larger society. When religious voices move to the center, they become co-opted by others who have no interest in religion and who use religion for their own purposes. . . . Marginalization gives the church freedom to do its business without worrying about how it will be received by the larger culture. From that vantage point, the church could critique a health care system and a profession gone seriously astray.[11]

Writing on stem cells and cloning, theologian Brent Waters resists the idea that theologians must acquiesce to "a bland or neutral public vocabulary," based on "a set of minimalist and largely unspoken values," in order to "deflect and neutralize potential conflict."[12] He is convinced that the best course for theologians is to "express in as clear and forthright a manner as possible the principal beliefs, convictions, and claims that inform their moral assessments."[13]

Complementary Modes of Discourse

Replying to the division between theological ethicists who favor public discourse and those who believe that theology's distinctive voice and agenda should be better protected, James Gustafson proposed, in the late '80s, a model for accommodating more and less distinctive types of speech in different contexts. His point was that different styles are appropriate on different occasions.

Gustafson identified four varieties of moral discourse in which theology participates: ethical, policy, prophetic, and narrative.[14] The worldviews and values that constitute particular religious identities are given most direct expression in narrative and prophetic discourse. Narratives shape communities and their members, while prophesy both recalls members to their highest commitments and speaks critically to the larger society on behalf of those commitments. "Narratives function to sustain the particular moral identity of a religious (or secular) community by rehearsing its history and traditional meanings, as these are portrayed in Scripture and other sources."[15] Narratives shape the ethos of a community and shape the moral character of participants so that they construe the world and envision appropriate action in ways that conform to the narrative. They do this not primarily by forming "concepts" and "ideas," but by construing and embodying a worldview that is constituted not only by "stories" told, but by emotions evoked, dispositions shaped, and practices engaged.

Prophetic discourse prioritizes certain values over others, especially in view of social situations that threaten core values, and attempts to see that these values are embodied in social practices and institutions. Prophetic discourse "sometimes uses narratives to make prophetic points."[16] Though their utopia is ultimately eschatological, prophets hold up a vision of a more equitable society characterized by virtues of solidarity, compassion, and justice inspired by love of God and neighbor. Narratives that convey these points include biblical accounts and stories, such as the ancient Israelite mandate to care for the widow and orphan (Isaiah 10:1-2), the Gospel of Matthew's parable of judgment (chap. 25), or Luke's story of the Good Samaritan (chap. 10). Like narrative, prophecy works by challenging the imaginative horizon of its audience more than by constructing logical rationales or arguments. This is not to say reflective analysis is not important as a test of the moral adequacy of images, stories, and moral demands.

By means of both prophetic and narrative discourse, theology engages the emotions and the imagination to illuminate what is at stake in a certain kind of moral choice or way of life. Through prophesy and narrative, theology helps reorient the worldviews of persons and communities and forms them in the virtues that will dispose them to act on their ethical understandings and conclusions. By recalling and living within the story of Yahweh's liberation of the people from bondage, or the sacrifice of Christ on the cross, a religiously and theologically informed people will become better prepared to take action on behalf of those without health care or dying of AIDS. Narrative and prophecy begin in practices, reinforce or challenge those practices, and hold up ideal practices that audiences are to cultivate.

According to Gustafson, the types of discourse that bring one's values and worldview down to the concrete level are ethical and policy discourse. Ethical discourse helps "to decide how one ought to act in particular circumstances."[17] It does so by linking moral justification to a basic theory of morality focused on such concepts as rights, duties, obligations, and justice, rather than distinctively religious narratives. In a theological theory, these concepts will be interpreted in relation to a concept of God and God's purposes or claims regarding humanity. Ethical discourse has a necessary reflective and deliberative component. At the same time, it too will always be embedded in a context in which certain issues or problems been identified for analysis. Moreover, "ethics" takes place within certain more or less formal practices with their own rules and limits, such as scholarly publications, academic conferences, college classrooms, or national commissions.

Policy discourse envisions decisions about what kinds of general practices, institutions, and laws should guide social behavior. Once again, a social context, along with existing institutions and practices, instigates a policy inquiry. Compared with ethical discourse, however, policy discourse must accommodate more overtly and extensively the conflicts and limitations inherent in any particular situation of decision, as well as to the fact that people from different moral traditions must resolve policy dilemmas together. "The 'ought' questions are answered within possibilities and limitations of what resources exist or can be accumulated or organized."[18] Theology can bring to policy discourse a sense that all human enterprises are relative and are marked by finitude and sinfulness, and a commitment to prioritize and defend some basic values, such as the value of human life, the dignity of every person, and the obligation to advocate for those who are most vulnerable and those who suffer most.

One might argue, as William Galston implies, that there should be a fairly clear line between prophesy and narrative, which are appropriate to guide convictions and behavior within religious communities, and policy based on publicly available ethics, which has to operate fairly and effectively across religious boundaries. Or one might argue, as Stephen Lammers implies, that theologians should stay away from policy and politics, because investment in the requisite kinds of discourse will dilute what is most important to a religious way of life.

In my view, neither analysis adequately envisions the potential role of religious communities and theologies in democratic politics. "Discourse" is an insufficient paradigm to capture the process of moral discernment, action, and change within communities, or within the public sphere. Religious communities are present and active in many additional dimensions of public life. As we have seen, Gustafson's descriptions of the modes of discourse actually imply more than speech, argument, verbal give-and-take, and rhetorical persuasion. Practices are constitutive sites of moral insight, understanding, emotional formation, socialization, motivation, behavioral training, and commitment. This need not imply either that moral argument is completely relative to those practices or that the discourse that emerges will be intelligible only to those sharing the practices of distinctive communities of faith or belief. Social practices, even religious ones—especially in democratic societies—are not locations in which participants are walled off from other communities in which they participate, or from other participants in the same practice whose identities are partly constituted by different practices. In fact, religious groups and organizations are active participants in civil society, and partner with many other kinds of entities to fulfill their public roles.[19]

Theology and "Public" Interaction

Brent Waters is correct when he observes that "public life" is not a neutral sphere beyond any particular traditions, but a complex reality made up of many overlapping types of association, and that any individual citizen will participate in many of these types. Public life takes place in all the institutions and relationships that make up civil society, such as "families, religious communities, charitable organizations, corporations and the like." One could add education systems; neighborhood associations; advocacy groups; clubs and sports teams;

political parties; local, state, and federal government; and more. It is within all of these that "virtues and values are formed which either serve us well or badly in forming the contours of our common, public life."[20]

Not only do most people belong to many such organizations, the associations themselves overlap and are interdependent components of society and the "public." Their value systems are not completely separate. Likewise, there is no strict or clear separation between a religious tradition and the realm of citizenship, or between medical professions and corporations, or between public policy on stem cells and political philosophies, or between the U.S. economic system of democratic capitalism and the altruistic norms that may guide a faith-based social service agency. "Value traditions" and convictions or background assumptions about "ultimate meaning" pervade all of these realms and interact together in all social life, including bioethics.

For example, within bioethics, rights language comes from Western political and constitutional traditions; cost-benefit language comes from market economics; the research imperative comes from Enlightenment science; and the call for scientific knowledge to be used for human benefit and the relief of suffering owes much to modern evolutionary views of society as well as modern democracy. The "preferential option for the poor" comes from religious traditions, is reflected in philosophical traditions about equal respect and solidarity, can be backed up by democratic politics, and has some roots in Karl Marx's critique of industrial capitalism, and others in Scripture. Even religiously indebted images such as "care for the poor" or "we are all children of God" can stimulate the imaginations of those from diverse traditions so that common ground can be amplified. To the degree that any one image, story, moral principle, or concrete moral analysis can appeal to a variety of values and commitments, it can have a chance to influence public life by raising the profile of one pattern of associational behavior over another. For instance, when reformers call for universal access to health care over our present market-based system, they are appealing to fellow citizens to prioritize solidaristic experiences of social life over those based on capitalism and class hierarchies, and they can use many rhetorical and symbolic incentives to do this.

Theological voices should not be ruled out of court simply because they emerge from traditions that are not those of all other participants in civil society. Even explicitly theological language and religious symbols or stories (like creation in the image of God, the story of the Fall, the healings performed by Jesus, the parable of the Good Samaritan, the ideal of covenant community) can evoke patterns of individual existence and social life that are shared, abhorred, or admired in interreligious or nonreligious associations. Examples are the universal human need for health and vulnerability to illness; the inevitability of death; the reality of social exploitation; democratic political traditions of equality, respect, and fairness; and multiple other religious and moral traditions of other-concern and altruism.

The ways that theology moves into the realm of public bioethics are extremely complex. As we have seen, "theology" can mean either references to distinctive and particular religious symbols and narratives or more general claims generated by those narratives; it can be directed at members of a religious community specifically, or it can aim at a more inclusive audience; it can aim to shape a worldview, or it can address concrete problems in medicine and research. Moreover, "theology" does not exist in the abstract or as a field of knowledge detached from the lives and commitments of its practitioners. Theologians participate in many circles of expression and influence, including teaching, academic and popular publishing, media commentary, conferences (theological and interdisciplinary, national and international), and membership on the bodies and committees that produce the "official" positions and teachings of religious traditions and denominations. Theology is mediated to the public in a variety of ways, including the representative positions of institutional religious bodies; pastors, teachers, and congregations; religiously sponsored educational systems; activist organizations and movements; and representation on public commissions. Theological language, and religious stories and images, can sometimes effectively move into public settings—not to dominate, alienate, or condemn, but to stimulate the emotions and imaginations of discussion partners, as they seek to move together toward better understanding of the human condition and more humane, just, and beneficent practices and policies of biomedicine.

Argument and Emotion in Public Ethics

Debates about whether it is appropriate for theology to speak in the public sphere often seem to assume that such "speech" will take the form of intellectual premises, propositions, and arguments. But arguments are conveyed by rhetoric, are supported by narratives, and are embedded in or confront specific practical arrangements. Hence they reach more than the intellect and achieve more than understanding. They also form the moral affections or emotions that motivate the will and even influence understanding. Today there is a large and growing literature on the role of the emotions in moral cognition. Rhetoric is said to "manipulate" emotion when it evokes emotional responses in order to motivate an audience to take unreflective action in the direction at which the rhetoric aims. Yet well-integrated emotions are an important part of morality and ethics. The emotions are essential to moral discernment and action. This is a fact that "liberal" and "neutral" discourse misses or at least occludes, but which religious ethics and activism recognize.

　　Theologians have argued,[21] for instance, that the cultivation of emotions like compassion is part of what it means to live a virtuous life, and that emotions help guide our desires and wills toward morally worthy aims and actions. Indeed, it is wrong to say that we first "know" the good, and then "will" it; our emotional response to good and evil and our corresponding desire for the good help make it possible to recognize and know the good intellectually. Conversely, we can avoid knowing a good to which we are not attracted and for which we have no desire. Therefore, images and stories that appeal to the imagination are important not only in moral formation, but also in moral knowledge. Intellectual recognition of a value, good action, or good practice can be impeded by competing and entrenched values and practices, whose hegemony is enabled by intellectual rationalizations that shore up their persuasiveness to those who gain from them or who are threatened by change. Debate at the intellectual level may not succeed in widening the established worldview. But an appeal to the emotions through story or symbol can sometimes provoke a new opening or a new insight, one that widens horizons, stimulates desires for a different ordering of values, and enables the intellect to recognize a different practical good. Intellectual arguments about morality make more sense once one is able to imagine and even to be attracted to a novel constellation of values, one in which goods and relationships are placed differently than in the arrangement to which one is accustomed and which has until now seemed most "logical."

A philosopher who has made major contributions to a theory of the role of the emotions in normative ethics is Martha Nussbaum. According to Nussbaum, emotions are "intelligent responses to the perceptions of value" and "part and parcel of the system of ethical reasoning."[22] Nussbaum attends particularly to the importance of compassion, an emotion that can "hook our imaginations to the good of others and to make them the object of our intense care."[23] She believes that appropriate cultivation of the emotion of compassion is necessary to "good citizenship," and that compassion, "the ability to participate in the experiences of others and to share in their suffering," should be publicly supported and taught.[24] Nussbaum recommends the arts as one way to do this. Works of art are, of course, culturally specific and are situated within particular traditions not only of artistic creation, but of social, moral, and religious practices and beliefs. Nonetheless, art can educate for compassionate membership in the public order, presumably even when the "public" or the realm of citizenship is pluralistic.

Religious narratives and images can serve a similar function. Moreover, accessing moral knowledge through the emotions highlights human interdependence, for emotions are essentially responses to persons, objects, and states to which the self is in relation. Margaret Farley notes that Judaism, Christianity, and Islam all "raise up compassion for those in need as a requirement for the human community and a command of God. . . . In each of these traditions the recording and retelling of stories and teachings have been aimed at awakening in hearers what the narratives and instructions advocate and depict."[25] Christian religious narratives, urging love of neighbor, humility before God, repentance for sin, and unity in the "body of Christ," can help form the emotion of compassion, and remind Christians and citizens that interdependence is part of the human moral condition.

Reproductive Technologies: A Case Study

One biomedical problem that has been around since the birth of bioethics is no less contentious today: reproductive technologies. At first focused on the birth of Louise Brown through in vitro fertilization in 1978, this area of biomedical debate moved to artificial insemination by donor, to surrogate motherhood and ovum donation, and most recently to reproductive cloning for otherwise infertile couples. A related area is therapeutic cloning for stem cell research. Theologians have been involved all along the spectrum, as has the *magisterium* (teaching authority) of the Roman Catholic Church. A brief review of some important contributors will make it clear that theologians from the beginning used religious symbols in advancing their views, though they (both Protestants and Catholics) also tended to employ more "tradition-neutral" language when addressing expressly "public" policy-making bodies. Both before and after the birth of Louise Brown, Paul Ramsey and Richard McCormick took on the problematic ethics of the creation of "test tube babies." Their theological resources were somewhat different, but their conclusions were similar. Both also interfaced with cultural and philosophical understandings of ethics itself and of procreation, borrowing some elements while subjecting others to criticism. Both aimed to influence a "public" and policy-oriented as well as a Christian audience.

Ramsey draws upon biblically derived covenant language, and especially an interpretation of the Creation stories refracted through Christian tradition and the Gospel of John. He tends to paraphrase rather than to quote the Bible directly, and he is not particularly concerned about what the narratives might have meant in their original contexts. Rather, he is searching for images that have defined the Christian understanding of procreation through the centuries and can help mold a wise and respectful use of medically assisted procreation today. For instance, in a proactive treatment of the ethics of cloning, he states:

> God created nothing apart from His love, and without the divine
> love was not anything made that was made (John 1). Neither should
> there be among men and women, whose man-womanhood (and not
> their minds or wills only) is in the image of God, any love-making
> set out of the context of responsibility for *pro*creation or any begetting apart from the sphere of human love and responsiveness. Thus
> is our man-womanhood created in covenant and for covenant—the
> covenant of marriage and the covenant of parenthood.[26]

For Ramsey, conception should take place only as a result of the embodied union of a man and a woman, a union expressing their mutual love and commitment, extended to the child-to-be. He was willing to accept the artificial insemination of a woman with her husband's sperm, but believed that techniques going further than that violated the embodied nature of human procreation or its role as an expression of love, or both. "To put radically asunder what God joined together in parenthood when He made love procreative, to procreate from beyond the sphere of responsible procreation (by definition, marriage), means a refusal of the image of God's creation in our own."[27]

In testimony given to the British government on *in vitro fertilization*, Ramsey's conclusions are equally definite but, though he does refer to the writings of the Christian author C. S. Lewis, his language is not overtly theological. On using artificial insemination to create a pregnancy in a surrogate mother, he predicts "objective results in promoting self-violation, further assaults upon the natural foundations of the integrity of the marriage relation, and new ways toward the manufacture of children."[28]

In 1978 and 1979, Richard McCormick also addressed in vitro fertilization and the use of donor gametes, as well as the moral treatment of embryos.[29] McCormick reviews other theological viewpoints on these matters, focusing especially on the birth of Louise Brown. He surveys the work of Paul Ramsey as well as of official Roman Catholic teaching, which had consistently ruled out any experimentation on or with embryos, along with any innovations in the reproductive process involving third parties outside a marriage and mas-turbation to acquire sperm for insemination, even from the husband of the woman to be inseminated. McCormick expresses agreement with what was the majority consensus of the time, that AID is morally wrong because it "sep-arates procreation from marriage, or the procreative sphere from the sphere of marital love, in a way that is either violative of the marriage covenant or likely to be destructive of it and the family."[30] On similar grounds, he accepts in vitro fertilization, but only if the gametes of wife and husband are used.[31]

McCormick draws on what he considers to be a human understanding of the meanings of marriage and parenthood, as well as on the "Christian con-viction that the same sexual love that generates ought to become *in principle* the parental love that nurtures." However, he acknowledges (following theo-logian Karl Rahner) that there is a certain "nondiscursive element" in moral reasoning that is important in making a final judgment in concrete questions. In other words, he does not claim to have conclusively "proven" on the basis of either theological or humanistic (natural law) arguments that there is only one acceptable solution to the problems he poses. Rather, evidence can be pulled from many sources, with the ultimate judgment dependent on the worldview of the judge, and on an integral grasp of values and goods that cannot be reduced to "analytic reasoning."[32]

In 1987, the Vatican Congregation for the Doctrine of the Faith published a document on reproductive technologies, *Donum vitae*.[33] This document is typical of official Catholic teaching on bioethics, in that it aims to address both a religious audience and public policy. It begins with references to the creation of "man" in God's image, to the redemption of fallen humanity by Christ, to the gospel of salvation as revealing the true dignity of the person, and to the responsibility of the Church to teach about morality and to make judgments about science and technology. Past teachings of the Church itself are also im-portant. According to *Donum vitae*, no methods of conception are legitimate that circumvent sexual intercourse between a married woman and man, who together becomes parents of a child. In addition, although it is conceded that the decision when personhood begins is a philosophical (not scientific) matter that has not been definitively settled by the Church, embryos should be given the benefit of the doubt and treated as persons.[34]

The ultimate aim is not only to influence Catholic belief and practice, but to have an impact on public policy and civil legislation. The action of public authorities with regard to the new reproductive technologies must be guided by "rational principles" and the "common good," "fundamental rights," and "the promotion of peace and public morality."[35] Therefore, the Vatican document defines as "fundamental rights" both "every human being's right to life and physical integrity from the moment of conception until death," and "the rights of the family and of marriage as an institution and, in this area, the child's right to be conceived, brought into the world and brought up by his parents."[36] The authors of the document evidently do not regard religious arguments as necessary to confirm this conclusion though they have in fact utilized appeals to religious symbols to create the context in which this final claim is made. They believe that most new reproductive technologies violate universal human nature and family relationships, and that any reasonable person and all legitimate governments should be able to discern that this is so.

Many contemporary readers will discern instead that neither the claims of Ramsey nor of the Vatican are "clinched" by the arguments they offer. Both raise legitimate concerns, as does McCormick, about the ideal nature of parenthood in marriage. Yet they have not demonstrated conclusively that only one answer to the problems raised by birth technologies is persuasive and acceptable. McCormick is right that more goes into the creation of moral convictions than "rational" arguments, and that arguments that may appear rational often owe a large debt to premises that can be questioned. An important factor in the persuasiveness of an argument offered is the ability of the advocate to address interlocutors on the basis of shared social situations, practices, or problems, in which an analysis "makes sense" because it corresponds to the values the practices instantiate—or to threats posed by practices that contravene shared values.

As if to underline this point, subsequent authors, including theologians, have questioned whether the bond between the "spheres" of love and biological cooperation for procreation was as tight as these early analyses made it seem. Paul Lauritzen, a Catholic theologian, defends donor insemination (and by extension other donor methods) on the basis that the love of a couple for a child is paramount, even if there is an asymmetry in their biological relation to it.[37] Lauritzen writes from a cultural situation in which many Christians have resorted to infertility therapies to build families, and from a time in which such procedures are increasingly well-accepted. From a Protestant and more biblical side, Ted Peters reappropriates the creation symbol to argue not that humans are limited in their authority over birth by God's design, but that they are "co-creators" with God, whose freedom permits and even requires them to explore and invent. "As created co-creators, we engage in creating, and this includes sponsoring the birth of new children . . . whether the child is conceived through sexual intercourse or carefully designed through genetic selection and engineering."[38]

A Catholic feminist theologian, Maura Ryan (to be discussed further below), pulls back somewhat, giving more weight to the use of reproductive technologies by committed couples to remedy infertility (usually of a committed heterosexual couple). She gives concerns about social justice a more central role.[39] The "Christian message" for our culture seems clearly to back a social justice approach to biomedicine. As Karen Lebacqz states, the "first thing" theology brings to policy discourse is "justice as a crucial category," assessed in terms of "the plight of the poor" and accompanied by "a willingness to let go of the landscape as we know it in order to permit justice to be done."[40] This means that an analysis of reproductive technologies must go beyond the decisions and relations of involved spouses, parents, donors, and children. It must look at social conditions and effects, broadening the scope of vision beyond individuals and couples that have access to medically assisted reproduction.

The earlier, perhaps more prevalent, concerns about protection of embryos and children, and concerns about instrumentalizing and commodifying procreation and human life, can also be interpreted as deriving from concerns about just relationships in society and about the danger of instituting practices that would help create a social ethos in which not all are treated fairly and with dignity. Recently, however, theologians have begun to accentuate economic justice, and the way in which control of health care and treatment resources are allocated according to economic status, social class, race, and gender.

An interesting example of a narratively informed and practice-directed prophetic use of discourse in public bioethics is the effort of Pope John Paul II to expand moral awareness in areas of reproduction beyond the rights of the embryo. In the summer of 2001, President George Bush met with John Paul II, just as the president was preparing to announce a policy on the federal funding of research using stem cells taken from embryos. The pope's remarks rejecting the destruction of embryos for research were widely cited. Less noted, however, were the pope's exhortations on the same occasion about social justice. He called for "a revolution of opportunity" for all the world's peoples, and asserted that "respect for human dignity and belief in the equal dignity of all the members of the human family demand policies aimed at enabling all peoples to have access to the means required to improve their lives."[41] The year before, John Paul had observed, "The many disturbing ways in which health and life are attacked should be courageously addressed by every person who truly respects human rights." He deplored the fact that "men and women, especially in the poorest countries, are unfortunately still deprived of access to health care services and the essential medicines for their treatment."[42] The pope had in view the transformation of national and international health care practices; he set his values against a horizon that was ultimately religious, but evidently hoped or trusted that these values would resonate across many moral traditions.

On the same occasion, John Paul II urged Catholic doctors, on the basis of their religious identity, to become more involved in providing services to the poor. Here he spoke out of a long-standing religious practice of offering care to the sick, and he directed his exhortations to those specifically engaged in this practice today, people who have Christian religious values but are not necessarily providing services in religious institutions. Catholic doctors exemplify the fact that religious persons and groups share membership in many communities of affiliation in which they interact with a variety of traditions, value systems, and practices, among which there can be common ground. The pope invoked the image of the Good Samaritan but did not neglect the big picture of professional responsibility, international justice, and the possibility of using legislative means to accomplish moral goals that are consistent with, but not dependent exclusively on, Christian ideals.

Philosophy, the social sciences, and practicality and prudence are indispensable links that take us in the public realm from theological convictions to concrete negotiations about laws and policies. In the process, religious participants can be nourished by religious and theological narratives, symbols, ideas, and formation. It is still important to emphasize, however, that theology's role is not confined behind "closed doors" at the "beginning" of a process that is initiated in faith but concluded in that ever-elusive "neutral" zone where traditions meet anonymously. Instead, the theological value reorientation must and can be engaged repeatedly throughout and within the public square of bioethics, even as policy debates are under way. The worldview context of ethics and of policy making needs to be constantly readjusted in response to economics and interest-group politics that continually threaten to pull policies out of alignment with justice and the common good.

Let me offer a couple of examples from my own experience. From 1992 to 1998, I was a member of a national ethics and policy advisory group (National Advisory Board on Ethics in Reproduction) established by the American College of Obstetricians and Gynecologists to help formulate positions on the new reproductive technologies, including ovum donation. Members were from very diverse backgrounds and the practices these imply: medicine, philosophy, law, and theology. The advisory group itself was a type of practice, governed generally by the "liberal consensus," and it aimed to affect national policy in a more "liberal" direction. Bringing with me faith-informed concerns about the beginning of human life, the commercialization of procreation, and the economic exploitation of women, I tended to engage in group debates in generally "philosophical" terms. One member who was much more open to all sorts of reproductive innovations than I was, a rabbi, repeatedly brought forward the story of Abraham and Sarah to justify his views. "Hagar—the first surrogate mother!" he would exclaim. I was not convinced—my sensibilities (Catholic and feminist) led me to a different interpretation of the story, one in which the moral is not approval but warning. I observed to the group that the arrangement had not worked out all that well for Hagar and her son.

In October 2002, I was invited to the Sixth World Congress of Bioethics (in Brazil), to present on a panel on reproductive technologies. The general theme of the congress—attended by only a small minority of theologians— was clear in its title, "Power and Injustice." The congress, too, was a form of practice, not just of academic argument. Unlike most professional venues, it was a site of quite energetic international interaction, engaging not only academics but activists from around the world, including many advocates for the poor. Many were from cultures where "secularization" has not taken hold to the extent that it has in the United States, and many were skeptical if not outright hostile to the "liberal consensus" in bioethics, politics, and economics.

I took the opportunity to think through a different rendition of the significance of Hagar for my presentation. Important factors in my interpretation are pressures, present in all cultures, on women to become mothers; the tendency of First World populations to rely on science and technology and to consume far more than their share of the world's health care resources; and the possibility of finding nonmedical solutions to childlessness, including adoption. My role as a theologian on the panel was primarily to try to get other participants and the audience to imagine reproductive technologies not always as a godsend, but as also a symptom of gender oppression and health care inequities. Although the conference in Brazil drew a very pluralistic audience ethnically, racially, religiously, and philosophically, the story of Abraham, Sarah, and Hagar (Genesis 16) was a provocative and apparently successful way to raise questions about the value systems within which anti-infertility technologies are usually advocated as "solutions." This story is a rich source of understanding of the human condition, revealing human aspirations and foibles, and offering insights into mixed motives and paradoxical situations.[43]

Abraham, of course, is the great patriarch to whom God made his promises of covenant and blessings, blessings passed on to the Israelites through Abraham's son and grandson, Isaac and Jacob. At the outset, however, Abraham's wife, Sarah, was "barren," seemingly an insuperable obstacle. Sarah tells Abraham to "go in to" her Egyptian maid, Hagar, so that Hagar can bear Abraham children in Sarah's name. But almost immediately, the situation begins to go awry, for Hagar, once pregnant, "looked with contempt on her mistress." Sarah complains to Abraham. He replies, " 'Behold, your maid is in your power; do to her as you please.' " So Sarah "dealt harshly" with Hagar, and Hagar runs away. In the only place in the Bible where God appears directly to a woman and speaks to her, God tells Hagar to go back to Sarah, which she does. She then bears a son by Abraham, and calls her son Ishmael.

Miraculously, Sarah, who is past the normal age of childbearing, has her own baby, Isaac. When Sarah sees Ishmael and Isaac play together, she becomes angry and jealous. She does not want Ishmael to share Isaac's inheritance. She has Abraham throw Ishmael and Hagar out. Abraham does not want to do this, because Ishmael is his son also. Yet Abraham gives Hagar some bread and water and sends her into the wilderness. When the water is all gone, she resigns herself to the baby's death. But God hears the baby crying and tells Hagar to pick him up—he is going to give Ishmael descendants, too. Ishmael is saved by the compassion of God, but Abraham and Sarah's childbearing strategy is not the means by which their destiny as parents is fulfilled, and Hagar and Ishmael do not fit into their plan in the way they had intended.

What is going on in this story? The story assumes certain practices of marriage and family—patriarchy, the urgency of marriage and childbearing for women, women's economic dependence on men, the enslavement of some for the benefit of others, and the sexual exploitation and abandonment of enslaved and unprotected women. The women are defined through the males, Abraham, Isaac, and Ishmael, though all three adults want sons above all else in life. Sarah and Hagar are living through their children; they have no other real life beyond motherhood. The women treat each other badly; Sarah is particularly guilty here, because she has more power than Hagar the slave. There is also conflict between Sarah and Abraham, largely because they do not have an equal relationship to the child they have planned to conceive by the surrogate. God is the only one who has the true interests of the surrogate's child at heart and saves him. God "hears the lad crying in the wilderness." God in the story never actually says that using Hagar as a surrogate mother was wrong, but it turns out that only God can end Sarah's infertility and rectify the troubled relations created by the surrogate arrangement.

Ultimately the story is about the need for trust in God and humility regarding human power. It illustrates how religious faith and worship bring human customs and moralities under criticism in radical and surprising ways. The story of Abraham, Sarah, and Hagar shows that human well-being and fulfillment of human destiny often depend on forces beyond our control, here symbolized by divine action. This does not mean that we should never try to take responsibility (which would wipe out all medical intervention and all social ethics, for that matter). However, we should be aware of hubris and of tunnel vision, and be conscious that good aims can get corrupted.

Maura Ryan expresses similar concerns in an analysis of "the ethics and economics of assisted reproduction." Ryan addresses social practices from an explicitly theological perspective, but she aims to communicate with all those interested in the institutionalization of reproductive technologies in Western societies. Ryan has written about her own experience of infertility and the effect it has had on her analysis. She is aware as a feminist of the pressures to use reproductive technologies. She also places these technologies in a social justice context. She speaks to all who endeavor to understand and implement a bioethics of reproduction that will respect individual needs but also be responsible to the common good.

Ryan argues that there should be a bias in favor of using medical resources to address needs that are truly medical (i.e., inability to become a biological parent because of a physical pathology or dysfunction) rather than using them to fulfill needs that arise from social circumstances (e.g., in vitro fertilization for single people) or from the normal aging process. She notes that it is important to consider whether the function can be restored by medical means, rather than simply replaced (e.g., by a surrogate mother or sperm donor).[44] This criterion still leaves some gray areas, but the basic idea that the criterion upholds is that we should avoid medicalizing social problems.

A second consideration is the success rate of the technology in question, balanced off against its expense and burdensomeness to the infertile individual, couple, or resulting child or children. For example, in vitro fertilization enjoys a success rate of only about 20 percent in producing "take-home babies," and both it and fertility drugs carry risks of multiple births and low birth weights. Prolonged courses of therapy also take a significant emotional and physical toll on individual patients, and the emotional toll extends to relationships and marriages.

A third criterion is social justice. Responsibility for justice should not fall disproportionately on the shoulders of those seeking treatment, nor on their individual caregivers. But social justice is still a criterion that should be applied in the formulation of social policies about the availability and funding of reproductive technologies. Ryan asks whether infertility is addressed by society and medicine chiefly or only when it is a disease of the middle and upper classes. Technological expertise regarding pregnancy is turned more to avoiding births when the situations of poor women are addressed. Allocation decisions reflect decisions about who is "fit to reproduce" and whose children are socially valued and deemed worthy to receive social investment. Moreover, the emphasis on high-tech interventions against infertility "deflects attention from the social and medical causes of infertility, some of which, such as untreated sexually transmitted diseases and undertreated endometriosis, disproportionately affect poor women and women of color."[45]

Part of the reorientation that theology can bring is a realignment of the desire for a child. Ryan describes and quotes women who have realized that their personal identity and happiness do not depend on motherhood. Another "realignment" is to redefine what motherhood or fatherhood means. Most cultural expectations about parenthood follow Abraham and Sarah in assuming that "our own" children are those we bear biologically—and that at least one "parent" must have that biological connection, even if they need to use a "surrogate mother" or gamete donor (whose own biological connection to the child is erased). It is the biological connection, it seems, that makes children truly "ours" in an irreplaceable and unparalleled way. The story of Abraham's dealings with God challenges this thinking. A familiar if terrifying sequel to the miraculous birth of Isaac is God's demand that Abraham be willing to sacrifice his son at the divine command (Genesis 22). Although God does not ultimately follow through on this command, this story makes the point that even our biological children do not belong to us as our property or as instruments through which we control our own destiny.

In the infertility context, theology can suggest and reinforce ethical and policy analysis that is more attuned to the "downside" of new technologies, and more open to nontechnological and even altruistic ways of dealing with biomedical problems. In Ryan's analysis, the justice criterion refers primarily to the distribution of health care resources. It can also turn our attention to the reality of already-existing children who need families. Certainly, adoption is not a special obligation of the infertile, but it can become an opportunity for adults who desire children and children who deserve parents.

Conclusion

In *The Contributions of Theology to Medical Ethics*, Gustafson points out that theology helps establish a "moral point of view," in which certain attitudes and dispositions inform the debate.[46] Among these are an attitude of respect for God and for human life, as well as an attitude of responsibility for creation that is not closed to new possibilities. Human interventions, however, must always proceed with due awareness of fault and failure, an appropriate attitude of self-criticism, and the acceptance of accountability for interventions and their risks. Although various of these attitudes and predispositions will be worth stressing in various social contexts, with their respective opportunities and dangers, public theological bioethics, in the First World at least, does well to keep the danger of exploitation and injustice on the near horizon of vision. An attitude of self-criticism "cautions human agents against insensitivity and blindness to their overweening desires for individual self-fulfillment or for the fulfillment of their professional or other communities by ignoring their obligations to others and engaging in actions which are costly to others."[47]

Theology is not only a viable but an indispensable conversation partner in the realm of public bioethics, for any society that aims to incorporate health care and health research within institutions and practices that serve justice and the common good. In an era of economic globalization, the theological agenda to seek justice in health care is defined generally by the biblical "option for the poor." Specifically, one of its most important and distinctive contributions to public discourse is a critique of the ways in which modern biomedicine and biotechnology have become luxury items marketed to economically privileged classes, while the world's poor majority lacks basic health needs.[48] Theological bioethics challenges such practices partly by its narratives and stories, and partly by its arguments. It does so partly by its advocacy for more just and compassionate health policies, and partly by enacting inclusive health care practices in religiously sponsored and other institutions. It also does so by mobilizing members of churches and faith traditions to engage the democratic process in favor of the poor.

NOTES

1. James R. Kelly, "Can Liberals Become Progressive Again?" Paper delivered at "Religion and the Future of Liberal Politics: A Post-Election Analysis Sponsored by the Fordham Center on Religion and Culture," Fordham University, Lincoln Center Campus, November 11, 2004, 7.

2. Ibid., 3. Kelly cites Laurie Goldstein and William Yardley, "President Benefits from Effort to Build a Coalition of Religious Voters, *New York Times*, November 5, 2004, A22.

3. Stephen Hart, *Cultural Dilemmas of Progressive Politics: Styles of Engagement among Grassroots Activists* (Chicago: University of Chicago Press), 13.

4. Ibid., 23.

5. Kelly, "Can Liberals Become Progressive Again?" 6.

6. James M. Gustafson, *The Contributions of Theology to Medical Ethics* (Milwaukee, Wis.: Marquette University Press, 1975), 67.

7. Paul Ramsey, *The Patient as Person: Explorations in Medical Ethics* (New Haven, Conn.: Yale University Press, 1970), xi.

8. Richard A. McCormick, "To Save or Let Die; The Dilemma of Modern Medicine," *Journal of the American Medical Association* 229 (1974): 174.

9. William A. Galston, "Catholics, Jews, and Stem Cells: When Believers Beg to Differ," *Commonweal*, May 20, 2005, 14.

10. Ibid., 17.

11. Stephen E. Lammers, "The Marginalization of Religious Voices in Bioethics," in *Religion and Medical Ethics: Looking Back, Looking Forward,* ed. Allen Verhey (Grand Rapids, Mich.: Eerdmans, 1996), 41.

12. Brent Waters, "What Is the Appropriate Contribution of Religious Communities in the Public Debate on Embryonic Stem Cell Research?" in *God and the Embryo: Religious Perspectives on Stem Cells and Cloning,* ed. Brent Waters and Ron Cole-Turner (forthcoming; read in manuscript), 28.

13. Ibid., 31.

14. James M. Gustafson, *Varieties of Moral Discourse: Prophetic, Narrative, Ethical, and Policy* (Grand Rapids, Mich.: Calvin College Press, 1988), and *Intersections: Science, Theology and Ethics* (Cleveland: Pilgrim Press, 1996).

15. Gustafson, *Varieties of Moral Discourse,* 19.

16. Ibid., 41.

17. Gustafson, *Intersections,* 39.

18. Ibid., 54.

19. On the civic participation of religious persons, groups, and organizations, see Mary Jo Bane, Brent Coffin, and Richard Higgins, eds., *Taking Faith Seriously* (Cambridge, Mass.: Harvard University Press, 2005).

20. Ibid., 29.

21. See, for example, Simon Harak, S. J., *Virtuous Passions: the Formation of Christian Character* (New York: Paulist Press, 1993); Diana Fritz Cates, *Choosing to Feel: Virtue, Friendship, and Compassion for Friends* (South Bend, Ind.: University of Notre Dame Press, 1997); Paul Lauritzen, *Religious Belief and Emotional Transformation: A Light in the Heart* (Cranbury, N.J.: Associated University Press, 1992).

22. Martha C. Nussbaum, *Upheavals of Thought: The Intelligence of Emotions* (Cambridge: Cambridge University Press, 2001), 1.

23. Ibid., 13.

24. Ibid., 425–26.

25. Margaret A. Farley, *Compassionate Respect; A Feminist Approach to Medical Ethics and Other Questions* (New York: Paulist Press, 2002), 48–49.

26. Paul Ramsey, *Fabricated Man: The Ethics of Genetic Control* (New Haven, Conn.: Yale University Press, 1970), 88.

27. Ibid., 39.

28. Paul Ramsey, "The Issues Facing Mankind," in *The Question of In Vitro Fertilization: Studies in Medicine, Law and Ethics,* by Jerome Lejeune, Paul Ramsey, and Gerard Wright (London: SPUC Educational Trust, 1984), 26.

29. For a composite synthesis, see Richard A. McCormick, S.J., "Ethics and Reproductive Interventions," in *How Brave a New World? Dilemmas in Bioethics* (New York: Doubleday, 1981), 306–335.

30. Ibid., 317.

31. Ibid., 326.

32. Ibid., 321.

33. Congregation for the Doctrine of the Faith, *Donum vitae* (*Instruction on Respect for Human Life in Its Origin and on the Dignity of Procreation* (Braintree, Mass.: Pope John XXIII Medical-Moral Center, 1987). Also published in *Origins* 16, no. 40 [1987]: 697–711.

34. Ibid., 10–11.

35. Ibid., 20.

36. Ibid.

37. Paul Lauritzen, *Pursuing Parenthood: Ethical Issues in Assisted Reproduction* (Bloomington: Indiana University Press, 1993), 89–97.

38. Ted Peters, *For the Love of Children: Genetic Technology and the Future of the Family* (Louisville, Ky.: Westminster John Knox Press, 1996), 181.

39. Maura A. Ryan, *The Ethics and Economics of Assisted Reproduction: The Cost of Longing* (Washington, D.C.: Georgetown University Press, 2001).

40. Karen Lebacqz, "Theology, Justice, and Health Care: An International Conundrum," paper presented at the University of Uppsala, Uppsala, Sweden, April 2002, 6. See also Karen Lebacqz, "Fair Shares: Is the Genome Project Just?" and "Genetic Privacy: No Deal for the Poor," in *Genetics: Issues of Social Justice*, ed. Ted Peters (Cleveland, Ohio: Pilgrim Press, 1998), 82–110 and 239–254.

41. "Remarks by John Paul," *New York Times*, July 24, 2001, A8.

42. John Paul II, "Address to Catholic Doctors' Congress," July 7, 2000, available at the Vatican Web site, www.Vatican.va.

43. The following interpretation is adapted from my presentation, "Putting Parenthood in Perspective." A revised version appeared as "Paternidade/maternidade em Perspectiva," in *Bioetica: Poder e Injusticia*, ed. Volnei Garrafa and Leo Pessini (Sao Paolo, Brazil: Sociedade Brasileira de Bioetica, Centro Universitario Sao Camilo, and Edicoes Loyola, 2003), 379–85.

44. Ryan, *Cost of Longing*, 138.

45. Ibid., 33.

46. Gustafson, *Contributions of Theology to Medical Ethics*, 25.

47. Ibid., 71–72.

48. Several examples of this trend are offered in Lisa Sowle Cahill, "Genetics, Ethics, and Feminist Theology: Some Recent Directions," *Journal of Feminist Studies in Religion* 18 (2002): 53–77.

PART II

Religion and the Terrain of Public Discourse

Discussions over the role of religion in the public square or in relation to public bioethics often fall prey to ambiguities and confusion created by inadequately defined terminology and misunderstandings over the nature and character of religion. What do we mean by the term "religion"? What is public bioethics? In what way can or should religion participate in public bioethics? Terms that initially appear self-evident will, upon closer examination, reveal a startling complexity. For example, many of the critiques against the participation of religion in the public domain, such as complaints over accessibility, authoritarianism, and the inhibition of public discussion, appear to assume that religion is a unique form of discourse incommensurate with others. As will be seen, that is not the case.

In this part we will attempt to start teasing out the meaning of these terms and concepts. Instead to seeking these answers within the context of religion, we will draw upon other disciplines. John Evans will provide a sociological perspective on the problem. Tod Chambers draws upon language theory and literary criticism. Therese Lysaught uses Foucauldian philosophy.

The first question might be, What do we mean by the term "religion"? Interestingly, none of the authors in this section explicitly tackles that question. Though John Evans notes the possibility of choosing between a substantive definition of religion (one that conforms to traditional understandings of religion associated with Christianity, Judaism, Islam, etc.) and a functional one (one that considers how a belief system functions in a manner similar to traditional religion), he specifically opts to adopt the substantive definition. (This is a task that will be left to me in my contribution, "The Heart of the Matter," chap. 16.) Nonetheless, what quickly becomes evident in these three pieces is that religion simply represents one category of discourse. It is subject to the same rules of authorization (what Chambers, drawing upon J. L. Austin, refers to as becoming "performatives") as other forms of discourse.

Second, what do we mean by the term "public bioethics"? John Evans adopts the definition I initially proposed in developing this volume, which defines public bioethics as ethical reflection directed toward the development of public policies regarding health and medicine. Under this understanding, public bioethics is distinct from clinical ethics—the practice of ethics to address moral concerns over individual treatment or research. Lysault challenges that definition and demonstrates that the line between public and clinical (or private) bioethics is not as clear at it first appears. Specifically, she argues that the discipline of bioethics is an exercise of power over the body—whether exercised in terms of broad public policy or individualized treatment. The role that religion or any ethical worldview plays within this political exercise is similar in both cases.

Third, we have the question of who speaks for religion. As Evans points out, there are three typical categories of religious spokespersons: theologians or scholars of religion; denominational officials or leaders; and the people in the pews. As emphasized by both Evans and Chambers, the authority and effectiveness of each varies according to a variety of circumstances. At a minimum, these authors challenge the tendency in conversation about religion and the public square to treat religion as a univocal phenomena. Each religious "speaker" stands in a unique position and speaks in a special way according to his or her discipline and standing within the faith.

Fourth is the question of how religion participates in and/or influences the development of public bioethics. Evans provides a basic outline of alternatives, ranging from theologians/religious scholars participating as experts within a technocratic model of public bioethics formation, to religions acting as a special interest under a pure politics model. Chambers builds on this, exploring the nature of authority within a religious bioethical discourse. Lysault pushes even further, raising critical questions about the grounding and political dynamics of public bioethics discourse itself as a form of social control driven by capitalist forces.

Though these authors provide an incisive analysis as to how religions have participated, normative questions remain. Who *should* speak for religion? In what type of discourse? What are the risks to religion of participating in public bioethics? If religion is to participate, how can we structure the conversation to avoid the many problems raised by the critics? These questions remain to be answered.

3

Who Legitimately Speaks for
Religion in Public Bioethics?

John H. Evans

The question embodied in the title of this chapter is a critical one
not only for scholars of religion and politics, but also for persons engaged in public bioethics. Religion is inevitably a part of American
public bioethics, because the public is very religious, at least compared to other Western nations. The perennial question is how to
(inevitably) fuse the two without coercing those from nonmajority
religions and those of no religion, while not requiring the religious
to bracket their actual beliefs when they enter the public square.
This is traditionally thought of as the place of First Amendment law,
but public bioethics is an arena that shows how much more complicated religion and politics is than commonly recognized by the
courts, and how more careful thought has to be given to how religion and politics work in practice.

Before starting, I must state that I am referring to institutional
religion here—the groups identified as having an organized presence in society who concern themselves with sacred or transcendent
matters—and not with personal religious belief that exists independent of these groups. I also am using a substantive definition of religion (i.e., one with recognizable normative content), not a functional
one in which those belief systems that serve the same function as
religion are defined as religion. Though in some theoretical discussions a "scientific worldview" could be considered the functional
equivalent of a religion, in this chapter I follow Berger's old admonition to use a substantive definition if for no other reason than this is
what everyone else thinks religion is.[1]

This chapter has a structure based simply on combining the various meanings of the two critical ideas in the title and comparing
them. The critical ideas are "who speaks for religion" and "public

bioethics." It is best to address the simpler distinction first. Who could legitimately speak for *religion* in public bioethics can be placed into useful, yet obviously simplified, categories.

Theologians. These are the professional interpreters of a religious tradition, those who work out the details of beliefs and figure out how to apply them to concrete situations. Often they do not have official authority from the members of the religion itself—an important distinction that I will raise below. I would also include in this category any scholar of religion, whether he or she would use the term "theologian" or has any recognized connection to the religion.

The members. These are the "people in the pews"—the members without which there would be no religion to represent for any practical purposes. Their connection to the theologians is typically distant at best.

The religious "authorities." The person authorized *by the religion* to speak for it. (A different question from who can legitimately speak in public bioethics.) This varies by religion, and this variance will be important below. A critical distinction to start with is how it is determined that what they say is "representative" of the beliefs of the religion. There are two ends of this spectrum. On the one end, some authorities have institutional standing to set religious truth (e.g., the pope in Roman Catholicism). On the other are those authorities who can speak only when what they have to say has been authorized by the members (e.g., mainline Protestant denominational officials).

The answer to the question that is the title of this chapter depends most of all not on the different religious roles, but on what we think "public bioethics" is or should be. First, public bioethics is distinct from "clinical bioethics," which consists of the ethical decisions made in individual treatment or research settings. It is also not "foundational bioethics," the study of the relationship of ethics to broader structures of metaphysics or political and social philosophy. (Actually, this book, by studying public bioethics, is an example of foundational bioethics.) Elsewhere, I define public bioethics as societal elites debating "over what society should do about a problem" having to do with science and/or medicine.[2] For the purposes of this chapter I will broaden this definition a bit, splitting it into two important strands that influenced my original definition. Let us consider "public policy bioethics" and "public opinion bioethics" to be important subcategories.

Public Policy Bioethics

Public policy bioethics asks what an ethical public policy is on a matter of science or medicine. There are many models of what public policy bioethics is or should be, and participants in these debates at best are unclear about their assumptions and at worst shift back and forth among models to give themselves tactical advantage in arguing against positions advocated by people they disagree with. The four models I will be discussing can be identified as the technocratic model, common morality model, pubic opinion model, and democracy model.

To anticipate a fuller discussion below, I'll define these briefly. The technocratic model is where elites—typically scientists—decide what is best for society and act accordingly. What I will call the "forwarding the common morality model" is similar to the first, except that instead of forwarding their own vision, experts forward what they consider to be the values of the public without consulting the public. In the third model bioethics is the adjudicator of public opinion, weighing the perspectives of different interest groups, including religion. The final model treats all bioethical issues as standard public policy questions that should simply be addressed by our elected officials without experts.

I would like to make two further observations about the role of the bioethicist within this system. First, Hannah Pitkin describes two models for an elected official in a representative democracy; a "delegate" and a "trustee."[3] A "delegate" tries to determine what the people they represent think about an issue, and votes accordingly. A "trustee" does what he or she considers to be the best, and if the voters don't like it, they can vote him or her out of office. How much the people making public policy should be delegates is a core tension in representative democracies and also within public bioethics. My four models of public bioethics will start with the "trustee" end of the spectrum and work their way toward the "delegate" end.

Second, historian Daniel Fox makes an analogy between nuclear weapons and medical research, noting that in both, there has been a tension between professional and civilian control. "Arms control intellectuals and bioethicists have been critically important mediators between the ideologies and the technical fantasies of the professionals on the one hand, and the most adamant and uninformed advocates of civilian control on the other," he argues.[4] Thus bioethics stands in the middle of this tension, with the important caveat that most participants in public bioethics are not elected officials themselves, but are advising—directly or indirectly—officials who are at least more closely legitimated by the democratic process.

I will describe each of these models for public policy bioethics, and who legitimately speaks for religion in each. I will then discuss how each type offers advantages to certain religions based upon their theology or their polity, and disadvantages to others. It must be remembered that these four models are ideal types, existing nowhere in reality in their pure form, but are rather analytic devices to forward our thinking.

The Technocratic Model

As previously noted, the technocratic model is one in which elites—typically scientists—decide what is best for society and act accordingly without further consultation. The technocratic model falls at the far end of the trustee side of the scale. It is somewhat out of fashion—although signs of its reappearance occur from time to time. It is not even quite right to say that this type of bioethics is about public policy because if the advocates of this tradition had their way, there would be no involvement of elected officials. The position taken in this model is that elites can decide what to do, without consulting or even considering what the public thinks, because these elites know best.

This represents a long political tradition. The idea that the wisest people in a society should rule goes back at least as far as Plato. In more recent formulations the term we use is "technocracy," in which technical experts make political decisions with the idea of guiding society to where they think it should be.

People familiar with the canonical histories of bioethics will recognize this as the position of the (arrogant) physician, and later scientist, that the bioethics enterprise dethroned.[5] Clinical ethics was invented to force physicians and scientists experimenting on people to surrender their technocratic privilege and let other people's opinions (specifically, the patient's) enter into the ethical decision-making process. In public bioethics, this position was represented by scientists who thought they knew best for society. For example, a scientist testifying before Congress in 1968 on possible government oversight of the ethics of medicine and science responded, when asked about having other professionals help the scientists to determine the ethical impact of their work: "I cannot see how they could help. . . . [T]he fellow who holds the apple can peel it best."[6] This technocratic view is also assumed in the simplistic "scientific freedom" argument—that scientists should be able to do any experiment they want to. (This absolutist version is obviously rhetorical, given that we would stop any scientist whose experiment involved torturing children.)

Though a technocracy could be led by theologians, in the context of U.S. public bioethics, technocratic decision making has historically been the preferred mode of scientists and their close allies. In a technocracy made up of scientists, there would probably not be any religious input, but we can imagine scenarios in which scientists would want to obtain the wisdom of elites from other fields, while still making the decisions and setting the ends that would be forwarded. For example, at the time the first criticisms of biological research were coming out, in vitro fertilization pioneer R. G. Edwards, noting that biologists must "invent a method of taking counsel of mankind" or "society will thrust its advice on biologists . . . in a manner or form seriously hampering to science," stated that what was needed was an organization "easily approached and consulted to advise and assist biologists and others to reach *their own* decisions."[7] The public would not be consulted. We could imagine that some who would help scientists make their own decisions could be people "representing" religion.

Finally, in this vision of public bioethics, who would speak for religion? A reflection on the constraints suggests that it would be theologians and not denominational officials or the members of religions. Since it would be scientists who would be making the ultimate decision, the discussion would occur on their terms. It is only the people who have the time to become extremely familiar with the technology under review who will be welcome at the table. Denominational officials, and certainly the members, do not have time to create the requisite expertise. But, a theologian, freed from other tasks, can learn about the technology. For example, Paul Ramsey, one of the first theologians involved in public bioethics, spent about a year observing life in a hospital before writing his influential book on medical ethics *The Patient as Person*.[8] A theologian would also be much more likely than the other possible religious voices to have a high degree of education, and therefore be capable of speaking and understanding the language of Enlightenment reason spoken by scientists, either as a first or second language.[9]

In this model, theologians will be preferred for another reason. In this model, what is important is the expression of religious wisdom, not any representation of the popular will of the religious people, so *who* can speak will be determined by the wisdom of what they say. Theologians will once again be the preferred group here, followed by denominational officials, whose wisdom is limited by the time spent on practical tasks. The average member has no role. This is indeed what occurred during the era in public bioethics when technocracy was the primary model. Scientific elites, in what Jonsen calls the "decade of conferences" in the 1960s,[10] would bring a religious voice in for commentary, and the voice was almost always a theologian.

Certain religious groups will be privileged in this conversation. First, and all else equal, religious groups with strong representation among the technocrats will have an advantage over nondominant groups because the other elites are more likely to be members of these religions and therefore see the dominant religions as more relevant. Second, and equally clearly, religious groups that are generally favorable toward science and technology will be preferred. This could, as in the case of Judaism, compensate for being a religion with few members, although overrepresented among scientists. To give an example that could be the punch line of a joke, old-order Amish theologians will not be asked to give advice on the ethics of human genetic engineering. More subtly, theologians from different traditions have a range of views on humanity's role in creation, with some emphasizing our "createdness" and some that we are "co-creators" with God.[11] Although I have not done the research, I believe it to be true that mainline Protestants, Catholics, and almost all Jews would fall toward the co-creator end of the spectrum, while evangelicals would fall on the "created" end. We would expect that evangelical theologians would not be welcome in a technocratic public policy bioethics discussion about germline human genetic engineering,[12] which has generally been the case.

Theologians from traditions that are capable of translating their claims to secular language will obviously be more likely to be invited to speak for religion. Some religious traditions not only are capable of translating their beliefs into secular languages, but require it or do not even acknowledge the secular/sacred distinction in these matters. Catholic natural law, for example, is in some ways the perfect "secular" language, and efforts at secular translation of theological ideas by liberal Protestants fits well here too. The greater concern with biblical justification found in evangelical theology leads to arguments peppered with theological ideas that will be like a foreign language to most scientists.

Finally, only certain religious groups would want to participate in such an elite enterprise. The religion must think that its views should be binding on the entire society because either it is the established guardian of society or its views are universally true. The mainline Protestants of the 1950s are often accused of having the first view, and a number of religions assume the second. (Indeed, while all religion involves believing in a metaphysical truth, empirically the members and theologians have different degrees of certitude about the uniqueness of their truth.) We can imagine religions that neither consider themselves to be the established guardians of societies nor possessors of universal truth (e.g., Reform Judaism, Unitarian Universalism) would be reluctant to participate in a purely technocratic enterprise.

It is important to point out that theologians who fit all of the above qualities are not necessarily shills for scientists. Rather, there are theologians who come to all of the above conclusions on their own and are selected by scientists over theologians who come to conclusions that will be less supportive of scientists' intentions.

Forwarding the Common Morality

The second type of public bioethics is actually quite similar to the first. The key difference is that what the experts are forwarding is not their own vision, but what is explicitly considered to be the general morality of society. It remains on the "trustee" side of the continuum because the public is actually not consulted about its views, but edges toward the delegate side because the interests of the public is derived from academic reflection.

This model of public bioethics is currently dominant in the debate. Indeed, it served as the basis for ousting the technocratic model. Up until the 1960s or early 1970s, physicians were treating their patients without consulting them, and scientists were experimenting on people without their permission. Critics were quick to point out how these practices violated what they took to be the common morality and, indeed, from the reaction of the public to the revelations about these practices, these critics were probably right.

Congress responded to news of the experiments done on people without their permission by setting up a commission that would, among other tasks, "conduct a comprehensive investigation and study to identify the basic ethical principles which should underlie the conduct of biomedical and behavioral research involving human subjects."[13] The resulting "Belmont Report," in what could be considered the first use of this model of public bioethics, identified three ends, values, or goals that are "among those generally accepted in our cultural tradition."[14] These ends, later expanded to four by subsequent scholars, are beneficence, nonmaleficence, autonomy, and justice.[15]

How did this commission determine what the preferred ends of the public are? Drawing on a strong tradition within political philosophy, it had a conference at which members reflected upon it. John Rawls, the political theorist and intellectual parent of public bioethics as it is currently construed, views this as determining the overlapping consensus around certain values or ends.[16] Beauchamp and Childress refer to the "common morality" as "the set of norms that all morally serious persons share."[17]

The way public policy bioethics works in this model is that the debate centers on whether a technology or practice forwards the "common morality" of the people. Within contemporary bioethics, the touchstone for that determination remains the Belmont Report. For example, the federal bioethics commission of the early 1980s, the President's Commission, created a report about human genetic engineering that made a number of ethical recommendations to policymakers and the public. This report essentially supported those acts that would maximize the ends identified in the Belmont Report, and argued against ends that were not in the report.[18]

To return to the religion question, *who* can speak for religion in this model of public policy bioethics is very different from the previous model. There are two possible answers: either nobody can speak for religion or everyone can, depending upon how one defines religion.

In the first case, *nobody* can speak for religion, because religion has been subsumed into the common morality. In fact, this model for bioethics seeks to replace religion and the conflicts that religions are perceived to cause. Consider this account of the growth of this model of public policy bioethics:

> The history of bioethics over the last two decades has been the story of the development of a secular ethic. Initially, individuals working from within particular religious traditions held the center of bioethical discussions. However, this focus was replaced by analyses that span traditions, including particular secular traditions. As a result, a special secular tradition that attempts to frame answers in terms of no particular tradition, but rather in ways open to rational individuals as such, has emerged. Bioethics is an element of a secular culture and the great-grandchild of the Enlightenment. . . . That is, the existence of open peaceable discussion among divergent groups, such as atheists, Catholics, Jews, Protestants, Marxists, heterosexuals and homosexuals, about public policy issues bearing on health care, will press unavoidably for a neutral common language. Bioethics is developing as the lingua franca of a world concerned with health care, but not possessing a common ethical viewpoint.[19]

In its pure form, this model of public bioethics does not allow any theological input, and theologians who participate must do so in a secular register, as interpreters of the common morality. Theologian James Gustafson noted this requirement of the new form of public bioethics as early as the early 1970s, saying that he was unsure what made someone a "religious ethicist" in debates over science and medicine. He quipped that "an ethicist is a former theologian who does not have the professional credentials of a moral philosopher."[20]

It is not the secularism of arguments from the common morality that excluded theology. Theologians—at least theologians of traditions that could engage in translation of theological ideas to secular terms—never had a problem with secular debate. Even Paul Ramsey, the intellectual founding father of evangelical theologians in contemporary public bioethics, engaged in this translation, translating *agape* and covenant with God into the autonomy or informed consent. Ramsey made use of consent because he "sought to find a language accessible to as many people as possible despite their theological convictions and 'consent' appeared to cross over communities and traditions."[21]

The problem for theology with this model of public bioethics is twofold. It is not the secular translation, but that there are only a limited number of ends allowed within this debate, all of which must be universally applicable across issues. For example, autonomy is to be forwarded in human genetic engineering, abortion, human subjects research, and all other issues in science and medicine. Theologians prefer to determine what to do from within their theological tradition, and then translate this into secular language. Having to then fit this secular language into four ends means that many theological ideas must be put aside as unimportant. Second, if theologians are truly arguing for universal principles, then what is the distinctive contribution of theology? Since, by definition, the universal preempts the particularistic, theologians are replaced by professionals who have less distinctive baggage.[22]

I mentioned above that this model could allow for a certain type of religious input. At the time that this model became dominant in public bioethics in the 1970s, there was a movement in both liberal Protestantism and Catholicism toward a form of theology that was accessible to all people, whether or not they believed in God.

The "death of God" theology in liberal Protestantism and situation ethics would both "eliminate any exclusively Christian conditions or terms" from what was also called "the new morality."[23] To slightly oversimplify the argument, there was nothing unique about Christian ethics that could not be obtained through secular sources. Theology could be expressed in secular terms. Among Catholics, a variant of natural law theology emerged that Vincent MacNamara calls "an autonomous ethic" theology.[24] This theology, according to one of its advocates, believes that "Christian morality, in so far as its categorical determination and materiality is concerned, is basically and substantially a human morality, that is a morality of true manhood. That means that truth, honesty and fidelity, in their materiality, are not specifically Christian but universally human values."[25]

As one critic at the time stated, "whereas a few years previously theologians regarded it as natural to demand that the teaching of morality should be theological, i.e., 'Conceived in terms of scripture and of salvation history,' things have been entirely reversed 'so that Christian morality is understood in rational, philosophical terms, i.e., in terms of empirical human science.' "[26]

It is not in my professional training to determine whether this is "truly" theology or not. Instead, I will limit myself to the following sociological observations. First, if this is theology, it would not be recognized as such by the majority of the people in the country who consider themselves religious. Second, the entities we call denominations would have no role *as denominations* in a public policy bioethics based upon this model. Third, members of religious groups would also have no input *as members of the religion*, but would rather be simply secular citizens. Therefore, if this approach is religious, the only people who could speak for religion would be the theologians. Moreover, and quite obviously, within the technocratic or common morality models of public bioethics, religious traditions having this conception of theology would be advantaged, those without it disadvantaged.

Bioethics as Adjudicator of Public Opinion Model

The common morality model was designed for development of public policy without the input of the public, meaning that it is toward the trustee end of the spectrum. This model is not unique to public bioethics. For example, debates among economists about macroeconomic policy do not involve the public either, but remain at the level of the experts who then make recommendations to unelected officials at the federal reserve. It works well when the audience for ethics is the bureaucratic state, such as decision makers at the National Institutes of Health.[27] In fact, as I show elsewhere, this model became prominent because it kept the decision making at this level, away from the public.[28] At the same time it answered the need that state decision making, particularly on issues construed as "ethical," require the articulation of a limited and concise morality, but also that it be portrayed as the morality of the citizens.[29]

However, what happens if the public begins paying attention to public bioethics? Because the public is largely religious, religious concepts will be used to define bioethical problems, putting public policy bioethics in conflict with the will of the people that it is supposedly forwarding through maximizing the common morality.

This is what happened in 1997 with the announcement of the birth of Dolly the cloned sheep. President Clinton, probably an incredibly average American in his relation to religious traditions, defined the problem with Dolly theologically: "Any discovery that touches upon human creation is not simply a matter of scientific inquiry, it is a matter of morality and spirituality as well."[30] A host of religious groups advocated restricting cloning, using religious language. The federal bioethics commission operating at the time, the National Bioethics Advisory Commission (NBAC), held a series of hearings and wrote a number of reports, which included the input of religious voices. The commission acted as an adjudicator, taking in the testimony of public representatives and determining public attitudes toward the morality of the act.

In this model, religious views cannot be considered to be sources of wisdom, which had been the case in the technocratic model. So many years of striving for the common morality had made this illegitimate. Rather, the input of religious groups entered into the debate as the positions of interest groups.

This is clear from an insider's summary of the process. After the NBAC created its final report on cloning, NBAC Commissioner James Childress offered five reasons why the NBAC had invited theological input. Childress's first reason was that religious communities "shape the moral positions taken by many U.S. citizens on new technological developments." The second was that religious traditions often make secular arguments. The third was that the NBAC wanted to know whether there was a consensus among religious groups about cloning. The fourth was that they wanted to start a national debate about cloning, and implicitly, it would be religious communities that would frame the debate. Finally, and most tellingly, noting that effective public policy requires assent from the governed, the NBAC wanted to gauge the "nature, extent, and depth of opposition to those policies" by religious groups.[31] In sum, although the third reason implies that theologians might have been able to offer insight to the process, the other four reasons suggest that theologians represent the views of interest groups that must be brought into any compromise position. To be fair, the NBAC was in a transition zone between models, because although the reasons for inviting religious voices into the debate had an interest-group quality to them, they also welcomed the testimony of scholars of religious groups that have very few members in the United States, such as Islam.

The model here is that public policy bioethics—NBAC in this case—would adjudicate between the religious and secular traditions in the United States to create a compromise position, just as Congress does on other issues. Who would speak for religion in this model of public policy bioethics? The first answer is any religious voice that is organized like an interest group, with the ability to make its views known to public policy bioethics through testimony, writing letters, and the like. Employees of denominational agencies become important here. For example, the Christian Life Commission of the Southern Baptist Convention and the Board of Church and Society of the United Methodist Church were involved in the cloning debate. In general, the most important voice would be anyone that could claim to represent the views of a bloc of (religious) citizens. It is in this model of public bioethics that the ubiquitous "denominational statement" takes on greater importance. Protestants, whose denominational leaders at least in theory take their direction from the laity, are quite fond of the practice of passing resolutions and policies that state the view of the denomination on issues.[32] For example, the Presbyterian Church (USA), at its general assembly in 2001, passed a resolution supporting embryonic stem cell research using embryos from in vitro fertilization clinics.[33] The Southern Baptist Convention, also meeting in 2001, passed a resolution opposing "therapeutic cloning."[34] To the extent these are viewed as representative of the views of the "people in the pews," they would have weight in this model of public policy bioethics. However, it is well known by people in politics that there is no religion in the United States of any size in which the leaders can induce bloc voting.[35]

In this model, theologians recede in importance unless they can demonstrate that their views are representative of the views of the members—not an easy feat. The views of the average members as identified through public opinion polling could be important, to the extent to which they can be identified as caring about the issue and having a cohesive position.

This model has obvious biases toward certain religious groups. First, the religions that are organized like interest groups benefit. Having a separate agency devoted toward representing the views of the religion in public affairs is obviously beneficial, and almost all of the larger denominations in the United States have such an operation. This is a disadvantage to large religious traditions that have low degrees of central organization, such as Pentecostals. Loosely organized religions do not have central spokespersons, and, unlike the more highly organized groups, they tend to not make official summaries of their beliefs on contemporary issues. Of course, in more loosely organized religions, social movement organizations whose constituency by and large comes from particular religious traditions, such as the Concerned Women for America,[36] make up for this weakness. Smaller religious groups are then doubly disadvantaged. First, they are unlikely to have interest-group entities within them. Second, even if they did, they do not represent very many people and can be safely ignored.

It is not just the larger groups that have an advantage in this model, but groups whose beliefs are broadly commensurable to the "middle" of U.S. opinion. Even if 20 percent of the United States were Hindu, it would be hard to create a compromise position with religious resonance between Christians and Hindus because they are not very similar religions. Within Christianity and Judaism there is at least a shared tradition that can be the basis of some sort of compromise position.

This model of public bioethics has not been institutionalized. Indeed, it is an unstable beast because the logical conclusion from it is that the public's views will directly set public policy on these sorts of issues. This stands in tension with the remaining technocratic influences. Public policy bioethics was created at the behest of scientists to be a buffer between their interests and the passions of the public—not to let the public directly make decisions.

Democratic Public Bioethics—The Standard Legislative Problem

As one would expect, the religious groups most aggrieved by the previously stated models of public bioethics have sought an end-run around them by making appeals directly to elected officials, instead of appealing to elected officials via public bioethics. Instead of (only) testifying before a government commission that will make a recommendation to the executive branch on fetal tissue research, they (also) engage in interest-group lobbying and mobilization to encourage our elected officials to follow their preferred version of ethics. For example, though evangelical and Catholic leaders are opposed to any use of fetal tissue, current public policy bioethics has repeatedly concluded that it is acceptable to use fetal tissue under certain conditions. Evangelicals and traditionalist Catholics have appealed directly to elected officials on this issue. Mainline Protestants and Jews have not gone this route, because their conclusions are generally supported by public policy bioethics as currently construed. (These groups *do* engage in direct politics when their views are ignored at bureaucratic levels. For example, mainline Protestants have advocated against U.S. policies in Central America when their views are ignored in the executive branch.)[37]

As this chapter is being drafted (summer 2002), Congress is debating a bill to ban both "therapeutic" and "reproductive" cloning. It is clear that the effort to ban "therapeutic" cloning is organized by evangelicals and Catholics, who have long been opposed to the destruction of human embryos. I think that it is incontestable that if this were left to a traditional public policy bioethics mechanism to decide, "therapeutic" cloning would be declared licit. Evangelical and Catholic elites seem well aware of this, and have made the Bush administration know that it expects the administration to ignore the mainstream public policy bioethics mechanisms on this and similar issues.

At its extreme, this model radically changes public bioethics because it makes all of the current participants—bioethicists, theologians, philosophers, scientists—change their audience from government advisory commissions and other elites to the public. In this model, public bioethical debate would be more like the abortion debate, a fact that illustrates the pros and cons of the model. On the one hand, the abortion debate is cantankerous, polarizing, and extreme, because everyone is invited to the debate, and the mediating institutions have an interest in increasing cantankerousness in order to raise motivations. In public bioethics, admission is limited, and the mediating institutions—primarily academia—have an interest in civility. On the other hand, the abortion debate is more democratic, in that this one issue about reproduction and the body is debated by the elected officials who are actually responsible to the electorate.

Who speaks for religion here is first and foremost the individual member of the religion: the voter in the eyes of the elected official. Interestingly, when we get to a purely individual form of advocacy like this, it doesn't really matter whether the individual member of the religion uses that religion in his or her advocacy; rather, this person need only state the conclusions upon which he or she will judge elected representatives. The second most influential speaker for religion would be religious leaders and theologians, to the extent they are perceived to be speaking for members who do not raise their own voices.

The religious groups that are advantaged by this model are most obviously the larger ones, or at least those whose members vote more frequently or, more realistically, give money to elected officials. Smaller religious groups that have distinctive views on these issues would not be able to muster the political clout that large religions could. Clearly, religious groups that are reluctant to engage in legislative advocacy—as evangelicals were before the 1980s—would be at a serious disadvantage as well. As with some of the other models, religious groups that have established advocacy arms would have an advantage. Finally, if there were a religious group in America in which the members faithfully followed the advice of their leaders on these issues, they would be at an advantage. As noted above, these religions are small and rare.

Public Opinion Bioethics

Public bioethics not only concerns proposing public policy. Part of its ambiguity—an ambiguity that can be strategically played at times—is that it is also about changing the opinion of the public that legitimates the public policy. In more academic terms, public bioethics is also an institution in the public sphere,[38] the set of institutions separate from the state "in which something approaching public opinion can be formed."[39] More formally, I will follow Charles Taylor in defining the public sphere as "a common space in which the members of society are deemed to meet through a variety of media: print, electronic, and also face-to-face encounters; to discuss matters of common interest; and thus to be able to form a common mind about these."[40] Participants in public bioethics are often found in this public sphere, forming the public opinion. Of course, the members of a religion are members of the public sphere, and religions try to communicate with their own members. I will not consider this further here, but will focus on religions communicating with nonmembers.

The question of *who* speaks for religion is in theory less important here, because any citizen is a legitimate contributor to the public sphere—all have authority. However, while all are authorized to represent religion, this very fact means that not all can effectively do so. This is because the debates over bioethical issues are not taking place in a society with 35 inhabitants, but rather in a modern differentiated society with hundreds of millions of inhabitants. Face-to face communication in the formation of public opinion is less important than the various forms of mediated conversation. Conversations are mediated by myriad institutions, most importantly the print and television media, the entertainment industry, and interest groups. Therefore, the question of *who* speaks for religion is transformed into *who will be able* to speak for religion in the court of public opinion. Or, put differently, who will be chosen by the gatekeepers of the public sphere to "speak for" religion.

First and most obviously, it helps a religious group if it has money to spread its views through commercial or professionally managed means. This may allow them to overwhelm the gatekeepers. For example, in the early 1990s the National Council of Catholic Bishops of the Roman Catholic Church hired the public relations firm Hill and Knowlton to create a campaign to teach the public the Catholic view about fetal life and abortion. The attention given to the Catholic perspective on these issues surged past the level the bishops had achieved by relying upon the gatekeepers of the media.

Second, as was the case in public policy bioethics, having a denominational agency dedicated to communicating with the public will also enhance the religious group's ability to form public opinion. For example, most mainline Protestant denominations have "church and society" units that are supposed to communicate the religion's views to elected officials and the public, as well as media offices. Of course, these are typically starved for money, at least in mainline Protestantism,[41] so the effectiveness of this mechanism has never seriously been tested. Once again, religious groups with little centralized organization will not fare well because they lack an ability to create and disseminate unified messages.

Finally, although all citizens are allowed to speak in the public square about their religious views on, say, cloning, in reality the gatekeepers of the communications mechanisms in the public sphere (e.g., newspaper editors) will look for people with "religious authority." With the exception of the very unusual religions, which they can safely brand as deviant (e.g., "cults") without much public opposition, most gatekeepers will not take positions on the legitimacy of the central beliefs of people attempting to speak for a religion. In not taking a position on the truth of a particular religion, what becomes more important is the "credibility" of the person speaking on behalf of other members of the public.

More generally, "representing" a religion in the public sphere is, sociologically speaking, actually the demonstration of non-idiosyncrasy. Non-idiosyncrasy is the demonstration that you are not just speaking of a religious idea that you invented, but that you speak in a way that is generally representative of a group of citizens. How does one claim to be non-idiosyncratic? There are a number of ways.

First, one can simply be reporting on a position that is literally representative of all of the members of a religion. In theory at least, when the executive presbyter of the Presbyterian Church (USA) says that the denomination is supportive of stem cell research, this is a position that was developed by democratically elected representatives of all members of the denomination at their last convention. Of course, in practice these processes are imperfect. Nonetheless, when someone can claim to be speaking for a group that has a process to create a collective view, it suggests a certain power in the public sphere because of the number of citizens who, at least in theory, agree. When the Southern Baptist Convention, which, like the Presbyterian Church,[42] is democratic, states its opposition to human cloning, it is assumed that this is a rough approximation of the views of Southern Baptists, who make up a large percent of the citizens in the public sphere.

One would think that religions that determine their views on bioethical issues through the authority of unelected officials (such as Roman Catholicism) would not fare as well here, given that the extent to which the official represents the views of the members must be demonstrated. However, officials in these religions are also let into the public sphere by gatekeepers. Although their representativeness is unclear, they have the ability to try to get the members to conform to their views because they also control the institutional communication mechanisms. If there were a hierarchical religion in which the hierarchy did not also control the means of communication, it presumably would not fare well.

Below the level of people who claim to represent the average members of a religion, other people can claim this role, probably with less success. On a more local level, any title that suggests that the spokesperson is respected by others in their community will give authority, such as someone being "chair of board of trustees, First Baptist Church" or "the Rev. Joe Smith, First Congregational Church." Theologians would fit into the mix about here. Although they generally cannot claim to be directly representative of anyone's views, they do have some legitimacy in that they were selected to their role by some group of people, presumably people concerned about the fidelity of the tradition.

The religious groups with an advantage in the public sphere are the religions of the gatekeepers. Though the religious makeup of the societal elites has become more representative of the American public in recent decades,[43] it is still the case that societal elites are disproportionately mainline Protestant and Jewish.[44]

Conclusion

Who speaks for religion in public policy bioethics largely depends upon what we think public policy bioethics *is* or what we think it should be. Who speaks for religion in public opinion bioethics largely depends upon who can make it past the gatekeepers of public discourse in the media. Each model of public bioethics offers certain advantages and disadvantages to particular religious groups. In conclusion, I will address the question of: What is to be done?

I will leave it to the reader to decide which version of public policy bioethics is best for American society. However, I will add one normative point about how one should decide. The choice of which model of public bioethics is best for society should be based on a principle such as believing that no religious discourse should be allowed in the policy process[45] or, conversely that all religions should be allowed free access. The choice should not be decided by whether the model one advocates will exclude those who oppose your conclusions on particular issues. For example, supporters of embryonic stem cell research should not advocate a model of public policy bioethics that tends to disadvantage religious groups that are opposed to this technology and advantage those who support it.

Picking one's model of public bioethics on these grounds is wrong for (at least) three reasons. First, and most simply, it is undemocratic to structure the system so that your opponents are not allowed equal standing in the debate. Second, even if this first principle is not motivating, there is a self-interested reason as well. It is self-defeating to structure a debate against your opponents because the excluded group will simply press their views in another arena that you do not have input on, resulting in less conversation, more posturing, and more polarization. This seems to have been the case in the early 1980s when the President's Commission for the Study of Ethical Problems in Medicine and Biomedical and Behavioral Research released a report on genetic engineering called *Splicing Life*.[46] The religious input to the report was structured so that only certain types of theologians could participate, and even their views were translated into a perspective that ended up removing fundamental objections to technologies such as germline human genetic engineering. A few days after the release of the report, a coalition of religious leaders and theologians, including many people from religious groups excluded from participation (such as fundamentalist Jerry Falwell), released a statement opposing germline human genetic engineering. The opposition statement probably earned more press coverage than the official document did, and, more important, it precluded conversation because the public was left to interpret rival statements.

A third reason makes sense only in the current political configuration, where people identified as being from religious groups tend to reach more conservative conclusions on technologies than scientists and bioethicists would like. For example, while a few liberal Protestant denominations and most of Judaism have come out in favor of embryonic stem cell research,[47] they are outnumbered by the religious groups opposed to this technology. Hence, the temptation to remove all religious voices from the debate in order to limit opposition.

In current public policy bioethics, it would be "conservative" religion that would be excluded. However, this is particular to this exact time in history and these particular issues. We can imagine situations in which secular conservatives might try to exclude all religion to get rid of religious liberals. (For example, religious liberals advocate positions in international relations that are anathema to the conservative international policy community.)[48]

Here is why people who reach "liberal" conclusions in public policy bioethics should not exclude all religion in the name of a short-term advantage: in the long run you will loose an ally on other issues that you care about. Liberals can be excused for thinking that it is only the conservative religions who operate in the public sphere because of all of the attention that the Religious Right has obtained since 1979. However, religious liberals have continued on in much less visible ways throughout the time period.[49]

Let us consider historically the campaigns of religious groups that "liberals" would agree with. Most apropos to public bioethics, I think it can be persuasively argued that without liberal Protestants and Jews advocating for the legalization of abortion before 1973, without their clergy smuggling women for illegal yet safe abortions during that period, and without these groups' defense of the *Roe* decision after 1973, abortion would not be legal today.[50]

More famously, religious motivations and discourse were so intertwined with the Civil Rights movement of the 1950s and 1960s that it is hard to say whether it was a religious movement or a social movement.[51] More important, here was religion in public discourse in the liberal cause. On the similar issue of abolitionism a century or more earlier, it was also religious liberals who were the leaders.

If religions were excluded from the public square, there would probably have been no Third World debt relief passed in the 2000 Congress,[52] and the largest funder of Saul Alinsky-style community organizing is the Catholic Church.[53] I believe that if the public sphere is structured to exclude religion, liberals will lose out in the end, having won a few battles and lost the war. For a self-interested liberal, it would be better to argue against "conservative" religious perspectives on the merits, instead of creating structures in the public sphere that exclude *all* religions in order to exclude one's enemies.

NOTES

1. Peter L. Berger, *The Sacred Canopy: Elements of a Sociological Theory of Religion* (New York: Doubleday, 1967), 175–77.

2. John H. Evans, *Playing God? Human Genetic Engineering and the Rationalization of Public Bioethical Debate* (Chicago: University of Chicago Press, 2002), 34.

3. Hanna Fenichel Pitkin, *The Concept of Representation* (Berkeley: University of California Press, 1967).

4. Daniel M. Fox, "View the Second," *Hastings Center Report* 23, no. 6 (1993): S13.

5. Albert R. Jonsen, *The Birth of Bioethics* (New York: Oxford University Press, 1998); David J. Rothman, *Strangers by the Bedside: A History of How Law and Bioethics Transformed Medical Decision Making* (New York: Basic Books, 1991).

6. Jonsen, *The Birth of Bioethics*, 93.

7. My emphasis. See Robert G. Edwards and David J. Sharpe, "Social Values and Research in Human Embryology," *Nature* 231, no. 14 (May 1971): 89, 90.

8. Paul Ramsey, *The Patient as Person* (New Haven, Conn.: Yale University Press, 1970), xx.

9. Jeffrey Stout, *Ethics after Babel* (Boston, Mass.: Beacon Press, 1988).

10. Jonsen, *The Birth of Bioethics*, 13.

11. Ronald Cole-Turner, ed., *Human Cloning: Religious Responses* (Louisville, Ky.: Westminster John Knox Press, 1997).

12. There are two ways of changing the genes of a human being, which I call human genetic engineering. The first is "somatic," where the genes of a person are changed, but those changes are not passed down to the next generation. The second is "germline," where the genes that are passed down to the next generation are changed. Germline engineering therefore would eventually change the genes of the species.

13. Jonsen, *The Birth of Bioethics*, xiv.

14. Ibid., 103.

15. Tom L. Beauchamp and James F. Childress, *Principles of Biomedical Ethics*, 5 (New York: Oxford University Press, 2001).

16. John Rawls, "The Idea of Overlapping Consensus," *Oxford Journal of Legal Studies* 7, no. 1 (1987): 1–25.

17. Beauchamp and Childress, *Principles of Biomedical Ethics*, 3.

18. Evans, *Playing God? Human Genetic Engineering and the Rationalization of Public Bioethical Debate*, chap. 4.

19. H. Tristram Engelhardt, *The Foundations of Bioethics* (New York: Oxford University Press, 1986), 5.

20. James M. Gustafson, "Theology Confronts Technology and the Life Sciences," *Commonweal* 105 (1978): 386.

21. D. Stephen Long, *Tragedy, Tradition, Transformism: The Ethics of Paul Ramsey* (Boulder, Colo.: Westview Press, 1993), 125–26.

22. Stout, *Ethics after Babel*.

23. James T. Laney, "The New Morality and the Religious Communities," *Annals of the American Academy of Political and Social Science* 387 (1970): 19.

24. Neo-scholasticism in Catholic ethics produced a stream of moral manuals which have, according to one account, "a great air of security and certainty," reflecting "a confident understanding of the identity of Christian morality." Oversimplifying, the whole point is to make sure people know the rules to get to heaven. See Vincent MacNamara, *Faith and Ethics: Recent Roman Catholicism* (Washington, D.C.: Georgetown University Press, 1985), 9, 10.

25. Josef Fuchs, writing in 1970, quoted in MacNamara, *Faith and Ethics: Recent Roman Catholicism*, 40.

26. Gustav Ermecke, writing in 1972, quoted in MacNamara, *Faith and Ethics*, 55.

27. Evans, *Playing God?*

28. Ibid., 80–92.

29. John H. Evans, "A Sociological Account of the Growth of Principlism," *The Hastings Center Report* 30, no. 5 (2000): 31–38; Evans, *Playing God?* 40–42.

30. President Clinton, quoted in James F. Childress, "The Challenges of Public Ethics: Reflections on NBAC's Report," *Hastings Center Report* 27, no. 5 (1997): 11.

31. Ibid.

32. Audrey R. Chapman, *Faith, Power, and Politics: Political Ministry in Mainline Churches* (New York: Pilgrim Press, 1991).

33. See "Attachment A: Statement on the Ethical and Moral Implications of Stem Cell and Fetal Tissue Research." Available at: http://www.pcusa.org/oga/actions -of-213.htm#attachment.

34. "Resolution No. 2 on Human Cloning," Southern Baptist Convention Annual Meeting. Available at http://sbcannualmeeting.org/sbc01/sbcresolution.asp ?ID=2

35. Allen D. Hertzke, *Representing God in Washington: The Role of Religious Lobbies in the American Polity* (Knoxville: University of Tennessee Press, 1988).

36. Ronnee Schreiber, "Playing 'Femball': Conservative Women's Organizations and Political Representation in the United States," in *Right-Wing Women: From Conservatives to Extremists Around the World*, ed. Paolo Bacchetta and Margaret Power (New York: Routledge, 2002), 211–224.

37. Lester Kurtz and Kelly Goran Fulton, "Love Your Enemies? Protestants and United States Foreign Policy," in *The Quiet Hand of God: Faith-Based Activism and the Public Role of Mainline Protestantism*, ed. Robert Wuthnow and John H. Evans (Berkeley: University of California Press, 2002), 364–80.

38. Charles Taylor, "Liberal Politics and the Public Sphere," in *The New Communitarian Thinking*, ed. Amitai Etzioni (Charlottesville: University Press of Virginia, 1995), 183–217; Jürgen Habermas, *The Structural Transformation of the Public Sphere* (Cambridge: MIT Press, 1989); Alan Wolfe, *Whose Keeper? Social Science and Moral Obligation* (Berkeley: University of California Press, 1989); Robert Wuthnow, *Between States and Markets: The Voluntary Sector in Comparative Perspective* (Princeton, N.J.: Princeton University Press, 1991).

39. Jürgen Habermas, "The Public Sphere: An Encyclopedia Article (1964)," *New German Critique* 1, no. 3 (1974): 49.

40. Taylor, "Liberal Politics and the Public Sphere," 185–86.

41. Robert Wuthnow and John H. Evans, *The Quiet Hand of God: Faith–Based Activism and the Public Role of Mainline Protestantism* (Berkeley: University of California Press, 2002), 19.

42. Although obviously the Presbyterians have a Presbyterian polity and the Baptists a congregational one. However, both sets of delegates to the decision-making body are elected by the members, albeit with different degrees of directness.

43. Robert Wuthnow, *The Restructuring of American Religion* (Princeton, N.J.: Princeton University Press, 1988).

44. James D. Davidson, Ralph E. Pyle, and David V. Reyes, "Persistence and Change in the Protestant Establishment," *Social Forces* 74, no. 1 (1995): 157–75.

45. Robert Audi, "Liberal Democracy and the Place of Religion in Politics," in *Religion in the Public Square*, ed. Robert Audi and Nicholas Wolterstorff (Lanham, Md.: Rowman & Littlefield, 1997), 1–66.

46. President's Commission for the Study of Ethical Problems in Medicine and Biomedical and Behavioral Research, *Splicing Life: A Report on the Social and Ethical*

Issues of Genetic Engineering with Human Beings (Washington, D.C.: GPO, 1983); Evans, *Playing God? Human Genetic Engineering and the Rationalization of Public Bioethical Debate*, chap. 4.

47. John H. Evans, "Religion and Human Cloning: An Exploratory Analysis of the First Available Opinion Data," *Journal for the Scientific Study of Religion* 41, no. 4 (2002): 749–60.

48. Kurtz and Fulton, "Love Your Enemies?"

49. Stephen Hart, *Cultural Dilemmas of Progressive Politics: Styles of Engagement among Grassroots Activists* (Chicago: University of Chicago Press, 2001); Wuthnow and Evans, *Quiet Hand of God*.

50. John H. Evans, "Multi–Organizational Fields and Social Movement Organization Frame Content: The Religious Pro–Choice Movement," *Sociological Inquiry* 67, no. 4 (1997): 451–69.

51. Doug McAdam, *Political Process and the Development of Black Insurgency, 1930–1970* (Chicago: University of Chicago Press, 1982).

52. Kurtz and Fulton, "Love Your Enemies?" 374.

53. Hart, *Cultural Dilemmas of Progressive Politics*, 50.

4

Bioethics, Religion, and Linguistic Capital

Tod Chambers

Everett McGill: It ain't the law!
Sheriff Cooley: The law? The law is a human institution.
—*O Brother, Where Art Thou?*

The Authority to Perform

In the Coen brothers' film *O Brother, Where Art Thou?* three escaped convicts stumble upon a mass baptism. Two of the prisoners, Pete and Delmar, carried away by the ceremony, decide to be baptized, and they believe this act means that the state of Mississippi has also forgiven them for their legal transgressions. Their leader, Everett, strives to straighten them out on this point:

> PETE: The preacher said it absolved us.
>
> EVERETT: For him, not for the law! I'm surprised at you, Pete. Hell, I gave you credit for more brains than Delmar.
>
> DELMAR: But there were witnesses, *saw* us redeemed!
>
> EVERETT: That's not the issue, Delmar. Even if it did put you square with the Lord, the State of Mississippi is more hardnosed.[1]

Pete and Delmar have confused the authority of the preacher to declare them absolved of their spiritual sins with a state judge's authority to declare them absolved of their legal troubles. They have confused the necessary conditions for what the English philosopher J. L. Austin refers to as "performatives."[2] Austin notes that language does not merely describe states of affairs but brings about actions.

Austin accordingly distinguishes between descriptive utterances, constatives, and performative utterances, and he observes that a successful performative is quite different from a successful constative. Take the two utterances "I now pronounce you husband and wife" and "They were married this morning." The second utterance "succeeds" to the degree that it accurately portrays the world. If we were to discover that that the marriage will actually occur tomorrow, then we would judge the constative unsuccessful. The first utterance does not describe the relationship between the couple but rather in its being uttered, transforms the couple's relationship to each other and to the state. When the preacher declared that Pete had been absolved of his sins, this was a constative utterance describing Pete's relationship with God, not a performative that altered his relationship with the state of Mississippi. Later in the film, when the governor of the state declares to an audience, "Why then *I* say, by the par vested in me, these boys is herby pardoned!"[3] his performative utterance truly does transform our heroes' relationship to the state. Austin reports that a "failed" performative is "not indeed false but in general *unhappy*," or, to use the term he adopts for such a failure, an "infelicity."[4]

In outlining the necessary conditions for a happy performative, Austin advanced that "the particular persons and circumstances in a given case must be appropriate for the invocation of the particular procedure invoked."[5] Such an insight into the dramaturgical nature of language, according to Pierre Bourdieu, should have compelled Austin to acknowledge the need for a sociological account of utterances. Austin instead attempted to determine "the relationship between the properties of discourses, the properties of the person who pronounces them and the properties of the institution which authorizes him to pronounce them."[6] Being a philosopher, Austin viewed the issue of infelicity as a philosophical problem, a problem that does not require understanding the social determinants of authorization. Bourdieu, a philosopher who converted into a sociologist, asserts that Austin's inattention to social dynamics prevents him from grasping what truly determines if a performative is felicitous: it is not words that perform actions but the speaker of words, or, rather, the authority given to particular speakers to perform actions. This authority is determined by particular discourse communities, which possess differing criteria for judging a particular individual's capability to perform certain acts. So performative acts are felicitous not simply when they are performed correctly but also when they are performed by those individuals who have the necessary social status to perform them.

A single individual can be recognized to hold the authority to conduct ritual performatives by differing communities. The preacher is not recognized by the state as able to pardon legal transgressions, but he may well be qualified to pronounce a couple "husband and wife." The preacher's authority is determined not solely by his religious community, however, but also by government agencies. The preacher could, of course, pronounce the couple married, and this act may very well be recognized by the religious community without its being seen as a valid performative by the state. Similarly, a judge may declare a couple to be married without the marriage being recognized by a particular religious community. In order to understand performatives, then, we need to attend to the conditions by which individuals acquire the authority to make things happen when they make utterances. As to what role religion has, if any, in making public policy, the condition we need to determine is how individuals are authorized to express a community's views, to represent its worldview.

Like the question of who can forgive transgressions, the question of who speaks for a religious tradition must be understood in relation to what Bourdieu refers to as "symbolic capital." In his sociological analysis of status, Bourdieu expands the traditional notion of wealth from being solely one of the acquisition of financial wealth to one in which wealth is measured in a variety of economies. We compete for status not simply through physical possessions but also through various symbolic economies. For Bourdieu, social life entailed a variety of "fields" of competition in which individuals battle over status within a particular socially constructed hierarchy through the acquisition of whatever capital is deemed to have value in that particular field's hierarchy. Every field— religious, artistic, political, academic—has different rules and standards by which individuals attain higher status. In the literary world, for example, one may mark status by the number of works an author has sold, but there are alternative economies of value. Thus, while one social class may prize a novelist for publishing bestsellers, another may value a novelist who had won particular literary prizes or the acclaim of noted critics. In the field of literary production, Stephen King may outsell Saul Bellow, but the value of Bellow's work is considered by academia to be considerably higher. This is nicely illustrated by distinguished Yale professor Harold Bloom's attack on the National Book Foundation's decision to award its "distinguished contribution" prize to King. Bloom argues that the award was not given in recognition of the aesthetic value of King's work—as the foundation had done in a prior year by awarding it to Bellow—but rather in recognition of "nothing but the commercial value of his [King's] books, which sell in the millions but do little more for humanity than keep the publishing world afloat."[7] Bloom possesses a differing hierarchy of literary value, one he believes far superior to any other.

From Bourdieu's perspective, Bloom's despair is more an example of class difference than of aesthetic difference. It is only those who have been educated to appreciate certain aspects of literary works who will value Bellow over King, and, likewise, their ability to do so gives them greater status within their particular class. Bloom is essentially accusing the foundation of shifting markets from the upper class to the lower class. Bloom's ability to write an article for the *Boston Globe* is itself representative of his acquisition of symbolic capital. His education, position, and writings add to his status and confer upon him the power to speak about the issue of literary merit, and the fact that his own books have been bestsellers makes him someone that the *Globe* would view as having value for its middle-class readers. Bloom possesses "linguistic capital," which John Guillory defines as "the means by which one attains to a socially credentialed and therefore valued speech."[8]

Linguistic capital is what is at issue when we ask who can speak for a religion. But asking who has the linguistic capital to speak *about* a religious community in public policy forums is different from asking who has linguistic capital *within* the religious community. The first question forces us to examine the acquisition of linguistic capital in three separate—yet at times over-lapping—fields of social discourse: academia, religion, and government. Each of these discourses entails distinctive ways of earning the necessary social capital to be authorized to speak. The issue of who has the status to speak for a religion in a political forum is essentially a question of what types of linguistic capital gained in one field are deemed legal tender within another field, what is the rate of exchange between the fields.

Charismatic Capital

In terms of religious communities, one can devise a rudimentary typology of linguistic capital by drawing on Max Weber's notion of "charisma,"[9] his global term for a particular quality of an individual's character "by virtue of which he is set apart from ordinary men and treated as endowed with supernatural, superhuman, or at least specifically exceptional powers or qualities."[10] For Weber, these powers or qualities, which Bourdieu refers to as "the economy of charisma,"[11] can be attained in a variety of ways. One of the oldest methods for obtaining charismatic capital is through shamanistic practices, which Mircea Eliade describes as "archaic techniques of ecstasy,"[12] and those who have direct access to the sacred through such practices in turn gain special religious authority within their communities. Charismatic capital can be a source for authority in other arenas of social economics. After discussing the way Hmong shamans acquire their spiritual power, Dwight Conquergood explains that the shaman's work in society entails "the combined roles of physician, spiritual minister, psychiatrist and elder statesman."[13] The shaman can exchange charismatic wealth with the currency of other symbolic economies.

Many religious traditions, especially those that are often referred to as "world religions," must respond to the death of initial charismatic individuals by routinizing charisma. This can occur through a variety of means, including the creation of ritual authority and canonical texts. Capital within the religious field thus can be acquired in the ways in which one attains authority within the routinization. Christianity, for example, has developed an extensive tradition of theological interpretation of its sacred texts; intimate knowledge of this material confers linguistic capital within the community. Thai Buddhist males can acquire a substantial amount of religious and social capital by undergoing temporary ordination as monks. The ritual of ordination confers on them a form of ritualized charisma that translates into a raised social status while in the monastic robes and afterward. Weber sees the creation of routinization as a binary split between prophetic and priestly roles, but it may be more accurate to describe this as a continuum from direct charismatic experiences to routin-ized ones. Some religious traditions permit a degree of direct contact with the sacred but also maintain clear boundaries by means of routinization.

One's symbolic capital outside a particular religious community is, of course, not necessarily the same as one's capital within the community. In fact, one's symbolic capital outside the community usually must be understood in relation to the religion's general symbolic capital within a particular society. In a Buddhist country, having capital within a Christian sect will not necessarily translate into having capital that can influence the state. The situation is similar in the United States. The state perceives Christian and Jewish sects as having higher degrees of capital than other religious communities have, and the differences are not directly related to their numbers. Of course, the symbolic capital one can achieve as an outsider must also be viewed in relation to other forms of capital. In particular, monetary capital can influence symbolic capital. In any case, routinized religious capital is an essential component to overlap capital in the secular sphere, and charismatic individuals are rarely thought to possess the same degree of capital as those who work within a routinized established church. It would be substantially easier for a small-town pastor to testify in front of a presidential council than, for example, it would be for the founder of a UFO cult to do the same.

Academic Capital

Linguistic capital in academia follows a very different set of rules. The difference in the types of status can perhaps best be illustrated in the manner in which religious studies became an acceptable subject within secular academia. In his history of the discipline, Eric Sharpe notes that in order for religious studies to be acceptable in the academy, scholars had to consciously disinherit theological methods and perspectives on the subject.[14] When other scholars accuse religionists of failing to maintain this separation, they are questioning the religionists' legitimacy within the academy. One of the severest attacks on religious studies came from anthropologist Edmund Leach, who in an article in the New York Review of Books challenged the scholarship of one of the central figures in comparative religion, Mircea Eliade. Leach compared Eliade's work to "sermons by a man on a ladder," accusing him of presenting his personal confessional ideas as if they were secular and objective claims.[15] In a comparable attack, Donald Wiebe accused religious studies of a "failure of nerve" for refusing to adopt appropriate methods of investigation within a secular institution.[16] In these criticisms, Leach and Wiebe were reevaluating the worth of religious studies. Wiebe, who comfortably plays both the role of secular academic and that of theologian in his work, believes that there can be a "scientific" study of religious phenomena, but he clearly also believes that the two roles he occupies should be kept separate. Within the economics of rhetoric, this means that Wiebe wishes to acquire linguistic capital within both the academic and theological marketplaces but thinks that there should be no equivalence in the currencies. A theologian's credentials are to be deemed worthless in a secular academic institution; his or her ideas should be of interest to the religionist only insofar as they provide material for study. For Wiebe, the fact that religionists are unable to make such a distinction discredits the academic field.

Perhaps a more interesting way to approach status within the academy is to look at what generally does not confer substantial status: teaching. In a recent article in the *Chronicle of Higher Education*, a professor who had been denied tenure writes that she felt as if she were at her own funeral as people expressed their condolences. The reason for the denial of tenure? "In a university that every year intensifies the chant of 'research, research, research,' I apparently spent too much time teaching and made the mistake of going up for tenure on the combined strengths of my research and my classroom skills."[17] The author suggests that the desire to achieve excellence in teaching was not considered to be important in the university's decisions about granting promotion. There is nothing unusual about this author's criticism of the American university system, for all academics know a tale similar to the one recounted in the *Chronicle*.

Of course, the central goal within academia is the creation of knowledge. In *Academic Tribes and Territories*, Tony Becher and Paul Trowler observe that "communication of all sorts and the partly socially constructed nature of disciplines that is associated with them are the forces that bind together the sociological and the epistemological, giving shape and substance to the links between knowledge forms and knowledge communities."[18] Being able to communicate successfully within a discipline furnishes one with academic capital. Though publishing is the most recognized form of capital, assessing a scholar's academic capital is not simply a matter of counting up his or her publications (although this can help). As a humanities scholar who works in a medical school, I experience ongoing struggles with the question of whether the scholarly capital I acquire will be recognized as exchangeable currency. Research in academic medical centers tends to be focused on data-driven research papers. Though books are viewed as a key source of capital in many humanities disciplines, they are not the dominant speech genre in medicine, articles are. Because these articles are usually multiauthored, one's position as first or second author is a key feature in determining one's worth. The number of publications considered to be acceptable also varies greatly from one academic discipline to another. In some disciplines, such as philosophy, a single article a year may be viewed as a productive output. Also, scholars measure each other's influence in the field; the coin of the realm is the number of citations to a particular scholar's work. The value of one's work is also determined by the status of the journal in which one publishes. In the medical world, publication in such journals as the *Journal of the American Medical Association* and the *New England Journal of Medicine* adds substantially to one's status.

Because of its relative youth as an academic discipline, bioethics has yet to reach a consensus about what exactly will—and, just as important, what will not—count as legal tender. Interestingly, many achievements that are prized in bioethics are not highly valued in traditional philosophy. Many bioethics scholars criticized the selection of members for George W. Bush's presidential bioethics council. Though its chair, Leon Kass, is usually thought of as being part of the "bioethics community," bioethics scholars did not consider most of those selected as being a part of mainstream bioethics. Kass acknowledged that the commission's members, "though not bioethicists per se, have bioethics-related training."[19] This controversy—and Kass's response to it—raises questions about what exactly is a bioethicist (and what is "bioethics-related training"). Determining what constitutes capital for the bioethics community is—as the controversy itself reveals—just becoming clear. Below I outline some of the forms that are recognized within this new field as legal tender.

Publication

Like other academic fields, bioethics has its series of ranked journals. For a long time, the *Hastings Center Report* had little competition in terms of its renown within the discipline. Bioethicists also can receive a great degree of intellectual capital by publishing in medical and scientific journals. Because many bioethicists hold jobs in medical academic centers, their status within their home institutions increases if they publish in such international medical journals as the *Journal of the American Medical Association*, the *New England Journal of Medicine*, the *British Medical Journal*, and *Lancet*. Another venue through which bioethicists can gain status is the more popular press, such as newspaper and magazine articles. These are not necessarily areas where a great deal of capital is gained within the community, but such publications do sometimes afford a great deal of symbolic capital within their institutional setting or with the general public.

Clinical Experience

Especially for those working in the area of clinical ethics, "clinical experience" can be a key source of symbolic capital. Such experience denotes having a working knowledge of the clinical setting, and it can be considered equivalent to the value anthropologists place on "fieldwork." The value placed on clinical experience represents a distinction between "armchair" ethicists (similar to the denigrated armchair anthropologists) and clinical bioethicists. I heard a bioethicist begin his lecture by reporting that he had performed more than 500 ethics consultations; this bioethicist was asserting that he had the necessary rhetorical capital to make assertions about the field.

Media Presence

One of the most controversial elements within bioethics is the kind of symbolic capital gained by media appearances. (Here I am distinguishing media presence from publication in the popular press, although I recognize that the two are often interrelated.) Because bioethicists as scholars of a form of applied humanities can comment about current issues in biomedicine, they can be a part of media stories or, as Art Caplan was in *People* magazine, the story itself. One could draw a parallel between the rise of bioethicists as media personalities and the rise of what is sometimes referred to as the "academic star system." In *Academic Instincts*, Marjorie Garber claims that there is an ongoing tension between academics and journalists.[20] To some degree, the same tension exists within bioethics, for although there is a desire to be relevant to current issues, traditional academic distrust of the media abides.

Academic Degrees

One source of bioethics capital that has been changing radically in recent years has been the importance of degrees. Like any new discipline, simply having "been there" at the start allows one to acquire capital. If a particular conversation continues, then the discipline must decide if it wants to professionalize it by creating a mechanism for accreditation or a series of degrees. Bioethics has begun to enter into that very discussion. A current issue within the largest bioethics association in the United States, the American Society for Bioethics and Humanities, is whether bioethics should be professionalized. At one time, the intensive bioethics course at Georgetown University's Kennedy Institute of Ethics conferred an informal accreditation to individuals wishing to become bioethicists at their home institutions. Similar symbolic capital was earned by holding a yearlong fellowship at the University of Chicago's MacLean Center for Clinical Medical Ethics. In recent years, the route of having "just fallen into bioethics" is becoming replaced with formal courses; thus, while the old guard retains its symbolic capital for having been around for a long time, new forms of degrees have begun to be created in various academic settings. The members of the old guard are able to maintain their symbolic status as the ones who now determine the degree by which the new guard has learned the knowledge.

Government Service

Unlike scholars in disciplines like English literature and traditional philosophy, bioethicists can earn symbolic capital by serving on government commissions. For some bioethicists, the lack of mainstream bioethicists on Kass's commission as opposed to the two prior presidential commissions represents a loss of a means to achieve this capital, akin to a sudden shift in currency. The degree by which there now exists two bioethics—a liberal and a conservative one—itself comes to represent whether the particular political sway of the government determines which bioethicists can use such commissions as a means for the acquisition of capital.

Censorship by Convention

In 1996, the Clinton administration inaugurated the National Bioethics Advisory Commission (NBAC) to analyze "the appropriateness of departmental, agency, or other governmental programs, policies, assignments, missions, guidelines, and regulations as they relate to bioethical issues arising from research on human biology and behavior, and applications, including the clinical applications, of that research." This commission was particularly interested in hearing from various religious perspectives. In its 1997 report, "Cloning Human Beings," an entire chapter is dedicated to religious perspectives: "NBAC solicited oral and written presentations from scholars in several religious traditions, contracted for a scholarly analysis of the views of these and other religious traditions, and received public testimony and written submissions from various other individuals and groups with religious orientations."[21] Religious studies scholar Courtney S. Campbell of Oregon State University wrote a commissioned paper titled "Religious Perspectives on Human Cloning." In this report, he presented ten religious traditions: African American churches, Buddhism, Hinduism, Islam, Judaism, Native American, Orthodox Christianity, Protestant Christianity (Conservative Evangelical), Protestant Christianity (Mainline), and Roman Catholic Christianity. Though at first glance, it seems that Campbell was presenting a quite catholic view of the range of traditions, prior to presenting these views he provided a "normative analysis" that seems a synthesis of Jewish and Christian views.

When NBAC requested religious perspectives on human stem cell research, it brought together particular representatives to present these perspectives. All of the individuals had university appointments. All save Edmund Pellegrino had Ph.D.s. Even within the range of world religious traditions, the speakers represented a relatively limited and highly conventional range of Christian, Jewish, and Muslim viewpoints. As representative of the status that various religions have within the United States, there were seven from the Christian tradition (three Protestants, three Roman Catholics, one Greek Orthodox), three from Judaism, and one from Islam. These individuals tend to be of high academic status and of high routinized charismatic status.

It is profitable to ask what kinds of individuals would not be considered to have adequate status to be considered to have linguistic capital. First, it would be difficult to imagine anyone being asked to testify whose religious capital was acquired through direct charismatic contact rather than through routinization. Routinization, including academic routinization, establishes a primarily conservative relationship to the sacred. Though some theologians may be considered "radical," their radical reinterpretation is still a routinization of some prior direct charismatic experience. To declare that one has status acquired through direct contact with the sacred would represent the construction of a novel tradition that broke in some manner from the revelations that already form the basis of the tradition, which would in turn place one outside the mainstream.

Second, as mentioned above, every religious community is not awarded the same degree of status in relation to its government. Buddhism is the official religion of Thailand, and the Muslims and Christians in the country have a secondary status and are not accorded the same degree of attention in the making of official policy for the country. In the United States, on the other hand, discussion of whether prayer should be permitted in public schools is always framed within a Judeo-Christian worldview without regard to religious traditions that do not practice prayer as a central tenet of their relationship to the sacred. When Bush declared his support of faith-based initiatives for social services, one cannot imagine that he thought that this would include support of Scientology, Hmong shamanism, or Wiccan religions. In a national survey conducted in 2001 by the Pew Research Center for the People and the Press, the kind of status that various religious traditions have among the American public is clearly demonstrated: though a clear majority of Americans believe that religious organizations should receive government funding for charitable work, they tend to be less generous when asked about their support of particular religious faiths. Catholic and Protestant churches were deemed by more than 60 percent to be favorable recipients of funding; Muslim and Buddhists were seen by only 38 percent to be worthy; the Church of Scientology gained only 26 percent support. The NBAC's emphasis on Judeo-Christian viewpoints thus accords with the sympathies of the nation at large.

In his analysis of linguistic capital, Bourdieu was particularly interested in the issue of censorship. For him, censorship meant not explicit decrees to govern speech acts but rather "the structure of the field itself," which determines what kind of expressions are deemed worthy of attention. Thus, he notes that "among the most effective and best concealed censorships are all those which consist in excluding certain agents from communication by excluding them from the groups which speak or the places which allow one to speak with authority."[22] NBAC, like all government agencies, and thus like all fields, structures itself so that only certain voices will be allowed to speak and will be recognized as authoritative. In attempting to broaden its view by bringing in religious voices, such commissions are destined to hear only what they already know. Those with high charismatic capital and low academic capital do not possess the necessary linguistic capital even to present their alternative views.

NOTES

1. Ethan Coen and Joel Coen, *O Brother, Where Art Thou?* (London: Faber and Faber, 2000), 25.

2. J. L. Austin, *How to Do Things with Words*, 2d ed. (Oxford: Clarendon Press, 1975).

3. Coen and Coen, *O Brother, Where Art Thou?* 97.

4. Austin, *How to Do Things with Words*, 14.

5. Ibid., 15.

6. Pierre Bourdieu, *Language and Symbolic Power* (Cambridge, Mass.: Harvard University Press, 1991), 111.

7. Harold Bloom, "Dumbing Down American Readers," *Boston Globe*, December 19, 2003. Available from http://www.boston.com/news/globe/editorial_opinion/oped/articles/2003/09/24/dumbing_down_american_readers.

8. John Guillory, *Cultural Capital: The Problem of Literary Canon Formation* (Chicago: University of Chicago Press, 1993), ix.

9. Max Weber, *The Sociology of Religion* (Boston: Beacon Press, 1963).

10. Max Weber, *The Theory of Social and Economic Organization: Being Part I of Wirtschaft Und Gesellschaft*, trans. A. M. Henderson and Talcott Parsons (London: W. Hodge, 1947), 358.

11. Pierre Bourdieu, "Genesis and Structure of the Religious Field," *Comparative Social Research* 13 (1991): 28.

12. Mircea Eliade, *Shamanism: Archaic Techniques of Ecstasy* (New York: Bollingen Foundation, 1964).

13. Dwight Conquergood, "Ethnographic Commentary," in Dwight Conquergood, Paja Thao, and Xa Thao, *I Am a Shaman: A Hmong Life Story with Ethnographic Commentary*, Southeast Asian Refugee Studies (Minneapolis: University of Minnesota, 1989), 51.

14. Eric J. Sharpe, *Comparative Religion: A History*, 2d ed. (La Salle, Ill.: Open Court, 1986).

15. Edmund Leach, "Sermons by a Man on a Ladder," *New York Review of Books* 7, no. 6 (1966).

16. Donald Wiebe, *The Politics of Religious Studies: The Continuing Conflict with Theology in the Academy* (New York: St. Martin's Press, 1998).

17. Maria Annunziata, "Dead Professor Walking," *Chronicle of Higher Education* 51, no. 2 (2004): C3.

18. Tony Becher and Paul Trowler, *Academic Tribes and Territories: Intellectual Enquiry and the Culture of Disciplines*, 2d ed. (Philadelphia: Open University Press, 2001), 104.

19. Eugene Russo, "Advice Fit for a President," *Scientist*, February 18, 2002, 22.

20. Marjorie B. Garber, *Academic Instincts* (Princeton, N.J.: Princeton University Press, 2001), 32–39.

21. National Bioethics Advisory Commission, Cloning Human Beings: Report and Recommendations of the National Bioethics Advisory Commission (Rockville, Md.: June 1997). The National Reference Center for Bioethics Literature at Georgetown University, 1996–2001, http://www.georgetown.edu/research/nrcbl/nbac/pubs.html, accessed December 21, 2004.

22. Bourdieu, *Language and Symbolic Power*, 138.

5

And Power Corrupts . . . : Religion and the Disciplinary Matrix of Bioethics

M. Therese Lysaught

Religion and Public Bioethics: Complicating the Received Narrative

"Public bioethics" is often positioned as a subfield in the discipline of bioethics. It is depicted as a public practice of deliberation or debate among professionals or a plurality of voices about how society should proceed in the face of a particular problem related to health care or biotechnology. Such debate seeks to produce some level of consensus *via* rationally coherent arguments useful for formulating guidelines to be promulgated by policymakers (aka public policy)[1] or for influencing the beliefs and values of the public. Daniel Callahan and others, in fact, differentiate this sense of "public" bioethics from other forms of bioethics that they variously label "foundational," "clinical," "pedagogical," "institutional," "community," "civic," and so on.[2]

Yet to limit "public" bioethics to the action of public panels, public conversations, or the crafting of government regulation and health policy is somewhat artificial and misleading. For contemporary images of the clinical setting are structured along similar lines. The clinical context is narrated as a pluralistic space where a diverse set of people—patients, physicians, nurses, allied health workers, families—come together as both strangers and moral strangers yet are bound to work together cooperatively. To resolve moral disagreement, various stakeholders must meet and, through reasoned conversation, craft a balance between the strictures of institutional/public authority and individuals' rights to pursue their own goods. In fact, Bette-Jane Crigger notes (with concern) that medicine (by which she means the clinical setting) is well on its way to becoming "a privileged domain—perhaps the preeminent domain—of public moral discourse in contemporary American society."[3] The public, it seems, is everywhere.

One could in fact argue that there is no subcategory of bioethics that is not public. One reason is that the bioethical architecture of what are deemed to be putatively distinct arenas draws on a shared narrative of public space, a narrative whose "core thesis," as Michael Sandel puts it, is this:

> Society, being composed of a plurality of persons, each with his own aims, interests, and conceptions of the good, is best arranged when it is governed by principles that do not themselves presuppose any particular conception of the good; what justifies these regulative principles above all is not that they maximize the social welfare or otherwise promote the good, but rather that they conform to the concept of right, a moral category given prior to the good and independent of it. This is the liberalism of Kant and of much contemporary moral and political philosophy.[4]

Again and again, the settings of particular subfields of bioethics as well as the ways in which they locate and choreograph agents within those settings reproduce this narrative.

Not only does this narrative give a particular shape to the practice of bioethics across contexts.[5] It tells a consistent story about religion. Across the board, from the pluralistic contexts of public to clinic, religion presents a problem.[6] Religions posit beliefs that are, by definition, not held in common and as such cannot provide a shared basis for moral exchange.[7] At best, they are denied intrinsic moral value.[8] At worst, they emerge as one of the primary sources of moral conflict. Belying their apparent neutrality toward religious convictions, Tom Beauchamp and James Childress in their highly influential *Principles of Biomedical Ethics* return again and again to a particular example of self-destructive behavior, "bizarre actions prompted by unorthodox religious beliefs."[9] One of the few other contexts in which religious convictions are mentioned in their text is in the conflictual situation of refusal of treatment.[10] In a similar fashion, H. Tristram Engelhardt, the once-despairing champion of the Enlightenment project in biomedical ethics, again and again rhetorically equates the terms "particular," "religious," "parochial," and "ideological."[11] Examples abound to demonstrate how the dominant mode of bioethics no longer takes theological or other substantively rational authors seriously but rather simply deems them irrational and outside the purview of legitimate argument.[12]

Yet it is not just that religious beliefs confound the canons of moral consensus and rationality. As problematic as religion can be in the clinical setting, to allow participation of religion within the practice of public bioethics can be even dicier. James Childress, in his account of the process behind the NBAC report on human cloning, names the fundamental issue:

> Arguments for and against a significant role for religious convictions in public policy appeal to two different fears, which may be

more or less plausible depending on the particular liberal, pluralistic democracy at a particular time. On the one hand, opponents often fear religion's divisiveness. John Rawls begins his book on political liberalism with the story of religious conflict in the West, and we know full well religion's role in conflicts around the world. Many who argue for a reduced role, or no role at all, for religious convictions in public policy share this fear, *and it is not unreasonable.*[13]

Religion, in other words, must be handled carefully vis-à-vis the public sphere because it is inherently dangerous and violent.

Childress's remarks echo one of the foundational myths that undergird the U.S. liberal social vision described earlier by Sandel. As Judith Sklar tells the story:

> Liberalism . . . was born out of the cruelties of the religious civil wars, which forever rendered the claims of Christian charity a rebuke to all religious institutions and parties. If the faith was to survive at all, it would do so privately. The alternative then set, and still before us, is not one between classical virtue and liberal self-indulgence, but between cruel military and moral repression and violence, and a self-restraining tolerance that fences in the powerful to protect the freedom and safety of very citizen.[14]

The modern state, in other words, arose out of what came to be known as the "wars of religion" of the sixteenth and seventeenth centuries, as that force necessary to make the peace. Behind the pluralist narrative outlined earlier, then, lies a vision of the state as the necessary hedge that protects individuals against the coercive tyranny of religious authority and the inevitable violence inherent in religious difference.

The story of the state as that which saves us from the violence of religious passion, as the agent of peace, has become canonical for both U.S. public policy and bioethics. More important, it is historically and theologically false. Theologian William Cavanaugh carefully displays that the received story that the liberal state emerged as a response to religious violence gets the matter backward.[15] Drawing on the work of social theorists and historians Charles Tilly, Quentin Skinner, and Richard Dunn, Cavanaugh compellingly argues that the modern liberal nation-state began to emerge well in advance of the wars of religion, documents how indeed most of these wars were not fought between Protestants and Catholics but rather between co-religionists (i.e., between Protestants and Protestants or Catholics and Catholics), and shows how emerging religious identities were manipulated as tools of unflinching *Politiques* in their quest for state power.

Cavanaugh argues that key to emerging states' ability to foment such wars was the very creation of the modern category of "religion." Through the Middle Ages, religion was understood as a virtue, deeply intertwined with bodily practices located within the institutional structure of the Roman Catholic Church. But in the sixteenth and seventeenth centuries, the term "religion" began to be used in a new way. It begins to refer to a system of beliefs, a set of propositions that could be held by newly minted modern "individuals" and that could exist separately from one's public loyalties to institutions of church or state.[16] Thus, as he notes: "To call these conflicts 'Wars of Religion' is an anachronism, for what was at issue in these wars was the very creation of religion as a set of privately held beliefs without direct political relevance."[17]

Cavanaugh convincingly demonstrates that this theoretical reconfiguration of Christianity as a now fractured diversity of religions fit not only with Enlightenment epistemological presuppositions but, more important, was employed as a tool for wresting power from the only institution strong enough to stand against the state, namely the church. "True religion," in Locke's words, found a new home not in a public, communally extended and authoritative institution but rather in the private and solitary confines of an individual's mind and conscience. As such, the medieval configuration of disciplinary authority split between church and state was dismantled: "What is left to the Church is increasingly the purely interior government of the souls of its members; their bodies are handed over to the secular authorities."[18] The state, in other words, assumed unchallenged disciplinary control over individuals' bodies as religion was brought into service of the sovereign.

Cavanaugh's account upends the foundational myth that sets the terms of debate in the conversation on religion and public bioethics. With others, it reveals the problematic nature of the concept of 'religion' as it functions within the field of bioethics.[19] It displays as mythical the fear that Childress identified as *not unreasonable*. And it unmasks the modern state's claim to be the keeper of peace rather than what it is—the purveyor of violence on a scale previously unimaginable.

But Cavanaugh's rereading of the historical record does more than challenge the very way 'religion' is conceptualized within bioethics; more fundamentally, it problematizes the very depiction of bioethics itself. Far from being an open, public deliberative practice that involves reasoning with other citizens or a limited set of procedural norms that facilitate the full range of individual value judgments, bioethics instead has become part of the disciplinary matrix of the modern social order, a key practice in the state's management of bodies within its purview.

For bioethics, like its ally medicine, is about nothing if it is not about bodies. Bioethics does an extraordinarily good job at masking this fact; rarely will one see bodies referred to, even obliquely, within the discipline of bioethics. The various distinctions between subfields of bioethics (especially distinctions between 'clinical bioethics' and other types) are but further attempts to distance the discipline from the bodies that it organizes.

It will be the burden of this essay to make this case, that bioethics ought properly be understood as a disciplinary matrix that serves the modern Leviathan of state and market. The purpose of doing so, of course, is to narrate a rather different vision of 'public bioethics.' For without a more accurate accounting of the nature and function of public bioethics, it will not be possible to begin to posit how 'religion' might even begin to position itself in relationship to it.

Cavanaugh's account of the reconfiguration of the relationships between religion, bodies, and the state is clearly indebted to the legacy of Michel Foucault, a debt I share. For those who are not familiar with Foucault, I begin with a brief overview of his analytic framework. The major work of the essay will be to display how bioethics fits the Foucauldian paradigm. So as to avoid the appearance of special pleading, I will turn not to theologians to develop this account[20] but rather to social scientists and bioethicists.

Bodies and Disciplinary Matrices

Robert Zussman and others have recently argued that bioethics can and ought to learn from sociology.[21] Foucault might well have concurred, holding as he did that medicine is a mode of applied sociology.[22] Although Foucault is not quite what Zussman has in mind, for those who have read his account of medicine as well as his work on power, knowledge, and discipline, it is but a small step from there to the field of bioethics.[23]

Central to Foucault's analysis is a recognition of the material reality of bodies and the politics that is nothing other than production and organization of bodies within culture.[24] Bryan Turner, one theorist who has attempted to systematize a theory of the body, summarizes Foucault's thesis: "The body as an object of power is produced in order to be controlled, identified, and reproduced."[25] Power, for Foucault, is not negative per se. Rather, it is essentially *productive*. As Anthony Giddens notes, "Power is actually the means whereby all things happen, the production of things, of knowledge and forms of discourse, and of pleasure."[26] Joanne Finkelstein extends this definition, capturing its more decentered, circulatory, weblike, operational sense:

> Power is a strategy of relations that gives some individuals and
> groups the ability to act and keep acting for their own advantage.
> Power is also the ability to bring about a desired situation and to
> prevent the actions of those who would thwart such desires.[27]

Key to the productivity of such power is the fact that it is wielded not in an overt, coercive manner but rather that individuals come to wield it over themselves. In other words, within a regime of disciplinary power, each person—by internalizing the norms and surveillance of the social order—effectively disciplines her or himself. As such, Finkelstein writes, this exercise of power is "extremely subtle as it can direct individuals toward actions the eventual outcome of which will not necessarily be to their advantage."[28] The basic goal of disciplinary power is to produce persons who are docile—persons, in other words, who do not have to be externally policed.[29]

But how does this occur? How does it happen that individuals—or rather

individuals vis-à-vis their bodies—become formed in such a way as to internalize the agenda of the wider social order? What, in other words, are the
mechanisms of governmentality?[30] Bodies are constituted, Foucault and others
argue, via disciplinary matrices consisting of the intersection of three key elements: discourses, practices, and institutions.[31]

A *discourse* is that body of concepts and statements that make possible the
appearance of objects at a particular historical moment and provide a language
for talking about them. Discourses define and produce objects of knowledge,
governing the ways a topic can be meaningfully talked about and reasoned
about. Variously put, nothing that is considered meaningful exists outside discourse, nothing has any meaning outside of discourse, and nothing outside of
discourse is considered meaningful.[32]

Social theorist Arthur Frank pushes this definition one step further, noting
how deeply allied discourses are to bodies. Discourses, he notes, are:

> cognitive mappings of the body's possibilities and limitations, which
> bodies experience as already there for their self-understanding. . . .
> These mappings form the normative parameters of how the body
> can understand itself. . . . Discourses only exist as they are instan-
> tiated in on-going practice or retained by actors as "memory
> traces."[33]

One example of such a discourse would be the modern scientific account of
anatomy. Arising in part out of the structures of the human body, it equally
arranges, depicts, defines, and describes the way in which inhabitants of Western culture literally "map" their bodies; bodies no longer consist of humors or
mime the structures of the heavens, but instead are composed of organs, systems, tissues, cells, DNA, and so on. Equally, the languages of disease and
illness are discourses mapping bodies' self-understandings.[34]

Dorothy Smith refers to discourses as "extralocal texts—texts created elsewhere—that organize action and relationships in local settings by instructing
actors in those settings as to what they should do and perhaps proscribing what
they cannot do."[35] Frank elaborates on Smith's reading of discourse with the
example of DRGs:

> In medicine, diagnostic-related groups (DRGs) . . . are a prime ex-
> ample of discourse. . . . DRGs are written documents, created by a
> group of specialists working on the basis of individual clinical expe-
> rience and aggregate data but working apart of any specific scene of
> clinical practice. These specialists produce a code of diagnosis—all
> illness must map into DRG categories to be treated—and detailed
> specifications of what count as reimbursable services for each cate-
> gory. DRGs, as a textual code created elsewhere, thus organize activ-
> ity in local clinics. People in local settings still make decisions and
> deliver care, but the text limits and directs what they can do.[36]

This particular example highlights a key feature of discourses—that the content
of the "extralocal text" is understood as technical or formal knowledge, knowl-

edge that is increasingly esoteric, the purview of specialists and elite professionals.

As such, knowledge associated with discourses becomes a mode of social power. As Finkelstein notes:

> Where knowledge becomes a source of power, as it does with technical or formal knowledge, it is the technocrat, the owner, the controller of knowledge, who gains social power. Significantly, when technical knowledge is the basis of power, the inequalities between provider and consumer are frequently concealed by the idea that a professional service is offered. . . . Indeed, the inherent power and domination of the situation are disguised insofar as the monopoly created by specialist knowledge has been legitimated by the sanction of law and professionalism.[37]

Disciplinary identity and professionalization are key markers of the development of discourse.

Discourses, of course, cannot float free. In order to do the work of constituting and disciplining bodies, of inscribing the meanings of the social order into bodies, they must be incarnated in social *practices*. Discourses and practices stand in reciprocal relationship: discourses define the rules for practices, which in turn embody those discourses.

Discourses, then, are reproduced into the social world by techniques of discipline, by the practices of bodies on which they are inscribed. As Frank notes:

> Theory needs to apprehend the body as both medium and outcome of social "body techniques," and society as both medium and outcome of the sum of these techniques. Body techniques are socially given—individuals may improvise on them but rarely make up any for themselves—but these techniques are only instantiated in their practical use by bodies, *on* bodies. Moreover, these techniques are as much resources *for* bodies as they are constraints *on* them; constraints enable as much as they restrict.[38]

In other words, through their enactment these techniques produce bodies that embody the commitments of the wider social order; they produce "docile bodies." And it is through the creation of such bodies, that then go on to act in the world in self-motivated ways, that practices further realize (make real) and reproduce the commitments of the discourses in the world.

Discourses are legitimated in part by being embedded in *institutions*, social organizations which have attained sufficient power to render their discourses true. Institutions, Frank writes, "have a specificity within both space and time. A discourse can only be spoken or enacted; it is nowhere but in that act or speech. An institution is a physical place where one can go, which may or may not be there any longer."[39]

Institutions, then, provide both a centralized social space for exponential consolidation of productive power as well as visible social sanction for the truths put forward in a particular discourse. Such institutionalization, at least in our culture, further reinforces the "scientific" character of the discourse's growing body of knowledge.

Further, institutions enable methods of surveillance that are crucial to the mapping of the bodies within their population as well as the process of normalization. Via disciplines like medicine, certain attitudes and practices come to prevail as normal and acceptable. Institutionally sanctioned discourses both define the "normal" and, through techniques and practices, encourage individuals to regulate and achieve her or his own conformity with the established rules.[40]

Disciplinary matrices of discourses, techniques, and institutions are able to exercise power in this decentralized manner insofar as the discourse is able to sustain a *regime of truth*. "Truth" in this sense points to the creation of knowledge as a function of power (power, as noted above, which is understood not negatively but as productive). Truth is a product of discursive practices understood to emerge only within a structure of rules, practices, and institutions that control the discourse and collaborate to establish a given claim as "true." Knowledge shaped by discourses, empowered by institutions, and wielded through techniques and practices thus has the power to make itself true.

Truth then is embodied and reproduced through "rituals of truth," practices shaped according to the rules of the discourse which then, not surprisingly, reinforce the truth claims of the discourse (one might think, for example, of the "truth" of the anthropological claim that we are autonomous individuals embodied and reproduced through the practice of advance directives). Through these many factors, the networks of productive power serve to produce, via inscribed bodies, particular styles of subjectivity. Subjects are both produced within discourses and simultaneously subjected to discourses. Such subject production is one component of the process of normalization.

These, then, are the components of a Foucauldian disciplinary matrix. By not allowing attention to be diverted from bodies, such an analysis seeks to unmask how particular discourses—particular fields of knowledge and truth claims—are used in conjunction with institutionalized practices to effect social and political ends, even while rhetorically claiming to be apolitical, neutral, and objective. It turns attention not to abstract ideas or disembodied "wills" but rather to the usually covert operations of productive power, power that produces particular kinds of embodied subject-citizens and in doing so reproduces the body of the state.

The Disciplinary Matrix of Bioethics

Equipped with an outline of disciplinary matrices and how they function, we can turn now to the field of bioethics itself. One might counter that the connection between bioethics and the state is already inferred in the phrase "public bioethics."[41] This analysis seeks not only to establish that fact but to display the intricate connections between the various types of bioethics, suggesting that they ought rather be understood as coordinated aspects of an overarching matrix rather than as conceptually and practically distinct activities. By narrating bioethics as an institutionally located set of discursive practices, its function as a normalizing discipline in service to state and market becomes disturbingly clear.

Bioethics as Discourse

In historical perspective, discursive formation entails a discontinuous trajectory in which one can plot the emergence of a new discourse and the decline of an old one. Although such a history will often be recounted as seamless, more often it is one of ruptures and radical breaks. As history is written by the winners, so "the persons and professions that rose to prominence will tend to write the history of the debate in a way that makes their rise seem somehow natural."[42]

Such a pattern indeed characterizes recent histories of the development of the field of bioethics. As per the standard narrative of the genesis of bioethics, its earliest origins lay among theologians, but substantive theological discourse was quickly replaced by the more advanced discourse of philosophy. Kevin Wildes narrates this standard account, that bioethics emerged because of the increased technologization of medicine in the 1960s and that theological ethics was pushed aside because "philosophical ethics offered the hope of resolving such questions without appealing to the faith of a particular community."[43] Wildes further proclaims the canonical narrative, highlighting the transition from theology to (in his own words) secular or civil religion:

> Bioethics has emerged as a field that is distinct from theological ethics and traditional physician ethics even though both disciplines were important to the development of the field. . . . [O]ne needs to understand why theological voices receded from the field. . . . The turn toward a secular bioethics became a search for a secular or civil religion that might bind the sentiment of citizens who were at least nominally divided by religions, cultures, or other differences.[44]

The transition here is cast as seamless, logical, necessary.

But is this the only way to reconstruct this history? Is this the most accurate way to tell this story? John Evans, in fact, narrates the same history quite differently.[45] He helpfully debunks the dominant myths that shape the recent histories of bioethics, including those that suggest that the principles' approach to bioethics was necessitated by expanding commitments to democracy or stories that plot such developments as "natural" progressions. Over against the accounts that claim that the dominant approach to bioethics is necessitated by the pluralistic nature of contemporary U.S. society, Evans convincingly demonstrates that the growth and institutional embodiment of bioethics in the

United States, via government advisory commissions, took shape precisely as a way to circumvent pluralism, to "avoid more direct democratic control."[46] As he demonstrates, the pluralist model of democracy was in fact "unacceptable to the scientists, who feared that an 'excitable' public would shut down not only [human genetic engineering] research, but other research in their home jurisdiction that the public did not understand."[47] They were fearful, in other words, of funding cuts,[48] pointing to the hidden economic substrate of all these discussions.

Bioethics, then, emerged as a mechanism for shaping and controlling the hoi polloi. A first step toward such an end would be to create a body of esoteric, technical, formal knowledge that would be portrayed as inaccessible to the common person while simultaneously constituting objects of knowledge and defining the acceptable parameters for discussion. Although many bioethicists protest the characterization of their field as one of specialized knowledge (a claim made most often by detractors) one finds such descriptions with relative frequency. Most often such claims arise within conversations about hospital-based ethics consultation. David Casarett and his colleagues note that some "contend that the ethicist is a specialist who possesses expertise in moral theory . . . [that] ethicists, like physicians possess a unique fund of knowledge, problem-solving techniques, experience and techniques that allows them to solve complex moral problems."[49] Nancy Dubler paternalistically states the claim in a *via negativa* when she maintains: "It is simply not within the purview of most patients and family members to understand the complex nature of the moral judgments facing them."[50]

Though the precise content of this knowledge base remains contested within the realms of hospital-based ethics consultation, it has become well established within the realm of public bioethics. Bioethics' specialized knowledge defines the acceptable parameters of discussion, prescribing certain ways of talking about topics and excluding others (i.e., rules of inclusion and exclusion). Substantively rational arguments and religious language have been systematically excluded, or at least carefully positioned so as to be mostly irrelevant within public bioethics. While dominated by a formal, instrumental rationality,[51] public bioethics privileges a particular point of view, a particular conception of "the good" and of the ends that society and individuals within it must necessarily pursue and preserve.[52] Evans captures it well when he notes that it operates "with a very constrained list of universal, commensurable ends that have become institutionalized by the dominant profession in the debate."[53] These ends are, of course, the principles of autonomy, beneficence, nonmaleficence, and justice.[54]

As the above accounts make clear, specialized, technical knowledge is inextricably intertwined with professionalization, the creation of experts or specialists.[55] Professions are defined, in fact, by their role as those who apply a distinct system of knowledge to a well-defined set of problems delimited within a particular jurisdiction. Insofar as such knowledge is abstract, professional training is necessary to know how it is to be applied.[56] That bioethics has become a "profession" is little contested.[57] Evans fleshes out the demographics of this shift:

> While the bioethics profession has been strengthening its jurisdiction over ethical decision making in public bioethical debates, it has grown even stronger in its other jurisdiction of decision making in hospitals (clinical bioethics). The bioethicists have also increasingly taken on the trappings of a classic profession, with a professional association of 1,500 members; 200 centers, departments, and programs; an academic degree (a master's in bioethics from the University of Pennsylvania and a Ph.D. in bioethics from various other universities). There is even a debate about licensing: who is qualified to be a clinical bioethicist and to offer ethical judgments in hospitals? Licensing, and other internal and external controls over who is a legitimate member of the profession, is the hallmark of an increasingly successful profession. The organization that accredits hospitals has required since 1998 that every hospital have a mechanism for resolving ethical problems that arise.[58]

In the words of Henk ten Have: "In a certain sense, ethics has become part and parcel of the technological order. It has been professionalized as an autonomous discipline external to medical practice. It is dominated by an engineering model of moral reasoning and impregnated with the idea of a technical rationality, applying principles to practices."[59]

In an interesting twist on the standard discussions of professionalization, Tod Chambers insightfully recounts how central the image of "centering" has been to the internal contests shaping the field over the past thirty-five years.[60] Centering narratives trace the "migration" of the practice of bioethics from the academic realm to that of the hospital or clinic; from the realm of "theory" into the realm of "action"; from philosophical training to medical training, with the rise of clinical bioethics. His story closes with more recent attempts to wrest bioethics from both philosophy and medicine by sociologists.[61] With each move, such centering strategies have functioned as attempts to establish authority, legitimacy, and jurisdiction within the field by defining which conceptual tools shape the field and who ought rightly be included as a conveyor of bioethical power.[62]

As Chambers notes, all these scholars and more use the metaphors of inside-outside to describe this shift in their work.[63] Intriguingly, the same metaphors shape the discussion on religion and bioethics. The conversation revolves around phrases such as whether religions should be "included" in public bioethics, how they might "contribute to" the debate, "how a religious community might enter into the discussions in bioethics,"[64] or how they might "influence" public bioethics. True to the founding myth, religion and theology must be located "outside" the public sphere in such a way that they must "enter" it, be "included" or "influence" it, as if from a distance. Yet perhaps a mark of how completely irrelevant theology has become to bioethics, the recentering of the field away from theology does not even enter into Chambers's account.

Evans's sociological analysis of the growth of bioethics also demonstrates how the discourse of bioethics clearly functions as an "extralocal text," in Smith's sense of the term. As he documents, once the Belmont principles were established, bioethicists began to apply them and their form of argumentation beyond their original focus in the ethics of human experimentation.[65] Capturing the work of Belmont in textbook form, Beauchamp and Childress's *Principles of Biomedical Ethics* expanded the form and content of this approach to apply to almost all ethical issues in science, medicine, and society.[66] The twin sanctions of public approval and an authoritative textbook fueled principlism's growth, creating an "enormous demand" for ethics training, spawning a new and ongoing industry of books, workshops and courses "designed to make 'the theories and methods of ethics' 'readily available to more people in a shorter period of time.'"[67] As a result, this particular method increasingly shaped bioethical discussion across localities—in the academy, the literature, the public forum, the media, and the clinic. As David Rothman notes, "the new rules for the laboratory permeated the examining room, circumscribing the discretionary authority of physicians. The doctor-patient relationship was modeled on the form of the researcher-subject; in therapy, as in experimentation, formal and informal mechanisms of control and a new language of patients' rights assumed unprecedented importance."[68] The long arm of state policy reaches into all levels of the social body.

Techniques and Practices of Bioethics

As James Lindemann Nelson notes, bioethicists "wield explicitly normative techniques."[69] The discipline of bioethics, in other words, comprises a distinct set of practices, techniques by which discourses are enacted, inscribed onto bodies, and thereby reproduced as truthful in the world. These techniques mediate the "extralocal texts" of the bioethics canon into local settings.

Bette-Jane Crigger, in her account of hospital-based ethics consultation, provides one of the most straightforward accounts of bioethics as a practice. Noting from the outset that bioethics has become "established as a particular form of practice," the intent of her essay is to explore the ways in which "bioethics does a further sort of cultural work that tends not to be recognized."[70] Although working with a slightly different sense of local and extralocal knowledge, Crigger's account of bioethics reflects Frank's account of how practices mediate extralocal texts, making it possible for abstract norms to shape local actions, to interpret individual bodies. Speaking first of medicine, she notes:

> Medicine operates as a paradigm of meanings on at least two levels: as a system of concrete, local, ready-made meanings, and as a system of abstract, global, negotiated meanings. As a system of local, that is clinical, meanings, medicine construes individuals' privately experienced sensations as symptoms and signs upon which to base

diagnosis, recommend treatment, and assess prognosis. That is, medicine names and thus confers a particular kind of socially recognized significance ("illness" or "disease" of a given sort) on personal bodily experience. . . . There is a fixed set of indicators to be deployed in construing embodied experience. . . . Overlaying this "local knowledge" of the clinic, however, is a system of more abstract and far-reaching meanings that link medicine—or better perhaps, patients' embodied relationship with medicine—to the wider social order.[71]

These higher order meanings, she notes, are "abstract and self-consciously normative" as well as "profoundly social."[72] Each moment of clinical practice— be it a practice of medicine or bioethics—realizes these higher order meanings in the world and serves to reproduce them, slowly working to transform the world into its image: "Each clinical encounter offers the prospect of incrementally transforming the set of meanings upon which not simply the immediate participants, but also the wider culture, may draw, refashioning the universe of discourse within which the next encounter will take place."[73] Ethics consultation stands as a vehicle for negotiating between the local and higher order meanings, offering, "the potential not only to 'discover' normative meanings in clinical decisions, but also actively to create new norms and values in the process of making those decisions."[74]

Such a dynamic could be displayed for each bioethics practice. One will suffice for our purposes. Consider the practice of informed consent. Rothman, above, has noted how the practice of informed consent has reshaped the clinical encounter in the direction of the politics of the laboratory; the patient-physician relationship now more closely resembles the subject-researcher relationship. Drawing on the normative anthropology captured in the primary end of bioethics—the principle of autonomy—the practice of informed consent constructs the patient as first and foremost, primarily, essentially an autonomous subject, even though the patient's autonomy may be severely compromised by illness or even though their own anthropology—should they hail from a non-Western culture—provides no space for contemporary U.S. concepts of autonomy. The practice of informed consent shapes patients by persuading them (or coercing them, since most medical procedures will not be performed without a signed document) to locate themselves under the rubric of autonomous consent, to understand their relationship with the physician as somewhat contractual (based on a signed document, one which waives many of their rights), as consumers who are "choosing" a particular course of medical treatment, having weighed the advantages and disadvantages of the options.

Institutionalization

Institutions, as noted earlier, are social organizations that have attained sufficient power to render their discourses true. The institutional dimension of bioethics takes two main forms. Clearly, the main institutional form of bioethics has been the U.S. government, in the form of government advisory commissions. Evans traces the dominance of principlism to the increased scope of state intervention in issues related to science and medicine. Pointing to an obvious but often overlooked fact: "A blunt indicator of this spread in state interest are the titles of the first and second government bioethics commissions. The 'National Commission' was 'for the Protection of Human Subjects of Biomedical and Behavioral Research.' The 'President's Commission' was 'for the Study of Ethical Problems in Medicine and Biomedical and Behavioral Research.' "[75]

Evans establishes the crucial role played by these commissions in establishing the parameters of truth. First, they determined which arguments would count as legitimate, thereby granting jurisdiction to some professions over others.[76] The replication of this mode of reasoning in subsequent government commissions reinforced those truth claims. Second, these parameters for argumentation were codified into law via government regulations. As Evans notes:

> The influence of this new profession grew rapidly. Through the influence of the first government advisory commission, its form of argumentation was written into public law as the proper method of making ethical decisions about research involving human subjects. Henceforward all researchers at institutions that receive federal funds would have to learn and adopt this form of argumentation.[77]

It is important to note that the power of law was reinforced by force of economics. The Belmont Report, by translating its reasoning into government regulation, which was tied to government funding, rendered the principles' approach and its formal rationality to be the 'truth' vis-à-vis public bioethics. This is the case now not only for human subjects research but for the clinical sector as well.[78] Indeed, bioethics has become a primary agent of the presence of the state in the practices of research and medicine.

From policy through law and economics, this new regime of truth has been further reinforced by the institutionalization of the theoretical apparatus supporting the discourse via the production of knowledge within the academic realm. The 'truth' of Belmont was first expanded—almost evangelically—by Beauchamp and Childress's *Principles of Biomedical Ethics* and its aftermath. Yet this dissemination, of course, was not accidental. As James Lindemann Nelson notes: "The birth of principlism itself is intertwined with the advent of state intervention in ethics. . . . It is also well known that the Belmont principles were created at the urging of the state, and enacted as regulations, with the help of Kennedy Institute members who were simultaneously writing *Principles of Biomedical Ethics*."[79]

One can trace additional links between the quiet hand of the state and the culture of academic bioethics. As Evans notes:

> Since journals refuse to publish results from research not reviewed by IRBs [Institutional Review Boards], the principles became the

standard not only for federally funded research, but for privately sponsored research as well. This was a huge resource given to the new profession of bioethics in its competition with other professions: the government was essentially requiring researchers at every re-search institution and hospital in the nation to learn its form of ar-gumentation.[80]

The linkage between the institutions of state, clinical research, and the academy render a clean distinction between "public bioethics" and other realms of ethics (i.e., foundational, clinical, institutional, community, etc.) problematic. Here we see the reification (one could say, the fetishization) of the substance of bioethics: its content and parameters "do not seem to have been created by anyone but is just 'common sense' or even 'fact'—and takes on a life indepen-dent of its creator."[81]

Thus, tracing the institutional infrastructure of bioethics begins to unmask the intimate relationship between bioethics and the state. Even if one was narrowly to construe public bioethics as concerned with the crafting of public policy, etymology would lead to the same conclusion. As Ruth Malone notes, the Greek origins of the word *policy* "link it to citizenship, government, polity, citizen, city. That is, the idea of policy arises originally from the relationship of citizens to one another in a common public space."[82] Indeed, as the literature on the rise of formal rationality indicates, the state is one of the foremost proponents of formal rationality.[83] Thus, the state appears not only as an his-torical factor in the rise of bioethics but indeed as so critically constitutive of the discourse itself that bioethics might rightly be construed as itself an ap-paratus of the state.

The State, Bioethics, and Normalization

Foucault's account of disciplinary matrices seeks in part to demonstrate how the state/social order effectively shapes the subjectivities of citizens within their purview to embody that social order's normative claims, in order to reproduce those norms toward the end of maintaining, furthering, or reproducing that state/social order.[84] As mentioned earlier, this process of producing docile bod-ies is known as normalization.

Evans, as we observed, debunks the claim made in the recent histories of bioethics that the principles approach was required by our society's increasing recognition of pluralism or what he calls the "expanding democracy" expla-nation.[85] Rather, as he notes, this story masks a deep disconnect between the objectives of the allied scientific-government complex and the populace. The first government advisory commission, the National Commission (1973), he argues, was "instructed by Congress to create a set of ends," ends that "had to be portrayed as universally held by the citizens, but had to be applied without a method of determining empirically what the ends of the citizens were."[86] Its subsequent task, as outlined in the previous section, was to establish these ends as truth, to diffuse them throughout the institutional infrastructure of research and patient care, and through the practices of bioethics to persuade the citizenry to adopt these as their own ends.

Crigger captures this normalizing function in the practice of hospital-based ethics consultations. For Crigger, bioethics consultation poses a paradox. On the one hand, bioethics' "peril" is that it may "work toward imposing on patients a particular, content-laden vision of what the dominant culture perceives to be morally most significant and most appropriate."[87] Yet its peril is equally its promise, as she notes.

> The practice of bioethics consultation in clinical settings not only guides individual decisions, but just as importantly announces the dominant culture's commitment to fashioning a common moral order in a pluralistic society. That commitment and the practices in which it is inscribed in the clinic hold both promise and peril. Promise in that ethics consultations may indeed promote a common moral idiom, if not also a stronger commonality of norms . . . [Bio-ethics] work(s) toward shaping some significant portion of a shared moral order.[88]

Indeed, for Crigger, "the moral and *political* authority of ethics consultation on this model are seen to derive from a societal mandate to foster shared decision making."[89]

Yet can this promise be fulfilled without imposing culturally dominant views of the good on patients? It is hard to see how it will be avoided. In fact, Casarett et al. obliquely point to this inevitability: "It is rare," they note, "that an ethics consultant can simply hand down an opinion. In fact, that typically happens only when the primary issue has been legally resolved, or, to put it another way, *when a national discourse has produced a consensus that is then imposed by the state.*"[90]

Thus, the normative claims of the liberal political philosophy that shapes the social order are, through the practices of bioethics, subtly prioritized. More powerfully, although claiming that particular goods are permitted to exist in their private spaces, an important component of the normative infrastructure is that such particular convictions ought not be held too tightly; all commitments must ultimately be negotiable. Casarett et al., in their reflections on the process of ethics consultation, highlight this dynamic:

> Often, the immediate obstacle to consensus is unwillingness to engage in dialogue. . . . Consensus is fragile and is easily disrupted when one or more participants hold tenaciously to a principle or value. The fragility of consensus requires that *all* participants, including the ethics consultant [though equally this would include the patient or physician], be willing to reconsider their own normative claims. Indeed, this is the only way normative validity can be evaluated. . . . Genuine understanding of the issues involved may threaten

deeply held beliefs about the values that make collaborative social life possible. Just as allocation decisions frequently require us to make choices that call into question certain fundamental values that hold society together, moral argumentation in clinical ethics highlights troubling choices that we might prefer to keep hidden. Ethical deliberation requires participants to examine deeply held values such as the sanctity of life, the primacy of autonomy, and the commonly held view that lives do not have a dollar value. These threads make up the fabric of our social existence. To bring them to the surface in order to examine and weigh them threatens the integrity of the view we have of ourselves and our society.[91]

In the end, all particular commitments must bow to the overarching norm of consensus.

But it is no longer only the common moral idiom of autonomy that bioethics serves to normalize among the citizenry through its practices; bioethics more recently appears to be serving as an agent for the increasingly powerful alliance between state and market. The standard portrayal of public interaction around questions of bioethics is one of discourse, argument, persuasion, and consensus. Yet often this image is bolstered by that bizarre fiction of "the marketplace of ideas" (a metaphor rendered even more absurd in these days of global capitalism). Can the capitalist resonances be accidental?[92]

Troyen Brennan abandons any pretense of bioethics' neutrality and maintains that the future of the field lies in embodying more consistently the commitments of political liberalism and, indeed, the market. Brennan calls for a new medical ethics that reflects "the public morality of liberalism" and respects the resource constraints of "market justice."[93] But although Brennan issues this as a call for bioethics to move toward, others acknowledge how deeply bioethics is indebted to and allied with market economics.[94] Ruth Malone focuses on the economic infrastructure of bioethics, noting that although medicine and bioethics once framed its discourse in military terms, more recent metaphors have shifted to the language of the market.[95] As she notes:

> The market metaphor has assumed a prominent place in U.S. discourse on medicine and health policy, displacing an earlier military metaphor ("battling disease," "doctor's orders") still in use but now considerably less prominent. . . . [T]his shift in language has been extremely effective in promoting a different understanding of medicine and health care. . . . [T]he metaphor has been taken up readily, perhaps due to its compatibility with the economism of much health services research methodology, such as cost-benefit and cost-effectiveness studies.[96]

Metaphors, of course, do not merely label things; they form our concepts, create the parameters for action, define what can even be seen as a problem or issue.[97] Market metaphors within bioethics function as extralocal texts, en-hancing bioethics' ability to mold health care institutions, practitioners, and patients as increasingly ideal consumers. Market metaphors embody particular philosophical presuppositions about the nature of the person and the nature of social interaction:

> In markets, the relationship to the other is primarily, if not solely, instrumental: the other is necessary only as a means to the end of purchase or sale of products. Buyers' and sellers' relations are based in contractual obligations of business that do not extend to concern for or dependence on one another. . . . The product-market metaphor relies on the self-interested utility-maximizer view of human agents that is congruent with neoclassical economics, in which individuals make choices based on their perceptions of what will benefit them most. Agency is reduced to rational choices made to buy or to sell, a matter of exerting preferences rather than of acting in accordance with constitutive values or concerns.[98]

Market metaphors are likewise deeply enmeshed with the images that shape standard displays of public bioethics. As Malone notes:

> The product-market metaphor works for talking about policy in sev-eral important ways: we understand policy at least partially in terms of political negotiation, which bears more than a passing resem-blance to negotiations for market goods. And we view the practice of policymaking as one in which choices must be made among differ-ent ideas or viewpoints, much as a shopper in a market must choose among competing brands of soap. Also, we sustain the cul-tural myth of "objectivity" as a desirable and achievable goal in policy-making, congruent with the moral impassivity of the market.[99]

Malone sees deep incongruities between such an anthropology and health care policy, which at least in theory "addresses how we as a society will deal with sick and injured people who must depend on the care and concern of others. . . . This view of human agency as instrumental rationality leaves little space for the kinds of actions that embody different values—for example, generosity, mercy, or solidarity."[100]

In reality, however, this is not an incongruity but rather a Foucauldian window into the operative but obscured foundations of bioethics, a window that Malone's own words suggest:

> The product-market conception of health policy (and health care) also helps to keep the experience of suffering safely at bay for us. . . . Sickness, as others have noted, represents a challenge to the social order. If the perceived need for policy solutions to social problems may be understood as a confrontation with uncontrolled elements, the product-market metaphor suggests a restoration of order: a rule-

based mechanism (the market) that both preserves and controls the autonomous self. In the quite recent past, this has been largely a function of medicine: we have a vast and illuminating literature on the medicalization of social problems. . . . The market has begun to supplant even medicine as a dominant mechanism of social control.[101]

Not coincidentally, Evans (evidencing his debt to Weber) traces the dominance of principlism to the development of double-entry bookkeeping in 1494, which paved the way for modern capitalism and formal rationality. The logic of principlism, he argues, is isomorphic with the logic of accounting. The principles of bioethics function as units of commensuration—akin to other commensurable metrics such as utility, risk-benefit analysis, profit, and money.[102]

In short, much of public bioethics functions as a normalizing practice that masks the economic interests and dynamics that are the real forces that shape public policy. As Ed Pellegrino notes: "In stem cell research, for example, commercial and technological imperatives dominate the decisions under the guise of a value-free agreement among 'reasonable' people who will not be so benighted as to invoke some transcendental source of morality in support of their position."[103] How metaphorical is it, we might ask, when Albert Jonsen refers to the principles of bioethics as "the common coin of moral discourse"?[104]

Theology and the Disciplinary Matrix of Public Bioethics

More could be said, but for now, we come to the end of a rather different narration of the practice of public bioethics.[105] Where, then, does this leave the question of religion? Clearly, a thoroughgoing constructive account of the relationship between religion and public bioethics would take me beyond the limits of this chapter. Let me indicate, instead, the direction such an account might take.

Over against standard responses to the question of religion and bioethics, this alternative construal of bioethics forces a question: Is it the proper task of religion to contribute to, support, undergird, disseminate, and so on, the disciplinary matrix of the modern social order? Is it the job of religion to assist the state in the management of bodies within its purview? Is it the task of Christianity to assist the state in normalizing its citizens according to particular canons of philosophical and economic "truths," especially norms such as autonomous individualism, adversarial rights, or utility, which are deeply at odds with the central truths of the faith? Is it proper to Christianity to aid the state in producing docile citizens, those who have internalized market paradigms of consumer choice so deeply that they apply them to all aspects of their lives, including the realm of moral discernment?

It is not clear that many authors—theologians and scholars of religion included—would not assent to the above questions, at least in their broad outlines. Time and again, religion is cast as instrumental to the ends and needs of bioethics.[106] Too many accounts of how to "relate" religion to public bioethics end up being little more than attempts to make a kinder and gentler Leviathan. But Leviathan it remains. And theologians do little to challenge the idolatrous and heretical claims of the state.[107]

To answer "no" to the above questions will be to issue a radical call. For to answer "no" will be a call to orient religion (or, more accurately, theological reflection on medicine and healing) toward a different social body. If Foucault's account is valid, truths (as known, as productive) do not exist apart from the discourses in which they are embedded, discourses that inscribe bodies into certain visible practices which are institutionally extended. Truth, in other words, sits in a complex relationship to power—the power to produce bodies and, more important, to reproduce particular social bodies. Theology, indeed, is such a discourse—a field of knowledge that forwards a regime of truth by aiming toward the reproduction of the social body of the church through concrete, embodied disciplinary practices. To answer "no" to the above questions is to issue a call for the church.

And this, of course, is why bioethics has left theology behind. For inextricable from substantive theological discourse is the one social body with the real potential to challenge the unbridled authority of the state, the one that the state has, since the sixteenth century, been trying to render powerless.[108] Is it indeed a coincidence that shortly after medical ethics emerged within theological circles, the state-biotech-market complex quickly mobilized to consolidate disciplinary oversight, deftly circumscribing religion to the sphere of autonomy/informed consent, thereby evacuating it of any independent power?[109]

Forty years later, any pretensions on the part of the church to encroach on the disciplinary authority of the state meets with fierce resistance. As Catholic hospitals find, their attempt to embody in their institutional practices particular visions of the good or common good (such as the sanctity and dignity of life) via a refusal of certain practices is increasingly considered unacceptable. The scathing invective with which Catholic hospitals are derided by organizations such as "MergerWatch" and the recent legislative assaults on Catholic hospitals' practices regarding emergency contraceptives (which are largely misrepresented in the popular press) and "conscience clauses" for health care professionals evidence that, indeed, bodies are the site upon which power is contested.[110]

In the end, the relationship between theology and the disciplinary matrix of public bioethics must remain both critical and constructive. If Christianity is to be truthful and liberatory, it must first "query and unmask the dynamics of power" embedded in the discipline of bioethics. The important critical task is to uncover the hidden processes—in its discourse, in its practices, in its institutional affiliations—by which medicine and bioethics seeks to normalize us not toward freedom and autonomy (as the rhetoric would suggest) but rather toward the ends of the state/biotech/market. Such was the work of this chapter.

And second, it must construct alternatives. In other words, the task of Christian theology is to help people live as Christians through illness, healing, dying, and medical care. Its task is to forward the countercultural claim that Christian convictions make a difference for who one is, for how one lives (i.e., how one is produced)—in short, to maintain the truthfulness of Christian convictions. To do so will require practical, visible, institutional embodiment—an embodiment in a church, not the state. To do so will require robust theological language, alternative discourses wedded to alternative practices and regimes of understanding self/body directed toward and sustained by a church that is able to produce bodies which em-body these truths. Such a claim will, indeed, strike fear into the hearts of those James Childress mentioned at the outset. Yet such fears would indeed, I abjure, be unfounded. In the words of William Cavanaugh:

> If we understand the unity of body and soul, we must understand that what is really at stake is not body-power versus soul-power, but competing types of soul/body disciplines, some violent and some peaceful. Christians must understand that the state's control of the body is a control of the soul as well. The church must see that is own disciplinary resources—Eucharist, penance, virtue, works of mercy, martyrdom—are not matters of the soul which may somehow "animate" the "real world" of bodies, but are rather body/soul disciplines meant to produce actions, practices, habits that are visible in the world. For the church to be a true social body it must reclaim not only its body but its soul from the state, and institute a discipline which is truly Christlike—a power based in compassion and martyrdom, suffering, and reconciliation, and not in a revived Christendom.[111]

Through the disciplines of the Christian tradition, bioethics could find in theology a very different kind of power, not the power of state violence but the power of peaceableness, a power made perfect through weakness. How fitting this is for a practice whose center is sick and broken bodies.

NOTES

1. Lisa Sowle Cahill at one point equates the two: "Public bioethical discourse (or public policy discourse) is actually a meeting ground" ("Can Theology Have a Role in 'Public' Bioethical Discourse?" *Hastings Center Report* 20, no. 4 [July–August 1990, special suppl.]: S11).

2. Daniel Callahan, "The Social Sciences and the Task of Bioethics," *Daedalus* 128, no. 4 (1999): 297; and Courtney S. Campbell, "Bearing Witness: Religious Resistance and Meaning," in *Notes from a Narrow Ridge: Religion and Bioethics*, edited by Dena S. Davis and Laurie Zoloth (Hagerstown, Md.: University Publishing Group, 1999), pp. 21–48.

3. Bette-Jane Crigger, "Negotiating the Moral Order: Paradoxes of Ethics Consultation," *Kennedy Institute of Ethics Journal* 5, no. 2 (1995): 90.

4. Michael Sandel, *Liberalism and the Limits of Justice* (London: Cambridge University Press, 1982), p. 1.

5. The vision of bioethics, and indeed of moral interaction, that emerges from this narrative is conflictual, intellectual, and pluralistic. Bioethics exists because of conflict of opinions among diverse and possibly irreconcilable points of view. The "stuff" of bioethics is primarily ideas and beliefs that are packaged into reasoned arguments and traded until one side is persuaded, consensus is reached, or an impasse is met. Moral reasons put forward must be accessible to all parties of the conversation (both as a matter of courtesy and as a matter of persuasion). And all meet on equal ground; the presumption is that "in [secular pluralist societies] there cannot be a privileged moral position or a dominant moral view. The realities of moral and political life demand that we respect the moral claims of others even when they differ fundamentally from our own" (David J. Casarett, Frona Daskal, and John Lantos, "Experts in Ethics? The Authority of the Clinical Ethicist," *Hastings Center Report* 28, no. 6 [November–December 1998]: 7).

6. In 1989, the Hastings Center held a symposium titled "Religion and Bioethics," the proceedings of which were subsequently published in a "Special Supplement" to the *Hastings Center Report* (July-August 1990). The fundamental perspective shaping the conversations asked, "What significance, *if any*, does [religion] hold for the ways we now do bioethics? What difference, finally, do religious perspectives make for bioethics?" (Daniel Callahan and Courtney S. Campbell, preface to "Theology, Religious Traditions and Bioethics," in *Hastings Center Report* 20, no. 4 [July/August 1990, special suppl.]: 1 [emphasis added]). Although rabbis and theologians asserted the indispensability of religious perspectives, many participants demonstrated a marked antagonism toward any religious influence on the field of biomedical ethics, hailing the "exorcism" of the theological as "rational" and realistic "progress."

7. In light of the foregoing analysis in this paper, it is interesting how religious and moral "beliefs" have come to be described in economic terms—as quantifiable, productlike propositions that are or are not "commensurable." We cannot have real moral discourse between particular communities, it is claimed, absent a more overarching transactional system which can determine the moral "exchange rate." In other words, we will get nowhere as long as we bring francs and lire to the table; what we need is a moral Euro.

8. In Tom L. Beauchamp and James F. Childress's classic *Principles of Biomedical Ethics*, religious beliefs are situated as "non-moral" (2nd ed., New York: Oxford University Press, 1983), pp. 6, 48.

9. Ibid., pp. 72, 175, and 295. See also Ruth Macklin's essay "Ethical Relativism in a Multicultural Society," *Kennedy Institute of Ethics Journal*, 8, no. 1 (1998): 1–22, which offers many examples of conflict that center on religion. It is instructive that in this essay, religious beliefs are conceptually equated with foreign "cultural" beliefs and practices.

10. Beauchamp and Childress, *Principles of Biomedical Ethics*, pp. 90–92.

11. His rhetoric is worth noting:

The balance—the tolerance, the *sophrosyne*, required by secular pluralist societies—is empty, insipid, and effete in comparison to the consuming commitment that can be felt as a member of the Baader-Meinhof gang, of the Communist party, of the National Socialist party, of the Inquisition, or for that matter of any religious or ideological group ready for consecration of self and of all to what is felt to be the truth." (*The Foundations of Bioethics* [New York: Oxford University Press, 1986], p. 52)

See also pp. viii, 3, 4, 10, 11, 12, 13, 80, 239.

12. John H. Evans (*Playing God: Human Genetic Engineering and the Rationalization of Public Bioethical Debate* [Chicago: University of Chicago Press, 2002]) captures such characterizations of theologians and religious thinkers in the work of bioethicists Eric Juengst and LeRoy Walters (p. 157). Further, a case could be made for what one might call the "feminization of religion/theology" within the dominant discourse of bioethics. For the characteristics now ascribed to religion or theology are those traditionally ascribed by modern rationalism to women—emotional, irrational, particular, private, embodied, and so on. Alternatively, one might refer to it as the impoverishment, indigenization, or ethnicization of religion or theology insofar as characteristics now ascribed to them are those ascribed to poor, ethnic persons, as depicted so well by Roberto Goizueta in his *Caminemos con Jesus: Toward a Hispanic/Latino Theology of Accompaniment* (New York: Orbis, 1995).

13. James F. Childress, "Religion, Morality, and Public Policy: The Controversy about Human Cloning," in *Notes from a Narrow Ridge: Religion and Bioethics*, edited by Dena S. Davis and Laurie Zoloth (Hagerstown, Md.: University Publishing Group, 1999), 74–75. Emphasis added.

14. Judith Sklar, *Ordinary Vices* (Cambridge, Mass.: Harvard University Press, 1984), p. 5. Rawls, as Childress notes, tells the same story.

15. William T. Cavanaugh, *Theopolitical Imagination* (New York: T & T Clark, 2002), pp. 15–31.

16. Ibid., pp. 31–42.

17. Ibid., p. 22.

18. Ibid., p. 25.

19. For further critique of this notion of religion, see also John Milbank, *Theology and Social Theory* (London: Blackwell, 1990); and Catherine Bell, *Ritual Theory, Ritual Practice* (New York: Oxford University Press, 1992).

20. For my own initial development of this account of bioethics, see my *Sharing Christ's Passion: A Critique of the Role of Suffering in the Discourse of Biomedical Ethics from the Perspective of the Theological Practice of Anointing of the Sick* (diss., Duke University, 1992). In employing a Foucauldian account of medicine, Gerald P. McKenny, in his *To Relieve the Human Condition: Bioethics, Technology, and the Body* (New York: SUNY Press, 1997) also suggests that "standard bioethics . . . participates in discursive formation" (p. 9). Joel James Shuman, in his *The Body of Compassion: Ethics, Medicine, and the Church* (Boulder, Colo.: Westview Press, 1999) displays even further how deeply captured the major approaches to bioethics are by "the politics of modernity" (pp. 52–57). Beyond us three, however, one is challenged to find another who explicitly discusses bioethics in Foucauldian terms (except Joanne Finkelstein, as noted below). It is not coincidental that McKenny, Shuman, and I focus particularly on the embodied dimension of medicine and technology, with attention to how bodies function as sites of formation and power. I also think it unlikely to be a chance event that all three of us are theologians.

21. Robert Zussman, "The Contributions of Sociology to Medical Ethics," *Hastings Center Report* 30, no. 1 (January–February 2000): 8. See also James Lindemann Nelson, "Moral Teachings from Unexpected Quarters: Lessons for Bioethics from the Social Sciences and Managed Care," *Hastings Center Report* 30, no. 1 (January–February 2000): 12–17. Renee Fox, of course, stands as a pioneer in bringing the social sciences into conversation with medical ethics.

22. Joanne L. Finkelstein, "Biomedicine and Technocratic Power," *Hastings Center Report* 20, no. 4 (July–August 1990): 16.

23. See Michel Foucault, *Madness and Civilization: A History of Insanity in the*

Age of Reason (London: Tavistock, 1971); *The Birth of the Clinic: An Archeology of Medical Perception* (New York: Vintage Books, 1973); *Discipline and Punish: The Birth of the Prison* (New York: Pantheon Books, 1977).

24. That Foucault might be relevant to bioethics is signaled first by the ideological erasure of bodies within the discourse of bioethics and the fact that bioethics is about nothing if it is not about the organization of bodies in contemporary culture.

25. Bryan S. Turner, *The Body and Society: Explorations in Social Theory* (New York: Basil Blackwell, 1984), p. 34.

26. Anthony Giddens, "From Marx to Nietzsche? Neoconservatism, Foucault, and Problems in Contemporary Political Theory," in *Profiles and Critiques in Social Theory* (Berkeley: University of California Press, 1982), p. 219. See also Finkelstein, "Biomedicine and Technocratic Power," p. 14.

27. Finkelstein, "Biomedicine and Technocratic Power," p. 14.

28. Ibid. She writes, "It is also an instance of 'structural violence' in that disadvantages are perpetuated by a legitimated social structure."

29. Turner suggests that in order to preserve its boundaries and thus reproduce itself, a society must negotiate four tasks: "the reproduction of populations in time, the regulation of bodies in space, the restraint of the 'interior' body through disciplines, and the representation of the 'exterior' body in social space" (p. 2; see also p. 91). It would be fruitful to display the many ways in which bioethics is involved with all four of these tasks.

30. While Foucault uses the word "governmentality," Dorothy Smith (*Reading the Social: Critique, Theory, and Investigations* [Toronto: University of Toronto Press, 1999]) refers to the mechanisms that connect the local and extralocal with the intriguing phrase "ruling relations." Governmentality or "ruling relations" does not ascribe agency to a class or any specific individuals, although some individuals and groups clearly benefit from a given system of ruling relations. They are not, per se, intentional, nor directly under control of particular individuals or groups. Rather, their power lies in that they are "pervasive and pervasively interconnected" (p. 49). Ruling relations organize local settings through the medium of discourses and are themselves the effects of that textual organization. Ruling relations make extralocal imperatives appear under such rubrics as *rationality, efficiency,* and perhaps most relevant to social sciences, *objectivity.* Cited in Arthur W. Frank, "Can We Research Suffering?" *Qualitative Health Research* 11, no. 3 (May 2001): 353–362, p. 357.

31. Most fundamentally, bodies are corporeal, physical, empirical: "Bodies, of course, do not emerge out of discourses and institutions; they emerge out of other bodies, specifically women's bodies" (Arthur W. Frank, "For a Sociology of the Body: An Analytical Review," in *The Body: Social Process and Cultural Theory*, edited by Mike Featherstone, Mike Hepworth, and Bryan S. Turner [Newbury Park, Calif.: Sage Publications, 1991], p. 48).

32. Stuart Hall, "The Work of Representation," in *Representation: Cultural Representations and Signifying Practices*, edited by Stuart Hall (London: Sage Publications, 1997), pp. 44ff.

33. Frank, "For a Sociology of the Body," p. 42. Turner adds: "Discourses are not linguistic machines which routinely and invariably produce the same effects but possible modes of social construction the consequences of which contain a large element of contingency" (p. 175).

34. As he further notes: "Bodies too exist within space and time, as physiologies. But 'physiology' is at any given time produced in a discourse which seeks some

'truth' of bodies, and the history of physiology proves only that this truth may be re-defined without apparent limit" (Frank, "For a Sociology of the Body," p. 48). Of course, not only social theorists see medicine in these terms.

35. Frank, "Can We Research Suffering?" p. 356.

36. Ibid., p. 357.

37. Finkelstein, "Biomedicine and Technocratic Power," p. 14. She continues: "In the normal transaction between consumer and provider the consumer does not feel exploited by the provider's monopolization of knowledge nor abused as his or her ex-perimental subject, because the desire for the product or service has been publicly cultivated while its cost, in monetary and moral terms, has not been so broadly de-bated or examined."

38. Frank, "For a Sociology of the Body," p. 48. He continues: "People construct and use their bodies, though they do not use them in conditions of their own choos-ing, and their constructions are overlaid with ideologies."

39. Ibid.

40. Finkelstein: "It is principally through discourse, that is, through the ways in which systems of knowledge are established, expectations of human abilities dis-cussed, and subjects and practices described in the working literature of a profes-sional group, that the 'normal' is defined" ("Biomedicine and Technocratic Power," p. 15).

41. The major definitions of "public" in the *Oxford English Dictionary* include references to national identity, nation, and state.

42. Evans, *Playing God*, p. 43.

43. Kevin Wm. Wildes, "Religion in Bioethics: A Rebirth," *Christian Bioethics* 8, no. 2 (August 2002): 169. In addition to the increase in technology, Wildes credits the eclipse of theological discourse to "the development of knowledge in the basic sci-ences along with the development of medical bureaucracy to deliver care" (p. 165), which, he says, "changed the fundamental ethos of medicine." The clear implication is that "traditional" loci of moral reflection (the Hippocratic ethos and religion) were superseded.

44. Ibid., pp. 163–164; similarly, see p. 168.

45. Clearly, my account of the discipline of bioethics relies significantly on John H. Evans's extraordinary sociological analysis of the development of the discourse surrounding genetics in *Playing God*. Though I find his Weberian reading of the de-velopment of bioethics to be extraordinarily insightful, it needs to be further devel-oped in three ways—economically, vis-à-vis the body, and sociologically. Ironically, al-though many of his findings highlight the reconfiguration of bioethics, he does not seem to detect the relationship between that reconfiguration and the growth of the biotech industry—for example, he does not attend to the connections between science and the economic dynamics underlying its growth, especially in the United States, be-tween 1970 and 1995. He is concerned, rather, with the reduction of the four princi-ples/ends to one, that of autonomy. He finds this to be a threat to the internal logic of the profession of bioethics and therefore a threat to the profession itself. However, linking bioethics to its economic substrate would clarify for Evans how the move to the single principle of autonomy actually furthers the internal logic of bioethics, inso-far as it is rooted in furthering the economic ends of a state—and a biotech profes-sion—committed to late capitalism: all becomes consumer choice directed toward the end of producing profit. Thus, the profession of bioethics is not threatened by the reduction of all ends to autonomy; it will simply become the profession that ensures

that no other ends come into competition with that of autonomy, so as to protect the unbridled operation of the marketplace within the realm of biotech research, application, and health care.

With regard to embodiment, he notes in a couple of places how, for example, in the arguments about human genetic engineering (HGE), the move to make it more acceptable was to "limit the claim to the application of HGE to the bodies of patients [and in doing so] they linked the new means with the means used in their safe home jurisdiction" (p. 75). But beyond this, he does not attend to the obvious relationship between the human genome project and the management/production of bodies. Which leads me to point three: he makes no reference to the work of Foucault, whose analysis of bodies and power is indispensable to developing a fully adequate account of the disciplinary role of bioethics. I, then, am employing his Weberian analysis of bioethics to undergird an allied but, I would argue, ultimately more compelling Weberian account.

46. Evans, *Playing God*, p. 73.

47. Ibid., p. 36; see pp. 72ff.

48. Ibid., p. 76.

49. Casarett et al., "The Authority of the Clinical Ethicist," p. 6. They concur that "technical expert" and specialized knowledge are part of the identity of the ethics consultant (p. 9). They prefer the language of "consensus building": "Our claim is that consensus building is precisely what ethics consultants do. . . . When she acts as an engineer of the consensus process, and guides the process according to the rules of discourse ethics, the ethics consultant is both a mediator *and* a moral expert" (p. 7). One might, of course, raise questions about the reality of such a consensus insofar as for the most part, after such a "consensus" is established, those involved will part company. It also fails to account for the power imbalance between parties within the clinic. For more on the topic of the specialized knowledge of the clinical ethicist, see also Scot D. Yoder, "Experts in Ethics? The Nature of Ethical Expertise," *Hastings Center Report* 28, no. 6 (1998): 11–19.

50. Nancy Dubler, *Ethics on Call* (New York, Random House, 1995). One might suggest against this position that in fact it is precisely the patients and their families, and only them, that have any idea of the true complexity and ramifications of the decisions that they face, since they—in their own bodies and in their own lives—are the ones who will bear the burden of the decision.

51. Evans, *Playing God*, p. 13.

52. Bioethics also privileges a particular conception of what counts as legitimate in moral discourse (the impersonal/public/universal/intellectual/rational/objective/secular as opposed to the personal/private/particular/bodily/affective/subjective/religious); of moral anthropology (autonomous individualism); of moral agency and authority (freedom to define, choose, and pursue one's own goods); of society (a composite or collection of discrete individuals who exist in competition and do not a priori hold goods in common); of rationality and knowledge (disembodied, mentalist, positivistic); and so on. These and related commitments are part of the extralocal apparatus that work via the practices of bioethics to produce particular sorts of persons, thereby reproducing the truth of these commitments in the world.

53. Evans, *Playing God*, p. 11. More specifically: "What became known as either the Belmont principles, principlism, or more pejoratively, the 'Georgetown mantra,' became the accepted form of argumentation in public bioethical debates about human experimentation. . . . In a hallmark of formal rationality, the ends came to be

taken as outside the realm of debate, leaving only thin debates about whether technologies (means) maximized these given ends" (pp. 88–89).

54. Although public bioethics is often referred to as "procedural," Evans characterizes the principles of autonomy and justice as "substantive ends" (*Playing God*, p. 90), a position shared by Bette-Jane Crigger ("Negotiating the Moral Order," p. 106). Most important, in a formally rational debate, the ends are either explicitly or implicitly assumed and considered no longer open to debate (see Evans, *Playing God*, p. 16).

55. The debate over the "expertise" of bioethicists dates back at least to the early 1980s. See the exchange in the *Hastings Center Report* 12, no. 3 (May–June 1982) between Cheryl N. Noble, "Ethics and Experts" (7–9), Peter Singer, "How Do We Decide?" (9–11); Jerry Avorn, "A Physician's Perspective" (11–12); Daniel Wikler, "Ethicists, Critics, and Expertise" (12–13); and Tom L. Beauchamp, "What Philosophers Can Offer" (13–14).

56. Evans: "This system is taught by the elite to the average members of the profession. . . . Elite bioethicists likewise perform a maintenance role (which Callahan calls 'foundational' bioethics). . . . The fact that principlism is also the legally required decisionmaking system for recipients of federal research funds also encourages this process" ("A Sociological Account of the Growth of Principlism," *Hastings Center Report* 30, no. 5 [September–October 2000]: 36). More to the point, esoteric, abstract knowledge is the essence of bioethics: "In the particular case of the work of ethics, the system of abstract knowledge is the form of argumentation typically used by the profession. An ethicist's work is precisely to make those arguments" (Evans, *Playing God*, p. 30). Evans in facts delimits those identified as "bioethicists" to those "professionals . . . who use the profession's form of argumentation" (p. 34).

57. As Edmund Pellegrino laments: "At its beginnings, bioethics was not a separate discipline; nor were its practitioners regarded as 'professional' bioethicists. Rather, bioethics was considered a branch of general or professional ethics as applied to medicine and biology. In the last two decades, however, 'bioethics' has become a specialized field of its own, with its own literature, professional societies, and practitioners" ("Secular Bioethics and the Catholic Conscience: The Growing Divide," *Newsletter of the Institute of Catholic Studies, John Carroll University*, April 10, 2003, p. 4).

58. Evans, *Playing God*, p. 193.

59. Henk A.M. ten Have, "Medical Technology Assessment and Ethics: Ambivalent Relations," *Hastings Center Report* 25, no. 5 (September–October 1995): 13–19.

60. Tod Chambers, "Centering Bioethics," *Hastings Center Report* 30, no. 1 (January–February 2000): 22–29.

61. Interestingly, Chambers marks Art Frank's work as the latest attempt to recenter bioethics, recentering it this time on patients, on bodies. Chambers question is telling: "Yet where does the ethicist fit into Frank's scheme, that is, besides being another person waiting his or her turn sooner or later to be another wounded storyteller? In his detailed analysis of Frank's argument, Howard Brody notes how in Frank's perspective it does not seem that 'bioethics does any better than modern medicine in helping rather than hindering' the liberation of the sick person" ("Centering Bioethics," p. 28). It is not clear that Chambers hears the power of Frank's critique.

62. "Metaphorically, bioethicists have been able to *center* their discipline and in doing so marginalize the academic philosopher and perhaps defend themselves as well against the charge leveled by academic philosophers that they are no longer doing 'real' philosophy" ("Centering Bioethics," p. 23).

63. Chambers, "Centering Bioethics," p. 23.

64. Wildes, "Religion in Bioethics: A Rebirth," p. 170.

65. Evans, *Playing God*, p. 89.

66. Ibid., p. 90. "Departing slightly from the commission, they derived four ends by splitting the principle of beneficence into nonmaleficence and beneficence." For my own analysis of the shift in the form of the principles from Belmont to Beauchamp and Childress—particularly the not insignificant transformation of the principle of "respect for persons" into the principle of "respect for autonomy," and the relocation of vulnerable subjects and patients from the principle of respect for persons to the principle of beneficence—see my "RESPECT, or How Respect for Persons Became Respect for Autonomy," *Journal of Medicine and Philosophy* 29 (December 2004): 665–680.

67. Evans, *Playing God*, p. 90.

68. Ibid., p. 91.

69. James Lindemann Nelson, "Moral Teachings from Unexpected Quarters: Lessons for Bioethics from the Social Sciences and Managed Care," *Hastings Center Report* 30, no. 1 (January–February 2000): 13.

70. Bette-Jane Crigger, "Negotiating the Moral Order: Paradoxes of Ethics Consultation," *Kennedy Institute of Ethics Journal* 5, no. 2 (1995): 89.

71. Ibid., pp. 91, 92.

72. Ibid., p. 92.

73. Ibid.

74. Ibid., p. 93.

75. Evans, "A Sociological Account of the Growth of Principlism," p. 36.

76. Ibid., pp. 36–37.

77. Evans, *Playing God*, p. 73. Although he is talking about the area of human subjects research, the same process could be displayed with regard to issues at the end of life.

78. Evans rightly notes that "hospitals lacking legitimate ethics mechanisms will be denied accreditation and thus Medicaid funds, while research institutions may be denied government research funding or may have such funding removed" (*Playing God*, p. 194). Carl E. Schneider writes in this regard: " 'Bioethics' is contesting medicine's power to influence the way doctors treat patients. If it follows the classic pattern, bioethics will solicit work and authority by recruiting government's power" ("Experts," *Hastings Center Report* [July–August 2001]: 11).

79. Nelson, "Moral Teachings," p. 34.

80. Evans, *Playing God*, p. 89.

81. Ibid., p. 26. Elsewhere Evans observes: "The reason for this further spread of principlism [into the realm of 'cultural bioethics'] is that principlism itself has become an institution. . . . [Institutions take] on a life of their own, independent of the social conditions of their founding, and are self-replicating. . . . Principlism has similarly taken on a life of its own, independent of the conditions that encouraged its early growth, although the continued appetite of the state and bureaucracies for bioethical decisions continues to encourage principlism directly. This independent life of principlism has been encouraged by the rise of bioethics as a profession" ("A Sociological Account of the Growth of Principlism," p. 36).

82. Ruth E. Malone, "Policy as Product: Morality and Metaphor in Health Policy Discourse," *Hastings Center Report* 29, no. 3 (May–June 1999): 18.

83. Nelson, "Moral Teachings," p. 34. Similarly, Evans, *Playing God*, p. 26.

84. Nelson describes the usefulness of social science to bioethics in terms of

surveillance: "How many people are willing to make out advance directives? How do chronically ill people experience their illness? What impact does shifting a state's Medicaid population to managed care have on health outcomes overall?" ("Moral Teachings," p. 13).

85. This story he labels "the Genesis narrative of the bioethics profession, a narrative that "retells the profession's founding as following the central themes of American democracy, thus legitimating its jurisdiction" (Evans, *Playing God*, p. 40).

86. Evans, *Playing God*, p. 83, also p. 85. Interestingly, lacking in most sociological accounts of the development of bioethics is the role played in the development of the field by the courts, a key agent in policing normalization.

87. Crigger, "Negotiating the Moral Order," p. 90. Nelson writes:

It might be interesting to ask, for example, why the chief values of mainstream bioethics—most conspicuously pride of place given to respect for autonomy—have remained relatively fixed despite countervailing theoretical ferment in other areas of ethics and even in the light of what seems to be rather disturbing empirical findings. . . . The social sciences might make a contribution to bioethics by helping the field's practitioners understand better what's behind its deeply installed respect for individual autonomy and whether it has assumed more the character of an ideology than a moral philosophy." ("Moral Teachings," p. 15)

More ominously: "If bioethicists can better understand how various moral understandings become practically effective, either in the world of medical practice or within the field itself, they clearly are in a better position to have the kinds of influence that they want" (pp. 15–16).

88. Crigger, "Negotiating the Moral Order," pp. 89, 90.

89. Ibid. Emphasis added. Or as she states equally clearly: "The public scrutiny of ethical analysis is softened and made more intimate, palatable, and accessible in the person of the consultant at the bedside. . . . That the intention is to serve the patient's interest in receiving the best possible care and that consultations may extend beyond the particular question brought for resolution and seek to educate the requesting physician do little to ameliorate the bald fact of medical control" (pp. 95, 98).

90. Casarett et al., "Experts in Ethics?" p. 7. Emphasis added.

91. Ibid., p. 9. All values—even the commitment that human life does not have a dollar value—are open to challenge.

92. The emphasis within biomedical ethics on public policy correlates with exponentially increasing financial investment in and control over biomedical sciences and medical care services by the private sector and government since the Second World War. Diana B. Dutton gives a fascinating historical account of how the biotechnology and medical industries have come to be seen as "critical to national security and a strong economy," in her book *Worse than the Disease: Pitfalls of Medical Progress* (New York: Cambridge University Press, 1988), p. 23. Paul Starr documents the beginning of this process in the public health movement of the 1800s, in his *The Social Transformation of American Medicine: The Rise of a Sovereign Profession and the Makings of a Vast Industry* (New York: Basic Books, 1982).

93. Troyen A. Brennan, *Just Doctoring: Medical Ethics in a Liberal State* (Los Angeles: University of California Press, 1991), p. 23.

94. As Joel Shuman notes: "Modernity—and this includes modern medicine—cannot be understood politically or philosophically apart from the development of capitalist markets. Not surprisingly, the market forces of capitalist political economy are a

significant influence in the emergence of bioethical expertise" (*Body of Compassion*, p. 54).

95. Malone, "Policy as Product," pp. 16–22. She does not explore, however, how deeply intertwined the military and markets are in late capitalist political economies. While she treats these notions as metaphors, she might well explore their concrete referents—the concrete embeddedness of medicine and bioethics in the military and economic infrastructure of the United States.

96. Ibid., pp. 17–18.

97. As Malone notes, metaphors "maintain and modify the kinds of common understandings that set up our possibilities for action in any situation. Words not only reflect, but shape what is real to us; they also shape us, as any wise parent knows. . . . [They] structure understanding and experience by bringing forth certain aspects of that experience and hiding or silencing others, and they do this so seamlessly and constitutively that we are often hard put to identify them as metaphors, much less to identify alternative metaphorical connections" ("Policy as Product," pp. 16, 17).

98. Malone, "Policy as Product," pp. 18, 19.

99. Ibid., p. 19.

100. Ibid., pp. 18, 19.

101. Ibid., p. 19.

102. Evans, "Sociological Account of the Growth of Principlism," p. 32. "This process is taken so much for granted," he notes, "it is hard to imagine an alternative" (p. 31). He recounts how before this, accounts were kept in narrative form:

> Double-entry bookkeeping was a major innovation in economic history. Two changes in the accounts system also transformed it into a procedure that allowed for calculability, efficiency, and predictability in human action, paving the way for modern capitalism. The first change was that the new system was a means of discarding information deemed to be extraneous to decisionmaking. . . . The second change was that these numbers took on a new degree of calculability . . . translated into a common metric called "profit." . . . A similar evolution, I suggest, has happened in bioethics. . . . The Babel of information formerly thought to be relevant to an ethical decision has been whittled down to a much more manageable level through the use of principles, and the principles give us a commensurable unit—akin to "profit" in bookkeeping—that also allows for much simpler decisions. Weber called the calculable logic of the new accounting system "formally rational." . . . The principles are a system of commensuration. . . . They are a method that takes the complexity of actually lived moral life and translates this information into four scales by discarding information that resists translation. . . . This calculability or simplicity is largely gained by discarding information about deeper epistemological or theoretical commitments."
> (pp. 32–33)

103. Pellegrino, "Secular Bioethics," p. 2.

104. Albert R. Jonsen, *The Birth of Bioethics* (New York: Oxford University Press, 1998), p. 333.

105. An even more complete account of the normalizing function of bioethics would necessarily include the ways in which the popular media have become part of the institutionalized practice of bioethics, an important vehicle for reproducing its truth claims and normalizing the public. A recommended starting point would be Pe-

ter Simonson's "Bioethics and the Rituals of the Media," *Hastings Center Report* 32, no. 1 (January–February 2002): 32–39.

106. See, for example, Dena S. Davis, who opens her essay " 'It Ain't Necessarily So,' " seeking to posit "some ways that religious ethics scholars can meet the needs of clinicians . . . [arguing] that clinicians' needs should translate into goals for at least some religious ethics scholars, or at least some of those who contribute regularly to the field of bioethics (" 'It Ain't Necessarily So': Clinicians, Bioethics, and Religious Studies," in *Notes from a Narrow Ridge: Religion and Bioethics* [Hagerstown, Md.: University Publishing Group, 1999], pp. 9–10). Or see Courtney Campbell's essay, which suggests that religion ought to "enable constructive civic discourse" ("Bearing Witness," p. 38); or James Childress, who finds it important to understand religious views so as to "gauge the[ir] intensity . . . as part of a cost-benefit analysis of different public policies (for instance, predictable serious and sustained opposition might count as a major cost)" ("Religion, Morality, and Public Policy," p. 73).

107. As Cavanaugh notes, the modern state is built on a false or heretical soteriology (account of salvation) insofar as it positions itself as that agent which can save humanity from violence (*Theopolitical Imagination*, p. 2). This is but one of a number of problematic claims of the state identified by Cavanaugh and Milbank.

108. In other words, if power (as productive) is tied through embodied disciplinary practices to truth, one can see how the dis-empowerment of the church as a public institution correlates with the evisceration of its ability to claim truth status for religious convictions. As the church loses disciplinary authority over bodies, religious truths simultaneously become located in subjectivity, not amenable to emerging epistemological canons, thereby rendered objectively meaningless.

109. A refrain that echoes throughout *Notes from a Narrow Ridge: Religion and Bioethics* is precisely that the proper space of religion is circumscribed by informed consent. See Davis (" 'It Ain't Necessarily So,' " p. 9), Campbell ("Bearing Witness," p. 26), Childress ("Religion, Morality, and Public Policy," p. 65), and so on. Stephen E. Lammers, in his essay "Bioethics and Religion: Some Unscientific Footnotes" in the same volume, masterfully deconstructs this position, problematizing voluntarist notions of religion as "choice" as well as the ogre of "choice" within bioethics (pp. 154–162).

110. Along these same lines, Edmund Pellegrino raises concerns about the policing of the medical profession. Questions are raised, he notes, about whether or not applicants who refuse to participate in certain practices—abortion, certain reproductive technologies, capital punishment—ought to be refused admission to medical school. What we see here is the placement of a binding set of norms and practices necessary to preserve our contemporary social order put forward as "value-free."

111. William T. Cavanaugh, *Torture and Eucharist: Theology, Politics, and the Body of Christ* (Malden, Mass.: Blackwell, 1998), p. 197.

PART III

Religion and Bioethics in the Public Square

In this part, Cynthia Cohen, Rabbi Elliot Dorff, and Tristram Engelhardt lay the groundwork for many of the arguments supporting religious participation in the public square and challenging the received wisdom of the arguments against religious participation in the public square. They start to answer the normative questions regarding the morality of religious participation in the public square and the formation of public bioethics.

Cynthia Cohen begins this effort in a piece that puts flesh to the skeleton of religious public bioethics discourse by linking it to a discussion of embryonic stem cell research. By doing so, she joins Lisa Sowle Cahill in refuting the tendency of secularists to flatten the religious landscape and treat it as a simplistic, monolithic phenomenon. Cohen illustrates the multivocal character of religious perspectives and the variety of theological and rhetorical techniques used by people of faith involved in bioethics. Within religion ethicists draw upon a variety of explicitly religious resources to support their arguments, including Scripture, history, precedent (the arguments of historic religious thinkers or leaders), dogma, and formal sectarian doctrine. However, people of faith also draw upon nonreligious resources, such as liberal secular values (dignity, justice, etc.), secular philosophic systems (e.g., utilitarianism) or prudential arguments.

In considering the role of religion in the public square, Cohen turns the tables on many liberal secularist critics. Instead of defending religion, she bases her analysis upon the very idea of a public square as a liberal value. "Ideas are set out in the public square to be tested and accepted, rejected, or reworked," she notes. Denying access to the public square to religious believers (or anyone else) defeats the very purpose of the public square. Instead of denying access, resort to the public square should be favored. Indeed, her commitment to the public square is so strong that she argues that people of faith should not resort to coercive practices (or what John Evans in chapter 3 referred to as pure demo-cratic models of policy formation) that would use heavy-handed political threats to advance their agenda.

Rabbi Dorff turns tables on the secularist critics in another direction. In-stead of arguing from an abstract position about religion in the public square, Rabbi Dorff moves to a position within the faith. Specifically, he refutes the critique that religion is an inappropriate participant in the public square be-cause it is uniquely intolerant (implicit in the arguments over violence, au-thoritarianism, divisiveness, etc.) by demonstrating how Jewish principles sup-port tolerance within moral discourse. Indeed, Dorff goes further by "argu[ing] that American public policy discussions should follow a Jewish model—open, frank, and even heated at times, but within an atmosphere of mutual respect."

Dorff's model of Jewish bioethical discourse clearly rebuts the charge of separationist critics that religion is not rational. His model is extremely rea-sonable and grounded in rational argument. So much so that the question arises as to what role emotion (as proposed earlier by Cahill) can and should play in this model of discourse. After all, as he describes the practice—as opposed to how he presents the model—this type of discourse can be "heated."

All of the authors to this point, with the exception of Lysault, have accepted to a greater or lesser extent the current Rawlsian liberal vision of the public square and public discourse as normative. They have simply tried to describe the ways it works in relation to religion and public bioethics (e.g., Jonsen, Evans, Chambers), critiqued the effectiveness of its operations and how ex-cluding religion weakens the public square (e.g., Cahill, Evans, Cohen) or noted how ideas of tolerance and equality are equally present in religion (Dorff). Tristram Engelhardt Jr., in his chapter, "Public Discourse and Reasonable Plu-ralism: Rethinking the Requirements of Neutrality," throws down the gaunt-let—challenging the primacy of the traditional liberal compact.

Engelhardt, a notoriously provocative thinker, has for many years chal-lenged the ideals of secular bioethics and its capacity to support the "thick" moral vision necessary for a serious bioethics.[1] He also rejects the tendency of many apologists to present only the tolerant, ecumenical face of religion. For Engelhardt Christianity is an authoritarian religion grounded in revelation. And not all who call themselves Christians qualify under his definition of Christianity—a sect that he refers to here as Traditional Christianity or what he has previously identified as a "born-again Texan Orthodox Catholo[cism]."[2] Given this strong nonmainstream religious perspective, Engelhardt has in the past argued for the adoption of a more libertarian society. He has attacked the Rawlsian project, as does Lysault, as an undertaking advancing a particular moral agenda that does not always accord with Traditional Christianity.

Here he again affirms his critique of the Rawlsian liberalism. However, he takes the next step, asking how Traditional Christians should respond. Spe-cifically, Engelhardt rejects the Rawlsian argument that participants in the public square should only make arguments based upon public reason accessible to all in favor of advocating that participants draw upon those arguments that *they* believe to be true.

NOTES

1. See, e.g., H. Tristram Engelhardt Jr., *Bioethics and Secular Humanism: The Search for a Common Morality* (London: SCM Press/Philadelphia: Trinity Press International, 1991); *The Foundations of Christian Bioethics* (Lisse: Swets & Zeitlinger, 2000.)

2. Engelhardt, *Foundations*, xvi.

6

Religion, Public Reason, and Embryonic Stem Cell Research

Cynthia B. Cohen

The discovery of human embryonic stem cells has raised the possibility of making significant advances in the treatment and cure of a variety of illnesses that afflict human beings. Medical scientists are attempting to redirect these cells to replace diseased cells in organs and tissues of the human body in hopes of overcoming such conditions as Parkinson's disease, diabetes, stroke, heart disease, and Alzheimer's disease. However, major ethical questions have been raised about this research, most of which center on the moral status of early human embryos. Some maintain that it is wrong to destroy embryos, which occurs in embryonic stem cell research. Others hold, to the contrary, that early human embryos can rightly be used in this research and that medical scientists have an obligation to proceed with it.

Several religious groups that object to embryonic stem cell research have been in the forefront of those speaking out publicly against it. Some have passed official resolutions against this research, brought representatives before legislative and executive bodies to testify against it, and written and phoned elected officials to urge them to reject it. Religious bodies that favor embryonic stem cell research have taken a less active public role in voicing support. Yet some have passed official resolutions in its favor, spoken out in support of it before legislative committees, and joined secular groups in petitioning the federal government to provide more federal funding for this research.

Questions have been raised, however, about whether groups and individuals should express their religious beliefs about public policy issues such as embryonic stem cell research in the public square. Critics of religious bodies and individuals who have done so maintain that as a matter of principle, religious beliefs should not be introduced into such public discussions in a constitutional democracy. Those who are religious, they insist, should keep their convictions within the walls of their houses of worship and allow public policy to be developed on the basis of commonly held secular reasons and values. Some among these critics hearken back to the church in Galileo's time to argue that religious views should not be allowed to dictate the direction of science. A growing number of religious commentators have responded that freedom of religion consists in the freedom to express one's religious views and the freedom to take a public stand on matters of public policy. These freedoms are of constitutional dimension, they declare. Indeed, some among them view their critics as complicit in a secularist ruse to reduce religion to insignificance.

What role, if any, should religious beliefs play in the development of public policy in a pluralistic democratic republic? Should those religious bodies and their members that wish to take a strong stance for or against embryonic stem cell research keep silent about their views as public debate about this research proceeds? Or should they be free in a constitutional democracy to express and explain publicly their views about such issues?

In this chapter I maintain that, although there are certain limits on how religious bodies and their members should attempt to insert their beliefs into public policy matters, religiously based arguments should, as a matter of principle, be allowed to enter into public debate in a pluralistic democratic republic. This is the case even when many participants in these debates do not accept the premises on which the arguments of religious believers are constructed. In the first part, I consider the stances that various religious bodies and commentators have taken publicly regarding embryonic stem cell research and the ways in which they have justified their views in the course of public discussion. I go on to examine why critics of religious bodies object to the introduction of religious views into public policy debates and offer several responses to these critics, using the responses of religious bodies and thinkers to embryonic stem cell research as examples. Finally, I set out an alternative view that offers a principled justification for allowing religious adherents to present their views in the public square, provided that they follow certain practices that allow fair and open debate that is free of coercion.

Arguments by Religious Bodies' Concerning Stem Cell Research

Many religious groups were caught by surprise when embryonic stem cell research was introduced as a promising new area of scientific endeavor at the end of the last century. Although several had teachings in place regarding the moral status of human embryos, they had not formally applied them to early embryos at approximately five days after fertilization, which is when stem cells are extracted for this research. Since the question of whether to allow the destruction of early embryos in stem cell research is a major bone of contention among religious groups, many considered it necessary to develop and present their positions regarding the moral legitimacy of this research in the public square. To assess whether religious bodies and commentators should have done so, we must first gain a sense of the positions that they took, the bases on which they justified them, and how they attempted to get them a foothold in the public square.

Some religious traditions, such as the Roman Catholic, Eastern Orthodox, and Southern Baptist, hold that from conception onward the embryo should be treated as a living human being. Therefore, representatives of these groups maintain that no research use of an embryo that is not for the benefit of that particular embryo should be allowed. This, in their view, rules out embryonic stem cell research. For instance, Roman Catholic layman Edmund Pellegrino explained to the National Bioethics Advisory Commission (NBAC): "In the Roman Catholic view, human life is a continuum from the one-cell stage to death. At every stage, human life has dignity and merits protection. Upon conception, the biological and ontological individuality of a human being is established."[1] This view is representative of those of several religious denominations that have publicly rejected embryonic stem cell research on grounds that the early embryo has the moral status of a human being.

Other religious bodies and commentators approach the question of the moral status of the human embryo in other ways. Some choose a certain point in the development of the embryo at which they maintain that it has become a potential human being and then elaborate their arguments for or against embryonic stem cell research on this basis. For instance, several commentators within the Anglican-Episcopal tradition have developed the view that the early embryo does not have the capacity to become a distinct individual with the potential to develop into a human being until the 14-day point when the primitive streak, the precursor of the spinal cord, develops and the embryo can no longer split into several individuals.[2] This view influenced a resolution adopted at the General Convention of the Episcopal Church in 2003 calling on Congress to fund research on embryonic stem cells no longer required for procreation that would otherwise be discarded.[3] Within the Jewish tradition, the generally accepted belief is that the embryo is owed protection after 40 days of gestation. Rabbi Moshe Dovid Tendler testified before NBAC that "[T]here are two prerequisites for the moral status of the embryo as a human being: implantation and 40 days of gestational development. The proposition that humanhood begins at zygote formation, even *in vitro*, is without basis in biblical moral theology."[4] Jewish commentators have therefore have been supportive of embryonic stem cell research. Still other religious thinkers put the time at which the embryo gains moral status at a later point. Many Islamic scholars, for instance, maintain that human embryos take on human life at 120 days after conception. Therefore, Abdulaziz Sachedina states, "It is correct to suggest that a majority of the Sunni and Shi'ite jurists will have little problem in endorsing ethically regulated research on the stem cells that promises potential therapeutic value."[5]

Some religious traditions do not choose a specific time in the development of the human embryo at which it gains special moral status, but speak more generally of the respect that is owed the embryo. This leads some to maintain that embryonic stem cell research is morally unobjectionable and others to reject this research altogether. For instance, a resolution of the 213th General Assembly of the Presbyterian Church (U.S.A.) of 2001 accepts embryonic stem cell research and states:

> We believe, as do most authorities that have addressed the issue, that human embryos do have the potential of personhood, and as such they deserve respect. That respect must be shown by requiring that the interests or goals to be accomplished by using human embryos be compelling and unreachable by other means. . . . Prohibition of the derivation of stem cells from embryos would elevate the showing of respect to human embryos above that of helping persons whose pain and suffering might be alleviated.[6]

An official of the United Methodist Church, who also held that human embryos are owed respect, reached the opposite conclusion about whether it is right to engage in embryonic stem cell research. In a letter to President Bush, Jim Winkler declared that the United Methodist Church objects to this research on grounds that it threatens to lead us to ignore "the sacred dimensions of life and personhood and turns life into a commodity to be manipulated, controlled, patented, and sold."[7]

It is important to recognize that religious bodies and speakers do not all base their conclusions about the morality of embryonic stem cell research on the same sorts of grounds. Within certain religious traditions, sacred writings provide the primary justification for their position. Southern Baptists, for instance, point to certain passages in the Bible that they take to prohibit the deliberate destruction of early human embryos as evidence that it is wrong to carry out embryonic stem cell research.[8] Other religious groups cite not only sacred scripture, but also various schools of thought within their tradition in discussing the morality of embryonic stem cell research. Muslim jurists, for instance, adhere to the Koran, but provide various interpretations of their sacred text that lead them to differ views about when "ensoulment," at which point the embryo takes on human life, takes place. However, all seem to agree that this occurs later than five days after conception.[9]

Some religious bodies explain their conclusions about the morality of embryonic stem cell research after reviewing a wide variety of secular and religious sources: relevant scriptural passages, historical understandings of the moral status of embryos within their tradition, theological commentaries, philosophical arguments, recent scientific information, and public policy considerations. Representatives of the Roman Catholic, Episcopal, and United Methodist churches, for instance, have each used these various resources to reach different conclusions about whether embryonic stem cell research should proceed. Thus, the United Methodist Church official cited above explained the grounds for his convictions about this research as follows: "I am moved by my faith, by careful reading of official United Methodist policy and teachings, and by my abiding concern for human dignity, justice, and the integrity of God's creation to urge you to impose an extended moratorium on the destruction of human embryos for the purpose of stem cell or other research."[10] He appealed primarily to values that are of significance in a secular liberal democratic republic, such as human dignity and justice and brought in his religious views as a sort of backup. Pellegrino also gave reasons for his conclusions that were not only religious, but philosophical and prudential. He explained, "My objections are grounded in the following: 1) my understanding of the teachings of the Roman Catholic Church about the moral status of the fetus and embryo, 2) the insufficiency of the utilitarian arguments that would justify destruction or discarding of embryos, and 3) the practical difficulties of effectively regulating the practice even if it were morally defensible."[11]

Still other religious commentators do not cite passages from sacred writings or the teachings of their church and theologians, but instead present only philosophical, public policy, and prudential reasons for opposing embryonic stem cell research. For instance, when Richard Doerflinger, who is affiliated with the United States Conference of Catholic Bishops, addressed embryonic stem cell research before the Senate Appropriations Committee in 2001, he analyzed the secular arguments of those who favor embryonic stem cell research with the aim of showing that they were self-contradictory. He went on to give reasons why he believed that it would be contrary to public policy to allow embryonic stem cell research to proceed.[12] Although Roman Catholic teachings enunciated in a 1987 document, "*Donum Vitae*," specifically condemn embryo research,[13] Doerflinger did not expressly bring them into his discussion.

Other individuals who are deeply committed to a religious tradition have also elected not to present the specific beliefs of their tradition in their public testimony. Instead they have appealed to generally held values. Thus, Gilbert Meilaender, whose roots are in the Lutheran Church–Missouri Synod, did not seek to convince his audience by presenting specific scriptural or theological grounds for his position against embryonic stem cell research in his statement before NBAC. Instead, he sought to discuss the issue in terms that resonate with both Protestant and secular thought, such as the need to protect the weakest members of the community, what it means to be a person with a history, and the dangers of making ourselves the objects of our own technological manipulations. He explained his approach as follows:

> I have tried not to think of what I am doing as an attempt by some Protestant "interest group" to put its oar into your deliberations. Although I will begin as best I can from somewhere rather than nowhere, that is, from within a particular tradition, its theological language seeks to uncover what is universal and human. It begins epistemologically from a particular place, but it opens up ontologically a vision of the human. You might, therefore, be interested in it not only because it articulates the view of a sizeable number of our fellow citizens but also because it seeks to uncover a vision of the life that we share.[14]

Further, when spokespersons for religious groups have addressed embryonic stem cell research before legislators, executive commissions, and other
groups involved in making public policy, they have not directly insisted that
those to whom they speak should embrace their tradition's view of the morality
of embryonic stem cell research. Jewish commentators have explained their
religious beliefs before national commissions without attempting to convert
their listeners to their position. Rabbi Elliott Dorff, for instance, told NBAC
that "genetic materials outside the uterus have no legal status in Jewish law,
for they are not even a part of a human being until implanted in a woman's
womb and even then, during the first 40 days of gestation, their status is 'as
if they were water.' " He went on to explain that because of this, the Jewish
tradition maintains that frozen embryos may be discarded or used for reasonable purposes, and so may stem cells be procured from them.[15] He did not ask
his listeners to accept the view of his branch of Judaism about the moral status
of early embryos, but only to understand it.

In an interesting twist, Southern Baptist speaker Richard Land has argued
against doing the reverse. That is, he has urged others not to impose their
religious and moral views on members of his denomination, declaring that "to
compel millions who find such research unconscionable to support it with our
tax money is abhorrent."[16] Instead, he wants readers to understand the religious beliefs of the Baptist tradition and to recognize why those adhering to it
are bound by these beliefs to oppose embryonic stem cell research.

At times, however, some religious figures have attempted to push legislators to vote a certain way on bills concerning embryonic stem cell research
by exerting strong political and religious pressure on them. Some legislators
have reported that they have been told by religious leaders that if they did not
vote in that way, the latter would urge followers to remove them from office.[17]
Some added that these legislators would be denied access to essential aspects
of their religious worship if they did not vote in the way that these religious
leaders maintained was correct. This seemed to these legislators to impinge
on their freedoms of religion and expression in that they had been subjected
to political and religious pressure verging on coercion to get them to vote in a
way that was contrary to their own conclusions regarding embryonic stem cell
research.

In short, religious groups, their representatives, and individuals who adhere to specific religious traditions have addressed the morality of embryonic
stem cell research in the public square in a variety of ways. Some have set
forth the distinctive resources of their faith, such as sacred writings and theological teachings, that support their view of the moral status of the early embryo. They have maintained that others should be informed about their beliefs
and their implications for the discussion of important public policy issues.
Others have elected not only to explain how their religious writings and teachings have affected their beliefs about the morality of embryonic stem cell research, but also to introduce other considerations, such as those of philosophy
and policy to explain their views. Still others have referred exclusively to secular
justifications that coincide with their religious visions and that resonate with

those who do not share their religious convictions. Finally, some have bypassed arguments entirely and have instead attempted to exert political and religious pressure on those making policy decisions about embryonic stem cell research in an effort to impel them to reach certain conclusions.

Objections to Voicing Religious Views in the Public Square

Several commentators have proposed that citizens should not appeal to their religious beliefs when they participate in public discussions about policy issues. Robert Audi, for instance, argues that one should have an adequate secular reason to support a stance about a public policy. By "secular reason," he means "one whose normative force . . . does not (evidentially) depend on the existence of God (for example, through appeals to divine command) or on theological considerations (such as interpretations of a sacred text), or on the pronouncements of a person or institution qua religious authority."[18] This would rule out many of the statements that religious groups and individuals have made in public discussions of embryonic stem cell research. He goes on to declare that one's secular reason must be adequate, by which he means that "its truth is sufficient to justify it. One should keep silent unless one has adequate secular reasons for supporting a particular policy." On this account, religious reasons for or against embryonic stem cell research do not qualify as among those that should be set out in public, since they are not "adequate secular reasons."

Presumably the secular reasons presented in public for their views of embryonic stem cell research by thinkers such as Pellegrino, Meilaender, and Doerflinger, if adequate, would be acceptable to Audi because they do not necessarily depend on specific religious grounds. However, the religious reasons of those such as Southern Baptists, who argue against embryonic stem cell research on biblical grounds that it is wrong, would disqualify them from speaking in the public square about their beliefs, according to Audi. In his view, Scripture does not provide adequate secular reason for public policy conclusions. Presumably a secular group that had no adequate secular reason for its stance about stem cell research—perhaps it reviewed photos of five-day-old embryos and had a negative emotional response to the thought of their destruction—would also have to keep silent in the public square, according to Audi, although he does not mention this.

Although prohibiting religious voices from speaking out in the public square would cut down on the noise level there considerably, it would also defeat the purpose of having such a square in the first place. Ideas are set out publicly to be tested and accepted, rejected, or reworked. If religious believers cannot express ideas that they consider relevant and adequate in the public square, the central democratic good of presenting one's views to others so that they can critically examine them and learn from them will be lost. If Audi were to broaden his view of what it means to have an adequate reason so that reasons are "adequate" when they appear to those holding them to be true and to justify the policy in question, that would still leave us with the following question:

Why must citizens who have religious reasons that seem to them to be true and to justify a certain public policy be excluded from stating them in the public square? Why discriminate against adequate religious, as opposed to secular, reasons? To presume from the start that religious reasons can never be "adequate" is to beg the question.

One response to this question is that religious reasons have the taint of being dangerously divisive. Audi remarks that "conflicting secular ideas, even when firmly held, can often be blended and harmonized in the crucible of free discussion: but a clash of gods is like a meeting of an irresistible force with an immovable object."[19] Audi's view here is prudential. That is, he maintains that things are likely to take a turn for the worse if people speak up about their religious beliefs in the public square.

Surely religious beliefs are at the basis of certain political conflicts in the political world today and, as history indicates, can be dangerous, destabilizing, and polarizing. Some religious theses have led to wars and murder. Yet these terrible consequences need not inevitably result from the expression of religious views in the public square. Although the embryonic stem cell debate between religious and secular forces has, at times, been heated, verbal conflict has not spilled over into violence and has not threatened the stability of our government. Moreover, not just religious, but also secular views, such as those behind Hitler's and Stalin's march to power, have led to war and devastation in the course of human history. It is erroneous to put the blame exclusively on the religious expression of belief.

A second, more principled, response that Audi gives to why religious individuals and groups must keep their beliefs to themselves is that in a pluralistic society, religious reasons cannot justify policies restricting the actions of all citizens in terms that those who are not religious can share. He states that "adherence to the principle of secular rationale helps to ensure that, in determining the scope of freedom in a society, the decisive principles and considerations can be shared by people of differing religious views, or even no religious convictions at all."[20] When some begin from sacred scripture and the teachings of religious sages or traditional doctrines, those who are of a different religion or no religion will not be able to join them in discussion on the same terms. How can those who do not believe in Jesus Christ or the teachings of the Torah or the Koran find meaning in and be convinced by statements about embryonic stem cell research policy premised on those convictions or teachings? Religious beliefs seem immune to processes of deliberation and debate and therefore not amenable to contributing to a well-thought-out position about such issues as embryonic stem cell research, in Audi's view.

However, if the fact that religious reasons are rejected by some in a pluralistic democracy is sufficient to warrant excluding them from discussions of public policies, then many other sorts of reasons should also be excluded from such discussions on the same grounds. Appeals to any secular ethical theory, such as utilitarianism or communitarianism, should be barred because every such theory includes beliefs that some in society do not share and can be reasonably rejected by them. Fairness requires that we either exclude all religious and secular reasons for or against a policy under consideration or admit them all into debate in the public square.

In response to this problem, the late John Rawls distinguished between public and nonpublic reasons, rather than secular and religious ones. He developed the notion of "public reason," by which he meant the body of generally accepted common sense beliefs and ways of reasoning, as well as uncontroversial scientific conclusions.[21] Public reason can be used to justify laws and policies regarding questions that involve "constitutional essentials and questions of basic justice." That is, public reason includes certain rights, liberties, and opportunities; assigns them special priority with respect to the general good; and affirms measures assuring all citizens the means to use their basic liberties and opportunities.[22] We are to appeal only to public reason and not to comprehensive religious and philosophical doctrines when participating in public policy matters in a constitutional democracy, according to Rawls. The views of Meilaender and Doerflinger, for instance, might well be taken to be a part of public reason, in Rawls's view, since they purport to be based on generally accepted commonsense beliefs. All reasonable comprehensive doctrines are treated in the same way on this approach—they are all barred. Thus, public reason will not be unfair in its exclusion of religion, for it will exclude secular comprehensive doctrines as well.

Rawls maintained that public reason must proceed from some consensus, "from premises that we and others recognize as true, or as reasonable for the purpose of reaching a working argument."[23] Public deliberation, he held, should be limited to "the shared methods of, and the public knowledge available to, common sense, and the procedures and conclusions of science when these are not controversial."[24] This, however, seems to rule out the possibility of making novel points in the course of political argument. Individuals, at times, propose ideas that no one has previously expressed in the public square, but which seem plausible once expressed and eventually are adopted. Waldron points out that Rawls's conception of public reason seems to assume an inherent limit in the human capacity for imagination and creativity.[25] It implies that something counts as a legitimate move in public debate and discussion only to the extent that it is consistent with existing premises that everybody already shares.

Yet this presents an extremely narrow view of public reason. Religious leaders, for instance, have fueled movements for social justice on the basis of novel ideas that were not a part of public reason in their time. The nineteenth-century abolitionists, the early-twentieth-century social gospelers, and the 1960s civil rights marchers, many of whom based their public positions on Scripture and religious traditions, played important roles in changing the direction of public policy in this country. If the sole acceptable basis for public policy decisions in a constitutional democracy is public reason, and if religious beliefs had been excluded from public reason in the past, slavery might not have been abolished, suffrage might not have been expanded to women, and the Civil Rights movement might not have been validated.[26] Each of these significant changes occurred when the prevailing public reason was challenged by religious figures who stated their beliefs in the public square and was over-thrown.

Rawls subsequently modified his view to say that reasonable comprehensive doctrines, including religious ones, may be introduced into public policy discussions provided that, "in due course, proper political reasons—and not reasons given solely by comprehensive doctrines—are presented" to support them.[27] That is, religious reasons have to show promise that they will be redeemed by secular ones in the future before they can be said to be a part of public reason.

This amendment, however, does not resolve the difficulty, for it would require citizens with religious views to engage in self-fulfilling prophecies before they could speak up in the public square. They would have to peer into the future to discern whether their views might subsequently be adopted as part of public reason. This would be an impossible task. If the abolitionist movement had failed, rather than prevailed, according to this argument, its policies would not have entered public reason, and its leaders would have spoken out against slavery wrongfully. Similarly, today Southern Baptists, Methodists, Roman Catholics, Jews, Presbyterians, Muslims, Episcopalians, and others whose views of the acceptability of embryonic stem cell research are drawn at least in part from religious reasons would have to know in advance whether nonreligious "proper political reasons" would ever be presented in the future to support their conclusions.

An underlying difficulty with Rawls's view is that the conclusions of common sense that are said to be incorporated into public reason will strike some as wrong. Moreover, scientific results that are considered to be established, and therefore to have entered public reason, will be challenged. There is no proposition that is a part of any putative public consensus that is immune from denial by someone. Further, public reason is said by Rawls to incorporate an "overlapping consensus," some common ground between different philosophical, ideological, and religious worldviews. Yet several sets of such worldviews may exist that exhibit no common ground or only partial and indeterminate common ground. Each of these different worldviews could claim to represent the public consensus. How would one be chosen over another as representing the "real" public consensus? On Rawls's approach, both religious and secular thinkers would be muzzled in the public square if they could appeal to no considerations other than those that are part of common secular knowledge of the day. Any attempts that they made to develop significant social change to bring about a more just society, to protect the vulnerable, or to promote human well-being would be stifled.

Warrants for Including Religious Views in Public Policy Debates

To ensure that citizens explain their positions to one another in terms that they can reasonably expect that others might endorse, Rawls restricts the content of public reason to common sense and uncontroversial scientific findings. However, common sense seems divided about such issues as whether to pursue embryonic stem cell research. Rawls cites as an important political value that enters into discussions of constitutional essentials "the due respect for human life."[28] Yet whether early embryos constitute "human life" and what it would mean to show them "due respect" are precisely what are at issue in the embryonic stem cell debate. Some will argue that the right to life of an early embryo overrides considerations of the health and well-being of living persons who might benefit from embryonic stem cell research. Others will hold that the early embryo has no such right and that the health and well-being of living persons has priority over early embryonic life. The disputants will be unable to appeal to comprehensive religious or metaphysical doctrines about the moral standing of the early embryo to support their intuitions, for these are outside the limits of Rawls's public reason. Moreover, embryonic stem cell research is scientifically controversial; some maintain that it is unlikely to live up to the hopes of its investigators and that adult stem cell research is more likely to lead to new therapies, whereas others disagree. Therefore, public reason cannot resolve the issue of whether to engage in embryonic stem cell research on the basis of widely accepted scientific conclusions.

In short, public reason cannot lead those debating about embryonic stem cell research in the public square to conclusions about whether to pursue this sort of research. There is no overlapping consensus among presently accepted general beliefs that participants in public discussion about this issue can bring to their aid. And it seems unlikely that some conclusion regarding the acceptability of this research will enter into public reason at some predictable time in the future to validate one of the major positions that some of the participants in the discussion have taken. The putative resolving power of public reason is brought to a standstill by this issue.

This leaves those engaging in public debate about embryonic stem cell research today wondering what modes of reasoning they can justifiably present in the public square. Indeed, it leaves them back where they started. Since public reason has foundered on the question of embryonic stem cell research, it provides no grounds for omitting religious views about the morality of this research from the public square. Rawls's claim that we must not appeal to considerations that are not shared in society, that we must begin from common premises and use shared modes of reasoning, is too narrow to resolve the question of whether to proceed with embryonic stem cell research.

Instead of insisting that we must be sure that a reason is part of an existing overlapping consensus before we can appeal to it, we can turn to an approach to public discourse advocated by Michael Perry. He urges that "we should accept the inclusivist ideal according to which neither any controversial moral belief nor supporting belief—including (and this is what I want to emphasize here) any supporting religious belief—is excluded."[29] The inclusivist ideal presumes that agreement may emerge from a public forum in which such agreement is not already presupposed.

A major reason to engage in pubic debate about such questions as those surrounding embryonic stem cell research is to expose citizens and legislators to perspectives and experiences with which they may be unfamiliar. It is to introduce into public debate enough of their comprehensive doctrines, including religious ones, to display to others the grounds on which they base their position and to allow others to assess whether these grounds are meaningful and supportable. It is to allow them to exchange reasons and insights about this matter that others may not have dreamed of prior to public debate. It is to encourage them to be open to new thinking and reasoning. Jeremy Waldron observes that "moves may be made in political argument that bear no relation to existing conventions or commonly held opinions, but which nevertheless gain a foothold as soon as they are considered and discussed by persons with open minds."[30] Rather than hearing "bland appeals to harmless nostrums that are accepted without question on all sides," he argues, citizens can gain new insights and reasons from hearing arguments that are novel and quite at odds with their own view.[31] The view of a citizen or group may be sharpened and better defined by hearing a different view that one may be prone to reject.

On an inclusivist approach, there appears to be no reason why religious discourse should be excluded from the public square. Religious belief has a place in public deliberation even when many of the participants in that debate do not accept the premises on which religious thinkers construct their arguments. An open and challenging form of debate in the public square, in which nothing is taken for granted, supports the underlying values that provide the justification for having such a square in the first place.

Citizens of a constitutional democracy have the right not only to make up their minds about public policy issues such as those involving embryonic stem cell research as they think best, but also to express their reasoning freely. The free expression of religious belief in the public square is morally grounded in the value that we assign to freedom of religion and to free expression generally. This, of course, presumes that such views are offered in a spirit of respect for others as free and equal persons. It requires that those presenting their views in the public square, be they religious or secular, not take a back-door route to attempting to write their views into public policy determinations but present their arguments and attempt to persuade others. That is, those speaking out in the public square should not attempt to exert overbearing pressure on legislators and citizens to adopt their views in lieu of presenting those views and engaging in discussion and argument about them.

There is evidence, some of which is briefly noted above, that some religious figures participating in the embryonic stem cell debate have attempted to bring undue pressure on elected officials to cast their legislative votes a certain way. Indeed, not only religious proponents, but also secular figures have done so. Those exerting such pressure risk undermining freedom of thought and expression by coercively pushing legislators to adopt certain public policies. The whole point of debate in the public square in a pluralistic democratic republic is to allow citizens, including legislators, to reason and argue with one another in order to justify policies. Such debate becomes tainted if those participating in it are unduly pressured or coerced to think, decide, or vote in a certain way.

In a constitutional democracy that places high value on the freedom of citizens to articulate their vision of significant public policy issues and to attempt to persuade others to share it, respect for others as free and equal persons is a basic requirement for those speaking out in the public square.

NOTES

1. Edmund D. Pellegrino, "Testimony," in *Ethical Issues in Human Stem Cell Research, Vol. 3. Religious Perspectives* (Rockville, Md.: National Bioethics Advisory Commission, 2000), F3–5

2. Cynthia B. Cohen, "The Moral Status of Early Embryos and New Genetic Interventions," in *A Christian Response to the New Genetics*, ed. David H. Smith and Cynthia B. Cohen (Lanham, Md.: Rowman and Littlefield, 2003), 105–30; *Report of a Working Party on Human Fertilisation and Embryology of the Board of Social Responsibility, Church of England, Personal Origins*, 2nd rev. ed. (London: Church House Publishing, 1996), 32–45.

3. General Convention of the Episcopal Church, *Reports to the 74th General Convention Otherwise Known as The Blue Book* (New York: Church Publishing, 2003), 68–69.

4. Moshe Dovid Tendler, "Stem Cell Research and Therapy: A Judeo-Biblical Perspective," in *Ethical Issues in Human Stem Cell Research, Vol. 3, Religious Perspectives* (Rockville, Md.: National Bioethics Advisory Commission, 2000), H3–4.

5. Abdulaziz Sachedina, "Islamic Perspectives on Research with Human Embryonic Stem Cells," in *Ethical Issues in Human Stem Cell Research, Vol. 3, Religious Perspectives* (Rockville, Md.: National Bioethics Advisory Commission, 2000), G3–6.

6. General Assembly, Presbyterian Church (USA), "Overture 01–50. On Adopting a Resolution Enunciating Ethical Guidelines for Fetal Tissue and Stem Cell Research—From the Presbytery of Baltimore. Attachment A: Statement on the Ethical and Moral Implications of Stem Cell and Fetal Tissue Research," at http://www.pcusa.org/oga/actions-of-213.htm. Accessed on August 27, 2004.

7. Jim Winkler, "GBCS General Secretary's Letter to President Bush to Extend Moratorium on Human Embryo Stem Cell Research," July 17, 2001, at http://www.umc-gbcs.org/gbpr118a.htm. Accessed on Sept. 11, 2004.

8. Southern Baptist Convention, "Resolution #7: On Human Embryonic and Stem Cell Research, adopted at the SBC Convention, 16 June 1999" at http://www.johnstonsarchive.net/baptist/sbcares.html. Accessed on Aug. 27, 2004.

9. Sachedina, "Islamic Perspectives," G3–5.

10. Winkler, "GBCS General Secretary's Letter."

11. Pellegrino, "Testimony."

12. Richard M. Doerflinger, "Testimony on Behalf of the Committee for Pro-Life Activities, United States Conference of Catholic Bishops before the Subcommittee on Labor, Health and Human Services, and Education, Senate Appropriations Committee, Hearing on Stem Cell Research, July 18, 2001" at http://www.usccb.org/prolife/issues/bioethic/stemcelltest71801.htm. Accessed on Sept. 11, 2004.

13. Congregation for the Doctrine of Faith, "*Donum vitae*," *Acta Apostolicae Sedis* 80 (1988), 70–102, para. 1, no. 1.

14. Gilbert C. Meilaender Jr., "Testimony," in *Ethical Issues in Human Stem Cell Research, Vol. 3, Religious Perspectives* (Rockville, Md.: National Bioethics Advisory Commission, 2000), E3–6.

15. Elliott N. Dorff, "Testimony," in *Ethical Issues in Human Stem Cell Research*,

Vol. 1, Report and Recommendations of the National Bioethics Advisory Commission (Rockville, Md.: National Bioethics Advisory Commission 1999), 50.

16. Jane Lampman, "Different Faiths, Different Views on Stem Cells," *Christian Science Monitor*, July 23, 2001, at http://www.csmonitor.com/durable/2001/07/23/pls2.htm. Accessed on Sept. 4, 2004.

17. Patrick Dobson, "Bills May Force Researchers to Relocate," *National Catholic Reporter*, June 18, 2004, 15.

18. Robert Audi, "The Separation of Church and State and the Obligations of Citizenship," *Philosophy and Public Affairs* 18 (1989): 278.

19. Ibid., 296.

20. Ibid., 290.

21. John Rawls. *Political Liberalism* (New York: Columbia University Press, 1993), 224–25.

22. Ibid., 223.

23. John Rawls, "The Idea of an Overlapping Consensus," *Oxford Journal of Legal Studies* 7 (1985): 1.

24. Ibid., 8.

25. Jeremy Waldron. "Religious Contributions in Public Deliberation," *San Diego Law Review* 30 (1993): 820.

26. Cynthia B. Cohen, "Religious Belief, Politics, and Public Bioethics: A Challenge to Political Liberalism," *Second Opinion* 6 (2001): 37–52.

27. John Rawls, "The Idea of Public Reason Revisited," *University of Chicago Law Review* 64 (1997): 767.

28. Rawls, *Political Liberalism*, 243–44.

29. Michael J. Perry, "Religious Morality and Political Choice: Further Thoughts—and Second Thoughts—on *Love and Power*," *San Diego Law Review* 30 (1993): 716.

30. Waldron, "Religious Contributions," 838.

31. Ibid., 842.

7

"These and Those Are the Words of the Living God": Talmudic Sound and Fury in Shaping National Policy

Elliot N. Dorff

Seated next to a woman on an airplane, I apparently made clear in the first several minutes of our encounter that I was Jewish. She turned to me and said: "You Jews do it right." "We do *what* right?" I asked warily. "When you Jews have an argument with each other," she said, "you yell and scream at each other, if you have to, until the argument is settled. When we Presbyterians disagree with each other, we stare at each other and glare."

I cannot vouch for her depiction of Presbyterians. A number of mainstream Protestants have since told me, though, that she was right: they would rather let bad feelings stand than risk being impolite. She was surely right about Jews, though. The standard Jewish joke, in fact, is that where there are two Jews, there are at least three opinions—and you can bet that they will argue about them all vigorously.

In this chapter I will argue that American public policy discussions should follow that Jewish model—open, frank, and even heated at times, but within an atmosphere of mutual respect. Moreover, I will argue that religious views should be part of the American public discussion. This is a departure for me from my long-standing belief in a strong wall of separation between church and state, and I will describe why I have shifted my stance.

Part of the reason for my change of views is my experience between 1993 and 2002 in several federal government commissions. During March and April 1993, I served on the Ethics Committee of Hillary Rodham Clinton's Health Care Task Force. Though I have a Ph.D. in philosophy with a dissertation in ethical theory, I was keenly aware that my role on the committee was primarily that of rabbi. The same was true when I gave testimony to the President's National Bioethics Advisory Committee (NBAC) on cloning in 1997 and on stem cell research in 1999, for in both cases I was specifically asked to describe a Jewish perspective on those issues. Similarly, I suspect that it was my role as a rabbi rather than as a philosopher that prompted my appointment to the Surgeon General's Task Force in 1999 and 2000 to create a national Call to Action for Responsible Sexual Behavior in order to diminish the spread of family violence and of sexually transmitted diseases. Most recently, when I served for the two-year charter of the National Human Resources Protections Advisory Commission of the Department of Health and Human Services, a body appointed to review the federal guidelines governing research on human beings and suggest revisions, my expertise in ethical theory and in practical ethics often came in handy, but repeatedly I was asked to articulate a religious—and sometimes a distinctly Jewish—point of view.

These opportunities to serve the U.S. government raised an important issue about which I had thought before, but never up close with immediate practical consequences. Specifically, how should I as an American Jew integrate my American and Jewish identities in helping to shape national policy? More broadly, what ought to be the role that Judaism plays in national affairs? Note that the question is not what role *Jews* should play in government; as American citizens, American Jews, like all other Americans, should be as active or inactive in government affairs as they choose to be. The harder question is the one to which this chapter is addressed: should Jews consciously invoke their Jewish heritage in the process of serving their government, and, if so, how?

Probing the Depth of the Wall between Church and State

These questions arise from both the American and Jewish contexts. On the American side, the First Amendment mandates that the government shall not establish any religion (the establishment clause) nor interfere in the free exercise thereof (the free exercise clause). Thomas Jefferson understood the establishment clause to erect a "wall of separation" between government and religion, a view articulated in several Supreme Court decisions of the mid-twentieth century[1] and discussed in detail in other chapters in this volume. But if church and state are to be strictly separated, how can I legitimately inject Jewish views into discussions of government activities? For that matter, how can the government ask me to do that, as NBAC expressly did?

On the Jewish side, a number of national Jewish organizations have been zealous in defending the wall of separation from all onslaughts. They have done this, in part, because they understand the establishment clause to require a complete separation of church and state, but also because they believe strongly that Jews and Judaism, as a minority people and a minority religion in the United States, can flourish only if the majority religion is not reenforced by government.[2] Many examples in Jewish history demonstrate that when there was a state religion, Jews were at best second-class citizens and, at worst, persecuted, executed, or exiled. As a result, one can readily understand why, on the one hand, the classical rabbis of the Mishnah, Talmud, and Midrash would say, "Pray for the welfare of the government, for without respect for it people would swallow each other alive;"[3] while, on the other hand, they would also say, "Love work, hate lordship, and seek no intimacy with the ruling power," and "Be on your guard against the ruling power, for they who exercise it draw no person near to them except for their own interests; appearing as friends when it is to their own advantage, they do not stand by a person in his hour of need."[4] The respect for authority but the simultaneous wariness of it, as embodied in these early rabbinic comments, shaped the attitude of Jews toward government in most times and places throughout the last two thousand years, and that would argue for Jews to defend a wall of separation in our day as well.

The reality in America, though, has never been as pure as the theory of a wall of separation would require. For example, national policy or law has long recognized Sunday as a day off for government workers and Christmas as a national holiday; government money supports chaplains in the armed services; tax law exempts religious institutions, not just as nonprofit enterprises but specifically as religious centers; and even the Senate and the House of Representatives hire a member of the clergy to begin each day's session. Though U.S. Supreme Court decisions in the 1940s, 1950s, and 1960s banned the use of public schools for religious instruction and prayer in the name of that wall of separation, more recent decisions and legislation have made the line more fuzzy. For example, the Supreme Court ruled that Navy regulations governing attire could legitimately prohibit a religious Jew in the Navy from wearing a skullcap (*kippah*), but Congress quickly overruled the Court through special legislation on that issue. The Equal Access Law, passed by Congress in 1984, established the right of high school students to use school facilities for meetings after school hours regardless of the intended religious, political, or philosophical content of the topic of the meeting as long as the meeting was voluntary, student initiated and with no school sponsorship, and not during regular school hours. The U.S. Supreme Court, in *Braunfeld v. Brown* (1961), upheld the constitutionality of Sunday closing laws, and in *Lynch v. Donnelly* (1984) it validated the right of a municipality to allow the display of a nativity scene in a public park during December, even though the mayor of Pawtucket, Rhode Island, specifically intended thereby "to put Christ back into Christmas." In *Wallace v. Jaffree* (1985) the Supreme Court declared unconstitutional an Alabama statute mandating a moment of silence at the beginning of the school day for "meditation or prayer," but several justices indicated that they would look favorably on a statute that designated such a moment of silence only for meditation. Most recently, on June 27, 2005, the Supreme Court issued two opinions, each 5–4, upholding in *Van Orden v. Perry* the constitutional legitimacy of a display of the Ten Commandments on government land in Texas, but declaring in *McCreary County v. ACLU* that a display of the Ten Commandments in a Kentucky courtroom was unconstitutional because its purpose was to make a religious statement. These and other breaches in the wall of separation are generally justified as permissible on the grounds that they assure the "free exercise" of religion without constituting government establishment of a particular religion and/or as measures that the government may properly take in providing for the citizens' welfare.[5]

Similarly, some Jews are questioning whether Jews should continue to support a strong wall of separation between church and state. In part that is because of practical considerations. For example, the number of Jewish parochial schools has increased dramatically in the last twenty years, and so some Jewish parents are interested in government vouchers to ease their tuition burden. A larger part of this reevaluation has been prompted not by practical interests but by changing sociological conditions—specifically, by the increased acceptance of Jews as Americans. Until the establishment of the state of Israel in 1948, the only times Jews have ruled themselves were during the First Temple period (c. 950 B.C.E. to 586 B.C.E.) and the time of the Maccabees (167 B.C.E. to 63 B.C.E.). Otherwise Jews have always lived in countries ruled by someone else, where they were at best tolerated as second-class citizens and at worst persecuted. The theory of religious freedom that emerged in the United States, though, would change that. In President George Washington's 1795 words to the Jewish congregation in Newport, Rhode Island:

> All possess alike liberty of conscience and immunities of citizen-ship. It is now no more that toleration is spoken of, as if it was by the indulgence of one class of people that another enjoyed the exercise of their inherent natural rights. For happily the government of the United States, which gives to bigotry no sanction, to persecution no assistance, requires only that they who live under its protection should demean themselves as good citizens, in giving it on all occasions their effectual support.[6]

It took more than 150 years for American reality to match American aspirations in this area, for Jews experienced discrimination in higher education, job placement, and in areas where they could live through the 1940s, a reality poignantly portrayed in Laura Hobson's 1947 novel and the movie made on the basis of it, *Gentleman's Agreement*.[7] Nevertheless, the founders' theory of full religious freedom has increasingly become a fact for Jews as it has for Catholics and others, graphically symbolized by the presidency of John F. Kennedy and the major-party candidacy for vice president in the 2000 election of Joseph Lieberman, a religiously committed Jew. But if Jews are now full-fledged citizens of the United States, the degree to which Jews should participate in government *as Jews* has become a wholly new issue.

Jews living under Enlightenment conditions in other countries have faced similar questions, sometimes very publicly and politically, as in the instance of the questions posed to Napoleon's French Sanhedrin,[8] and sometimes in the writings of specific philosophers, such as Hermann Cohen's equation in the early twentieth century of the German and the Jewish ethos.[9] The American context, though, is different even from those times and places for two reasons, one legal and one sociological. Other countries whose laws reflect Enlightenment principles have extended full citizenship to Jews, but they have also given special legal status to one particular branch of Christianity. It was the United States that first declined to establish a national church by constitution, and it still is one of very few countries that does so. Moreover, from a sociological point of view, nowhere has the multiplicity of religions and, indeed, the freedom to affirm no religion been so consciously part of national identity as they have been in the United States.

Since other chapters in this volume deal with changes in American ideology, law, and practice on the broad question of the proper separation between church and state and one of its corollaries, namely, the degree to which, and the ways in which, Americans may or should allow their religious convictions to influence their government service, I shall not address those matters here. Suffice it to say that American Jews, like all other Americans, are certainly asking those questions in our time and proposing various responses. Instead, I will ask two questions: (1) Can Jews derive any guidance from Jewish sources as to how to play a role in American government, given that the American context of Jewish equal citizenship is one that those sources never knew?[10] (2) Can talmudic debate be a model for how Americans should conduct public policy debates with the aim of achieving the wisest public policy without fracturing the body politic? As I shall demonstrate, the answer to the first question depends on one's view of what should be the relationship between Jews and non-Jews, and the answer to that and to the second question ultimately depends on one's view of revelation.

The Role of Religion in Conceiving of Public Issues

First, we need to build some philosophical foundations. Aside from the political fact that many Americans espouse a religion, why should religion play any role in public decisions? The etymology of the very word, "religion," can help us understand that. The "lig" in that word comes from the Latin word for link or tie—the same root from which we get the word "ligament," connective tissue. Religions link us to the broader context of things. They spell out the ways in which we are related to our family, our community, our environment, and to the transcendent. They articulate a philosophy of life, a coordinated view of all the pieces of our experience and of the relationships among them, together with a description of what we should aspire to be and do. In other words, each religion gives us a comprehensive picture of who we are and who we should strive to be, both as individuals and as communities.

Secular philosophies such as Western liberalism and Marxism do this, too, but they are the product of one or several people whose views may or may not be adopted by a group; religions, in contrast, from the outset teach their specific philosophy and its implications through story, ritual, prayer, custom, and law within the context of a living community. They are therefore much more powerful influences on humanity than philosophies are by themselves. They share with philosophy, however, the ability to portray an approach to life, and it is in such a broad view of the larger scheme of things that our specific moral judgments are rooted.

All religions provide such a broad picture of the world and a set of moral norms that result from it. Religions differ from each other, however, not only in the region of the world in which they are most commonly found, and not only in their ritual practices, but also in their concepts and values. Contrasting the views of Judaism, Christianity, and the American version of Western liberalism, for instance, will reveal some overlapping features but also some major differences.[11] These factors play a critical role in determining concrete questions as, for example, the kinds of medical research that should be prohibited, permitted but not publicly funded, or permitted and funded.

A Philosophy of Judaism on Government Service

How should Jews interpret and apply their tradition to understand government service in a free, democratic country?[12] As I mentioned above, historical considerations prompt Jews to be suspicious of any interaction with non-Jews. Echoing the rabbi's prayer in *Fiddler on the Roof*, some Jews would say, "May God keep the czar—far away from us!" Such sentiments were well founded in countries where Jews qua Jews had to fear for their lives. In a free and democratic country like the United States, however, the question goes beyond simple self-defense and becomes this: Can one develop a theology of Judaism that would permit or even encourage Jews to interact with non-Jews in the shaping of national policy? Such a theology would justify interaction with non-Jews and government not only from the pragmatic motives of protecting Jewish interests, but also from a genuine appreciation of plural avenues of truth and wisdom while still retaining one's Jewish convictions about what is true, right, and good.

In my view, the grounds for such a pluralistic approach are historical, philosophical, and theological:

1. *History*. Historically, Christianity and other religions have been subject to change and redefinition at least as much as Judaism has. Even within the same denomination, creeds created centuries ago are continually changed, sometimes through outright amendment and sometimes through new interpretations, emphases, and/or applications. This constantly evolving nature of the world's religions makes some of the faithful uneasy; they long for certainty and stability. At the same time, though, each religion retains its relevance and its dynamism only by opening itself to change.

In any case, whatever the pluses and minuses, the historical fact is that religions *have* changed and continue to do so. The certainties of today, *even within the boundaries of one's own faith*, are not necessarily the convictions of tomorrow. History does not undermine one's ability to take a strong stand on what one believes. Similarly, historical roots and the fact of historical development do not rob religious communities of the right to define their criteria for belonging; so, for example, the contemporary Jewish community can and has definitely determined that the religion espoused by groups like Jews for Jesus or Messianic Jews is decidedly *not* Judaism. The historically evolutionary nature of religious faiths should, however, help people get beyond the feeling that the present articulation of their own religion is the only possible faith for a decent person to have; on the contrary, historical change in one's own faith should teach us all that no statement of faith is absolute and that people of intelligence, morality, and sensitivity most likely exist in other faiths, too—an understanding of critical importance for a country as multicultural as the United States is.

2. *Philosophy*. This realization is only reinforced when one turns from historical considerations to philosophical ones. All human beings, whatever their background or creed, suffer from the same limitations on human knowledge. Many of us have sacred texts and traditions which, for us, reveal God's nature and will as clearly and fully as we think possible. Religious adherents who do not speak in terms of God, a description that includes Hindus and Buddhists, nevertheless have documents which, in their view, articulate truth, goodness, and wisdom. When we recognize that other people make the same claim to ultimate authority that our own group does, however, we must either resort to vacuous and disingenuous debates like those of the Middle Ages as to which is correct, or we must confront the fact that none of us can know God's nature or will—or truth, goodness, or wisdom—with complete certainty.

At the same time, as with historical considerations, philosophical thinking does not make it rationally impossible or inadvisable to affirm a specific faith. To see this, Van Harvey's distinction between "non-perspectivists," "hard perspectivists," and "soft perspectivists" will be helpful. Non-perspectivists claim that we look at the world through epistemologically transparent eyeglasses, and so all of us should ultimately see the world in the same way if we only are sufficiently intelligent and attentive. On the other end of the spectrum, hard perspectivists claim that one's own specific view of the world is so entrenched in one's thinking and acting that it makes it impossible for one person to understand, let alone learn from, the views of others. In between these approaches to knowledge is soft perspectivism, which claims that we each have a perspective that influences how we think and act, but that it is not so hard and fast that it blinds us to the views of others or makes it impossible to learn from them.[13] It is interesting to note that even a medieval, hard-line antirationalist like Judah Halevi was open to considering the claims of other faiths and recognized that part of his inability to accept them stemmed from the fact that they were not *his* faiths, that he had not had personal experience with them.[14]

Those who take a non-perspectivist or hard-perspectivist approach to human knowledge will likely affirm their own view of things and think that alternative views are simply incorrect. Since non-perspectivists think that we should all see the same truth, they would advance a number of arguments in an attempt to convince those who disagree with them. Hard perspectivists, on the other hand, might give up on such a project fairly early, convinced that those who disagree are simply too blind to see the truth and that no rational argument will help (although force may). As long as we acknowledge ahead of time, though, that no human argument on these matters can be conclusive, and as long as we assert that our particular understanding of God (and/or truth, goodness, wisdom) is the correct one for all people *as far as we can tell*, we may still leave room for a kind of pluralism in which we appreciate the intelligence and moral sensitivity of others, even if we disagree with their views on specific issues. One need not deny cognitive meaning to religion to take such a position, as A. J. Ayer, R. B. Braithwaite, and others did in the middle of the last century;[15] one need only be humble enough to recognize that none of us is omniscient and that we are all trying to articulate the truth, the good, and the wise.

Alternatively, we may take the more "live and let live" approach embodied in soft perspectivism. That is, we would recognize that part of the reason that the arguments for my faith seem most persuasive to me is because it is, after all, *my* faith and that of my family and my people. This view has the advantage of recognizing not only that none of us is omniscient, but also that none of us is an objective observer, that we all view the world from one or another vantage point, and that our autobiographical backgrounds inevitably do, and perhaps should, play a role in determining the content of our particular views. Such soft perspectivism, aside from being, in my view, philosophically most astute, affords the strongest foundation for mutually respectful relations among Jews, Christians, and advocates of all sorts of other religious and secular stances. It accomplishes that by acknowledging the critical role that our particular view-point has in shaping our knowledge while yet affirming our continuing ability to learn from others who come from other traditions and who hold other views. At the same time, soft perspectivism enables us to affirm what we believe as our perspective *of the truth*—whether that be understood in theological or in non-theological terms—and so it does not dissolve into relativism or nihilism. It is rather a form of relativity, one that recognizes that there is an objective truth to be known but grasps also that we can know it only through the lenses of our own vantage point. This is exactly what Einstein showed us to be true in science as well. That is, just as in Einstein's physics there probably is some absolute vision of the truth but we can only know it from our own vantage point, so too there probably is an absolutely valid way of thinking about human life and the values that should inhere in it, but we human beings can know it only through our particular standpoints and lenses. And that means that we must understand our own vision of the true and the good as one possible version of it, just as everyone else's is, each to be evaluated for its strengths and weaknesses.

3. *Theology.* Some Orthodox rabbis reject pluralism completely, both within the Jewish community and between Jews and non-Jews. So, for example, Rabbi Walter Wurzburger, past editor of the modern Orthodox journal *Tradition* and hardly among the hardliners within the Orthodox world, has said this:

> Religious pluralism borders on religious relativism, if not outright
> nihilism. It rests on the assumption that no religion can be true and
> that it does not really matter what kind of myth we invoke in order
> to provide us with a sense of meaning and purpose.[16]

Other Orthodox rabbis, including Rabbis Joseph Soloveitchik, Irving Greenberg, and David Hartman, have suggested ways in which Orthodox Jews can
understand other Jews more appreciatively,[17] but none of their models would
open the door to dialogue with non-Jews on national issues except on the most
pragmatic of bases. However, Simon Greenberg (1901–1993), a Conservative
rabbi, has pointed out some features of Jewish theology that warrant pluralism
not only among Jews, but between Jews and non-Jews, and I will mention some
others. My goal is to explore the *theological* grounding for Jewish involvement
in national policy formation.

Rabbi Simon Greenberg defines pluralism as "the ability to say that 'your
ideas are spiritually and ethically as valid—that is, as capable of being justified,
supported, and defended—as mine' and yet remain firmly committed to your
own ideas and practices."[18] But what bestows legitimacy upon varying views
such that a person should be pluralistic in outlook? Political pluralism, as
mandated in the U.S. Bill of Rights, can be justified by pragmatic considerations, as James Madison does: the state needs to accommodate differing beliefs
in order to promote the peace and welfare of its citizens. What, however, legitimizes a spiritual or ethical pluralism?

Greenberg says that he knows of no philosophic justification for pluralism,
for that would entail the legitimation of accepting a position and its contrary
or contradictory. There is, however, a religious justification: God *intended* that
we all think differently.

Greenberg learns this from, among other sources, the Mishnah, the most
authoritative collection of rabbinic law from the first and second centuries.
Why, the Mishnah asks, did God initiate the human species by creating only
one man? One reason, the Mishnah suggests, is to impress upon us the greatness of the Holy One, blessed be he, for when human beings mint coins, they
all come out the same, but God made one mold (Adam) and yet no human
being looks exactly like another. This physical pluralism is matched by an
intellectual pluralism for which, the rabbis say, God is to be blessed: "When
one sees a crowd of people, one is to say, 'Blessed is the Master of mysteries,'
for just as their faces are not alike, so are their thoughts not alike."

The Midrash, the written record of rabbinic lore, supports this further. It
says that when Moses was about to die, he said to the Lord: "Master of the
Universe, You know the opinions of everyone, and that there are no two among
Your children who think alike. I beg of You that after I die, when You appoint
a leader for them, appoint one who will bear with (accept, *sovel*) each one of
them as he thinks (on his own terms, *lefi da'ato*)." We know that Moses said
this, the rabbis claim, because Moses describes God as "God of the *ruhot* (spirits [in the plural]) of all flesh" (Numbers 27:16).[19] Thus God *wants* pluralism
so that people will constantly be reminded of his grandeur.

In addition to these sources mentioned by Greenberg, other elements of the tradition would also support a pluralistic attitude. God intentionally, according to the rabbis, reveals only a part of his truth in the Torah, and the rest must come from study and debate.[20] Study, though, can never remove the ultimate limits to human knowledge, for, as the medieval Jewish philosopher Joseph Albo said, "If I knew Him, I would be He."[21] Moses himself could not see God directly but only through a lens, and the other biblical prophets, although accepted as true by the tradition, saw God only through nine lenses, and cloudy ones at that:

> What was the distinction between Moses and the other prophets?
> The latter looked through nine lenses, whereas Moses looked only
> through one. They looked through a cloudy lens, but Moses through
> one that was clear.[22]

Ultimately, according to the rabbis, even those who stood at Sinai understood the revelation given there through their own individual abilities and perspectives;[23] the Torah was not clear and transparent to everyone even at the moment God revealed it. Those who come generations after that event are all the more limited to their own capacities and vantage point in understanding the Torah that resulted from it.

God as understood in the Jewish tradition thus wants pluralism not only to demonstrate his grandeur in creating humanity with diversity, but also to force human beings to realize their epistemological creatureliness, the limits of human knowledge in comparison to that of God. One is commanded to study Torah; one *is* supposed to be committed to learning as much of God, his world, and his will as possible. One must recognize, though, that a passion for truth does not mean that one has full or exclusive possession of it; indeed, both of those are humanly impossible.

Moreover, one should understand that everyone's quest for religious knowledge is aided by discussion with others, for different views force all concerned to evaluate and refine their own positions. Thus the School of Hillel reverses its position a number of times in the Talmud, in contrast to the School of Shammai, which did so at most once. The Hillelites understood the epistemological and theological value of plural views and the need to learn from others. As a result, the School of Hillel was privileged to have the law established according to its views:

> Rabbi Abba stated in the name of Samuel: For three years there was
> a dispute between the School of Shammai and the School of Hillel,
> the former asserting, "The law agrees with us," and the latter con-
> tending, "The law agrees with us." Then a Heavenly Voice an-
> nounced, "These and those [i.e., the utterances of both] are the
> words of the living God, but the law agrees with the School of Hil-
> lel." Since "these and those are the words of the living God," what
> was it that entitled the School of Hillel to have the law fixed accord-
> ing to them? Because they were kindly and modest, they studied

their own rulings and those of the School of Shammai, and they [were even so humble as to] mention the opinions of the School of Shammai before theirs.[24]

Diversity of opinion may be very frustrating to those who would like a definitive answer, but God, according to the classical rabbis, refuses to provide such answers and instead instructs us to engage in vigorous debate and learn how to listen to other people's views:

> If the Torah had been given in a fixed form, the situation would have been intolerable. What is the meaning of the oft-recurring phrase, "The Lord *spoke* to Moses"? Moses said before Him, "Sovereign of the Universe! Cause me to know what the final decision is on each matter of law." He replied, "The majority [of the judges] must be followed: when the majority declares a thing permitted, it is permissible; when the majority declares it forbidden, it is not allowed; so that the Torah may be capable of interpretation with forty-nine points *for* and forty-nine points *against*."[25]

Thus an appropriate degree of religious humility should lead one to engage in spirited argumentation; one should not assume that one knows the truth and attempt to exclude others by fiat or by social pressure. One can and must take stands, but one should do so while remaining open to being convinced to the contrary. One should also recognize that others may intelligently, morally, and theologically think and act differently. And, indeed, virtually every page of the Talmud is filled with the sound and the fury of heated—but respectful—arguments. That is as it should be, for from the standpoint of Jewish piety, a vigorous pluralism does not require polytheism, atheism, or agnosticism, but rather can and should emerge from a deeply held and aptly humble monotheism.

These sources indicate that pluralism is a divine creation; as such, human beings should try to imitate it, but they have difficulty doing so. To achieve the ability to be pluralistic is, in fact, the ultimate ethical and spiritual challenge, according to Greenberg. Just as "love your neighbor as yourself"—which, for Rabbi Akiba, is the underlying principle of all the commandments[26]—requires a person to go beyond biologically rooted self-love, pluralism requires a person to escape egocentricity. It is not possible for human beings totally to love their neighbors as themselves, and neither is it possible to be totally pluralistic. We are, by nature, too self-centered fully to achieve either goal. The Jewish tradition, however, prescribes methods to bring us closer to these aims. Many of the biblical directions to learn love of neighbor appear in that same chapter 19 of Leviticus in which the commandment itself appears, and that would be a good starting point to learn pluralism as well.

If it is difficult to convince some Jews of these theological reasons to tolerate and, indeed, to rejoice in plural views *within* the Jewish community, one can readily understand that such Jews—largely within the Orthodox camp—would have even more difficulty applying this mentality to non-Jews. Moreover, most of the above sources were clearly intended only for intra-Jewish dialogue. Nevertheless, it seems to me that some of these same considerations can form the foundation for a mutually respectful interaction among Jews, Christians, the other religions that various Americans espouse, and secularists.

In some ways, the theological considerations mentioned above that govern debates within the Jewish community can apply quite straightforwardly to a Jewish understanding of Christian and other views of matters that are part of a national policy debate. If all the Israelites at Sinai heard God according to their individual abilities and perspectives, those who came after Sinai—Jews, Christians, Muslims, and even those who adhere to East Asian religions or to no religion—must surely have heard God and/or understand the world in a variety of ways as well. This should open us to listen to other people's understanding of truth and goodness even if we assert and live by our own tradition's view of them. Moreover, if no two Israelites think alike, how much the more must we expect that people from different backgrounds will vary in their thoughts. If the Eternal is to be blessed for the former, God certainly should be blessed for the latter as well.

Furthermore, as master of the spirits of all flesh, God could clearly have created all human beings to think alike. The fact that God did not do this underscores the divine intention that people vary in their beliefs. The rabbis already drew one significant implication from this: non-Jews can attain salvation (however understood) outside the bounds of Jewish law,[27] and so Jews need not missionize and historically have not done so.

Finally, it definitely is just as hard—if not harder—to extend one's empathy and sympathy not only to those within one's own group, but also to those with different affiliations, backgrounds, patterns of living, and aims. One needs all of the qualities ascribed to the School of Hillel, and more. To act in this way surely partakes of the divine.

And yet there are some limitations to this line of reasoning as the basis for Jewish participation in discussion with non-Jews on matters of national policy. It may be the case that God wants people to think independently, but ultimately the biblical prophets assert that Judaism's Torah is God's true teaching, the one that all nations will ultimately learn and adopt.

One should note that Micah, a younger contemporary of Isaiah, copies the latter's messianic vision of universal adherence to the God of Israel but then adds a line of his own that effectively changes it: "Though all the peoples walk each in the names of its gods, we will walk in the name of the Lord our God forever and ever."[28] This is a decidedly pluralistic vision of messianic times: every people shall continue to follow its own god. Even so, Micah added this line *after* quoting Isaiah's vision that "the many peoples shall go and say: 'Come, let us go up to the Mount of the Lord, to the House of the God of Jacob, that He may instruct us in His ways, and that we may walk in His paths.' For instruction shall come forth from Zion, the word of the Lord from Jerusalem" (Isaiah 2:3; Micah 4:2). Thus even for Micah, apparently, other gods and other visions of the good life might exist, but only Israel has the true understanding of God's will.

God, then, may indeed want multiple conceptions of the divine, as Greenberg maintains, but traditional sources assign non-Jewish views to a clearly secondary status. God may like variety among His creatures, and He may even hold people responsible only for what they could be expected to know (the seven laws given, according to the rabbis, to all descendants of Noah);[29] but ultimately only the Jews know what is objectively correct. This is liberal toleration—and it should be appreciated as such—but it certainly is not a validation of others' views. In that sense, it falls short of Greenberg's criterion that "your ideas are spiritually and ethically as valid—that is, as capable of being justified, supported, and defended—as mine." And, indeed, Greenberg himself may not have wanted to extend his thesis beyond disagreements among Jews.

I would take a somewhat broader view. It is only natural that Jewish sources should reflect a tension between nationalism and universalism.[30] God is, according to Jewish belief, the God of all creatures, but, at the same time, God chose the Jews to exemplify ideal standards for human life. This is how *Jews* understand God's will, the reason why Jews commit all their energies and, indeed, their very lives to Jewish belief and practice.

Despite this nationalistic side of the Jewish tradition, however, what ultimately rings through it is the rabbis' assertion that non-Jews fully meet God's expectations by abiding by the Seven Noahide Laws and the rabbis' statement that "The pious and virtuous of all nations participate in eternal bliss."[31] Jewish sources, then, that speak about God wanting plural approaches to the Eternal within the Jewish community can apparently be applied, without too much tampering, to intercommunal relations as well. Of course, the same segments of the Jewish community that have difficulty with the former would undoubtedly have difficulty with the latter, but even some pluralists within the Jewish community would need to stretch their understanding and sensitivity to apply Jewish theology in this way. Nevertheless, a firm basis for this kind of theology exists within the Jewish tradition.

Rabbinic Approaches to Diversity

Even if one accepts the historical, philosophical, and theological grounds for admitting of multiple approaches to a problem, though, how can a society that respects a broad range of opinions arrive at a shared decision on anything? And how can it avoid splintering into multiple groups?

Here the rabbinic sources may be helpful as a model for how Americans can carry on vigorous debates and nevertheless be able to make decisions that do not stymie or break up American society but rather strengthen its bonds and make its decisions wiser. The context in which the rabbis were establishing their model was, of course, very different from the contemporary, multiethnic society that is the United States, but some of the methods, limitations, and rationales for the rabbinic mode of discourse seem remarkably apt for modern America.

1. *The Need for Unity.* A play on the Hebrew words of Deuteronomy 14:1 leads the rabbis to the principle that Jews should not split into factions.[32] The need for unity is, in part, political and social. Only a cohesive community can prevent anarchy and plan joint action to protect and enhance life. For the rabbis, though, the motivation is also theological: "When Israel is of one mind below, God's great name is exalted above, as it says, 'He became King in Jeshurun when the heads of the people assembled, the tribes of Israel together' (Deuteronomy 33:5)."[33] If communities are splintered, the various groups look as if they are guided by two different Torahs or even by two different gods.[34] This can undermine respect for religious institutions and, ultimately, for religion itself. Furthermore, a divided Jewish community cannot effectively accomplish its religious mission of being "a light unto the nations" in perfecting the world under the dominion of God.[35]

Those for whom unity is the exclusive or paramount goal sometimes seek to attain that by claiming that there is only one correct view and that all others should be shunned or even attacked. Unfortunately, there is ample precedent for this approach in Jewish history. One account of the relationships between the first-century School of Shammai and its rival School of Hillel, for example, depicts the former as ambushing and killing all but six of the latter,[36] and in the eighteenth century, Eastern European Jewry was split between Hasidim and Mitnaggedim, who issued bans of excommunication against each other prohibiting members of each group from engaging in communication or commerce with members of the other.

2. *Rabbinic Endorsements of Pluralism.* But that is not the only—and certainly not the predominant—model for attaining unity. Deuteronomy's commandment of not deviating from the words of the court—the basis for judicial authority and communal conformity—is effectively balanced by Deuteronomy's command to "fear no man, for judgment is God's."[37] Traditional sources accordingly document a dynamic pluralism *within* the Jewish community. There are 70 faces to each passage in the Torah, according to the rabbis, and so nobody can claim that their interpretation is the only possible one.[38] Furthermore, the rabbis say, Moses was not told the final decision on each matter of law "so that the Torah may be capable of interpretation with forty-nine points *pro* and forty-nine points *contra.*"[39] People should listen to each other and be prepared to change their minds on legal matters, says the Mishnah, and the opinion of a dissenting judge is recorded because in a later generation the court may revise the law to agree with him.[40] Just as the manna that the Israelites ate in the wilderness tasted different to each person, so too, say the rabbis, each person hears God's revelation according to his own ability.[41] The long tradition of finding varying rationales for the laws and varying interpretations of the biblical stories is the sum and substance of the Midrash Aggadah, an extensive and rich body of classical Jewish literature, and the very methodology used in Jewish law encourages debate.[42] That may be frustrating at times, but one must learn to live with that and open one's mind to the multiplicity of meanings inherent in the Torah:

Lest a man should say, "Since some scholars declare a thing impure and others declare it pure, some pronounce it to be permitted while others declare it forbidden, some disqualify an object while others uphold its fitness, how can I study Torah under such circumstances?" Scripture states, "They are given from one shepherd" (Ecclesiastes 12:11): One God has given them, one leader [Moses] has uttered them at the command of the Lord of all creation, blessed be He, as it says, "And God spoke *all* these words" (Exodus 20:1). You, then, should make your ear like a grain receiver and acquire a heart that can understand the words of the scholars who declare a thing impure as well as those who declare it pure, the words of those who declare a thing forbidden as well as those who pronounce it permitted, and the words of those who disqualify an object as well as those who uphold its fitness.... Although one scholar offers his view and another scholar offers his, the words of both are all derived from what Moses, the shepherd, received from the One Lord of the universe.[43]

Indeed, people should intentionally expose themselves to diverse approaches by studying with at least two rabbis, for "One who studies Torah from [only] one teacher will never achieve great success [literally, "a sign of blessing]."[44]

Some, of course, did not like diversity of opinion. In the second century, Rabbi Jose complains that multiple views on the meaning of biblical verses make the Torah seem like many Torahs, and he attributes the lack of conformity on the meaning of each verse to insufficient study and/or overweening pride on the part of contemporary scholars there.[45] Ten centuries later, though, Maimonides (1135–1204) pointed out that multiple interpretations are inevitable because of the varying temperaments and intellectual capabilities of the Torah's many interpreters.[46] Rabbi Menahem ben Solomon Meiri (1249–1316) maintained that disagreement is not only inevitable but desirable as an integral part of establishing the truth, for without dispute people are not challenged to test and refine their positions.[47] The talmudic section most quoted on this issue is =the one cited earlier, according to which scholarly arguments are not only rationally, but *theologically* necessary, for all sides bespeak "the words of the living God."[48] (Incidentally, this source presents a totally different view of how the schools of Shammai and Hillel handled their disputes from the one cited above, and it is probably accurate: sometimes people literally or figuratively kill each other over their disagreements, and at other times they act in a much more adult manner and appreciate each other for the challenges and refinement of thinking that they provide.)

The goal, then, is to educate people to be open to learning from others, similar to the School of Hillel, and to respect those with whom they disagree— so much so as to cite them first. In other words, we must strive to have learning with manners, commitment to finding the truth together with respect for others and love of peace.[49]

If each answer is the word of God, though, why exert oneself in pursuit of truth? Vigorous study of the classical texts is required, according to the rabbis, because that is the way one learns and applies God's will. That is, study and interpretation of the Torah is the post-biblical form of God's revelation[50] and one important way in which a person comes into contact with God; it is a religious experience as well as a legal one. Moreover, Jewish law obligates Jews to study the Torah throughout their lives, even if they are poor, and even if such study involves them in debates with their teachers or parents—although there are rules of propriety governing how such debates should be held.[51] So, for example, in addition to the characteristics that the School of Hillel demonstrated in its debates with the School of Shammai, the rabbis maintain that students need to honor their teachers by not, for instance, calling them by their first name, that teachers must be conscientious in preparing their lessons for their students and stand before them as a mark of respect, and that fellow students must honor one another, for "He who learns from his fellow a single chapter, a single rule, a single verse, a single expression, or even a single letter ought to pay him honor." Again, "Let the honor of your student be as dear to you as your own, and the honor of your associate be like your reverence for your teacher, and the reverence for your teacher like your fear of Heaven."[52]

3. *Rabbinic Limitations on Pluralism.* The Talmud is full of fractious disputes in which virtually anything could be questioned. There were some limits, though, to this general picture of uninhibited debate. When the Sanhedrin existed, rabbis could challenge decisions in debate, but in practice they had to conform to the Sanhedrin's majority ruling.[53] Rabbinic sources strive to differentiate the high level of dissent to which the rabbis were accustomed and which they thought healthy from that of the biblical figure Korah, whose rebellion the Torah condemns. Korah's dissent, the rabbis said, was not "for the sake of Heaven" but rather for his own power and love of victory, whereas the disputes of Hillel and Shammai were for the sake of heaven—to seek the truth. Because that was the case, rabbinic disputes will continue for all time, but Korah's dispute died with him.[54] Thus disputants must argue for the right reasons while following the practice determined by the majority.

Rabbinic literature speaks of Jews whose mode of dissent led the community to exclude them. These include the *min* (sectarian) and the *apikoros* (heretic). In view of the wide latitude of rabbinic debate, one can understand why there is considerable discussion in classical and contemporary literature about exactly what these people held or did that made their modes of dissent unacceptable.[55] Rashi, for example, says that one feature of admissible debate is that "Neither side of the conflict cites an argument from the Torah of another god, but only from the Torah of our God."[56]

In addition to such individuals, there have been groups that splintered off from the Jewish people. These include Christians, Hebrew Christians (from the first through the fifth centuries), Karaites (from the eighth century to the present), and Sabbetaians (in the late seventeenth and early eighteenth centuries).

4. *Rabbinic Modes of Accommodation in Practice.* The groups mentioned in

the last two paragraphs Jews ruled to be outside the bounds of the Jewish community. For those who remained part of the Jewish people, though, there was a need to determine how the various individuals and factions should interact with those with whom they disagreed.

One rabbinic source addresses the degree to which a community can tolerate diversity of practice. As mentioned earlier, a play on words in Deuteronomy 14:1 leads the rabbis to the principle that Jews should not split into factions.[57] For Rabbi Johanon (third century, Israel) and Abayye (fourth century, Babylonia), that principle precludes multiple practices in one locale, but communities in distinct areas could follow disparate rulings in observing the law. Rava, Abayye's contemporary and sparring partner, is more permissive. For him the principle only prohibits the members of a given court from issuing conflicting rulings; they may disagree in discussion, but they ultimately have to make one, coherent decision. Two courts, however, even within the same city, could issue conflicting rulings without violating the principle. In tolerating this, Rava may be thinking of the circumstances in large cities, where differing groups of Jews may live in close proximity to each other but practice Jewish law in varying ways.[58]

Members of the schools of Shammai and Hillel, however, served on the same courts. How did they agree upon a ruling—and even permit each others' children to marry one another? According to one talmudic opinion, since the Hillelites were in the majority, the Shammaites accepted their authority in practice while remaining opposed in theory. Pluralism, on this model, stops with thought; uniformity is necessary in action, and that must be determined by the majority of the rabbis charged with making the decision. A second talmudic solution is that God prevented any cases prohibited in one view but not in the other from occurring. The third explanation is that both parties kept each other informed of problematic cases, and thus marriages between the families associated with the two schools could continue.[59] In other words, they trusted the majority, they trusted God, or they trusted each other.[60]

Creating National Policy in a Diverse Society

How, then, can one apply this rabbinic model to a pluralistic country like the United States in order to make wise and shared concrete policy decisions without rending itself apart? In more monolithic countries, one might expect general agreement on most moral issues—although even there such agreement is sometimes more theoretical than actual as, for example, in the case of Italy's sanction of abortions under some circumstances, despite heavy Roman Catholic influence there. In a country like the United States, though, where pluralism is both a fact and a principle embedded in the Constitution, does its plethora of views make it impossible to make coherent social policy? Put even more strongly, if so many varying views exist on moral questions, does it make any sense to ask what we *should* do as a nation with regard to any specific issue at all? Or is it all a matter of "might makes right," politically, if not militarily?

And how can the talmudic model of debate help the United States come to a national consensus?

There are fundamentally two different approaches as to how to make decisions in communal affairs. Some would claim that we can identify a common public viewpoint. Then the various religious traditions within the nation (or state or city) are simply vehicles for transmitting the values of that view, and the common public theory sets the limits within which the various religions may vary in thought and practice. This approach assumes that there are either absolute values held by all human beings or at least a set of values held by a given society (moral absolutism or relativism), and it assumes that we can know this list of values with considerable certainty; only then does the society have the moral authority (quite apart from its military power) to restrict variations of individuals and groups with such assuredness. Within Judaism, the early Reform Movement, as articulated by the Pittsburgh Platform of 1885, and some right-wing, contemporary Orthodox rabbis are examples of people who take this approach, based, in these two cases, on their assertions of absolute values—although very different ones!

The second model is based on much greater humility about what we can know about the right and the good. It therefore leads people to anticipate and to respect much more variation on those questions. It is, in a word, more pluralistic. It does not even expect to find a single, common moral ideal to which all or even most citizens subscribe, for people differ too much for that to be possible. Our epistemological position as limited and fallible human beings makes that so. People may have strong moral convictions, even ones for which they would give up their lives, but they never have total moral knowledge; only God has that, if anyone does. The various individuals and groups within a given nation may nevertheless negotiate agreements on specific matters, and so social policies can be formulated even if people support them for different reasons.

This second view, to which I subscribe, does *not* entail that we human beings are totally bereft of moral knowledge; we have, after all, the benefit of the moral thought and experience of all human beings in the past and present as well as what we learn with our own moral faculties from our own experience. It is just that we are not omniscient as God is, and so we must be satisfied with knowing that our knowledge of moral matters—like our knowledge of science—is partial and flawed. I am not claiming that every person or every society should just state what it likes and dislikes when it formulates its moral code and ethical views. The right position is not moral relativism; it is moral relativity. Pluralism, then, is the only position that makes sense epistemologically—and, for reasons I discussed above, theologically as well.

How, then, do we rise above our varying views of life to come to some kind of social policy on concrete issues that face us all? In some societies, of course, the decision is made by decree of a tyrant or tribal leader, and that is the end of the matter. In others, a high degree of ethnic homogeneity leads a nation to use its heritage to make moral decisions with little, if any, awareness of, or regard for, alternative views.

The hard contexts for this question, however, are those like Israel and the United States. The methodological problems in those two countries, though, are different, and they serve as models for other nations of the two sorts that they represent. In Israel, avowedly a Jewish state but also a democratic one, Israeli Jews must find a method to apply the Jewish heritage to contemporary concerns in a way that leaves room for the pluralism that inheres in Judaism and in the Jewish community and for the varying views of Muslims, Christians, secularists, and others who are citizens of the Jewish state. Similarly structured states include France, Italy, and England, with Catholicism or Anglicanism rather than Judaism as the dominant (and in some ways official) religion.

In the United States the context is even more complicated. An overwhelmingly Christian country that nevertheless by constitution separates church and state and that includes citizens of virtually every world religion and view, the United States must find a way to engender social discourse and decision making in a thoroughly multicultural format. Canada, Australia, and New Zealand face similar problems, although with much less demographic diversity and with a different legal structure to frame the issue.

How can moral decisions be made in such contexts? Frankly, only if people are willing to discuss issues in a multicultural setting in which one's own view of things will be challenged and not necessarily adopted; only if people have sufficient perspicacity and flexibility to see and seize areas of agreement; only if people have respect for the varying points of view presented and for those who hold them; and only if people are resolved to live together not only peacefully, but cooperatively, despite their differing views and practices. No society— and certainly not all of the world's people—can succeed in attaining this high level of civility, humanity, and philosophical appropriateness at all times. The new technology in medicine and engineering, however, has brought us together as a global village with the need to get to know each other and to make decisions together on the many issues that transcend borders and affect every one of us. Under these circumstances, the cocky assuredness that some might have had when living in isolated conclaves of people who think and act like themselves must give way to greater openness to other views and respect for those who hold them. This is not moral laxity or indifference; people should— and, one hopes, would—still argue forcefully for their convictions. They must, however, come to recognize that their own way of seeing and doing things is not the only possible way that a person of intelligence and moral character might adopt.

This is not as utopian as it may sound, as illustrated by the two major national discussions on health care—that of the President's Commission on Health Care in the early 1980s, and that of the national Clinton Task Force on Health Care of 1993. Quite remarkably, a surprising degree of civility and even coherence prevailed in those discussions. Daniel Wikler noted this about the essays produced during and for the President's Commission:

> It is true that each essay provides a different account of equity in
> access to health care and insists that rival accounts are mistaken. Yet

there is one policy recommendation supported by each of these essays: Every person ought to be assured of access to some decent
minimum of health care services. This conclusion cannot be said to
have been "proved" by this collection of arguments, but the fact that
a recommendation of universal access to (at least some) health care
follows from such disparate sets of premises suggests that the recommendation is "insensitive" to choice of moral theory. Even if we
do not know which moral theory is correct, then, and thus cannot
provide a ground-level-up proof that all should have access to a minimum of health care, such a belief has been rendered reasonable
and perhaps even compelling. In this sense, this diverse and inconsistent collection of theories of justice in health care delivery supports the consensus reached by members of the President's Commission concerning the moral obligation of our society to ensure
access to health care for all its people.[61]

I can report that the Ethics Committee of the Clinton Health Care Task Force
produced similar results. The theoretical debates were many and, in some
instances, heated. For example, in formulating the underlying moral principles that argue for universal health care guaranteed by the government, all of
us agreed that the moral grounds for such a system included principles en-
shrined in the nation's constitutive documents, specifically, equality, justice,
and "providing for the general welfare." The religious among us, though,
wanted to include what the Protestants call "our obligations of stewardship"—
that is, our duty to take care of God's property, including our bodies. Even
though the subcommittee writing the preamble to the legislation specifically
said that religious Americans understand our obligation to provide for health
care in those terms *in addition to* the secular values Americans all hold, the
secularists on the Ethics Committee argued strenuously and heatedly to drop
the religious language altogether. Ultimately, the committee presented two
different versions of the preamble to President and Mrs. Clinton, one with
the religious language and one without, leaving it to them to decide. With all
this controversy, though, the policy advocated by both sides was the same,
namely, that we as an American community have the duty to provide health
care for at least all American citizens and perhaps even for undocumented
aliens.

Sometimes, of course, religious differences made for differences in policy
as well. Early in its deliberations the Ethics Committee decided not even to talk
about whether the benchmark health plan would include abortion services,
knowing full well that that decision would ultimately be made on the basis of
the political consideration of what could get through Congress. I am personally
sorry, though, that we did not have that discussion. The varying stances on
abortion taken by religious and secular groups in America are well known, but
the issue raises an important question about American democratic theory—
namely, whether freedom of religion should extend to an issue like this where

there is significant moral debate among America's religious and secular communities.

I think that it should, but President Reagan and both Presidents Bush have thought otherwise. Until now, the freedom to have an abortion has been granted, but the government has refused to pay for abortions for those who cannot otherwise afford them. A national health care plan, though, would force us to confront the question of whether the government should pay for abortions for the indigent and, indeed, for all Americans who want one together with the underlying theoretical issue in American democratic theory of the role of religion in such discussions.

Thomas Jefferson understood the matter this way:

> The practice of morality [is] necessary for the well-being of society.
> ... The interests of society require observation of those moral principles only in which all religions agree.[62]

What would this mean, though, when the issue is not only granting people the freedom to do as they think right, but also the monetary support to carry out their convictions? Jefferson and Madison did not deal with that ripple of the question because they did not conceive of the government providing the many services it now does and the even greater scope of health care services that the government has periodically considered in the last decade.

We, however, must test the limits of the principles on which Madison and Jefferson founded this nation as we construct a new health care system. With abortion as a particularly poignant example, then, what does freedom of religion entail when a particular medical procedure is required by some religions under at least some circumstances (usually to save the life or health of the mother), permitted by others or seen as a matter for individual conscience, and forbidden by others? Methodologically, should that question be decided on the basis of political power in a vote of Congress, or should it instead be treated as a matter of individual rights guaranteed by the Constitution and affirmed by the courts?

Either way, the broader point should not be lost. Even if a particular religious argument does not win the day in public debate, it should not be denied simply because it comes from a religious source and uses religious language and reasoning. In his book, *The Culture of Disbelief*, Professor Stephen Carter has made this point eloquently with regard to court cases,[63] and I would like to extend it to public policy discussions as well. In my view, built into the First Amendment is not only the right but the duty for all of America's religions to articulate their views and advance the arguments for those views in the public forum. Only then can America benefit in forming its public policy from the variety of peoples who constitute America. This effectively imposes an *American* duty on Americans to learn more about their own religion's views so that they can participate in an informed, intelligent, and distinctly religious way in the shaping of American public policy.

Bringing Religion and Nation Closer Together

I grew up in the 1950s and 1960s, when Jews like me roundly applauded each new brick being added by the Supreme Court to the wall of separation between church and state. As a result, my advocacy in this chapter for people of all religious persuasions to get involved in American public policy debates actively and from their own religious vantage point represents somewhat of a change for me. My experience with several federal arms of government, however, together with the historical, philosophical, and theological musings recorded above, have convinced me that although Americans should ever be on their guard to prevent undue entanglement of church and state, a healthy relationship between the two, as defined by both American and Jewish sources, demands open discussion of matters of national policy with full-throated religious and nonreligious voices being heard at the public table. That discussion should not be overly polite, with people holding back what they really feel in the name of not offending anyone. For the good of all, people instead should feel the duty to bring their views to the fore as cogently and articulately as possible so that they can be understood and considered in the fullness of wisdom and conviction that support them in an atmosphere of respect for all. American public debate, then, should definitely *not* take place in a "naked public square" devoid of religious convictions; it should rather resemble the sound and the fury of talmudic debates, where values and conceptions are openly discussed along with the practical and political aspects of any given issue. Only then can Americans be true to their religious or secular commitments while at the same time giving America the broad basis for the wise public policy it deserves.

NOTES

In the following notes, M. = Mishnah (edited c. 200 C.E.); T. = Tosefta (edited c. 200 C.E.); J. = Jerusalem Talmud (edited c. 400 C.E.); B. = Babylonian Talmud (edited c. 500 C.E.); M.T. = Maimonides's *Mishneh Torah* (1177) ; S.A. = Karo's *Shulhan Arukh* (1565).

1. See note 5 below.
2. See Joshua Skoff, *Religion in the Public Schools*. Los Angeles: University of Judaism (Vol. 7, no. 1, in the *University Papers* series, 1988), pp. 3–5, 14–15.
3. M. *Avot* 3:2; B. *Avodah Zarah* 4a; B. *Zevahim* 102a. One was even supposed to pray for the welfare for non-Jewish (as well as Jewish) kings: B. *Berakhot* 58a.
4. M. *Avot* 1:10; 2:3.
5. For a summary of the development of the relationship between church and state in the United States on issues regarding public schools and the role of Jewish organizations in establishing that relationship, see Skoff, *Religion in the Public Schools*, n. 2. For a somewhat dated, but exhaustive presentation of the materials until 1977 relevant to this issue in all of its forms, see Robert T. Miller and Ronald B. Flowers, *Toward Benevolent Neutrality: Church, State, and the Supreme Court* (Waco, Tex.: Baylor University Press, 1977).

The major Supreme Court cases separating church and state include these: *Everson v. Board of Education* (1947), according to which "laws which aid one religion, aid all religions, or prefer one religion over another [are invalid]. . . . In the words of Jefferson, . . . [there is erected] 'a wall of separation between Church and State.' " *McCollum v. Board of Education* (1948) forbade "released time" for religious instruction within public schools during regular school hours, but *Zorach v. Clauson* (1952) upheld the constitutionality of released time off school grounds. *Engel v. Vitale* (1962) banned even non-denominational, "non-preferential" prayer in the public schools, and *Abington Township v. Schempp* (1963) banned Bible reading in public schools. In *Lemon v. Kurzman* (1971), the Supreme Court established a three-prong test for a statute to be constitutional under the establishment clause of the First Amendment: (1) it must have a secular legislative purpose; (2) its primary or principal effect must neither advance nor inhibit religion; and (3) it must not foster excessive government entanglement with religion. Numerous attempts to overturn these decisions through constitutional amendment have been made, including President Ronald Reagan's efforts in 1982, 1983, and 1984.

6. George Washington, "A Reply to the Hebrew Congregation of Newport," in Lewis Abraham, "Correspondence between Washington and Jewish Citizens," *Proceedings of the American Jewish Historical Society* 3 (1895): 91–92; reprinted in *The Jew in the Modern World: A Documentary History*, ed. Paul R. Mendes-Flohr and Jehuda Reinharz (New York: Oxford University Press, 1980), p. 363.

7. Laura Z. Hobson, *Gentleman's Agreement* (New York: Simon & Schuster, 1947).

8. For a thorough treatment of this episode from the point of view of Jewish sources, see Gil Graff, *Separation of Church and State: Dina de-Malkhuta Dina in Jewish Law, 1750–1848* (Birmingham: University of Alabama Press, 1985).

9. Hermann Cohen, "The German and the Jewish Ethos," in *Reason and Hope*, ed. E. Jospe (New York: W. W. Norton, 1971), pp. 176–184.

10. On the general issue of how Jewish sources can be read to give moral guidance on issues it never knew or contemplated, see Elliot Dorff, *Matters of Life and Death: A Jewish Approach to Modern Medical Ethics* (Philadelphia: Jewish Publication Society, 1998), pp. 395–423, and Elliot Dorff, *To Do the Right and the Good: A Jewish Approach to Modern Social Ethics* (Philadelphia: Jewish Publication Society, 2002), pp. 262–282.

11. I discuss these differences at some length in *To Do the Right and the Good* (at note 10), pp. 1–35.

12. I first developed these themes in Dorff, "The Covenant: How Jews Understand Themselves and Others," *Anglican Theological Review* 64, no. 4 (1982): 481–501. Reprinted in revised form as "The Covenant as the Key: A Jewish Theology of Jewish-Christian Relations," in *Toward a Theological Encounter: Jewish Understandings of Christianity*, ed. Leon Klenicki (New York: Paulist Press, 1991), pp. 43–66; and in Dorff, "Pluralism," in *Frontiers of Jewish Thought*, ed. Steven T. Katz. (Washington, D.C.: B'nai Brith Books, 1992), pp. 213–234; reprinted with further revisions in Dorff, *To Do the Right and the Good* (at note 10), pp. 36–60. What follows below draws on some of the thought in those essays as it applies it to the specific issue of government service.

13. For the terms "hard" and "soft" perspectivism, see Van A. Harvey, *The Historian and the Believer* (New York: Macmillan, 1966), pp. 205–230; see also James Wm. McClendon Jr. and James M. Smith, *Understanding Religious Convictions* (Notre Dame, Ind.: University of Notre Dame Press, 1975), pp. 6–8.

14. See Judah Halevi, *Kuzari*, Book I, Sections 5, 6, 25, 63–65, 80–91; Isaak

Heinemann, trans. and ed., *Three Jewish Philosophers* (Philadelphia: Jewish Publication Society, 1960), pp. 31–32, 35, 37–38, 41–45.

15. The two non-perspectivists mentioned, A. J. Ayer and R. B. Braithwaite, share the view that religion does not make true or false assertions but rather motivates one emotionally, but the former thinker sees this as a major limitation on religion, whereas the latter thinks that this description is both accurate and laudatory of religion's role in life. See A. J. Ayer *Language, Truth, and Logic* (London: Dover, 1936), pp. 114–120; and R. B. Braithwaite, *An Empiricist's View of the Nature of Religious Belief* (The Eddington Memorial Lecture for 1955) (Cambridge: Cambridge University Press, 1955). Reprinted in *Christian Ethics and Contemporary Philosophy*, ed. Ian T. Ramsey (New York: Macmillan, 1966), pp. 53–73.

16. Walter Wurzburger, In *A CAJE Symposium: Division, Pluralism, and Unity among Jews* (New York: Conference for Alternatives in Jewish Education, 1986), p. 11.

17. For a discussion of these various approaches, see Dorff, "Pluralism" (at note 12 above), pp. 219–229.

18. Simon Greenberg, "Pluralism and Jewish Education," *Religious Education* 81, no. 1 (1986): 19–28, at 23. See also p. 27, where he links pluralism to the absence of violence in transforming another person's opinion.

19. Ibid., pp. 24, 26. The Mishnah cited is M. *Sanhedrin* 4:5; the blessing cited is in B. *Berakhot* 58a; and the Midrash cited is in *Numbers Rabbah* 21:2 and *Midrash Tanhuma*, Pinchas, #10, on Numbers 26:16.

20. J. *Sanhedrin* 22a; *Numbers Rabbah* 19:6.

21. Joseph Albo, *Sefer Ha-Ikkarim*, Vol. 2, trans. Isaac Husik (Philadelphia: Jewish Publication Society of America, 1946), Part II, chap. 30, p. 206.

22. *Leviticus Rabbah* 1:14.

23. *Exodus Rabbah* 29:1; see also 5:1; *Mekhilta*, "Yitro," chap. 9; *Pesikta d'Rav Kahana*, "Bahodesh Hashlishi," end of chap. 12, on Exodus 20:2 (Mandelbaum ed., Vol. 1, p. 224); *Tanhuma*, "Shemot," #22 (Buber ed., p. 7b); "Yitro," #17 (Buber ed., p. 40b).

24. B. *Eruvin* 13b.

25. J. *Sanhedrin* 22a.

26. *Sifra* to Leviticus 19:18. Ben Azzai instead cites "This is the book of the generations of Adam . . . in the likeness of God He made him" (Genesis 5:1)—a principle that extends love beyond Jews ("your neighbor") and ties it directly to God, whose image should be appreciated in every person.

27. *Sifra* on Leviticus 19:18.

28. Micah 4:5. Compare Micah 4:1–3 with Isaiah 2:2–4.

29. T. *Avodah Zarah* 8:4; B. *Sanhedrin* 56a, 60a. The seven laws consist of prohibitions against murder, idolatry, incest/adultery, theft, blasphemy, and eating a limb from a living animal, together with the positive commandment to establish a system of justice. This doctrine is thoroughly discussed in David Novak, *The Image of the Non-Jew in Judaism: An Historical and Constructive Study of the Noahide Laws* (New York: Edwin Mellen Press, 1983).

30. See Dorff, "The Covenant: How Jews Understand Themselves and Others" (at note 12 above), pp. 482–484; reprint, "The Covenant as the Key" (at note 12 above), pp. 45–48.

31. See note 29 for the doctrine of the Seven Noahide Laws. The doctrine that righteous non-Jews inherit a place in the world to come appears in the *Sifra* on Leviticus 19:18.

32. *Sifre Deuteronomy* 96, 346.

33. Ibid., 346.

34. Rashi (Rabbi Shlomo Yitzhaki, 1040–1105) ascribes the fear to the appearance of two Torahs on B. *Yevamot* 13b, s.v. *lo ta'aseh aggudot aggudot*; Ritba (Rabbi Yom Tov ben Abraham Ishbili, c. 1250–1330) fears the appearance of two gods in *Hiddushei Haritba* on B. *Yevamot* 13b.

35. The image of Israel as a light to the nations is in Isaiah 42:6; 49:6; cf. 60:3. The mission of Israel to perfect the world under the dominion of God is repeated three times daily in the *Alenu* prayer. For more on this central Jewish mission, see Elliot N. Dorff, *The Way into Tikkun Olam (Repairing the World)* (Woodstock, Vt.: Jewish Lights Publishing, 2005).

36. M. *Shabbat* 1:4; J. *Shabbat* 1:4 (3c); cf. also B. *Shabbat* 17a, and Josephus, *The Jewish War*, Book IV.

37. Deuteronomy 17:11; 1:17. David Dishon suggests this juxtaposition, and he collected and analyzed many of the rabbinic sources discussed in Sections 2–4. See Dishon's *Tarbut Ha–Mahloket B'Yisrael* (Tel Aviv: Schocken, 1984 [Hebrew]).

38. *Numbers Rabbah* 13:15–16.

39. J. *Sanhedrin* 4:2 (22a).

40. M. *Eduyot* 1:4–5.

41. *Pesikta d'Rav Kahana*, Massekhet Bahodesh Ha–shlishi, on Exodus 20:2. Cf. also *Exodus Rabbah* 29:1.

42. David Hartman stresses these features of the Aggadah and the Halakhah in demonstrating the acceptability of pluralism. See David Hartman, *Joy and Responsibility* (Jerusalem: Ben–Zvi Posner, 1978), pp. 130–161.

43. *Avot d'Rabbi Natan* 18:3; T. *Sotah* 7:7; B. *Hagigah* 3b; *Numbers Rabbah* 14:4.

44. B. *Avodah Zarah* 19a.

45. T. *Hagigah* 2:9; B. *Hullin* 7b, and see Rashi's commentary on this there. Cf. also T. *Sotah* 14:9 (Erport MSS).

46. Maimonides, introduction to *Commentary to the Mishnah*, ed. Kafah, Vol. I, pp. 11–12 (Hebrew).

47. Meiri, *Commentary to Ethics of the Fathers* on M. *Ethics of the Fathers* 5:17.

48. B. *Eruvin* 13b.

49. M. *Ethics of the Fathers* 1:12; 3:21; B. *Berakhot* 64a.

50. B. *Bava Batra* 12a.

51. B. *Kiddushin* 29a–b, 40b; *Arukh Ha–Shulhan, Yoreh De'ah* 240:12ff. See Israel M Goldman, *Life-Long Learning Among Jews* (New York: KTAV, 1975), esp. pp. 50–68.

52. M. *Avot (Ethics of the Fathers)* 6:3; 4:15. That a student should not call his teacher by name (and is actually a heretic if he does so): B. *Sanhedrin* 100a. That a teacher must stand before his students to show them honor: B. *Megillah* 21a.

53. See, for example, M. *Rosh Hashanah* 2:8–9.

54. Numbers 16:1–35; M. *Avot (Ethics of the Fathers)* 5:17, and see the commentaries of Rabbi Obadiah of Bertinoro (c. 1450–before 1516) and Rabbenu Jonah ben Abraham Gerondi (c. 1200–1263) to that Mishnah.

55. For example, A. Buchler, "The Minim of Sepphoris and Tiberias in the Second and Third Centuries," in *Studies in Jewish History*, ed. Israel Brodie and J. Rabbinovits (Oxford: Oxford University Press, 1956), pp. 245–274.

56. Rashi on B. *Hagigah* 3b, s.v. *kulan*.

57. *Sifre Deuteronomy* 96; 346.

58. J. *Pesahim* 4:1 (30d); B. *Yevamot* 14a.

59. J. *Yevamot* 1:6 (3b); B. *Yevamot* 14a–b. See also T. *Yevamot* 1:12.

60. Reuven Kimelman put it this way in Kimmelman, "Judaism and Pluralism," *Modern Judaism* 7, no. 2 (May 1987): 131–150, at 136.

61. Daniel Wikler, "Philosophical Perspectives on Access to Health Care: An Introduction," in Vol. 2 of *Securing Access to Health Care* (Washington, D.C.: U.S. Government Printing Office 1983), p. 48.

62. Cited by Earl Raab, untitled essay, in *American Jews and the Separationist Faith*, ed. David G. Dalin (Washington, D.C.: Ethics and Public Policy Center, 1993), pp. 110–111.

63. Stephen L. Carter, *The Culture of Disbelief* (New York: Basic Books, 1993). On p. 21, he says specifically:

> I speak here not simply of arguments for or against the adoption of any *government* policy, although that will, of necessity, be part of my subject. My concern, more broadly, is with the question of what religiously devout people should do when they confront state policies that require them to act counter to what they believe is the will of God, or to acquiesce in conduct by others that they believe God forbids.

My chapter here, in contrast, concentrates on the former issue—that is, the shaping of government policy in the first place.

8

Public Discourse and Reasonable Pluralism: Rethinking the Requirements of Neutrality

H. Tristram Engelhardt Jr.

May Christians Licitly Be Silent about the Truth of Christianity?

This chapter explores the view that religious claims have no legitimate place in the public forum. In great measure, this exploration involves a critical reexamination of the so-called public versus private distinction that would place religious commitments and grounds for action in a sphere isolated from that of public discourse and public choice. In the process, this chapter brings into question John Rawls's defense of a public discourse that claims to have an integrity of its own and that seeks to marginalize religious commitments. At stake is the place of various frankly religious considerations into both public discussions and governmental decision making, ranging from individual Christians on religious grounds publicly condemning such evils as abortion to legislators, representatives, and senators announcing that they are voting in accordance with religious obligations (e.g., in opposition to such issues as the public funding of abortion). These reflections are focused on this guiding question: Under what circumstances should traditional Christians hold it reasonable to abide by a neutrality requirement that demands they closet the transcendentally grounded character of their claims regarding proper public conduct and government decision making?

If one knows that God exists and that His only-begotten Son, Jesus Christ, is the Messiah of Israel and the fulfillment of the Law and the Prophets through Whose Incarnation and Resurrection mankind is redeemed, what would one also need to believe to hold it appropriate to withhold this truth with its watershed moral, metaphysical, and existential implications from one's remarks, decisions, and actions in the public forum? If one is a rightly believing Christian, how could one fail to take the great commission seriously: "Go into all the world and preach the good news to all creation. Whoever believes and is baptized will be saved, but whoever does not believe will be condemned" (Mark 16:15–16) and, like St. Paul, enter the Agora and the Areopagus to preach the Gospel (Acts 17:18–31)? Under what circumstances should Christians agree to abide by a religious and metaphysical neutrality requirement for public discourse, especially if such a requirement is understood in somewhat the following fashion?

> All public claims regarding political decisions and acceptable social structures should only be made in terms of those moral commitments ingredient to a public rationality in which all can share, given the premises and rules of evidence manifestly available to all; these public claims should avoid reference to an ultimate reality or to moral constraints accessible only through special forms of knowledge, as for example those of a religious nature.

Such a neutrality requirement excludes publicly making moral and metaphysical claims bearing on political choices in terms understandable only in the context of Christian commitments (e.g., voicing objections grounded in the insights of Christianity to the evils of abortion, research on human embryos, homosexual acts, and physician-assisted suicide).

Traditionally, Christians are obliged never to deny the claims of Christ: "If anyone is ashamed of Me and My words in this adulterous and sinful generation, the Son of Man will be ashamed of him when He comes in His Father's glory with the holy angels" (Mark 8:38). Indeed, if one knows the deep origin and goal of all being, and given the great commission, what would justify not making reference to this crucial truth in public discussions concerning the human good and the nature of human flourishing? Would one not be required, even as a member of the legislature, executive branch, or judiciary, to exploit whatever discretionary authority available to support human well-being and human flourishing, even if one's justifications are robustly grounded in sectarian commitments (e.g., "as a Christian I am opposed to abortion because it is the killing of unborn children, and therefore as a member of the legislature I am voting against the bill to provide public funds for abortion; moreover, I hope for the support of not only fellow Christians, but all persons, religious or not, who understand the truth of this moral insight")? As a citizen, must one not make such choices, while acknowledging one's sectarian grounds? That is, should not Christians agree with the very position Rawls rejects, namely, "that fundamental political questions should be decided by what they regard as the best reasons according to their own idea of the whole truth, including their religious or secular comprehensive doctrine and not by reasons that might be shared by all citizens as free and equal"?[1] This issue of proper public discourse and choice is of concern not just for Christians, but for all who must share a society with Christians who by their sectarian behavior may bring into question the normative secular moral rationality of public discourse. If Christians will not abide by a neutrality requirement, then they will bring to the public forum considerations opaque to many non-Christians. Worse yet, if the public contentions of Christians prove influential, public policy will be established with a character foreign to the commitments of many non-Christians. This outcome will tend to disestablish the secular character of public discourse and public policy.

Concern with the sectarian character of Christian claims raises the issue of the meaning of the secular and secularity.[2] Four different understandings must be noted. First, there is secularity in the sense of an absence of ecclesiastical control over public discourse, individual choice, and community life, as would obtain in a limited democracy. The second sense of the secular requires not only that ecclesiastical control be absent, but that all public discourse and choice be guided by a practical agnosticism, that is, by acting as if God did not exist. The third sense of the secular requires not just the absence of ecclesiastical control, as well as acting and speaking in public as if God did not exist. In addition, all public choices must be in harmony with reasons defensible in terms of a particular social structure that will affirmatively transform the public space, in the case of Rawls, that of a social democratic constitutional framework.[3] As long as one defends this general framework in reasons congenial to its commitments, one can make reference to religious grounds motivating this defense. In this third understanding, the sectarian character of religious claims must be redeemed through specifically supporting a particular social structure such as a social democratic constitutional polity whose general structure is liberal and agnostic. The fourth sense of the secular is aggressively laicist[4] and requires all spheres of life, private and public, to be transformed by its demands. It excludes public reference to religious grounds in support of the secular social structure, even if they are publicly defended in secular terms. Insofar as one holds public discourse to be normatively secular, then one must not only forbid legislators and those in the executive branch and the judiciary from stating that they are acting on sectarian grounds, but also discourage citizens from voicing sectarian religious opinions as the basis for public policy or from voting on such grounds.

There are many objections to the intrusion of Christian moral and metaphysical claims into the public forum beyond threatening the secular character of society, ranging from specific concerns regarding particular traditional Christian doctrines (e.g., that such doctrines will create impediments to medical progress as by condemning promising research on human embryos, failing to give equal respect to divergent sexual lifestyles, as by condemning homosexual unions, affirming sexism by defending the headship of men in the church and family, and causing needless suffering by condemning physician-assisted suicide and euthanasia) to special disutilities held to be associated with religious discourse itself (e.g., that religious discourse will discourage the pursuit of human flourishing in this world in favor of the pursuit of bliss in an afterlife). In addition, there are objections based on the consideration that if Christians speak in religious terms in the public forum, they will come to vote as a Christian bloc, religiously polarizing society and constituting a threat to civil peace, as well as other concerns (e.g., that the public salience of a religious worldview will marginalize interests in empirical science).

In this chapter, Christianity's relationship to moral and political claims, and to how one might plausibly appreciate the nature of the public forum, is explored to determine what a Christian must hold regarding Christianity to consider improper the intrusion of Christian claims qua Christian into the public forum and public policy. First, a brief categorization is offered of different understandings of Christianity and their implications for intrusions into public discourse. The plausibility of construing the public forum and its discourse as normatively secular is then critically assessed. This will be done by exploring a range of considerations drawn from Immanuel Kant and John Rawls. Kant is selected because his recasting of religion in order to establish a public forum defined in terms of critical rationality exemplifies the Enlightenment's commitment to marginalizing traditional Christianity. Rawls is selected in having provided the most influential late-twentieth-century defense, at least in the English language, of a public forum independent of particular religious commitments yet tolerant of religious views as long as they indirectly serve as a basis for affirming social democratic constitutionalism. As such, Christian commitments transformed by the public forum become functionally agnostic in being primarily oriented to proper constitutional government rather than to right worship and right belief. The elements of this secular liberal agnostic ethos are examined.

This chapter shows why secular moral rationality cannot provide the content claimed for the secular public forum's moral discourse in a way any less arbitrary than Christian claims. That religious considerations are no less rationally compelling than appeals supplying the content of secular moral understandings brings into question the supposed universal character of secular reciprocal reason-giving. The chapter concludes with observations as to why one should reject the liberal cosmopolitan ethos and instead affirm a libertarian cosmopolitan framework for the public forum (thus affirming the first sense of secularity), while accepting the introduction of religious claims in public discourse and the framing of public policy.

Whose Rationality? Which Christianity?

To determine what Christians must hold to consider themselves legitimately silent about the special claims of Christ on persons, societies, and states, one must first recognize the diversity of Christianities. Each understanding carries with it its own implications for public discourse. For the purpose of this chapter, the Christianities can be procrusteanly placed in three categories.

A. Christianity as a cultural perspective. As one of the major global cultural traditions, Christianity is accepted as offering an influential narrative of love, mercy, and justice, which inspires and sustains images of concern for others, a tradition that has transformed not only the West, but the world. Without making exclusive claims, Christianity can motivate moral conduct, establishing

Christianity as part of the universal human cultural heritage. As a cultural tradition it can critically revise its own moral understandings (e.g., with respect to the place of women in the church and the family, as well as the licitness of homosexual relations), being guided by what is considered general progress in moral reflection. Strictly speaking, there is no peculiarly Christian morality or bioethics, only special motivations for moral conduct provided by Christianity's culture and inspirational myths. An example of this Christianity is offered by elements of Unitarian Universalism that recognize the positive cultural force of Christianity.[5] This genre of Christianity does not introduce moral and political claims into the public forum at odds with social democratic commitments; but instead it affirms the intellectual consensus of the day (i.e., that which is taken to be morally normative by the dominant intellectual culture).

Indeed, in stepping back from many of the traditional moral prohibitions of Christianity (e.g., in not generally condemning artificial insemination from donors, abortion, fornication, homosexual acts, and physician-assisted suicide), as well as by not insisting on literal adherence to traditional Christian beliefs (e.g., the Virgin Birth, the bodily Resurrection of Christ, and the Trinity), this genre of Christianity seeks to avoid moralism and dogmatism. Unlike Kantian Christianity and Reform Judaism,[6] which sought a reduction of the dogmatic and rational elements of Christianity to a set of moral commitments, this genre of Christianity tends to reduce the moral and the dogmatic to the inspirational (e.g., engaging a reimaged Christ to inspire social justice), the cultural (without doctrinal substance, e.g., Christmas celebrations), and well-staged rituals (considered as cultural events, e.g., Anglican high church services).[7]

B. Christianity as good philosophy. Christianity is accepted as possessing the fullness of God's revelation to man, offering unique insight into the importance of love, mercy, and justice. Though this revelation provides special grounds for moral conduct, the content of morality is considered amenable to full disclosure by rational inquiry, analysis, and reflection. Since a good moral life is taken to be a sufficient condition for salvation, Christianity should not make exclusivist claims (e.g., the claim that Christianity is the privileged way to moral/metaphysical truth or salvation). Because the rationality (i.e., basic moral premises and rules of evidence) of Christian morality is held to be the same rationality shared by humans generally, this Christianity develops its moral doctrines guided by general secular "progress" in moral insight (e.g., with respect to the place of women in the church and the family, as well as the licitness of homosexual relations). Strictly speaking, this Christianity has no peculiarly Christian morality or bioethics, only a special ground or motivation for moral conduct disclosed through revelation (e.g., the promise of heavenly reward). An example of this account of Christianity is provided by many contemporary Roman Catholic moral theologians.[8]

This genre of Christianity often attempts to recast secular moral viewpoints by advancing religious insights in the guise of forwarding general rational considerations, which considerations, protests to the contrary notwithstanding, are grounded in particular religious insights (e.g., by attacking the contraceptive ethos through putatively general, philosophical natural law arguments against the use of artificial contraception, which can be appreciated only within the context of the Roman church). Because this genre of Christianity gives centrality to moral philosophy, and because the dominant account of moral philosophy tends to be shaped by the dominant cultural "consensus" (which supplies the moral premises and rules of evidence), this Christianity will be inclined, given its identification of its moral rationality with the moral rationality of public discourse, to adapt its own claims to the generally received moral commitments and conceits of the day. It tends to consider its rituals not simply as communal bonds (e.g., baptism), though the moral tends to have precedence over the ritual.

C. Christianity as the unique experience of the Truth. Christianity is recognized as the only complete revelation of God to man, fulfilling the Law and the Prophets of Israel. Christianity not only offers a special motivation for moral conduct, but the full content of the canonical morality that reliably leads to salvation. Because a necessary condition for moral knowledge is right worship (see St. Paul's account in Romans 1:18–32 of how the worship of idols leads to morally perverse sexual inclinations), and because living a good moral life for virtue's sake is recognized as insufficient for salvation, in that salvation requires holiness achieved through rightly loving God ("Thou shalt love the Lord thy God with all thy heart, and with all thy soul, and with all thy mind" [Matt 22:37]), Christianity is appreciated as the only secure avenue to true human flourishing. Since moral progress is achieved by bringing the world to affirm what is disclosed by grace, not merely that disclosed by secular reason acting apart from a rightly ordered experience of God,[9] Christian morality has always disclosed right conduct in its fullness. Moral progress is achieved insofar as secular morality comes to conform to Christian morality (e.g., by forbidding abortion, by affirming the headship of men in the family and the church, and by condemning homosexual relations).[10] This account of Christianity is exemplified by Orthodox Christianity.[11]

This traditional Christian perspective (i.e., the perspective of the first half millennium of Christianity) appreciates that moral theological truth is fully realized only in a noetic experience of that which truly is (where Truth is a Who, not a what), which encounter with Truth is the result of neither sensory empirical evidence nor deductive reason. Truth as a rightly ordered relationship with a transcendent God is beyond discursive rationality. As a result, its traditional commitments cannot be brought into question by supposed moral theological progress grounded in developments in philosophical reflection.[12] Finally, it recognizes its rituals (e.g., baptism) as effective, somewhat as medicine and surgery are effective.

These three accounts are not exhaustive, and among actual persons and particular denominations there is much overlap. These three categories rather shed light on the source of religious conflicts with the neutrality requirement for public discourse. It is those Christians that understand their identity apart from their surrounding secular culture that will be most troublesome for a public forum that aspires to bind persons apart from any sectarian commitments. It is the third genre that poses the most significant threat to the secular neutrality of public discourse.

Domesticating Christianity: The Moral Reduction of Religious Concerns and the Reasonableness of Public Rationality

It is not simply that one must be clear about the kind of Christianity at stake in considerations of sectarian intrusions into the public forum and its discourse; one must be clear as well about the character of the secular culture that attempts to define the public forum and its discourse. In social democratic states, the dominant intellectual culture is that of a secular liberal agnosticism. As such, this culture is set over against the Christianity of Europe's past, as well as other secular frameworks that could have defined these polities, such as a limited democratic framework (the assumptions of this latter framework defined the U.S. Constitution and in part continue to sustain one of the positions in the constitutional debates of contemporary America). This secular liberal agnostic culture is marked not only by a radical reduction of the religious to the moral, but by an affirmation of the priority of liberty as a value, as well as by an affirmation of equality of opportunity as a central societal goal. These commitments are set within an assertive operational agnosticism: a requirement that public discourse and public choices be undertaken as if God did not exist. All of this is nested in an account of rational discourse and reciprocal rationality, which is forwarded in order to define the character of proper public discourse. In the public forum, reasons, considerations, and interests must be articulated in general secular terms involving no claims to special knowledge (e.g., Divine revelation) or transcendent considerations (e.g., the will of God), so that legal, consensual actions may not be condemned as sinful (e.g., condemning homosexual acts as offensive to God).

This rationality in the fourth sense of secularity not only asserts sovereignty over discourse in the public forum, but also aspires to transform all religion into its image and likeness. Religious discourse is to be neutralized by recasting its substance into moral commitments materially equivalent to those of secular morality so that it will no longer pose a sectarian threat to the universalist aspirations of the new secular liberal agnostic morality. This project has deep roots in the Enlightenment's commitment to setting aside ecclesiastical power, superstitious conceits, and irrational religious particularity. Immanuel Kant exemplifies this approach by holding that the truth of Christianity and for that matter of any religion can be fully captured by secular moral rationality. The critical perspective of public reason is the avenue for securing a moral vision independent of parochial and denominational understandings. As grounded in reason, this moral vision is an expression of appropriate reciprocal human relations and is therefore morally normative through representing how persons ought to give reasons to each other for their actions.

In his thoroughgoing moral reduction of religion to morality, Kant argues that the real content of religion is that secured by the rational requirements of a universal morality. As Kant puts it, "There is only *one* (true) *religion*; but there can be *faiths* of several kinds."[13] This one true religion, the kingdom of God within us, is the universal religion of reason, "the pure faith of reason [which] stands in need of no . . . documentary authentication, but proves itself."[14] The goal is to enlighten and reshape a Christianity that traditionally claims by grace a privileged access to moral and metaphysical truth. In this respect, Kant's account of religion, morality, and community is paradigmatic. Morality is identified with rationality (i.e., acting on reasons grounded in discursive reflection), which for its part is identified with those claims endorsable by anonymous secular moral legislators and judges of conduct. The authority of rightly ordered political structures is rationality itself and the true human community is that of all persons bound implicitly by the constraints of rightly ordered rationality. Morality and moral community are thus appreciated from the perspective of rational moral agents who construe their duties outside of particular cultural, historical, and communal commitments. All moral communities that affirm a morality whose content is not justifiable in such hypothetical secular rational perspectives are to that extent morally deviant and defective. Christian moral claims, insofar as they cannot be grounded in this moral perspective, and Christian communities insofar as they are not at one with this ideal moral community, should be reshaped to meet the demands of this moral rationality. In this fashion, critical rationality, philosophy proper, transforms Christianity into a religion of the public forum by grounding its morality not in grace or in a special revelation, but instead in a secular moral rationality. It is this standpoint of the secular reduction of the religious to the moral that grounds the now widely accepted claim: it does not matter to what religion one belongs as long as one lives a good life.

This moral understanding has cast long shadows. In many post-Kantian accounts, the requirement for appropriate public discourse is articulated with reference to the possibility of reciprocal reason-giving, such that Christians as citizens are asked to think of themselves and deport themselves according to the demands of secular rationality, not grounds particular to Christianity. As Rawls puts it:

> Ideally citizens are to think of themselves as if they were legislators and ask themselves what statutes, supported by what reasons satisfying the criterion of reciprocity, they would think it most reasonable to enact. When firm and widespread, the disposition of citizens to view themselves as ideal legislators, and to repudiate government officials and candidates for public office who violate public reason, is one of the political and social roots of democracy, and is vital to its enduring strength and vigor.[15]

At the very least, deviant moral claims (i.e., reasons for conduct not articulable in this context) are to be radically privatized so that they do not enter into the discourse of the public forum as grounds for choices as a citizen, much less as a legislator, judge, or public administrator.

Because the focus is on considerations articulable within the secular rational discourse of the public forum, claims made on the basis of the particular requirements of Christianity are fundamentally illicit. Such claims disrupt the reciprocity of reason-giving which defines the character of appropriate public discourse. All such "God talk," and most especially "Christ talk," must be privatized within contexts that do not disrupt the integrity of the discourse of the public forum. "Christ talk," when it introduces particular religious claims, is particularly at variance with the canonical rationality of the public space and threatens that which is, in this later account, normatively human: a nonsectarian rationality. The Christianities that regard their faith as a cultural tradition will have no difficulty in complying with these requirements. The case is more complex with those Christianities that embed their moral theologies in moral philosophy. Although on the surface this genre of Christianity may seem to constitute a substantial threat to public discourse, there is a tendency, as already noted, for the moral theology of this Christianity to embrace the culturally dominant moral rationality, thus reducing the commitments of its faith to the requirements of the secular public forum and its normative public discourse, in the process relieving Christians of the burden of counterculturally forwarding their sectarian claims.

In this regard, Kant's arguments can be appreciated as an intermediate stage between contemporary commitments to a secular moral rationality and the natural law commitments that began to emerge in the Western Christianity of the thirteenth century[16] leading in the end to an affirmation of a view of social justice that functions as an analogue of social democratic aspirations. As a consequence, Christianity in the second genre can be supportive of, and assimilated to, the aspirations of a social democratic cultural perspective. Here one can understand Hayek's observation:

> [Social justice] seems in particular to have been embraced by a large section of the clergy of all Christian denominations, who, while increasingly losing their faith in a supernatural revelation, appear to have sought a refuge and consolation in a new "social" religion which substitutes a temporal for a celestial promise of justice, and who hope that they can thus continue their striving to do good.[17]

There is a deep consanguinity binding Thomas Aquinas (and many of the ancients) with Immanuel Kant, John Rawls, and Jürgen Habermas, when they hold out the possibility of providing an adequate account of right reason and right action in the absence of right belief and right worship. The affirmation of the possibility of a common moral discourse unanchored in special knowledge secured by grace (including grace through right worship), and which supposedly can sustain a common moral rationality that not only has content, but that is not sectarian, that is, indeed, universally justifiable, bridges the high Middle Ages and contemporary social democratic aspirations. This is the aspiration, though the purchase price for securing moral content always requires embracing a particular moral perspective, a view from somewhere rather than everywhere (and therefore nowhere).

This Enlightenment faith in, and commitment to, rationality shows a continued influence in positions taken by many contemporary moral and political theorists, ranging from John Rawls to Jürgen Habermas. Each in his own way requires that claims made in the public forum be fully grounded in a public secular rationality, in reasons comprehensible to all. Excluded are claims of special religious or cultural insight requiring a privileged grace, revelation, or particular experience (e.g., "only physicians from their engagement in clinical practice can truly know the good of patients"). Knowledge claims must be grounded in empirical experience open to all, the possibility of such experience, or in the requirements of valid reasoning. These various considerations can be summarized in the requirement of public moral rationality.

> All public moral and political claims should be articulated within a reciprocity or dialogue of reason-giving comprehensible to all persons without appeal to special knowledge of moral and metaphysical truths.

This requirement excludes appeals to special knowledge gained through religious experience or grounded in faith.

Such approaches, characteristic of much of the contemporary dominant culture, abound. For example, Habermas pursues the hope for a secular moral perspective with content but yet with universality through his account of discourse.

> I shall speak of "discourse" only when the meaning of the problematic validity claim conceptually forces participants to suppose that a rationally motivated agreement could in principle be achieved, whereby the phrase "in principle" expresses the idealizing proviso: if only the argumentation could be conducted openly enough and continued long enough.[18]

> Thus every valid norm has to fulfill the following condition: (U) *All* affected can accept the consequences and the side effects its *general* observance can be anticipated to have for the satisfaction of *everyone's* interests (and these consequences are preferred to those of known alternative possibilities for regulation).[19]

Thomas Scanlon makes a similar point in his account of contractualism. As he argues, contractualism "holds that an act is wrong if its performance under the circumstances would be disallowed by any set of principles for the general regulation of behavior that no one could reasonably reject as a basis for informed, unforced general agreement."[20] Here as elsewhere, all turns on the nature of reasonableness, of proper reason-giving in moral discourse, and therefore on a particular understanding of reciprocal rationality, on what Rawls calls "a reasonable public basis of justification on fundamental political questions."[21] Indeed, Rawls introduces a concept of the politically reasonable to replace the strong claims of the morally rational (e.g., as advanced by Kant) not only in recognition of the difficulty of providing a rational foundation or justification for his particular views, but also as a means of coming to terms with moral diversity. As we will see, the third genre of Christianity will collide with this particular, nevertheless content-rich account of the reasonable.[22] The moral rationality or reasonableness that is to guide political discourse (e.g., when in the political forum one gives substance to the requirements of fair and equal cooperation) must reflect special conditions, such as rightly turning to the Creator.

The Secular Liberal Agnostic Cultural Project

More than two centuries after the French Revolution, not only has the role of Christian institutions been marginalized, but even the Enlightenment's faith in reason has been significantly undermined. Appeals to rationality have turned out to be appeals to a particular form and way of life asserted to hold the convictions of most contemporary, educated persons. The argument then is made not from a timeless understanding of rationality, but rather from a particular understanding of proper, common governance embedded in a particular view of the reasonable. Undergirding the enterprise of the later Rawls is a Rortian realization that reason cannot by sound rational argument secure either Kant, Rawls, or anyone else's content-full moral vision of morality or justice.[23] Faced with the choice of either arguing in a circle, engaging an infinite regress, or begging the question, the choice is made to beg the question in a way that seems contingently to carry conviction: the political conceits of the dominant intellectual elite are confirmed as normative. In the case of Rawls, these commitments are found to be equivalent to the essentials of a liberal social democratic constitutional framework (even though, for example, America has a limited constitutional framework rather than a social-democratic constitutional framework).[24] It is out of commitment to this social democratic standpoint inter alia that Christianity must be radically domesticated.

This position may at first blush appear modest, as when Rawls claims, "Political liberalism looks for a political conception of justice that we hope can gain the support of an overlapping consensus of reasonable religious, philosophical, and moral doctrines in a society regulated by it."[25] The answer to Rawls's question, "What are the fair terms of social cooperation between citizens characterized as free and equal yet divided by profound doctrinal conflict?"[26] is a totalizing social democracy that requires reforming communal institutions, even if their members are committed to living peaceably with those who peaceably affirm perverse moral visions (e.g., euthanasia as an appropriate element of end-of-life care). Rawls assumes that a reasonable pluralism will sustain a public culture committed to social democratic ideals defining political relationships in terms of what he styles the "criterion of reciprocity, viewed as applied between free and equal citizens, themselves seen as reasonable and rational."[27] Packed into his account of the reasonable and the rational is what he styles the third characterization of this criterion of reciprocity. This characterization requires "measures ensuring for all citizens adequate all-purpose means to make effective use of their freedoms."[28] Among the many difficulties with this requirement is that it legitimates the use of state manipulation and coercion in order to ensure that persons are free not as they wish to be free, but as this particular conception of liberty holds that they ought to be free.

For this reason Rawls must regard Christians who freely recognize the headship of men in the family and in the church (therefore inter alia restricting the priesthood and church authority to males) as an example of perverse false consciousness. No matter how peaceable such undertakings, there will be a liberal social democratic commitment to use the force of law to thwart the illiberal policies of churches and religiously affiliated institutions, as when they refuse to hire and when they fire individuals for involvement in activities the churches recognize as immoral (e.g., cohabitating without benefit of clergy, or engaging in homosexual acts) or for publicly supporting views at odds with traditional Christian teachings (e.g., denying the bodily Resurrection of Jesus Christ). The term "liberal" in the phrase "secular liberal agnostic culture" thus identifies a particular understanding of freedom at odds not only with that of traditional Christians but that of limited democracies as well. When Rawls regards authentic Christian claims, he is not so much concerned that they may introduce doctrinal concerns in the public forum, but rather that they will affirm a moral rationality at odds with social democratic constitutional commitments.

This particular moral vision affirms the lexical priority of liberty as self-determination in the sense of not submitting to another (e.g., rule by another such as by God), and then fair equality of opportunity[29] as necessary elements of a political view that should be freed from traditional, antiliberal and antiegalitarian moral, political, ecclesial, and familial commitments. Secular rationality thus establishes an enlightened ethos aimed at realizing human flourishing immanently understood within a key, liberal egalitarian requirement:

> All humans must be treated as free and equal moral agents oriented to their self-realization and self-satisfaction, the content of which is fully specifiable without appeal to special knowledge acquired through grace or the commitments of faith, whose liberty is not expressed in humbly submitting to another (e.g., God), and whose equality should be pursued through an affirmative commitment to equality of opportunity.

Because the focus is on a constraining account of free choice (i.e., one should freely choose only those relationships that avoid submission to others and that accord with an affirmative equality of opportunity) and self-realization understood in immanent terms, this ethos invites the deconstruction or at least the restructuring of any traditional moral and communal commitments that challenge this ethos (e.g., patriarchal and heterosexist, as well as aristocratic moral commitments and communal structures). The result is that this ideology is committed affirmatively to pursue equality of opportunity, even if this pursuit is incompatible with traditional commitments to the family, in that families tend unfairly to advantage their own members.[30]

Thus, Rawls notes that "Mill held that the family in his day was a school for male despotism: it inculcated habits of thought and ways of feeling and conduct incompatible with democracy. If so, the principles of justice enjoining a reasonable constitutional democratic society can plainly be invoked to reform the family."[31] The morality that should be justified in the discourse of public forum ought to transform and set aside many traditional Christian moral claims (e.g., the headship of the husband and father). This is the case even if such claims are made within spheres customarily held to be within zones of privacy (e.g., the family). As John Rawls stresses,

> The spheres of the political and the public, of the nonpublic and the
> private, fall out from the content and application of the conception
> of justice and its principles. If the so-called private sphere is alleged
> to be a space exempt from justice [read here Rawlsian justice], then
> there is no such thing.[32]

The claims of this moral rationality are totalizing. They reach into all public speech and private association. The totalizing character is hidden in a notion of the reasonable, which thickly incorporates particular social democratic ideals. In terms of these ideals, all social structures are to be rendered reasonable, that is, thoroughly reshaped, in the image and likeness of this understanding of justice as fairness.

Rawls and others, but not all others,[33] downplay their hostility to actual moral diversity. Rawls admits that his account of fairness involves "a comprehensive philosophical doctrine,"[34] thus distinguishing this from "comprehensive liberalism"[35] which would involve more moral-theoretical and/or metaphysical commitments and which would directly exclude doctrines that might nevertheless support a social democratic constitutionalism. Rawls will allow the confession of a religious basis for one's support in reasonable terms of social democratic constitutionalism, as long as the reasons forwarded are articulated in terms of his account of the reasonable. However, no one should in the public forum advocate policies contrary to social democratic ideals. In addition, one is not freely to choose communal structures contrary to those ideals. Most especially, one's religious commitments may never justify civil disobedience on behalf of one's faith, that is, acting "to resist or to disobey laws that they think undermine their positions."[36] "A modern democratic society is characterized not simply by a pluralism of comprehensive religious, philosophical, and moral doctrines but by a pluralism of incompatible yet reasonable comprehensive doctrines."[37] As already noted, "reasonable" here embraces only those understandings of interaction that comport with the requirements of a social democratic understanding of fairness, thus excluding those of libertarians and religious fundamentalists,[38] whose communities and families would need to be refashioned according to the requirements of social democratic commitments. Rawls finds himself required by social democratic justice and fairness to reform communities, even if they are peaceable, when they are grounded in reasonable but peaceable moral rationalities.[39] Pluralism is tolerated only if it is a pluralism that conforms to the substantive side constraints of social democratic constitutional commitments.

God and the Coherence of Morality

Though in many ways indebted to Kant, Rawls significantly separates himself from Kant, who recognized that the rationality of morality requires one to act as if God existed and as if one were immortal, so as to guarantee the harmony of the right and the good, as well as of the rationality of the motivation to be moral in accord with the justification of morality.[40] Without God and immortality, the summum bonum of happiness in proportion to worthiness of happiness could not be assured. As a consequence, Kant held that "it is morally necessary to assume the existence of God,"[41] because he recognized that the full rationality of morality requires God as its cardinal source of unity. In the absence of a recognition of the Deity, the pursuit of the good in numerous circumstances will involve profound collisions with deontological, right-making conditions.[42] Thus, even when lying would save the lives of thousands, one could not within Kantian terms both achieve the good and avoid acting wrongly.

To take a step beyond Kant, prudential rationality and moral rationality can also be in deep tension. Consider if an individual were asked to murder a person painlessly or face the cruel, prolonged, and painful death of all the individual's family and friends, while the reward for cooperating was $100 million in a secret bank account under circumstances in which it is very unlikely that there would be legal sanctions or other adverse consequences. In the absence of an understanding of God securing a harmony of the right and the good, it is impossible to show that it would be irrational to choose to act prudently. This point is captured by Elisabeth Anscombe in noting that when God's existence is no longer recognized, moral concerns can no longer be tied to divine commandments attached to reliable consequences for disobedience. The result is that the character of morality is fundamentally changed. "It is as if the notion 'criminal' were to remain when criminal law and criminal courts had been abolished and forgotten."[43]

Though Kant did not acknowledge it, without God as the perspective from which morality is defined, morality also fragments into a polytheism of competing moral views, each with its own ranking of cardinal moral values. Given different cardinal intuitions, moral premises, and rules of moral evidence, different moralities will be affirmed. Within the sphere of immanence, there can be no escape from the resultant polytheism of moral perspectives. As Gianni Vattimo aptly puts it, "Atheism appears in this light as another catastrophic Tower of Babel."[44] In addition, absent God, all ultimate orientation is lost. That is, absent at least a deistic account similar to that of Christianity, an appreciation of an ultimate direction to cosmic and human history collapses. Everything goes from nowhere to nothing and for no ultimate purpose. In contrast, the Christian recognizes that all of time goes from the Creation and the Fall through the Incarnation and Redemption to the restoration of all things. The only protection against these outcomes is an as-if pretense of God's existence so that the rationality, unity, and meaningfulness of morality can be preserved. It is for this reason that Kant requires us to act as if we knew God existed and as if we were immortal (*Critique of Practical Reason* AK V 132).

The difficulty is that Kant's as-if appeal to God has proven far from compelling. Instead, it becomes rational to recognize the limited scope and reasonableness of morality. As a result, a deep tension emerges between the right and the good, as well as between moral and prudential rationality. Worse yet, it proves impossible to avoid a plurality of moral visions each incompatible with the other. The result is that the morality of the secular liberal agnostic moral vision and the reasonableness at the roots of social democratic constitutional concerns must be recognized as at bottom arbitrary. The recognition of this problem has great antiquity.[45] It finds one of its classical summaries attributed by Diogenes Laertius (third century A.D.) to a Greek skeptic of the later Academy, Agrippa. In his *pente tropoi*, Agrippa summarized the impossibility of securing any particular, content-full, philosophical conclusion and therefore any particular moral claims.[46] Sextus Empiricus (also probably third century A.D.) summarized these *pente tropoi* or five modes as "the first based on discrepancy, the second on regress ad infinitum, the third on relativity, the fourth on hypothesis, the fifth on circular reasoning."[47] The implication of the *pente tropoi* for moral discourse is that an appeal to reason-giving cannot establish a principled, adequate guide to a common moral rationality or even reasonableness, as Immanuel Kant, Habermas, Rawls, and others assume, without begging the question, arguing in a circle, or engaging an infinite regress.[48]

Moral Intuitions and the Truth as Personal

A central moral space has been emptied by the failure of sound rational argument to establish a particular canonical moral or political view as normatively entitled to define proper public discourse and proper public deportment. By default, space opens for many voices, including those of traditional Christians. Secular moral or political theorists may endorse their particular understandings of morality or political structure, but they cannot by sound rational argument justify establishing their understandings as *the* canonical understanding. Indeed, the rationality of their claims fragments, and their force is domesticated to the sphere of one particular moral or ideological perspective. As a result, totalizing constraints on public discourse and reciprocal reason-giving in the public forum become arbitrary, in the sense that they cannot be justified by sound rational argument. By default, one is left with a multitude of approaches and a thousand contending voices, each defined by its own ranking of values, moral premises, and rules of moral evidence.[49] Within the bounds of discursive rational reflection, save for considerations of coherence and clear misunderstandings of empirical facts (as well as, as we shall see, the requirements that persons be used only with their consent), no particular understanding can conclusively show itself to have more secular authority than another. One might even note that traditional Christian appeals to grace and noetic knowledge are no more arbitrary than invoking particular moral intuitions, engaging particular modes of balancing moral appeals, and so on, in securing a particular moral or political vision. Indeed, Kant's reflections indicate a deep rational plausibility to the Christian invocation of God and ultimate purpose. Nevertheless, given this chapter's critical reflections, not to mention ordinary experience, such appeals to grace (since many have a closed heart) will not resolve the interminable moral and political controversies that mark the human condition. In the face of substantive moral pluralism as well as the inability to agree as to what God requires, not only is space cleared for all parties to advance the best considerations at their disposal, but there is a special rationality that the religious voice can claim in integrating the good and the right, though in the absence of a heart open to God that appeal will by no means be conclusive. The human condition is as many recognize it to be: there are numerous competing moral, political, and religious visions with no basis through sound rational argument within the sphere of immanence to choose *the* normative account.

In this circumstance (i.e., in the face of numerous competing moral, political, and religious accounts), the only source for securing a general moral authority that all can accept without appeal to particular disputed moral premises or rules of evidence is the authoritative permission of those who peaceably collaborate. That is, even if one cannot agree whether there is a canonical moral rationality to authorize action, or whether God exists and what He demands, at least one can recognize those individuals willing to join in particular collaborative ventures. To agree to collaborate, one need not agree regarding anything except who will cooperate with whom regarding which projects. If the authority for common interaction cannot be grounded in a canonical understanding of moral rationality or in the will of God, the authority for interaction can at least be grounded in the permission of those who freely associate. It is this expedient that by default allows the free market to bind moral strangers across the world. It is this expedient that undergirds the plausibility of limited democratic, rather than social democratic constitutional frameworks.[50] A limited democratic framework can only, and need only, claim that authority that can be derived from the actual persons who constitute a polity. The exemplar for public conversation ceases to be that of rational discourse and becomes instead peaceable, limited exchanges of opportunities to realize interests, moral and otherwise.

It is for this reason that such a democracy is limited in its authority, including lacking the authority to constrain peaceable public discourse and association, as well as to control the character of peaceable public debates and decisions. In the absence of the ability to discriminate in a justified fashion between peaceable secular ideologies (e.g., social democratic commitments) and peaceable religious understandings (e.g., traditional Christian commitments), the emphasis falls by default on limiting the authority of the majority over peaceable individuals and consensual communities. Peaceable individuals and consensual communities are protected against the majority, including being protected against the imposition of particular, content-rich views of justice. In this context, each can attempt peaceably to convert others to his moral-metaphysical understanding, including to a rightly ordered Christian understanding.

Speaking One's Mind, Voting One's Conscience

Where are we left? To begin with, we possess a set of important constraining conclusions. This chapter's reflections show the implausibility of (1) restricting religious discourse from the public forum, (2) limiting the grounds on which a public official may act and make decisions (as long as the decisions and acts fall within constitutionally established limits and scope of office), or (3) reforming the peaceable interaction of persons in associations or communities (e.g., the Amish, hedonic communes, the Hassidim, and the Boy Scouts). Space is made for individuals and communities peaceably to do with consenting collaborators what others may understand (often rightly) to be deeply morally misguided, imprudent, and perverse. It also means that religious considerations in their own terms can be advanced in bioethics and health care policy. Thus, religious opposition to funding abortion or forms of reproduction such as cloning can appropriately be made in terms of refusing to pay for that which is sinful. By publicly acknowledging when such opposition is based in faithfulness to God, rather than grounding the opposition in more generic moral considerations, all are called to their obligation to God. In so doing, the point of ultimate direction for all human and cosmic history is acknowledged.

Christian claims in bioethics and health care policy offer to all knowledge about human history and the human condition: that all comes from creation by a personal God, that there has been a Fall because of the sin of Adam and Eve, that mankind has been redeemed by Jesus Christ, the Son of God, and that creation will eventually be restored at Christ's Second Coming. In disclosing these truths, Christians can bring orientation in an otherwise seemingly meaningless universe and ultimate sense to the human encounter with sexuality, reproduction, suffering, dying, and death. Otherwise, all these cardinal elements of human life lose their true ultimate significance. Within the horizon of the immanent, they can have only the superficial meanings acquired within particular human narratives. Christian physicians and nurses can aid patients and their families by nesting all bioethical concerns and therapeutic decisions within that narrative into which God has effectively told all creation. In particular, Christian physicians and nurses can provide crucial information about the meaning of life and death, in the process expanding the scope of appropriate behaviors on the part of health care professionals. After all, because death leads to judgment and eternal life, a failure to provide crucial information about this circumstance deprives patients and their families of knowledge essential to informed medical decisions (e.g., the eternal dangers involved in having an abortion), not to mention the proper focus of decision making at the end of life.

The result is that not just different values (e.g., the priority of the holy over the good) enter into private and public decision making, but that crucial knowledge becomes available regarding the nature of the human condition. Such knowledge can legitimately guide not just the decisions of physicians, nurses, families, and patients, but even those in public office, as when a legislator votes against a bill that would require religious hospitals to provide abortifacients after rape to those brought to emergency rooms. Grounded in the limits of the secular moral authority of the state, this affirmation of a right of the religious to give public voice to their insights and to act on their special knowledge radically limits the aspiration to establish a public discourse that excludes claims about God, sin, and eternal life. Even those who are blind to the truth of Christianity, if they are religious, can nevertheless celebrate the space made for an authentic Christian voice because it defends space for all believers. Even the unbelieving can recognize an enriched discourse that appreciates the irreducible moral and metaphysical diversity that characterizes human conversation within the horizon of the environment. Human conversation in general, and that in health care in particular, should give place for concerns about the ultimate interests that break through the horizon of the immanent and the bounds of public discourse and public decision-making as set by contemporary moral and political theorists from Rawls to Habermas.

Conclusions: Facing Controversy and the Philosophy of Ultimate Meaning

This chapter's reflections show the secular moral implausibility of the attempt to form society into one community united around a particular, thick understanding of justice, especially one that requires inter alia the moral and/or political reformation of peaceable individuals, communities, and associations. We are left with an important conclusion regarding the place of intrusions by traditional Christians into the public forum: their claims are no less plausible or less admissible into the public forum than secular moral understandings, including social democratic moral views. Because of the failure of secular moral foundationalism, morality fragments into a plurality of perspectives so that no single content-full secular moral understanding can be established as canonical by sound rational argument. This state of affairs has profound implications for a reasonable understanding of public discourse and the public forum. Totalizing constraints on public speech, public actions, and public decisions cannot be justified. Traditional Christians are from a secular perspective free peaceably to speak and act as they wish.

Traditional Christians have no secular ground for hesitation when advancing their moral and religious views in the public forum. Indeed, they have no general secular grounds for failing to make their views the basis for how they vote and encourage others to vote. Within a limited democracy, religious commitments can properly guide the decisions of citizens, legislators, judges, and even presidents as long as they are within the constraints set by law and the authority of an office. Traditional Christians will have no grounds to comply with neutrality requirements that seek to constrain their public claims and choices in terms of demands by particular notions of public rationality that require that religious claims be advanced in ways open to be appreciated by all. Given the plurality of secular moral rationalities and senses of the reasonable, there will be an opacity separating secular accounts from each other, similar to that which separates religious accounts from the secular. If anything, religious accounts and understandings have a deep plausibility in indicating the possibility of recognizing a unity in God that can reinstate the fragmented dimensions of morality. In particular, traditional Christians will also have very good reasons both secular and religious for not only rejecting but vigorously resisting the totalizing demands of social democratic constitutionalism to reform families, associations, and communities. Justifiable secular commitments will at best support a limited democracy, where in the marketplace of ideas all will be at liberty to advance their pleadings peaceably in the hope of converting others to their perspective. In this context, which is that of the human condition as we find it, traditional Christians will have no grounds for failing publicly to obey the great commission by Christ, to preach the gospel to all peoples.

Those who are culturally Christian will likely be directed by the dominant culture of the time and therefore act according to its expectations. They will recast Christian images into mythlike narratives so as better to achieve human flourishing, understood within the horizon of the finite and the immanent. Theirs will be a reform Christianity in which dogma (e.g., Christ's Resurrection) and particular Christian moral commitments (e.g., the recognition of the immorality of homosexual acts) will be set aside in favor of an affirmation of image, inspiration, and ritual that excludes any claim of the truth of Christianity vis-à-vis other religions. Those of the second genre of Christianity will internalize the basic moral and metaphysical premises and rules of inference of the dominant culture. They will recognize a tension between the traditional commitments of Christianity and those of the surrounding culture and then try to resolve this tension not by invoking grace, but by engaging sound rational arguments that will tend to be hostage to the premises and rules of evidence of the surrounding culture. Their engagement will be intellectual rather than ascetic and hierological. Like John Paul II, they may call for philosophers ever more boldly to take seriously their commitments critically to analyze concepts and frame arguments. In the process they will further internalize the commitments of the surrounding culture within their own religious commitments, thereby transforming their religious commitments.[51]

Postmodernity discloses the moral-epistemological cul-de-sac of attempting to live without grace. It is not simply that under such circumstances all final orientation is lost so that it must appear as if ultimately all of human and cosmic history goes from nowhere, to nothing, and for no purpose. In addition, one is left with moral intuitions, sentiments, hunches, and moral feelings disengaged from any enduring metaphysical framework. One finds a moral world hungering for a noetic apprehension, an immediate unity with the Truth that can only be restored by grace. The way out of this sea of conflicting intuitions lies beyond the market and Socratic dialogue. It is found in opening the human heart to the Truth Who is ultimately personal.

NOTES

1. John Rawls, "The Idea of Public Reason Revisited," *University of Chicago Law Review* 64 (1997): 771.

2. The concept of secularity is rich and multivalent. For a study of the range of its meanings, see H. T. Engelhardt Jr., *Bioethics and Secular Humanism* (Philadelphia: Trinity Press International, 1991), esp. pp. 20–31.

3. John Rawls affirms a constitutional scheme characterized by two fundamental ideas, the substance of which forms the basis of his social democratic constitutionalism, all of which Rawls packs into the concept of free and equal persons. The two fundamental ideas are "the idea of citizens (those engaged in cooperation) as free and equal persons . . . [and] the idea of a well-ordered society as a society effectively regulated by a political conception of justice" (*Political Liberalism* [New York: Columbia University Press, 1993], p. 14).

4. Rawls declares that his position is not secular (e.g., "A view often expressed is that while religious reasons and sectarian doctrines should not be invoked to justify legislation in a democratic society, sound secular arguments may be" ("Idea of Public Reason Revisited," p. 779). By this he apparently means to claim that his position is not aggressively laicist, as for example was the position of Jules Ferry (1832–1893). See, for example, Maurice Reclus, *Jules Ferry* (Paris: Flammarion, 1947). That is, Rawls's position does not forbid Christians, Jews, Moslems, and others from pleading issues of public concern because of their religious commitment, as long as their arguments are made on the basis of considerations open to all within the constraints of liberal social democratic political assumptions. In this Rawls puts both fundamentalist Christian supporters of limited constitutional regimes and libertarians on the same footing, excluding their basic commitments and requiring them to advance their considerations within the constraints of "a reasonable political conception of justice specifying . . . civil rights" (p. 780), which turn out to include substantive social democratic constitutional claims, beyond the formal constitutional rights as embodied, for example, in the U.S. Constitution.

5. The Unitarian Universalist positions led to a broad progressivist understanding. See Stow Parsons in *Free Religion* (New Haven: Yale University Press, 1949). The connection between Unitarian Universalism and the progressivist hopes of the nineteenth and twentieth centuries is significant. Consider:

> Brothers and sisters, we want to work for humanity. We have a new gospel to proclaim—the gospel of religion and science, two in one—the gospel of faith in man carried out to its extremest consequences. . . . We have a new gospel of good news, a radical gospel, the gospel of the "enthusiasm of humanity." God grant us . . . a new Pentecostal outpouring of courage and fidelity to truth! (Francis Abbot, *Report of Addresses at a Meeting Held in Bos-*

ton, May 30, 1867, to Consider the Conditions, Wants, and Prospects of Free Religion in America [Boston, 1867], pp. 37–40, quoted in Stow Persons, *Free Religion* [New Haven, Conn.: Yale University Press, 1947], pp. 47–48)

6. See, for example, Hermann Cohen (1842–1918), *Religion of Reason*, trans. Simon Kaplan (Atlanta: Scholars Press, 1995); *Religion der Vernunft aus den Quellen des Judentums* (1919).

7. Mario Perniola, *Ritual Thinking*, trans. Massimo Verdicchio (Amherst, N.Y.: Humanity Books, 2001).

8. J.-M. Aubert, "La spécificité de la morale chrétienne selon saint Thomas," *Supplément* 92 (1970): 55–73; F. Böckle, "Was ist das Proprium einer christlichen Ethik?" *Heythrop Journal* 13 (1972): 27–43; James F. Bresnahan, S. J., "Rahner's Christian Ethics," *America* 23 (1970): 351–54; Joseph Fuchs, S. J., "Gibt es eine spezifische christliche Moral?" *Stimmen der Zeit* 185 (1970): 99–112; John Macquarrie, *Three Issues in Ethics* (New York: Harper & Row, 1970).

9. In his commentary on Romans, St. John Chrysostom emphasizes that those non-Jews and non-Christians who nevertheless keep the law of God (Romans 2:10–16) are not like the great masses of persons who, living and worshiping wrongly, have obscured the energy of the law in their hearts. St. Paul means "not them that worshipped idols, but them that adored God, that obeyed the law of nature, that strictly kept all things, save the Jewish observances, which attribute to piety, such as were Melchizedek and his, such as was Job, such as were the Ninevites, such as was Cornelius" (St. John Chrysostom, "Homily V on Romans I.28," in *Nicene and Post-Nicene Fathers*, Vol. 11, ed. Philip Schaff and Henry Wace [Peabody, Mass.: Hendrickson, 1994], p. 363). The important connection is recognized between right worship and rightly ordered moral commitments (Romans 1:18–32).

10. Orthodox Christianity does not regard its moral task as progressively revising its commitments in light of alleged secular moral advances, but rather as preserving the truth in terms of which all putative advances are to be judged. "But we, in all things holding the doctrines and precepts of the same, our God-bearing Fathers, make a proclamation with one mouth and one heart, neither adding anything, not taking anything away from those things which have been delivered to us by them [p. 541]. . . . To make our confession short, we keep unchanged all the ecclesiastical traditions handed down to us, whether in writing or verbally" ("The Seventh Ecumenical Council," in *Nicene and Post-Nicene Fathers*, Vol. 14, *The Seven Ecumenical Councils*, ed. Philip Schaff and Henry Wace [Peabody, Mass.: Hendrickson, 1994], p. 550).

11. In his account of religion, John Rawls focuses primarily on Western Christianity, rightly regarding the Roman Catholic religion of the High Middle Ages as robustly illiberal. Although Orthodox Christianity and traditionally oriented fundamentalist Christians are in numerous regards significantly different from Roman Catholicism in their commitments, traditional Christians affirm at least three commitments that, as Rawls notes, disbar them from constituting a civic religion, namely, that their religion is recognized as [1] "a religion of salvation, a way to eternal life, and salvation required true belief as the Church taught it. . . . [2] a doctrinal religion with a creed that was to be believed. . . . [3] an expansionist religion of conversion that recognized no territorial limits to its authority short of the world as a whole" (*Political Liberalism*, p. xxiii).

12. St. John Chrysostom argues that it is noetic apprehension of reality through the grace of the Spirit, not disengaged moral philosophical reasoning, that brings us

to the Truth. Rational reflection on morality when separated from grace leads to false-hood. "Therefore they who inquire by reasonings, it is they who perish" ("Homily IV on I Corinthians I.18–20, IV.2," in *Nicene and Post-Nicene Fathers*, Vol. 12, ed. Philip Schaff and Henry Wace [Peabody, Mass.: Hendrickson, 1994], p. 16). St. John Chrysostom argues further that it is lamentable to have to rely on the Scripture rather than to know immediately through the grace of the Spirit. "It were indeed meet for us not at all to require the aid of the written Word, but to exhibit a life so pure, that the grace of the Spirit should be instead of books to our souls, and that as these are inscribed with ink, even so should our hearts be with the Spirit. But, since we have utterly put away from us this grace, come, let us at any rate embrace the second best course. . . . [God] discoursed [to Noah, Abraham, Job, and Moses] not by writings, but Himself by Himself, finding their minds pure" ("Homily on the Gospel of St. Matthew I.1," in *Nicene and Post-Nicene Fathers*, Vol. 10, ed. Philip Schaff [Peabody, Mass.: Hendrickson, 1994], p. 1).

13. Immanuel Kant, *Religion within the Limits of Reason Alone*, trans. T. M. Greene and H. H. Hudson (New York: Harper, 1960), p. 98, AK VI 107.

14. Ibid., p. 120, AK VI 129.

15. Rawls, "Idea of Public Reason Revisited," p. 769.

16. For an account of the tie between the Western Christian commitments to reason, in particular to discursive philosophical reflection, which eventually led to a condemnation of fideism and the affirmation of a philosophical grounding of theology, all of which produced modernity with its agnostic culture, see Michael Buckley, *On the Origins of Modern Atheism* (New Haven, Conn.: Yale University Press, 1987).

17. Friedrich Hayek, *The Mirage of Social Justice* (Chicago: University of Chicago Press, 1976), p. 66.

18. Habermas, *The Theory of Communicative Action*, Vol. 1, trans. Thomas McCarthy (Boston: Beacon, 1984), p. 42.

19. Habermas, *Moral Consciousness and Communicative Action*, trans. Christian Lenhardt and S. Nicholsen (Cambridge: MIT Press, 1990), p. 65.

20. T. M. Scanlon, *What We Owe to Each Other* (Cambridge, Mass.: Belknap, 1998), p. 153.

21. Rawls, *Political Liberalism*, p. xix.

22. Rawls seeks to replace a moral and metaphysical sense of justice with a political sense of justice that will ensure stability as well as "fair terms of social cooperation," in the process replacing the true with the political commitments of a secular, social-democratic vision. See Rawls, *Political Liberalism*, p. xxv.

23. Richard Rorty frankly acknowledges the arbitrary character of any foundational secular moral commitments. Morality is for any group of people simply that which its moral community endorses, and nothing more.

> We can keep the notion of "morality" just insofar as we can cease to think of morality as the voice of the divine part of ourselves and instead think of it as the voice of ourselves as members of a community, speakers of a common language. We can keep the morality-prudence distinction if we think of it not as the difference between an appeal to the unconditioned and an appeal to the conditioned but as the difference between an appeal to the interests of our community and the appeal to our own, possibly conflicting, private interests. The importance of this shift is that it makes it impossible to ask the question "Is ours a moral society?" (Richard Rorty, *Contingency, Irony, and Solidarity* [Cambridge: Cambridge University Press, 1989], p. 59)

Rawls, in a similar vein, affirms that view which will in the long run be affirmed. "Such a consensus consists of all the reasonable opposing religious, philosophical, and moral doctrines likely to persist over generations and to gain a sizable body of adherents in a more or less just constitutional regime, a regime in which the criterion of justice is that political conception itself" (Rawls, *Political Liberalism*, p. 15). The normative character of his claim regarding the reasonableness of his view of the reasonable turns out to be grounded in an empirical claim regarding the future.

24. The U.S. Constitution not only does not require fair equality of opportunity but also eschews any material rights, guaranteeing only bare procedural fairness.

25. Rawls, *Political Liberalism*, p. 10.

26. Ibid., p. xxv.

27. Rawls, "Idea of Public Reason Revisited," p. 774.

28. Rawls, *Political Liberalism*, p. xxv.

29. The secular liberal social democratic ethos presupposes something like John Rawls's thin theory of the good. (See, for example, John Rawls, *A Theory of Justice*, rev. ed. [Cambridge, Mass.: Belknap, 1999], #60, pp. 347–350.)

30. James S. Fishkin, *Justice, Equal Opportunity and the Family* (New Haven, Conn.: Yale University Press, 1984).

31. Rawls, "Idea of Public Reason Revisited," pp. 790–791.

32. Ibid., 791.

33. See, for example, Amy Gutmann, *Democratic Education* (New Haven, Conn.: Princeton University Press, 1987) and *Identity in Democracy* (New Haven, Conn.: Princeton University Press, 2003); and Will Kymlicka, *Politics in the Vernacular: Nationalism, Multiculturalism, and Citizenship* (New York: Oxford University Press, 2001).

34. Rawls, *Political Liberalism*, p. xvi.

35. Rawls, *Political Liberalism*, p. xxvii.

36. Rawls, "Idea of Public Reason Revisited," p. 781.

37. Rawls, *Political Liberalism*, p. xvi.

38. Rawls defines as fundamentalist those who "assert that the religiously true, or the philosophically true, overrides the politically reasonable" ("Idea of Public Reason Revisited," p. 806). That is, fundamentalism for Rawls is the view that religious commitments trump social democratic constitutional commitments. Following this account, libertarians and others who support limited democracies are also fundamentalists.

39. "Of course, a society may also contain unreasonable and irrational, and even mad, comprehensive doctrines. In their case the problem is to contain them so that they do not undermine the unity and justice of society" (Rawls, *Political Liberalism*, pp. xvi–xvii).

40. Kant introduces his "als-ob" or as-if perspective regarding God's existence in the "Appendix to the Transcendental Dialectic" of the *Critique of Pure Reason*. See A673 701 and A685 713. This assumption allows Kant to appreciate nature as having a purposive unity, which can in turn allow him to assume that a single moral perspective exists. See also A816 844 to A819 847.

41. Immanuel Kant, *Critique of Practical Reason*, trans. Lewis White Beck (Indianapolis: Bobbs-Merrill, 1956), p. 130, AK V 125.

42. Kant writes:

Thus God and a future life are two postulates which, according to the principles of pure reason, are inseparable from the obligation which that same reason imposes upon us. Morality, by itself, constitutes a system. Happiness, however, does not do so, save in so far as it is distributed in exact proportion to morality. But this is possible only in the intelligible world, under a wise Author and Ruler. Such a Ruler, together with life in such a world, which we must regard as a future world, reason finds itself constrained to assume; otherwise it would have to regard the moral laws as empty figments of the brain, since without this postulate the necessary consequence which it itself connects with these laws could not follow. (*Immanuel Kant's Critique of Pure Reason*, trans. Norman Kemp Smith [New York: Macmillan, 1964], A811 839, p. 639)

43. G. E. M. Anscombe, "Modern Moral Philosophy," *Philosophy* 33 (January 1958): 6.

44. Gianni Vattimo, *The End of Modernity*, trans. Jon R. Snyder (Baltimore, Md.: Johns Hopkins University Press, 1991), p. 31.

45. There are summaries of the difficulty of providing a foundation for moral or general philosophical accounts antecedent to that of Agrippa as recorded by Diogenes Laertius and Sextus Empiricus. For example, Clement of Alexandria observes, "Should one say that Knowledge is founded on demonstration by a process of reasoning let him hear that first principles are incapable of demonstration; for they are known neither by art nor sagacity" (Clement of Alexandria, "The Stromata," Book 2, chap. 4, in *Ante-Nicene Fathers*, Vol. 2, ed. Alexander Roberts and James Donaldson [Peabody, Mass.: Hendrickson, 1994], p. 350).

46. "But Agrippa and his school [affirm five] modes, resulting respectively from disagreement, extension *ad infinitum*, relativity, hypothesis and reciprocal inference" (Diogenes Laertius, *Lives of Eminent Philosophers*, Vol. 2, trans. R. D. Hicks [Cambridge, Mass.: Harvard University Press, 1931], IX.88, p. 501).

47. "Outlines of Pyrrhonism," I.164, in *Sextus Empiricus*, Vol. 1, trans. R.G. Bury (Cambridge, Mass.: Harvard University Press, 1976), p. 95.

48. The first trope identifies the difficulty that, after centuries of effort, philosophical reflection has not succeeded in conclusively justifying a particular canonical moral view. This record of persistent failure on the part of moral philosophy strongly suggests that the affirmation of any particular moral position is unsecured by sound rational argument. The third trope identifies the circumstance that all philosophical arguments are made from the perspective of a particular knower conditioned by (i.e., biased by) that particular knower's circumstances, commitments, and assumptions, including his particular moral framework, with the result that disputants, unless they share a lifeworld framed by the same moral and metaphysical assumptions, will inevitably speak past each other, thus accounting for the de facto irresolvability of philosophical and moral controversies noted in the first trope. The debates may be impassioned, but they are interminable, with no principal basis for their resolution in sight. The second, fourth, and fifth tropes indicate the impossibility of coming to a particular moral conclusion without already having in hand common moral premises and rules of moral evidence. As the second trope indicates, arguments will involve an infinite regress or, as the fourth trope indicates, begging the question or, as the fifth trope notes, arguing in a circle. The hope to secure within the bounds of immanence a general rational foundation for a particular moral view fails. The contemporary fashion is to respond to these challenges by boldly appealing to, and then embracing, some particular point of departure, which is accepted as a secure foundation for all that follows. This device is usually at bottom simply an invocation to a particular cluster of intuitions, or some particular set of putative moral insights. Often, the

procedure is rendered more complex by orchestrating numerous such appeals within a framework as if the concatenation of a number of arbitrary assumptions would convey greater authority than a single arbitrary foundation. Thus, one encounters various attempts to balance moral appeals, to engage wide reflective equilibria between intuitions and moral principles, or to develop a cluster of arguments (no one of which escapes the difficulties noted by Agrippa), as if such a pluralist casuistry or project of reflection could by relying on a number of inadequate arguments produce a more reliable conclusion (rather than more confusion) than would be secured by reliance on only one inadequate argument (perhaps the confusion generated serves strategically to obscure the failure of this approach). At some juncture, there is always a crucial affirmation of particular moral intuitions, sentiments, or supposedly manifest initial moral premises. At no place do the arguments proceed without begging the question, arguing in a circle, or engaging in infinite regress. One confronts the moral theoretic difficulty that unless one can noetically apprehend the truth such that it is truly self-evident, Agrippa wins, and one is left with a polytheism of competing moral visions, of which John Rawls's thin theory of the good is one among many. See Rawls, *Theory of Justice*, #60, pp. 347–350.

This challenge to moral and political theory is acknowledged by Rawls in his retreat from the somewhat stronger claims in *A Theory of Justice* toward the more theoretically cautious claims in *Political Liberalism*. For this reason, Rawls conceded that his account of justice as fairness is political-theoretical, not metaphysical or foundationally moral-theoretical (see John Rawls, "Justice as Fairness: Political not Metaphysical," *Philosophy and Public Affairs* 14 [summer 1985]: 223–251). Though he admits that his account involves only the explication of a political structure one has already affirmed (i.e., the normativity of a particular understanding of democratic constitutionalism, which turns out to be social-democratic constitutionalism), he fails to acknowledge how much content is smuggled in the luggage of seemingly harmless terms such as "reasonable." As Rawls frankly puts it, "Political liberalism . . . supposes that a reasonable comprehensive doctrine does not reject the essentials of a democratic regime" (*Political Liberalism*, p. xvi). Reasonableness is here defined in terms of those principles necessary to support a particular set of moral intuitions and principles. The problem thus remains: why *this* moral rationality, why *this* understanding of justice? The attempt to establish a particular normative rationality or reasonableness goes aground at least on the second, fourth, and fifth trope of Agrippa. Social democratic constraints on the public forum and public discourse turn out to be arbitrary at best. Although these conclusions do not endorse a metaphysical moral skepticism (i.e., one is not forced to deny the existence of moral truth), one is confronted with good grounds for a moral-epistemological skepticism: sound rational argument cannot within the horizon of immanence establish a canonical understanding of morality.

49. Ruiping Fan, "Reconstructionist Confucianism and Health Care: An Asian Moral Account of Health Care Resource Allocation," *Journal of Medicine and Philosophy* 27 (2002): 675–682, and "Reconstructionist Confucianism and Bioethics: A Note on Moral Difference," in *Bioethics and Moral Content: National Traditions of Health Care Morality*, ed. H. T. Engelhardt Jr., and L. Rasmussen (Dordrecht: Kluwer, 2002), pp. 281–287.

50. H. Tristram Engelhardt Jr., *Foundations of Bioethics*, chaps. 1–4; and *Bioethics and Secular Humanism*, chap. 5.

51. "I appeal now to philosophers to explore more comprehensively the dimensions of the true, the good and the beautiful to which the word of God gives access.

. . . I appeal also to philosophers, and to all teachers of philosophy, asking them to have the courage to recover, in the flow of an enduringly valid philosophical tradition, the range of authentic wisdom and truth—metaphysical truth included—which is proper to philosophical enquiry" (Pope John Paul II, *Fides et Ratio* [Vatican City: Libreria Editrice Vaticana, 1998], § 103, pp. 148, 151).

PART IV

Religion and Official Discourse

If religion has a place in the public square and can be used as a basis upon which to advocate for public policy decisions on bioethical matters, what happens to religion when those policies are adopted by the state? How is the state to address the idea of religious justification?

As previously suggested, for many people sensitive to religious freedom issues, the use of religious justifications in the public square by private individuals is a matter of political morality rather than constitutional law. While such use of religion is allowed, it may or may not be ethical. The dynamic shifts when the state begins to use religion and religious justifications. When the state, which is expected to speak for all, adopts a religious position—does that not discriminate against those that do not hold that belief? Clearly, every law "discriminates" against those who do not support it. Is a religious grounding different?

As a constitutional matter, the U.S. Supreme Court has held that although the presence of a religious justification for a law does not automatically make the law unconstitutional for violating the First Amendment, states must be able to offer strong and legitimate secular justifications for that law.[1] Moreover, the courts will very carefully review statutes that are drafted in a strictly secular manner if it appears that the statute is discriminatory and was motivated by religious animus.[2] The Court has not, however, gone so far as to preclude the inclusion of religious reasoning or justifications in addition to secular reasons.

The question then becomes, How can the state use religion? In arguing against the use of religious justifications, many critics appear to assume that religious and secular justifications are either interchangeable or that people of faith are able to adopt secular rationales at will. Moreover, presumably the goal is to distinguish religion to make sure that the law does not in fact impose religious beliefs.

In "Law and Bioethics in *Rodriguez v. Canada*," I and my coauthors, Edward Keyserlingk and Wendy Morton, challenge the legitimacy of this distinction. Specifically, when courts address a novel bioethical policy decision, all judges would certainly assert, as the *Rodriguez* court does, that they are a drawing upon secular legal resources rather than religion or personal values and beliefs. (Since religion is the primary source of moral values for most believers, the two may be considered synonymous for people of faith for purposes of this discussion.) Using *Rodriguez* as a case study, we explore what "legal resources" are relied upon by the justices of the Canadian Supreme Court and demonstrate that ultimately these resources are little more than veiled moral-political beliefs. In this case these moral-political beliefs are described according to secular norms. However, a religious source of values could be equally brought into the law via the same ratio-legal process.

If this analysis is correct, then the demand for a secular justification to screen out strictly religious values loses force. Though it may offer some comfort by making public discourse less offensive to those that do not hold the religious view being expressed, this practice may in fact allow for greater intrusion of religious beliefs unchecked by secular forces because they are unacknowledged and potentially unrecognized. Moreover, we must ask whether demanding the use of secular justifications and the repression of religious views that may be much more persuasive to the speaker does not breed a troubling level of cynicism and hypocrisy. Honoring form over substance does not necessarily advance sincere engagement with the issues. Finally, repressing religious justifications may have consequences for the public. People of faith will not receive the justifications that might be most persuasive to them; they will suffer the silence of the marginalized because their voice—the values they find persuasive—is not considered legitimate or acceptable; and the religious justifications that may be motivating the policy statement will not be subjected to the challenges of the public marketplace of ideas (as described by Cynthia Cohen in chapter 5).

Simply adding religion to the mix, however, is not in and of itself adequate. As M. Cathleen Kaveny points out in her chapter, "The NBAC Report on Cloning," although the NBAC specifically included a religious perspective in its hearing and in its report, the manner in which it did so was very troubling. First, it distorted the religious perspective that it presented by advancing a conclusion that there was greater disagreement and conflict within the religious community than was in fact the case. Clearly, encouraging public officials to include religious perspectives gathered during the course of developing public policy and/or public policy proposals puts that perspective at risk of being distorted. However, what is more troubling in this case is that this distortion, along with some other rhetorical strategies, allowed NBAC to effectively marginalize religion from having any influence in the debate. It in effect adopted the suspicions prevalent about religion in the public square (e.g., that it was divisive and irrational) and reinforced them.

The NBAC case does not prove that religion cannot be included in the public policy arena. One way of viewing the problem is that religion was included without altering or addressing those normative assumptions within traditional liberalism that had previously augured against including religion. Nonetheless, this chapter does raise questions about how and whether appropriate cultural changes can be expected that might promote religious participation. On the other hand, are there structural adjustments that can be made? These remain open questions.

NOTES

1. See, e.g., *Everson v. Board of Education*, 330 U.S. 1 (1947); *McGowan v. Maryland*, 366 U.S. 420 (1961); and *Griswold v. Connecticut*, 381 U.S. 479 (1965).

2. See, e.g., *Church of the Lukumi Babalu Aye, Inc. and Ernesto Pichardo v. City of Hialeah*, 508 U.S. 520 (1993).

9

Law and Bioethics in
Rodriguez v. Canada

David E. Guinn, Edward W. Keyserlingk, and Wendy Morton

There is a voluminous body of literature on the relation between law and morals, a hotly debated topic over the last five decades.[1] There is an equally significant body of literature that uses the law as one of the sources for bioethics.[2] There is, however, a paucity of material examining how lawmakers, particularly the courts, use ethics in the process of making laws. Moreover, since a vast majority of people in the United States draw upon religion as the source for their ethical reflections and values and believe that others should as well,[3] understanding the role ethics plays in judicial decision making may similarly illuminate the role that religion may explicitly or implicitly play in the formation of bioethical law.

This chapter will attempt to address this topic through a close reading of the Supreme Court of Canada's decision *Rodriguez v. Canada (A.G.)*,[4] considered within the broader context of jurisprudential practice in countries with common-law traditions like Canada and the United States. In *Rodriguez*, the court sustained the federal government's criminal law against assisted suicide, an issue with clear ethical dimensions. By a vote of 5 to 4, including three minority dissents, the Supreme Court upheld the constitutionality of the federal criminal code's prohibition against assisted suicide.

In this chapter we will attempt to demonstrate that ethics plays an extremely important role in decision making and lawmaking in bioethics issues. These decisions are not simple case-by-case judgments; rather, they rest upon rich, comprehensive ethical perspectives. We will also consider the implications of this epistemic grounding for bioethics and its use of case law materials as an ethical resource. Finally, as previously noted, since many people base

their moral judgments on religious beliefs, we will consider the religious implications of this legal-moral relationship.

Background

Sue Rodriguez was a 42-year-old woman suffering from amyotrophic lateral
sclerosis (Lou Gehrig's disease) with a life expectancy of two to fourteen
months. Her condition was rapidly deteriorating, and doctors expected that she
would soon lose her ability to speak, walk, move her body, breathe, swallow, or
eat without increasing levels of assistance and intervention. Rodriguez, anticipating her deteriorating condition, wanted the assistance of a "qualified physician . . . to set up technological means by which she might, when she was no
longer able to enjoy life, by her own hand, at the time of her choosing, end
her life."[5]

In seeking to have the law against assisted suicide (s.241 (b) of the criminal code)[6] invalidated so as to allow her this option, Rodriguez asserted
three interrelated claims under the Canadian Charter of Rights and Freedoms.[7] First, she asserted that the law against assisted suicide violated her
interests in liberty and security of the person (protected under s.7 of the
Charter[8]) by denying her right to make important choices concerning her
own body. Second, she asserted that by denying her the option of assisted suicide, the state would be subjecting her to "cruel and unusual treatment" in
violation of s.12 of the Charter.[9] The law would force her to endure treatment
she did not wish to receive and to suffer the type of death caused by her disease. Finally, insofar as suicide has been decriminalized in Canada, Rodriguez argued that the assisted suicide law discriminated against her, in violation of s.15 of the Charter,[10] because her anticipated physical disability would
preclude her from committing suicide whereas an non-disabled person
would not be precluded.

In terms of studying the relationship between bioethics and law, *Rodriguez*
provides an excellent case study. First, it deals with an important and timely
issue in bioethics and public policy. Second, this issue is confronted directly
by the court. There were no intervening issues complicating the case, such
as questions regarding Rodriguez's competency to make such a choice or
doubts about the motives or actions of a third party. The issue was solely
whether or not a competent, rational person should be allowed the assistance
of a qualified physician in carrying out her desire to commit suicide. Finally,
the dispute was framed strictly as a question of law based upon specific provisions of the Charter of Rights and Freedoms and a statute directly addressed to the situation. The court was not being asked to create a new right
based upon its powers at equity without prior legal precedent. This case
clearly falls within the norms of the judicial lawmaking system and provides
a good illustration of it.

The Courts and Judicial Law Making

In attempting to discern the role of ethics in judicial law making in a primarily common law tradition such as Canada[11] the first and most obvious difficulty is that the courts do not identify ethical theories and moral values as a resource for their decision making. Indeed, the use of ethics is often explicitly denied, and, instead, the assertion is made that the court should adhere solely to principles of law,[12] a point explicitly raised by Chief Justice Lamer in his dissent.[13] Though not often articulated, this claim appears to rest upon three grounds. First, it reflects a particular arguably erroneous understanding of ethics and morals. Second, it entails a particular understanding of legal process and judicial reasoning. Third, it places great emphasis upon the sources used in judicial lawmaking.

As a preliminary matter, it is necessary to discuss these three grounds in some detail.

Ethics and Morals

In *Rodriguez v. Canada*, Chief Justice Lamer, in his dissent, is the only justice who specifically raises the issue of ethics in relation to law. In denying that use of ethics is appropriate in judicial decision making, Lamer writes:

> In my opinion, the Court should answer this question [before the court] without reference to the philosophical and theological considerations fueling the debate on the morality of suicide or euthanasia. It should consider the question before it from a legal perspective.[14]

It appears that what he is denying is the appropriateness of using arguments or conclusions drawn from ethics texts. This is, however, a very narrow and distorted understanding of ethics.

The understanding of ethics that will be applied in this chapter is as follows: Ethics is the disciplined reflection upon human character, actions, values, and institutions in relation to conceptions of the "good" human life.[15] The "good" refers to "the interest, purpose, or set of interests, or purposes that an individual or group does or should seek to realize."[16] The good thus reflects an understanding of what it means to be human and the type of life one should lead as a human being. Ethics provides the tools or framework by which we may seek to understand the implications of the good.

Morals refer to the norms or values actually held by a society. For example, the understanding that one should not lie, cheat, or commit murders are all moral norms or values. It should be noted that in many cases these norms are also included in the law. Thus, the distinction between ethics and morals can be described as one of procedure or process on the one hand and substance or normative values on the other.

In applying these definitions to Lamer's opinion in particular, it can be argued that his opinion is in fact an exercise in ethics. In the opinion, he identifies certain legal principles which embody strong social norms or values, including the ideas of equality,[17] the "dignity" of the individual, the autonomy of the individual in making decisions in relation to his or her own person,[18] and the idea that the statute against suicide was intended to protect "vulnerable" individuals.[19] The former two ideas clearly relate to a particular understanding of human character (i.e., that the person possesses and should be accorded dignity and should be treated as autonomous), and the latter relates to "actions" in relation to the human "good" of life itself. As Lamer's analysis indicates, though the legislation against assisted suicide targets specific actions, it is predicated upon moral values.

Legal Process and Judicial Reasoning

Assuming that the foregoing analysis is correct, that the subject matter of law and ethics is to a greater or lesser extent the same (i.e., understandings of the human good in relation to "character" or "acts"), the next question is whether the nature of the disciplined reflection applied to this subject is fundamentally different. That is to say, Are the logical processes of reasoning or analysis different for law and ethics (recognizing, of course, that there is no single definitive form of ethical reasoning)? In approaching this question, there are two prominent theories of legal reasoning identified by legal theorists that must be considered: reasoning by rules and reasoning by cases or analogy.

Judicial reasoning by rules is based upon the idea that law is a system of rules of behavior that are identified by the lawmaking process (i.e., the legislature or judiciary) and then applied to specific cases or controversies.[20] Insofar as there is a conflict between identified rules or principles, the principle of reasoning by rules requires the Court to seek a balance between those principles as a way of resolving the case. The process of reasoning by rules is arguably the dominant form of reasoning used by the Court in *Rodriguez*. It can be seen in both Justice Sopinka's majority opinion and Chief Justice Lamer's dissent in their efforts to identify the principles (i.e., rules) presented in the various provisions of the Charter, and the rule protecting vulnerable individuals in the assisted suicide statute, and attempting to apply those principles to the specifics of the case at hand.

The idea of seeking balance among conflicting rules can be seen in the argument over the principle of protecting vulnerable individuals found in the statute against assisted suicide as against the right of autonomy and self-control asserted by Rodriguez (see, e.g., Lamer's approach to the issue of vulnerability discussed below).

This reasoning process is not, however, unique to the law. Indeed, it is almost identical to the ethical method known as principle ethics. As identified by Beauchamp and Childress,[21] principle ethics involves the identification of certain principles (i.e., rules) rooted in commonsense morality that are then applied to the specifics of a case. Where two or more principles are in conflict in a specific case, the moral reasoner is expected to balance those principles in resolving the case.

A second form of legal reasoning identified by legal theorists may be identified as analogical or case-based reasoning.[22] Under this theory, courts start with the assumption that all citizens must be treated equally under the law and that similar cases should yield similar results. In reaching its decision, however, the court must focus not only upon similarities between particular cases (what may be identified as common principles) but also upon specific differences that would justify differing results. One can find an example of this process in Lamer's attention to the decriminalization of suicide[23] as providing a legal basis for distinguishing the application of the assisted suicide statute to a person in Sue Rodriguez's position. Her disability is the distinguishing factor relevant to his decision.

Again, this reasoning process is not unique to the law. It is a process of reasoning that Alan Goldman has argued should be adopted by ethicists.[24] This is almost identical to the process used by casuists and bioethicists who adhere to the case method of analysis.[25] Indeed, the case method familiar to common law and used in this opinion shares a common root from the time of the Middle Ages with the ethical system known as casuistry.[26] Thus it can be concluded that the process of disciplined reflection does not fundamentally vary between the law and some schools of ethics.

Legal Perspectives and Sources

The third component of Lamer's argument is that the courts are constrained to apply a legal perspective. "[The Court] should consider the question before it from a legal perspective," he writes.[27] The Chief Justice does not explain what this means, but a review of his opinion suggests that this requires that the Court confine its analysis to legal texts and resources such as statutes, the national Constitution, and prior court decisions. It would appear that the distinction he is trying to make here is that the Court is not to develop or apply a new moral norm in its lawmaking function but rather that it is constrained to work within the framework of the law and the principles and standards embodied in it. This would conform to the distinction Goldman makes between legal reasoning and moral reasoning.[28] However, this limitation to legal texts and resources is not as restrictive as it might first appear.

For example, reliance upon prior court decisions would fulfill Lamer's requirement that the Court restrict itself to legal perspectives. However, those prior court decisions may themselves embody ethical decisions that are in some ways independent of the legal perspective. In asserting "the central place of freedom of conscience [a moral value or good]," Lamer quotes with approval the statement of Justice Robert George Brian Dickson in *R. v. Big M Drug Mart Ltd.*:

> A truly free society is one that can accommodate a wide variety of beliefs, diversity of tastes and pursuits, customs and modes of conduct. A free society is one which aims at equality with respect to the enjoyment of fundamental freedoms, *and I say this without reliance upon s.15 of the Charter.* (Emphasis added.)[29]

If this judgment is independent of the Charter, then what is its source?

Again, in order to buttress his contention that personal autonomy is a fundamental legal right and to link it more closely to the facts of *Rodriguez*, Lamer focuses attention on the common law:

> In medical matters, the common law recognizes to a very large degree the right of each individual to make decisions regarding his [sic] own person.[30]

And again:

> Like the Charter itself in several of its provisions, therefore, the common law recognized the fundamental importance of individual autonomy and self-determination in our legal system.[31]

The fact that this "right" exists within the common law may absolve the present Court from the charge of making a "new" value judgment. However, it does not absolve the Court as an institution from the adoption of new values—it merely places that adoption as occurring within the past actions of the Court. Reliance upon common law means, by definition, that this law is judicially created as opposed to having its source in legislative action.

Two additional justifications may be offered for the distinctions that Lamer is making between law and morality. First, the chief justice may be attempting to distinguish between general norms or values that are found pervasively in the law and specific moral judgments drawn from particular value systems, which John Rawls has described as comprehensive worldviews.[32] As suggested by political philosopher Charles Larmore, the goal of a liberal society is to avoid the adoption of controversial notions of the good in order to respect the right of each individual to determine and pursue their own "good."[33] Thus, Lamer's reliance upon legal precedent reflects an effort to find common or uncontested values upon which to base his decision.

Alternately, he may be attempting to avoid a moral judgment about this specific act (assisted suicide) by seeking a higher, political value. Thus, if freedom is a primary legal value, how one exercises that freedom is irrelevant.

Ultimately, both efforts fail as an attempt to avoid moral judgment or to distinguish between law and morality. With respect to the first, identifying common or overarching values simply ignores the potential that those values are not universal but rather are hegemonic—the worldview of a majority that has found expression in legal tradition and judgments. The mere existence of the case demonstrates that the specific moral or legal judgment to be made remains contested. With respect to the latter, it attempts to hide the moral judgment that freedom, according to Lamer, is a superior moral value to that codified in the law against assisted suicide.

In attempting to present a legal basis, Lamer's opinion also relies upon statutory sources. On its face, this would appear to be the clearest example of a strictly legal perspective freed from the claim that the Court is involved in making ethical judgments. The Court could, in this situation, legitimately claim that if an ethical judgment is being made, it is being made by the legislative branch of government. As suggested by Justice Hollinrake of the Supreme Court of British Columbia in the lower court ruling in this case, which rejected the notion that one has a right to assisted suicide:

> In areas with public opinion at either extreme, and which involves
> basically philosophical and not legal consideration, it is proper that
> the matter be left in the hands of Parliament as historically has been
> the case.[34]

Yet upon closer analysis, this legal resource as used by the Court is also problematic.

Statutory adjudication of a law such as the statute against assisted suicide S.241 (b) or the decriminalization of suicide can be adjudicated in two ways. These may be characterized as (1) statutory construction or (2) statutory interpretation.

Statutory construction involves the court attempting to determine and articulate the intended meaning of a statute through a close reading of the text, legislative records relating to its enactment and any prior court decisions relating to that statute. This arguably embodies the most "legal" type of judicial decision making in that it places the greatest constraint upon judicial discretion by demanding that the courts not only adhere to the text of the statute, but, in the face of ambiguity, that they determine the actual intent of the legislators through the legislative history. Canada, however, rejects this jurisprudential theory. In Canada, statutory construction is limited to the plain meaning of the text of the statute. Even in the face of textual ambiguity, the courts do not seek to identify the intent of a statute from the records of those individuals that enact the law.[35] Hence, since the text of the statute clearly prohibits assisted suicide, this technique is irrelevant to Lamer's decision.

The second method, as reflected in Chief Justice Lamer's opinion, may be identified as statutory interpretation. Here, for example, he interprets the "intent" of the statute against assisted suicide as being the protection of vulnerable individuals.[36] He does so without significant discussion, apparently because this characterization was not disputed by the appellant (Rodriguez) and was accepted by the trial judge.[37] These sources would fit in with his required legal perspectives as sources of authority. Nonetheless, one must ask whether this is, in fact, a legitimate interpretation of "statutory intent" as some kind of objective standard or an interpretation into the statute to promote the moral values of the interpreter.

For example, Lamer does not consider the alternative possibility that the law was directed not at the person seeking assistance but against the person assisting in the suicide (the actual party that is the subject of the law). It is not the "victim" but the abettor that the legislators determined to be criminally culpable. A direct reading of the statute, as noted by Justice Sopinka, specifies that "the active participation by one individual in the death of another is intrinsically morally and legally wrong."[38] Moreover, because this alternative reading of the statute's intent is present in Justice Sopinka's majority opinion, one cannot say that Lamer was unaware of it. Instead, one must assume that Lamer is rejecting this interpretation (without explicit comment) because it doesn't fit in with his overall argument supporting Sue Rodriguez's right to assisted suicide.

One can also discern this intent in Lamer's linkage of his interpretation of the purpose behind the assisted suicide statute and his interpretation of the decriminalization of suicide. Without reference to other legal sources, the most that one can say in that by its actions, Parliament decriminalized suicide. As noted by Justice Sopinka (also without citation to other legal sources):

> Parliament's repeal of the offence of attempted suicide from the Criminal Code was not a recognition that suicide was to be accepted within Canadian society. Rather, this action merely reflected the recognition that the criminal law was an ineffectual and inappropriate tool for dealing with suicide attempts.[39]

This limited interpretation is in fact the only interpretation that can be logically made upon the available facts.

By contrast, Lamer interprets this decriminalization as conferring in essence, if not in fact, a right to commit suicide.

> I . . . take the repeal of the offence of attempted suicide to indicate Parliament's unwillingness to enforce the protection of a group containing many vulnerable people (i.e., those contemplating suicide) over and against the freely determined will of an individual set on terminating his or her life. *Self-determination was now considered the paramount factor in the state regulation of suicide.* (Emphasis added.)[40]

The logical fault in this interpretation privileging self-determination can be readily demonstrated by the fact that this law did not alter legal precedent that someone who is suicidal can be prevented from suicide through involuntary commitment nor the fact that individuals may be required to intervene to prevent a suicide.[41] Thus, self-determination can be legally frustrated (hence regulated) even though the act of attempting suicide may not be punished.

In this sequence of linked statutory interpretations, it is very clear that Lamer's attention is so tightly focused upon the issue of individual self-determination that he ignores the roles that others have to play in an individual's life (i.e., the assistor to the suicide, or the ability and/or duty of others to prevent suicide). Thus, even if one argues that self-determination or autonomy is a "legal" perspective, the weight or value that Lamer gives this value at the expense of other legal perspectives suggests a particular understanding of the good. That is to say, his "interpretation" of the law embodies an ethical understanding that human autonomy is a paramount good.

Lamer's use of the provisions of the Charter is similarly interpretive. He ostensibly relies upon a significant number of prior decisions. Nevertheless, value judgments, independent of legal resources, can be identified in two respects. First, there is the issue of which decisions to cite. As demonstrated in the opinion by Justice Sopinka, there are decisions not cited by Lamer that counter his opinion. He is, therefore, expressing value judgments in relation to the decisions he elects to cite. Second, in interpreting "security of the person" as a central provision of section 7, he is making a value judgment in opposition to Justice Sopinka's determination that the sanctity of life is the central value. Here again is a value judgment.

Lamer cannot escape the assertion that these value judgments are in fact ethical judgments because these judgments cannot be said to rest simply upon reliance on legal resources (as might be the case with statutory construction as noted above). There is no effort to explicitly shift the burden of these judgments upon the legislative process—either in terms of the statute or the Charter. They are, therefore, judicially made, ethical value judgments.

General Theories of Law and Ethics

As the foregoing analysis demonstrates, there is a significant ethical component in judicial decision making. There is, however, a second level of ethical analysis to consider. What are the general theories of law and morals that may be said to underlie the approaches taken by the justices?

In the North American context there are two primary competing theories in this regard. The first, which may be referred to as the communitarian theory, is popularly associated with Lord Patrick Devlin.[42] Devlin argues that liberal society may legitimately legislate and enforce moral standards. He argues that morals reflect a community's self-understanding and provide a source of community adhesion.

> What makes a society of any sort is community of ideas, not only
> political ideas but also ideas about the way its members should be-
> have and govern their lives; these latter ideas are its morals. . . .
> [Moreover] without shared ideas on politics, morals and ethics no
> society can exist. . . . [S]ociety is not something that is kept together
> physically; it is held by the invisible bonds of common thought.[43]

The state is empowered to enforce these moral standards in its function as a guardian of the community and as a means of community support and maintenance.

> An established morality is as necessary as good government to the
> welfare of society. Societies disintegrate from within more frequently
> than they are broken up by external pressures. There is disintegra-

tion when no common morality is observed and history shows that
the loosening of moral bonds is often the first stage of disintegra-
tion, so that society is justified in taking the same steps to preserve
its moral code as it does to preserve its government and other essential institutions.[44]

Thus, for Devlin, violation of a society's public morality is a subversive activity
that can and should be repressed by the state to the same extent as any other
subversive activity.

Although Devlin argues for the support of morals, he denies them any
independent standing. That is to say, morals are not independently determin-
able—they simply embody the standards held by a particular society. Devlin
writes that "morals and religion are inextricably joined," and insofar as a society
deems itself secular and leaves matters of religion to the private judgment of
its citizens, it is precluded from justifying its laws "by reference to the moral
law."[45] Instead, the morality, which the law is competent to regulate, is

> what Pollack called "practical morality," which is based not on theo-
> logical or philosophical foundations but "in the mass of continuous
> experience half-consciously accumulated and embodied in the mo-
> rality of common sense." He called it also "a certain way of thinking
> on questions of morality which we expect to find in a reasonable civ-
> ilized man . . . taken at random."[46]

Devlin then builds on this to argue that the markers of this morality are intolerance, indignation, and disgust:

> Not everything is to be tolerated. No society can do without intoler-
> ance, indignation and disgust; they are the forces behind the moral
> law, and indeed it can be argued that if they or something like them
> are not present, the feelings of society cannot be weighty enough to
> deprive the individual of freedom of choice.[47]

Again, the key is not the truth of the moral law, but its effect on one's feeling
of community that is essential.

The second general theory denies the legitimacy of a liberal state attempting to legislate the area of morals. While this theory is most popularly identified
with H. L. A. Hart,[48] based upon his published debates with Lord Devlin, it
finds its most rigorous application in the so-called theories of "procedural justice" by such thinkers as John Rawls,[49] Jürgen Habermas,[50] and Brian Barry[51]
and in theories of procedural liberalism by such thinkers as Ronald Dworkin[52]
and Charles Larmore.[53]

In articulating this theory, Dworkin begins by distinguishing between two
moral commitments.[54] One is that we all hold particular "substantive" views
of the nature of human life, what constitutes the "good" and the goals for which
we should all strive. The second commitment is that we have a duty to deal
fairly and equally with everyone irrespective of their views of the good and the

values that view entails. Dworkin argues that a liberal society is one that is strongly united around this latter "procedural" commitment. Such a society is precluded from adopting any substantive views of the good because in any pluralistic society, such a substantive view would not be accepted by all of the citizens of that society. Adopting such a view would deny equal recognition of those who reject the validity of that substantive view. It would be an assertion by that society that their views were not as valuable as the views of those whose views were in accord with the favored substantive view.

In these theories, an effort is made to distinguish the "just," which is a proper concern of the state, and the "good," which is a private concern of each individual. Here the nature or truth of the good is understood as being indeterminable, and the proper role of the state is to promote each individual's identification and pursuit of the good without favoring one over the other. And within this theory there is significant emphasis upon the rights of the individual and the value of individual autonomy.

When looking at *Rodriguez* in light of these theories, one finds both theories represented in the various opinions in the decision. The communitarian theory can be discerned as underlying Sopinka's majority opinion, and the procedural theory appears to underlie Lamer's dissent.

Justice Sopinka's Communitarian Analysis

Justice Sopinka bases his opinion upon his determination that "sanctity of life" is the principle of fundamental justice that supports the state's regulation of assisted suicide (608). The state has a legitimate interest is preserving life under this fundamental principle, and the statute reflects this interest whereas Rodriguez's claim to autonomy in choosing to end her life would violate it. Principles of fundamental justice, of which sanctity of life is only one, are not explicitly identified in the Charter. Indeed, section 7 of the Charter, upon which Justice Sopinka's analysis is ultimately based, reads as follows:

> Everyone has the right to life, liberty and security of the person and the right not to be deprived thereof *except in accordance with the principles of fundamental justice.* (Emphasis added.)

While recognizing the existence of fundamental principles of justice, the Charter itself does not enumerate them. This is left to the courts. As noted by Sopinka:

> Discerning the principles of fundamental justice . . . is not an easy task. A mere common law rule does not suffice to constitute a principle of fundamental justice, rather, as the term implies, principles upon which there is some consensus that they are *fundamental to our societal notion of justice* is required. (Emphasis added.)[55]

In determining principles of fundamental justice, Sopinka J. stresses that the court should not seek to supply "its own view of the wisdom of legislation."[56]

The principle of fundamental justice cannot be created for the occasion to reflect the court's dislike or distaste of a particular statute.
. . . [They] are "fundamental" in the sense that they would have general acceptance among reasonable people.[57]

Ultimately, what makes these principles operative is that there is a "consensus"
in support of them.[58]

Interestingly, while Sopinka argues that "sanctity of life" is the principle
of fundamental justice that supports the state's regulation of assisted suicide,
this principle does not *require* the state to act in this way. Sopinka quotes with
apparent approval the statement by Lord Goff of the British House of Lords in
Airedale N.H.S. Trust v. Bland:

> It is of course well known that there are many responsible members
> of our society who believe that euthanasia should be lawful; but that
> result could, I believe, only be achieved by legislation which ex-
> presses the democratic will that so fundamental a change should be
> made in our law.[59]

In determining this consensus on principles of fundamental justice, Sopinka
relies upon four sources which he identifies in his opinion: laws and court
decisions of Canada and other Western countries,[60] legal commentators,[61] the
opinions of professional medical associations[62] and, somewhat ambiguously,
the standard that it be acceptable to "reasonable people."[63] It is unclear as to
how this last source is to be determined and whether he does so except insofar
as this source was expressed within the other three sources as legal principles.[64]

While Justice Sopinka does not attempt to justify the legal regulation of
what he acknowledges to be a moral concern,[65] it is clear that he believes the
state to have a right to do so based upon the perceived consensus that it should
do so. This is what Devlin refers to as "public morality." Also, like Devlin,
Sopinka appears to deny that principles of fundamental justice have any independent status as moral laws; they merely reflect the existing status of consensus in Canadian society which may be subject to change.[66]

Sopinka's communitarian orientation also leads him to be more open to
recognizing society's interests.

> The principles of fundamental justice are concerned not only with
> the interest of the person who claims his liberty has been limited,
> but with the protection of society. Fundamental justice requires that
> a fair balance be struck between these interests.[67]

Thus, it is Sopinka and not Lamer who recognizes that one of the interests
behind the assisted suicide statute is to address the behavior of the assistor of
the suicide.[68]

Sopinka is also more open to the communitarian idea that individuals are
not atomistic but rather, are powerfully influenced by their social context.[69]
Thus, he notes that society's prohibition of assisted suicide can itself be sup-

portive of vulnerable individuals in times of distress in which they may be contemplating suicide.[70]

It should be noted that one can identify similar communitarian features in Sopinka's treatment of the issues of causality in which he seeks to distinguish "passive" euthanasia (the withholding of life-saving treatment) and active euthanasia as would occur in Rodriguez's proposal for assistance. It is the consensus that the withholding of life-saving treatment does not represent the "cause" of death, the underlying illness being the real cause, that is determinative for him.[71] (Though Sopinka's theoretical orientation is closely in accord with Devlin's model for the legal enforcement of morals, he is very careful to limit the court's discretion in identifying and propounding moral positions. He focuses his attention primarily upon legal sources and is generally deferential to Parliament's judgments in these matters.[72])

Lamer's Procedural Justice Analysis

Similarly, Lamer's opinion appears to be profoundly influenced by the procedural understanding of the relation between law and morals. Indeed, the distinction he draws between ethics and the law, his assertion that the Court must apply the law, and his approving recitation of Justice Dickson's opinion in *Big M Drug Mart* (cited above) can be described as a legal articulation of this theory.[73] To assert that "a truly free society is one which can accommodate a wide variety of beliefs, diversity of tastes and pursuits, customs and codes of conduct" is nothing more than an effort to distinguish between the "just ("a truly free") society" and the "good" determined by the individual citizens of that society.[74]

One can also see his procedural justice orientation in his effort to focus upon Sue Rodriguez's right of "choice" independent of the ends or goods which are the object of that choice.

> It should be pointed out that the advantage which the appellant
> claims to be deprived of is not the option of committing suicide as
> such. She does not argue that suicide is a benefit which she is de-
> prived of by the effect of s.241(b) of the Criminal Code. What the
> appellant is arguing is that she will be deprived of the right to
> choose suicide, of her ability to decide on the conduct of her life
> herself.[75]

Then, later, in his own evaluation of her right to choose, Lamer specifically exempts his "opinion on the moral value of suicide" as irrelevant to this inquiry.[76] The ends of the choice are considered solely within the purview of the individual.

Finally, there is a noticeable lack of concern for community values (with the possible exception of the law seeking to protect vulnerable individuals, to be discussed below). Lamer's attention in this opinion is focused solely upon the rights of the individual against the state and upon the rights of the autonomous individual.

It appears noteworthy that these two competing general theories are reflected in opposing opinions. A fair conclusion would be that the theoretical approach is determinative of the result. That is to say, the theoretical approach is not adopted as a way of supporting the decision reached, but the theoretical understanding shapes the analysis that leads to the decision. By focusing upon the communal nature of human life, and the communal nature of determining the good of human life, someone taking Sopinka's position will naturally gravitate toward supporting the state in this type of controversy, unless the government grossly overextends itself against the recognized rights of the individual. In that Parliament is the natural forum for consensus, his or her tendency will normally lie in favor of determinations made by it.

By contrast, Lamer's emphasis upon individual rights and individual autonomy orients him against the state. For him, the state must always justify its actions according to the highest possible standard. Moreover, given his skepticism toward the state's determining the "good," there is little room for the state to justify its actions upon any understanding of values, such as the value of human life. Instead, justification must be found in an analysis of harm to others (such as the protection of individuals who can be shown to be "vulnerable" in an identifiable, measurable sense).[77]

The Issue of the Vulnerable Individual

In identifying the purpose behind the case against assisted suicide, Sopinka identifies the protection of vulnerable individuals as the primary purpose of the law[78] though he also notes that the law may be intended to prohibit the development of the "macabre specialty" of the professional assister of suicide.[79] His choice to focus upon the protection of the vulnerable rests in large part upon his identification of the "sanctity of life" as the principle of fundamental justice which supports the provisions of the assisted suicide statute.[80]

Though Sopinka starts his analysis by recognizing the state's interest in protecting "the vulnerable who might be induced in moments of weakness to commit suicide,"[81] his communitarian orientation allows him to take a broader perspective on this issue. For example, he is cognizant of the law's interest in the person assisting in the suicide and the effects of that action on the social value of the sanctity of life. Here he can assert that assisting a suicide is itself a transgression of this value[82] and that a policy allowing assisted suicide would itself "deprecate" this value.[83] Moreover, he can take the position that a policy against assisted suicide can be supportive of the vulnerable individual.

> In upholding the respect for life, it may discourage those who consider that life is unbearable at a particular moment, or who perceive themselves to be a burden upon others, from committing suicide.

To permit a physician to lawfully participate in taking life would
send a signal that there are circumstances in which the state approves of suicide.[84]

His analysis recognizes the complex interaction of individuals, the contexts in
which they reside, and the relation of each to society as a whole. The law, in
Sopinka's view, can serve not only the function of protecting individuals from
the depredation of others but can also serve a supportive function for that
individual in her or his confrontation with one of the great challenges of life
at the limits.

Lamer's individualist, procedural theoretical perspective leads him to emphasize that the purpose of the law is to protect the individual.[85] However, his
individualist perspective leads him to focus upon the term "vulnerable." Instead of seeing vulnerability as being linked to the context (i.e., of being terminally ill and suicidal), he views it as descriptive of particular individuals.[86]
He does so in two steps. First, he interprets the decriminalization of suicide
as establishing the primacy of self-determination as against the protection of
a group containing many vulnerable members (a questionable interpretation,
as has been suggested above). Second, he then links this to the law against
assisted suicide as applied to those who are physically incapable of committing
suicide themselves and asks if this group is "more likely to be vulnerable than
the physically able?"[87] He then takes the further step of asserting that a physically incapacitated individual should be exempt from the coverage of s. 241
(b) where it can be demonstrated that they are not vulnerable.[88] He relies upon
the court's ability to determine whether or not "the free and independent consent" of the person seeking assisted suicide as the test of whether or not the
person is vulnerable.

One can question Lamer's logic and argumentation at virtually every point
in this line of reasoning, including asking such fundamental questions as to
whether the court is in fact capable of determining whether the choice of suicide is freely made by the individual. What is more important for our purposes
here, however, is the fact that Lamer's opinion is profoundly shaped by a particular understanding of the nature of being human. That is, humans are "atomistic," to use Charles Taylor's term,[89] and the role of government is to protect
and defend the autonomy and freedom of the individual. This is a profoundly
moral point of view, the validity of which many communitarian theorists question.[90] Nonetheless, it shapes Lamer's understanding of what it means to be
vulnerable and the relative value to be placed upon the protection of the vulnerable as against the "freedom" of the self-determined individual.

To a certain extent, Sopinka's decision might be criticized on the basis that
his theoretical orientation is not clearly developed and expressed. This failure
may be because the pressure and importance of these ethical theoretical perspectives is largely denied within the judicial system. Nonetheless, the vague-
ness of his analysis of vulnerability opens this position to the attack leveled by
Lamar.

Conclusions

Though the presence of ethics in judicial decision making has been explicitly denied, a close reading of *Rodriguez* reveals its presence as an important element within the process. Indeed, general ethical theoretical perspectives may be determinative of the decisions reached by the Court.

In some ways, these findings are not surprising. It is to be expected that the fundamental values of a society will be embedded in that society's laws. Nonetheless, there are some important implications to be drawn from this study in relation to the discipline of bioethics.

The authors of this paper have on occasion wondered if bioethics is not at risk of being subsumed under the domain of health law. This is a concern shared with other thinkers.[91] Some bioethicists place extraordinary significance upon health law[92] and such reliance is quite understandable. Medical doctors, by virtue of their training, are oriented toward seeking practical answers to their question about treatment. As such, it is not surprising that they bring this attitude into their ethics consultations. Health law, in certain areas, can give the kind of firm, decisive answers that doctors expect: either something is legal, or it is not. Insofar as bioethics tracks health law, it can give equally decisive answers. The question is whether this congruence between health law and bioethics is legitimate.

The foregoing analysis of *Rodriguez* suggests that case law can serve as a normative source for bioethics. At the same time, it suggests that there are some limits to the degree of reliance that bioethicists should place upon court decisions.

First, it must be recognized that court decisions do incorporate and articulate certain widely recognized norms or mores. In the case of *Rodriguez*, it seems fair to conclude that not only is assisted suicide illegal in Canada at the present time, it is equally immoral according to the dominant morality of Canadian society. When viewed in connection with other cases such as *R. v Latimer*,[93] and the fact that there has been no significant effort to reform or change the law, this legal and moral standard would appear to be fairly absolute. At the same time, circumstances may mitigate the level of censure that will be directed toward the performer of an assisted suicide. For example, there has been little or no effort to identify and prosecute the person who illegally assisted Sue Rodriguez in her successful suicide subsequent to the conclusion of this litigation. Public sympathy for Sue Rodriguez, as a result of publicity associated with her case, appears to have headed off public outrage toward the person who assisted her suicide.

Some might challenge the idea that the court in *Rodriguez* accurately expressed the dominant Canadian morality on this position by noting that public opinion polls suggest that a majority of Canadians support the idea of a right to physician assisted suicide.[94] However, it is suggested that such polls are unreliable barometers of people's actual beliefs in that they may be reporting unreflective opinions. For example, although the idea of assisted suicide has some popular acceptance in the United States and has been adopted in Oregon, in at least one case when assisted suicide statutes more restrictive (i.e., limited) than the right of assisted suicide suggested in *Rodriguez* were publicly debated and voted upon in a public referendum in California, the proposed law was roundly defeated.[95] Insofar as morals embody deeply held beliefs, it would appear that the law may be a more reliable resource for identifying values that are strongly held and that are likely to come to the fore when those individuals are called upon to make choices which will have identifiable consequences.

At the same time, the existence of these contradictory polls raises two additional problems. As suggested by Carl Schneider, one of the qualities of law is that it tends to end debate.[96] Indeed, that is one of its virtues. One of the purposes of law is to resolve controversies. The problem is that by ending debate, one loses the capacity to publicly articulate the issues involved and thereby educate the public in relation to that issue. Thus, the confusion expressed in Canadian opinion polls on assisted suicide may reflect the fact that public debate was ended before the public was in a position to fully understand the terms of that debate.

Of related concern, this debate-ending quality may end discussion of an issue in which there is in fact no genuine consensus or where such a consensus is in transition. This may lead to three possible results: it may simply leave the issue as one in which the law exists but receives little support; it may result in a law that is widely circumvented or ignored; or it may result in a political war in which consensus itself is precluded because the law has divided the public into conflicting camps. The decision of Roe v. Wade,[97] legalizing abortion in the United States, may be illustrative of this latter result.

In using the law as a resource, bioethicists must be cognizant of this debate-ending quality. They must be sensitive not only as to whether the law has ended the debate at the appropriate place (i.e., that it does reflect the deeply held position of the people) but also as to whether the debate has been ended at the appropriate time. Has the debate in fact educated the community to the degree necessary to inform and support them when they are confronted by that issue in their lives and in the lives of their loved ones?

As demonstrated in our analysis of *Rodriguez*, in considering court decisions as an ethical resource or authority, bioethicists also need to be aware of the importance of conceptualizing those decisions in relation to the theoretical orientation of the court and the justices in question. For example, Justice Sopinka's communitarian orientation provides a fairly strong interpretation of legal and moral understanding. Specific values are identified and strongly affirmed by the court in Sopinka's decisions. On the other hand, a court operating out of the liberal democratic orientation demonstrated by Chief Justice Lamer would identify and affirm some values, but in some sense, those values must be understood as minimum values or standards. There would remain open the question of the ethical standards of the individual in question who, liberal theory posits, is still free to pursue his or her own understandings of the good. Indeed, given the dominance of liberal theory in the North American context, this latter approach is the more likely to occur in most cases arising in health law. Bioethicists must recognize this constraint or risk limiting their ethical work to the level of an artificially imposed minimal standard as opposed to being open to the full range of human activities and understandings of the good.

It is also important to consider the ethical standard being applied by the court, particularly if one is attempting to use a case by analogy to apply to another situation. For example, while Sopinka identifies sanctity of life as a strong moral value, the ethical standard he applies is one of consensus. Thus consensus may not exist or may lead to a different result in another situation even though the same value of sanctity of life may arguably arise in that situation in an analogous way. Alternately, consensus may change subsequent to the original decision. Hence, analogical use of these cases is made more problematic.

By contrast, although Lamer makes a much more limited assertion of moral values, that of individual freedom and autonomy, he is more absolutist in its application as a social political norm. An analogy based upon an opinion following Lamer's theoretical orientation would undoubtedly be somewhat more predictive (while not absolutely) of what a subsequent court might find. However, the moral weight of that decision would be analogous only in the minimalist sense discussed above. That is to say, the law would reflect only the values that are uncontested—not necessarily those held by most people.

Finally, since many people base their ethical judgments upon their religious beliefs, these findings have significance with respect to the question of religion in public bioethics. First, and foremost, it undercuts the popular argument that religion can and should be absolutely separated from the state or state action.[98] As we have demonstrated, ethical beliefs, whether acknowledged or not, enter the law through the actions of judges. Insofar as most people ground their moral judgments upon religious beliefs, religious beliefs will similarly find their way into law.[99] So although it may be possible to artificially restrict judicial or public legal reasoning to using secular-legal language, that language may in fact be nothing more than a mask for an underlying religious-ethical belief or argument. Bioethicists need to be aware of this potential religious dimension.

Of perhaps greater importance, those interested in supporting religious freedom need to be aware of this potential for religious influence insofar as the most likely influence on the law will be the dominant religion(s) in that society. This could result in discrimination against minority religions where the religious beliefs of the majority have migrated into the general legal discourse under the guise of religiously neutral secular standards.[100] Thus, in considering objections raised by people of faith to the standards set forth in the law, ethicists and the courts need to carefully examine the justifications offered for the law for possible religious bias hidden within the dominant norm.

In summary, this analysis suggests that court cases can serve as a legitimate source for bioethics. At the same time, their use must be made subject to the constraints within the judicial decision-making process. Bioethicists must be sensitive to those constraints and not limit themselves to a rigid adherence to the finding of the courts as definitive ethical statements.

NOTES

1. Simon Lee, *Law and Morals* (Oxford: Oxford University Press, 1986); Robert T. George, *Making Men Moral: Civil Liberties and Public Morality* (Oxford: Clarendon Press, 1993); Harry M. Clor, *Public Morality and Liberal Society* (Notre Dame, Ind.: University of Notre Dame Press, 1996).

2. George J. Annas, *Standard of Care: The Law of American Bioethics* (New York: Oxford University Press, 1993); Thomas L. Beauchamp and James F. Childress, *Principles of Biomedical Ethics*, 4th ed. (New York: Oxford University Press, 1994).

3. See David E. Guinn, "Religion in Public Ethics," *Second Opinion* (January 2002): 15.

4. *Rodriguez v. Canada*, 3 S.C.R.519 (1993). Note: While Canada has a mixed common law/civil law tradition, this case can best be understood as falling within the domain of common law.

5. Ibid., 520.

6. The relevant provision of which is as follows: "2. Everyone who (a) Counsels a person to commit suicide, or (b) *aids or abets a person to commit suicide*, whether suicide ensues or not, is guilty of an indictable offence and liable to imprisonment for a term not exceeding fourteen years" (emphasis added).

7. Part I of the Constitution Act, 1982, being Schedule B to the Canada Act (U.K., 1982), c.11.

8. Section 7 reads as follows: "(4) Everyone has the right to life, liberty and security of the person and the right not to be deprived thereof except in accordance with the principles of fundamental justice."

9. Which reads: "5. Everyone has the right not to be subjected to any cruel and unusual treatment of punishment."

10. Which reads in relevant part: "Every individual is equal before and under the law and has the right to the equal protection and equal benefit of the law without discrimination and, in particular, without discrimination based on race, national or ethnic origin, color, religion, sex, age or mental or physical disability."

11. Though Quebec, a province of Canada, operates under a civil law tradition, that tradition played no part in this decision.

12. Patrick Devlin, *The Enforcement of Morals* (London: Oxford University Press, 1965).

13. *Rodriguez*, 553.

14. Ibid.

15. We are grateful to Karen Lebacqz for this definition, which she provided in a lecture for a course (Sexual Ethics) that she taught at McGill University in 1996.

16. I. Franklin Gamwell, "The Compound Conception of Justice," in *Religion and Law in the Global Village*, ed. David E. Guinn, Chris Berrigar, and Katherine Young (Atlanta: Scholars Press, 1999).

17. *Rodriguez*, 545.

18. Ibid., 554.

19. Ibid., 558.

20. H. L. A. Hart, *The Concept of Law* (Oxford: Clarendon Press, 1961).

21. Beauchamp and Childress, *Principles*.

22. George Christie, *Law, Norms, and Authority* (London: Duckworth, 1982); Alan H. Goldman, "Legal Reasoning as a Model for Moral Reasoning," *Law and Philosophy* 8 (1989): 131–149; Cass R. Sunstein, *Legal Reasoning and Political Conflict* (New York: Oxford University Press, 1996).

23. *Rodriguez*, 558–569.

24. Goldman, "Legal Reasoning."

25. A. R. Jonsen and Stephen Toulmin, *The Abuse of Casuistry: A History of Moral Reasoning* (Berkeley: University of California Press, 1988).

26. Ibid.

27. *Rodriguez*, 553.

28. Goldman, "Legal Reasoning."

29. *R. v. Big M Drug Mart, Ltd.*, 1 S.C.R. 295 (1985) at 336.

30. *Rodriguez*, 554.

31. Ibid.

32. John Rawls, *Political Liberalism* (New York: Columbia University Press, 1993), p. xvi.

33. Charles Larmore, *Patterns of Moral Complexity* (New York: Cambridge University Press, 1987).

34. *Rodriquez v. Canada*, B.C.L.R. (2d, 1993), 145 at 171.

35. *Regina v. Vasil*, 58 C.C.C. (2d., 1981), 97–122; G. Parker, "Comments on Legislation and Judicial Decisions," *Canadian Bar Review* 60 (1982): 502–533.

36. *Rodriguez*, 558.

37. Ibid.

38. Ibid., 601.

39. Ibid., 522.

40. Ibid., 559.

41. Gerald B. Robertson, *Mental Disability and the Law in Canada*, 2nd ed. (Toronto: Carswell, 1994); Harvey S. Savage, *Mental Health Law in Canada* (Toronto: Butterworths, 1987).

42. Devlin, *The Enforcement of Morals*.

43. Ibid., 13.

44. Ibid., 4–5.

45. Ibid.

46. Ibid., 15.

47. Ibid., 17.

48. Hart, *The Concept of Law*.

49. John Rawls, *A Theory of Justice* (Cambridge, Mass.: Harvard University Press, 1971).

50. Jürgen Habermas, *Moral Consciousness and Communicative Action* (Cambridge: MIT Press, 1990); Jürgen Habermas, *Justification and Application* (Cambridge: MIT Press, 1993).

51. Brian Barry, *Justice as Impartiality* (Oxford: Clarendon Press, 1995).

52. Ronald Dworkin, "Liberalism," in *Public and Private Morality*, ed. Stuart Hampshire (Cambridge: Cambridge University Press, 1978).

53. Charles Larmore, *Patterns of Moral Complexity* (London: Cambridge University Press, 1987).

54. Dworkin, "Liberalism."

55. *Rodriguez*, 590.

56. Ibid.

57. Ibid., 607.

58. Ibid., 608.

59. *Airedale N.H.S. Trust v. Bland*, 2 W.L.R. 316 (1993), at 368–369.

60. *Rodriguez*, 596–605.

61. Ibid., 606.

62. Ibid., 608.

63. Ibid., 607.

64. Ibid., 590–591; Edward W. Keyserlingk, "Assisted Suicide, Causality, and the Supreme Court of Canada," *McGill Law Journal* 39, no. 3 (1994): 708–718, n. 27.

65. *Rodriguez*, 601, 604.

66. Ibid., 596.

67. Ibid., 593, quoting J. McLachlin, in *R. v. Cunningham* 2 S.C.R.143 (1993), at 151–152.

68. Ibid., 601.

69. Katherine P. Addelson, *Moral Passages: Toward a Collectivist Moral Theory* (New York: Routledge, 1994); Charles Taylor, "Atomism," in *Philosophy and the Human Sciences: Philosophical Papers 2* (Cambridge: Cambridge University Press, 1985); Iris M. Young, *Justice and the Politics of Difference* (Princeton, N.J.: Princeton University Press, 1990).

70. *Rodriguez*, 608.

71. See Keyserlingk, "Assisted Suicide," for a detailed discussion and critique of this issue and view.

72. *Rodriguez*, 589–590, 614.

73. *Big M Drug Mart*, 589–590, 614.

74. *Rodriguez*, 553 n. 3.

75. Ibid., 552.

76. Ibid.

77. Ibid., 562.

78. Ibid., 595, 601.

79. Ibid., 582.

80. Ibid., 595–96.

81. Ibid., 595.

82. Ibid., 601.

83. Ibid., 608.

84. Ibid.

85. Ibid., 558–559.

86. Ibid., 560–561.

87. Ibid., 559.

88. Ibid., 569.

89. Taylor, "Atomism."

90. Addelson, *Moral Passages*; Young, *Justice and the Politics of Difference*.

91. C. Barry Hoffmaster, "Comments on 'Legalism and Medical Ethics,' " in *Contemporary Issues in Biomedical Ethics*, ed. John W. Davis, Barry Hoffmaster, and Sarah Shorten, pp. 37–42 (Clifton, N.J.: Humana, 1978); J. Ladd, "Legalism and Medical Ethics," in *Contemporary Issues in Biomedical Ethics*, ed. John W. Davis, Barry Hoffmaster, and Sarah Shorten, pp. 1–36 (Clifton, N.J.: Humana, 1978); Carl E. Schneider, "Bioethics in the Language of the Law." *Hastings Center Report* 24, no. 4 (July–August 1994): 16–22.

92. See Annas, *Standard of Care*.

93. *R. v. Latimer*, 8 W.W.R. 609, 99 C.C.C. (3d, 1995), 481; 126 D.L.R. (4th) 203 (Sask. C.A.)

94. Anonymous editorial, "Time to Empower Angels of Mercy," *Globe and Mail*, April 6, 1996, D6.

95. N. Clark and P. S. Liebig, "The Politics of Physician-Assisted Death: California's Proposition 161 and Attitudes of the Elderly," *Politics and the Life Sciences* 15 (September 1996): 273–280.

96. Schneider, "Bioethics in the Language of Law."

97. *Roe v. Wade*, 410 U.S. 113 (1973)

98. See, e.g., Robert Audi, *Religious Commitment and Secular Reason* (New York: Oxford University Press, 2000); Isaac Kramnick and R. Laurence Moore, *The Godless Constitution* (New York: W. W. Norton, 1996).

99. Since up to 90 percent of U.S. legislators say they draw upon their religion in enacting major legislation, the same argument applies to all lawmakers. Stephen Carter, *The Culture of Disbelief* 111 (New York: Basic Books, 1993).

100. See, e.g., *Goldman v. Weinberger* 475 U.S. 503, 511 (1986), Brennan (dissent).

IO

The NBAC Report on Cloning: A Case Study in Religion, Public Policy, and Bioethics

M. Cathleen Kaveny

Reflecting upon his field of specialization in 1990, the prominent bioethicist Daniel Callahan observed that "the most striking change over the past two decades or so has been the secularization of bioethics."[1] Callahan wrote that in the minds of many secular bioethicists, "Whatever place it [religion] might have in the private lives of individuals, it simply did not count as one of the available common resources for setting public policy."[2] In addition, he noted, "There was (and still is) a lurking fear of religion, often seen as a source of deep and unresolvable moral conflict as well as single-minded political pressure when aroused."[3]

Although no longer a religious believer himself, Callahan did not look upon this development in the character of the field as entirely positive. More specifically, he claimed that the exclusion of religion from the realm of bioethics distorts moral reflection in three ways. First, it "leaves us too heavily dependent upon the law as the working source of morality." Second, it renders us "bereft of the accumulated wisdom and knowledge that are the fruit of long-established religious traditions." Third, it forces us "to pretend that we are not creatures both of particular moral communities and the more sprawling, inchoate general community that we celebrate as the expression of our pluralism."[4]

What is the situation today, well over a decade after Callahan published his article in the *Hastings Center Report*? On the one hand, one could say that he was overly pessimistic. None of his worries about the consequences of excluding religion from the discipline of bioethics have materialized, because in some sense religion has remained a key participant in the discussion. On the other hand, he may not have been pessimistic enough. It is also true to say that the role of religion in bioethics has not expanded in the slightest in the time since he wrote. How can Callahan have been both right and wrong about the place of religion in bioethics? In my view, the key to answering this question lies in one's definition of the term "bioethics."

If one uses the term broadly, to encompass all scholarly consideration of bioethical issues, then religious voices in the field are strong and vigorous. Books and journal articles examining medical-moral questions from a religious perspective regularly appear, and many departments of theology or religious studies offer popular courses on medical ethics from the perspective of particular religious traditions. Consequently, none of Callahan's worries predicated on the exclusion of religion from the field have come to pass. In contrast, if one uses the term "bioethics" narrowly, to cover only the formulation and justification of law and public policy, then religiously informed perspectives seem to be as marginalized as they were when Callahan wrote, for precisely the reasons that he identifies.

In my view, the situation that we have today is one that Callahan may not have contemplated, probably because he did not fully appreciate that his very real worries about the consequences of excluding religious perspectives from bioethics operate over a somewhat different sphere than does the rationale for that exclusion. It is possible to affirm the importance of including religious voices in the realm of bioethics *broadly construed*, for precisely the reasons Callahan identifies, while at the same time keeping religion at arm's length in the *narrower context* of bioethics and public policy. In my view, this two-pronged approach, which simultaneously affirms and marginalizes the role of religion in bioethics, describes the current situation more accurately than terms such as "secularization" or "exclusion" do.

The report produced by the National Bioethics Advisory Commission at the request of President Bill Clinton, titled *Cloning Human Beings*,[5] provides a powerful example of the two-pronged approach to the place of religion in bioethics. Some may wonder why it is worthwhile to scrutinize the report of a now-defunct commission, whose charter expired after President George W. Bush took office and whose functions were largely assumed by a new President's Council of Bioethics appointed by Bush. In my view, doing so is worthwhile for three reasons. First, although the commission itself may no longer exist, its analysis and approach to the regulation of controverted bioethical issues is of enduring value. Second is a related point: the membership of that commission was largely composed of extremely prominent self-identified "bioethicists."[6] The approach taken by the commission still wields enormous influence in the field of bioethics in general. Third, and more pragmatically, it is not inconceivable that a Democrat could retake the White House, in which case the general approach of the commission to these issues might gain more political sway.

In February 1997, news broke that Scottish scientists had successfully cloned an adult sheep, causing great public apprehension that human cloning would soon follow. In order to quell this apprehension, President Bill Clinton asked the commission to prepare a report on human cloning, giving it ninety days in which to do so. The report paid great attention to religious concerns about cloning; doing so was a political necessity, because religious voices were a major force in the public debate. Soon after the unveiling of "Dolly" (the name given to the cloned sheep), "private" questions of the ultimate meaning and value of human life began to dominate the front pages of newspapers and the covers of weekly magazines in ways that would previously have been unimaginable.[7] Would a human clone be a new unique person, or just a soulless copy of the person cloned? Was cloning an activity permissible to mere mortals, or did its radical break with the nature of human reproduction count as "playing God" in an unacceptable way? Religious thinkers and religious viewpoints were key figures in the public discussion, as Americans turned to their deepest sources of meaning to make sense of this newly revealed scientific and medical leap.

Nonetheless, at the same time that the report took religious viewpoints seriously, it also "tamed" them by insulating them from direct influence on public policy and law. A close analysis of the report reveals that it is deeply influenced by the same reservations Callahan identified about allowing religion significant influence in this arena. Consequently, the report's recommendations for changes in policy and law are not indebted to the normative viewpoints of any of the religious views it articulates; instead, they reflect an almost total reliance on a particular version of liberal legal theory.

More specifically, the commission advocated the following three steps in the realm of law and public policy: (1) a continuation of the moratorium initiated by President Clinton on the use of federal funding "in support of any attempt to create a child by somatic cell nuclear transfer";[8] (2) the issuance of an immediate request to scientists and clinicians who do not receive federal funds, asking them to refrain voluntarily from such attempts;[9] and (3) the enactment of federal legislation (with a sunset clause) prohibiting anyone from attempting to create a child through somatic cell nuclear transfer (109). The commission anchored its proposed restrictions in its finding that any attempt to clone a human being might at that time result in real harm to the cloned child or to its mother (108). In both the target of and rationale for its proposed restrictions, the commission complied with the requirements of the "harm principle," a linchpin of liberal legal theory which maintains that the law, particularly criminal law, may legitimately prohibit only those actions that wrongfully harm others.

How successful was the report in achieving its goals? If one views those goals both narrowly and straightforwardly, as directing the formulation of U.S. public policy on the cloning of human beings, then its success was at best mixed. More than seven years after Dolly's unveiling, no federal law banning the creation of a human child through the cloning process has yet been passed, although political efforts to do so have been intense from time to time. Nonetheless, the commission's vision of appropriate public policy regarding human cloning has carried the day, albeit in an indirect manner. The Food and Drug Administration eventually asserted its jurisdiction over any effort to produce a live-born human being through the process of cloning.[10] By statutory mandate, the FDA's sole focus is the safety and efficacy of the process in question; its approach to the issue would likely coincide with the report's emphasis on the risk of tangible harm to the cloned child as a basis for its proposed prohibition.

It is possible, however, to take a broader view of the report's function by looking at its place within the politics and rhetoric of the public discussion prompted by the appearance of Dolly. The public crisis of meaning generated by the specter of human cloning threatened to overturn the two-pronged approach to the role of religion in bioethics that I described above. The report played a crucial role in circumventing this disruption. Its ultimate effect, if not its ultimate goal, was to restore the two-pronged approach to its former stability, thereby affirming religion's value even as it limits its sphere of operations. Religious believers reading the report would recognize that their attitudes were taken seriously in articulating the moral "attitude" or "atmosphere" surrounding human cloning, and scientists and secularists would appreciate the fact that religious attitudes played virtually no role in justifying the restrictions ultimately supported by the commission.

In my view, the report merits careful scrutiny precisely because of the deftness with which it appears to negotiate the thorny questions surrounding the role of religion in public policy. As I hope to show in the next section of this chapter, close analysis of the structure, arguments, and rhetoric of the report reveals the theoretical and practical inadequacy of the currently reigning two-pronged approach to the role of religious perspectives in the field of bioethics. Unfortunately, there is no ready-made and clearly preferable substitute for that approach. In the years to come, a major task for both religious and secular bioethicists will be to bring the specific concerns of their discipline into conversation with the general discussion currently taking place in political philosophy on the role of religion in the public square. In the final section of this chapter, I will identify key questions that must be addressed in the course of this conversation.

The Report

On Human Cloning comprises six chapters, which total 110 pages. The first chapter is introductory, and the second offers a clear and highly accessible description of the science and application of cloning. Religious perspectives are addressed in chapter 3, and chapter 4 separately addresses ethical considerations. Chapter 5 covers legal and policy considerations, and chapter 6 summarizes the commission's recommendations. A key function of this organizational structure is to segregate and neutralize religiously based moral concerns about cloning before using the chapter devoted to secular ethics to set up the philosophically liberal policy analysis that follows in chapter 5.

Exaggerating Religious Division

It is apparent even to the casual reader of the report that the subject matter of chapter 3 overlaps a great deal with that of chapter 4. A cursory review of their respective tables of contents reveals that both chapters cover two broad themes: the implications of cloning for issues pertaining to human dignity and equality, and the ramifications of cloning for family life and society. The most obvious principle for dividing and organizing this material would have been on the basis of content, dedicating a chapter to each set of themes. In contrast, the source-based division actually chosen by the commission seems structurally unjustifiable, since it leads to a fair amount of redundancy in exposition. One might attempt to justify the division by claiming that the religious thinkers are likely to raise esoteric and idiosyncratic perspectives on these topics; such a claim, however, would be patently false. The vast majority of the thinkers whose views are summarized in chapter 3 express concerns that are relevant to all those concerned with the issue, no matter what, if any, religious beliefs they profess. The fact that their concerns may be rooted in metaphysical views of the world not shared by each and every American does not prevent many of them from being broadly intelligible and broadly addressed, as the commission itself seems to acknowledge (54).[11]

The function of the division of material chosen by the commission becomes apparent when one considers the significant dissonance between the evidence of a variety of religious perspectives on human cloning presented in the body of chapter 3 and the interpretation of that evidence that is offered in the conclusion to that chapter. More specifically, a careful reading of the body of chapter 3 supports the judgment that a wide range of religious thinkers are in general agreement that cloning poses unprecedented risks for human well-being. Many such thinkers believe it is a practice that can never be justified. A few maintain that there are highly exceptional cases in which cloning would be morally acceptable.[12] Even they, however, are acutely aware of the possibilities for abuse. No religious thinker from any denomination is brought forward who thinks that human cloning is an unambiguously positive development for human well-being. In short, the testimony amassed in chapter 3 supports the conclusion that representatives of a range of religious traditions are generally negative about the practical and moral ramifications of human cloning, for reasons that are broadly intelligible to all Americans, no matter what their belief system.[13] Astonishingly, however, the commission supplies the chapter with a very different conclusion which contradicts the weight of its own evidence. That conclusion seems to be rooted not in the specific testimony it heard, or even in the broader facts that it considered, but rather in its own strongly held presuppositions about the influence and role of religion in the United States. According to the commission:

> The wide variety of religious traditions and beliefs epitomizes the pluralism of American culture. Moreover, religious perspectives on cloning differ in fundamental premises, modes of reasoning, and

conclusions. As a result, there is no single "religious" view on cloning humans, any more than for most moral issues in biomedicine.
(57)

The inaccuracy of this presupposition—or prejudice—is demonstrated by
an examination of the relevant data. If the term "most moral issues in biomedicine" is meant to apply to abortion and euthanasia, then the comparison
it includes is patently false. Polling data reveal that public opinion on abortion[14]
and euthanasia[15] is significantly divided. The percentage of persons favoring
and opposing the legality of such practices were about the same with respect
to Catholics and Protestants; in fact, the divisions appear to be stronger within
the two major branches of Christianity than between it. At the same time, there
appears to be an appreciable divergence of opinion on abortion and euthanasia
between Christians and Jews, with a significantly higher percentage of the latter
group finding both practices to be morally acceptable. None of these divisions
is apparent in the case of cloning. In fact, a Roper poll taken at the time of
Dolly's appearance demonstrated overwhelming moral opposition to cloning
among all Americans; moreover, it revealed little divergence of opinion in the
overall responses given by Catholics, Protestants, and Jews.[16] On the question
of cloning, as opposed to abortion and euthanasia, Americans appeared to have
reached a consensus.

It is impossible to speculate about the commission's motivations for advancing a conclusion to chapter 3 that is so markedly at odds both with the
material developed in the body of the chapter and with readily available polling
data. It is not, however, difficult to determine the practical effect of that conclusion. Functionally, it serves to marginalize religious perspectives on cloning,
by depicting them as canceling each other out in a cacophony of hopelessly
competing views. In short, the conclusion to chapter 3 quietly but inexorably
renders religious perspectives irrelevant to the ongoing debate. Subtly invoking
the widespread American fear of religiously motivated political battles, it ex-
aggerates the division between religious thinkers opposed to cloning and those
who believe it is morally acceptable only in highly limited circumstances. Rhetorically, it sparks in the reader the desire to begin the discussion again on
different terms, and in a way that will not increase the substantial political
tension surrounding the brave new world of cloning by allowing it to be taken
hostage by rationally irresolvable religious debates.

Reducing Ethics to Law

Consequently, the commission's attempt to grapple with the moral concerns
involved in cloning begins anew and in earnest in chapter 4. Viewed in this
light, it is not surprising that this chapter, titled "Ethical Concerns," manifests
a fair amount of redundancy.[17] Many of the reservations that religious thinkers
express in chapter 3 about the negative effect of human cloning on personal
dignity and family and social relations are replicated here. In fact, a theologian
(Gilbert Meilaender) is invoked to articulate the common fear that cloning will

erode our sense of human uniqueness and individuality (67). Another theologian (Nancy Duff) gives voice to the concern that devoting resources to cloning rather than to projects likely to benefit many more persons could violate the demands of social justice (72). This redundancy should not be surprising. Although Christian moralists ultimately draw upon a distinctive view of the source of human moral obligations, their concerns about the ethical ramifications of concrete social practices frequently overlap with those of secular moralists.

The "seepage" of religious voices into chapter 4, along with the substantial overlap between chapters 3 and 4, raise a fundamental methodological question that the report sidesteps. Why exactly are "religious" and "ethical" voices being treated separately? Does the report assume that religious perspectives on ethics are more epistemologically contestable than secular ethical perspectives per se? Obviously, this assumption is subject to serious challenge on philosophical grounds. Not only postliberal philosophers such as Alasdair MacIntyre,[18] but even liberal philosophers such as John Rawls[19] admit that a philosophically liberal comprehensive worldview is subject to epistemological challenge in much the same way as a religious comprehensive worldview.

Nonetheless, the commission clearly means for chapter 4 to stand alone as an articulation of the considerations pertaining to the morality of creating a child through somatic cell nuclear transfer. Moreover, a careful reading of the summary inserted at the beginning of the chapter reveals that purpose is not to undertake a thorough analysis of the moral issues considered in themselves; instead, it sees moral analysis as a necessary means to the far more significant topics of the formulation of public policy and law.

More specifically, as the summary makes perfectly clear, chapter 4 adopts a two-pronged approach designed to support and promote the legal and policy analysis ultimately set forth in chapter 5. First, the summary describes the relationship between the reasons supporting the claim that human cloning is morally permissible under some circumstances and the reasons opposing that claim in a noteworthy way; it maintains that the two sets of reasons are "arrayed against" each other (63). Second, it points toward a particular framework for resolving the claims of these competing sets of reasons, which is firmly rooted in one particular version of liberal legal theory. As I argue below, both elements of this two-step approach are subject to dispute in a way that the report does not acknowledge, let alone adequately address.

An "Array" of Opposing Considerations?

The first part of chapter 4 outlines the reasons for opposition to human cloning, focusing largely on potential harms that could come to pass if cloning were to become an accepted procedure. The chapter treats the risk of physical harm to the cloned child as a negative factor that is different in kind, not merely in degree, from the other potential harms at issue (65–66). These other potential harms include the risk of psychological harm to the child caused by a loss of her sense of uniqueness (66–67), as well as the erosion of her right to an "open future" by the clear or subtle imposition of parental and societal expectations based on the track record of her older genetic "twin" (67–68). Also at risk is her relationship with her parents, who might be tempted to view her as a mere "product" of their own "making," rather than a mysterious being of transcendent value whom they "begot" (69).

Chapter 4 also acknowledges that concern about these risks bears upon broader values to which our society is deeply committed, include the fear of treating children as objects who are less worthy of moral respect than their progenitors (69–70), the related worry that we will be tempted to view children as made-to-order commodities, and the concern that the practice of cloning will diminish the rich virtues of nurturing and unconditional acceptance that sustain healthy relationships among family members (70–71). Many of these concerns converge in the specter of the implementation of eugenics programs, which history reveals to be a perennial temptation. Until now, the effects of this temptation were blunted by the fact that the techniques involved were generally ineffective and inefficient. With the advent of the new genetics, this extrinsic restraint to evildoing will lose much of its force (74–75).

After its lucid and sympathetic expositions of the factors supporting moral opposition to human cloning, the report presents the factors "arrayed against" them, stating that they encompass "five separate grounds."

> First, that there is a general presumption in favor of human liberty; second, that certain actions, such as human reproduction, are particularly personal and should remain free of constraint; third, as a society, we ought not limit the freedom of scientific inquiry; fourth, that there are some reasons to create a child through somatic cell nuclear transfer so compelling they should transcend objections to the practice even if it should otherwise be prohibited; and finally, that many of the objections to the use of this technique are largely speculative and unproven. (76)

What can be said about the five reasons adduced to support a positive assessment of the practice of human cloning? Most significant, with the exception of the fourth reason (dealing with compelling exceptional cases) they are *not* directly "arrayed against" the reasons to oppose human cloning explicated earlier in the chapter. In fact, they occupy an entirely different plane of moral argumentation. The reasons the report articulates against cloning are specifically and substantively focused on the practice of human cloning; they suggest that this particular practice is likely to harm the particular parties who are involved in it, as well as to erode institutions and values of importance to the society at large. In contrast, four out of the five reasons articulated in support of cloning are general and procedural in character. They do not *defend* the moral acceptability of cloning per se, but *attack* the propriety of prohibiting it as a matter of public policy. Subtly but surely, they shift the debate from the morality of *the specific practice* of cloning to the morality of a *general legal prohibition* against cloning in the American political context. The report's rhetoric on these issues, powerful though it is, masks argumentation that is highly flawed.

First, general presumptions in favor of human liberty, reproductive freedom, and scientific inquiry tell us nothing about the regulation of particular actions and practices, which require a nuanced assessment of costs and benefits in order to evaluate whether the presumption holds in a particular case. The report does not provide the requisite assessment with respect either to the costs or the benefits of cloning. For example, it is not clear what to make of the report's observation that the objections to cloning are largely speculative and unproven. No one can deny its truth, since no one has yet brought a cloned child to term, much less successfully raised one. But what are its implications? Does it mean that we have to allow the practice of cloning to go forward in order to demonstrate its deleterious consequences, even though it will be too late to reverse them once the practice is established? How, if at all, does the claim take into account the fact that judgments about the effects of changes in social practices and policy always involve some element of conjecture? Policymakers implement such judgments all the time, on matters ranging from the effects of an aging population on the nation's Medicare program to the effect that a lack of strong male role modes will have on an entire generation of economically deprived African Americans. Taken literally, this objection would paralyze practical reasoning in all areas of political, social, and economic life. In most of these spheres, the fact that a projected "cost" has not yet materialized does not make it irrelevant to moral and political analysis.

What about the potential benefits of cloning? Here, again, the report is strikingly reticent. Only one of the factors "arrayed" in favor of human cloning alludes to substantive moral consideration, namely, the human suffering that arguably could be alleviated by its availability in certain "hard cases." Even with respect to this factor, however, the focus of the report shifts subtly but surely from moral judgments about specific acts to moral judgments about the appropriate state of the law. Rather than using these hard cases as the basis for a focused discussion about whether or not cloning may be morally justified in exceptional instances, the report uses them to generate a pervasive moral agnosticism about the practice, which inevitably gravitates toward a nonrestrictive legal policy across the board.

The three exceptional cases mentioned in the chapter include: (1) a couple who are both carriers of a lethal recessive gene who wish to have healthy children without resorting to donor gametes or selective abortion; (2) a woman whose family is in a terrible accident, and who wishes to clone her dying only child in order to have a child genetically related to her late husband; and (3) the parents of a terminally ill child who wish to clone her in order to produce a perfectly matched bone marrow donor (79–81). In response to objections that neither of the first two cases is compelling because fertility and grief are in inescapable part of human experience, the report offers a non sequitur that sends us back into the vagaries of procedurally based protections for individual action: "The intensely personal nature of that infertility or grief argues for an equally personal decision about how to respond" (80). Nowhere, for example, does the report explain why availing oneself of the complicated array of reproductive technologies that is so dependent for its existence upon an intricate and socially powerful network of medical and scientific professionals counts as more "personal" than, say, a decision to steal another couple's baby. The response to the third situation, which the report takes to be the most compelling case for cloning, is a moral platitude, not a moral argument. "Indeed, the tragedy of allowing the sick child to die because of a moral or political objection to such cloning overall merely points up the difficulty of making policy in this area" (80). There is *no* area of law in which forging sound public policy to further the common good may not demand the adoption of rules that will work considerable grief in individual cases. As hard as it sounds, the maxim "hard cases make bad law" holds in bioethics as well as in other areas of law and policy—a fact that the report appears to acknowledge at other points in the analysis (82).[20]

A Method for Managing the "Array"

In the first prong of chapter 4's approach to the ethical analysis of human cloning, the commission articulates two sets of competing moral considerations that it depicts as "arrayed against" one another. As we saw above, that depiction is not accurate. Unlike the arguments against cloning recounted by the report, the arguments adduced in favor of cloning are generally not straightforward moral arguments at all. Instead, they are fundamentally jurisprudential in nature, offering considerations why legal restrictions on cloning are not morally appropriate. Moreover, the arguments opposed to human cloning proceed at a different level of generality than those in favor of it. For the most part the former narrowly target the activity of cloning itself, and the latter defend general principles that should animate a liberal society, such as freedom of inquiry and respect for autonomy.

Precisely because they remain at the level of moral truisms, one would expect the general arguments in favor of cloning to make a rather weak showing against the vivid and particular objections to the practice outlined in the first part of chapter 4. They are fortified in their effect, however, by the second prong of the chapter's approach to ethical analysis: the framework of presumptions it adopts for adjudicating the competing considerations it has elaborated. Astonishingly, the framework's soundness and appropriateness is not defended in any detail in the body of the chapter; instead, its validity is assumed from the outset, from the point at which it is described in the following manner in the summary at the beginning of the chapter.

> As somatic cell nuclear transfer cloning could represent a means of
> human reproduction for some people, limitations on that choice
> must be made only when the societal benefits of the prohibition
> *clearly outweigh* the value of maintaining the private nature of such
> highly personal decisions. Especially in light of some arguably com-

pelling cases for attempting to create a child through somatic cell nuclear transfer, the ethics of policy making must strike a balance between the values we, as a society, wish to reflect and the freedom of individual choice and any liberties we propose to limit. (63, emphasis added)

Several features of this framework are worth noting. First, it is apparent that the commission has determined the salient issue to be addressed in this chapter to be the morality of *restrictions* on cloning, rather than the morality of cloning itself. This determination is puzzling, since the fifth chapter of the report is entirely devoted to the question of law and policy, which would be the natural place in which to air the former issue. It demonstrates, however, just how uncomfortable the commissioners are in formulating first-order ethical judgments about cloning, rather than limiting themselves to second-order judgments about the morality of restrictions upon cloning.

Second, there is a marked disparity between the conclusions announced in the summary and the arguments adduced for those conclusions in the body of the chapter. More specifically, the body of the chapter presents the three "hard cases" in a way that does not straightforwardly address, let alone resolve, the many questions that can be asked about their appropriate ethical resolution, let alone their implications for public policy. Nonetheless, the summary's description of these cases as "arguably compelling" completely ignores these ambiguities and doubts. Moreover, the summary makes clear that these three cases have been conscripted to support a liberal public policy. The summary goes forward with this conscription despite the failure of the commission explicitly to consider anywhere in the chapter how likely they are to occur, and how typical they are to be of the cases in which cloning will take place. In addition, it ignores a crucial and related question of public policy that is addressed in the chapter, which is whether it is workable to adopt a policy that prohibits human cloning in all but a few hard cases.

Third, the summary's assertion that decisions to resort to human cloning are "personal" and "private" is a linchpin of the policy argument, despite the fact that it is neither explained at length nor defended against obvious objections in the body of the chapter. More specifically, one might argue that the desire to have a child is "personal" and "private," but that the decision to avail oneself of scientific and medical techniques that have made it possible to do so in this manner is inherently deeply social.

Fourth and finally, not only have the arguments against cloning been misleadingly depicted as directly "arrayed against" those in favor of a liberal public policy, they have been charged in the summary with carrying a substantial burden of proof before they can be allowed to hold sway. This is surprising. Nowhere in the chapter does the commission state why the factors leading to a negative assessment of human cloning must "clearly outweigh" their positive counterparts before guiding American public policy. Indeed, it is not apparent what, if anything, the commission would consider to "clearly outweigh" the value of individual liberty on these matters, particularly in light of its inclusion in the body of the chapter of a comment suggesting that *all* views on the harmful consequences of cloning can be viewed as summary and speculative before they actually come to pass (68)!

Shaping Policy and Law

Despite its serious shortcomings as a balanced account of the ethical issues raised by the possibility of human cloning, chapter 4 in fact succeeds admirably well in its fulfilling its structural, rhetorical, and logical function within the report, which is to provide support for its heart and soul—chapter 5, "Legal and Policy Considerations." Unfortunately, the open-minded pluralism that characterized the commission's rhetoric—if not its stance—with respect to religious and ethical perspectives on human cloning is essentially invisible in chapter 5. In considering constitutional and jurisprudential issues, the commission adopts a one-sided perspective emphasizing the priority of individual liberty.

Although President Clinton directed the commission to undertake "a thorough review of the legal and ethical issues associated with this technology,"[21] the sole scholar with legal expertise invited to testify was John Robertson, an eminent bioethicist whose own views are firmly rooted in a constitutional theory and legal theory that gives maximum sway to individual liberty. The commission adopts Robertson's views on these matters quite unselfconsciously, not appearing to appreciate their highly controversial nature. For example, eminent legal scholars such as John Hart Ely, Michael Perry, Kent Greenawalt, or John Noonan would have all been able to provide a different perspective on the appropriate constitutional and legal theory to undergird the fifth chapter of the report. None of these scholars, however, were asked to testify. In the paragraphs below, I will attempt to illustrate some of the controversies in constitutional theory and philosophy of law that the report ignored or suppressed.

Constitutional Theory

The commission concedes that "the collective force of these objections [against cloning] make a strong prima facie case for a political judgment that creating a child in this manner would violate the deeply held views of many Americans" (93). It immediately goes on to state correctly, however, that U.S. law "demands more" to justify a legal prohibition in cases where fundamental liberties are at stake. Not surprisingly, it then turns to the analytical framework of contemporary constitutional law in order to determine whether such liberties are at stake in this situation.

> Specifically, while any rational reason will suffice for government limitation of ordinary individual liberties, such as the right to drive or operate a business, the Constitution demands a more compelling reason when a more important kind of right is infringed. Then, any

limitation must serve a compelling purpose and must be drawn as narrowly as possible, so as to infringe upon individuals only as needed. (93–94)[22]

The text of the report then goes on to create the strong impression that cloning indeed involves a "fundamental right" meriting heightened constitutional protection. The commission writes that "since such cloning, if successful, would involve bringing children into the world, it is quite possible that one could characterize it as a form of procreation, for which the courts have carved out areas of special protection since the 'bearing and begetting' of children has been characterized as a fundamental right" (94). Embedded in this statement, and in the commission's constitutional analysis more generally, is a two-step argument: (1) The Constitution protects an individual's positive right to avail herself of reproductive technology as a "fundamental right." (2) Cloning counts as a form of reproduction that triggers constitutional protection. Appearing to assume that the first point is generally uncontroversial, the report suggests that the real argument arises over the second: it cites the work of Leon Kass and others who contend that cloning is not a form of "reproduction," but a novel method of "replication" (95).

This assumption about the uncontroversial nature of the first point is not only incorrect, it verges on being irresponsible. Without legal training, only a very careful reader would be able to infer from the text of the report that the U.S. Supreme Court has *never* found that there is a right of positive reproductive liberty. Moreover, even such a reader would be led to believe that although the Supreme Court has not yet had the opportunity to consider the issue, it will likely rule in a manner protecting such a right when the occasion arises. However, even a cursory review of the Court's fundamental rights jurisprudence demonstrates that such a prediction rests on very shaky grounds.

The overall narrative of the report suggests that Supreme Court decisions protecting a right *not* to assume the responsibilities of childbearing and childrearing by availing oneself of contraception and abortion can easily and unproblematically be translated into a right of access to reproductive technologies in order to have a child. This suggestion, however, is unwarranted. As its judicial authority in this matter, the report cites only a lone federal district court decision, *Lifchez v. Hartigan*. In *Lifchez*, the court held unconstitutional an Illinois statute prohibiting the sale or experimentation upon a fetus produced by the fertilization of a human ovum by a human sperm.[23] The grounds of the holding were two: First, the statute was unconstitutionally vague. Second, the statute unconstitutionally restricted a woman's right to make reproductive choices without interference from the government. More specifically, *Lifchez* held that the restrictions the statute would place upon certain types of fertility treatment would violate a woman's right to privacy as recognized in *Roe v. Wade*: "It takes no great leap of logic to see that within the cluster of constitutionally protected choices that includes the right to have access to contraceptives, there must be included within that cluster the right to submit to a medical procedure that may bring about, rather than prevent, pregnancy."[24]

The report is correct in stating that *Lifchez* articulates a right to positive reproductive liberty—a right to avail oneself of technologies that can overcome infertility. Yet it was incorrect, or at least highly misleading, in presenting the case as exemplifying mainline American jurisprudence regarding reproductive privacy. First, the precedential value of the case is quite weak. While the U.S. Court of Appeals for the Seventh Circuit affirmed the decision in Lifchez, it did so without issuing an opinion. Technically, therefore, it did not endorse either ground upon which the district court found the Illinois statute to be unconstitutional.[25] Standing on its own, a district court opinion does not bind any other court; its sole authority is persuasive. To date, no other federal court has adopted *Lifchez's* articulation of a right to positive reproductive liberty.

Second, less than a month after the report was issued, the Supreme Court issued opinions in two cases dealing with assisted suicide, overturning the decision of two federal courts of appeals that took an expansive role to the creation of rights in substantive due process. In *Vacco v. Quill*[26] and *Washington v. Glucksberg*,[27] the Court rejected attempts made in different ways by the Second and Ninth Circuits to extend a competent adult's *negative* right to refuse medical treatment, including life-saving medical treatment,[28] to encompass a positive right to seek a physician's assistance in *bringing about* her death. In response to the Ninth Circuit's argument that assisted suicide is an "intimate and personal" decision, *Glucksberg* observes: "That many of the rights and liberties protected by the Due Process Clause sound in personal autonomy does not warrant the sweeping conclusion that any and all important, intimate, and personal decisions are so protected [citation omitted] and *Casey* did not suggest otherwise."[29]

In the last paragraph before chapter 5 turns to specific policy analysis, the report observes that "it is impossible to say with certainty whether somatic cell nuclear transfer would be treated in law as a fundamental right" (95). In my view, that statement was incorrect when made and it is clearly untenable after *Glucksberg* and *Quill*. The mode of analysis adopted by the Supreme Court in the assisted suicide cases strongly suggests that the recognition of a positive right to have children through the use of alternative reproductive technologies will not be forthcoming.[30]

It would be wrong, of course, to expect the commission to have read the minds of nine Supreme Court justices about the nature and grounds of a pending case. Nonetheless, the normative trajectory followed by the justices in the assisted suicide decisions was by no means unexpected or without theoretical justification.[31] Though the commission admits that "others take a narrower view of the Supreme Court's decisions about reproductive liberty" (94) than that embodied in *Lifchez*, it fails to acknowledge that these "others" include the justices of the Supreme Court—which has been backing away for years from the expansive "substantive due process" jurisprudence that *Lifchez* embodies.[32]

The Harm Principle

Suppose, as is likely, that it would be constitutionally permissible to ban human cloning. The question still remains, however, whether it would be morally appropriate to enact such a ban. The second prong of the Commission's analysis of the legal and policy issues is concerned with this question. In addressing it, the Commission draws heavily upon a particular strand of Anglo-American liberal legal theory, which has its roots in the thought of John Stuart Mill and finds powerful contemporary expression in the works of theorists such as H. L. A. Hart,[33] Joel Feinberg,[34] and Joseph Raz.[35] In order to protect autonomy, liberal legal philosophers emphasize the necessity of placing stringent limits on the ability of the state to impose legal restrictions on the free activities of those within its sphere of authority. Those limits are frequently expressed in some version of what has come to be known as the "harm principle," which in general terms holds that the state cannot place legal restrictions (particularly criminal restrictions) on an agent's activity unless it wrongfully causes harm to another.

Although liberal legal theorists are united in their insistence on the importance of individual autonomy, there are also significant differences among them, including different ways of understanding the harm principle. The analytical structure of the report bespeaks an inheritance to a rather stringent understanding of the harm principle, most powerfully and coherently defended by Joel Feinberg in his four-volume series, *The Moral Limits of the Criminal Law*.[36] Feinberg's interpretation of "harm" is very narrow; it consists only of a setback to a person's interests that is at the same time a violation of her rights.[37] For Feinberg, this definition excludes harms to which a person consented, moral harms (he denies that a person has a prior interest in being good), free-floating evils (i.e., violation of taboos, discrete and harmless sexual immoralities, religiously tabooed practices, evil and impure thoughts, false beliefs, the wanton, capricious squishing of small wriggly things, and social or cultural change, including the disappearance of important and valued institutions).[38] Feinberg also excludes psychological hurt that is not rooted in a more tangible prior or concurrent harm or result in a more tangible subsequent harm, such as a mental breakdown.[39]

In my view, Feinberg would at most accept criminal restrictions against cloning only if they were necessary to prevent physical harm to cloned children (presumably their mothers would have consented to the procedure, so they would not be wrongfully harmed if some damage occurred to them).[40] He would dismiss broader social concerns about eroding respect for individuality as "free-floating evils." In addition, he would not be especially sympathetic to attempts to preserve the values of American family life if doing so required altering the requirements of the harm principle. He writes: "Even if the family as we now know it should in time become extinct, however, and even if that would not be an evil, it doesn't follow that any given individual would be wrongfully harmed in the process."[41]

The report does not state its theoretical dependence upon (a particular version of) liberal legal theory with the same forthrightness that it expresses its indebtedness to its controversial version of the American constitutional tradition. In fact, some passages in the report appear designed to distance it from such dependence. Chapter 4 acknowledges that "while personal autonomy is upheld rhetorically as an ideal, it is often also constrained on behalf of the common good, even in the absence of harm to others, both in personal and public life" (76). At this point in the argument, the report recounts, and seemingly endorses, three guidelines for determining when moral arguments ought to be able to constrain personal liberty that are more lenient than most liberal legal theorists would allow. These guidelines, formulated by political theorists Amy Gutmann and Dennis Thompson, are as follows:

> (1) A convincing argument that a particular action is wrong, independent of whatever specific harms it might cause, because it violates, for example, natural law, social convention, or fundamental social values; (2) that the wrong is serious enough to warrant public attention and is otherwise eligible for public regulation; and (3) that regulation or prohibition will not cause more harm than the action that opponents seek to prohibit. (77)

Nonetheless, in the end it appears that the stringent liberal harm principle analysis carries the day. In making its normative recommendations, the report frames the issue in terms most congenial to a strict version of the harm principle. More specifically, those recommendations set up a sharp distinction between the risk of physical harm to children born as a result of somatic cell nuclear transfer, on the one hand, and the risk of psychological harms to such children and the erosion of important social values, on the other. Quite firm in its conviction that the first danger justifies the prohibition of cloning at the present time, the report also intimates that once cloning has been proven to be safe and effective for the child (and the surrogate mother) involved, none of the other concerns will be sufficiently weighty to justify continued prohibition.

The conclusion does state that "more speculative psychological harms to the child, and effects on the moral, religious, and cultural values of society may be enough to justify continued prohibitions in the future, but more time is needed for discussion and evaluation of these concerns" (108). Read in the context of the whole report, however, the call for discussion and evaluation appears slightly disingenuous. For example, summaries prominently included at the beginning of chapter 4 ("Ethical Considerations") and chapter 5 ("Legal and Policy Considerations") do not even acknowledge the existence of a way of understanding law's relationship to society that legitimate restricting cloning on the basis of social harms, even the Gutmann/Thompson theory.

Moreover, the committee's adoption of the harm principle is consistent with the constitutional jurisprudence that it adopts in the report. As noted above, that jurisprudence promotes a broad understanding of constitutionally protected reproductive freedom. The substantial prospect of physical harm to the cloned child is likely to satisfy these constitutional tests; it is less likely that the other "more speculative" objections to cloning will do so. Thus, if cloning is determined to be an aspect of a constitutionally protected freedom to reproduce, then the "strict scrutiny" applied to legislation restricting the practice will yield results that more closely resemble the application of (a strict version of) the liberal harm principle than the application of the Gutmann/Thompson criteria. In fact, on the first page of the conclusion, the committee seamlessly blends a strong reading of the harm principle with an expansive understanding of the likely constitutional protection to be afforded to human cloning.[42]

Finally, if the Gutmann/Thompson approach had exerted any real influence on the commission's formulation of public policy and law, the results would have been very different. More specifically, the commission probably would have adopted a presumption against legalizing cloning, even after it is proven to be safe and effective. The strong array of public sentiment against cloning, the weighty moral arguments elaborated in chapters 3 and 4 that cloning does violate "natural law, social convention, and other social values," and the difficulty of identifying any more than a few isolated instances in which cloning seems a justifiable course of action all combine to produce a solid prima facie case for a legal prohibition under the Gutmann/Thompson criteria, even though they fall short of the mark under the liberal harm principle.

Thus a careful review of the report, particularly chapter 5, indicates that the commission's superficial openness to the views of religious thinkers on matters of public policy is deeply misleading. A close reading of the text indicates a concerted effort to separate religious perspectives on ethics from those that are rooted in nonreligious worldviews and to segregate religion from any influence on public policy. Furthermore, attentive consideration of chapter 5, "Legal and Policy Considerations," reveals no serious attempt to analyze the question of whether and how to restrict human cloning from the perspective of differing views of constitutional law or legal theory, including those more sympathetic to religious or even broadly communal values. Instead, a view that gives maximum weight to individual liberty at the expense of other values dominates the discussion of policy and law.

Outstanding Questions

The National Bioethics Advisory Commission's report *Cloning Human Beings* furnishes a vivid demonstration of how to welcome religion into the public conversation on the meaning of cloning (and other bioethical questions) while at the same time ensuring that it has virtually no effect on the formation of law and public policy. The report exemplifies, therefore, how religion can have an important place in the field of bioethics broadly construed, even as its influence is strictly limited with respect to the field of bioethics construed narrowly. What the report does not do, however, is provide a justification of the two-pronged approach that it adopts, or address the theoretical difficulties inherent in it. On the other hand, my detailed critique of the report admittedly does not supply a positive, alternative account of how religious voices can appropriately be involved in the formulation of law and public policy.

Making progress in this area will require, I think, concerted efforts to integrate bioethics more fully with an important subfield in political philosophy: the vigorous debate about "public reason" that has grown up around John Rawls's work on this topic, which includes religious and secular thinkers reflecting upon the role of religious belief in the public square.[43] It is significant that this debate also includes reflection on the role of other "comprehensive worldviews," because participants on both sides of that debate have acknowledged that "secular" visions of the nature and purpose of life are as contested and contestable as religious ones.[44]

As an initial matter, it seems to me that the body of writing on public reason raises four basic questions, two directed primarily at those who support the current restrictions on the role of religion in bioethics narrowly construed and two directed primarily at those who would like to see a more expanded role for religious perspectives even in the arena of public policy and law.

Two Questions for Those Defending the Status Quo

I. WHY SHOULD WE CONSIDER RELIGIOUS PERSPECTIVES ON BIOETHICAL ISSUES AT ALL? The answer to this question is, of course, obvious to those who adhere to a particular religious tradition: they believe it offers a true perspective on the nature and purpose of human life, which provides the proper framework for consideration of those issues. The answer is not as clear for those that adopt the perspective toward religion, bioethics, and public policy dominating the report. More specifically, a careful reading of the report reveals that the commission has not developed a coherent view about why the consideration of religious views is important. This becomes apparent when one considers three possible answers to the question, and how each answer would have affected the structure of the report if it had been adopted by the commission.

First, one could say that it is important to consider religious perspectives on cloning because many people in the United States are religious, and laws are made by the democratically elected representatives of the people. If this were the reason adopted by the commission, however, one would expect to find some statistical breakdown of the U.S. population by religious belief. In addition, one would likely give attention to various religious viewpoints in proportion to the percentage of the population they represent. Furthermore, in choosing representatives of various religious traditions, one would seek those who represented the views of the majority of the American adherents of those traditions, not necessarily the "official teaching." The report does not proceed in this manner. It gives no sense of the demographic breakdown of Americans by religious belief, and it makes no attempt to claim that the religious thinkers it cites are in any way representative of any particular constituency of believers.

Second, one could say that religious perspectives are important because, as Daniel Callahan suggested, they offer the wisdom of long traditions of reflection on the meaning of human life. If this were the rationale for including religious perspectives, one would need to situate each tradition's view on cloning within its broader theological and anthropological perspective. Ideally, one would also need to allow each tradition to speak for itself, presenting its viewpoint in its own words. It would be impossible, of course, for the report to adopt this approach wholeheartedly, given its space and organizational constraints. Nonetheless, particularly with respect to minority traditions such as Judaism and Islam, it appears that the report presents snippets of their thought in a way that leaves the reader devoid of any kind of broader context within which that tradition's perspective on cloning could be evaluated.

A third approach to the question would be to draw explicitly on Rawlsian themes, arguing that we should seek and foster an emerging "overlapping consensus" among the various religious traditions on cloning. Such an approach would have been buttressed by the polling data surrounding human cloning, which strongly suggest that a good deal of agreement may exist regarding its immorality. Doing so would require, for example, uncovering shared basic commitments regarding the nature of God and the purpose of human life, as well as an attempt to evaluate the source of disagreements regarding cloning, differentiating between differences rooted in theoretical commitments and those rooted in different prudential judgments. Assessing the report in terms of this objective, we find the result is far more mixed. On the one hand, chapter 3 is largely organized around common themes that are addressed from a number of different religious perspectives. On the other hand, as noted earlier in this chapter, the authors of the report frame their analysis in a way that highlights—even assumes—disagreement rather than agreement.

2. WHY IS RELIGION DANGEROUS? The second question to be posed to those who would segregate religious claims far from public policy and law is *why* they think it important and beneficial to do so. As I have argued elsewhere,[45] a review of the "public reason" debate indicates that two rationales are most often used to justify this segregation of religion, which track those that Daniel Callahan identified in the article on religion and bioethics I cited at the beginning of this chapter. The first rationale is that it is somehow unfair for religious believers to use their specifically religious premises in the decisions they make as citizens because those decisions will forge the political framework and restrictions under which nonbelievers will live as well.

Several difficulties can be posed for this justification for segregation of religion from public policy. First, there is no comprehensive view, religious or secular, that is shared by everyone. There is no neutral Archimedean point of decision. Moreover, as the debate about cloning shows, there are points at which law will have to move beyond pragmatic questions and deal with fundamental questions that straightforwardly engage comprehensive worldviews.

Moreover, it is not clear how this reason can be implemented without active discrimination against religious believers. The focus of this reason for restriction is substantive; it concentrates attention on the manner in which believers actually deliberate and formulate their judgments about matters of public concern. We cannot peer inside the minds of other persons, discerning their "real reasons" for adopting the positions they hold. There is nothing to prevent religious theorists from translating commitments rooted in particular belief systems into secular, pragmatic concerns that are then held out as decisive to the general public. What can be done about that? If the fundamental worry is the normative framework used to generate the positions, not the way they happen to be articulated, the only remedy is to insulate theorists working from a religious perspective, and to keep them as far away as possible from direct effectiveness on public policy and law. In fact, as I argued above, this is precisely the strategy exemplified in the report. In my view, this phenomenon is deeply disturbing, and without justification either philosophically or constitutionally.

A second rationale frequently offered for restricting the role of religion in the public square is its potential divisiveness. On this view, offering controvertible religious premises as justifications for views on policy or law can be dangerous to public peace and civic friendship. Here, the focus is the *expression* of arguments in religious terms; the invocation of a distinctively religious premises or reasons can be seen as "fighting words," at least in a pluralistic culture such as our own. But this rationale for restricting religion is also open to question on two grounds.

First, it is not clear that the American situation is radically and divisively pluralistic about all issues, as I argued above. It may be the case that the vast majority of persons have converging opinions on certain issues, although they reach them from a number of different comprehensive worldviews. In this sort of situation, it may be that the case that articulating these different but converging worldviews will foster mutual respect, not division.[46] In my view, the polling data reveal that cloning might well have been just this sort of case.

Second, it is not at all clear that civic peace will be fostered by refraining from expression of religious perspectives, even in controversial cases. Will social peace be promoted by restricting discourse in situations in which it is impossible to restrain discernment? Will not such restraint sometimes lead to ad hominem strategies that involve "outing" speakers' religious affiliation in order to discredit their positions?[47] Moreover, in other cases, the requirement to use public language may have unacceptably elitist implications. Well-educated believers may have no difficulty translating faith-based positions into a more secular vocabulary. But what of believers who are not well educated? Are they to be put under moral pressure to remain silent in the public square?

In sum, the two reasons offered for minimizing religious premises or modes of argumentation in the public square are not above reproach. This does not mean, however, that religious thinkers who wish to participate more fully in discussion of key medical-moral issues bear no responsibility for addressing the situation. Two questions can be posed to them in turn, which in some sense are parallel to the two questions addressed to those who are more sympathetic to the status quo.

Two Questions for Those Who Want an Expanded Role for
Religious Perspectives

I. FOR WHOM DO RELIGIOUS ETHICISTS SPEAK? When religious ethicists are invited to testify before congressional bodies or other public entities such as the National Bioethics Advisory Commission, whom are they representing? What is their task? This question is related to the first question that I addressed to those who are sympathetic to the status quo; before we can determine the role of religious thinkers in this sort of setting, we need to figure out why it is important that they speak. For example, suppose we say that they are invited as representatives of the views held by their respective religious bodies. How, then, do we determine those views, by reference to the position taken by the members who are citizens or by reference to the position taken by the official "church"? Both approaches have their problems. With respect to the Roman Catholic Church, for example, many of its official teachings on medical-moral issues are both clear and clearly inconsistent with the positions held by the majority of American Catholics. With respect to Protestant, Jewish, and Muslim communities of faith, it is not clear who, if anyone, is authorized to speak for the tradition. In some cases, it is evident that no one thinker is authorized to do so.

We could say that it is the view of the congregation, not the official teaching, that is relevant for "public" bioethics. Yet this approach has its problems as well. If we adopt an undifferentiated "direct democracy" approach, why not eliminate religious ethicists altogether? In fact, this approach would also suggest the elimination of secular ethicists as well—most people do not have a consistent philosophy of life but approach issues in an ad hoc manner that may involve numerous logical inconsistencies when taken as a whole.

At this point, we might switch our focus to another justification that might be given for selecting and inviting certain religious ethicists to speak before the commission—the intrinsic coherence and power of their arguments. At first glance, this seems to be a more promising approach, since it neatly sidesteps the problem of considering any and all democratically powerful viewpoints, no matter how internally inconsistent they may be. But who will judge the "intrinsic coherence and power of argument," and what standards will they apply? Who will decide whether a particular thinker is an appropriate representative of a particular religious tradition? It may be unavoidable that the decision makers are those who run the committees and the commissions, and that they will choose the representatives of various traditions who make them most comfortable. This may not be a real problem in the case of "assimilated" religions that have made sense of and made peace with the American political system. But this approach may stifle the voices of more marginalized religious traditions or those that have developed a more radical stance toward the prevailing value system.

2. WHAT DO RELIGIOUS BELIEVERS OWE TO THEIR FELLOW CITIZENS? As I observed at the very beginning of the chapter, bioethics in a narrow sense

pertains to the formulation of law and policy. Most religious ethicists work in the field of bioethics broadly defined; they explore and extend the frameworks of meaning that determine our first-order moral judgments. Many, if not all, are reluctant to wade too deeply into the realm of bioethics narrowly defined; while they may offer considerations that bear on the formulation of law and public policy, they frequently do not advocate a normative vision they believe should guide judgments in this area.

Therefore, the next step for religious ethicists who wish to participate more extensively in bioethics is to address this realm of discussion in a more explicit and self-conscious manner. The fundamental issue that arises in this area, of course, are political fairness and prudent lawmaking. When is it appropriate to impose coercive regulations—or more broadly, to adopt a regulative scheme designed to forward some versions of flourishing and exclude others—when some elements of the lawmaker's vision are not shared by those who live under it?

As I suggested above, Feinberg's version of liberal legal theory gives but one answer to this question. Other answers have been proffered, including answers by those working in a way that is sensitive to the political thought of various religious traditions.[48] Unfortunately, because of the currents of academic life, discussions in bioethics (including religious bioethics) and political-legal theory all too frequently proceed independently of one another. General reflections about the nature of our polity and the scope of wise law in a pluralistic society need to inform and be informed by the highly detailed understanding of biological science and medical technology increasingly required of bioethicists, religious and secular. It seems to me that more overlap might be beneficial not only to the bioethicists, but also to the political and legal theorists.

I would like to conclude where I began, with Daniel Callahan's observations of some of the distorted reflection that has come from the exclusion of religion from bioethics. The first distortion he identified was that the exclusion made us too dependent upon law for morality; the second was that it deprived us of accumulated wisdom found in religious traditions; and the third was that it forced us to remember that we are creatures of particular communities as well as of an all-embracing secular culture. The thrust of my chapter has been to refocus his worries in a slightly different direction: Because we do not remember that we are creatures of particular communities who have forged a common culture that reflects our particularities, because we do not draw upon the accumulated wisdom of religious traditions, we have come to be dependent upon a view of law that is far too impoverished—both culturally and morally.

NOTES

1. Daniel Callahan, "Religion and the Secularization of Bioethics," *Hastings Center Report* 20:4 (July/August 1990, special supp.): 2.

2. Ibid., 3.

3. Ibid.

4. Ibid., 4.

5. National Bioethics Advisory Commission, *Cloning Human Beings* (Rockville, Md., 1997). All citations to this report will be given parenthetically in the text.

6. In contrast, the composition of President Bush's commission was deliberately designed so as not to be dominated by self-identified bioethicists, with the aim of situating its deliberation within a broader field of humanistic and scientific concerns.

7. See, e.g., Diana Butler, "Once Again, Science Challenges Religion: Cloning Raises Theological Issues," *Austin American-Statesman*, 27 February 1997, A15; Kenneth L. Woodward and Anne Woodward, "Today the Sheep . . . ," *Newsweek*, 10 March 1997, 60; Wray Herbert, Jeffery L. Sheler, and Traci Watson, "The World After Cloning: A Reader's Guide to What Dolly Hath Wrought," *U.S. News and World Report*, 10 March 1997, 50; Robert Wright, "Can Souls Be Xeroxed? Your Clone Might Be Eerily Like You. Or Perhaps Eerily Like Someone Else," *Time*, 10 March 1997, 73; Vincent Kiernan, "The Morality of Cloning Humans: Theologians and Philosophers Offer Provocative Arguments," *Chronicle of Higher Education* 18 July 1997, A13.

8. The question of cloning for biomedical research, which would not involve any attempt to bring the cloned embryo to a live birth, was not addressed in *Cloning Human Beings*; it was, however, addressed in the report prepared by the President's Council on Bioethics, *Human Cloning and Human Dignity: The Report of the President's Council on Bioethics* (with foreword by Leon R. Kass, M.D., chairman) (New York: Public Affairs, 2002).

9. Organizations that supported the voluntary moratorium included the American Society for Reproductive Medicine, the Biotechnology Industry Organization, the American Medical Association, the Federation of American Society of Experimental Biology, RESOLVE (the National Infertility Association), and the Society for Developmental Biology.

10. See Rick Weiss, "Human Clone Research Will Be Regulated; FDA Asserts It Has Statutory Authority to Regulate Attempts at Human Cloning," *Washington Post*, 20 January 1998, A1.

11. For example, some religious thinkers worry that cloning would violate human dignity, which they believe to be rooted in the transcendent reality that each person is created in the image and likeness of God. Yet the manner in which they fear that cloning will work such violations is practical, not metaphysical: "by the denial of such rights and protections [given to all human beings], for instance, through enslavement to others and other forms of 'man's mastery over man' " (49). The same broad intelligibility characterizes the religious concerns raised with respect to the effects that cloning might have on the human family. Protestant theologian Allen Verhey focuses on how cloning "risks transforming children into 'products' of technological achievement rather than 'gifts' created in love. As products, children become objects, and objectification violates what it means to treat a child as a gift" (53).

12. For example, one case put forward by a Jewish rabbi involved the cloning of a "young man who is sterile, whose family was wiped out in the Holocaust, and who is the last of a genetic line" (55). A second hypothetical, supported by some Jewish and Protestant thinkers, involves parents who clone a child who has leukemia in order to produce a compatible bone marrow donor.

13. Indeed, immediately before the concluding section of the chapter, the commission acknowledges that "most religious thinkers who recommend public policies on cloning propose either a ban or restrictive regulation" (56).

14. The General Social Survey Database (cumulative data file 1972–2000), assembled by the National Opinion Research Center, gives the following data with respect to abortion. In response to the question, "Please tell me whether or not you

think it should be possible for a pregnant woman to obtain a legal abortion if the woman wants it for any reason," the following answers were obtained:

	Yes	No
Protestant	36%	64%
Catholic	35%	65%
Jewish	79%	21%

An introduction to the database is available at http://www.icpsr.umich.edu/GSS/about/gss/about.htm

15. The General Social Survey Database (cumulative data file 1972–2000), assembled by the National Opinion Research Center, gives the following data with respect to euthanasia. In response to the question, "When a person has a disease that cannot be cured, do you think doctors should be allowed by law to end the patient's life by some painless means if the patient and his family request it?" the following answers were obtained:

	Yes	No
Protestant	63%	37%
Catholic	68%	32%
Jewish	86%	14%

An introduction to the database is available at http://www.icpsr.umich.edu/GSS/about/gss/about.htm.

16. Roper Center for Public Opinion, Question ID: USYANKP. 97FEB26 R27 (available online through Westlaw). In response to the question "Do you think it is morally acceptable to clone human beings, or don't you feel this way?" 7 percent of Americans said it was morally acceptable, 89 percent said it was not morally acceptable, and 4 percent said they were not sure. Breakdown according to religion is as follows:

	Morally Acceptable	Morally Unacceptable	Not Sure
Protestant	7%	91%	2%
Catholic	10%	85%	5%
Jewish	13%	87%	0%

17. The two major moral considerations *against* cloning that appear in chapter 4 but that are not elaborated in chapter 3 are first, that cloning will lead to the widespread practice of an invidious biological eugenics and second, that the cloning process will cause physical harm to the ensuing child. To anyone familiar with the history of the religious discussion of cloning and other developments in reproductive technology over the last thirty years, the omission of those concerns from the chapter devoted to religious perspectives seems rather arbitrary.

18. See especially MacIntyre's *Whose Justice? Which Rationality?* (Notre Dame, Ind.: University of Notre Dame, 1988).

19. See, e.g., John Rawls, "The Idea of Public Reason Revisited," *University of Chicago Law Review* 64:3 (summer 1997): 765–807.

20. As David Guinn has pointed out to me, it is arguable that none of these three "hard cases" can be justified against the basic maxim of Kantian morality that it is never permissible to treat persons as means only, rather than also as ends in themselves.

21. Letter from President Bill Clinton to Dr. Harold Shapiro (24 February 1997), included in the introductory materials to the report.

22. In addition, the constitutional test applied by the commission is rather outdated and indicates a lack of familiarity with the evolving formulation of such standards in contemporary constitutional jurisprudence. The commission invokes the "tiered" approach, according to which there are two (or three) tiers of judicial scrutiny corresponding to two (or three) levels of rights. More specifically, it suggested that cloning might be a "fundamental right" whose existence would then trigger the highest level of constitutional protection, known as "strict scrutiny." In recent years, however, the Supreme Court has been more inclined to speak of due process "liberty interests" rather than fundamental rights. Moreover, it appears to be headed toward a "continuum" approach, in which the strength of the state interest required in order to prevail varies with the importance of the liberty interest threatened by its protection. This important shift in the Court's due process jurisprudence was explicitly noted and summarized in the two *appellate court* cases that unsuccessfully attempted to work around this shift in order to confer constitutional protection on physician-assisted suicide. See *Compassion in Dying v. State of Washington*, 73 F.2d 790 (1996) at 799–806 and *Quill v. Vacco*, 80 F.3d 716 (1996) at 723–725.

23. *Lifchez v. Hartigan*, 735 F.Supp. 1361 (N.D. Ill.) aff'd without opinion, *Lifchez v. Hartigan*, 914 F.2d 260 (7th Cir. 1990), *cert. denied*, 498 U.S. 1069 (1991). The Illinois statute made an exception for experimentation that was "therapeutic to the fetus thereby produced." Ill.Rev.Stat., Ch. 38, ¶ 81–26, § 6(7) (1989).

24. Ibid., 1377.

25. Technically speaking, this aspect of the district court's analysis is dicta, because it was the second of two alternative grounds that the court offered for its decision in the case. Furthermore, because it was affirmed by the Seventh Circuit without opinion, we have no reason to believe even that the circuit court in which it was generated endorses the reasoning upon which the district court depended.

26. *Vacco v. Quill*, 521 U.S. 793 (1997).

27. *Washington v. Glucksberg*, 521 U.S. 702 (1997).

28. The Court assumed but did not decide upon the existence of such a right in *Cruzan v. Director, Missouri Dept. of Health*, 497 U.S. 261 (1990).

29. *Glucksberg*, 521 U.S. at 727–728.

30. In *Glucksberg*, the Supreme Court articulated two stringent criteria that limit the recognition of any new fundamental rights or liberty interests. First, the content of any alleged right must be carefully and specifically described. Second, the right must be "objectively, deeply rooted in this Nation's history and tradition." It is doubtful that these criteria would confer constitutional protection on attempts to create a child by somatic cell nuclear transfer.

31. In my view, *Lawrence v. Texas*, 539 U.S. 558 (2003), does not undermine this analysis. Fundamentally, *Lawrence* does no more than extend the right to sexual privacy already recognized in the case of married couples to all couples, heterosexual and homosexual. It protects a negative right of sexual privacy, not a positive right of reproductive freedom. According to the Court, "to say that the issue in *Bowers* was

simply the right to engage in certain sexual conduct demeans the claim the individual put forward, just as it would demean a married couple were it to be said marriage is simply about the right to have sexual intercourse. The laws involved in *Bowers* and here are, to be sure, statutes that purport to do no more than prohibit a particular sexual act. Their penalties and purposes, though, have more far-reaching consequences, touching upon the most private human conduct, sexual behavior, and in the most private of places, the home. The statutes do seek to control a personal relationship that, whether or not entitled to formal recognition in the law, is within the liberty of persons to choose without being punished as criminals." 539 U.S. at 567.

32. See n. 16 above. Citing *Collins v. City of Harker Heights, Tex.*, 503 U.S. 115 at 123, the Ninth Circuit explicitly acknowledged that "the Court has also recently expressed a strong reluctance to find new fundamental rights," *Compassion in Dying*, 79 F.3d at 803.

33. H. L. A. Hart, *Law, Liberty and Morality* (Stanford, Calif.: Stanford University Press, 1963).

34. Joel Feinberg, *Harm to Others* (New York: Oxford University Press, 1984), *Offense to Others* (New York: Oxford University Press, 1985), *Harm to Self* (New York: Oxford University Press, 1986), *Harmless Wrongdoing* (New York: Oxford University Press, 1988).

35. Joseph Raz, *The Morality of Freedom* (Oxford: Clarendon Press, 1986).

36. Feinberg also allows the milder penalties of the criminal law to be used to prohibit offensive behavior; that qualification, however, would not be relevant in this case, since the behavior in question must be performed in a public place, from which unwilling witnesses cannot or should not have to escape, in order to qualify as an offense appropriately targeted by the criminal law.

37. Feinberg, *Harmless Wrongdoing*, x.

38. Ibid., chaps. 28–29.

39. Feinberg, *Harm to Others*, 48–49.

40. Feinberg is sympathetic to the more liberal position considered and rejected by the commission, namely, that it is impossible to claim that a cloned child has been "harmed" since so doing requires one to compare the value of existence with nonexistence (66). Nonetheless, he does acknowledge that the harm principle could be modified to encompass "wrongfully bringing other persons into existence in an initially harmful (handicapped) position." Feinberg, *Harm to Others*, 104.

41. Feinberg, *Harmless Wrongdoing*, 73.

42. The two key paragraphs read as follows:

> In addition to concerns about specific harms to children, people have frequently expressed fears that a widespread practice of somatic cell nuclear transfer cloning would undermine important social values by opening the door to a form of eugenics or by tempting some to manipulate others as if they were objects instead of persons. Arrayed against these concerns are other important social values, such as protecting personal choice particularly in matters pertaining to procreation and child rearing, maintaining privacy and the freedom of scientific inquiry, and encouraging the possible development of new biomedical breakthroughs.
>
> As somatic cell nuclear transfer cloning could represent a means of human reproduction for some people, limitations on that choice must be made only when the societal benefits of the prohibition clearly outweigh the value of

maintaining the private nature of such highly personal decisions. Especially in light of some arguably compelling cases for attempting to clone a human being using somatic cell nuclear transfer, the ethics of policy must strike a balance between the values society wishes to reflect and issues of privacy and the freedom of individual choice. (107)

43. John Rawls, *Political Liberalism* (New York: Columbia University Press, 1993), and "The Idea of Public Reason Revisited," *University of Chicago Law Review* 64:3 (summer 1997): 768. Key works in the debate include: Kent Greenawalt, *Religious Convictions and Political Choice* (New York: Oxford University Press, 1988), and *Private Consciences and Public Reasons* (New York: Oxford University Press, 1995); Michael Perry, *Morality, Politics, and Law* (New York: Oxford University Press, 1988) and *Love and Power* (New York: Oxford University Press, 1991); and John Finnis, "Public Reason, Abortion, and Cloning," *Valparaiso University Law Review* 32:2 (1998): 361–82. An important anthology is Paul J. Weithman, ed., *Religion and Contemporary Liberalism* (Notre Dame, Ind.: University of Notre Dame Press: 1997). Michael Perry also organized a conference on the topic, the papers for which were published in *Wake Forest Law Review* 36:2 (summer 2001).

44. See, e.g., Rawls, "The Idea of Public Reason Revisited."

45. M. Cathleen Kaveny, "Religious Claims and the Dynamics of Argument," *Wake Forest Law Review*, 36:2 (summer 2001): 423–448.

46. Ibid., 429–434.

47. Ibid., 446–447.

48. In my view, helpful theoretical alternatives can be found in both the perfectionist liberal legal theory of Joseph Raz, *The Morality of Freedom*, and the analytic natural law approach of John Finnis, *Natural Law and Natural Rights* (Oxford: Clarendon Press, 1980), and *Aquinas* (Oxford University Press, 1998).

PART V

Religion and Ethical Praxis

To this point, we have explored the law and morality of religion's participating in public bioethics—specifically, whether religion should participate. The next critical question is, What difference does religion make if it does participate? Does it offer anything different from current secular-oriented bioethics? Will it lead to different results in terms of policy or practice? If so, are they of concern?

In the short term, the answer is that probably not much would change if religion were admitted as a full participant at the table. There is no evidence of a massive schism between religions and religious values on the one hand and bioethical practice and policy on the other. As Jonsen (chap. 1) pointed out, contemporary bioethics grew out of prior religious ethical traditions and were elaborated and developed by many of the new bioethicists who were themselves initially trained as religious ethicists. This did not represent a disjuncture, but a continuity. Moreover, as Cahill notes in chapter 2, in the lives of individuals, there are no clear divisions between religious faith and secular life. " 'Value traditions' and convictions or background assumptions about 'ultimate meaning' pervade all of these realms and interact together in all social life, including bioethics." As I noted in the general introduction, more than 90 percent of the members of Congress said they consulted their religious beliefs before voting on important matters, and 80 percent of all Americans said they take guidance in living their own lives from the Bible. If this is so, it is likely that religious perspectives have already been incorporated into public policies.

Moreover, the diversity of religious perspectives suggests that accepting them into public bioethics will not change existing pluralistic policies. Even when we look at a topic like abortion, which many identify as a religiously divisive issue and in which religious affiliation is considered predictive, studies generally indicate that the range of positions held by people of faith (both pro-life and pro-choice and everything in between) largely mirrors the overall demographics of the debate.[1]

To say that it will not change public policies on bioethical issues abruptly does not mean that it will not change them over time, however. Moral standards and values clearly have evolved. What inclusion of religious perspectives will do is allow religious arguments greater attention and focus. One area that will receive enhanced attention, according to Karen Lebacqz, is justice. Justice is one of the "principles" in bioethical principlism that grew out of the Belmont Report (following the principles of autonomy, beneficence, and nonmaleficence).[2] It should be noted that Lebacqz may even be in part responsible for its inclusion, as she was a member of the commission that produced this report, and, according to one participant, the idea of developing a set of Kantian principles arose out of a suggestion she made.[3]

Though justice was among the founding principles in the new bioethics, as Lebacqz notes, the current focus in bioethics is on principles of autonomy and consent. Religion—in her example, specifically Christian theology—will push to make justice a primary concern rather than an afterthought. As Lebacqz notes, and Cahill (chap. 2) agrees, Christian theology is uniquely qualified to speak of justice.

In anticipating the effects of religion on bioethics, many may view the effort to include religion with the suspicion that religion will be a "conservative" force. At present, in most political conversations about religion, the focus is upon the Religious Right. And indeed, a number of chapters in this book have thus far justified religious engagement by highlighting the liberal or progressive aspects of religion throughout history in order to rebut the fears of liberal secularists (see, e.g., Evans's chap. 3, Cohen's chap. 5, and others). However, conclusions about the potential political direction of religious engagement is problematic. First, regardless of the political beliefs of the participants, political orientation cannot disqualify a person from participating in the public square. Moreover, one cannot necessarily judge the direction of a policy argument based upon the political reputation of the religious speaker. For example, both Lebacqz (a member of the liberal United Church of Christ), and Cahill (a Roman Catholic) both agree on the theological importance if not primacy of justice. Similarly, despite the popular perception of Islam as a very conservative religion, Abdulaziz Sachedina presents a very strong argument on how Islamic principles support many of the same ideas expressed in principlism and modern bioethical discourse.

Another argument in favor of engaging religion is that religion provides additional tools or techniques for ethical reflection. One tool or technique, as suggested by Lebacqz and Cahill, is that theology provides a unique perspective that focuses on justice in ways not prevalent in secular bioethics. Sachedina, Nakasone, and Cameron provide illustrations as to how other religious traditions can be engaged in public bioethics. These chapters also rebut the biased and simplistic critique that the sole task of religion is "theological hermeneutics—the interpretation of sacred texts" and that religion "abolish[es] the hard ethical questions" because the answers are to be found in the texts of revelation.[4] Cameron, who writes from an Evangelical perspective, and Sachedina, who writes from an Islamic perspective, both operate from perspectives that might be thought to illustrate this "texts of revelation" critique. In fact, while drawing upon sacred texts, they illustrate how religious ethicists in practice have to develop strong ethical arguments building on revelation—because the answers are not obvious.

Finally, involving religious perspectives broadens the audience for ethical reflection, engages points of potential resistance, and potentially helps build stronger political constituencies necessary to support the new policy. As Nakasone's chapter on the Japanese organ transplant law illustrates, religious beliefs can profoundly affect not only the development of public bioethics, but also its implementation. Failure to engage the religious belief may ultimately defeat the ostensible objective of the policy. (This point will also be addressed by Michele Goodwin in chap. 17.)

NOTES

1. See the National Opinion Research Center's General Social Survey "Public Opinion on Abortion" at http://www.norc.uchicago.edu/library/abortion.htm. (Accessed on May 20, 2005.)

2. The National Commission for the Protection of Human Subjects of Biomedical and Behavioral Research, *The Belmont Report: Ethical Principles and Guidelines for the Protection of Human Subjects of Research*, DHEW Publication No. (OS) 78–0012, 1978.

3. Conversation with a participant.

4. R. C. Lewontin, "The Confusion over Cloning," *New York Review of Books*, Oct. 23, 1997, p. 7.

11

Philosophy, Theology, and the Claims of Justice

Karen Lebacqz

Thirty years ago, both the National Commission for the Protection of Human Subjects of Biomedical and Behavioral Research and the collaborative team of Tom L. Beauchamp and James Childress placed justice on a short list of principles that should undergird medical treatment and research in a pluralistic society. *Principles of Biomedical Ethics*[1] by Beauchamp and Childress, the leading text in bioethics, continues to list justice as one of the necessary ethical principles for biomedicine. Appeals to justice are becoming increasingly common in the public arena of bioethics, and several recent essays focus specifically on issues of justice in development of new technologies such as stem cells.[2]

It is a bit difficult to sort out the specific contributions of religious or theological ethics to justice theory in bioethics. Nonetheless, I believe that some claims can be made both for the influence of religious ethics on the public discussion of bioethics and for the distinctive voice of religious or theological ethics in matters of justice.

Taking a biblically based view of justice, I argue that a religious view (1) extends the *scope* of justice; (2) makes *oppression* and *liberation* primary categories for understanding justice; and (3) makes justice the *first principle* rather than the second or third.

It is my conviction that the Hebrew Scriptures and the Christian New Testament portray a God who is a God of justice. It is further my conviction that the demands of justice seen through a biblical lens differ from the demands of justice that the West has inherited from its dominant secular philosophical tradition. The view of justice developed here is therefore particular, but it is one that may find resonances within American culture. MacIntyre argues that contemporary culture retains "fragments" of a tradition that no longer dominates the landscape but may nonetheless intrude into our everyday thinking.[3] Grant argues that English-speaking peoples attain their understanding of justice in part from the legacy of Jewish and Christian (especially Protestant) theological traditions.[4] If MacIntyre and Grant are correct, then religious traditions on justice may differ from the dominant philosophical tradition yet make sense to many in the American public. I believe this is the case. Indeed, I would argue that as recognition of the centrality of justice grows in the field of bioethics, the legacy of the biblically based theological tradition becomes more evident. Though a fully developed argument to this effect is beyond the scope of this chapter, the following reflections will suggest avenues for further exploration.

The Scope and Content of Justice

Two rhetorical moves distinguish the early work of the National Commission for the Protection of Human Subjects of Biomedical and Behavioral Research (as evidenced in its Belmont Report)[5] and the ongoing work of Beauchamp and Childress. First, they treat justice primarily as a philosophical concept; though both sets of authors had theological training, it is philosophical notions that were and still are used to portray the demands of justice. Following Western philosophical tradition, then, justice is understood largely within a *distributive* or *allocative* framework. In keeping with dominant theories of justice,[6] justice is conceptualized largely in terms of specific requirements for distribution of the burdens and benefits of social living.[7] Beauchamp and Childress are clear about this delineation: "the term *distributive justice* refers to fair, equitable, and appropriate distribution. . . . Its scope includes policies that allot diverse benefits and burdens."[8] Hence, questions of justice typically include: How should scarce goods be allocated? Who should bear burdens and who should get benefits in medical research and treatment? Who should get scarce organs, such as kidneys?[9]

Different philosophical traditions will answer these questions differently. Some will stress equality of access, some will stress doing the greatest good overall, and so on. But as Beauchamp and Childress note, all assume a minimal formal requirement traditionally attributed to Aristotle: similar cases must be treated similarly. Injustice consists in the first place in treating people dissimilarly if they are similar in relevant respects. Arguments arise over what constitutes such relevant respects. For example, is an early embryo fully a "person" in the way a newborn infant or an adult is? Does the vulnerability of prisoners suffice to make them dissimilar to free-living populations? The question then becomes: When are inequalities warranted, and on what grounds?[10]

Different grounds have been proposed: need, effort, contribution to society, ability to pay, and so on. Many authors stress need as a relevant criterion for distribution of benefits. But some accept more than one criterion. Utilitarian theories focus on creating the greatest good overall; Marxist theories focus specifically on addressing needs. In all cases, however, the theories tend to assume that health care is a benefit to be distributed, that participation in research is a burden to be borne by some, and that the important question is what characteristics qualify someone for receiving a benefit or bearing a burden. Justice is primarily a matter of distributing benefits and burdens.

The biblical view extends this approach to justice in two ways. First, it "implodes" justice. In theological ethics, justice becomes a concern of *character* as well as a requirement for social action. Some contemporary writers have argued that bioethics in general needs to be seen as a matter of character or virtue, and there are strong roots of this move in the philosophical system of Aristotle, which was elaborated by Thomas Aquinas. Nonetheless, James Drane was correct to assert a decade ago that "to suggest that character and virtue have a place in contemporary medical ethics comes across as strange to most U.S. ethicists."[11] The influence of the theological tradition on some of those arguments is evident, however, as several of the strongest arguments for character issues in bioethics come from those with theological backgrounds or religious affiliations.[12] As Drane notes, historically, religion influenced medicine with considerable attention to virtue and character. In the contemporary scene, "religion does not guarantee character and virtue, but the loss of religion can explain a perceived loss of character and virtue considerations in contemporary professional life."[13]

The theological tradition has been clear in its development of justice as a necessary virtue.[14] In a biblical perspective, justice is first and foremost *relational*; the requirements of justice emerge out of a history of God's interaction with God's people. Justice is therefore fidelity to the demands of a relationship.[15] Those who know God will do justice. This means concretely a change of heart and a desire to bring about justice for the oppressed. Justice is therefore not simply a demand for fair treatment of others, but a human "excellence" to be cultivated as a fundamental character trait. Roman Catholic tradition in particular has stressed justice as one of the four cardinal virtues (along with prudence, temperance, and fortitude). To be a good person, one must be above all a *just* person, and hence justice is the highest of the moral virtues.[16]

Taking this view seriously, justice would not be limited to a consideration of what qualities make people sufficiently similar or different to justify different treatment. Rather, justice would be seen as a characteristic to be cultivated through training and habit. Such theological insights about justice as a matter of character have not received a great deal of attention in the bioethics literature.

More important and influential has been the second way in which theological views extend the concept of justice. Theological views of justice "explode" justice from questions of allocation or distribution into questions of social structure and system. Concerns about distribution or allocation of goods do not disappear. Indeed, in biblical language, justice takes one form in the demands of *mishpat*—the requirements for living together in community. Under this rubric, theology asks about what is "owed" to whom, and how humans are to meet their obligations.[17] Thus, for example, Christian ethicists as well as philosophers have puzzled over the allocation of scarce organs and the minimal requirements of access to health care.[18]

But there is another understanding of justice in the Bible that has become primary for many theological thinkers. Justice appears in the Hebrew scriptures not simply as *mishpat* but also as *sedakah,* the ultimate righteousness of God. *Sedakah* is captured in poetic images such as Amos's vision of justice rolling down like a mighty stream that washes everything away and requires new beginnings (Amos 5:24). It is captured in the notion of the Jubilee year in which debts are remitted and people are returned to their original lands.[19] It is captured in the Magnificat: the image of God bringing down the mighty and lifting up the lowly (Luke 1:46–55). It is captured in Handel's powerful use of Scripture in the *Messiah:* ". . . and the rough places [will be made] plain." It is captured in Carter Heyward's notion of "right relationship," which has become a standard phrase in feminist theological ethics.[20] The notion of *sedakah* goes beyond the specifics of allocative justice to ask about entire systems—about what William Coats once called "the shape of the age."[21]

In other words, the scope of justice is extended beyond concerns for fair treatment of individuals or allocation of specific goods to look at *systemic* issues. "Religious ethicists are more likely [than secular theorists] to view justice as constitutive of systems as well as individual relationships."[22] To be sure, secular ethicists have addressed systemic issues. Rawls's massive *A Theory of Justice* begins with a concern for how the *basic structure* of society privileges some and disadvantages others.[23] Nonetheless, secular ethicists tend to focus on formal principles of justice, ignoring how historical injustices affect people's options and opportunities. By contrast, religious ethicists have focused on *oppression* as a primary category of injustice. This has been particularly true in liberation theology. This issue of oppression will be elaborated further below. What is important here is to recognize that justice, "exploded" into questions of systems and structures, may require social upheaval that goes beyond mere concerns of distribution. Distribution works *within* systems; *sedakah* may require subversive activities *outside* systems or the overthrow *of* systems. In this regard, it is significant that feminist theologians such as Mary Daly have called for massive change in the very symbol system by which women are identified.[24] Changes of language are rarely addressed in mainstream bioethics, but they are a central justice issue for many feminist theologians.

The first extension in theological notions of justice, then, is an implosion of justice into the arena of character; the second is an explosion into the social arena, with attention to histories of oppression, to structures and symbol systems and their contributions to oppression, and to the ways in which social changes such as new technologies affect categories of people.

The Centrality of Oppression

Precisely because justice gets exploded into the social arena, religious views on justice often make *oppression* a primary category. Here, contemporary theology is deeply indebted to a thirty-year history of liberation theology. Though the term "liberation theology" specifically designates certain Latin American theologies, the same marks are borne by theologies of struggle in Africa, "minjung" theologies in Korea,[25] and theologies of suffering around the world. Liberation theology takes the exodus theme as central: the God of the Hebrew scriptures is a God of the oppressed who desires liberation for the poor, the marginalized, the outcast, the oppressed. As African theologian Allan Aubrey Boesak puts it, "the all-surpassing characteristic" of God is God's acts in history "as the God of justice and liberation for the sake of those who are weak and oppressed."[26] Liberation is not about salvation from personal sin, but about restructuring those aspects of social life that create gaps between the rich and the poor. Hence, in biblically based theologies of justice, themes of liberation and oppression loom large.[27]

To be sure, theologians are not the only theorists concerned about oppression. In *Justice and the Politics of Difference*, Iris Marion Young elaborated five "faces" of oppression: exploitation, marginalization, powerlessness, cultural imperialism, and violence.[28] Taking seriously the ways in which we live as members of *groups* and the ways in which groups are oppressed in one or more of these dimensions, Young makes a strong argument for the centrality of oppression as a concept in theories of justice. Joining cause with many theologians, she is also critical of the emphasis on distributive justice that tends to permeate mainstream secular theories of justice. Thus, it is clear that some philosophers do take seriously the same concerns for oppression that have permeated liberation theology. But development in the theological literature of arguments about justice as liberation from oppression predates Young's contribution.[29]

That the language of oppression has entered into discourse on bioethics can be seen from the recent essay by Ruth Faden et al. on justice in stem cell research and therapy. In arguing for an "ethnic representation" approach to therapy, the group notes that the history of oppression of minority groups in the United States is a relevant consideration.[30] But I would argue that religious ethicists have been the first and foremost to apply this language.[31]

Moreover, religious ethicists not only make oppression a central category, they also argue explicitly for an "epistemological privilege" of the oppressed. This means that the experiences, perspectives, and views of oppressed people should be given priority in determining what is fair or just.[32] To date, I have not seen such an assertion in the mainstream philosophical literature on bioethics.

Connected to the epistemological privilege of the oppressed is a "hermeneutic of suspicion"—a skepticism toward the voices of those in power. Long ago, theologian Reinhold Niebuhr cautioned that those in power rarely give up their power voluntarily.[33] Taking this insight seriously, many theologians believe that the views of those with power are distorted and that truth will be more readily gained by looking to the views of those who are oppressed. Thus, justice demands attention to power differentials. Feminists in both theological and philosophical bioethics have been adamant about the need for suspicion

of power structures.[34] As noted above, this suspicion extends to the very language with which we approach issues. Because attention to power structures
has permeated feminist bioethics in both the theological and philosophical
arenas, it is a bit difficult to distinguish the theological voice. However, it is
clear that attention to oppression and liberation has been and continues to be
a strong theme in theological ethics that influences the philosophical arena.

The Priority of Justice

The second rhetorical move that distinguished the work of both the National
Commission and the team of Beauchamp and Childress was the placement of
justice *last* on the short list of ethical principles. Although both teams elevated
justice to the status of a primary ethical principle, it followed, in terms of
priority, "respect for persons" (as the commission called the first principle) or
"respect for autonomy" (as it is called by Beauchamp and Childress) and beneficence and non-maleficence.[35] One rather striking result of this placement
is that the demands of autonomy have often come first in ethical analysis. For
instance, the Geron Ethics Advisory Board cited a concern for global justice as
a requirement for research on stem cells, but lists that concern *after* requirements for informed consent.[36] Indeed, it may be fair to say that autonomy—
and its derivative requirement for informed consent—has dominated bioethical discourse in the United States.[37] The demands of informed consent in
biomedicine have received sustained attention and elaboration, while the demands of justice have been relatively neglected.

There is reason to believe, however, that a religious, specifically biblical,
view of justice would place justice in a primary rather than secondary position.[38] For example, in Roman Catholic social teachings, humans are understood as social beings whose "ends" are intimately connected to the common
good. Though the tradition supports many rights of people, these rights cannot
be conceived apart from the demands of justice. Even so fundamental a right
as the right to hold property may give way to the demands of justice seen in
the needs of others. For example, *Gaudium et Spes* reports the consensus of
Vatican II that a person in extreme necessity may take from the riches of others
to meet basic needs.[39] Thus, in the dominant Roman Catholic tradition, the
demands of justice can take priority over individual desires, autonomy, and
rights.

Another example comes from the rich tradition, extant in both Roman
Catholic and in Protestant circles, known as liberation theology. Latin American liberation theologians from Gutierrez on have stressed the importance of
justice—and its requirement of liberation—as a primary theme for understanding the will of God and the requirements of human living.[40] A particularly
strong proponent of the priority of justice is Jose Porfirio Miranda. Miranda
argues bluntly that the God of the Bible is a God of justice.[41] Therefore, to
know and to love God is to do justice for our neighbor. Hence, the demands

of justice and liberation for the poor and oppressed become central for any faithful follower of God.

Protestant theologians from the mainstream have also contributed to the increasing stress on the priority of justice and its importance in social policy.[42] The stress on justice in recent theology has found its way into reflections in bioethics. In a recent essay, Audrey Chapman recommends "that the justice implications of inheritable genetic modifications should be in the forefront of any evaluation."[43] Similarly, in addressing matters of cross-cultural bioethics, Lebacqz states: "Every practice must be judged by how it deals with the poor and oppressed. . . . Hence, I begin by asking about justice, and by requiring that justice be done."[44] As Chapman notes, "From the beginnings of the genetic revolution, religious communities and thinkers have been sensitive to the justice implications of these new technologies."[45] Hence, a number of religious thinkers from Jewish and Christian traditions make justice a primary concern in assessing matters of technology and bioethics.

Thus, where mainstream and philosophically oriented public discourse on bioethics often attends first to issues of consent and autonomy, and relegates justice to a subsidiary position, there is reason to think that in some biblically based traditions, the requirements of justice would get pride of place. Justice would not be the last principle, but the first.[46]

Implications

Because the field of bioethics in general has gained such an interest in questions of justice, it is difficult to know whether the voice of religious bioethics can contribute something distinctive. Perhaps the most important contribution lies in the fact that secular and philosophical bioethicists have increasingly emphasized the importance of justice and have expanded the arena of justice questions. To those who have long advocated for justice as a central category of bioethics, it is heartening to find that justice language is permeating bioethical thinking.[47]

Still, I believe that attention to religious voices might bring something new into public discussion. In this chapter I try to illustrate that with attention to biblically based approaches to justice. Where mainstream bioethics still tends to relegate justice to questions of allocation of scarce resources or questions of access to new technologies, the biblical image of *sedakah* suggests that a major overhaul of the system might be needed. If justice requires not simply treating equals equally, but treating the marginalized and oppressed with special consideration, then some approaches to health care should get priority. For example, preventive medicine, which gets very little attention in bioethics today, might emerge as the preferred option. Basic nutrition and sanitation might be deemed more important than the building of neonatal intensive care units.[48] Further, if the epistemological privilege of the oppressed is taken seriously, the perspective from which biomedical practices are assessed would have to change.

The language of liberation and oppression that is central to biblically based theological understandings of justice has not yet permeated philosophical discussions in bioethics. There, justice is still understood within the rubrics of equality of treatment and justification of inequalities. Attention to liberation as a central category might also affect public policy; rather than focusing on patients' "rights," for example, the discussion might attend to structures that oppress patients and how to liberate them from such oppression. Such discussions do occur in feminist philosophical discussions of bioethics, and there is mutual enrichment between theological views and these feminist views.

Though the entire field of bioethics has begun to use the language of justice with some seriousness, therefore, the religious voice may contribute a particular emphasis that would influence public policy in certain directions. This can be seen, for example, in the strong advocacy for the disadvantaged in studies such as Robert Veatch's *The Foundations of Justice*.[49] It is a distinctive theological contribution that all systems and structures must be assessed by how they impact on the "poorest of the poor." To be sure, the perspective that takes the disadvantaged as a baseline for measuring justice is not missing altogether in contemporary philosophy. It is no mistake that theologians have found resonances with their concerns in the so-called difference principle of Rawls's massive *A Theory of Justice*. Rawls's proposal for a principle that would require that differences in income or wealth work to the benefit of the least advantaged bears resemblances to the theological concern for the oppressed. But it is not clear in Rawls's work whether the difference principle requires only that the least advantaged have more in "absolute" terms than they had before, or whether they must be advantaged in *relative* terms, thus closing the gap between rich and poor. In the biblical tradition, the standard for justice is very clear: gaps between the rich and poor are taken as ipso facto signs of injustice that require rectification.[50] Justice takes priority, and justice requires nothing less than full "right relationship," even if that means an overthrow of the current system. Thus, in the ongoing discussion of justice in bioethics, the field is indebted to the insights of theology and might yet benefit from attention to categories that are not uniquely theological but have received more emphasis and attention in theological circles than in mainstream philosophical bioethics.

NOTES

1. Tom L. Beauchamp and James F. Childress, *Principles of Biomedical Ethics*, 5th ed. (New York: Oxford University Press, 2001).

2. Lisa Sowle Cahill, "The New Biotech World Order," *Hastings Center Report* 29, no.2 (1999): 45–48; Ruth R. Faden et al., "Public Stem Cell Banks: Considerations of Justice in Stem Cell Research and Therapy," *Hastings Center Report* 33, no. 6 (2003): 13–27.

3. Alasdair MacIntyre, *After Virtue* (Notre Dame, Ind.: University of Notre Dame Press, 1981), p. 2.

4. See George Parkin Grant, *English-Speaking Justice* (Notre Dame, Ind.: University of Notre Dame Press, 1985).

5. The National Commission for the Protection of Human Subjects of Biomedi-

cal and Behavioral Research, *The Belmont Report: Ethical Principles and Guidelines for the Protection of Human Subjects of Research*, DHEW Publication No. (OS) 78–0012, 1978.

6. John Rawls, *A Theory of Justice*, rev. ed. (Cambridge, Mass.: Harvard University Press, 1999); Robert Nozick, *Anarchy, State, and Utopia* (New York: Basic Books, 1974); Michael Walzer, *Spheres of Justice: A Defense of Pluralism and Equality* (New York: Basic Books, 1983).

7. See, for example, the President's Commission for the Study of Ethical Problems in Medicine and Biomedical and Behavioral Research, *Securing Access to Health Care: A Report on the Ethical Implications of Differences in the Availability of Health Services, Vol. 1: Report* (Washington, D.C.: U.S. Government Printing Office, 1983).

8. Beauchamp and Childress, *Principles of Biomedical Ethics*, p. 226.

9. See, for example, John F. Kilner, *Who Lives? Who Dies? Ethical Criteria in Patient Selection* (New Haven, Conn.: Yale University Press, 1990).

10. Beauchamp and Childress, *Principles of Biomedical Ethics*, p. 227.

11. James F. Drane, "Character and the Moral Life: A Virtue Approach to Biomedical Ethics," in *A Matter of Principles: Ferment in U.S. Bioethics*, ed. Edwin R. Dubose et al. (Valley Forge, Pa.: Trinity, 1994), p. 286.

12. See, for example, Edmund D. Pellegrino and David C. Thomasma, *For the Patient's Good: The Restoration of Beneficence in Health Care* (New York: Oxford University Press, 1988).

13. Drane, "Character and the Moral Life," p. 304.

14. Josef Pieper, *The Four Cardinal Virtues* (Notre Dame, Ind.: University of Notre Dame, 1966).

15. John R. Donahue, S. J., "Biblical Perspectives on Justice," in *The Faith that Does Justice: Examining the Christian Sources for Social Change*, ed. John C. Haughey (New York: Paulist Press, 1977).

16. Pieper, *The Four Cardinal Virtues*, p. 64.

17. Benjamin Freedman, *Duty and Healing: Foundations of a Jewish Bioethics* (New York: Routledge, 1999). It is particularly noteworthy that Western philosophical traditions often stress *rights* whereas religious traditions have often stressed *duties*. However, there is also a strong stress on human rights in Catholic social teachings.

18. Gene Outka, "Social Justice and Equal Access to Health Care," in *On Moral Medicine: Theological Perspectives in Medical Ethics*, ed. Stephen E. Lammers and Allen Verhey (Grand Rapids, Mich.: Eerdmans, 1987).

19. Sharon Ringe, *Jesus, Liberation, and the Biblical Jubilee* (Philadelphia: Fortress, 1985).

20. Carter Heyward, *The Redemption of God: A Theology of Mutual Relation* (New York: University Press of America, 1982).

21. William Coats, *God in Public: Political Theology beyond Niebuhr* (Grand Rapids, Mich.: Eerdmans, 1974), p. 43.

22. Audrey R. Chapman, "Should We Design Our Dependents?" *Journal of the Society of Christian Ethics* 23, no. 2 (fall/winter 2003): 201.

23. Rawls, *A Theory of Justice*, p. 7.

24. Mary Daly, *Gyn/Ecology: The Metaethics of Radical Feminism* (Boston: Beacon, 1978).

25. See, for example, Jong-Sun Noh, *Liberating God for Minjung* (Seoul, Korea: Hanul Academy, 1994).

26. Allan Aubrey Boesak, *Farewell to Innocence* (Maryknoll, N.Y.: Orbis, 1977), p. 19.

27. See Donal Dorr, *Option for the Poor: A Hundred Years of Vatican Social Teaching* (Maryknoll, N.Y.: Orbis, 1983); Karen Lebacqz, *Justice in an Unjust World* (Minneapolis: Augsburg, 1987). See also Karen Lebacqz, "Justice," in *Christian Ethics: An Introduction*, ed. Bernard Hoose (London: Cassell, 1998).

28. Iris Marion Young, *Justice and the Politics of Difference* (Princeton, N.J.: Princeton University Press, 1990).

29. See, for example, Lebacqz, *Justice in an Unjust World*. An early and outspoken theologian who linked justice with oppression was Martin Luther King Jr. See *A Testament of Hope: The Essential Writings of Martin Luther King, Jr.* (New York: HarperCollins, 1991).

30. Faden et al., "Public Stem Cell Banks," p. 23.

31. For example, see Karen Lebacqz, "Bio-Ethics: Some Challenges from a Liberation Perspective," in *Faith and Science in an Unjust World: Report of the World Council of Churches Conference on Faith, Science, and the Future, Vol. 1: Plenary Presentations*, ed. Roger Shinn, (Geneva: World Council of Churches, 1980); see also Emilie M. Townes, *Breaking the Fine Rain of Death: African-American Health Issues and a Womanist Ethic of Care* (New York: Continuum, 1998).

In the fifth edition of Beauchamp and Childress's massively successful and influential *Principles of Biomedical Ethics*, "oppression" gets only two mentions, both in passing.

32. Lebacqz, *Justice in an Unjust World*.

33. Reinhold Niebuhr, *Moral Man and Immoral Society* (New York: Charles Scribner's Sons, 1932).

34. See, for example, Rosemarie Tong, *Feminist Approaches to Bioethics: Theoretical Reflections and Practical Applications* (Boulder, Colo.: Westview, 1997). Feminists are not the only ones who have attended to issues of power, however; see Alastair V. Campbell, *Health as Liberation: Medicine, Theology, and the Quest for Justice* (Cleveland, Ohio: Pilgrim, 1995).

35. In more recent editions, Beauchamp and Childress have added a discussion of concepts such as veracity, confidentiality, and fidelity; however, these have not gained the same status as the primary principles. The tendency to list justice last is followed by Robert M. Veatch in *A Theory of Medical Ethics* (New York: Basic Books, 1981). H. Tristram Engelhardt, in *The Foundations of Bioethics* (New York: Oxford University Press, 1996), p. 121, presents bioethics as a clash between beneficence and autonomy and views justice as at root a concern for beneficence.

36. Geron Ethics Advisory Board, "Research with Human Embryonic Stem Cells: Ethical Considerations," *Hastings Center Report* 29, no. 2 (1999): 31–36.

37. Ruth R. Faden and Tom L. Beauchamp, *A History and Theory of Informed Consent* (New York: Oxford University Press, 1986).

38. It is important to note here that Buddhist tradition might differ significantly from Jewish and Christian traditions. All three traditions emphasize compassion, but the stress on justice may be more peculiar to biblical traditions. Hence, I am offering a theological view rather than a general religious view, and I do not presume that my view is compatible with all religious traditions.

39. Pope Paul VI, Pastoral Constitution on the Church in the Modern World (*Gaudium et Spes*), 1965, #69 (www.vatican.va/archive/hist_councils/II_vatical _council/documents/vat-II_cons_19651207_gaudium-et-spes_en.html).

40. Gustavo Gutierrez is often credited with being the father of Latin American liberation theology. See Gustavo Gutierrez, *A Theology of Liberation* (Maryknoll, N.Y.:

Orbis, 1973); see also Robert McAfee Brown, *Gustavo Gutierrez: An Introduction to Liberation Theology* (Maryknoll, N.Y.: Orbis, 1990).

41. Jose Porfirio Miranda, *Marx and the Bible: A Critique of the Philosophy of Oppression* (Maryknoll, N.Y.: Orbis, 1974).

42. See Stephen Charles Mott, *Biblical Ethics and Social Change* (New York: Oxford University Press, 1982); and Nicholas Wolterstorff, *Until Justice and Peace Embrace* (Grand Rapids, Mich.: Eerdmans, 1983).

43. Chapman, "Should We Design Our Dependents?" p. 201.

44. Karen Lebacqz, "Theology, Justice, and Health Care: An International Conundrum," in *The Relevance of Theology: Nathan Soderblom and the Development of an Academic Discipline*, ed. Carl Reinhold Brakenhielm and Gunhild Winqvist Hollman (Uppsala, Sweden: Uppsala University Press), p. 118.

45. Chapman, "Should We Design Our Dependents?" p. 201.

46. At the same time, it must be acknowledged that theological thinkers do not always place justice first. Some key works in theological bioethics follow the mainstream in placing justice last. For example, in the massive and important collection *On Moral Medicine: Theological Perspectives in Medical Ethics* (Grand Rapids, Mich.: Eerdmans, 1987), editors Stephen E. Lammers and Allen Verhey place the section on considerations of justice last in the volume. It is possible that differences in the stress on justice are attributable to a growing recognition of the importance of justice in both philosophical and theological ethics.

47. For example, when I did a study of ethical dimensions in clinical studies under the auspices of the Program for the Study of Health Care Relationships, a collaborative program of Yale University and the University of Connecticut, I found that justice issues, and particularly concerns for the marginalized and oppressed, appeared to underlie the convictions and design of the clinical studies in almost all studies included in the program.

48. A strong argument for shifting priorities emerges in Townes's *Breaking the Fine Rain of Death*.

49. Robert M. Veatch, *The Foundations of Justice: Why the Retarded and the Rest of Us Have Claims to Equality* (New York: Oxford University Press, 1986). Veatch draws on theological ethics and attends to questions of oppression; by contrast, ten years later, the study by Daniels et al., drawing only on philosophical notions of justice, does not attend to oppression as a category. See Norman Daniels et al., *Benchmarks of Fairness for Health Care Reform* (New York: Oxford University Press, 1996).

50. For example, in *Ownership: Early Christian Teaching* (Maryknoll, N.Y.: Orbis, 1983), Charles Avila notes that, almost without exception, the early church "fathers" saw almsgiving as a matter of *justice*, not simply of mercy. Later church fathers concur: in *Quadragesimo Anno*, Part II, Section 3, Pope Pius XI asserted that the immense numbers of poor people and the superabundant riches of the few provide "an unanswerable argument" that goods are "far from rightly distributed and equitably shared."

12

"No Harm, No Harassment": Major Principles of Health Care Ethics in Islam

Abdulaziz Sachedina

Islam as a comprehensive religious-moral system does not divide the public space in terms of spiritual and secular domains with separate jurisdictions. Rather, it strives to integrate the two realms to provide total guidance about the way human beings ought to live with one another and with themselves as citizens, or professionals, or workers of one kind or another, or simply as human beings. Muslim ethics tries to make sense of human moral instincts, institutions, and traditions in order to provide a plausible perspective on the making of moral judgments, the fashioning of rules and principles, and devising of a virtuous life. Its judgments are ethical in the sense that they deal with the sense of what reasonable people count as good and bad, praiseworthy and blameworthy, in human relationships and human institutions. Ultimate questions connected with human suffering through illness and other afflictions, reproduction and abortion, death and dying are within the purview of its religiously based ethics. Human beings are essentially God's creatures, and, hence, their total welfare related to this and the next world is within the domain of religious deliberations.

How do Muslims solve their ethical problems in biomedicine? Are there any distinctive theories or principles in Islamic ethics that Muslims apply in deriving moral judgments in bioethics? Is the sacred law, the Shari'a, which is regarded as an integral part of Islamic ethics, the only recognized source of ethical judgments in Islam? What is the role of human experience/intuitive reasoning in moral justification? This chapter will be devoted to an exploration of these questions and their answers.

The Nature of Islamic Juridical-Ethical Discourse

Legal-ethical decisions in Islamic law are determined by concerns of justice and public good. The problem arises as to the authority that can define the parameters of justice and public good. Since there is no organized "church" in Islam, the responsibility falls on Muslim scholars of legal tradition. In dealing with immediate questions about issues in biomedicine, Muslim jurists draw on legal doctrines and rules in addition to analogical reasoning based on paradigm cases. The practical judgments or legal opinions, known as *fatāwa*, reflect the insights of a jurist who has been able to connect cases to an appropriate set of linguistic and rational principles and rules that actually provide keys to a valid conclusion of a case under consideration.

Undoubtedly, the enunciation of underlying ethical principles and rules that govern practical ethical decisions is crucial for making any religious perspective an intellectually insightful voice in the ongoing debate about a morally defensible ethics of biomedicine cross-culturally. Given that all cultures share such moral principles as beneficence or nonmaleficence, all require rules including truthfulness and confidentiality as essential elements in regulating responsible physician-patient relationship, yet there are major issues that generate controversy on a global scale such as the right of a woman to decide about terminating her pregnancy, discrimination against ethnic and religious minorities, recognition of respect for individual autonomy against competing moral considerations of the community, and so on. What kind of ethical resources do different traditions possess to provide internationally collaborative efforts in creating a common ethical discourse to resolve issues in biomedicine?[1]

The Question of Cultural Relativism in Ethical Values

To be sure, ethical values seek cultural legitimacy by adapting themselves in prevailing economic and political circumstances. Accordingly, these values can hardly be expected to be free from cultural relativity. Since human reason depends on information gleaned from experience to make correct ethical judgments, moral presuppositions operative in society interact with the specific experience to provide culturally conditioned moral justification.[2] In fact most objectivist ethical theories, which affirm that value has a real existence in particular things or acts, regardless of the opinion of any judge or observer, include a certain aspect of social or conventional relativism. In the highly politicized debates about the applicability of the International Bill of Human Rights, cultural relativism figures prominently in the arguments made by the non-Western nations against the charter's ethnocentric language that defies its absolute application across cultures.[3] Similar arguments against universalizability of a single bioethical theory in the inherently pluralistic ethical discourse are commonly heard in national and international biomedical ethics conferences.

However, there is already an intellectual movement to search for "metacultural" ethics, which can ameliorate the negative effects of the overemphasis laid on cultural relativism in the areas of human rights as well as medical ethics. There is a growing effort in the international community to adopt a more or less transcultural framework of ethical principles and rules that could engage theologians, scholars, and policymakers in the health profession in a dialogical mode to search for solutions to the ethical problems in biomedical technology and research across nations. Is such an ethical framework and dialogue among traditions to enunciate underlying moral principles and applicable rules feasible?

In this chapter, my purpose is not merely to search for Islamic equivalents of the primary principles of autonomy, nonmaleficence, beneficence (including utility), and justice expounded by Beauchamp and Childress in the context of Western-American culture characterized by deeply ingrained with distinctly Western values of empirical science, principle-based ethics, and the democratic political philosophy. Rather, I intend to make a strong case for distinctly Islamic, and yet cross-culturally communicable, principle-based deontological-teleological ethics[4] that is operative within the Muslim social-cultural context in assessing moral problems in Islamic biomedical ethics.

The process has already begun in Egypt and Iran, where religious scholars, medical professionals, and the government are searching for ontological foundations of Islamic law to enable them to make authentic choices of what is morally and legally justifiable conduct in biomedical research and practice and its application in the Muslim society. I mention Egypt and Iran only because these are the only Muslim countries where religious scholars (ulema) are engaged in formulating national policies related to health care. In Iran, one can even observe the relative independence enjoyed by religious scholars from government interference in formulating their judicial decisions. Accordingly, there the function of the Muslim jurists is not merely to provide endorsement of the decisions made by the government, as happens in Saudi Arabia or, to a lesser extent, in Egypt, for instance. In these latter countries, since the religious authority is under the direct control of the government, usually the dissenting opinion against the fait accompli is repressed. In the case of Pakistan,[5] there seems to be a wide gulf between medical professionals and the religious scholars, to allow for practical Islamic guidance to emerge in the area of imported medical technology and the government policy to that effect.

The important thing that deserves serious consideration in Islamic context is that even when the source of normative life was believed to have been revealed by God in the Shari'a, the procuring of a judgment and its application was dependent upon reasons used in moral deliberation. This moral deliberation took into account particular human conditions, which affected the way Muslims justified an action to be moral. In other words, Islamic law developed its rulings within the pluralistic cultural and historical experience of Muslims and non-Muslims living in the different parts of the Islamic world. It recognized the autonomy of other moral systems within its sphere of influence, without imposing its judgments on peoples whose cultural beliefs and practices were at variance with its own. More important, it recognized the validity of differing interpretations of the same revealed system within the community, thereby giving rise to different schools of legal thought and practice in Islam. In the absence of an organized "church," or a theological body that speaks for the entire tradition or the community, as a source for the normative and paradigmatic religious system, Islam was and remains inherently discursive and pluralistic in its methods of deliberation and justification of moral actions. Hence, on the basis of particular application of principles and rules to emerging ethical issues, like a woman's right to abortion following a rape or incest, it is possible to observe differing judicial opinions toward which speculation over the interpretation of scriptural sources that preserve paradigm cases and the principles that were applied to discover them has led.

Islamic Ethical Discourse

When one considers the normative Islamic tradition for standards of conduct and character, it becomes obvious that besides the scriptural sources like the Qur'an and the Tradition (*sunna*) ascribed to the founder of Islam, which prescribe many rules of law and morality for humans, Muslim scholars recognized the value of decisions derived from specific human conditions as equally valid source for social ethics in Islam. But how exactly was human intellectual endeavor to be directed to discover the effective cause, the philosophy and the purpose behind certain paradigm rulings provided in divine commandments, in order to utilize these to formulate rational deductive principles for future decisions?

The question had important implications for the jurists who were faced with practical necessity to make justifiable legal rulings, which could be defended against accusations of making arbitrary decisions. There was a fear of reason in deriving the details of law. The fear was based on the presumption that if independent human reason could judge what is right and wrong, it could rule on what God could rightly prescribe for humans. In other words, human reasoning could arrogate the function that was in large measure within the jurisdiction of revelation. However, it was admitted that although revealed law can be known through reason and can aid human beings in cultivating the moral life, human intelligence was not capable enough to discover what the reason for a particular law is, let alone demonstrate the truth of a particular assertion of the divine commandment. In fact, as these theologian jurists asserted, the divine commandments to which one must adhere if one is to achieve specific end prescribed in the revealed law are not objectively accessible to human beings through reason. Moreover, judgments of reason were arbitrary, as demonstrated by the fact of their contradicting each other, and reflected personal desire of the legal expert.

Besides the problem of resolving substantive role of reason in understanding the implicit effective cause of a paradigm case and elaborating the juridical dimension of revelation as it relates to the conduct of human affairs in public and private spheres, there was a problem of situating the credible religious authority empowered to provide validation to the ethical-legal reasoning associated with the derived philosophy behind legal rulings. On the one hand, following the lead of the Sunni jurists like Shāfiʿī and Ibn Ḥanbal in the tenth and eleventh centuries C.E., Sunni Islam located that authority in the Qurʾan and the Tradition. These scholars represented the predominant schools of Sunni theology that held that in deciding questions of Islamic law one could work out an entire system based on juridical elaboration of Islamic revelation and the Tradition. On the other hand, following the line of thought maintained by the Shiʿite Imams, Shiʿite Islam located that authority in the rightful successors of the Prophet. The Shiʿite Imams maintained that there was an ongoing revelatory guidance available in the expository ability of human reason in comprehending the divine revelation exemplified by the solutions offered by the Shiʿite religious leadership.

In general, Muslim theologians paid more attention to the nature of God and of creation and of human beings' relation to God as the Creator, Lawgiver, and Judge. They were also interested in the extent of divine power and human freedom of will as it affected the search for right prescription for human behavior. In the final analysis, in view of the absence of the institutionalized religious body that could provide the necessary validation of the legal-moral decisions on all matters pertaining to human existence, the problem of determining the Sacred Lawgiver's intent behind juridical-ethical rulings that had direct relevance to the social life of the community was not an easy task. The entire intellectual activity related to Islamic law can be summed up as a jurist's attempt to relate specific moral-legal rulings to the divine purposes expressed in the form of norms and rules in the Qurʾan and the Tradition, but this did not proceed without ambiguities. In view of incomplete state of their knowledge about present circumstances and future contingencies of human conditions, in most cases of ethical judgment, the jurists proceeded with a cautious attitude on the basis of what seemed most likely to be the case. Such ethical judgments were appended with a clear, pious statement that the ruling lacked certainty because only God was aware of the circumstances and consequences affecting human beings.[6]

Sometimes the effective causes that discovered the rulings were derived directly from the explicit statements of the Qurʾan and the Tradition that set forth the purpose of legislation. At other times, human reasoning discovered the relationship between the ruling and the effective cause, in order to provide sound theoretical basis for jurisprudence. However, the jurists admitted and determined the substantive role of human reasoning in making valid legal or moral decisions. Moreover, admission of reasoning as a discoverer of a legal-ethical judgment depended upon the jurist's comprehension of the nature of ethical knowledge and the means by which humans can access information about good and evil. In other words, legal reasoning depended upon the way the human act was defined in terms of human ethical discernment about good and evil and the relation of human act to God's will. In an important way, any advocacy of reason as a substantive rather than formal source for procuring moral-legal verdicts required authorization derived from religious sources like the Qur'an and the Tradition. In the Qur'an, a teleological view of human being with the very ability to use reason to discover God's will is possible to maintain, more particularly when the revelation itself endorses reflection on the reasons for revealed laws as well as obeying them. Without the endorsement of the revelation, reason could not become an independent source of moral-legal decisions.

This precautious attitude toward reason has its roots in the belief that God's knowledge of the circumstances and of the consequences in any situation of ethical dilemma confronted by human existence is exhaustive and infallible. Whereas the Qur'an and the Tradition had provided the underlying justification for some moral-legal rulings when declaring them obligatory or prohibited, on a number of issues the rulings were expressed as divine commands which had to be obeyed without knowing the reasons behind them. Thus, for instance, the effective cause for the duty of seeking medical treatment is to avoid grave and irremediable harm to oneself, whereas the reason for prohibition against taking human life is the sanctity of life as declared by the revelation. The commandments were simply part of God's prerogative as the Creator to demand unquestioning obedience to them. To act in a manner contrary to divine commands is to act both immorally and unlawfully. The major issue in legal thought, then, was related to the defining of the admissibility and the parameters of human reasoning as a substantive source for legal-moral decisions. Can reason discover the divine will in confronting emerging legal-ethical issues without succumbing to human self-interest?

Rationalist and Traditionalist Ethical Reasoning in the Sacred Law—the Shari'a

The enunciation of legal-ethical principles thus begins with the jurists' elaboration of the sources of Islamic law. Central to this discussion was the analytical treatment of the twin concepts of justice ('adāla, usually defined as "putting something in its appropriate place") and obligation (wujūb, sometimes defined as "promulgation of divine command and prohibition"). The concept of justice provided a theoretical stance on the question of human obedience to divine commands and the extent of human capacity in carrying out the moral-religious obligations. The concept of obligation defined the nature of divine command and provided deontological grounds for complying with it. The commandments have reasons of their own that can be explained in terms of the function they fulfill for the good of humankind.

Gradually, two responses emerged to the pressing need of providing consistent and authentic guidance in the matter of social ethics. Some prominent jurists of the tenth and eleventh centuries C.E. maintained that in deciding questions on which there was no specific guidance available from the normative sources of Islamic law and ethics, judges and lawyers had to make their own rational judgments independently of the revelation. This was certainly the case when the law, being stated in general terms, did not provide for the peculiarity of situations. Other jurists disapproved of this rational method not adequately anchored in the normative writings, and insisted that no legal or moral judgment was valid if not based on the revelation, both the Qur'an and the Tradition. There was no way for humanity to know the meaning of justice outside the divine revelation. In fact, they contended, justice is nothing but carrying out the requirements of the revealed law. It was the revealed law, the Shari'a, that provided the scales for justice in all those actions that were declared as morally and legally obligatory. At the end of the day, the latter traditionalist thesis became the standard view held by the majority of the Sunni Muslims. The Shi'ite Muslims, on the other hand, maintained the rationalist thesis about the fundamentality of intuitive reason in ethical epistemology with some adjustment in conformity to their doctrine about supreme religious authority of the Imam, who could and did arbitrate in cases that confounded human intellect in offering a resolution.

However, the role of ethical principles in deriving moral judgments was articulated in greater detail by the theologians who, too, were divided on the same lines as the jurists: those who supported the substantive role of reason in knowing what is right and obligatory; and those who argued in favor of the revelation as the primary source of ethical knowledge. In other words, ethical reasoning is directly related to religious epistemology in Islamic thought. Ethical objectivism or deontological theory, with its thesis that human being can know much of what is right and wrong because of the intrinsic goodness or badness of actions is connected with the rationalist ethicist Mu'tazilite theologians; whereas ethical voluntarism, the traditionalist ethics, which denied that anything objective in human acts themselves that would make them right or wrong, is connected with Ash'arite theologians.[7]

Very early on, scholars of jurisprudence were led to distinguish between duties to God (*'ibādāt* = "ritual duties") and duties to fellow human beings (*mu'āmalāt* = "social transactions"). Ritual duties were not conditioned by specific human conditions, and hence were absolutely binding. Social transactions were necessarily conditioned by human existence in specific social and political context, and, hence, adjustable to the needs of time. It was in the latter sphere of interpersonal relations that the jurists needed to provide fresh rulings generated by the changing human conditions. The entire area of social ethics in Islam falls under the *mu'āmalāt* sections of jurisprudence. However, authoritative decisions in matters of social ethics could not be derived without first determining the nature of human acts under obligation (*taklīf*). The divine command, understood in terms of religious-moral obligation (*taklīf*), provided the entire ethical code of conduct and a teleological view of human and the world. More pertinent, violation of divine command, as Muslim jurists taught, is immoral on the grounds that it interferes with the pursuit of human goal of achieving perfection that would guarantee salvation in the Hereafter. Ultimately, human salvation is directly connected with human conduct—the subject matter of legal-theological ethics.

Legal and Theological Ethics in Islam

Islamic law is concerned with human conduct. It pertains to the total welfare of human being. Human perfection involves having a correct belief and a noble moral quality. This perfection guarantees the good end in this and the next world. In this latter sense, human perfection is salvific because it strengthens the bond between God and humanity. Hence, the revealed law of Islam is concerned with apprehending the divine wisdom through the study of rules derived from revelatory sources for the acts of people under legal-moral obligation.

Every class of act, whether incumbent, recommended, permitted, disapproved, or forbidden by God, is founded upon explicit or implicit rules in the Qur'an or the Tradition. Thus, Islamic law, as a religious science, is theoretically able to discover the divine judgment on every class of human act in the area of ritual duties and social transactions. But Islamic law also investigates the revelatory sources, the Qur'an, the Tradition, and the consensus of the learned for their validity and evidentiary use in deducing fresh legal-moral prescriptions. This part of the law is concerned with the science of legal principles (*uṣūl al-fiqh*) or jurisprudence. Islamic jurisprudence is an inquiry into the principles of normative ethical judgments on external human acts. The philosophical aspects of ethics of action are concerned with fundamental questions about whether reason on its own can rule things necessary, good, or evil.[8]

The Principles and Rules in Islamic Juristic Ethics

Theological debates about ethical evaluation of human actions and of the nature of human beings as moral agents were foundational to the development of Islamic jurisprudence. The consideration of ethical good and prevention of evil as known to the sound mind made the legal doctrines adaptable to the contemporary legal problems and issues. The ultimate purpose of the legal deliberations entailed doing justice and preserving people's best interest on earth and in the hereafter. How was that purpose to be fulfilled when all possible human contingencies in the future were not covered in the revelation, whether the Qur'an or the Tradition?

Here paradigm cases (preserved in the form of a *ḥadīth*) played a critical role as discoverers of divine purposes for human institutions. Contrary to commonsense expectations that the application of judicial decisions must be posterior to the prior elaboration of legal theory, Islamic jurisprudence actually antedated the genre of paradigm cases. Muslim scholars were able to appropriate these paradigm cases to resolve more immediate cases because these cases had the backing of the consensus built upon the practice of the community. The legal decisions preserved in the paradigm cases marks a transition point wherein the cumulative tradition, the Sunna, was utilized to document substantive law. As precedents for subsequent legal decisions, these cases indicated the underlying effective cause upon which depended the final judgment in those cases. Such cases became the sources for the development of juridical principles and rules. The novel issues were then settled through the evocation of these principles and rules.

At other times principles like justice and equity that were stated directly and in most general terms in the revelation were to be applied to concrete situations in Muslim society to determine the level of culpability in cases of violation of justice. The intellectual responsibility of a Muslim legal expert included providing the definition of the nature of religiously prescribed justice and its determination in the given context of a particular case whether it was distributive or corrective. Moreover, he had to determine whether the scale of violation necessitated financial or other forms of compensations recognized in the penal system. Undoubtedly, a major part of a Muslim jurist's training dealt with learning these principles and rules in the context of the Qur'an and the Tradition to offer new methods of approach to problem solving in the society.

In the context of this chapter we need to determine the most important juridical doctrines and principles that have been evoked in the contemporary situation to provide the necessary solutions to novel issues in biomedicine.

Islamic Principles of Bioethics

In our discussion about the ethical theories known among the Muslims, human reason and its substantive role in deriving legal-ethical decisions, whether through the references to the relevant principles or prescriptive precedents, occupied a central place. Sunni Muslim ethicists assigned a minimal and, to a certain extent, formal role for reason to discover the correlation between divine command and human good. Here, precedents derived from the revelation served as paradigmatic cases for casuistic decisions. Moreover, ethical reflection occurred within the Tradition as a process of discernment of principles that were embedded in propositional statements in the form of rulings (fatāwa) as well as approved practice of the earlier jurists. The relationship between legal-ethical judgments and the principles in such cases is overshadowed by reference to revelation, however far-fetched it might appear. It is important to keep in mind that for Sunni Muslims, knowledge of rules of law and ethics is anchored in divine revelation and not in human intuitive reason ('aql). The process of deriving rules from revelation is founded upon interpretation of texts. In this sense, Islamic law is a body of positive rules by virtue of the formulations of jurists based on the revealed texts rather than the dictates of their own intuition. The exposition of law depended on text-oriented approach, although a great deal of positive law in the area of interpersonal relations was derived from individual discretion in employing intuitive reasoning.

The substantive role for reason was maintained by Muslim ethicists belonging to the Shi'ite school of thought who saw human reason capable of not only discovering the divine purposes for human society, but also establishing the correlation between human moral judgment and the divine commandment. They identified the major principles and rules ensuing from both revelation and rational sources that could be used to make fresh decisions in all areas of interpersonal relationships. In other words, these principles and rules became general action guides to determine the ethical valuation of an act and declare it as incumbent or necessary, prohibited, permitted, recommended, or reprehensible in the context of specific circumstances. But the process of ethical reflection did not necessarily involve unchanging norms from which other rules or judgments were deduced. Rather, it involved a dialectical progression between the insights and beliefs of the jurists and the paradigmatic cases in the revelation that embedded principles and rules for solving particular cases. Nevertheless, there were certain principles that transcended relative circumstances in history and tradition and which became the source for solving contemporary moral problems.

However, there was no unanimity among representatives of four major schools of Sunni legal thought (Mālikī, Ḥanafī, Shāfi'ī, and Ḥanbalī) regarding the principles nor that these principles were derived from foundational, rationalistically established moral theories from which other principles and legal-moral judgments were deduced. Rather, scholars from different legal schools identified several principles, often but not always the same ones. Since the language of Shari'a is the language of obligation or duty the primary principles (qawā'id uṣūl) and rules (qawā'id fiqhī) in Islamic ethics are stated as obligations and their derivatives, respectively. Some jurists have identified principles to encompass both principles and rules and have indicated the primary and the subsidiary distinction in their application to particular cases.

Two such intellectual sources in Muslim jurisprudence were: istiḥsān (prioritization of two or more equally valid judgments through juristic practice) and istiṣlāḥ (promoting and securing benefits and preventing and removing harms in public sphere). These represented independent juristic judgment of expedience or public utility. However, the legitimacy of employing these reason-based sources depended upon their assimilation into the textual sources.

Thus, for instance, the duty to avoid literal enforcement of the existing law, which may prove detrimental in certain situations, has given rise to the principle of "juristic preference."[9] This juridical method of prioritization of legal rulings taking into account the concrete circumstances of a case at hand has played a significant role in providing the necessary adaptability to Islamic law to meet the changing needs of society. However, the methodology is founded upon an important principle derived from the directive of "circumventing of hardship," stated in the Qur'an in no uncertain terms: "God intends facility for you, and He does not want to put you in hardship"(2:185). This directive is further reinforced by the tradition that states: "The best of your law (dīn) is that which brings ease to the people." In other words, the principle of "juristic preference" allows formulating a decision that sidesteps an established precedent in order to uphold a higher obligation of implementing the ideals of fairness and justice without causing unnecessary hardship to the people involved. The obvious conclusion to be drawn from God's intention to provide help and remove hardship is that the essence of these principles is their adaptability to meet the exigencies of every time and place on the basis of public interest. In the absence of any textual injunction in the Qur'an and the Tradition, the principle of "necessity overrides prohibition" furnishes an authoritative basis for deriving a fresh ruling.

The limited scope of this chapter does not permit us to undertake to identify all the principles that are applied to make juridical decisions in various fields of interpersonal relations in Islamic law. What seems to be most useful and feasible is to identify a number of fundamental Islamic principles that are in some direct and indirect ways discerned through the general principle of *maṣlaḥa*, that is, "public good." This principle is evoked in providing solutions to majority of novel issues in biomedical ethics. The rational obligation to weigh and balance an action's possible benefits against its cost and possible harms is central to social transactions in general and biomedical ethics in particular. As stated earlier, Islamic juridical studies are undertaken to understand the effective causes that underlie some juridical decisions that deal with primary and fundamental moral obligations. The principles to be elaborated in this chapter are not necessarily the same in priority or significance as those recognized, for instance, in Western bioethics, namely, respect for autonomy, nonmaleficence, beneficence (including utility), and justice. In comparison, Islamic principles overlap in important respects but differ in others. For instance, the two distinct obligations of beneficence and nonmaleficence in some Western systems are viewed as a single principle of nonmaleficence in Islam on the basis of the overlapping between the two obligations in the Tradition: "In Islam there shall be no harm inflicted or reciprocated" (*lā ḍarar wa lā ḍirār fī al-islām*). This is the principle of "No harm, no harassment."[10] Moreover, the principle of "Protection against distress and constriction" (*'usr wa al-ḥaraj*) applies to social relations and transactions, which must be performed in good faith but are independent of religion. There are also a number of derivative rules that are an important part of the Islamic system but are underemphasized in secular bioethics. Thus, among the derivative obligation is the rule of consultation (*shūrā*) as part of the Islamic communitarian ethics, against the dominant principle of autonomy based on liberal individualism.

Moreover, although this research is based on the rulings compiled from four major Sunni and one Shi'ite legal schools, I have attempted to identify only the most commonly referred principles or rules in biomedical jurisprudence without necessarily attributing them to one or the other school except when there has been fundamental disagreement on their inclusion in one or the other legal theory. These are the principles that have made possible the derivation of fresh rulings in bioethics by seeking to identify and balance probable outcomes in order to protect society from harms. In the last two decades, jurists belonging to all the Muslim legal schools have met regularly under the auspices of the Ministry of Health of their respective countries to formulate

their decisions as a collective body. Some of these new rulings have been published through the *Majma' al-fiqhī al-islāmī* (Islamic Juridical Council). A close
examination of the juridical decisions made in this council reveal the balancing
of likely benefits and harms to society as a whole. In addition, these decisions
indicate the search for proportionality (*tanāsub*) between individual and social
interests of the community and the need, in certain cases, to allow collective
interests to override individual interests and rights. The inherent tension in
such decisions is sometimes resolved by reference to a critical principle regarding the right of an individual to reject harm and harassment ("No harm,
no harassment"), which constrains unlimited application of the principle of
common good.

The Principle of Public Interest/Common Good (*Maṣlaḥa*)

Consideration of public interest or common good of the people has been an
important principle utilized by Muslim jurists for accommodating and incorporating new issues confronting the community. *Maṣlaḥa* has been admitted
as a principle of reasoning to derive new rulings or as a method of suspending
earlier rulings out of consideration for the interest and welfare of the community. However, its admission as an independent source for legislation has
been contested by some Sunni and Shi'ite legal scholars. To be sure, *maṣlaḥa*
is based on the notion that the ultimate goal of the Shari'a necessitates doing
justice and preserving people's best interests in this and the next world. But
who defines justice, and what is the most salutary for the people? Here theological ethics defines the parameters of *maṣlaḥa*.

Looking at the majority of the Muslims, who belong to the Sunni-Ash'ari
school of thought in its understanding of God's plan for humanity, one needs
to understand the Ash'arite view of what is the best for people. The Ash'arites,
who maintained the divine command ethics (the theistic subjectivism), confined the derivation of *maṣlaḥa* strictly from the revelatory sources, that is, the
Qur'an and the Tradition. Ghazzali (d. 1111), as an Ash'ari theologian-jurist,
elucidates this position in his legal theory:

> *Maṣlaḥa* is actually an expression for bringing about benefit
> (*manfa'a*) or forestalling harm (*maḍarra*). We do not consider [*maṣ-
> laḥa*] in the meaning of bringing about benefit or forestalling harm
> as part of [God's] purposes for the people or [God's] concern for the
> people, in order for them to achieve those purposes. Rather, we take
> *maṣlaḥa* in the meaning of protecting the ends of the Revelation (*al-
> shar'*). The ends of the Revelation for the people are five: To protect
> for them (1) their religion, (2) their lives (*nufūs*), (3) their reason
> (*'uqūl*), (4) their lineage (*nasl*), and, (5) their property (*māl*). All that
> guarantees the protection of these five purposes is *maṣlaḥa*; and all
> that undermines these purposes is *mafasada* (a source of detri-
> ment).[11]

Hence, justice, according to the Ash'arites, lies in the commission and application of what God had declared to be good and the avoidance of that which God had forbidden in these sacred sources. Moreover, ruling an action good or evil depends on the consideration of the general principles laid down in the revelation. Consequently, human responsibility is confined to the course ordained by God by seeking to institute what God declares good and shunning what God declares evil. Moreover, as far as the derivation of fresh rulings is concerned, the Ash'arites maintain that the principle of *maṣlaḥa* is internally operational in the rulings that reveal with certainty that in legislating them God has the welfare of humankind in mind.[12]

The estimation of the Mu'tazilite Sunni thinkers, who maintained objectivist rationalist ethics, was understandably at variance with the Ash'arites. Their thesis was founded upon human reason as capable of knowing *maṣlaḥa*—the consideration of public interest that promoted benefit and prevented harm. For them, *maṣlaḥa* was an inductive principle for the derivation of fresh decisions in an area for which the scriptural sources provided little or no guidance at all, and in which judgments had to depend upon an evolving moral life that takes into consideration previous moral struggles and reflection derived from particular cases and circumstances.

In the context of matters connected with social ethics, which deal with everyday contingencies of human life, it is important to keep in mind that whether the principle of common good originates internally in the scriptural sources or externally through intuitive reason, no jurist questions the conclusion that legal-ethical judgments are founded upon concern for human welfare and in order to protect people from corruption and harm. In other words, they maintain that God provides the guidance with a purpose of doing the most salutary for people, even when the exact method of deducing this general principle is in dispute.[13]

Some jurists have, for all intents and purposes, related all the ordinances back to the principle of common good by employing case-based reasoning that compared cases and analogically deduced moral-legal conclusions. Hence, for example, Shāṭibī (d. 1388 C.E.) maintained that promulgation of the ordinances took place by referring to the paradigm cases in the scriptural sources like the Qur'an and the Tradition that took into consideration the welfare of the people in this world and the next. This assertion that God has the interest of people in mind is dependent upon an authoritative proof that could determine the validity of the claim that the paradigm case reflects an underlying doctrine that God is bound to do the most salutary thing for his creatures. However, as Shāṭibī correctly points out, regardless of the doctrinal aspects of the principle of common good that are treated in theology proper, it is important to emphasize that the application of this principle in the legal theory permits and even fosters new moral insights and judgments in the Shari'a. The majority of contemporary jurists maintain the latter view and have produced evidence in their works on legal theory in support of the specific legal decisions analogically derived on the basis of the principle of public good.[14]

Shāṭibī provides several examples of ordinances from the Qur'an and the

Tradition that were instituted by God in keeping with people's good in this and the next world. Thus in justifying the rules of purity and ablutions, God says in the Qur'an: "God does not intend to make any impediment (*ḥaraj*) for you; but He desires to purify you, and that He may complete His blessings upon you" (Q. 5:6). In addition, the scriptural sources have made the corruptive aspects of this and the next world known to humanity so that it can protect itself from them. If one investigates the Tradition, one will find nothing but the fact that all religious and moral duties point to God's concern for the welfare of humanity.[15]

The Types of Issues Covered under the Principle of Public Good

In view of the above explanation about public good, this principle consists of each and every benefit that has been made known by the purposes stated in the divine revelation,[16] and because some jurists have essentially regarded public good as safeguarding the Lawgiver's purposes,[17] the jurists have discussed the principle both in terms of types and the purposes they serve. Some have classified public good in terms of types, while others have resorted to purposes for classification. For instance, among the Sunni jurists, Shāṭibī has treated the principle and its corollaries in great detail in his legal theory by pointing out that religious duties have been imposed on the people for their own good in view of the fulfillment of God's purposes for them. These purposes are discussed under three headings:

1. The Essentials or the Primary Needs (*al-ḍarūriyāt*): These are things that are promulgated for the good of this and the next world, such as providing health care to the poor and downtrodden. Such actions are necessary for maintaining public health and the good of people in this life and for earning reward in the next. Moreover, without them, life would be threatened, resulting in further suffering for people who cannot afford even the basic necessities of life. According to Muslim thinkers, the necessity to protect the essentials is felt across traditions among the followers of other religions, too. The good of the people is such a fundamental issue among all peoples that there is a consensus among them that when one member of a society suffers, others must work to relieve the afflicted.[18] Some jurists have claimed unanimity among all religions that among the essentials is the protection of all these five indispensable things (religion, life, reason, lineage, and property) that human beings need to maintain a good order and the prohibition against ignoring them.[19]

2. The General Needs (*al-ḥājiyāt*): These are things that enable human beings to improve their life and to remove those conditions which lead to chaos in one's familial and societal life in order to achieve higher standards of living, even though these necessities do not reach the level of essentials. These benefits are such that, if not attended, they lead to hardship and disorder, but not to corruption. This kind of common good is materialized in matters of religious duties, everyday life situations, interpersonal relationships, and a penal system

that prevents people from causing harm to others. As an example of religious duties, the Shari'a exempts a sick person or a traveler from performing certain obligations under those conditions; under the category of everyday situations the law permits undertaking transactions that are beneficial for one's advancement in life; under the category of interpersonal relationships the law allows all those dealings that are justly executed; and, under the penal system, the law imposes various penalties that deter people from committing crimes that hurt one and all.[20]

3. The Secondary Needs (*al-Tahsināt*): These are the things that are commonly regarded as praiseworthy in society, which also lead to the avoidance of those things that are regarded as blameworthy. They are also known as "noble virtues."[21] In other words, although these things do not qualify as "primary" or "general" needs, their goal is to improve the quality of life, to make them easily accessible to average member of a society, and even to embellish these noble virtues in order to render them more desirable.[22]

In terms of the principle's application, when a number of beneficial or corruptive aspects converge or when public good and corruption appear in the same instance, it gives rise to disagreement. For example, one of the issues in the Muslim world is assisted reproduction is sex selection. Sex selection is any practice, technique, or intervention intended to increase the likelihood of the conception, gestation, and birth of a child of one sex rather than the other. In the Muslim world, some parents prefer one sex above the other for cultural or financial reasons. Some jurists have argued in favor of sex selection, as long as no one, including the resulting child, is harmed. However, others have disputed the claim that it is possible for no harm to be done in sex selection. They point to violations of divine law, natural justice, and the inherent dignity of human beings. More important, permitting sex selection for nonmedical reasons involves or leads to unacceptable discrimination on grounds of sex and disability, potential psychological damage to the resulting children, and an inability to prevent a slide down the slippery slope toward permitting designer babies. In such cases, it becomes critical to assess the important criteria for the public good, or to lead the jurists to prioritize criteria that lead to public good or corruption, and provide the requisite ruling.

The Change of *Maṣlaḥa* and the Change of Rulings

One of the consequences of considering the public good is the inevitable change of laws in accord with changes of circumstances that require reassessment of what serves the people's interests and what causes corruption among them. Many precedents in the early history of the community, which serve as documentation in support of public good, and which have been used as paradigm cases by the jurists to extrapolate fresh decisions, are rooted in this principle. If it is accepted that religious ordinances are based on considerations that look into increasing positive value and minimizing evil, especially in matters that deal with social transactions, then we must also regard these ordinances as relative to the situations, mutable, and hence specific to the logic of time and space. A number of prominent jurists have accepted this relative dimension of the ordinances dealing with all matters connected with intersubjective relationships. They have also asserted that alteration and adaptation are permissible, even if they go against the religious texts or if there is an agreement among the jurists advocating contrary to the terms of the text. However, a large number of jurists permit modification and adaptation in the ordinances dealing with specific topics about which there does not appear to be a textual proof or an agreement among scholars.[23]

In general, Sunni jurists were connected with the day-to-day workings of the government. Accordingly, they were required to provide solutions to every new problem that emerged in the society. In order to do this they devised methodological stratagems based on analogical reasoning, sound opinion, efforts to promote the good of the people, selection of the most beneficial of several rulings, removal of obstructions to resolving a problem, conventions and customs of the region, and, different forms of reasoning. Through these methodological tools they were, to a large extent, able to respond to the situations that arose in the medical practice. The Shi'ite jurists did not admit public good as a principle of problem resolution until more recently. Not until the Iranian revolution in 1978–79 did Shi'ite jurists take up the question of admitting public good as an important source for legal-ethical decision making. The direction followed by these jurists in Iran is not very different from the one followed by their Sunni counterparts throughout the political history of Sunni Islam.[24]

The Rule of "No Harm, No Harassment"

The rule of "No harm, no harassment" is regarded as one of the most fundamental rules for deducing rulings dealing with social ethics in Islam. Muslim jurists have discussed and debated the validity of this principle because it is regarded as one of the critical proofs in support of numerous decisions that were made in different periods of juridical development. What makes the rule authentic is its ascription to the Prophet himself. Jurists belonging to different legal schools are in agreement that the rule was set by no less a person than the founder of Islam. Hence, whether from the point of its transmission or from the congruity in the sense conveyed by it, the jurists have endorsed its admission among the rules that are employed in making all decisions that pertain to social and political life of the community. In fact, the Shāfi'i-Sunni jurist Suyūṭī regards "No harm, no harassment" as one of the five major traditions that served as authoritative sources for the derivation of the rules on which depended the deduction of legal-ethical decisions in the Shari'a.[25] In addition, he affirms that the majority of juridical rubrics were founded on the principle of "No harm, no harassment," and that closely related to this principle are a number of other rules, among them this one: "Necessities make forbidden permissible, as long as it does not lead to any detriment."[26] Some jurists include "No harm, no harassment" among the five major rules that shaped the new rulings in the area of interpersonal relations. These are as follows:

1. "Action depends upon intention." This rule is deduced from the tradition related by the Prophet: "Indeed, actions depend upon intentions."
2. "Hardship necessitates relief." This rule is inferred from the tradition that says: "No harm should be inflicted or reciprocated."
3. "One needs certainty." To continue an action requires linking the present situation with the past. This rule is rationally deduced on the basis of a juristic practice that links present doubtful condition to the previously held certain situation to resolve the case.
4. "Harm must be rejected." This rule is deduced on the basis of the need to promote benefit and institute it in order to remove causes of corruption or reduce their impact upon the possibility of having to choose the lesser of the two evils.
5. "Custom determines course of action." The rule acknowledges the need to take local custom into account when making relevant rulings.[27]

"No harm, no harassment" functions both as a principle and a source for the rule that states "hardship necessitates relief." As such, it connotes that there can be no legislation, promulgation or execution of any law that leads to harm of anyone in society. For that reason, in derivation of a legal-ethical judgment the rule is given priority over all primary obligations in the Shari'a. In fact, it functions as a check on all other ordinances to make sure that their fulfillment does not lead to harm. In case of dispute in any situation, the final resolution is derived by applying the rule of "No harm, no harassment." For instance, the primary obligation of seeking medical treatment becomes prohibited if it aggravates the affliction suffered under certain medical conditions.

It is important to keep in mind that "No harm, no harassment" functions most effectively when a rule that recognizes the absolute "right of discretion" (taslīṭ) of an owner over all his possessions is in competition with "No harm" rule. Simply stated, the problem is: How to protect the owner's interests when excercising one party's discretion leads to thwart another's interests. In situations in which the lack of owner's discretion may harm his interests, the jurists bypass the rule of "No harm" and simply adhere to the rule of "Right of discretion." However, if exercising one party's discretion leads to thwart another's interests, then the deliberations are faced with competing and conflicting interests. In such a case, admitting the "Rule of discretion" to the exclusion of the rule of "No harm" actually results in promoting the owner's interests only. If this occurs. some jurists prioritize the "Rule of discretion" in order to rule in favor of the owner's right to promote his legitimate interests. At the same time, the rule of "No harm" also becomes pertinent in promoting the owner's interests by considering the probable harm that can occur if the right of discretion is denied.

One more instance of competing interests is provided in a case in which the owner exercises his discretion without any justification to promote or pre-vent benefit. He simply undertakes something for amusement. Here the rule of "No harm" becomes preponderant in providing the ruling, regardless whether that action causes or reciprocates harm. Actually the tradition that bears the rule narrates a story of a man who had a legitimate right to pass through his own property in order to get into the garden where his neighbor's house was located. But this passing through, done frequently and even for exercise of his discretion over his property, invaded the privacy of his neighbor, making it uncomfortable for that family. Hence, the "Rule of discretion" was sidestepped, and the fact of harm caused by this intrusion in the privacy of the neighbor prompted the use of the rule of "No harm, no harassment." In other words, the "Rule of discretion" is made ineffective by "No harm," because exercise of discretion is restricted by consideration of harm and harassment. Any unreasonable exercise of discretion, which neither promotes nor thwarts the agent's interests, is forbidden. But who defines what is reasonable or un-reasonable in the matter of exercise of discretion? At this point, custom and culture provide the guidelines.

In the Shari'a, the definition "No harm" in to derive negative rulings de-pends upon custom (al-'urf), which determines its parameters. Custom also establishes whether harm to oneself or to another party has been done in a given situation. If custom does not construe a matter to be harmful, then it cannot be admitted as such by applying the rule itself, nor can it be considered as forbidden according to the Shari'a, even if the matter is lexically designated as "harmful." It is important to keep in mind that ultimately it is the Sacred Lawgiver who defines the parameters of harm. However, if custom regards as harmful something for which revelation offers no specific evidence against, the harm in that situation becomes more broadly defined as conditions that mediate injustice and violation of someone's rights. Moreover, harms differ as to who is causing the harm, as with self-harm and harm caused by another party. Hence, one's social status, culture, and the time in which one lives play a role in defining harm. Harm is relative to the person who experiences it. Therefore, what appears to be wrong prima facie and is regarded by one party as a harmful act may not be considered wrong or unjustified by another. Hu-man experience, although subjective, attains considerable importance in the evaluation of the kind of harm that is to be rejected in the rule of "No harm, no harassment." The context in which the Prophet gave the rule clearly leaves the matter of harm to be determined by the situation. In the report that speaks about the harm caused by an inconsiderate neighbor who violated the privacy of his neighbor, it was a case of harmful invasion by one party of another's interest. To be sure, the rule "No harm, no harassment" allows for the ruling that one must not become a cause for harm.[28]

The application of the ruling to reject harm has no bearing on the assess-ment of the actual situation when a person is going through the setbacks to his interests. Nor does the Lawgiver's admission of harm in certain situations as a mediating causation for some rulings that require reparation or compen-sation. In the final analysis, it is the personal assessment of harm that functions as an important consideration in determining related obligations. Hence, for instance, when a person is sick, she determines whether she can keep the fast of Ramadan as required by the Shari'a in consideration of the harm that fasting can cause. Regardless of the criteria one applies to determine the level of harm, whether it is less or more, once custom establishes its existence, then the Shari'a endorses it as equally so, even when there might be a difference of opinion as to what forms of harm are more detrimental. In any case, when such a difference of opinion occurs, the law requires following the decision that leads to least harm and that causes the least damage to one's total well-being. Hence, in the case of a terminally ill patient, if the decision to prolong life leads to more harm for the patient and his immediate family, then to keep him on life-saving equipment is regarded as causing further harm to the patient's and his family's well-being, and hence forbidden.

A number of subsidiary rules are related to the rule "No harm, no harassment," including the second rule, "Hardship necessitates relief," which becomes almost part of this rule. In addition, a number of traditions and verses of the Qur'an are cited to support its admission as a source of legal-ethical decision making in order to seek benefits and avert sources of harm, or to choose the lesser of two plausible evils. In general, Muslim jurists mention subsidiary rules in various other contexts dealing with interpersonal relations to correlate the establishment of good in order to avert malevolence. Moreover, they provide guidelines that govern situations in which a person has to choose between two evils that appear to be equal, or a situation in which one of the two equal evils has preponderance because of the external or internal causes. It is important to keep in mind that although the jurists do not mention or allude to any traditions in support of the rule directly, in different contexts when applying the five rules they assert that these are figured out on the basis of the four principal sources of Islamic jurisprudence: the Qur'an, the Tradition, consensus, and arguments based on reason.[29]

Moreover, some jurists justify the rule "Hardship necessitates relief" on the basis of the same tradition that sets up the rule "No harm, no harassment," that is, "No harm shall be inflicted nor reciprocated."[30]

However, the question remains as to when the rule was promoted to the status of a principle that had wider application in matters related to social ethics. The problem in applying the rule was connected with the determination of actual harm. Was this harm objective enough to overcome assumptions about it? As discussed above, the tradition uses the word "harm" in its broadest sense to include any setback suffered by a person, whether physical or psychological. At the same time, human experience of harm is key to its actual assessment as such. However, there is evidence in the juridical assessment of the concept, which suggests that even when certain acts appear prima facie wrong and unjustifiable, it is not possible to attach absolute meaning to them. Obviously, there are acts that are regarded as being detrimental, which stop being so as soon as their negative aspect is overcome. This was particularly true in matters that dealt with acts that were classified as being harmful in the area of both God-human and interhuman relationships.[31] Following this dif-

ficulty in determining its reality as harmful, there was the other difficulty arising from consideration that the Lawgiver does not legislate anything harmful
to people. In other words, God does not require people to do anything that
would necessitate inflicting harm on oneself or on others. There are two verses
in the Qur'an that refer to the rule as a negative injunction, in the situation
related to conflict between two harms or between harm and benefit, and the
Lawgiver's giving preponderance to the weightier among them:

> They will question you concerning wine, and arrow-shuffling. Say:
> 'In both is heinous sin (*ithm*), and uses (*manāfi'*) for men, but the
> sin in them is more heinous than the usefulness.' (Q. 2:219)

> If it had not been for certain men believers and certain women be-
> lievers whom you know not, lest you should trample them, and
> there befall you guilt unwittingly on their account . . . (Q. 48:25)

These two passages are interpreted to convey the negative injunction against
inflicting or reciprocating harm. There is no normative ranking proposed in
them. In cases of conflict, not to harm is given preponderance, but the guidelines vary in different circumstances, providing no a priori rule that requires
avoiding harm over providing benefit. They simply require weighing an action
in a circumstance of conflict in terms of its potential in preventing and removing harm and promoting good.

Some Shi'ite jurists regard the tradition that states the rule "No harm, no
harassment" as the source for a juristic principle among principles that are
applied to derive laws of the Shari'a. They report several other traditions that
speak about negation of harm in all matters related to human interaction to
support this view.[32] In fact, as these scholars maintain, since the tradition "No
harm, no harassment" is reported by all schools of thought among Muslims,
it should be accorded the status of a principle that is a source of a large number
of ordinances regarding intersubjective relationships.[33]

Other Shi'ite scholars have permitted carving out a precedence by including the rule about rejection of harm in their discussion about the legal theory.
They have afforded it a prominence that is enjoyed by other principal sources
like the Qur'an and the Tradition in deriving new rulings. The question of
compensation looms large in the rulings that regard the person causing harm
responsible for appropriate compensation. Once legal authority establishes that
harm has occurred, application of a rule that relieves a person of responsibility
for compensating the victim becomes pointless, especially when the person is
definitely responsible for the compensation. Using a rational argument, these
jurists have contended that it is reasonable and even natural to expect the
person who has caused the harm to another be held responsible for the compensation. In fact, both, causing harm or reciprocating it, require restitution
in the Shari'a. In other words, one cannot escape paying the compensation by
resorting to the rule of "Relief from responsibility" when the rule of "No harm"
holds him responsible for compensation. In line with the necessity to com-

pensate the victim of harm, some Shi'ite jurists have ruled that although causing any kind of harm to oneself or to another person is forbidden, one should definitely avoid those harms in which the victim cannot be compensated, as specified in the sacred law. The responsibility to compensate in cases of harm and harassment is ingrained in human nature and confirmed by the Sacred Lawgiver, who has not ruled anything that might cause harm without taking into consideration due compensation. For various situations in which an agent might suffer a setback to his interests the Shari'a has determined a fixed level of compensation. And, in situations that are not covered there, the Shari'a has permitted a fair settlement through arbitration as long as the validity of the claim is indisputable.[34]

In sum, most of the jurists have accepted the rule as being one of the principle sources of legal-ethical decision making. Some others have regarded the rule as being closely related to another rule that states: "No constriction, no distress," regardless of whether constriction or distress is caused by God or by human being. They mention three significations of the tradition "No harm, no harassment":

1. It simply signifies the proscription (al-nahy).
2. It simply signifies proscription of harm without compensation.
3. It means that God does not wish harm for his creatures, neither from him nor from human beings.

An obligation not to inflict harm (nafy al-ḍarar) intentionally has been closely associated in Muslim social ethics to an obligation to promote good (istiṣlāḥ). As a matter of fact, obligations of nonmaleficence and beneficence are treated under a single principle of istiṣlāḥ (promoting good). Obligations to promote good cannot be fulfilled without taking stringent measures not to harm others, including not killing them or treating them cruelly, obligations to take full account of proportionality in order to produce net balance of benefits over harms, and obligations to honor contractual agreements. Accordingly, Islamic bioethics regards the principle of "No harm, no harassment" as central to the Islamic conceptions of health care. It is for this reason that there is a constant evaluation of the situation to prioritize obligations of preventing harm in order to make a final ethical decision. In cases of conflict between probable harm and probable benefit, each individual case of such a conflict requires careful weighing of the rule that states, "Preventing or removing harm has a priority over promoting good." To be sure, the principle of "No harm, no harassment" has as its source in both the revelation and reason. Reasonable people are capable of recognizing the sources of good life in the sacred texts and human intellection.

However, whether the obligation not to inflict harm can be regarded as one of the principles or rules of the bioethical system is contested by the Muslim jurists. To be sure, even the rationalist-objectivists, that is, the Shi'ites and the Mu'tazilite Sunnites, who regard human reason to be the sole judge in determining harm or benefit, have debated the centrality of this obligation in ethical deliberations in all fields of human interaction, including the biomedical conditions. In almost 90 percent of cases confronting health care providers in the Muslim world, the issue of inflicting or reciprocating harm is at the heart of the ethical deliberations. In addition, in the rulings studied for the present work, the jurists almost unanimously provided reasons based on the obligation not to inflict harm. For example, in the rulings against human cloning, most jurists refer to the infliction of harm on the well-being of an offspring who will be deprived of normal parentage, regarded as a necessary condition in the healthy upbringing of a child. Or in the rulings about population control through abortion, the references all point to the harm that could be done to the moral fabric of society through legalization of abortion.

As a subsidiary rule, "Preventing harm has a priority over promoting good" also provides the jurists with the principle of proportionality. This principle is a source for careful analysis of harm and benefit when, for example, a medical procedure prolongs the life of a terminally ill patient without advancing long-term cure. The principle also allows for reasoned choices about appropriate benefits in proportion to costs and risks for not only the patient but also his or her family. It is well known that in many complicated cases, decisions about most effective medical treatments are based on probable benefits and harms for the patients and their families. Islamic bioethics require that medical professionals and health care providers ascertain the implications of a given course of medical procedure for a patient's overall well-being by fully accounting for the probable harm or benefit. The principle of "No harm, no harassment" thus is critical in clinical settings where procedural decisions need to be made in consultation with all parties to a case and with a sense of humility in the presence of God: There is nothing for humans but to strive to do their best.

NOTES

1. To speak about such a possibility in the highly politicized "theology" of international relations is not without problems. Like development language for which modern Western society provides the model that all peoples in the world must follow, any suggestion to create a "metacultural" language of bioethics runs the risk of being suspected as another hegemonic ploy from Western nations. However, there is a fundamental difference in the way development language is employed to connote Western scientific, technological, and social advancement, and biomedical vocabulary that essentially captures universal ends of medicine as they relate to human conditions and human happiness and fulfillment across nations. It is not difficult to legitimize bioethical language cross-culturally if we keep in mind the cultural presuppositions of a given region in assessing the generalizability of moral principles and rules.

2. Contemporary moral discourse has been aptly described as "a minefield of incommensurable disagreements." Such disagreements are believed to be the result of secularization marked by a retreat of religion from the public arena. Privatization of religion has been regarded as a necessary condition for ethical pluralism. The essentially liberal vision of community founded on radical autonomy of the individual moral agent runs contrary to other-regarding communitarian values of shared ideas of justice and of public good. There is a sense that modern, secular, individualistic society is no longer a community founded on commonly held beliefs of social good and its relation to responsibilities and freedoms in a pluralistic society. See David

Heyd, ed., *Toleration: An Elusive Virtue* (Princeton, N.J.: Princeton University Press, 1996).

3. See Ann Elizabeth Mayer, *Islam and Human Rights: Tradition and Politics* (Boulder, Colo: Westview, 1991). Chapter 1, "Comparisons of Rights Across Countries," has endeavored to analyze charges of cultural relativism against the Universal Declaration of Human Rights made by Muslim governments guilty of violating human rights of their peoples. However, in the process of arguing for the universal application of the UDHR document, she has paradoxically led to the relativization of the same by ignoring the historical context that actually produced the UDHR. See my review of her book in the *Journal of Church and State* 34, no. 3 (summer 1992): 614–616.

4. The deontological ethical norm determines the rightness (or wrongness) of actions without regard to the consequences produced by performing such actions. By contrast, the teleological norm determines the rightness (or wrongness) of actions on the basis of their consequences. Deontological norms can further be subdivided into objectivist and subjectivist norms: objectivist because the ethical value is intrinsic to the action independently of anyone's decision or opinion; subjectivist because the action derives value in relation to the view of a judge who decides its rightness (or wrongness). George Hourani, *Reason and Tradition in Islamic Ethics* (New York: Cambridge University Press, 1985), p. 17, introduces the latter distinction in deontological norms.

5. See K. Zaki Hasan's contribution in *Principles of Health Care Ethics*, ed. Raanan Gillon (John Wiley & Sons, 1994), pp. 93–103. Recent publications in Urdu on the subject of new rulings in Islamic jurisprudence indicate a growing interest in the deliberations of the *Majma' āl-fiqhi al-islamī* (Islamic Juridical Council) in Saudi Arabia, with chapters in India and Pakistan, and in growing interest of ulema in these two countries in formulating fresh juridical decisions in bioethics. *Jadīd fiqhī mabāḥith* (Karachi, n.d.), Vol. 1, deals with the proceedings of the seminar in which Indian and Pakistani ulema presented papers on various new issues, including organ transplant and birth control.

6. The usual practice among Muslim jurists is to end their judicial opinion (*fatwā*) with a statement *allāh 'ālim*, that is, "God knows best," indicating that the opinion was given on the basis of what seemed most likely to be the case (*ẓann*), rather than claiming that this was an absolute and unrebuttable (*qaṭ'*) opinion, which could be derived only from the revelatory sources like the Qur'an and the Tradition.

7. George F. Hourani, *Islamic Rationalism: The Ethics of 'Abd al-Jabbar* (Oxford: Clarendon, 1971), calls the Mu'tazilite theory of ethics "rationalist objectivism" because natural human reason is capable of knowing real characteristic of the acts, without the aid of revelation. Majid Fakhry, *Ethical Theories of Islam* (Leiden: E. J. Brill, 1991), pp. 35–43, regards this as quasi-deontological theory of right and wrong in which the intrinsic goodness or badness of actions can be established on purely rational grounds. Hourani calls the Ash'arite theory of ethics "theistic subjectivism" rather than "ethical voluntarism" because the value of action is defined by God as the judge and observer. However, since it is the divine will that is the determinant of right and wrong, it would be more meaningful to retain "voluntarism" in this particular type of divine command ethical theory. See Majid Fakhry, "The Mu'tazilite View of Man," in *Philosophy, Dogma, and the Impact of Greek Thought in Islam* (Brookfield, Vt.: Variorium, 1994), pp. 107–121, and his *Ethical Theories*, pp. 46–55. Further refinement in specifying the Ash'arite theory on the basis of Fakhry's discussions is provided by Richard M. Frank, "Moral Obligation in Classical Muslim Theology," in *Journal of*

Religious Ethics 11 (1983): 207, where he regards Ash'arite ethics "a very pure kind of voluntaristic occasionalism."

8. Madkūr, *Mabāḥith*, Vol. 1, p. 162.

9. Mohammad Hashim Kamali, *Principles of Islamic Jurisprudence* (Cambridge: Islamic Texts Society, 1991), chap. 12.

10. Literally, the principle translates: "There shall be no harming, injuring, or hurting, [of one person by another] in the first instance, nor in return, or requital, in Islam" (see Edward William Lane, *An Arabic-English Lexicon*, Part 5, p. 1775). Although based on a famous Prophetic tradition, in this work I will refer to this principle as the principle or rule of "No harm, no harassment."

11. Ghazālī, *Mustaṣfā*, Vol. 1, pp. 286–287.

12. Shāṭibī, *al-Muwāfiqāt*, Vol. 2, pp. 4–5, believes that legislating laws and promulgating religions have the welfare of humanity as their main purpose. Furthermore, he maintains that even when theologians have disputed this doctrine pointing out, as the Ash'arite theologian Rāzī has done, that God's actions are not informed by any purpose, the same scholars in their discussions on legal theory have conceded to the notion, however in different terms, that divine injunctions are informed by God's purpose for humanity. Shāṭibī clearly indicates that deduction of divine injunctions provides evidence about their being founded upon the doctrine of human welfare, to which Rāzī and other Ash'arites are not opposed.

13. Subkī, *al-Ibhāj fī sharḥ al-minhāj* (Beirut: Dār al-kutub al-'ilmiya, 1404/19), Vol. 3, p. 62.

14. Ḥusayn Ṣābirī, "Istiṣlāḥ va pūyāyī-yi fiqh," in *Majalla-yi Dānishkada-yi Ilāhiyāt Mashhad*, Year 1379 Shamsī, No. 49–50, pp. 235–286, gives an overview of the principle and its acceptance or rejection among the Sunni and Shi'ite jurists.

15. Shāṭibī, *al-Muwāfiqāt*, Vol. 2, pp. 6–7.

16. Muḥammad Sa'īd Ramaḍān al-Būṭī, *Ḍawābit al-maṣlaḥa fī al-sharī'at al-islāmiyya* (Beirut: Mu'assasa al-Risāla, 1410/1990), Vol. 3, p. 288.

17. Ghazālī, *al-Mustaṣfā*, p. 174.

18. Ghazālī, *al-Mustaṣfā*, p. 174ff.; Shāṭibī, *al-Muwāfiqāt*, Vol. 2, p. 8ff.; Ibn Badrān al-Dimashqī, *al-Madkhal*, p. 295; Ibn Qudāma, *Rawḍat al-nāẓir*, Vol. 1, p. 170.

19. Ibn Amīr Ḥāj, *al-Taqrīr wa al-taḥbīr*, Vol. 3, p. 213; Shāṭibī, *al-Muwāfiqāt*, Vol. 2, pp. 7–8, regards performance of all duties under the category of God-human relationship ('*ibādāt*) as fulfilling the need to protect one's religion; eating and drinking as fulfilling the need to protect one's life; performance of all duties under the category of interhuman relationship (*mu'āmalāt*) as fulfilling the need to protect future generation and wealth; and implementation of penal code and laws of retribution and restitution as fulfilling the need to protect all five essentials.

20. *Al-Muwāfiqāt*, Vol. 2, p. 9. Other jurists have mentioned these categories in different order, with different examples in each category. See, for instance, al-Ghazālī, *al-Mustaṣfā*, p. 175.

21. Shāṭibī, *al-Muwāfiqāt*, Vol. 2, p. 9.

22. Ghazālī, *al-Mustaṣfā*, p. 175.

23. Madkūr, *Madkhal al-fiqh al-islaāmī*, p. 102.

24. It is important to note that since the establishment of the Shi'ite ideological state in Iran, the question of public good has become an important source of legal thinking and problem solving, similar to the Sunni states in premodern days. Under the leadership of Ayatollah Khomeini, Shi'ite jurisprudence has once again become research oriented. A number of conferences have been held since the revolution in 1978–79 to discuss the role of time and place in shaping the rulings through inde-

pendent reasoning. The proceedings have been published in several volumes under the title *Naqsh-e zamān va makān dar ijtihād*.

25. Suyūṭī, *Tanwīr al-Ḥawālik: is'āf al-mubatta' bi-rijāl al-Muwaṭṭa'* (Beirut: al-Maktaba al-Thiqāfīya, 1969), Vol. 2, pp. 122, 218.

26. Suyūṭī, *al-Ashbāh wa al-naẓā'ir fī qawā'id wa furu' fiqh al-Shāfi'īya* (Mekkah: Maktabat Nizār Muṣṭafā al-Bāz, 1990), p. 92.

27. Shahīd Awwal, *al-Qawā'id*, Vol. 1, pp. 27–28.

28. There is a sustained discussion among jurists about the nature of harm that this tradition conveys. Undoubtedly, *ḍarar* refers to general forms of harm that include setbacks to reputation, property, privacy, and specific ones that include setbacks to physical and psychological needs. See 'Alī al-Ḥusaynī al-Sīstānī, *Qā'ida lā ḍarar wa lā ḍirār* (Qumm: Lithographie Ḥamīd, 1414/1993), pp. 134–141.

29. Shahīd Awwal, *al-Qawa'id*, Vol. 1, p. 123.

30. Ibid.

31. Ḍiya al-Dīn al-'Iraqī, *Qā'ida lā ḍarar wa lā ḍirār*, ed. and commented upon by al-Sayyid Murtaḍā al-Mūsawī al-Khalkhālī (Qumm: Intishārāt Daftar Tablīghāt Islamī, 1418/1997), p. 135.

32. Majlisī, *Biḥār al-anwār*, Vol. 2, p. 277.

33. Majlisī, *Mir'āt al-'uqūl*, Vol. 19, p. 395.

34. Ḥakīm, Sayyid Mundhir al-, "Qāi'dat nafy al-ḍarar: Ta'rīkh-ha—Taṭawwur-ha ḥatta 'aṣr al-Shaykh al-Anṣārī," in *al-Fikr al-Islāmī*, No. 7, 1415/1994, pp. 264–290.

13

Ethics of Ambiguity: A Buddhist Reflection on the Japanese Organ Transplant Law

Ronald Y. Nakasone

Japanese doctors performed their first legal heart transplant on 28 February 1999, twenty-one months after the passage of the Organ Transplantation Law (*Zōki isshoku hō*);[1] supporters of the legislation had hoped that its approval on 17 June 1997 would end the discussion and ease the procurement of organs after more than thirty years of national debate and reflection. It has not. Though the Japanese possess the technology, medical expertise, and legal sanction to carry out organ transplants, as of April 2004 only 29 cases fulfilled the legal requirements and medical criteria for donor eligibility; approximately 7,000 persons are determined to be brain-dead every year and 13,072 persons are on waiting lists to receive organs.

The Japanese ambivalence toward organ transplants is reflected in the ambiguity of the law; it does not provide a uniform answer to the question, What is human death? The "family consent" provision also contributes to law's ambiguity by allowing the family to override a close relative's directive of organ donation. The Organ Transplant Law and the Japanese public's hesitancy toward organ transplants reflects the character of *jūsōsei* or "porously laminated nature," an expression coined by Watsuji Tetsurō[2] (1889–1960) to describe the various traditions and cultures—Shintōism, Confucianism, Daoism, Chinese and Indian Buddhism, Neo-Confucianism, Christianity, and a variety of Western thought and attitudes—that inform the Japanese. Add to these layers a number of other influences on the Japanese attempt to come to grips with brain death and organ transplants: common folk beliefs; emotional, social, historical and current events; personal proclivities and experiences; and recent advances in biotechnology and the culture that it has spawned.

"*Jūsōsei*" articulates a cognitive texture that informs families when they are approached to consider donating the organs of a close relative who has been diagnosed with irreversible loss of consciousness; it is also a useful paradigm for understanding the ambiguities inherent in positing alternative notions of what constitutes human death and the primacy of "family consent" in the Organ Transplant Law. The law essentially accepts three separate concepts of death: (1) the traditional cardiopulmonary notions of human death; (2) the psychological, that is the absence of brain activity measured by the presence of brain waves; and as we shall presently learn, (3) social death.

The basis for this ambiguity and the practical implications inherent in the law merit a closer examination. To this end, this chapter will examine the structure and role of ambiguity in the Japanese Organ Transplant Law by appealing to the Chinese Huayen Buddhist doctrine of *dharmadhātu-pratītyasamutpāda* (*fajie yuanqi shuo*) or universal dependent "coarising," a major interpretation of the Buddha's original insight of *pratītyasamutpāda*, dependent-coarising or interdependence. Specifically, I will examine the nature of ambiguity through the *zhuban yuanming jude men* or "the attribute of the complete accommodation of principal and secondary dharmas"[3] that Fazang (643–712) has formulated. The interdependent and evolving Buddhist vision of reality provides the rationale for ambiguity in decision making and action. I begin with an outline of the Buddhist posture, proceed to summarize the first Japanese Organ Transplant Law, and employ Buddhist ideas to unpack and interpret attitudes that informed the first organ transplant experience in Japan.

The Buddhist Posture

The doctrine of *dharmadhātu-pratītyasamutpāda* (universal dependent coarising) articulates the Buddhist vision of an interdependent world and that all spatial and temporal dharma or existents (beings, things, thoughts, feelings, and sentiments) are mutually dependent and supportive; it asserts the Buddhist view of reality, humanity's place in the universe, and relationship between and among individuals. As the basis for Buddhist thinking and ethics, *dharmadhātu-pratītyasamutpāda* provides Buddhists with a vision of identity of, responsibility to, and gratitude for all things and beings. Envisioning the universe to be an organic whole, *dharmadhātu-pratītyasamutpāda* does not posit a single absolute center or first cause. The universe evolves through the interaction among all its constitute parts. Each and every existent reality is mutually dependent and mutually supportive; each individual functions to establish the whole; the whole in turn supports and defines the individual.

Pratītyasamutpāda is an extension and expansion of the law of karma. The idea of *karma*, literally, "action," appeared during the early Upanishad period (800–200 B.C.E.), approximately two to three centuries before the birth of Siddhartha Gautama (563–483 B.C.E.[4]), the historical Buddha. *Karma* took on a moral tone when it became associated with the idea of *samsara* or "passage."

The moral quality of action an individual generated in the past determined an individual's present station in life; present action will determine the quality of one's future rebirth. However, although karma may adequately describe the effects of an individual's karmic life, it fails to consider the interaction of conflicting karmic forces and the complexity and multiplicity of causes and conditions that affect an individual's life and the effects it can have on others and the world. Mahāyāna documents that appeared during the first century of the common era interpret *pratītyasamutpāda* to be compassionate and morally purposeful.

An interpretation of life grounded in the belief of an interdependent world wherein we are intertwined with the destinies of all beings dictates the various virtues and ends to be considered when reflecting on ethical and bioethical questions. Buddhist ethics thus contemplates an individual's conduct, responsibilities, and obligations within the context of his or her sociohistorical context, the needs and feelings of other persons, the natural environment, and other such considerations. For the moment we are specifically interested in obligations and concerns that arise between and among persons. Though an individual is completely autonomous, he or she exists with, is defined by, and molded by other persons and his or her community. Other persons and the community, in turn, are defined and transformed by the thoughts and acts of individuals who belong to the community. Ethical conduct and deliberation in an interdependent world places a premium on fair play, compassion, gratitude, humility, and patience. These virtues provide clues as to how we should reflect upon such questions as the definition of human death, organ donations and transplants, and decision making. They exemplify attitudes one should cultivate and exercise when relating to others and our responsibilities to the most vulnerable among us. Since Buddhists aspire for all beings to be free from suffering, they promote laws, policies, and decisions that minimize all manner of suffering.

On the Structure and Use of Ambiguity

Fazang explored in great detail how individual existents relate in an interdependent world through *shixuan yuanqi wuai famen* the "ten attributes of the unimpeded fusion of dharmas of interdependence." The tenth attribute, or "the complete accommodation of principal and secondary dharmas," illuminates the structure of ambiguity. This attribute explains that in an interdependent world in which every dharma is mutually supportive and mutually dependent, each dharma is of primary importance. When a dharma is arbitrarily singled out for special consideration, that dharma becomes the principal dharma and the remaining dharmas take on a secondary role. In postmodern terminology, the principal dharma is the center, and the remaining dharmas are marginalized. Yet at the next instant, another dharma can assume the central role, and the once-principal dharma is relegated to a supporting role. These changes can be seen in our shifting conversation with friends. When one friend is speaking, all of our attention is focused on that person, but suddenly a second friend may shift the conversation by picking up on a minor point. The locus of attention constantly shifts.

Centers shift also with a change in perspective. Shifting centers and perspectives illustrate the openness and fluidity to include everyone and every point of view. Though no one person or viewpoint commands the central position at every moment, each person or viewpoint is of absolute value in relation to other persons and viewpoints. The most obvious value of including varying viewpoints is evident in scientific investigations. The chemist, the physicist, and the atomic scientist look at an atom of helium through their respective training and practice, and they are interested in and see different aspects of the same phenomenon. To the chemist, the helium is a molecule because it behaves as a gas; to the physicist, on the other hand, it is not a molecule because it does not display a molecular spectrum. The atomic scientist, on the other hand, is interested in the energy that is produced when hydrogen atoms fuse to produce helium. Each specialist, by his or her training and professional methodology, understands the same phenomenon from a specific perspective. The chemist's view does not discount the physicist's understanding; both contribute to our knowledge of this simple atom. A specific discipline illuminates one facet of reality, never its totality. Shifting centers affirm the validity of varying viewpoints and allow for openness to new discoveries. It is unlikely that scientists will ever have a complete understanding of a single phenomenon. Their knowledge is forever evolving, and it remains incomplete and ambiguous.

Ambiguity is cinematically illustrated by Kurosawa's film *Rashōmon*. The "truth" is relative to a particular storyteller, the samurai who speaks through a medium, his violated wife, the bandit, and the woodcutter who witnessed the event. Each retelling gives one version of the events that transpired, thereby discounting other versions. *Rashōmon* asks the viewer to determine "truth," that is, what actually happened, and to infer from the various testimonies what actually transpired. Whose story are we to believe? "Reality" is what each storyteller makes it out to be. The facts of the woman's abduction and the death of her samurai husband are not in dispute, but Kurosawa links the event inward. How we think about the event colors our perceptions of the "truth" that transpired. Our thinking in turn is colored by our sociohistorical past and present location.

Organ Transplant and Brain Death: The Japanese Experience

The first heart transplant in Japan was performed by Dr. Wada Jurō (1922–?) in August 1968. The eighteen-year-old recipient, Miyazaki Nobuo, initially seemed to make good medical progress, but his condition took a turn for the worse, and he died eighty-three days after receiving the heart of Yamaguchi Yoshimasa. The Japanese media heralded the event as a medical triumph and

the doctor a national hero; but subsequent revelations clouded the feat in ethical and legal controversy. Dr. Wada was accused of human experimentation
and poor judgment in the determination of death. In December of that year,
he was charged with homicide and professional negligence in the deaths of
the donor and the recipient. This and other charges were eventually dropped.
But the Wada case spawned a national debate that included a search for a
medical definition of death. In 1983 the Japanese Ministry of Health and Welfare formed a committee to establish the criteria for brain death. The committee issued its final report in 1992 and concluded that brain death *is* human
death; a minority objected and issued a statement that brain death should not
be considered human death.

The current law attempts to accommodate both opinions. It allows a person with irreversible loss of consciousness to be legally declared dead but recognizes the traditional cardiopulomary death as the default standard; it also
makes a distinction between a clinical diagnosis and a legal determination of
brain death. Should the occasion arise, the definition of death as brain death
would be applicable to an individual who has previously agreed to this definition and who wishes to donate his or her organs for transplantation. However,
before the organs can be removed, a transplant coordinator must consult with
members of the family to ascertain whether they agree with their loved one's
desire and with the legal determination of brain death. Though an individual
may be clinically brain-dead, a physician is not allowed to make a legal determination unless the family's permission is obtained. If the family agrees, the
physician then proceeds to make such a determination in accordance to the
Japanese criteria for brain death, which includes an apnea test.[5] Once brain
death is legally established, the transplant team can begin its work. The "family
consent" provision allows the family to void any prior directive a brain-dead
person may have made concerning the disposition of his or her organs. If the
individual does not have a donor card or has declared against organ removal,
he or she is considered to be alive until the heart expires. Persons under the
age of fifteen are not allowed to be donors.

"Family" in "family consent" refers to close relatives who cohabit the same
dwelling, but not exclusively. "Consent" means that the family does not object
to the wishes of a close relative's desire to be legally declared brain-dead for
the purposes of organ donation. The family-consent requirement in effect introduces a third concept of death: social death. Only when the family accepts
the reality that one of their own has passed away is that individual considered
to be dead. Social death initiates mourning and mortuary rituals; brain death
does not. Finally, family consent means that a patient's wishes are not absolute.
In contrast, in the United States an individual essentially determines his or
her course of action even if it may involve serious risk, unless such action
infringes on the liberty of others. An individual's desire and intent to have his
or her organs retrieved for transplants is to be respected and honored (although
in practice organs are not removed if the family objects). It is perhaps for this
reason that U.S. law permits a physician to unilaterally declare a person brain-

dead. This difference in the notion of individual autonomy may explain the relative ease with which the United States has accepted brain death and organ transplants.

The plural definitions of death and the provision of family consent in Organ Transplant Law essentially means that the determination of brain death is negotiated between the donor and his or her family; family consent is a "wild card." Alternative concepts of death in the Japanese Organ Transplant Law crystallizes the difficulties of formulating an overarching vision that lends itself to legal clarity as to what should be done and what consequences follow "right" or "wrong" actions.[6] By avoiding an overarching definition that guarantees all meaning and values, the law recognizes the alternative claims and legitimate concerns; it does not criminalize, ignore, or marginalize alternative views. In essence the law reflects the Japanese experience and its attempt to accommodate the recent concept of brain death to accommodate organ transplants. It is a legal experiment that validates ambiguous, indeterminate, and changing realities in advancing the public good.

Jūsōsei

Four days after Miyazaki's diseased heart was replaced with Yamaguchi's, the *Asahi Shimbun* reported on 11 August 1968 that the families of the donor and the recipient met. The article noted that although Yamaguchi's parents were initially hesitant to donate their son's organs, they were now happy that their son was able to make a contribution to society. Miyazaki's father responded that he had no words to express his gratitude, and that he would like, if the Yamaguchi's were amenable, for both families to continue their relationship as relatives. Like her parents, the Yamaguchi's teenage daughter initially opposed the organ donation; though she now agrees with the decision, she said tearfully that she wished her brother's body had been left alone.

Ms. Yamaguchi's lament at the news conference hinted at the intensity of the family discussion and mirrors the Japanese public's ambivalence toward the concept of brain death and organ transplants. The family consent provision gives each member of the family an opportunity to participate in forming a response that the family must present to the transplant coordinator before the legal requirements are met and the medical procedure can proceed. If the family does not consent, the individual is considered to be alive. Morioka Masahiro made an interesting comment about the family consent provision in the 23 October 2000 *Nikkei Weekly:* "I think the Japanese organ-transplant law is more democratic that Western ones, because it allows people to have different opinions on the matter, which is closely linked to each individual's personal understanding of what constitutes the essence of human life."[7] Morioka understands the family consent provision to give families an opportunity to reflect on "the essence of human life" and voice their approval or disapproval for the legal determination of brain dead. Such reflections are existentially poignant because they can determine the physical life or death of a close relative. Further, these reflections, I venture, are not on the fine points of law, but recall deeply ingrained, if only vaguely understood, notions of life and death, and reactions are emotional rather than rational. Though each member of the family may have a different vision of life and death and his or her own special relations with the patient, the law formalizes the opportunity for personal reflection.

The expression "brain-dead person," thus, aptly describes a common Japanese attitude toward the irreversible loss of consciousness, a liminal state between life and death created by recent medical technology. Though the Japanese may rationally accept the notion of brain death and the medical logic of organ transplants, many are reluctant to acknowledge the death of a family member while the heart is still beating and the body is warm. Consequently, though a person may be clinically brain dead, persuading every member of the family to acknowledge his death vis-à-vis the definition of brain death meant the abandonment of the traditional cardiopulmonary understanding of death with its supporting rationale and rituals. Morioka Masahiro reflects:

> If a brain dead body is equal to a mere pencil or a cup, it would
> never put the family members into emotional crisis. For family
> members, the brain dead body must be some special "being" that
> can never be reduced to a mere "thing." If so, what sort of being
> should it be? This is the very question we are faced with when we
> encounter people who do not accept their family member's death
> until his/her heart beat stops. In my book in 1989, I used the term
> "brain dead person." This wording seems very strange from the
> view point of mainstream bioethics because it insists that a human
> being can be "brain dead" and "a person" at the same time. But
> from a philosophical/relational-oriented perspective, a human being
> can be a person, and at the same time, brain dead. He/she is brain
> dead in a medical sense, and may be a person in a sense that he/she
> can make his/her father say, by the door, "Do your best!" Our bio-
> ethics, or lifestudies, must not miss this point.[8]

We know from this passage that the common Japanese do not equate irreversible loss of consciousness with biological death or death of the person. An individual in the liminal space between life and lifelessness is still regarded as a person. The physical absence and/or loss of cognitive ability do not sever an individual's familial and social relationships. Thus Morioka concludes that this sentiment should be part of Japanese bioethical deliberation.

The liminal status of brain death is cause for great anguish. Brain death sharply demarcates life and death. In contrast, the complex and extended mortuary and memorial rituals most Japanese observe support the belief that the transition between corporal life and death is not abrupt or bipolar, but a process. This liminal and transitional period is marked by rituals that pleads with the spirit to return to the body, eases the transition into the next life, and helps the deceased to cultivate his or her spiritual life and transformation into ancesterhood.[9] These rituals are antithetical to organ transplants, which require a sharp divide between life and death. Defining death as the absence of brain activity, which often occurs before the heart stops beating, is crucial because doctors must remove organs before the cessation of cardiopulmonary activity damages them and precludes their use in transplantation. This clear distinction does not define the death as a process, but as an event. Such a demarcation also dispenses with the need for rituals that have traditionally marked transitions in human life. The absence of religious or other rituals (at least I am not aware of any, or of any being developed) to mark this passage is a further indication that the Japanese have not fully grasped the concept of brain death. Should the Japanese become more comfortable with the brain death concept, a ritual will likely emerge to mark this transition from life to death.

Buddhist opposition to organ transplantation is not absolute; it lays in the timing of organ removal. A sentient being has no fixed ontological reality, since it is a temporary aggregate of the fortuitous conjunction of psychophysical elements and consciousness whose relationships are constantly changing. Nonetheless Buddhism associates life with sentience in its broadest sense. Though the brain may have ceased to function, the individual with a beating heart is believed to be pained by being cut and having his or her organs removed. Pain and other feelings are features of sentience.

Additional traditional beliefs contribute to this concern. Confucians and Shintōists object to the deliberate desecration of the body. Confucian objections to organ transplant are based on the notion of filial piety. The opening lines of the *Hsiao-ching* (Classic on Filiality) states: "Filial piety is the basis of virtue and the source of our teachings. We receive our body, our hair, and skin from our parents, and we dare not destroy them."[10] The deliberate removal of vital organs would thus constitute a most unfilial act. Similarly, when Buddhism first entered China, the Chinese were appalled that men and women had to shave their hair when entering the Buddhist order. Traditional Chinese and Japanese notions of the body were influenced by Daoist concepts. Basically, Daoists understand the body to be a model of the universe in which all of the parts work in harmony. Spirits (*shen*) reside in critical areas of the body and coordinate the vital functions. Thus, replacing a vital organ destabilizes the inner harmony of the body.

Another question to be resolved is location of the different spirits that leave the physical body at death. Restless spirits are angry spirits that can cause misfortune. Chinese and Japanese mortuary rites require that an individual be buried or cremated with all of his or her body parts. I vaguely recall that one of the last Chinese eunuchs lamenting that he will be buried incomplete, his male organs were lost during the Cultural Revolution. Indigenous Shintō beliefs require that a person be buried with all of his or her body intact; burial without all of his or her physical remains angers the spirit (*reikon*), who will wreak havoc for the living and complicate the transformation into ancestorhood (*sosen*) and becoming a *kami* or ancestral spirit.

There are other difficulties. Miyazaki's father relayed long-held beliefs of personhood and human relationships, when he proposed that he would like their families to continue their relationship as relatives. Such an attitude can be attributed to Confucian notions of filial piety that defines the obligations between parent and child, including relations between spouses, siblings, friends, the individual and the community. Organ transplantation raises significant conceptual problems with reference to the idea of the family, i.e., as a single unbroken line, including the living and the dead, that extends into the future. Personal identity is defined by the multiple roles he or she may have within the family—Yoshimasa is simultaneously a son, a brother, and grandson; he is the product of prior generations. He will be an uncle to his sister children. In the *ie* system, donating and receiving organs raise the question of identity and the fidelity of family lineage. Though Yamaguchi Yoshimasa is dead, his heart is still alive and is now part of another person. This situation raises questions of personal identity by confusing an individual's relational role and temporal location in the family structure. To which family lineage does the person Yoshimasa belong to? How has he been memorialized in the long and complex Buddhist-Confucian-Shintō memorial cycle? (I am assuming that he is not a Christian). The Buddhist belief that personal identity is located in both the mind and body further complicates the question of personal identity.

The decision to accept brain death and agree to proceed with organ transplant or to observe the traditional cardiopulmonary notion of death is a highly personal decision for a family. Whichever decision is made carries within it its own justification and logic.

Organ transplants mean life, in its broadest sense, that rejects long-held beliefs of family lineage and mutual obligation, ideas of personhood that continue after physical death and their respective rationales. Any decision generates unforeseen rewards and consequences. One decision may not be preferable to another.

Ethics of Ambiguity

What is the best decision for a family contemplating the donation of the organs of a close relative who is brain-dead? What decision will minimize suffering? What guidelines can a vision of an interdependent world offer? A macroscopic view of the world can rationalize our predicaments and subsume them under an all encompassing vision. Yet such a vision does not always address our immediate and existential predicaments; nor does it prioritize values and needs. Fazang's vision of a symphonic and interdependent world of shifting viewpoints often fails to reconcile individual karmic choices that conflict with others. *Zhuban yuanming jude men* or "the attribute of the complete accommodation of principal and secondary dharmas" is useful in understanding the ambiguities posed by the competing definition of human death and role of "family consent" that allow space for the family sentiments to emerge. But it does not offer firm guidelines. How can the exercise of decision making, ethical deliberation, and conduct within the context of an interdependent world ask that we see ourselves as parts of a larger whole that gives us value and worth? Decisions and judgments prioritize conflicting wishes and needs. The plurality of the definition of death and the necessity of family consent highlight the ambiguity inherent in the Japanese Organ Transplant Law. Ambiguity arises primarily from attempts to reconcile sentiments and obligations that emerge from being part of a family, in the Japanese culture. This reciprocity, supported by the Huayen vision of *dharmadhātu-pratītyasamutpāda* that links our individual lives to each thing and each being in the universe, can be a beacon that directs our ethical energies, conduct, and deliberations.

The exercise of ethical deliberation and conduct, grounded in a vision of an interdependent world, includes a microscopic view along side a macroscopic one. In the appreciation of the integrity of a Noh performance, for example, it is not enough to listen to the individual instruments and acting sequentially. The instruments and the acting must be appreciated together, as each musician modulates his or her instrument and timing in response to the other instruments, the performer, and the audience. Each instrument participates in creating a greater whole. The whole in turn gives value to each instrument. The microscopic and the macroscopic resonate together. The appreciative response by the audience adds to the entire experience. Like the experience of a Noh performance, we must see ourselves as parts of a larger whole. The whole in turn gives each part value and worth. The idea of interdependence links our individual lives to each thing and each being in the universe. To act according to this vision is to work to nurture the lives and relationships that sustain life, my own and all others. James Gustafson, a Christian theologian, also shares this idea. He writes:

> Man [individual persons, communities, and species] is a participant
> in the patterns and processes of interdependence of life in the
> world. Man is not simply a spectator. . . . Man is part of a whole, in-
> deed part of various "wholes" that can be designated. The past
> brings us to where we are in time and space, providing both limita-
> tions and opportunities for new achievements. In the present we are
> interdependent with many factors, and in our actions are respond-
> ing to and interacting with the natural order. Man has capacities to
> affect subsequent courses of events and states of affairs, whether in
> the lives of friends and family members, the conduct of political af-
> fairs, or the ways in which nature itself will be developed.[11]

Gustafson's thinking is infused with the spirit of reciprocity between individuals who are part of a whole and who are participants in the life of the world, and the notion that each individual has the capacity to affect the subsequent development of the world. He goes on to say, "The concept of man as participant in the patterns and processes of interdependence, and reasons given to back it, have consequences for how one thinks about ethics itself."[12] The notion of "man as participant" emphasizes the importance of an ethic of involvement. Alternating between an immersion in and distancing from events strikes a balance between blind participation ("feeling one's way through judgments and choices") and ethical behavior ("rational activity to determine what man ought to be and do"). He bridges the ethical ideal with the practical realities of living. Gustafson's proposed ethics is based on an interpretation of God and divinity's relations to the world, particularly human beings. "In the religious consciousness the patterns and processes of interdependence of life in the world (and not merely in nature) are signs or indications of the divine power and ordering."[13] Buddhists can accept Gustafson's view that human beings are participants in the patterns and processes of interdependence. The core of the Huayen doctrine of *dharmadhātu-pratītyasamutpāda* is precisely the "vital involvement" in the mutual evolution of the world and the "becoming of all things."[14] Fazang would, however, object to attributing the "processes of interdependence" to divine power. Buddhism is a nontheistic tradition and *pratītyasamutpāda* posits a multicentered and evolving reality. *Pratītyasamutpāda* is a reality to be accepted and related to in practical ways. There is no need to probe the origins of the universe or its ultimate purpose.[15] To give life to the truth of interdependence, the devotee must act out the reality of that vision. The acting out of the vision is to take on the mantle of the bodhisattva, who forgoes enlightenment until all others are enlightened. I am reminded of Thich Nhat Hanh, who writes:

> The problem is whether we are determined to go in the direction of compassion or not. If we are, then can we reduce the suffering to a minimum? If I lose my direction, I have to look for the North Star, and I go to the north. That does not mean that I expect to arrive at the North Star. I just want to go in that direction.[16]

Thich Nhat Hanh articulates an important point by saying that by moving in "the direction of compassion . . . we can reduce suffering to a minimum." The decision to move in the direction of compassion may have only an incremental impact. But only by making this decision and acting on this decision can we hope to realize this vision of reducing suffering.

The difficulty of ethical deliberation and action lies in the fact that individuals do not have the same vision of what may be best for all or the means of realizing this vision. Disparate individuals could probably never achieve a common vision. The best that could reasonably be achieved would be a limited consensus of what needs to be done and how it is to be done by those who are directly involved. Decision makers must resolve dilemmas within the context, along the lines all sides have designed, and have a stake in the outcome. The thoughts of a trial judge, who sits in judgment of others, offers some insight into the nature of the goal:

> The person with the responsibility of judgment, whether in a court of in some other forum, must bring to the present moment an empty and impartial mind open not only to the history of the disputed event but also to the teachings of those lawgivers, masters, and poets who have helped us define what the community stands

for. "Save all sentient beings," encouraged the Buddha. "Do justly, but love mercy," says the Book of Micah. Should we who judge do anything less than strive our best to fulfill these imperatives?[17]

Concluding Remarks

Alternative perceptions of death that are written into the current Japanese Organ Transplant Law attempt to accommodate long-held Japanese notions of life and death and modern scientific ideas of life and brain death that are operative in Japanese thinking and emotional life. The law explicitly allows for different definitions of death, brain death and cardiopulmonary death, and it tacitly assumes a third kind of death: social death. Alternative paradigms of death and the need for securing family approval for organs to be harvested make for cumbersome decision making and implementation of organ transplantation. Yet, living and working in ambiguity is often the most productive way of proceeding with ethical reflection and scientific investigation. Such a method permits us to consider other points of view and thoughts. Knowing that we live in an interdependent world means that we may never fully discover all the relevant viewpoints and resolve issues with satisfaction to all people. Appreciating the complexity of personal dilemmas and decision making, and working within that limitation to minimize suffering are, undoubtedly, the most powerful exercises in deepening our understanding of the human condition. With the awareness that good intentions may often be thwarted, the Buddhist experience suggests that we should continue to exercise our compassionate aspirations in the belief that no matter how insignificant, an act of kindness resonates throughout the farthest reaches of the universe.

NOTES

1. Japan Organ Transplantation Network. Available at: http://www.jotnw.or.jp/news.news.hrml.

2. Japanese names in this chapter follow the normal convention: family name precedes given names.

3. This tenth attribute is the tenth and final attribute of the *shixuan yuanqi wuai famen*. Ten attributes of the unimpeded fusion of dharmas of interdependence describe and justify the ideas of mutual identity and mutual interfusion. The first principle states the Huayen position of *pratītyasamutpāda*. The fourth and fifth discuss identity. The second, third, sixth, and seventh attributes discuss facets of mutual fusion. The seventh clarifies the idea of the inexhaustible influence of all dharmas. The eighth explains the identity of phenomena and reality. The ninth speaks of the identity of the three time periods. The tenth is concerned with the identity of the one and the many. The second attribute is concerned with the pervasive influence a single dharma has on the entire universe; the one enters the all. In contrast, the sixth attribute explains how a single dharma can hold all dharmas. The third attribute discusses how the functions of dissimilar dharmas contain and interfuse with each other without losing their identities. The seventh attribute clarifies how dharmas mutually, repeatedly and inexhaustibly influence each other.

4. The most widely accepted dates, 563–483 B.C.E., are based on the Sri Lankan chronicles *Dīpavamasa* and *Mahāvamsa*. Hakuju Ui (1882–1963), a prominent Japanese scholar, disputed these dates based on Northern or Mahāyāna sources. Thus, according to Ui, the Buddha's dates are 466–386 B.C.E.

5. The Japanese criteria for whole-brain death are: (a) deep coma; (b) cessation for spontaneous breathing; (c) fixed and enlarged pupils; (d) absence of brain-stem reflexes; (e) flat brain waves; and (f) the continuation of the above four conditions for at least six hours. Children under six are not subject to the criteria. Two physicians with no vested interest in the harvesting of the individual's organs, in addition to the attending physician, are required to make the diagnosis.

6. On a less universal scale, nationalism requires a degree of homogeneity. To cite an extreme case, leaders of the post-French Revolution wanted the citizens to read the same books and identify with the same history. Similarly, the Japanese national building project required Okinawans and other people on the fringes of its cultural and political sphere to assimilate and become Japanese.

7. Morioka Masahiro, quoted in *Nikkei Weekly*, 23 October 2000.

8. Masahiro Morioka, "Two Aspects of Brain Dead Being," *Eubios Journal of Asian and International Bioethics* 10: 10–11 (2000): 11.

9. *Hsiao-ching*, 4.

10. See "Buddhist Issues in End-of-Life Decision Making," in *Cultural Issues in End-of-Life Decision Making*, ed. Kathryn L. Braun, James H. Pietsch, and Patricia L. Blanchette (New York: Sage, 1999), 213–28.

11. James M. Gustafson, *Ethics from a Theocentric Perspective: Ethics and Theology* (Chicago: University of Chicago Press 1984), 145.

12. Ibid., 146.

13. Ibid., 145–146.

14. Junjirō Takakusu, *The Essentials of Buddhist Philosophy* (Honolulu: Office Appliance, 1956), 39–40.

15. The Parable of the Poison Arrow rebukes the need to uncover the ultimate source of the poison arrow. The physician need only know the kind of poison to effectively prevent the wounded from dying.

16. Thich Nhat Hahn, *Being Peace*, ed. Arnold Kotler (Berkeley, Calif.: Parallax, 1987), 98.

17. Stephen J. Furtunato, "Judging with a Nonjudgmental Mind," *Tricycle, the Buddhist Review* (winter 2002): 21.

14

"On One Path or the Other": Cloning, Religion, and the Making of U.S. Biopolicy

Nigel M. de S. Cameron

Science has set before us decisions of immense consequence. We can pursue medical research with a clear sense of moral purpose or we can travel without an ethical compass into a world we could live to regret. Science now presses forward the issue of human cloning. How we answer the question of human cloning will place us on one path or the other.

—President George W. Bush, the White House,
April 2002

It does not follow that the theology of a few should be allowed to forestall the health and well-being of the many.

—Ron Reagan Jr., Democratic National
Convention, August 2004

If, as historians tell us, the nineteenth century opened in 1789 with the storming of the Bastille and closed in 1914 with the assassination of Archduke Franz Ferdinand, there is little doubt where their successors will locate the beginnings of the "biotech century."

The coincidence in 1997 of three events of vast strategic significance, one in bioscience and two in the emergent arena of biopolicy, announced four years early the opening of the twenty-first century and, with it, the third millennium *Anno Domini*. The event that transfixed the imagination of the globe was the announcement, on February 24, 1997, of the cloning of Dolly the sheep—whose features soon filled the covers of newsmagazines with a blandness to match the title of Ian Wilmut's epoch-making paper, "Viable Offspring Derived from Fetal and Adult Mammalian Cells."[1] Of less media interest, but perhaps of potentially greater significance, was the formalization of the first international convention intended to regulate biotechnology. The European Convention on Human Rights and Biomedicine was opened for signature at Oviedo in Italy, the fruit in brief compass of a decade of consultation among the 40-plus member states of the Council of Europe (to which process the United States was one of four observer parties). In parallel, and with putatively broader significance, the International Bioethics Committee of the United Nations Educational, Scientific, and Cultural Organization gained the approval of the UNESCO General Conference for the first stage in its ambitious development of a "universal instrument in bioethics," with its Universal Declaration on the Human Genome and Human Rights.[2]

Christian Religion and Public Bioethics

Others in this volume and elsewhere have wrestled with the curious predicament in which Christians who are engaged in bioethics find themselves at the opening of the twenty-first century. For one thing, they know well that Christian thinkers played a determinative role in the early development of the field. This is not true simply of Paul Ramsey, the most distinguished of them all,[3] and others who sought a cautious and critical approach to the emerging agenda of biotechnology for human dignity. And as far back as the early 1950s, Joseph Fletcher, soon to be the architect of "situation ethics," in his groundbreaking *Morals and Medicine*—which deserves greater recognition as one of the harbingers of the bioethics enterprise—engaged in a radical reassessment of the Christian tradition as the basis for a public bioethics.[4] Ramsey's settled affirmation of the centrality of a Christian understanding of human nature and human obligations which should be translated into public language offered a paradigm that is now little reflected in the participation of Christian thinkers in the bioethics community.[5] Moreover, Christians are keenly aware that the subject matter of the bioethics agenda lies in theological anthropology—the theological understanding of human nature. The very structure of Christian anthropology is at stake, as technologies are developed that entail capacities to reshape the nature of *Homo sapiens* itself. In a culture that has long been defined by a Christian view of human nature, and whose current character is significantly shaped by the slow death throes of that tradition, the emergence of technologies that grant to us powers over our own selves and our own kind at the most fundamental level raises in stark terms the need for a Christian critique of these possibilities, and the question how a culture that is thus defined will respond.

That is to say, for Christian anthropology the stakes could hardly be higher. The Christian tradition, with its admixture of classical and other elements and mediated since the Enlightenment of the eighteenth century in generally secular categories, has profoundly shaped the culture's understanding of what it means to be human. Yet, in its determination to reinvent itself in post-Christian terms, the culture will always tend to repudiate the Christian voice. Though this is true in general of the legatees of Western Christendom, in Europe and its diaspora around the globe, it is preeminently true in the United States, where the language and ethos of church-state separation enables one of the most religious nations on the planet to keep faith with the incremental Enlightenment secularism of its self-understanding. The nearest parallel, of course, is with France, and its determined Enlightenment principle of *laicite* (separation of church and state). Yet the French are as personally irreligious as the Americans are religious, so *laicite* fits post-Catholic, post-Christian France in a way that church-state separationism is mismatched by the deep-rooted religious conviction and devotion of the American people and so causes continual ructions in the vastly religious American body politic and has, among other things, made the question of abortion the single most significant issue in American culture for more than a generation.[6]

Though mainstream bioethics has tended to sidestep substantive questions such as abortion and focus instead on procedural approaches to decision making with a central interest in autonomy, the policy dimensions of the abortion question and its so far surprisingly quiescent sibling euthanasia have framed for conservative Christians, both Catholic and Protestant, a sanctity-of-life paradigm for engagement in biopolicy. One of the effects of this paradigm has been to discourage their engagement in the broader agenda of bioethics and, ironically, to encourage the rapid secularization of the field. The secularizing process has also been driven by the steady demand, among a generation who knew not Ramsey (or, for that matter, Fletcher), for exclusively public language to be employed in the bioethics conversation. With remarkably few exceptions, therefore, whatever their own religious convictions, religious scholars and thinkers qua bioethicists have tended to adopt the language and, with it, the general assumptions of their secular contemporaries, to such a degree that there is scarcely a recognizable tradition of Christian bioethics in the United States. That does not mean there are no Christians writing qua Christians on these questions, Catholic and Protestant, but they tend to operate within their religious communities and have little influence on the mainstream. For a number of reasons, Catholic writers have been more engaged in mainstream bioethics than Protestant, but their tendency to "go native" has been pronounced.

Though methodological secularism may at one level appear a reasonable expectation of participants in the deliberations of American public culture, if only on the part of those who are desirous of a hearing, the effect of the tail here has been thoroughly to wag the dog. It has essentially destroyed the possibility of a vibrant religious-based public bioethics in the tradition of Ramsey, and it has rendered Christian theology seemingly impotent to critique the emergent technologies of biomedicine whose power to transform the culture and finally human nature itself has emerged—for those with eyes to see—as the dominant question of the age. That this should have happened in the homeland of bioethics, where some three-quarters of the world's biotechnology research and development is located—and that this country is also by far the most religious of all the major Western nations—is something that will at least

be appreciated by lovers of irony. Yet religious, and specifically Christian, bioethics is not quite dead, and it may be that some of the developments chron-
icled in this volume will aid in its revivification.

One fact of particular interest is the manner in which developments in
biotechnology have themselves begun to transform the landscape of critical
bioethics reflection. Two aspects of this transformation should be noted, since
taken together they could yet have dramatic effects both on the possibility for
a public, Christian bioethics, and for the capacity of such a bioethics to influence the culture in its reception of new biotechnologies and, with them, the
most profound questions of human identity. For bioethics is at root anthropology, an exploration of the generally tacit assumptions of individuals and
communities as to what it means to be human. As technology ratchets up the
powers at our disposal, it raises the demands it makes on our self-
understanding, and challenges our will to address fundamental questions
about ourselves, our children, our families, our very species. The opportunity
is still open for intellectual and policy leadership on the part of Christians in
the public square. This will plainly involve a renewed intellectual vision that
will, in turn, lead to mastery of the questions that arise where anthropology
and biotechnology meet within and across distinctively Christian communities.
And we should note that one of the unintended consequences of the pro-life
movement has been its de facto unifying of both activity and reflection across
the fast-diminishing evangelical-Catholic divide in a manner that mainline
Protestant ecumenism should envy.

The developments, briefly, are these. First, the pro-life movement, which
over a generation has been steadily built around abortion as its single focus
(with tangential engagement in the cognate questions raised by euthanasia),
has begun to be pulled into the biotech century.[7] The policy narrative that
follows illustrates the context in which this has taken place. The issues of
research cloning and the patenting of human embryos have served to bridge
the divide between abortion and the moral and policy significance of biotechnology. Both have brought the pro-life movement into energetic engagement
in questions that are only analogically related to abortion and are no part of
the struggle over *Roe v. Wade*. With whatever caveats the pro-life movement
has crossed the bridge, there will be no going back. We may expect to see the
steady emergence of a fresh paradigm in which the taking of life is framed
within a broader fundamental context of the improper manipulation of the
"sanctity" of life, whether through destruction, manipulation, or putative enhancement.

Second, in a development that some have found hard to understand, we
have seen the beginnings of cooperation between those divided by the question of abortion. They have discovered that once abortion itself is taken off
the table, a surprising degree of agreement emerges on matters as varied as
cloning (whether for research or to produce a live-born baby), genetic discrimination, the patenting of embryos and genes, the prospect of "designer
babies," and broader issues affecting the integrity of the human condition,

including the potential significance of new technologies such as nanotech-nology and cybernetics to "enhance" and thereby demean human dignity. The specter of a new eugenics hangs ineluctably over this new century, pow-ered by technologies of vastly greater power for blessing and bane than the primitive barbarities of eugenic sterilization, widely practiced in the United States in the early twentieth century, and, in the more consequent hands of the Nazis, eugenic killing.[8]

The challenge faced by Christian thinkers since the Enlightenment, as the self-evident assumptions of the Western mind began to shift, and key defaults were reset, has been to think and write in Christian terms and public terms at one and the same time—without permitting the assumptions of the secular public square to determine the parameters of thought. In the nineteenth cen-tury, there was understandable confusion, at a time when the assumptions of Christendom seemed still to be in the ascendant, and yet their validity in the public mind was in question. The greatness of such interpreters of the Chris-tian tradition as John Henry Newman (who converted to Roman Catholicism from Anglicanism) and, at the seeming other end of the theological spectrum, Dutch prime minister, newspaper editor, and theologian Abraham Kuyper, lay precisely in their capacity to work within the confines of theological fidelity without permitting them to emasculate their engagement of the public mind. Paul Ramsey stands in that same tradition, as did C. S. Lewis. At a time when the Christian mind is found at a greater discount than for many centuries, the difficulty confronting the would-be Christian bioethics thinker is very great. The temptation to live and die within his or her faith community is strong. The counter-temptation, to live and die within the mainstream of the bioethics community, accepting its premises, is greater. The challenge is to live "in the world and not of it," vigorously engaging the theological tradition—in this context, its implications for anthropology and our use of technology—while translating our thinking into the language of public culture. The growing rap-prochement between Christian thinkers and activists and their colleagues in the generally secular progressive political community could prove a fruitful stimulant to growing bilingualism on their part.

Moreover, it is important to recognize that the making of common cause on the bioeugenics agenda arises from substantial commonalities that have long existed between the two major centers of conscience in Western culture (conservative and progressive), in respect of their anthropology and their view of the "givenness" of nature. In both cases, these communities of conscience find themselves ranged against the corrosive effects of incipient libertarianism, which is no respecter of the conventional left-right topography of Western politics. If the corrosion continues, it may not be too much to speculate on the possibility of a long-term realignment that will radically reshape our culture and its politics, and of which collaboration on the increasingly dominant bio-policy agenda is an eloquent harbinger.

The Biopolicy Debates

The Background: History of Policy on Embryo Research

Four flashpoint policy debates have characterized the formation of U.S. bio-policy during the opening years of this century. Though they have a common focus in the question of the human embryo and its use, each has a different character. In what follows I will review these policy debates. Before doing so, I should note that U.S. engagement in the discussion of policy in respect of research on the human embryo has a long history. Years before technical terms from biology jumped into the headlines and became household words, a series of federal documents offered policy proposals to guide the emerging field of human embryo experimentation that had been opened up by the development of in vitro technology which, for the first time, made available the early embryo ex utero as a potential object, and subject, of experimentation. The significance of these documents has been largely eclipsed in recent debate, and it is worth briefly revisiting their positions, for two reasons.

First, the National Bioethics Advisory Commission (NBAC) and other advisory panels were constituted as broadly representative bodies—but representative of the "bioethics community," which tends to be politically and culturally liberal in its general disposition (a fact dramatically illustrated in its cloning report) and tends also to be secular in its assumptions. That does not entail an absence of culturally conservative and religious participants in the discussion of bioethics, but, as I said above, they tend to accept the secular ground rules of the field. Certainly they were not much in evidence at NBAC and its cognates in the 1980s. The contrast with the President's Council on Bioethics (PCOB), appointed by President George W. Bush in 2001, has been overdrawn in much press comment. But there is no doubt that the PCOB, chaired by cultural conservative Leon Kass, has been widely perceived as taking a very different approach to the question of reflection on the significance of developments in biotechnology. One key difference lies in the composition of the council, which includes members (such as Francis Fukuyama and Kass himself) who have made distinguished contributions to the discussion of questions in bioethics[9] but has no member who is a professional bioethicist. To that extent, the PCOB takes the bioethics discussion back to a stage when it was more genuinely interdisciplinary and there was no bioethics "profession." Criticism of the council for its supposed monochrome approach to the questions on its agenda has been common but misinformed. There would seem, for example, to be a much wider spread of opinion among council members on some key questions than there was on NBAC. Certainly, there is (more) representation of culturally and ethically conservative opinion, but the wrongheadedness of much of the criticism attracted by the council on this ground was evident in its early failure (little noticed in the press, since it would have undermined representation of the council as an administration lapdog, though noted caustically by the White House) to endorse the position of the Bush administration on cloning.[10]

Second, the positions taken by NBAC on embryo research issues were reached before a combination of discovery and speculation fueled a massive inflation of expectation in respect of the "therapeutic" potential of embryonic stem cell research. Though these issues have always been controversial, never before has it been suggested—as was being said before 9/11—that the embryonic stem cell issue was of such significance that it might be seen as the defining issue of the Bush presidency. In the run-up to the 2004 presidential election it reemerged as a dominant political-cultural question.

The central thrust of these early biopolicy documents was to seek middle ground by approving embryonic research under strict conditions and, more significant, with candid recognition of the unique character of the human embryo.[11] Though not ruling out deleterious experimentation on the early embryo, the positions adopted were surrounded by ethical caveats, and centered in the clearly articulated conviction that the human embryo deserves "profound respect," even if not "the full legal and moral rights attributed to persons." So in 1994 the NIH Embryo Research Panel agreed that "the preimplantation human embryo warrants serious moral consideration as a developing form of human life" even though "it does not have the same moral status as infants and children."[12] Moreover, what the panel refers to as "the respect due to the preimplantation embryo" is listed as one of the reasons why certain research proposals should not be funded, "even if claims were made for their scientific or therapeutic value." Five years later, the National Bioethics Advisory Commission (NBAC), appointed by President Clinton, commented that there was wide agreement that "human embryos deserve respect as a form of human life."[13] These positions reflect a general approach that was perhaps most influentially articulated in the United Kingdom's *Warnock Report* (1984), to the effect that the research use of human embryos might be approved but only in a situation of great moral seriousness since the human embryo is unlike any other laboratory material.[14] This language stands in marked contrast both to the mass-production techniques envisaged for "therapeutic cloning" and the decisive triumph of ends over means that has, in most public debate, used the prospect of "cures" to quash even the simulacrum of serious ethical reflection.

Policy discussion and development on general questions of embryo research, which of course predated the development of cloning technology (by somatic cell nuclear transfer), set the immediate context for responses to the announcement that Dolly had been cloned. Although federal law did not already prohibit cloning (some other states, such as the Federal Republic of Germany, had passed prohibitions in anticipation of such a development in technology), it restricted the availability of federal funds for cloning-related research. Since 1996, Congress has included riders in appropriations measures for the Departments of Labor, Health and Human Services, and Education that prohibit the use of appropriated funds for the creation of human embryos for research purposes or for research in which human embryos are destroyed (the so-called Dickey Amendment). In general, the riders define the human embryo as any organism "derived by fertilization, parthenogenesis, cloning, or any other means from one or more human gametes or human diploid cells."[15]

In fact, while federal advisory bodies reflective of the bioethics mainstream were offering cautious encouragement to limited research on human embryos, federal funding of *any* type of research involving human embryos, starting with in vitro fertilization, has been blocked by various policy decisions dating back 25 years. Following the birth in England of Louise Brown, the first baby to result from in vitro fertilization, in July 1978, the Ethics Advisory Board of the Department of Health and Human Services (HHS) was tasked with considering the scientific, ethical, legal, and social issues surrounding the technology.[16] The ethics board released its report on May 4, 1979, finding that research on in vitro fertilization was acceptable from an ethical standpoint and could be supported with federal funds. Those recommendations were never adopted by the department, and the board was dissolved in 1980; no other ethics board has been chartered. Because federal regulations that govern human subject research (45 CFR 46) stipulated that, at the time, federally supported research involving human in vitro fertilization must be reviewed by the department's ethics board, a *de facto* moratorium on funding that research and other related embryo research resulted. The National Institutes of Health Revitalization Act of 1993 (P.L. 193–43, Section 121(c)) nullified the regulatory provision (45 CFR 46.204(d)) requiring the review and thereby lifted the *de facto* moratorium.

In response, the National Institutes of Health (NIH) established the Human Embryo Research Panel to assess the ethical issues raised by this research and to develop recommendations for the agency's review and for conduct of human embryo research. The panel released a report providing guidelines and recommendations on human embryo research in September 1994. It recommended that some areas of human embryo research be considered for federal funding, including somatic cell nuclear transfer (SCNT), stem cells, and (under certain limited conditions) embryos created solely for the purpose of research.[17] The panel also identified areas of human embryo research it considered to be unacceptable or to warrant additional review. It determined that certain types of cloning without transfer to the uterus warranted additional review before the panel could recommend whether the research should be federally funded. However, the panel concluded that federal funding for cloning techniques followed by transfer to the uterus should be unacceptable into the foreseeable future. The panel's report was unanimously accepted by the NIH's Advisory Committee to the Director on December 2, 1994.

After that committee's action, President Clinton directed the NIH not to allocate resources to "support the creation of human embryos for research purposes."[18] The president's directive did not apply to research involving so-called spare embryos resulting from clinical in vitro fertilization procedures. Following the directive, the agency proceeded with plans to develop guidelines to support research using spare embryos.

But the agency's plans to develop guidelines on the funding of embryo research were halted when P.L. 104–99, with the Dickey Amendment attached to it, was enacted on January 26, 1996. The same rider has been attached to the Labor, HHS, and Education Appropriations Acts for fiscal years 1997

through 2002. For 2003, the provision prohibits HHS from using appropriations for: (1) the creation of a human embryo or embryos for research purposes;
or, (2) research in which a human embryo or embryos are destroyed, discarded,
or knowingly subjected to risk of injury or death greater than that allowed for
research on fetuses *in utero* under 45 CFR 46.208(a)(2) and Section 498(b) of
the Public Health Service Act (42 U.S.C. 289g(b)). For purposes of this section,
the term "human embryo or embryos" includes any organism, not protected
as a human subject under 45 CFR 46 (Human Subject Protection regulations)
that is derived by fertilization, parthenogenesis, cloning, or any other means
from one or more human gametes or human diploid cells. The rider language
has not changed significantly over the years.

On March 4, 1997, shortly after the Dolly announcement, President Clinton sent a memorandum to the heads of all executive departments and agencies
making it "absolutely clear that no federal funds will be used for human cloning." This action extended the congressional ban beyond the HHS to all federally supported research. He also urged the private sector to adopt a voluntary
ban on the cloning of human beings. The *NIH Guidelines on Stem Cell Research*,
published by the Clinton administration in August 2000, would not have
funded research in which human stem cells are used for reproductive cloning
of a human; human stem cells are *derived* using SCNT; or human stem cells
that were derived using SCNT are *utilized* in a research project.

Advances in medical science proceeded, and in 1998 critical developments
were recognized by scientists at the University of Wisconsin. These researchers
were able to isolate human embryonic stem cells and coax them to grow into
specialized cells. Harriet Rabb, the general counsel for the HHS, concluded
that then-current law prohibiting the use of appropriated funds for human
embryo research would not apply to research using embryonic stem cells "because such cells are not a human embryo within the statutory definition."[19]
The department concluded that the NIH could fund research that uses stem
cells derived from the embryo by private funds. But because of the language
in the rider, the NIH could not fund research that, with federal funds, derived
the stem cells from embryos.

Some members of Congress strongly opposed HHS's view and believed
that the legislative ban that would continue through fiscal year 2001 covered
and prohibited such research. In response, Secretary Shalala stated in a letter
that the definition of embryo used in the HHS legal opinion relied on the
definition of embryo in the statute and that the ban applied only to research
in which human embryos are discarded or destroyed but not to research pre-
ceding or following "on such projects."[20] The letter stated: "Moreover . . . there
is nothing in the legislative history to suggest that the provision was intended
to prohibit funding for research in which embryos—organisms—are not involved." The NIH indicated that it would fund research on pluripotent stem
cells derived from human embryos and fetal tissue once guidelines were issued
and an oversight committee was established. Draft guidelines were published
in the *Federal Register* in December 1999, and final guidelines were issued in
August 2000.[21] The guidelines provided that studies using pluripotent stem

cells derived from human embryos may be conducted using NIH funds only if the cells were derived, without federal funds, from human embryos that were created for the purposes of fertility treatment and were in excess of the clinical need of the individuals seeking such treatment. The NIH initiated the applications process, which was running when the Bush administration took office at the start of 2001, and in the early months of 2001 was left in place. It emerged as the major issue in pre-9/11 American politics.

EMBRYONIC STEM CELL RESEARCH FUNDING. Subsequent debate over the use of embryonic stem cells for research has been intertwined with the question of cloning as a means of producing embryos, often as two aspects to the same question. Though cloning may be used for other research purposes than to generate stem cells (for example, disease models), and while embryonic stem cells may be produced without the employment of cloning, the idea of "therapeutic cloning" has proved a powerful driver for the debate. In a striking example of the rhetorical strategy being employed by advocates of research cloning, in a speech to the 2004 Democratic National Convention, Ron Reagan Jr., son of the late president, made a forceful case for research on therapeutic cloning, describing in detail how it could work, without once using the term.

Though the Bush administration has favored a statutory ban on human cloning for all purposes, its policy on embryonic stem cell research has been focused on federal research funding, in the context of the Dickey Amendment. In his first televised broadcast to the American people, President Bush responded to public and political debate over HHS plans to fund embryonic stem cell research and announced on August 9, 2001, that for the first time federal funds would indeed be used to support research on human embryonic stem cells. However, funding would be limited to "existing stem cell lines." President Bush indicated his strong opposition to human cloning; federal funds will not be used for the cloning of human embryos for any purpose, including the derivation of stem cells for research. Federal funds would be used to conduct research on human embryonic stem cells, but only those derived from embryos that had already been destroyed by that date, and subject to certain criteria: they must be obtained (1) with the informed consent of the donors; (2) from excess embryos created solely for reproductive purposes;[22] and (3) without any financial inducements to the donors. No federal funds will be used for the derivation or use of stem cell lines derived from newly destroyed embryos; the creation of any human embryos for research purposes; or cloning of human embryos for any purposes.[23] In the same televised speech, President Bush announced his intention to create a President's Council on Bioethics to evaluate the ethical implications of biomedical innovation, with Leon Kass as its chairman.[24] The council was established in November of that year.

Public debate about stem cells has been handicapped by the general inclination of the press to distil every major question into two basic viewpoints, a tendency aided by readiness to read every new bioethics question in light of its relation to abortion. Yet there is a wide range of ethical and policy options in embryonic stem-cell research, as the Bush administration's funding policy—neither a prohibition nor an open-ended endorsement—illustrates. There are at least five basic permutations. (1) All use of human embryos for research should be prohibited; (2) excess embryos derived from clinical in vitro programs may be used, but others should not be created for the purpose; (3) embryos may be created with the intent of using them for research; (4) only certain excess embryos should be used, such as those destroyed before August 9, 2001; (5) embryos may be cloned using somatic cell nuclear transfer for research purposes as a source for embryonic stem cells. Moreover, in each of these cases a position could be taken in respect of research funding, or in respect of criminal sanctions on unapproved research. In cases where research is permitted, two further issues arise: questions of consent on the part of donors, and the age limit to embryo development.

Among these various positions, the administration's funding of cell-lines from existing embryos represents an accommodation to the pressure for research funding that does not encourage the destruction of any further embryos, and does not countenance the creation of embryos—by in vitro techniques or cloning—for the express purpose of research in which they will be destroyed. The announcement was met with divided responses from conservative Christians; some were highly critical, and others praised it as a conscientious compromise.

HUMAN CLONING IN FEDERAL POLICY. When the cloning of Dolly the sheep was announced in February of 1997 it elicited a speedy response from President Clinton, who issued a memorandum to the heads of the executive departments and agencies that addressed the funding of human cloning stating that federal funds would not be used for the cloning of human beings. In remarks to the press, President Clinton urged the private sector to take a similar stance. His vigorous response stands in sharp and somewhat curious contrast to the NBAC report that he commissioned, which after high-profile and hurried meetings (it was asked to report within 90 days), published a lengthy document that included extensive discussion of religious and other views on the subject. NBAC reported its findings and recommendations on June 9, 1997. While concern was expressed about the impact of cloning on even a physically healthy child, in respect of issues of autonomy and individuality, the only "ethical" argument that finally carried weight with NBAC was, as it were, the ethics of safety. So its recommendation was for a three- to five-year moratorium on cloning to produce babies—a position that with hindsight appears extraordinarily permissive, since there is near unanimity in public and political circles that this practice should simply be prohibited.[25]

By contrast, the Bush administration has sought a legislative ban on human cloning for any purpose. In the Senate, a comprehensive cloning ban is proposed in S. 245, sponsored by Senators Brownback (Republican) and Landrieu (Democrat).[26] The bill parallels the House bill passed twice by large majorities, proposed by Dr. Dave Weldon (Republican) and Bart Stupak (Democrat), and mandates a civil penalty of at least $1 million and a criminal penalty of imprisonment of up to 10 years.[27]

Cloning has gripped the public imagination and offers a model of the fateful possibilities of biotechnology that may prove as potent as the enduring image of Mary Shelley's *Frankenstein*. While for some its use to mass produce embryos for purposes of research is benign and to be distinguished radically from the gestation and birth of cloned babies, for others these uses are conjoined. Its hold on the imagination has led to strenuous efforts on the part of those who favor research cloning to redefine the terms of the debate in a manner that avoids the use of the word, and instead employs such obscure alternatives as "nuclear transplantation." A bipartisan bill in the U.S. Senate that seeks to prohibit baby cloning and, in the process, protect cloning for research goes so far as to define cloning formally as the implantation of a clonal embryo. The sponsors of S. 303[28] include Sen. Orrin Hatch, a conservative Republican who is against abortion, as well as pro-choice Democrats. The bill's novel definition of cloning is this: "implanting or attempting to implant the product of nuclear transplantation into a uterus or the functional equivalent of a uterus." Its supporters can therefore claim that it opposes all "cloning," while permitting and thereby protecting cloning for research purposes. Furthermore, the bill offers an abstract, new term for the clonal embryo, referring to it as an "unfertilized blastocyst," that is, "an intact cellular structure that is the product of nuclear transplantation." This creative neologism is curious, since blastocysts do not get fertilized; oocytes are fertilized and thereupon become blastocysts. The purpose of this coinage is plainly to seek to redefine the terms of the debate and deflect attention from the clonal embryo, which it seeks to protect as a subject of deleterious experimentation.

A New Jersey state statute goes further, by defining cloning not even as implantation, but as live birth of the clonal fetus. In January 2004, New Jersey signed into law a bill that authorizes cloning for research and permits the gestation of an implanted embryo clone in the womb until birth. While claiming to "permit human stem cell research," it protects the experimental use of the implanted clonal fetus during pregnancy. All that is forbidden is for the baby to be born and survive.[29]

Perhaps the most bizarre example of these attempts at linguistic gerrymandering came to a head in the campaign around California's Proposition 71, intended to fund stem cell research and cloning. Proponents of the measure denied that it would fund cloning and asked a judge to deny its opponents the right to use the term, but the judge declined. Yet Proposition 71, as described in *Section 2, Purpose and Intent*, is unambiguous; and whether "somatic cell nuclear transfer" is used for the purpose of implantation or, as in Proposition 71, for research, the product of SCNT is a cloned human embryo.[30]

The President's Council on Bioethics, though divided on the issue of cloning for research, was unanimous in seeking honest language in the debate. The council specifically voiced concern about "the temptation to solve the moral questions by artful redefinition or by denying to some morally crucial element a name that makes clear that there is a moral question to be faced." The report adopted the terminology "cloning-to-produce-children" and "cloning-for-biomedical-research" and defined "cloned human embryo" as "the immediate (and developing) product of the initial act of cloning, accomplished by successful SCNT, whether used subsequently in attempts to produce children or in biomedical research."[31]

CLONING AT THE UNITED NATIONS GENERAL ASSEMBLY. The United States has pressed for a parallel cloning prohibition through the U.N. General Assembly. In response to a joint initiative from Germany and France in 2001 to initiate a process to write a convention to prohibit "human reproductive cloning," the United States and other governments sought to expand the intended terms of the convention to include human cloning for any purpose. The United States argued that all cloning is in fact reproductive, and that the only way to ensure that there would be no birth of clonal babies would be to forbid the development of human cloning technology and the manufacture of large numbers of clonal embryos. The United States worked in the Sixth (legal) Committee of the General Assembly meeting in February 2002 to build support for a wider convention, noting (a) that all cloning is in fact "reproductive"; and (b) that to secure a comprehensive prohibition on the birth of live-born cloned babies the use of somatic-cell nuclear transfer in human beings should be prohibited.[32]

The initial round of discussion in the Sixth Committee in 2002 led to a series of debates in which Costa Rica emerged as the formal sponsor of a ban on all cloning, with 66 cosponsors, against a Belgian proposal that superseded the German-French initiative and secured 22 cosponsors after Germany was forced to withdraw from its leading role by severe domestic pressure. In November 2003, the Sixth Committee voted by the narrowest of margins (80–79, with 15 abstentions) for a procedural motion to suspend the discussion until 2005, proposed by Iran on behalf of the Organization of the Islamic Conference.[33] In turn, this decision was revised by the General Assembly, where after concentrated diplomatic debate, it was agreed to address the matter in the fifty-ninth session of the General Assembly in the fall of 2004. In September 2004, President Bush addressed the General Assembly and called for support for the Costa Rican resolution. On March 8, 2005, the United Nations General Assembly approved the Declaration on Human Cloning, which calls on all member states to ban all forms of human cloning as incompatible with human dignity and the protection of human life.[34]

THE PATENTABILITY OF HUMAN EMBRYOS. In July 2003, U.S. Rep. Dave Weldon (R-Pa.) whose bill to ban human cloning for any purpose has twice passed the House, offered an amendment to the 2004 Commerce/Justice/State appropriations bill which stated, "None of the funds appropriated or otherwise made available under the act may be used to issue patents on claims directed to or encompassing a human organism."[35] As the United States Patent and Trademark Office cannot issue patents apart from funds allotted during the appropriations process, the amendment essentially functioned as a ban on the patenting of human organisms as products of cloning or any other biotechnological patented process. Though hailing the great benefits in health and knowledge that accrue to society through biotechnological advances, Weldon cautioned that the precipitous pace of developments coupled with the activity of "rogue scientists" who will not place ethical restraints upon their research demands the collective action of civilized society. Weldon cited as example the report presented before the European Society of Human Reproduction and Embryology of the creation and subsequent growth for six days of the first male-female hybrid human embryos—research almost universally condemned as unnecessary and unethical. The researcher in this instance reportedly indicated intent to obtain a patent for his human hybrid product. Noting that the monopoly of patent protection lasts for 20 years, Weldon asserted that Congress should take immediate action to ensure that our nation would not bestow upon this researcher or others like him an opportunity to gain financially by an "exclusive right to practice such ghoulish research."[36] Weldon called upon Congress to affirm the existing, bipartisan policy of the patent office against granting patents on human beings at any stage of development under.[37] He reassured his colleagues that the amendment would not bear upon stem cell research or gene patenting and delineated the subject matter prohibited from patentability to be "human organisms, human embryos, human fetuses or human beings."

The trade association of the biotechnology industry, the Biotechnology Industry Organization, initially opposed the amendment. Its cognate advocacy group the Coalition for the Advancement of Medical Research sent out alerts to the parents of children with devastating diseases[38] encouraging them to contact their legislators and warning them that the amendment may prevent development of treatments for their diseases—including "cancer, Alzheimer's, diabetes, Parkinson's, spinal cord injuries, heart disease, ALS [Amyotrophic Lateral Sclerosis], and other debilitating conditions."[39] Four primary reasons for objection to the amendment were cited: (1) the absence of a definition for the phrase "human organism" would preclude many biotechnology inventions and impede the development of life-saving products; (2) investment and research would halt; (3) the language is unnecessary as the patent office maintains an administrative policy not to issue patents on humans; and (4) the amendment would preclude patents on "an organism of human species at any stage of development produced by any method, a living organism made by human cloning, and a process of human cloning." In addition, the Biotechnology Industry Organization feared the possible ramifications of dealing with ethical concerns through proscribing certain subject matter to be outside the scope of patentability.[40] Finally, the industry group concluded by noting that the patent office justifies its policy under the Constitutional prohibition against slavery and involuntary servitude present in the Thirteenth Amendment with the implication that the same constitutional prohibition would also be found by the courts should the policy be challenged in a legal action.[41]

The administration joined the debate by issuing a letter from James Rogan, the director of the patent office, that welcomed the amendment as offering support to existing internal policy. The amendment was easily passed by the House, and agreed in conference committee. When it became clear that it would be accepted, the industry organization withdrew its objections and said that its concerns had been clarified.

Toward a Christian Anthropology for the Twenty-First Century

Though it is possible to argue that the political and broader cultural signifi-cance that these debates have attracted in the United States is to some degree the result of coincidence, we can be in no doubt as to the larger importance of the biotechnology agenda for the human community, reaching as it does deep into our sense of identity as individuals and a species, and holding out to us opportunities that may remind us less of Frankenstein than of Faust. The prospects of agelessness, of enhancement, of children designed with features of our choosing, of changes in the germline that will affect every generation to come, of an unholy matrimony of human and machine and, finally, the option of a posthuman future reached more by accident than design, as these manipulative possibilities accumulate and our new powers are let loose to re-shape the kind of beings we are—it is hard to grant this debate anything less than center stage in the human theater. More immediately, we can see in the debate over "therapeutic" cloning and the patenting of embryos what one re-cent writer has put in these terms: "that medicine has become, for us at the turn of the millennium, a primary (perhaps *the* primary) discourse and practice through which we articulate and pursue views of the good." He continues: "One would think, therefore, that Christian bioethicists would be interested in the question of whether and/or to what extent the ways in which we articulate and pursue the good through enhancements is compatible with the ways in which the good is articulated and pursued through Christian faith and practice. Yet Christian ethicists of all traditions have said surprisingly little about this question."[42]

Indeed, it has been left to Leon Kass, longtime critic of potential abuses of genetic technology and current chairman of the President's Council on Bio-ethics, to articulate such concerns sans pareil. Arguing that advances in ge-netics "cannot be treated in isolation," Kass maintains that these must be cor-related with "other advances in reproductive and developmental biology, in neurobiology, and in the genetics of behavior—indeed, with all the techniques now and soon to be marshaled to intervene ever more directly and precisely into the bodies and minds of human beings."[43] While scientists like to portray such questioning as arising from "scientific ignorance or else to outmoded moral and religious notions," a theme that has been depressingly dominant in the course of the controversies we have outlined, Kass goes to the heart of the question. The very success of our technology has given fresh impetus to a materialistic reduction of human nature that goes far beyond the rejection of this or that religious conviction or moral boundary. "Hence our peculiar moral crisis: we adhere more and more to a view of human life that gives us enormous power and that, *at the same time*, denies every possibility of nonarbitrary standards for guiding the use of this power." In consequence, he says, "we are doomed to become its creatures if not its slaves."[44]

Kass here alludes to a famous essay of C. S. Lewis, "The Abolition of Man," an occasional piece first published in 1943. Lewis—English literary scholar, novelist, and lay theologian—addresses from afar the coming challenges of human genetics.[45] Lewis's essay opens with a potent quotation from the English Puritan John Bunyan's *Pilgrim's Progress*: "It came burning hot into my mind, whatever he said and however he flattered, when he got me home to his house, he would sell me for a slave." That, in essence, is Lewis's percipient response to the prospect of the genetic revolution and what lies beyond.

Lewis argues that all technology, which is said to extend the power of the human race, is in fact a means of extending the power of "some men over other men." He instances the radio and the airplane as typical products of technology that, like all other consumer items, can be bought by some, not afforded by others, and could be withheld by some from others who have the resources to buy. Writing after four years of war in Europe, Lewis is peculiarly aware of the capacities of these technologies to be used to subject some to the power of others, whether in dropping bombs or broadcasting propaganda. But his third example, the bridge to the potentials of biotechnology, lies in contraception. Here some special features attach to the more general problems of use and abuse, since "there is a paradoxical, negative sense in which all possible future generations are the patients or subjects of a power wielded by those already alive." This is true at two levels. "By contraception simply, they are denied existence; by contraception used as a means of selective breeding, they are, without their concurring voice, made to be what one generation, for its own reasons, may choose to prefer." In light of the pervasive influence of eugenic thinking and practice, in the United States and the United Kingdom as well as Germany, in which enforced sterilization was widely employed for selective breeding purposes, Lewis is building his argument on the technology of the early twentieth century even as he anticipates that of the twenty-first. As a result, he continues, "From this point of view, what we call Man's power over Nature turns out to be a power exercised by some men over other men with Nature as its instrument." He hastens to add that while it can be easily said that "men have hitherto used badly, and against their fellows, the powers that science has given them," that is not his point. He is not addressing "particular corruptions and abuses which an increase of moral virtue would cure," but rather "what the thing called 'Man's power over Nature' must always and essentially be." For "all long-term exercises of power, especially in breeding, must mean the power of earlier generations over later ones."

What Lewis is here drawing attention to is, at it were, the genetic equivalent of what in another field is termed intergenerational economics. In the nature of the case, the genetic accounting is of a yet higher level of significance than economic relationships run through time, although the principle is the same: the effects of one generation's decisions on subsequent generations. So Lewis states: "We must picture the race extended through time from the date of its emergence to that of its extinction. Each generation exercises power over its successors: and each, in so far as it modifies the environment bequeathed to it and rebels against tradition, resists and limits the power of its predecessors." There can be no

> increase in power on Man's side. Each new power won *by* man is a power *over* man as well. Each advance leaves him weaker as well as stronger. In every victory, besides the general who triumphs, he is a prisoner who follows the triumphal car. . . .*Human* nature will be the last part of Nature to surrender to Man. The battle will then be won. We shall have "taken the thread of life out of the hand of Clotho" and be henceforth free to make our species whatever we wish it to be. The battle will indeed be won. But who, precisely, will have won it?[46]

Because "the power of Man to make himself what he pleases means, as we have seen, the power of some men to make other men what *they* please . . . [m]an's final conquest has proved to be the abolition of Man."[47]

Though much of Lewis's analysis is directed at the possibility of germline (inheritable) genetic interventions, his twofold thesis is of wider application: first, he sets out the fundamental problematic of biotechnology and its affiliates as a vast challenge that must be addressed; and, second, he frames its significance precisely in the context of anthropology. Though his argument uses public language, his starting point is the Christian understanding of what it means to be human, an understanding built deep into the Western cultural tradition.

The foundations of Christian anthropology lie in two of the most central Christian doctrines, those of Creation and Incarnation.

First, Creation. Genesis 1 unambiguously lays out a taxonomy of the created order, in which humankind—male and female—is set at its head, as "God's last work" (Tennyson), made "in his image." The contrast with the other creatures is striking, since in the repeated refrain they are to reproduce "after their kind." That phrase is not used of humankind, which is made, as it were, after "God's kind," in the maker's very likeness, even if also unlike him in the warp and woof of space and time. The bearing of the divine image and likeness is coterminous with humankind; membership in *Homo sapiens* entails nothing less. Every product of human conception is therefore a being after God's kind.

This foundation for human dignity offers a radical starting point for every discussion of human dignity and rights—especially of the equal dignity of women, and of men and women of all races and conditions. Yet it has remarkable application to the context of bioethics. Though not addressing every problem in contemporary bioethics debate, its radical assertion of the unity and common dignity of the human race in the Maker's image establishes a framework of understanding within which all questions may be addressed, and many are immediately resolved.

Second, Incarnation. The preeminent significance among Christian beliefs of the extraordinary doctrine of the Incarnation offers a second key to our understanding of a distinctively Christian bioethics, since it undergirds the creation anthropology with one rooted in Christology. And its teaching of God in human form, in humiliation in the Palestine of the first century and in glory today, lies at the heart of the highly distinctive character of the Christian vision of God. So it is also rich in significance for the questions addressed in contemporary bioethics. For not only did God take human form, he did so in the form of a blastocyst, as an early embryo. Not only did he sanctify human nature by his life as a Palestinian Jew, he sanctifies it forever in his continuing, glorified humanity.

With cloning, we take the first decisive step across the line that separates the kind of beings we are from the kind of things we make; thus *Homo sapiens*, in his character of *Homo faber*, man the maker, turns his making on himself—and in the sublimest of ironies in a single fateful act both elevates himself to the role of creator and degrades that same self to the status of a manufacture. This act is stupefying in its scope. Humankind simultaneously claims the role of God while being reduced to playing the part of a mere thing, the dust of the earth out of which we were made and to which we foolish creatures choose to return ourselves; in Lewis's classicism, we take the thread out of the hand of Clotho.

From a theological perspective, the significance of both these sides of the coin is plain. In our attempt to serve as our own creator, we are revealed as usurpers, capable only of manufacture. That Faustian bargain is the only one on offer. For the task of creator is personal to God, and his election of the interpersonal mystery of human sexuality as the context for procreation preserves his creatorhood absolutely. The most that his human creatures can do is, as we say, to "ape" his role, parody it, and reduce it to the mechanistic and industrial processes at which we are so good and for which indeed—among other things—we were made. The ambiguity of the clonal human, as both creature and product, *Homo sapiens* hijacked by *Homo faber*, moves us decisively toward what the posthumanists call the "singularity"—that state they envisage in which the distinction between human being and manufactured being is over, and a seamless dress weaves together humankind and what humankind has made. It anticipates the union of *mecha* and *orga*.[48] Yet within the Christian tradition, the rationale is clear. The technological imperative that we read out of the "dominion mandate" in Genesis 1 lies in the context of the kind of being that God has made his human creatures to be.

What is more, the incarnation of Jesus Christ, in which God takes human nature for his own, declares unambiguously that *Homo sapiens* is no mere accident of history but God's own image impressed into space and time. The fact of his continuing humanity offers the surest possible guide to Christians who are perplexed in the face of technologies that have the power to reshape human nature itself. The Jesus who died, rose, and ascended is seated in his divine-human form at the right hand of the Father; "this supreme ruler of the universe," as Charles Hodge, the greatest American theologian of the nineteenth century, stated it boldly, "is a perfect man as well as a perfect God."[49]

In Conclusion

The series of interrelated policy positions adopted by the U.S. administration in the opening years of the "biotech century" in respect of cloning, embryonic stem cell research, and the patenting of human embryos offer a case study in the development of public policy that, though it has been developed in the context of secular argument, reflects distinctive concerns of Christian theology. Through several circumstances (including the development of mammalian cloning by somatic cell nuclear transfer in 1996, the pursuit in the final months of the Clinton administration of a workaround for congressional bans on embryo research, the Franco-German cloning initiative at the United Nations, and rising concerns over intellectual property claims on human nature), the Bush administration in the opening years of the twenty-first century confronted a series of interconnected policy decisions affecting the ethical-legal framework for biotechnology. Though there has been little explicitly Christian reflection within the bioethics community, Christians together with other thinkers have recognized that these questions reflect a struggle for the anthropology that will determine the scope and course of developments in biotechnology. The distinctively Christian vision for human nature, founded deep in the doctrines of Creation and Incarnation, is in important aspects echoed more widely in the culture. So liberal and conservative Christians and progressive secular voices alike have taken broadly similar approaches to the need to contain biotechnology within a framework of human dignity, and thereby offered either endorsement or significant levels of support for this clutch of policy positions.

The challenge to Christian thinkers is to follow the example of Lewis and, while continuing to think as Christians, to speak in public language and seek allies for their distinctive positions in the wider culture. When they do that, they face a serious opportunity to influence and perhaps shape the biopolicy of the coming generation. If they withdraw into religious language, or, conversely, if their distinctive concerns amalgamate with the broad assumptions of the cultural elite—as has tended to be the way when they have become part of the professional bioethics community—then their influence and that of their distinctive view of the world will wither. The fact that broad consonances have become evident between highly distinctive, Christian ways of thinking about technology and human nature, and assumptions widely held in progressive political-cultural circles (among environmentalists, feminists, and others) suggests that a pattern of distinctive thinking accompanied by fluent translation into the cultural vernacular, a pattern sampled in these opening rounds of the great twenty-first-century biopolicy debate, may bring together into a common task the two most potent forces in Western culture, and finally render the struggle for the future of human nature one which, under God, may be won.

I am pleased to acknowledge the aid of my research assistants Dawn M. Willow and Amber Standridge in preparing parts of this essay.

NOTES

1. *Nature* 385, February 27, 1997, 810–813. Available at http://biocrs.biomed
.brown.edu/books/chapters/ch%209/clones/Nature/Sheep-NATURE.html.

2. Available at http://portal.unesco.org/shs/en/ev.php-URL_ID=1881&URL_DO
=DO_TOPIC&URL_SECTION=201.html.

3. In books such as *Fabricated Man: The Ethics of Genetic Control* (New Haven,
Conn.: Yale University Press, 1970); *The Patient as Person* (New Haven, Conn.: Yale
University Press, 1970); *Ethics at the Edges of Life: Medical and Legal Intersections* (New
Haven, Conn.: Yale University Press, 1978).

4. Joseph Fletcher, *Morals and Medicine* (Boston: Beacon, 1960).

5. I have outlined this problem in my article "Bioethics in Christianity," in *The
Encyclopedia of Bioethics*, 3rd ed., ed. Stephen G. Post (New York: Macmillan, 2003).

6. For the French, of course, the flash point of this doctrine does not lie with
Christians but with Islam and the wearing of the chador in public schools

7. What I have elsewhere referred to as "Bioethics II." Bioethics I focuses on the
traditional issues of medical ethics, and III the emerging agenda in cybernetics and
nanotechnology and other avenues with the potential for human enhancement. See
my article "Bioethics in Christianity."

8. The fullest and most recent account of this devastating story, which focuses
especially on the connections between U.S. and Nazi eugenics, is Edwin Black's *The
War against the Weak* (New York: Four Walls Eight Windows, 2003).

9. E.g., Francis Fukuyama, *Our Posthuman Future: Consequences of the Biotechnology Revolution* (New York: Farrar, Straus, & Giroux, 2002); Leon R. Kass, *Life, Liberty,
and the Defense of Dignity* (New York: Free Press, 2002).

10. President's Council on Bioethics, *Human Cloning and Human Dignity: An
Ethical Inquiry*, 2002. Available at www.bioethics.gov/reports/cloningreport.

11. This approach epitomizes the general method of mainstream bioethics, in essentially preparing the way for new technologies by a mixture of approval, delay, and
regulation, as has been eloquently argued by M. L. Tina Stevens in her narrative *Bioethics in America* (Baltimore: Johns Hopkins University Press, 2000).

12. NIH Embryo Research Panel, September 27, 1994, *Report*.

13. Ethics Advisory Board to the Department of Health, Education and Welfare,
Federal Register 44 (June 18, 1979), 35056; National Bioethics Advisory Commission,
Ethical Issues in Human Stem Cell Research (Rockville, Md., 1999). I am indebted for
these references to Richard M. Doerflinger, "Confronting Technology at the Begin-
ning of Life," in *Human Dignity in the Biotech Century*, ed. Charles W. Colson and
Nigel M. de S. Cameron (Downers Grove, Ill.: InterVarsity Press, 2004).

14. *Report of the Committee of Inquiry into Human Fertilisation and Embryology*,
Cmnd. 9314, 1984.

15. The Dickey amendment language has been added to each of the Labor, HHS,
and Education appropriations acts for FY1997 through FY2004. The original rider
can be found in Section 128 of P.L. 104–99.

16. This ethics board was created in 1978 by the Department of Health Educa-
tion and Welfare, the forerunner of the Department of Health and Human Services.
The board was formed at the recommendation of the National Commission for the
Protection of Human Subjects of Biomedical and Behavioral Research. The National
Commission operated from 1974 to 1978 and issued ten reports, many of which
formed the basis of federal regulations for research involving human subjects (45
CFR 46).

17. National Institutes of Health, *Report of the Human Embryo Research Panel*, September 27, 1994.

18. Statement, 30 Weekly Comp. Pres. Doc. 2459, December 2, 1994.

19. Letter from HHS General Counsel Harriet Rabb to Harold Varmus, director of the NIH, January 15, 1999.

20. Letter from Secretary Shalala to the Honorable Jay Dickey, February 23, 1999.

21. 64 Fed. Reg. 67576 (1999); 65 Fed. Reg. 51976 (2000), respectively.

22. This has involved the use of "spare" embryos. A furor resulted when, in July 2001, the Jones Institute for Reproductive Medicine, located in Norfolk, Virginia, announced that it had created human embryos through in vitro fertilization for the specific purpose of deriving human embryonic stem cells. A total of 162 oocytes (eggs) from 12 women were collected and fertilized with sperm donated by two men; 110 fertilized eggs developed, of which 40 developed to the blastocyst stage. The inner cell masses were removed from the blastocysts, resulting in three healthy embryonic stem cell lines. Each woman was paid from $1,500 to $2,000 for undergoing the egg donation procedure. It is thought to be the first time in the United States that a human embryo had been created solely for the purpose of harvesting stem cells for research rather than for the treatment of infertility. A representative of the Jones Institute, Dr. William E. Gibbons, stated that several ethics panels approved the work, and he contended that such "fresh" embryos may have advantages over the frozen embryos remaining after infertility treatment. Unlike couples using fertility clinics, the egg donors were younger, "possibly yielding more robust embryos." In January 2002, Dr. Gibbons announced that although the Jones Institute intends to continue to study stem cells, because of political pressure it will no longer recruit human egg donors in order to produce stem cells. Sheryl Gay Stolberg, "Scientists Create Scores of Embryos to Harvest Cells," *New York Times*, July 11, 2001, A1, A15; Deborah Josefson, "Embryos Created for Stem Cell Research," *British Medical Journal* 323, July 21, 2001, 127.

23. President's embryonic stem cell research policy, Fact Sheet, White House, Office of the Press Secretary, August 9, 2001, http://www.whitehouse.gov/news/releases/2001.

24. In July 2002, the council released its report on human cloning, which unanimously recommended a ban on "reproductive cloning" and, by a vote of 10-7, a four-year moratorium on cloning for medical research purposes. In January 2004, the council released its second report, *Monitoring Stem Cell Research*.

25. National Bioethics Advisory Commission report, available at www.bioethics.gov.

26. S.245: A bill to amend the Public Health Service Act to prohibit human cloning. Sponsor: Sen. Sam Brownback (Kan.); introduced January 29, 2003; cosponsors: 28. Action, January 29, 2003: referred to Senate committee. Available at http://thomas.loc.gov. On March 17, 2005, Sen. Brownback introduced S.658 to amend the Public Health Service Act to prohibit human cloning.

27. Two striking examples of private projects that are actively pursuing cloning research are to be found in Advanced Cell Technologies, the Massachusetts private company that announced in November 2001 that it had successfully cloned the first human embryos, and Stanford University, which in December 2002 announced plans to establish a privately funded institute that will use expertise in stem cell biology and cancer biology to develop novel treatments for cancer and other diseases. See http://mednews.stanford.edu/news_releases_html/2002/decreleases/stem-cell-QandA.html.

28. S.303: A bill to prohibit human cloning and protect stem cell research. Sponsor: Sen. Orrin G. Hatch (Utah); introduced February 5, 2003; cosponsors: 10. Action, February 5, 2003: referred to Senate committee. Available at http://thomas.loc.gov.

29. Gov. James E. McGreevey signed the "Stem Cell Research" bill A.2840/ S.1909. The bill establishes that "research involving the derivation and use of human embryonic stem cells, human embryonic germ cells and human adult stem cells, including somatic cell nuclear transplantation, shall . . . be permitted." The "cloning of a human being" is prohibited but is defined as "the replication of a human individual by cultivating a cell with genetic material through the egg, embryo, fetal and newborn stages into a new human individual." This takes the redefinition of the term "cloning" to a new level: the Hatch bill in the U.S. Senate defines it as the implantation of the clonal embryo; this New Jersey bill effectively defines it as the birth of the clonal baby.

30. Text, arguments and rebuttals available at http://www.ss.ca.gov/elections/bp _nov04/prop_71_entire.pdf; see also www.cloningproposition.org and www .noonprop71.org.

31. President's Council on Bioethics, *Human Cloning and Human Dignity*, xiv.

32. International convention against the reproductive cloning of human beings: Report of the Ad Hoc Committee, Official Records of the General Assembly, Fifty-Seventh Session, Supplement No. 51 (A/57/51); revised information document prepared by the Secretariat (A/AC.263/2002/INF/1/Rev.1). The writer served as bioethics adviser on the U.S. delegation, but these comments are made in his personal capacity.

33. On November 6, 2003, the delegation of Iran, on behalf of the member states of this organization, moved, under rule 116 of the Rules of Procedure of the General Assembly, to adjourn the debate on the agenda item until the sixtieth session of the General Assembly (i.e., September 2005). No action was taken on the proposals before the committee. It should be noted that some 15 states in the Organization of the Islamic Conference had co-sponsored the Costa Rican resolution, against only one (Turkey) on the Belgian list of sponsors.

34. G.A. Res. 59/280, U.N. Doc. A/RES 59/208 (Mar. 8, 2005), available at http://daccessdds.un.org/doc/UNDOC/GEN/N04/493/06/PDF/N0449306.pdf ?OpenElement.

35. Consolidated Appropriations Act of 2004, Pub. L. No. 108–199, 118 Stat. 3, Division B, Title VI, Section 634 (2004).

36. 109 Cong. Rec. H7274 (daily ed. July 22, 2003) (statement of Representative Weldon).

37. 35 U.S.C. § 101 (2004).

38. Richard Doerflinger, "Congressional Impasses on Human Cloning," LifeIssues.net: Clear Thinking about Crucial Issues, available at http://www.lifeissues .net/writers/doer/doer_01congresscloning.html; last visited July 20, 2004.

39. Stem Cell Action Alert, "Is Your Senator a Swing Vote?" CAMR, sent November 19, 2003 (on file with author).

40. Biotechnology Industry Organization, "New Patent Legislation Sets Dangerous Precedent and Stifles Research" 1–2, available at http://www.bio.org/ip/ cloningfactsheet.asp.

41. Amendment Thirteen: "Neither slavery nor involuntary servitude, except as a punishment for crime whereof the party shall have been duly convicted, shall exist within the United States, or any place subject to their jurisdiction."

42. Gerald P. McKenny, "Enhancements and the Quest for Perfection," *Christian Bioethics* 5, no. 2 (1999): 99, 100.

43. Leon R. Kass, "The Moral Meaning of Genetic Technology," *Commentary*, September 1999, 34, 35.

44. Ibid., 38.

45. "The Abolition of Man" was first published in 1943 as part of collection of three essays, under the same overall title, directed specifically at the improvement of teaching in English high schools. C. S. Lewis, "The Abolition of Man" (Oxford 1943), available at http://www.columbia.edu/cu/augustine/arch/lewis/abolition3.htm.

46. Ibid.

47. Ibid.

48. These useful terms are from Steven Spielberg's movie *AI: Artificial Intelligence*, generally memorable only for its special effects.

49. Charles Hodge, *Systematic Theology* (London: James Clarke, repr. 1960), vol. 2, p. 634.

PART VI

Instrumentalizing Religion

In reflecting on the role of religion in public bioethics, one naturally thinks of the public debate and discourses directed toward the formation of public policy. Clearly, that's the conception examined up to this point. However, the public square embodies more than simple conversation—it encompasses institutions and activities that either shape or are the product of public policy. One aspect of religion in the public square that deserves attention in this regard is the place of religion within the practice of health care.

There has always been a strong affinity between religion and health. In many ways, the medical profession itself grew out of religion, not just from the witch doctor–religious healer tradition, but also the religious ministry to provide help and comfort to the sick and downtrodden. Modern medicine as practiced in the hospital setting grew out of religiously sponsored institutions.[1] However, though religion continued to be associated with institutional medicine (in the form of hospital ownership and management), modern biomedicine adopted the scientific model and moved away from what it came to perceive as the superstitions of religion and religious healing. Faith healing was relegated to the revival tent.

Then, in the 1990s, partly out of a reaction against the depersonalization of modern medicine and partly out of a revived interest in alternative medicine practices, scientific medicine began to investigate religion as a therapeutic treatment. It effectively began to "instrumentalize" religion as a tool of modern medicine through research on such religious practices as prayer for the sick and the role of religion in health as forms of healing technology.[2]

This raises a whole host of very serious questions about the place of religion in the public square. Of particular concern to scholars and lawyers of religious freedom is whether the use of religion in publicly funded programs transgresses the limits of appropriate state action, moving from neutrality to endorsement—if not proselytization. Particularly in therapeutic programs in which religion is used as a motivation for behavioral reform, does not the state funding of that religious indoctrination for therapeutic purposes represent an establishment of religion—even if it is not restricted to one sect or religious tradition?[3]

Similarly, the medicalization of religion may present serious risks for faith. For example, within traditional Christian understandings of the healing services, the objective was not necessarily targeted exclusively toward a medical cure but rather toward an acceptance of God's will.[4] If the medical focus upon religion as a treatment becomes dominant, there is some risk that the practice itself will shift its broader religious objectives to mirror the medical goals. Similarly, what happens to faith if science finds the practice has limited or no medical efficacy?

These questions deserve extended exploration that unfortunately goes beyond the capacity of an overview of religion in the public domain such as this volume. Instead, we will explore this issue through a much more limited exploration of issues of concern relating to the science involved and the implementation of religious engagement at the clinical level.

In "Apples and Oranges: A Critique of Current Trends in the Study of Religion, Spirituality, and Health," Rabbi Gail Glicksman and Allen Glicksman challenge the current popularity of spirituality as a sui generis panacea for all psychosocial ills. Their analysis reveals the Christian bias in the term "spirituality" when scientists attempt to apply it to Jewish seniors. What is more troubling is that the rapid growth and acceptance of the spirituality concept within medical science as a valid therapeutic concept reveals how weak the science really is. Moreover, the prominence of the spirituality discourse threatens our understanding of religion itself by giving voice to "official" (i.e., medical) interpretations of religious concepts. Stanley Hauerwas has suggested that medicine is the new religion of the modern age.[5] Again, by standing behind medicine, the government may also be effectively establishing this new religion of medicine.

"The Heart of the Matter: Religion and Spirituality at the End of Life" seeks to establish some clarity about the place of religion and spirituality in clinical setting. Building on the insight provided by Therese Lysaught (chap. 5) that the line between public policy bioethics and clinical practice is permeable, if not illusory, the chapter discusses how public attitudes toward religion can shape how doctors engage with the religious needs of their patients. The chapter is both an ethical reflection on the place of religion and spirituality in the clinic and a normative and descriptive effort to consider an appropriate public ecumenical religious discourse.

NOTES

1. See, e.g., Paul Starr, *Social Transformation of American Medicine* (New York: Basic Books, 1984).

2. See, e.g., John A. Astin, Elaine Harkness, and Edzard Ernst, "The Efficacy of 'Distant Healing': A Systematic Review of Randomized Trials," *Annals of Internal Medicine* 132, no. 11 (2000): 903–910; Michael E. McCollough, William T. Hoyt, David B. Larson, Harold G. Koenig, and Carl Thoresen, "Religious Involvement and Mortality: A Meta-Analytic Review," *Health Psychology* 19, no. 3 (2000): 211–222.

3. See Ira C. Lupu and Robert W. Tuttle, *The State of the Law 2004: Partnerships between Government and Faith-Based Organizations* (Albany, N.Y.: Nelson A. Rockefeller Institute of Government, State University of New York, 2004).

4. Joel James Shuman and Keith G. Meador, *Heal Thyself: Spirituality, Medicine, and the Distortion of Christianity* (New York: Oxford University Press, 2003).

5. Stanley Hauerwas, "Sin Sick," in *Sin, Death and the Devil*, ed. Carl E. Braaten and Robert W. Jenson (Grand Rapids, Mich.: Eerdmans, 2000).

15

Apples and Oranges: A Critique of Current Trends in the Study of Religion, Spirituality, and Health

Gail Gaisin Glicksman and Allen Glicksman

Introduction

The intersections of religion and health, both physical and mental, have been an enduring concern of the social and behavioral sciences. This interest has usually been expressed in studies of the effect of specific religious traditions on the everyday lives of their adherents. Many classic texts in social science, such as *Suicide* by Emile Durkheim[1] and *The Protestant Ethic and the Sprit of Capitalism* by Max Weber[2] considered the effects of specific faith traditions such as Protestantism, Catholicism, and Judaism (Durkheim) and Calvinism (Weber) on every level, from the individual to entire societies. These authors insisted that to understand the effect of religion on individuals and societies, it was necessary to study individual religious traditions and examine how each tradition's beliefs influenced human behavior.

In recent years a new approach to the study of religion in the social sciences has emerged[3] which differs from the classical approach in four important ways. First, it treats all specific religious traditions as subsets or specific expressions of some underlying domain that is universal and shared across all groups. That domain is often referred to as "religiousness" and/or "spirituality." This new approach does not recognize differences between religious traditions or differences within religious traditions as important for the study of religion and health. Second, this new approach treats religion as generally beneficent, and in this way it differs from both those theoreticians like Durkheim and Weber, who saw a more complex relationship between religion and society, and those such as Marx and

Freud, who generally took a negative view of the effect of religion. Third, ad-herents of this new approach claim to be able to identify a therapeutic effect of religion on the physical and mental health of individuals, treating religion as a "health behavior." Though the classical theorists acknowledged that reli-gion could affect the individual, they also perceived this influence as complex, usually filtered through intermediary sources such as family. Finally, propo-nents of this new approach claim to be able to measure religiousness and its companion concept, "spirituality," with quantitative scales that can correlate scores on these domains with scores on measures of physical and mental health. For the classical theorists, who preferred an historical approach to the study of religion—as in *Ancient Judaism*[4]—and rarely used quantitative meth-ods, the idea of precisely quantifying religiousness would have seemed odd indeed.

The proponents of this new approach to the social and scientific study of religion claim several advantages over the classical approach to the study of religion and health. They point to the development of the previously mentioned scales and measures they use, claiming these are more scientifically valid than the methods used by the classical theoreticians, such as case studies. Repre-sentative samples and tests of statistical significance are presented as proof that these studies are more reliable representations of the role of religion in human life than research—such as *Protestant Ethic*[5]—based primarily on ser-mon material since we cannot gauge the response of the congregants to the messages in the sermons. Proponents argue that since persons from many religious backgrounds seem to comprehend and respond to the questions in the scales, the scales provide valid measures of these concepts across religious and spiritual traditions. Finally, it is also suggested that these measures of religiosity and spirituality could be used to help understand other domains of life, such as social networks.

We find it necessary to consider whether this new approach is better than the classical approach to the study of the relation between religion and health or, for that matter, of the general study of religion. There are several reasons we feel that this question needs to be asked. First, the development of these ideas, and especially the scales and measures, occurred in an almost exclusively Christian and more specifically Protestant milieu. Data taken from these stud-ies have already been used to argue that certain forms of religion, especially evangelical Protestantism, lead to a healthy lifestyle.[6] On the other hand, there has been almost no research that systematically applies these models specifi-cally to non-Protestant or non-Christian groups to determine whether they work as effectively as with evangelical Protestants. Second, we wonder whether religion and spirituality can be treated as similar to functional health for re-search purposes. That is, are there clearly identifiable beliefs and behaviors that are scientifically "valid" measures of religiousness and spirituality for all persons, irrespective of differences between and within faith traditions? Third, treating religion almost as a "health behavior," such as exercise and eating a balanced diet, limits the effect of religion to its positive elements and obscures the negative and ambiguous aspects of religious belief that can have equally strong effects on human life. Finally, this approach ignores the role of religion in shaping values and worldviews that in turn helps define the individuals' attitudes toward health behaviors and other types of daily life decisions.

In this chapter we ask whether this new approach accomplishes the goals of its proponents. We will examine the Jewish identities of American Jews 65 years of age and older as a test case. We will examine this group through a review of three studies, two using quantitative and one using qualitative research methods. There are four reasons we selected older Jews as a test of the value of the new approach to the study of the relation of religion to health. First, they are not Evangelical Protestant or even Christian, so they are therefore unlike the respondents who formed the core sample for many of the studies on which the claims regarding religion and health are based. Second, although they are not evangelical Protestants, older Jews are assumed to be part of the general religious tradition (Judeo-Christian or Abrahamic) of most Americans. Most Jews in the United States were born and socialized here, and so they have a common national culture as well as some part of a more general religious tradition with the Evangelical Protestants. Thus the two groups share enough characteristics that they are somewhat comparable, but they differ sufficiently to enable us to discern whether the model works outside the Protestant community. Third, issues of physical and mental health often appear in studies of older persons, so these studies provide more information on health and religion than those that focus on younger persons. Fourth, much of the research in this area started in social gerontology, so many of the materials use older persons as the focus of their analysis.

Methods and Data

The general method of this chapter will be to take American Jewish elderly's self-definition of Jewish identity and compare that to the assumptions in the new approach to research on religion. Data are taken from the 1990 and 2000–2001 National Jewish Population Surveys[7] and many other sources, including research conducted by the authors. The scales are taken from a work produced by the Fetzer Institute/National Institute on Aging Working Group in 1999 that provides a wide range of scales and measures of religiousness and spirituality.[8]

Analysis

We begin our discussion by asking: "What does being Jewish mean to older American Jews?" We will then move to a more general discussion of Jewish spirituality and finally turn to a consideration of the spiritual lives of older persons.

Traditionally, there are three aspects to Jewish identity—family, nation, and faith. In the biblical account, the Jewish people began as a family, became a nation when they left Egypt, and emerged as a faith at Mt. Sinai. Even if one does not accept the traditional view, it is clear that all three aspects are part of traditional Jewish civilization's understanding of what it means to be a Jew. For example, when a person converts to Judaism, he or she also assumes a new family lineage in the religious context. In the context of religious ritual, the Jew by choice has become a child of Abraham and Sarah, whom the biblical narrative identified as the father and mother of the Jews. The national aspect is also interwoven into the daily fabric of Jewish life. Every meal in a traditional household ends with a psalm—either one lamenting the exile from the land of Israel or one celebrating the return to the land. These expressions of family and nation both occur within the context of the practice of the faith. Although nation, faith, and family are all integral parts of traditional Jewish life, these three aspects of Jewish identity have assumed different weight in different contexts. The social environment has always decisively influenced the way Jews define themselves. In biblical Israel, the national aspect of Jewish life was paramount. In the medieval world, the Jews were treated as a corporate religious community, combining nation and faith. In the modern world, which of these three key aspects of Jewish identity was most prominent depended on how the host nation saw the Jewish people. For example, in nineteenth-century Germany, the Jews were a corporate religious group. In nineteenth-century Russia, the Jews were a "national minority." In the nineteenth and early twentieth centuries, the Jews were often described as a "race," that is, as having a common ancestry. This use of the term "race"—which lacks a pejorative connotation—can be traced to the idea of a common family origin for the Jewish people. Since the Second World War, the term "race" is no longer accepted as appropriate, especially in the United States, partly because of the way the term was used by the Nazis and in part because "race" in postwar America has come to refer to skin color rather than ethnic heritage.

The American Jewish community is a complex tapestry of threads from Western and Eastern European Jewry, which means that some combination of family, faith, and nation form the basis of American Jewish identity. The core institutions of American Jewish life—the synagogue and the coordinated charity structure—are products of the early waves of Jewish immigrants from western and central Europe, where Jewish identity was defined as religious and was synagogue-based, and charity was one of the major activities of the community. However, the vast majority of American Jews trace their ancestry to eastern Europe, where Jewish identity was based on an understanding that the Jews were first and foremost a "nation." The continued influence of that national (or, in American terms, "ethnic") identity can be neatly seen in the fact that virtually every synagogue in the United States—except for the very Orthodox, a complex issue beyond the scope of this chapter—has an American *and* an Israeli flag on the *bimah*, the podium where services are led. Also in contemporary American Jewry, individuals who oppose the state of Israel are more likely to be marginalized by the community than those who marry out of the faith, although in traditional Judaism, intermarriage is the more serious violation of religious norms. This demonstrates that one form of Jewish nationalism, Zionism, is a shared norm among most American Jews.

In 1990 and again in 2000, national probability surveys were completed of American Jewry called the National Jewish Population Surveys (NJPS). These surveys were conducted by a national Jewish organization (the Council of Jewish Federations in 1990 and United Jewish Communities, the successor organization to the Council, in 2000). The studies were undertaken for a number of reasons, mostly to determine the social, religious, and demographic characteristics of the American Jewish community. In each survey, respondents were asked who the Jews are. The question was "Please tell me if you think being a Jew in American means being a member of each of the following."[9] In NJPS 1990, four separate questions were asked, so that each respondent could answer positively to none, or one through four of the questions. The questions asked if the Jews were a religion, a culture, an ethnicity, or a nationality. Older Jews ranked the options in the following order: culture, ethnicity, religion, and nationality. In NJPS 2000, the same set of questions was asked, with a fifth option—"worldwide people." The responses in descending order were: (1) worldwide people, 70.4 percent; (2) culture, 68.1 percent; (3) religion, 62.7 percent; (4) ethnicity, 61.9 percent; and (5) nation, 44.0 percent. It is as interesting to note that religion was third on the list as the fact that nation was selected so frequently (more than a third) in the United States, where Jews virtually never refer to themselves publicly as a "nation." As in 1990, culture and a sense of peoplehood were more prevalent than religion as defining characteristics of Jewish identity.

The respondents in the 2000 survey were offered 15 items to express "what being Jewish" meant to them. The question was, "Personally, how much does being Jewish involve (insert item). Would you say a lot, some, a little, or not at all?" From this list of 15 possible items the three questions that were most frequently answered "a lot" were (1) remembering the Holocaust, (2) leading an ethical and moral life, and (3) fighting anti-Semitism. The three questions that were least often answered "a lot" were (13) leading a rich spiritual life, (14) observing the *halacha* (Jewish law), and (15) going to synagogue. Though 85 percent said they felt very positive about being Jewish, and 59 percent said that being Jewish was very important to them, only 27 percent said that Judaism guided their life decisions. Seventy-three percent said that they had a strong sense of belonging to the Jewish people, and 81 percent said that they had a very clear sense of what being Jewish means to them. Only 76 percent said that they believed in God, a lower percentage than the American public as a whole. Only 30 percent said that religion was important in their lives. But what of traditional belief? Only 14 percent of older respondents in the 2000–2001 NJPS stated they believed that the Torah (Five Books of Moses) was written by God. This belief in revelation at Sinai is the dividing line between traditional and liberal Judaism. Thus these elders, who feel that being Jewish is very important to them, still reject the core belief that defines traditional Judaism.

How did they express their Jewish identity? It is interesting that on the 15-

item list, family heritage was more frequently cited as important to being Jewish than believing in God, caring for Israel, or any type of Jewish religious observance or membership in a Jewish organization. In research by one of the authors of this chapter on Philadelphia-area older Jews, many study participants indicated that they liked the Jewish holidays because these occasions brought family together.[10] The value of religion to these elders was defined by the role that religion played in bringing family together. When religion brought family together, they perceived it as having a positive function. When it split family apart, as in intermarriage, they perceived it as functioning in a negative way. Therefore, the familial aspect of Jewish identify emerged as more important than the dimension of faith.

Proponents of the new approach to the study of religiousness and spirituality could respond to the materials presented above by arguing that even if part of Jewish identity, the ethnic/national part, might not be well measured by the scales they have developed, the religious part of that identity is well measured by these scales. We must then ask whether Jewish spirituality is well measured by these scales.

To begin with, we need to ask, What is the nature of Jewish spirituality and how does it differ from Christian spirituality? Spirituality in some religious traditions—including Christianity—has a focus on accepting God's will, whatever that will might be. A comparison with Christianity is particularly relevant because the scales and measures emerged from a Christian context, and even those intended for broader application retain deeply Christian language and concepts.

Jewish spirituality is characterized by a more active interaction with the divine—constant dialogue with and even arguing with God—in contrast to passive acceptance. Indeed, arguing with God is a hallmark of Jewish spirituality. In contrast, the questions on these scales and measures identify religiousness and spirituality as an acceptance of God's will, rather than a struggle with it. For example, the scale designed to measure daily spiritual experiences contains domains including connection with the transcendent, sense of support from the transcendent, strength and comfort, perceived love, inspiration/discernment, sense of wholeness/internal integration, transcendent sense of self, sense of awe, sense of gratitude, sense of compassion, sense of mercy, and longing for the transcendent.[11] All these domains reflect an acceptance of God's love and caring (especially the sense of gratitude, compassion and mercy) without any sense of being in dialogue with the divine or otherwise questioning or challenging the divine will. There is also no sense that ritual might be important to make a link to the divine.

There are several classic examples of Jewish figures who "argue with God." In the Book of Genesis, when Abraham learned that God planned to destroy Sodom, he advocated for the residents of Sodom, trying to dissuade God from this plan (Genesis 18:22–32).[12] Even Moses, whom God favored and selected as a leader, argued with the Almighty (Exodus 32:9–14).[13] Among the Hasidim, who have been embraced by some adherents of New Age religion as exemplars of spirituality, the struggle with the Almighty is characteristic of their ethos.

One Yom Kippur (the Day of Atonement), when according to Jewish tradition, God was passing final judgment on each individual, the Hasidic master, Rabbi Levi Yitzhak of Berditchev, challenged God for having allowed so much suffering to strike the Jewish people. There are various versions of this story, which include individuals speaking about their misery and their sins, and assessing God's sins, but in none of these versions is Levi Yitzhak portrayed as blasphemous.[14]

Beyond that, expressions of Jewish spirituality are often rooted in communal rituals. Even certain basic prayers cannot be recited without the presence of 10 Jewish adults, or in the case of traditional Judaism, 10 adult Jewish males. Private Bible study is discouraged in favor of study with at least one other person. Again, the scales focus on the individual rather than the group and on faith rather than ritual as measures of genuine spirituality, appropriate measures for certain Christian groups but not for Jews, whose understanding of genuine religiosity or religious expression differs in significant ways.

To further demonstrate that point, we will cite an example from the fieldwork of one of the authors in a synagogue whose congregants were primarily elderly. The fieldwork revealed that ritual and community are critical elements in the ability of these older Jews to express their spirituality, and the expression of that spirituality includes elements of doubt and struggle.

A study of a congregation completed by one of the authors[15] highlights the ways that the congregants used a specific ritual—the *Mi Sheberah Le'Holim* (a prayer for the restoration of health)—to engage in deep questioning about the meaning of their lives. In focusing on the *Mi Sheberah Le'Holim* and developing a ritual around it, these elderly Jews were engaging in deeply "religious" acts. However, this would not be apparent from the standard scales designed to measure religiousness. They were not accepting tradition passively, but were appropriating it to meet their needs. They did so in a public and communal context, one that was far from private and contemplative.

The project was completed while the author was a rabbinic intern at a congregation we'll call *Makom Tikvah*. At the time, the group's 200 members, primarily immigrants and first-generation Americans in the 65+ age range, devoted significant attention to the *Mi Sheberah Le'Holim* prayer. Congregants initiated the elaborations of the ritual surrounding the prayer. The congregation's ritual committee approved the changes, which were implemented by the committee chair. Thus, the ritual reveals the congregants' strategies for coping with the stress and uncertainty fostered by illness and loss.

Mi Sheberah prayers are benedictions offered when a person is called to the public reading of the *Torah* during a prayer service. There is a standard version for the individual honoree's well-being, with variations for special situations. The prayer derives its name from its first few words, "*Mi Sheberah Le'Holim*," "He who blessed." As suggested by the term, *L'Holim* ("for the sick"), the *Mi Sheberah Le'Holim* prayers focus on the hope of recovery from illness.

During the medieval period, the prayer caught the popular imagination, and the number of requests for the prayer multiplied, overshadowing other parts of the service. Over the generations, some prayer book editors have omitted the *Mi Sheberah Le'Holim* either because they discovered that it undermined decorum and lengthened the service or because they feared that it fostered magical thinking about prayer.

Initially at *Makom Tikvah*, the ritual chair followed the traditional custom, reciting two versions of the prayer—one for all men who are ill and one prayer for all women who are ill, including the individual names within their gender group. At one point, the congregants realized that many of their family and friends were ill. Inspired to try to help those struggling with illness, some congregants began to offer to include a specific individual in the prayer. When trying to support those facing particularly formidable challenges, occasionally the congregants convened a special service as an opportunity to recite the *Mi Sheberah Le'Holim* or they requested that a separate prayer be said for a specific individual. Soon, the ritual chair began to recite the entire *Mi Sheberah Le'Holim* prayer for *each* person who was ill. The congregation developed a ritual surrounding the prayer. They were proud of the time and devotion they lavished on the prayer and, by extension, on those who were ill.

After a number of years, unable to bear the awareness of the scope of the suffering highlighted by the great number of individual prayers, the congregants resumed the traditional approach. In deciding to recite one prayer for all the sick men and one for all the sick women, the congregants were also expressing disgust with the pervasiveness of illness. They tended to channel the despair as "anger at God" or as "anger at physicians." Many congregants identified with God in a personal way. If they had not expected anything from their relationship with God and their involvement with religious ritual, they would not have felt so disappointed. Although some congregants felt awkward or uncomfortable expressing anger at God, this "sacred rage" served as a socially appropriate way to express anger without blasphemy.

Discussion

The religious and spiritual lives of older Jews are rich, complex, and nuanced. They do not fit neatly into the precise measures offered by the new approaches to the study of religion. In transforming the *Mi Sheberah Le'Holim* prayer, the older Jews in the study engaged in a religious practice that revealed both faith and doubt at the same moment. The classical theorists recognized that religious rituals can play multiple roles. The ambiguities of faith are not easily captured by the scales and measures.

The scales present other challenges as well. First, the scales fail to recognize the importance of community, which is a hallmark of Jewish religious identity. Second, they focus on accepting God's decisions rather than struggling with them. Being angry at God is considered negative coping. In Jewish tradition, from Abraham's argument with God over the fate of Sodom to the present day, such active questioning of God's decisions has been an integral part of spirituality. Love, a key concept in Christianity but not in Judaism, is central to many of the questions on these scales. Forgiveness is another prominent theme in these scales. However, according to Jewish tradition, God can forgive sins only in the realms of ritual and belief, and forgiveness in the interpersonal realm is possible only when the aggrieved person expresses forgiveness. Finally, family, ethnicity, and other dimensions that can create a stronger bond with one's faith are totally absent in these scales. Instead the focus is almost entirely on the relation of the individual to God. Conspicuously absent from the scales is a consideration of whether the individual's beliefs match those of the faith community and whether he or she participates in the community's religious institutions. Traditional ways of evaluating religious behavior and participation—such as adherence to the official belief system and participating in official institutions—are absent from these scales.

Judaism is a religion of community. A male cannot fully participate in some aspects of religious life, such as wearing the prayer shawl, unless he is married. Even within liberal Judaism, which has been deeply influenced by Protestant American notions of individuality, the commitment to community persists. For example, many liberal versions of the Haggadah, the text read in Jewish homes on the first night of Passover, retain the traditional version of the story of the four sons. In that story, one son is considered to be evil because he fails to identify with the Jewish community.[16] The essence of Judaism is a commitment to that community. Entire areas of Jewish life are defined in terms of community and family, without reference to supernatural or theological concepts. The majority of early Zionist settlers clearly defined themselves in national and cultural terms only, and the only reference to God in Israel's Declaration of Independence is an oblique one at the end, inserted under pressure from the Orthodox community. The declaration itself defines the right of the Jewish people to the land of Israel as "natural and historic," without any reference to religious claims.

Our discussion of the nature of Jewish identity among older American Jews identified two issues that must be taken into account when considering the value of the new approach to the study of religiousness/spirituality and health. The first issue is that not all groups we might classify as a "religion" understand religiousness and spirituality in the same terms that underlie the scales proposed to measure these domains. Mark Zborowski noted differences in the roles that Catholicism played among Irish and Italian Catholics as they experienced pain and suffering. Although they had a common religious tradition, ethnic and national differences mattered, as it does in many other situations.[17] The second issue is that understandings of religion—as experienced on the individual level—can be ambiguous, complex, multidimensional, syncretistic, and generally difficult to categorize in ways easily amenable to scaling. Though the Jews are a small religious group within American society, the issues raised are ones that apply broadly.

The ambiguities and complexities shown by the members of Makom Tikvah are in no way restricted to older Jews; members of every faith and community struggle with many of the same issues of decline and loss.

The participant observer method used in the study of Makom Tikvah was perhaps the only way to gain a deep understanding of the meaning of the prayer for healing in that congregation. This fact brings us full circle to the beginning of this chapter. The classical study of the relation between religion and health included a wide variety of methodologies because no one approach could be used to explore all aspects of this phenomenon. Quantitative methods and survey research constituted but one approach among many employed in the classical works on the social scientific study of religion and health.

What final conclusions can we draw? Classical understandings of religiousness and spirituality, which treated these terms as organizing concepts rather than as "real" measurable things, fit the reality of religious diversity in a way that scales and measures that assume conformity and shared values and norms across faith traditions do not. These classical tools enable researchers to draw from the norms and values of each religious community, and in doing so, enrich our understanding of the human experience.

NOTES

1. Emile Durkheim, *Suicide: A Study in Sociology*, with an introduction by George Simpson (New York: Free Press, 1951).

2. Max Weber, *The Protestant Ethic and the Spirit of Capitalism*, with an introduction by Anthony Giddens (New York: Routledge, 1992).

3. Lynda H. Powell, Leila Shahabi, and Carl E. Thoresen, "Religion and Spirituality: Linkages to Physical Health," *American Psychologist* 58, no. 1 (January 2003): 36–52.

4. Max Weber, *Ancient Judaism* (New York: Free Press, 1967).

5. Weber, *Protestant Ethic.*

6. Harold Koenig, with Gregg Lewis, *The Healing Connection: A World Renowned Medical Scientist Explores the Powerful Link between Christian Faith and Health* (Nashville: Word Publishing, 2000).

7. National Jewish Population Studies 1990, 2000–2001. Available at http://www.jewishdatabank.org.

8. *Multidimensional Measurement of Religiousness/Spirituality for Use in Health Research* (John E. Fetzer Institute, January 1999).

9. National Jewish Population Studies 1990, 2000–2001. Available at http://www.jewishdatabank.org/.

10. Allen Glicksman, "Style versus Substance: The Cross-Cultural Study of Well-Being," In *The Many Dimensions of Aging*, ed. Robert L. Rubinstein, Miriam Moss, and Morton H. Kleban (New York: Springer Publishing, 2000).

11. Ellen Idler, "Daily Spiritual Experience Scale," in *Multidimensional Measurement of Religiousness/Spirituality for Use in Health Research*, pp. 11–18 (John E. Fetzer Institute, January 1999).

12. Genesis, 18:22–32. *Tanakh: The Holy Scriptures* (Philadelphia: Jewish Publication Society, 1985).

13. Exodus 32:9–14. *Tanakh: The Holy Scriptures* (Philadelphia: Jewish Publication Society, 1985).

14. "Levi Yitzhak," In *Encyclopedia Judaica*, vol. 11, pp. 102–103 (Jerusalem: Keter, 1972).

15. Gail G. Glicksman, "It Couldn't Hurt: An Ethnographic Study of a Ritual for Healing," in *Society and Medicine: Essays in Honor of Renée C. Fox*, ed. Carla Messiko-

mer, Judith Swazey, and Allen Glicksman (New Brunswick, N.J.: Transaction Publishers, 2003).

16. *The Passover Haggadah*, with a commentary by Rabbi Shlomo Riskin, pp. 54–60 (Ktav: New York, 1983).

17. Mark Zborowski, *People in Pain* (New York: Free Press, 1969).

16

The Heart of the Matter: Religion and Spirituality at the End of Life

David E. Guinn

The patient lies in the middle of the hospital bed amid the frightening machines of modern medicine, a small, quiet figure in a field of white starched sheets. She has been admitted for tests, and her doctor has just given her the results: the worst that can be imagined. She hesitates for a moment, then takes a deep breath and says: "Doctor. Will you pray with me?"

Religion and spirituality have become the buzzwords of the new millennium in health care. The curative power of intercessory prayer regularly makes headlines. The benefits of religious belief for health are noted in countless studies.[1] Treatment of patients at the end of life is no exception. Most experts agree that "attention to spiritual, existential and religious issues is a crucial component of palliative care."[2] However, despite this favorable attention, controversy surrounds the role of physicians and other health care workers in providing spiritual and religious care. Caregivers hesitate; many feel incompetent or uncomfortable.[3] Critics worry that caregivers may cross the bounds of their professional role, imposing their beliefs and values on the patient.[4] Yet, if caregivers do not address this need, it may go unmet. In the absence of a religious community or as a result of a patient's own alienation from organized religion, the physician or other provider may be the only person available to help the patient address her spiritual and religious concerns.

Concerns about caregivers providing religious or spiritual care arise, in large part, out of a misunderstanding about religion and spirituality and what those terms really mean. Many people treat religion and spirituality as special and unique. In this chapter, I will argue that religion and spirituality are basic human facts as inseparable from what it means to be human as are our sex, our age, our ethnicity or the countless other social and cultural factors that physicians and other caregivers routinely address.

I will begin by offering a functionalist definition of religion and spirituality. The significance of religion and spirituality for health care rests in the purpose they serve for the individual.[5] Understanding the purposes or functions of religion and spirituality provides guidance as to how to meet a patient's religious or spiritual need. I then examine research about the needs of patients at the end of life and suggest how those concerns express religious and spiritual concerns. Finally, I offer guidelines as to how the individual medical caregiver may attempt to meet those needs of a patient.

Like any other form of psychosocial patient care, of which religion and spirituality is one form, there are limits. Caregivers may unintentionally overstep their roles by imposing their values on their patients. They also may confront issues beyond their competence requiring specialized professional assistance. Nonetheless, physicians and bedside caregivers have a special role to play. They have a unique relationship with the patient. Patients have entrusted their health into the hands of the doctors and nurses at their sides. They look to them not only for treatment, but also for care.

Defining Religion and Spirituality

Most people don't really think about what they mean when they use terms like "religion" and "spirituality." Like Justice Stewart's statement about pornography, they know it when they see it. People often equate religion with the forms of traditional organized religion they are familiar with: Christianity, Judaism, Islam, and so on. Spirituality, on the other hand, is an individual, religionlike experience freed from the dogma and ritual of traditional religion. Many people make the statement that they are spiritual but not religious.

Though using these two terms to distinguish between organized, traditional understandings of faith (religion) and individual religionlike experience (spirituality) is useful, the distinction should not be taken too far. The two concepts are closely related. Religion clearly includes a spiritual dimension, and spirituality includes religious features.

In attempting to define these two terms, two possible approaches exist. First, one may begin with an intuition or insight drawn from within the experience of faith. For example, many religious studies scholars start with ideas of the sacred[6] or the holy.[7] Alternatively, we may start as outsiders to the faith, observers of how what is acknowledged as religion functions psychologically and sociologically for the individual. We can observe the purpose it serves or the need it fulfills—what I refer to as its functionalist definition.

Though the former approach offers many insights, the latter is uniquely appropriate for health care. The objective of the health care provider is not to evangelize or proselytize about the true or best expression of religion. It is to meet the needs of the patient in distress. To do so, the provider needs to understand the purpose religion or spirituality serves for that patient within the health care context.

Religion

William James argued that the attempt to define religion is futile: "The word 'religion' cannot stand for any single principle or essence, but is rather a collective name."[8] Most philosophers and theologians understand religion as a social system centered upon the relationship between the human and the "sacred,"[9] the supernatural,[10] or Ultimate Reality.[11] As suggested by David Tracy, religion orients believers toward "the one Reality that, as Ultimate, must be radically other and different, however that Reality is named—Emptiness, the One, G-d, Suchness"—which grants us "hope."[12] As noted above, these definitions draw on insights from within what we commonly recognize as religion.

By contrast, sociologists and anthropologists have taken a different tack, looking at how religion functions in the individual and social life of the religious believer. From this perspective, religion is seen as a psychological and/ or social mechanism by which the individual understands and gives meaning to the world and their life within it.[13] Religion responds to inescapable features of human existence: contingency, powerlessness, and scarcity.[14] Individuals use their religious beliefs to answer questions about life and death, suffering and evil. As suggested by David Tracy, they seek hope—but it is a hope sustained not so much by a belief that the source of their fear may be conquered but that life is not meaningless.[15]

Anthropologist Clifford Geertz defines religion as: "(1) a system of symbols which acts to (2) establish powerful, pervasive and long-lasting moods and motivations in men by (3) formulating conceptions of a general order of existence and (4) clothing these conceptions with such an aura of factuality that (5) the motivations seem uniquely realistic."[16] What is particularly noteworthy about this sociological, functionalist definition of religion is that it does not require belief in a transcendent reality or a notion of God. Any comprehensive or explanatory worldview (such as Marxism, psychoanalysis, or secular humanism) can function as a religion for that individual. A committed Marxist uses economic analysis to understand society; she draws on symbols of the class war to explain and justify her political actions, to describe how society functions and came to be; and, for the most part, she assumes that her observations and the basis for them are obviously true. Consequently, the distinction that many caregivers make between religion (which they may hesitate to address) and secular or cultural norms (which they will address) fails. The two epistemic systems are not fundamentally different.

Other features of a sociological, functionalist definition of religion reveal the following. First, though religion includes a social, collective meaning, it is inevitably shaped and formed by the individual believer in the process of incorporating it into her individual worldview. We create our sense of self in dialogue with our significant others, including those within our religious tradition.[17] In order to understand ourselves and our world, we have to find a way to integrate all of these important influences of family, culture, and belief—all of the diverse communities of meaning of which we are a part.[18] Each individual will accomplish this integration in a slightly different way. Hence, to some extent, the content of religion will invariably be different for different people.[19]

Second, religion is not a monolithic or unitary phenomenon. It is a multivocal tradition spanning a variety of cultures in space and in time. Indeed, as argued by Alasdair MacIntyre, the definition of a tradition is that it is an argument carried out over time.[20] Though a religion like the Roman Catholic Church may have a hierarchy with a strong body of dogma and religious instruction, the Vatican cannot speak for all believers who identify themselves as Catholic. Not only does faith differ at the individual level, it diverges greatly at both the national and historic levels. American Catholicism differs sharply from Irish Catholicism, which differs from Italian or Polish Catholicism. The same applies to other religions.[21]

Spirituality

As previously suggested, for many people spirituality may be described as religion without the formal trappings of dogma, ritual, and teachings of its organized counterpart. As described by John Hardwig, "*spiritual* refers to concerns about the ultimate meaning and values in life. It has to do with our deepest sense of who we are and what life is all about. *Spiritual* does not imply any belief in a supreme being or in a life after this."[22] Or, as described by Lynn Underwood-Gordon, spirituality is associated with Van Kaam's understanding of heart: it is at the core of the human. It helps us integrate all of the aspects of our life: the relationships we have with the world, with each other, and with the transcendent.[23]

One of the important features of the efforts to define spirituality is its linkage to emotions and feeling. Spirituality is a "state of being"[24]—the part of our being that "involves the intangible nonphysical world."[25] In speaking of the spiritual, people talk of feelings of connection and completeness and unity. It is a reminder that faith is more than an intellectual belief or a rational argument. The spiritual provides a visceral connection with the world that is in some way greater than the self—a movement beyond the isolated existence of the individual.

Spirituality is a universal human characteristic. "Spirituality is a lot like health," Father Jerome Dollard said. "We all have health; we may have good health or poor health, but it is something we can't avoid having. The same is true of spirituality: every human being is a spiritual being."[26]

Religion and Spirituality in the Clinical Setting

Any illness can raise religious or spiritual concerns. One of the major themes of religion is that of explaining suffering. Death is, of course, the ultimate challenge, the ultimate existential question. "Facing death brings to the surface questions about what life is about. Long-buried assumptions and commitments are revealed."[27] Hard questions must be asked and answered.

In the clinical setting, concerns about religion and spirituality arise in one of two ways. First, it arises as a specific issue of care. Death is a liminal experience, one that provokes a fundamental challenge to our human existence. Caregivers must consider their role in providing spiritual care for the patient facing the end of their life. Second, religion may affect the patient's approach to treatment and the decisions they make about the type of treatment to accept or reject.

Spiritual Care

Saying that the end of life represents an existential challenge that religion and spirituality are well suited to address does not mean that it presents a crisis to every patient. Some patients may be secure in their faith and religious understanding. We have all heard the stories of elderly or sickly patients ready to "go home" or "to be with God." Nor does saying that a patient is in spiritual distress mean that the caregiver should be the person to provide spiritual care. The challenge is finding out what patients need and what the caregiver can do to meet that need.

In fact, patients are willing to tell us. All that is necessary is for us to listen.

A number of recent research studies have considered what issues are important to the dying. In one recent study a vast majority of patients were concerned about a number of obviously religious and spiritual issues.[28] Far more than 80 percent thought it important to be a peace with God (89%), to pray (85%), and to feel prepared to die (84%). Equally high numbers were concerned with their family: worrying about having their financial affairs in order (94%), wanting to say good-bye to important people (90%), wanting to resolve unfinished business with family or friends (86%), hoping one's family is prepared for one's death (84%), and wanting to have the family present (81%). Finally, patients are concerned about feeling in control of the lives that remains to them. They want to make sure that decision makers are named (98%), know what to expect about their physical condition (96%), and have their financial affairs in order (94%).

These desires and concerns can be directly translated into the language of religion and spirituality. First, patients are struggling with the religious question of the meaning of life and death. They are concerned with their relationship with God and are pursuing those practices appropriate to advancing that relationship (e.g., prayer.) At the same time, they are expressing spiritual concerns. They are concerned with "wholeness" and "completion." They want to feel in control of their lives as reflected in their efforts to control their health care decision making. They want to resolve outstanding life issues such as finances and existing unresolved family conflicts. And they want to reaffirm their connection with their loved ones, not only by having the chance to say good-bye but also by having them present.

In addition to telling us of their religiospiritual needs, patients also tell us what they expect and want from their caregivers. What is most important to patients is that their physician be someone who will listen (95%), be someone with whom they can discuss their fears (90%) and be someone who knows them as a whole person (88%).[29] They may or may not translate these concerns into the language of religion and spirituality.[30]

Patients do not necessarily expect the physician to "fix" their spiritual concerns or distress. Less than half of the patients surveyed in two different studies worried about having a doctor who is spiritually in tune with them (39%) or having the doctor pray with them (44%–48%).[31] Even in a healthy population, patients are often more concerned with a physician trying to understand them and their beliefs than they are concerned about receiving a prescription as a treatment.[32]

In looking at these data, two questions arise. First, even if we assume that patients face a spiritual challenge at times of physical crisis, does that mean that medical caregivers should be the ones to provide it? And second, how are medical caregivers to provide such spiritual care?

WHAT PATIENTS WANT FROM CAREGIVERS. In looking at what patients want from their physicians, it might be possible to argue that most patients are not looking for religious or spiritual care. While admittedly a large number in itself, less than half of all patients identify their expectations of doctors in terms of explicitly religious concerns (i.e., spiritual resonance or praying with the doctor.) Nonetheless, careful reflection reveals that what they do want from their doctors ultimately reflects a desire for spiritual care.

First, as noted above, many of the most significant concerns expressed by patients involve religious or spiritual issues, either in terms of seeking meaning or seeking spiritual completion and wholeness. As such, when patients want a caregiver who listens and with whom they can discuss their fears, it makes no sense to suggest that they don't want to discuss those issues that are of most importance to them. For example, when a patient wants to discuss her fears with the attending doctor, these undoubtedly include fears about pain and the medical processes of dying. However, to say that this is patients' only fear dichotomizes the process of dying between physical and spiritual concerns in ways that patients do not. In ranking their concerns, these studies indicate that patients blend their concerns, including both religiospiritual and physical concerns, without necessarily ranking one category of concerns higher than the other.

Second, when patients say they want a caregiver who knows them as a whole person, it is highly unlikely that this would exclude acknowledgment of their religious and spiritual nature. As defined above, religion and spirituality are fundamental aspects of one's personhood. They shape who we are and how we perceive ourselves. How can a caregiver know us and not know anything about this core element of who we are?

Finally, the very nature of medical care argues that patients particularly want spiritual care from their caregivers. Modern medical treatment is a deeply humiliating process. We are striped of our clothes and dignity the minute we enter a clinic. We are exposed and prodded in terribly intimate places by relative strangers. These intimate strangers hold the powers of life and death—the tools of caring and curing—and the keys to controlling pain and suffering. Is it any wonder that patients long for a sense of connection with their caregiver? Even if it is a false intimacy—an illusion of connection, intimate knowledge, and caring—nonetheless, the desire to feel that connection as a sense of spiritual completion attaches to the caregiver in unique ways.

Other caregivers may also serve the spiritual needs of the patient. Families and friends are important. Trained clergy not only offer structured normative care, they are trained to address the serious spiritual problems that may arise. No one would suggest that physicians or other medical caregivers can or should attempt to replace the care offered by these other patient supporters. Nonetheless, none of these spiritual caregivers can substitute for the care of the medical caregiver.

ADDRESSING THE PATIENT'S RELIGIOUS AND SPIRITUAL NEEDS. Medical caregivers are not trained religious or spiritual counselors. They cannot be expected to provide expert guidance on religious issues, nor should they attempt to proselytize their own faith. Additionally, they cannot be expected to offer spiritual support if they are uncomfortable doing so. Nonetheless, the functionalist definitions of religion and spirituality offer some guidance on how the medical caregiver may provide spiritual care.

First, though religion and spirituality are often described as efforts to provide answers to the existential questions of life, the meaning of religion is individualistic. It is created by individual believers in dialogue with their tradition, their significant others, and their own experience. Though a caregiver may be invited to enter into the substance of this dialogue, the greater service would be the caregiver's willingness to be an audience to the patient's effort to work out her belief by talking about it. Second, as stressed above, though the concept of spirituality has an intellectual component, of equal or greater importance is its emotional role. For many people, it is not the content of the prayer that is important; it is the ritual and the sharing of it with the caregiver that matters.

The role of the physician and caregiver is not to cure the spiritual concern but rather to help patients address the concern themselves. The tactic for the caregiver must be to support the patient as the patient draws upon her own religious or spiritual resources to address a spiritual or religious concern. The technique advocated by most practitioners is the open-ended question.[33] As illustrated by the sample questions provided for the SPIRITual History by Todd A. Maugans,[34] the task for the caregiver is to help the patient identify her own religious or spiritual resources that may be applicable to end-of-life care (in terms of belief systems, ritual practices, and the individuals or community members that may be helpful) and direct the patient's attention to the types of questions about health care with religious implications that she must confront and answer. Whereas it would be inappropriate for a physician to lecture a patient on her understanding of God or the meaning of suffering and death, it is appropriate for the physician to raise the issue and allow the patient the opportunity to reflect upon her understanding of those subjects. The value for the patient is in having a willing listener who is providing the patient with an opportunity to talk through her concerns. A patient who is in profound crisis, unable to draw upon their personal religious or spiritual experience may require the assistance of a professional clergy member who is trained to counsel people in issues of faith. However, most patients do not suffer such a profound crisis. For them, it is more the need to resolve the feelings, to mourn their loss, and to bring their spiritual life to closure—a task well within their means if they are given the opportunity to address it. In short, the goal of the caregiver is to bring the patient's own spiritual and religious resources to bear upon her spiritual suffering.

Religion as an Obstacle to Care

Though religion may be a therapeutic option to address spiritual suffering, it may also prove to be a barrier to what the caregiver believes to be appropriate care. A Jehovah's Witness refuses a life-saving (or at least life-prolonging) blood transfusion. A Christian Scientist refuses antibiotics for a treatable bacterial infection. A fundamentalist Christian insists upon increasingly futile life support efforts in hopes that a miracle will cure her loved one. Though it is possible (though not necessarily advisable) for the caregiver to ignore her role in providing spiritual comfort to the patient at the end of their life, in these situations confronting religion is unavoidable. The caregiver cannot practice good medicine (as it is now understood) without coming to grips with a patient's religious beliefs.

In some cases, this simply requires acquiescence by the physician. Competent patients are allowed to make their own treatment decisions. The obligation of the physician is simply to make sure that the patient understands the physical medical consequences of the decision. That would typically be the case with the Jehovah's Witness or Christian Scientist mentioned above. There are, however, instances where the religious response raises certain concerns. The religious justification offered by the patient may appear to be unconventional or unusual in that a community of faith does not support it. Or the religious argument may suggest that the patient does not understand the limits of medicine, resulting in requests for inappropriate treatment.

How should the physician/caregiver address these concerns? Health professionals have a duty of beneficence: an obligation to do their best for their patients. It is not enough to simply allow the patient to make her own decision. Physicians/caregivers must reach out and offer their best advice, including guidance as to what they believe to be the best course of treatment.[35] How can they do this when the patient argues that she is acting according to a deeply held religious belief?

This problem with religion arises when caregivers think of religion as something profoundly different from other forms of human belief and interaction—when they treat religion as irrational. However, as described above, this belief is inaccurate. Religion is simply one of a variety of possible belief systems and is no more irrational than nonreligious belief systems (which may or may not be irrational.)

Religious belief expresses a form of personal theology. As such, the tools of theology provide a method for addressing religious beliefs. In Christian theology, a common methodology is that religious beliefs are the result of the integration of three sources: revelation (either in the form of scriptures or other sources), reason, and experience.[36] While drawn from Christian theology, this methodology applies to any religious belief. The believer will have some acknowledge grounding for her belief (e.g., a passage from Scripture, the guidance of a religious leader, etc.); she will draw upon personal experience or the experience of others to understand what the grounding source means in relation to situation at hand; and the believer will apply that knowledge and interpretation of grounding source to reach a conclusion about how to act.

In attempting to understand the arguments of the person of faith, caregivers must reconstruct this theological method. They should start by having patients describe the sources of their belief (both those grounded in revelation and experience) and then how they apply those sources to the particular problem. The caregiver is not required to know those sources in advance. Indeed, thinking that one knows the sources of belief of another may be misleading. As noted above, just because a person is Catholic or Jewish does not mean that she believes in everything popularly identified with that tradition. The patient therefore provides the basis for the conversation concerning their health care decision making.

Once this baseline is in place, the caregiver may address the concern by following certain guidelines.

1. *Assume that the religious belief is rational.* A person of faith uses the same rules of grammar and discussion as her secular counterpart. The rules of logic apply just as rigorously as they apply to any discussion by a nonphilosopher. Many religious beliefs appear irrational to an outsider because the outsider does not understand where the belief comes from and how it is explained by the religious worldview. For example, talking about eating the flesh and drinking the blood of one's father sounds barbaric until you understand the meaning of these symbols within the Christian Eucharist. Though it is possible to disagree with a person's faith because you disagree with her grounding understanding, that does not mean you cannot understand why she believes as she does.

2. *Never assume that you know the meaning of a term or concept.* As noted above, religious belief is a complex integration of influences, including those drawn from within a tradition and those that are idiosyncratic to the individual. While you may think you understand what the terms "miracle" or "God's will" means within a particular tradition, it is always possible that the individual believer brings a unique

interpretation to that term. Clergy members are often surprised by what the people in the pews think their tradition says about something. Simple terms can lead to significant misunderstandings. For example in the case of an elderly Irish-Catholic woman, doctors were very frustrated when the patient refused to have a potentially life-saving heart surgery. Though she acknowledged the risks that she might die by refusing treatment, she was adamant. Finally, after the doctors left, the chaplain asked why she didn't want the surgery. She replied, "Honey, the heart is where the soul is. I'd rather go to heaven than risk my soul!"[37]

3. *Accept the patient's understandings as the basis for discussion.* Many people seem to believe that it is impossible to carry on a conversation unless you share common beliefs. That is to say that only a Baptist can talk to a Baptist—or a Jew to a Jew—about issues of faith. However, that is no more the case than that it is impossible for a capitalist to talk to a Marxist, or a deontologist to talk to a consequentialist. The task for the caregiver is to adopt the terms given by the patient for purposes of discussion. The physician doesn't have to believe in them. She must simply respect the fact that the patient does believe and then use that belief as a basis for discussion. Using the common tools of discussion and argument, she can explore the patient's beliefs. What do the terms the patient uses mean? Are they being used consistently? Are there unarticulated assumptions that might offer an alternative approach?

4. *Acknowledgment of internal religious difference is not proselytization.* As described above, religion is not univocal. There are many strands of thought within a single tradition: the orthodox and the dissenter. Pointing out the existence of diversity within the tradition professed by a patient does not violate her beliefs. The physician need not advocate that the patient adopt the alternative position from within the tradition. However, the existence of an alternative can be presented to the patient as a call for her to consider alternatives and why the tradition might appear to support what may appear to be two mutually contradictory positions. For example, Orthodox Jews have had to struggle with a tradition that demands almost absolute reverence for life, but a majority of Jews support abortion and avoid end-of-life treatments that do little more than extend the process of dying.[38]

5. *Religion is more than reason—it is also faith and feeling.* At first glance, this appears to contradict the first guideline—that religion is not irrational. However, as religion demonstrates, reason and feeling are two different ways of understanding the world. Rationality rests upon how that understanding is articulated and argued—not its source. Consequently, the caregiver has to be alert to patient's feelings and intuition and how those feelings and intuitions may be affecting the patient's decisions and judgment. Does the patient's expectation of a miracle reflect a specific religious belief—or a denial of reality? The

task for the caregiver is not to attack the expression of religious belief but to address the denial, just the way she would address the denial of any other patient or patient's family.

Conclusions

Religion and spiritual concerns are important to patients as they confront the end of their life. Good patient care requires that physicians and caregivers address these concerns in a sensitive, nonjudgmental, and nonproselytizing way. A proper understanding of what religion and spirituality are—the functions and purposes they serve in the life of the patient—provides caregivers with important insights in how to meet these concerns and needs of their patients. At its heart, religious and spiritual care is fundamentally an expression of empathetic caring: a willingness to listen combined with a profound respect for the individual patient and an appreciation of our human interconnection.

NOTES

1. See, e.g., John A. Astin, Elaine Harkness, and Edzard Ernst, "The Efficacy of 'Distant Healing': A Systematic Review of Randomized Trials," *Annals of Internal Medicine* 132, 11 (2000): 903–910; Michael E. McCollough, William T. Hoyt, David B. Larson, Harold G. Koenig, and Carl Thoresen, "Religious Involvement and Mortality: A Meta-Analytic Review," *Health Psychology* 19, 3 (2000): 211–222.

2. Bernard Lo, Timothy Quill, and James Tulsky, for ACP-ASIM End-of-Life Care Consensus Panel, "Discussing Palliative Care with Patients," *Annals of Internal Medicine* 130, 9 (1999): 744–749, at 746.

3. Ibid.

4. See, e.g., Stephen G. Post, Christina M. Puchalski, and David B. Larson, "Physicians and Patient Spirituality: Professional Boundaries, Competency, and Ethics," *Annals of Internal Medicine* 132, 7 (2000): 578–583, at 581.

5. Though it is my argument that the two are fundamentally related, they do stress slightly different aspects of the religiospiritual impulse that deserve attention.

6. Mircea Eliade, *The Sacred and the Profane* (New York: Harper & Row, 1959).

7. Rudolf Otto, *The Idea of the Holy*, trans. John Harvey (London: Oxford University Press, 1923).

8. William James, *The Varieties of Religious Experience* (New York: NAL, 1958), p. 39.

9. Eliade, *Sacred and the Profane*; Otto, *Idea of the Holy*.

10. Melford E. Spiro, "Religion, Problems of Definition and Explanation." In *Anthropological Approaches to the Study of Religion*, ed. Michael Banton (New York: Praeger, 1966); Rodney Stark, "A Sociological Definition of Religion." In *Religion and Society in Tension*, ed. Charles Glock and Rodney Stark (Chicago: Rand MacNally, 1965).

11. Paul Tillich, *Dynamics of Faith* (New York: Harper & Row, 1957).

12. David Tracy, *Plurality and Ambiguity: Hermeneutics, Religion, Hope* (San Francisco: Harper & Row, 1987), p. 85.

13. Peter L. Berger, *The Sacred Canopy* (Garden City, N.Y.: Doubleday, 1967).

14. Thomas F. O'Dea and Janet Avaid, *The Sociology of Religion*, 2nd ed. (Englewood Cliffs, N.J.: Prentice Hall, 1983), p. 6.

15. Post et al., "Physicians and Patient Spirituality," p. 579.

16. Geertz, "Religion as a Cultural System," in *The Interpretation of Cultures* (New York: Basic Books, 1973), p. 90.

17. See, e.g., Charles Taylor, "Atomism." In *Philosophy and the Human Sciences: Philosophical Papers 2* (Cambridge: Cambridge University Press, 1985).

18. Iris Marion Young, *Justice and the Politics of Difference* (Princeton, N.J.: Princeton University Press, 1990).

19. Such as the well-known religion of Sheila. Robert Bellah, Richard Madsen, William M. Sullivan, Ann Swidler, and Steven Tipton, *Habits of the Heart: Individualism and Commitment in American Life* (Berkeley: University of California Press, 1985), p. 221.

20. Alasdair C. MacIntyre, *After Virtue* (Notre Dame, Ind.: University of Notre Dame Press, 1981).

21. See, e.g., Ronald M. Green, "Religions' 'Bioethical Sensibility': A Research Agenda." In *Notes from a Narrow Ridge: Religion and Bioethics*, ed. Dena S. Davis and Laurie Zoloth (Hagerstown, Md.: University Publishing Group, 1999), pp. 165–182.

22. John Hardwig, "Spiritual Issues at the End of Life: A Call for Discussion," *Hastings Center Report* 30, 2 (2000): 28–30.

23. Lynn Underwood-Gordon, "A Working Model of Health: Spirituality and Religiousness as Resources: Applications to Persons with Disability," *Journal of Religion in Disability and Rehabilitation* (1999).

24. Carol J. Farran, George Fitchett, Julia D. Quiring-Emblen, and J. Russell Burck, "Development of a Model for Spiritual Assessment and Intervention," *Journal of Religion and Health* 28, 3 (1989): 185–194, at 187.

25. Robert Thomsen, "Spirituality in Medical Practice," *Archives of Dermatology* 34 (1998): 1443–1446, at 1443.

26. Jerome Dollard, quoted by Thomas Prough, "Alcohol, Spirituality, and Recovery," *Alcohol, Health and Research World* 10, 2 (winter 1985–86): 28–33.

27. Hardwig, "Spiritual Issues," p. 28.

28. Karen E. Steinhauser, Nicholas A. Christakis, Elizabeth C. Clipp, Maya McNeilly, Lauren McIntyre, and James A. Tulsky, "Factors Considered Important at the End of Life by Patients, Family, Physicians, and Other Care Providers," *Journal of the American Medical Association* 284, 19 (2000): 2476–2482.

29. The George H. Gallup International Institute, "Spiritual Beliefs and the Dying Process" (The Nathan Cummings Foundation and Fetzer Institute, 1997).

30. Compare Gallup, ibid., with D. E. King and B. Bushwick, "Beliefs and Attitudes of Hospital Inpatients about Faith Healing and Prayer," *Journal of Family Practice* 39 (1994): 349–352.

31. Ibid.

32. Paul Little, Hazel Everitt, Ian Williamson, Greg Warner, Michael Moore, Clare Gould, Kate Ferrier, and Sheila Payne, "Preferences of Patients for Patient Centered Approach to Consultation in Primary Care: Observational Study," *British Medical Journal* 322 (February 21, 2001): 1–7.

33. See, e.g., Lo et al., "Discussing Palliative Care."

34. Todd A. Maugans, "The SPIRITual History," *Archives of Family Medicine* 1 (1996): 11.

35. Timothy E. Quill and Howard Brody, "Physician Recommendations and Pa-

tient Autonomy: Finding a Balance between Physician Power and Patient Choice," *Annals of Internal Medicine* 129 (1996): 441–449.

36. See, e.g., Schubert M. Ogden, *On Theology* (San Francisco: Harper & Row, 1986).

37. An anecdote told by Margaret McClauskey.

38. Ronald Green, "Religion's Bioethical Sensibility,' " pp. 167–170.

PART VII

Institutional Religion

Despite the best efforts of traditional liberal theory to relegate religion to the private realm of individual faith,[1] the reality is that religion is a communal activity. It is not simply the "relationship between man and his God" described by Thomas Jefferson[2] but between humans, God, and their community of faith. Moreover, it is a community that is often engaged in a social ministry of outreach and service—in effect, putting into action morals and values that reflect or influence public policies.

The first point to be made from this observation is that religion cannot be excluded in public bioethics and in the public square because it is already there and active. Ignoring it will not make it go away—and may in fact create its own problems. In the United States, most people of faith participate in formal, organized religion. And organized religion is a strong and important part of civil society. The church, the mosque, the synagogue, or the temple serves as an organizing force for the community of believers. In many cases it will mediate the relationships between the members of the community of faith and the larger world—including the believer's relationship with the government.[3] Policies that fail to account for this mediating influence risk failure.

Michele Goodwin demonstrates this point in her chapter on HIV and the black church: "Bioethical Entanglements of Race, Religion, and AIDS." As previously noted, though it is currently popular to glorify the place of religion in healing, religion also has a problematic side that can lead to poor health outcomes. The Jehovah's Witnesses' refusal of blood transfusions is just one illustration of the point. It is not fair to judge religion solely on the basis of health outcomes. Ultimately, who can say that the values of physical health outweigh all other concerns? Nonetheless, to the extent that the state adopts a public policy to address a particular public health concern, such as the spread of AIDS in the black community, failure to recognize the critical role played by the black church in the community may doom that policy to failure.

Admittedly, public policy may not be able to overcome the obstacles thrown up by religion. The religious freedom of the black church cannot be legislated against. However, failure to raise the issues in public debate certainly guarantees failure. Moreover, failure to air the issue in the public square may deny the black church itself the opportunity to reflect upon the problem of AIDS in the black community. The natural conservatism of the black church and its denial of the sexual may result in an inability to see the nature and extent of a problem that it has shoved into a darkened corner. The public square is the only avenue through which to shine light on that darkened corner.

The second major concern of public bioethics is the effect of organized religion upon the delivery of health care services. The problem is epitomized by Catholic health care and the delivery of reproductive health services (including abortion, birth control, and sterilization services) or, rather, the refusal to provide those services. This problem has become particularly acute because in the recent restructuring within hospital health care brought on by the efforts to restrain public funding for health care in the 1990s, Catholic health care has been unusually successful. Many public hospitals have been forced out of business or forced into mergers with Catholic hospitals, leaving the Catholic hospital as the sole provider in that area. When it refuses to provide reproductive health services, women can be effectively denied total access to those services.

Given the significance of this issue and how it illustrates this dilemma, we have two chapters specifically addressing this topic: Maura A. Ryan's "The Delivery of Controversial Services: Reproductive Health and Ethical Religious Directives" and Clarke E. Cochran's "Catholic Health Care in the Public Square: Tension on the Frontier."

In reflecting upon this issue, the first question for institutional religion is what is it that makes an institution sponsored by a community of faith a faith-based organization and how can it live its life of faith in the community? It is certainly not enough to simply apply the name. There must be some congruence between the beliefs and values of the religion and the faith-based organization. In terms of public bioethics, religion, and health, the struggle is how to deliver contested health care services while respecting the religious integrity of the faith-based provider. Maura Ryan takes us inside Catholic health care, with its ethical religious directives, as it struggles with this problem. She discusses prior attempts at compromise and the ethical process by which Catholicism struggles to achieve an ethical result.

Clarke Cochran situates the struggle within Catholic health care in the larger political context of the public square. Cochran acknowledges that some of the problems relating to health care delivery may be intractable—and the solution may not be compromise but rather a decision by Catholic health care to withdraw from hospital health care delivery.

It seems appropriate to end this collection with Cochran's chapter. Not only does he address the specific conflicts within Catholic health care, he reminds us that there are no simple solutions to the challenges and problems presented by religion's involvement in the public square. As he formulates it, religion and secular society exist in a dynamic tension that, though it may be stressful, also brings with it the potential to energize and provoke creative responses to the challenges of an ever-changing and evolving health care system. The goal of this book has been to bring that tension forward and seek to engage it in creative dialogue.

NOTES

1. See, e.g., David E. Guinn, *Faith on Trial: Communities of Faith, the First Amendment, and the Theory of Deep Diversity* (Latham, Md.: Lexington, 2002).

2. Thomas Jefferson, "Letter of January 1, 1802," in *Writings of Thomas Jefferson*, 20 vols., ed. Albert E. Bergh (Washington, D.C.: 1904–1905).

3. Guinn, *Faith on Trial*, esp. 101–103.

17

Bioethical Entanglements of Race, Religion, and AIDS

Michele Goodwin

Black same gender loving individuals have been beaten so terribly
by "the saints" and "the ain'ts" that we have had no other choice but
to turn to alcohol, drugs, and elicit sexual behavior for comfort (even
though those things only offer temporary relief before making our
problems worse—and we know it!). The church has preached hate,
and meted out abuse so long that they have made the very "lifestyle"
we are said to live the only place we have to go for acceptance and
love.

—Tuan N' Gai, Operation Rebirth

Double bind:(n). A situation in which a person is confronted with
two irreconcilable demands or a choice between two undesirable
courses of action.

—*The New Oxford American Dictionary* (2001)

During the last half of the twentieth century, double bind theory described the psychological impasse created when contradictory demands are made on an individual with vulnerable social status or
with weaker power within a relationship. The contradictory demands are such that no matter which command is followed, the response will inevitably be construed as incorrect. According to the renowned critical psychologist and existentialist researcher R. D.
Laing, the double bind is a "meta-communicative tangle" where "the
victim is caught in a tangle of paradoxical injunctions . . . in which
he cannot do the right thing."[1] In the double bind, the disempowered actor is without a true or unburdened choice because whichever directive is followed invites negative consequences. The classic
clinical examples apply to psychoanalytic clinical research on schizo-

phrenia that involves patterns of communications, primarily at the interpersonal level.

Religious discourse is often visited by paradoxes and conflicting social, moral, and medical demands. This chapter examines the AIDS double bind in the African American community. African American women are diagnosed with AIDS at a rate twenty times that of white women. AIDS is the leading cause of death among black women ages 25–34.[2] How does this happen? From where do we begin to examine this crisis? How is the church involved? Because most of these women attribute their disease to heterosexual contact, researchers are beginning to suggest, albeit with little evidence, that black men on the "down low" are hiding their secret sexual lives for fear of stigmatization and rejection from their communities.[3] Most important, it seems, is the trade between inclusion in the black church and silence on lifestyle, which could also mean treatment for AIDS, versus living openly gay with AIDS but without community support.

Double binds frequently occur at the intersections of religion, medicine, and the law. To pursue a particular religious directive over a medical option could lead to spiritual (after) life, but result in physical death. The practice of Jehovah's Witnesses to forgo blood transfusions even in the most critical cases demonstrates this double bind all too well. Thus the paradox within more orthodox or conservative religious denominations, saving the soul may supersede and be perceived as far more important than the physical life. Saving the soul could necessarily require the death of the physical life or, in the case of the black church, silence about the earthly life if it is incompatible with church principles.

Surely, declining medical treatment because it conflicts with religious teachings is not an easy decision to be made. Relationships, including those with spouses, children, and parents, are permanently interrupted by such ultimatums. For parents, then, the double bind is not only expressed through the decision of a medical choice versus religious doctrine or practice, but is also complicated by the duties of parenting and the knowledge that choosing salvation over medical intervention could mean the stark reality of orphaning children. The double bind for the congregant or religious follower is deciding which directive, the medical or the religious, to follow. The threat of jeopardizing salvation by following a medical directive over a religious philosophy remains a vital aspect of health care decision making.

Thus, the domains of religious doctrine and practice are fertile spaces for double bind analysis, particularly as applied to race, religion, and bioethics. In these spheres, reconciling church doctrine with social or medical practice is oftentimes challenging; the demands from each sphere are unique and sometimes perceived as irreconcilable. This chapter uses double bind theory as a framework to engage in a dialogue at the intersection of race, religion, and bioethics. I offer a dialogue that scrutinizes conservative religious thought in what is colloquially known as the "black church" with the challenges of medical ethics and race.

For purposes of this chapter, the terms "black" and "African American" are used interchangeably to describe members of the African diaspora who share the common legacy of slavery and post-antebellum life in the United States. By referring to various Christian denominations primarily serving African American congregants as the "black church," this chapter does not intend to foster essentialism or reduce the diversity of black religious thought, particularly given the introduction of Islamic faith in black communities over the past half-century and blacks turning to other religious institutions, including Judaism, Catholicism, and more traditional African practices. Rather, this chapter observes the uniquely joined expressions of the black church and attributes the very strong similarities to culture, the politics of segregation, and the design of Christian faith to black life in the United States.

However, challenges to double bind research and analysis in general must also be acknowledged. Though I attempt to avoid these pitfalls in this chapter, I am not unwise to their existence and the possibility that this article raises uncomfortable questions. First, this type of research invites criticism that authors tend to overstate coincidences as being exclusively derived from one cause. Second, double bind theory offers generalizations based on sociological observations that can be perceived as tenuous at times. Third, few bioethicists write and research about black life, and only recently have federal funds been earmarked for exploring health care disparities among African Americans. Therefore, data may not always be available to support the conclusions that researchers may wish to draw. Yet there is enormous value to studying the intersections of race, religion, and bioethics. This chapter attempts to expand traditional bioethics discourse to a health crisis in the African American community and seeks to overcome some of these traditional pitfalls to double bind theory.

Parts 1 and 2 briefly establish the backdrop to my thesis: that individual autonomy with regard to medical decision making may be subordinated to clerical and congregational values, thus creating the double bind of physical health versus spiritual health in the African American community. Most often, the values may be similar, creating no conflict and resulting in tremendous support from the church to the individual and family. To be clear, clerical values in the African American community refers not only to the identity and practices of charismatic leaders, but rather a combination of sectarian and general religious values. For example, the larger sects of African American churches are hewn from the Christian tradition, which has always been intolerant to homosexuality. The African American church, as discussed later, greatly influences the culture of black life in the United States more so it appears than any other institution. Keeping this in mind, exploring the clerical response to health crises in the black community that involve digressions from perceived religious values may prove incredibly relevant. This hypothesis is tested by the African American church's response to AIDS in the African American community.

The rapid spread of AIDS in the black community and the relatively limited responses—from silence to intolerance of its victims—by black clergy indicate an untenable double bind. The results of which have an impact on the health of black Americans. To be clear, the intolerance described in this article, and its very premise of the double bind, does not apply to all black churches. However, with the rapid spread of AIDS and the outspoken condemnation of homosexuals by popular black church leaders, patterns have emerged that should give rise to bioethical inquiry, at least and perhaps appropriately among black scholars. What exactly motivates the stigmatization that leads to the church's disengagement on the issue of AIDS is unknown. However, I speculate two causes. The first possible cause is found within the shaping of religious thought in the black community. The black church is traditionally conservative and was born out of evangelistic teachings emanating during slavery. The second possible explanation for the intolerance and silence about AIDS within the black church has to do with cultural identity, political space, and institutional legitimacy. In sum, the church is concerned about its credibility, stigmatization, and race. The pathologization of African Americans was a profitable enterprise that had economic and political power during Jim Crow and beyond. This does not explain, however, why African Americans have tolerated the church's silence and more intolerant teachings with regard to AIDS and homosexuality. This chapter offers some reflections on these questions and invites greater scrutiny, discourse, and research.

Part 1 uses double bind theory to establish the framework for this article. It provides a history and application of double bind theory, exploring the work of Bateson and his fellow researchers to shed light on the applicability of double bind analysis in non-psychoanalytic discourses. Part 2 locates the African American church as a multifaceted and textured entity within African American life. It scrutinizes the influence of the African American church in black life; in particular, the section explores how the church influences health care decision making. Part 3 describes double bind health crises in the African American community, focusing on HIV/AIDS and using empirical data to illustrate the significant consequences those health issues have for the African American community. It examines the often underestimated or overlooked religious conservatism within the African American church that may result in narrowed biblical readings and interpretations. Among the questions central for this discourse is: how have conservative religious teachings influenced health care decision making among African Americans? Such teachings may be increasingly difficult to reconcile with the contemporary health status of blacks. Part 4 forecasts the epidemic spread of AIDS in the African American community if black clergy fail to heed warnings.

Part 1: The Double Bind

Double bind theory was first advanced by an interdisciplinary group of scholars including Gregory Bateson, Don Jackson, Jay Healy, and John Weakland, who examined schizophrenia in families through intersectional research in mental health, anthropology, psychiatry, and genetics.[4] They theorized that paradoxical or contradictory behavior in family relationships predisposed its members to schizophrenia.[5] The classic and often-cited example that characterizes the theory involves a male child returning home after recovering from a "mental breakdown."[6]

> As he approaches her, she opens her arms for them to embrace but then, as he gets nearer, she freezes and stiffens. Upon seeing this he stops. She asks "don't you want to kiss your mummy?" and, as he is still standing irresolutely, she adds "you know, you shouldn't be afraid of your feelings."[7]

Rupesh Shah describes the "effect" of the child perceiving the mother's discomfort as providing "an analogic piece of communication that conflicts with the words that she speaks."[8] The child is thus trapped in a paradox; to move forward and embrace could lead to rejection. Yet, if the child does not embrace, it too could lead to emotional stress and possible punishment. The scenario describes conflicting messages within the mother/son relationship; one message vitiates the other. Mathijis Koopmans argues that "the child's ability to respond to the mother is incapacitated by such contradictions across communicative levels, because one message invalidates the other."[9] The child's voice is also reduced, if not eclipsed entirely, because he is unable to mention and critique the contradiction due to his subordinate status and reliance on the mother for all vital needs.[10]

According to Laing, both actors in this scenario are potentially vulnerable. As mother and child, both traditionally possessed a compromised or weaker legal and social status. Nonetheless, the power relationship between parent and child is clear.[11] The inversion of this scenario would equally hold true if, as the son approached, he indicated anger or fear of closeness.[12] The dependency of the child on the mother is delineated in the nature of all parent-child relationships. In this relationship, power is vertical, from parent over child. The child cannot escape the relationship, and to try invites other potential harms and dangers. There is no "common ground" between the two actors; their relationships are fixed in a hierarchical paradigm. This is equally apparent in other relationships, including that of the employer-employee and that within systems—social, economic, and political.[13]

Less addressed in the double bind scholarship, however, are the ways in which identity can be manipulated or fixed, causing double bind pitfalls to occur.[14] This is particularly true and problematic for any groups with "othered" status. Those who are "othered" often lack the political, economic, or even legal clout or status to shape their public identity. Examples of this abound in twentieth-century caricatures of blonde-haired women being perceived as lacking intelligence, or more directly with blacks in the roles of mammies, samboes, thieves and rapists in popular culture through magazines, newspapers, films, and even court transcripts. The very successful film Birth of a Nation depicted each of these stereotypes and is still considered one of the greatest masterpieces of the last century.[15] For black gay men in particular, the double bind is illustrated by the black church seeming to embrace "all" but imposing a "don't-ask-don't-tell standard," which has contributed in part to HIV/AIDS to becoming a "secret epidemic." In essence, the directive is "come unto us, but leave your disease, lifestyle, and identity at home."[16]

Thus, those who are "othered" live under the stereotype status imposed by a "dominant" group. If one cannot control his identity, he is always to bump up against notions of what his "ideal" behavior and image should be as a man, father, worker, son, and caregiver.[17] In essence, contradicting the notion of the ideal or *essential* man by being homosexual or bisexual when one is expected to *act* "manly," can have serious consequences. Those consequences include rejection from the church, and to the extent that one believes that salvation is found only through the church, then one's spiritual life is also cut off. Double bind theory aptly applies to the paradoxical circumstances in which black congregants may find themselves. For example, the African American church constructively and historically was a reliable safety net for blacks during and post antebellum.[18] Consider that the African American church can be credited with spearheading civil rights agendas, voting rights, housing, and integration.[19] However, church doctrines have historically been conservative, imposing standards on blacks unlike those of white churches with their congregants.

Ironically, African American religious ideology has generally held fast to more conservative roots, and while erasing oppressive racist ideology, has nonetheless in some instances continued a rigid path. To place this notion in context, let's consider the black church and the plight of African Americans and HIV/AIDS.

Part 2: The Black Church

Because of their ability to command the respect, trust, and loyalty of both the congregation and the community at large, they are able to guide their people in interpreting their political affairs and in marshalling their resources to accomplish social change. As charismatic leaders and the Lord's spokespersons, pastors command the rapt attention of their people. With an air of authority and confidence, they shape their worldviews, they inform their opinions, and they create their sense of right and wrong—a status that makes them indisputably well-qualified to popularize counter ruling-class ideas.

—Rupe Simms, "Christ Is Black with a Capital 'B' "

Double binds are particularly acute in African American religious communities where reliance on and loyalty to the church predates the past century and is entangled with the slave narrative. Yet for African Americans, loyalty and devotion to "the church" must be placed in context with their legal and social history in the United States. The black church is a political as well as religious institution.[20] As such, its practices and methodologies have not always been liberal; they more frequently have been conservative. Christianity was introduced to most American blacks during slavery. Inasmuch as churches provided religious education, which was almost exclusively Christian, they also served social and political functions. Churches provided an opportunity for the enslaved to come together outside of plantations and other labor environments. Parents separated from their children on other nearby plantations could visit with their offspring in the safety of church; communications could be passed with less fear of interception in the sacred confines of religious places (which may or may not have been in building). Communications were always more difficult on plantations with official "overseers" who patrolled and policed behavior and communications. Over time, churches provided the opportunity for organizing, planning, and politicizing the plight of blacks in the United States. In short, despite white religious thinkers endorsing slavery, black slaves used the church for purposes that would eventually support their communities.

Religious Endorsement of Slavery

African American communities, though internally varied by education, wealth, and employment, had a common geographical dimension and cultural expression that was uniquely defined by black life for most of the twentieth century. African American churches grew out of a unique history that involved the involuntary servitude of millions of Africans in the United States. According to African Methodist Episcopal (AME) scholars, that church and others which serve millions of African Americans grew out of a sociological rather than theological movement. Slavery, practiced primarily in southern states by the nineteenth century, and conservative religious dogma had the common denominator of southern geography. The backdrop of that enslavement involved Christian philosophy that endorsed slavery on southern plantations.[21] Whether Catholicism in Louisiana or the Baptist tradition in Mississippi, evangelism was originally imposed upon slaves to reinforce submissiveness. That African American Churches branched out on their own after the Civil War, creating the AME and Colored Methodist Episcopal (CME) and other churches, was a reflection of the desire to proactively address the crisis created by the color line.[22]

All the subspheres of black life described in pathbreaking studies on race by John H. Franklin,[23] E. Franklin Frazier,[24] Withrop Jordan,[25] Thomas Gossett,[26] Mary E. Goodman,[27] and Frantz Fanon[28] were affected by diminished legal and social status. Robert Fogel and Stanley Engerman attribute the accepted existence of slavery among religious thinkers as "part of the natural scheme of things" that predated slavery in the United States. Jesuits encouraged the importation of Africans to the New World, and the Catholic Church "actively promoted slavery."[29] Thomas More endorsed slavery for "vyle drudge" of society, including poor laborers and criminals. Blacks were depicted as "cursed" people with a heightened propensity for sexual depravity, vile behavior, and immoral conduct.[30] Slavery, thus, was a natural order for people who required private and state control in order to check their "unnatural" yearnings.

Ironically, the political and legal liberation of blacks would in some ways rely on the very rhetoric that justified African bondage. Cassius Marcellus Clay provided a stinging indictment against slavery. His abolitionist efforts, however, reinforced stereotypes about the indolence, laziness, and poor moral habits of Africans. Clay, cousin to the more famous Henry Clay who served in the United States Senate, rejected slavery as a poor economic institution. According to a letter he wrote in the *True American* that was reprinted in the *New York Tribune* in 1843, slavery was inefficient because blacks were "not so skilful, so energetic, and above all, have not the stimulus of self-interest."[31]

Nonetheless, the legitimacy of involuntary servitude was reinforced by its acceptance among religious thinkers and denominations in the New World. Slaves were expected to "keep their place" and aim for redemption in the afterlife. Such teachings attempted to reduce the significance of an earthly life with inalienable rights and legal protections for blacks. The clever juxtaposition of earthly ruler in contrast with a heavenly savior for purposes of creating a psychology to further bind the enslaved was seemingly effective. Hope and fear were powerful motivators that must be examined and understood in context. Robert Engerman, Stanley Foley, Richard Wade, and others document the horrible conditions of slavery in America. The brutality of plantation life included unpaid labor; deplorable living conditions; inadequate food; sexual exploitation of men, women, and children; rape; abductions; whipping; brining; and the excising of limbs. Because laws reinforced the legitimacy of such conditions, thereby supporting slave owners, planters were revered nearly as much as they were despised by their slaves.

Yet the "power" of planters was seductively packaged as second to and far inferior to that of God. What were slaves to make of this, particularly given religious instruction that demanded respect and obedience to God through submissiveness to masters? If the wrath of a slave owner was to sell one's children, whip until scarring occurred, or sever fingers and toes, what might the vengeance of God resemble? In a famous exegesis, Thomas Bacon reminds slaves that disobedience to masters is equal to sinning against God:

> Poor creatures! You little consider, when you are vile and neglectful of your master's business—when you steal, and waste, and hurt any of their substance—when you are saucy and impudent—when you are telling them lies, and deceiving them . . . [that] what faults you are guilty of towards your masters and mistresses, are faults done against God himself, who hat set your masters and mistresses over you in His own stead, and expects that you will do for them just as you would do for Him. And pray do not think that I want to deceive you when I tell you that your masters and mistresses are God's Overseers, and that, if you are faulty towards them, God himself will punish you severely for it in the next world . . . for God himself hath declared the same.[32]

Thus, early religious evangelizing to blacks with a slave experience delivered a vision of liberation through a shattered lens. Liberation and autonomy existed, but they were reserved for a romantic afterlife. Faith could not tolerate questioning or doubt, and given the deplorable conditions of the earthly life, the promised afterlife for obedience to masters held out hope of a better existence in the eternal.

So, what purpose did churches serve for blacks in bondage and out? According to Richard Wade, churches provided the "most acceptable" opportunity for blacks to unite.[33] Initially, slaveholders saw religious instruction in the lives of slaves as being in their political and economic best interest. Scriptures could be interpreted to support, condone, and even bless the institution of slavery. Sermons were powerful psychological tools, reminding slaves of their appalling conditions and reinforcing the threat of God should they attempt to overthrow their shackles.

Indeed, southern states at times sought to enforce Sabbath day practices for slaves even at risk of angering and fining their plantation owners.[34] It was a common belief among masters that religious doctrines interpreted "properly" supported the institution of slavery. Thus, religious teachings were thought to reaffirm rather than condemn slavery. Because most plantation owners and even state laws forbade educating slaves, most slaves would have been illiterate and unable to challenge select scriptures used in sermons with other passages.

Psychologically, however, churches were the fronts for liberation in a certain way. Unlike all other policed spaces, churches provided an opportunity to congregate, discuss, and plot. It was perhaps these functions of the church that proved most meaningful in the long term to African Americans. For this reason, shifts in how plantation owners embraced religious teachings for slaves became noticeable. In the mid-1800s, whites in Charleston, New Orleans, and other highly populated slave cities decried religious instruction for slaves, suggesting in local newspapers that churches had become "public nuisances and den for hatching plots against" masters.[35] In *United States v. Brooks* and similar cases initiated by prosecutors, blacks were chided for "loud," "disruptive," "irreverent" behavior in churches.[36]

Thus, the use of church and what church represented for African Americans evolved during the nineteenth and twentieth centuries. Plantation owners were shortsighted in two ways. First, they failed to appreciate the limitations of pro-slavery theology. Though Africans were certainly aware of the deplorable conditions in which they lived, blaming slaves for those conditions because they had "doomed" souls or were predisposed to hypersexuality, theft, laziness, and immorality would prove too strong a rhetoric—easily challenged within the enslaved community. Second, slave owners failed to appreciate that African Americans could reinterpret their church experiences and claim those aspects that spoke to them while rejecting the more derisive teachings promoted by plantation owners and white clergy.[37] In addition, blacks would come to rebel against the popular pro-slavery imagery that served to pathologize them. This rebellion would find its origins in the antebellum period, but would prevail long after.

African American Churches in the Twentieth and Twenty-First Centuries

Religion in black communities (or at least the church experience) was defined by race. The ways in which the churches identified their institutions indicated a broader mission and purposes beyond the hegemonic practices once imposed upon enslaved Africans. Consider the African Methodist Episcopal Church,[38] the Colored Methodist Episcopal Church,[39] and the Black Baptist Church,[40] all churches located within segregated communities populated by African Americans. These churches were so greatly influenced by the political and social needs of the black community that religious denomination was perhaps far less significant than a common mission to address the ubiquitous psychological and social threat of prejudice and discrimination against blacks. These churches acknowledged racism and rejected antebellum-derived stereotypes.

Churches, though distinctive by denomination, were often and continue to be considered the "black church" as a shorthand moniker that described their common goals, roles, and mission to serve as a priority, uplifting blacks from the legacy of slavery and the shackles of Jim Crow discrimination.[41] Largely because of this unique history and the collaborative efforts that marked various churches as speaking as "one" with regard to key issues in black life, churches serving African American communities were often called the "black church," without regard to specific religious affiliation. In this way, the churches were also equally positioned (for better or worse), unable to open doors outside of black communities, and equally threatened during the rise and height of the Civil Rights movement.

Segregation's geopolitical influence in the lives of black people influenced the Church's ability to easily reach and serve populations contained by the physical barriers of racism and housing discrimination. Segregation laws and practices constrained the movement of African Americans outside of black neighborhoods and within white communities. Except for the labor of maids, cooks, child-care providers, and other menial wage workers, access to white communities was strictly limited and actively policed. Thus, although not a homogenous community, African Americans to some extent were a captive audience for the black church because of the geopolitical nature of segregation: there was nowhere else to go.

According to religious scholar Dr. Charles Taylor, "the church was more than a safe house," and its importance to the African American community "can not be overstated."[42] The black church was significant in the life of the black community for several reasons. It is the single most identified and stable institution within the African American experience.[43] No other institutions in the African American community have survived threats, bombings, and other acts of targeted racism than has the black church. Furthermore, community and political leaders were created within the church. Even today, endorsement by the church can essentially create a political career. Taylor argues that blacks "were able to use their churches to hone organization and leadership skills useful in the economic, social and political development of their communities."[44] Indeed, mayors, judges, legislators, and even presidential candidates were products of the black church.[45] Thus, while the "black church" represented a place of respite and cleansing, a sacred space that rejected pro-slavery (and black emasculation) antebellum evangelism, its mission was larger. Segregation created a shared synergy for churches located in black communities—a shared interest in lives of a similarly situated community. In other words, the black community was "one" space with common language, experience, and resources. Finally, with the power that it wields, the black church is also the pathway to legitimacy in the African American community.

Thus, it is through the lens of a political body that black churches and their responses to sexuality and AIDS must be viewed. Those "speaking out" about the religious double binds in the African American Church provocatively describe how the "streets" have provided a more solicitous home than the church. For them, being true to their church communities is the equivalent of silencing their medical conditions and lifestyles. This choice may provide spiritual support, but does little to reconcile their lifestyles or treat their illnesses.

Part 3 provides an empirical overview of AIDS in Black America and analyzes the role the more conservative elements of the black church in shaping the dialogue about HIV. In particular, I argue, that because homosexuality and diseases connected with sexuality are largely taboo topics for the church, sick congregants face alienation, reprisal, and rejection. Indeed, sex remains part of the dark closet of black life. Incest, rape, and sexual exploitation are treated as sensitive issues—regarded as far too delicate for church consumption or greater community acknowledgment. Yet these realities are a part of American life, and without exception, a part of the African American experience. George Woods suggests that the external pressures of racism and the need to avoid further pathologizing cause African Americans to silence such harms. To give voice to these issues, according to Woods, is perceived as giving life to the harms that fester internally among African Americans, uncaused by the direct effects of racism.[46] In other words, to acknowledge any perceived weakness or deviancy in the African American community is to invite stereotyping and discrimination. This notion is highlighted in the scholarship of Mario Barnes, who provides a powerful analysis about silence and African Americans, suggesting that blacks hide emotional harms even from family members.

Part 3: AIDS, the Black Church, and Homophobia

To say there is such a thing as a gay Christian is saying there's an honest thief. Today, we look back with scorn at those who twisted the law to make marriage serve a racist agenda, and I believe our descendants will look back the same way at us if we yield to the same kind of pressure a radical sexual agenda is placing on us today.

—Bishop Gilbert A. Thompson Jr., pastor of New Covenant Christian Church in Cambridge, Mass.

In May 1999, Alveda King, the niece of Dr. Martin Luther King Jr., traveled to Massachusetts for what was to be a showdown about gays and the "protection" of heterosexual marriage. She testified before the joint House-Senate Judiciary Committee of the Massachusetts legislature in favor of a Massachusetts version of the Defense of Marriage Act (DOMA). According to Janet Jakobsen and Ann Pellegrini, her visit was arranged by conservative groups backing the bill. In her testimony, King "cited scripture to make her case for DOMA" and "the biblical passages she selected were, in her view, unambiguous condemnations of homosexuality and by implication of same-sex marriage."[47]

A few years after King's testimony, using some of the same scriptures that conservatives embraced against blacks, three major associations of Boston's black clergy issued not only a joint statement against gay marriage, but a stinging indictment that characterized homosexuality as an abominable sin.[48] Cast in such a light, and with the church as the gateway to legitimacy and acceptance within the black community, what homosexual, bisexual, or "down-low" explorer will choose to come out? Thus, indicted and conflated by such criticisms is not only the question of gay marriage, which is a separate legal issue, but the "quality of human beings," which is a uniquely answered within the religious context.

In effect, the impact of this type of public condemnation is that those suffering from the "homosexual" disease, male or not, will stay closeted and silent. The September 2002 issue of AIDS Impact, a publication by the Office of Minority Health in the U.S. Department of Health and Human Services, highlighted the black church and HIV.[49] The issue described one of a number of encounters in which black parishioners, even women, have been ostracized and rejected by their churches. Tiffany White describes a lonely journey with her black church, the first place she turned to when she learned about her HIV status. "I loved my church and it loved me. But it didn't love my disease. I told one of the other parishioners after worship and by the next week, I could see that a lot of people were looking at me funny."[50] By the next week, her pew was empty. Within a month, she was replaced as the Sunday school teacher. According to White, "no one said anything. They aren't mean people, they just aren't loving either."[51]

Conservative commentators, though, disagree with the notion that homophobia in the church affects AIDS in the black community. Their point, that risky sexual behavior, and not the word of God, causes AIDS addresses only the surface of the medical crisis. With rejoinders such as "God made Adam and Eve, not Adam and Steve," some black church leaders have abrogated a larger responsibility by reducing the medical crisis to one exclusively about sexuality.

Ultimately, the church's stand on homosexuality interferes with dialogues about HIV and AIDS. The effect of homophobia in black churches is a public health concern to the extent that the majority of those diagnosed with AIDS in the United States happen to be African American men, women, and children. Given the black church's influence in the African America community, denial of homosexuality and refusal to address the disease mean that more children, women, and men will forgo testing, counseling, and any type of medical treatment that could lead to being "exposed" or "outed." Jacob Levenson spent several years chronicling the lives of African Americans in the South who felt unable to tell their communities about their illness. The stories, involving fifteen-year-old girls, young men right out of college, and others, offered a glimpse into the lives of those who understood all too well that any acknowledgment of their illness would result in being ostracized and kicked out of their churches.[52]

The stigma associated with certain types of diseases in African American religious communities, particularly AIDS, is largely overlooked in legal and bioethical scholarship. Few scholars explore these intersections, although admirable scholarship has been written exploring connected discourses (queer theory, sex politics, critical race feminism jurisprudence). Even among critical race theorists, observes Richard Delgado in a compelling law review article, empirical research and analysis on issues such as health care often are under the radar.[53] Thus, the question of bioethics and religion in the African American community is a largely neglected enterprise. Yet, these questions of double binds with regard to HIV and many other medical questions in African American religious thought are important for our times. As an example, African Americans experience the highest rates of AIDS infection among all U.S. populations. More than half of all new AIDS cases are African Americans.[54]

Intragroup silence and covering have contributed to the rapid spread of sexual diseases among youth and adults in the African American community. Kenji Yoshino speaks of covering as being a secondary aspect of closeting behavior. To silence the disempowered is not enough, as acceptance within the desired group also means disavowing certain relationships and behaviors and appearing to assimilate within the dominant culture. For black gay men, assimilation and "covering" is expressed through stereotypically "manly" acts and donning the guise of heterosexuality. According to some commentators, this means being "on the down low." Although this notion of "down low" has been challenged as being a relatively small phenomenon, even critics recognize that Black gay and bisexual men are forced to "cover" their sexuality in order to win acceptance in the African American community—and the church is the center of African American life. Some critics and physicians have long attributed the rapid growth of AIDS and its devastating effects on heterosexual, non–drug using women to the fact that black men are covering their sexuality through active sexual engagement with black women.[55]

This chapter advances the case that essentialism or the perception of the "ideal" within the black community, particularly within traditional, conservative doctrine, causes double binds to occur that harm the health of those who otherwise view the black church as a place of security and respite. The purpose of this contribution is not to stereotype the African American church or to overlook its tremendous influence in liberating America from oppressive Jim Crow practices, but rather to bring forward dialogue. This part challenges the divide wedged between culture, technology, religion, and bioethics in African American religious thought. In keeping with the purpose of this chapter, it argues that the African American church influences black decision making regarding health. It uses AIDS as speaking points to examine how the church wrestles with contemporary social problems affecting health. It concludes by assessing whether the church's role has been more effective in healing, or whether it has unwittingly aided or exacerbated health care crises in the African American community.

Empirical Overview

It didn't take an epidemiologist to see that rural Alabama was a potential tin-derbox for an AIDS epidemic. It had some of the worst rates of gonorrhea, syphilis, and Chlamydia in the country; those diseases, the Centers for Disease Control said, helped facilitate HIV transmission.

—Jacob Levenson, *The Secret Epidemic: The Story of AIDS and Black America*

Despite efforts to control the spread of HIV/AIDS in the 1980s and '90s, its precipitous rise foretells a new human tragedy with devastating consequences for the African American community. In the African American community, AIDS is now the leading cause of death among women ages 25–34.[56] Nearly 70 percent of newly reported pediatric AIDS cases are African American children and babies.[57] The rapid spread of AIDS and its devastating effects in the African American community are undeniable. In 2003, the most recent year for which census data are available, African Americans constituted nearly 13 percent of the U.S. population, but they accounted from nearly 50 percent of the estimated AIDS cases.[58]

An aspect of the AIDS tragedy in the African American community is marked by its devastating death toll and subsphere effects on families and children. Yet the real "black" tragedy of AIDS predates postmillennium statistics, because HIV is a preventable disease, and its modes of infection have long been known. Lack of information is not the issue: HIV and AIDS have been a part of international nomenclature and words of common usage among even the least informed and most impoverished. Why, then, have African Americans, including black teenagers, been so disproportionately infected, and why have black churches failed to respond?

In the 1980s, when the first HIV cases were diagnosed, AIDS was considered a white, gay male disease. The stigma of homosexuality and the underlying denial of gay life in the black community ostensibly gave clergy the power to shut the door on homosexuality and the disease itself. In fact, AIDS was and continues to be regarded as a plague from God to punish those who violate Scripture by engaging in homosexual practice.[59] The Reverend Jerry Falwell and Reverend Albert Mohler (president of the Southern Baptist Theological Seminary) "characterized homosexuality as a willfully chosen behavior."[60] Black pastors have also taken up the homophobic call. Outspoken black ministers decry any claims that homosexuality is anything but chosen behavior. "They have the nerve to say they are a minority," says the Reverend Sikes of St. James

AME church in Tampa, Florida.[61] "Minorities are people with inborn traits. We have no choice of what we are. It is not immoral to be black, female or handicapped, but it is immoral to be homosexual."[62] Thus, depending upon the political position regarding homosexuality in the black church, the empirical data could be read as a call to action and breaking silence—or proof that punishment is at hand.

By the end of 2003 (the latest data sets available), the U.S. government reports that more than 42 percent (42.4%) of those living with AIDS in the United States were black.[63] This figure represents an increase from the prior year based on data from 2002. The AIDS rate, defined as the "number of people living with AIDS per 100,000 individuals" was 58.2 for African Americans compared with 14.5 for the total U.S. population.[64] These figures stand in stark juxtaposition to the AIDS denial within the dominant sphere of African American life. By the end of 2003, nearly 200,000 African Americans had died of AIDS. Nearly 38 percent of the total deaths from AIDS were among African Americans in 2002, and for 2003 it was more than 50 percent (50.2%).[65] As for African American children, they constitute 62.7 percent of the children under 13 living with AIDS.[66]

Consider the data in figure 17.1, which depicts the number of AIDS cases per 100,000 in the United States. The rate for African Americans is nearly three times that of the next highest group, Latinos. The AIDS rate for African Americans is now more than seven times that of U.S. whites and nearly sixteen times that of Asian Americans. With statistics such as these, can the black church afford to be quiet? Is there a responsibility to address the crisis?

Some commentators attribute the rapid spread of HIV to the tension between religious ideology and public health. Figure 17.2 shows that nearly 70 percent of women diagnosed with AIDS in 2003 were African American. African American women accounted for four times the rate of AIDS diagnoses of Latinas. What the figures do not convey were the number of women who were infected but unaware. The stigmatization of AIDS in the black church may affect such medical decisions as whether to be tested or to seek counseling and support.

Part 4: The Double Bind Applied

The tales of homophobia in the black church speak directly to the question about the role of religion in bioethics. Few other examples of the double bind of bioethics and religion are as clear as the case of AIDS and the church. Some commentators suggest that the true cause of AIDS has little to do with religious philosophy and more to do with risky behavior and rejection of religious teachings. They argue that homosexuality is an abomination and sin. AIDS, according to their analysis, is divine punishment for failure to follow biblical teachings. To discount their rhetoric as the homophobic rants of a small minority would be naïve. Rather this rhetoric reflects the realities of the black church. Certainly within the African American community, the black church is the

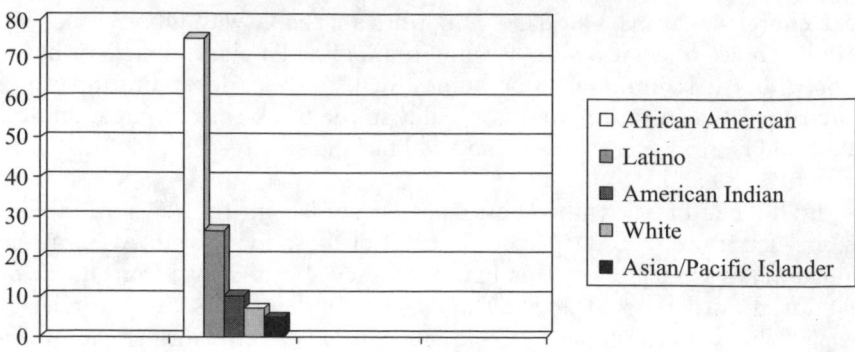

FIGURE 17.1. AIDS Case/Rate by Race/Ethnicity

cornerstone of racial, political, and cultural ideology and identity. Moreover, it is the single most established institution within the black community. Given the demonstrated strength of the black church, which has wielded incredible power over the past century, tackling AIDS would seem to be a winnable proposition. However, without the church's support, tackling even so much as the question of how AIDS is transmitted seems an uphill battle.

Ultimately, sex is at the center of this double bind. If homosexuals or men on the "down low" reveal their sexual identities or sexuality, they stand the risk of being alienated and ostracized within their church communities, representations of the larger black communities. Being silent in order to belong is not a new social phenomenon. Indeed, history is replete with examples of groups who followed "orders" spoken or not in order to avoid persecution or simply to fit in—even when compromising their own moral beliefs. Thus, the behavior of those who engage in "down low" sex or "toss the salad" (another euphemism for dating heterosexually and sleeping homosexually),[67] in order to maintain cultural and social legitimacy should not come as a surprise. On the other hand, perhaps what is at stake for them is something more. To the extent that salvation is offered only through religious contact controlled by black pastors, one must fit through the pastor's needle in order to gain the gates of heaven.

Thus, the double bind for a rapidly growing population of black Americans will be how to reconcile (if at all possible) black identity, medical identity, and religious identity. In the center of this double bind is the question about whether one can openly possess coexisting identities such as HIV status, or homosexuality and yet be a part of the black church. To the extent that religious leaders condemn those who are homosexual, relatively fewer gays and those who happen to be HIV infected will be willing to expose themselves to condemnation in order to move the church. Ironically, outside the black church, black gay men have fewer cultural options. Scholars such as Darren Hutchinson and Pamela Bridgewater have written about the double binds of black gay life and racism within the white gay community. Wanda Jean Allen's plight

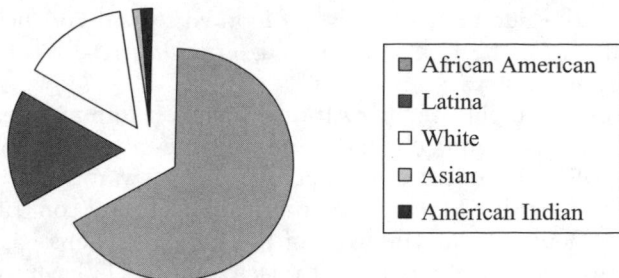

FIGURE 17.2. AIDS Rate among U.S. Women by Race (2003)

shortly before her execution in Oklahoma for killing her lover demonstrates far too well how gay persons of color struggle between identities without support from any. In her case, although black, woman, gay, and mentally disabled, only the Reverend Jesse Jackson was at her side before the state of Oklahoma put her to death. She was essentially abandoned by the very communities with which she could identify, and Reverend Jackson was the only black religious leader willing to crusade to save her life. Black churches and gay organizations were not to be found on the nights before her death.

Choosing the church over health is a calculated choice, but perhaps not a real one. True choices are not burdened by physical health versus spiritual death. Choosing the church over identity and even health (by revealing that one has a sexually related illness) is an illusory choice, but not one that is free from the avoidance of stigma. To be clear, I am not suggesting that there is no room for personal responsibility. That would hardly be the case. However, given the health crisis in which the black community has now plunged, it seems important that the dialogue move beyond conversations of abstinence. Indeed, by comparison, the white gay community has done exceedingly well in combating AIDS. There, success can be attributed to political, family, and community support of their plight. Unlike their gay white counterparts, African Americans continue to rely primarily on the church for support and guidance.

Conclusion: Lessons

What are the options for black churches and the communities they serve? Does embracing HIV+ parishioners and developing a proactive policy on AIDS signify a rejection of Scripture? How are these issues to be reconciled? These questions are worthy of serious address. The civil rights movements of various minority groups have demonstrated far too well the destructive power of labeling. Thus, "calling out" the black church for its less than sensitive stand on the issue of AIDS does little without proactive engagement. Indeed, without the support of the most important force in African American communities, efforts to stem the tide of AIDS may be doomed to fail. For these reason, exploring options for the black church and proposing research models are necessarily the better steps.

Indeed, some churches serving African American communities have engaged in proactive community-building and dialogues about HIV/AIDS. Gospel against AIDS in Detroit and Balm of Gilead in New York are two highly visible organizations that have designed ministries around combating AIDS and the values double bind. The work of these organizations has not been without challenges as they attempt to put a "face" on AIDS by having volunteers disclose their personal stories about living with AIDS. One of the volunteers for Gospel against AIDS, Tiffany Oliver, tells her story with congregations:

> I went to school. I went to work. I was engaged. I did all I thought I was supposed to do. I was raised in the church. My mother was a nurse. My grandmother, assistant pastor. I didn't do drugs. I wasn't a lesbian or a homosexual. Please don't stereotype anybody. HIV doesn't discriminate.[68]

Messages like Tiffany Oliver's have been powerful testimonials to African American congregations, if they can get in the door and past the ministers of the churches to give the message. The effects of the work of these organizations has yet to be measured, but a void is surely filled by their efforts.

Other steps worth pursuing involve research studies and grants to African American churches and scholars working in African American communities. Questions worth testing include whether the African American church's involvement with proactive programs acknowledging AIDS and promoting healthy sexual behaviors would reduce sexual disease transmissions in the communities they serve. Developing such research models would be challenging on a number of levels, but the design flaws could be overcome. For example, not all churches would be equally situated. Perhaps based on socioeconomic and education factors, some African American churches would experience far less of medical crisis surrounding the sexual transmission of diseases, and others would have a different experience. As well, fully engaging in such research may compromise privacy, and the stigma barriers may be difficult to overcome.

Nevertheless, the time has come to help African American churches address AIDS through federal programs that encourage testing and monitor health habits, including follow-up medical visits. Only through greater awareness and dialogue can those concerned about the health of the African American community begin to make a difference.

NOTES

1. R. D. Laing, *Self and Others*, 2nd ed. (London: Penguin, 1969), 125.
2. Centers for Disease Control and Prevention (CDC), "HIV/AIDS Surveillance Report," 2003, available at http://www.cdc.gov/hiv/stats/2003surveillancereport.pdf.

3. See, e.g., Jason B. Johnson, "Secret Gay Encounters of Black Men Could Be Raising Women's Infection Rate," *San Francisco Chronicle*, May 1, 2005, A1.

4. See Gregory Bateson, Don Jackson, Jay Healy, and John Weakland, "Towards a Theory of Schizophrenia," *Behavioral Science* 1 (1956): 4. See also Mathijis Koopmans, "Schizophrenia and the Family: Double Bind Theory Revisited" (1997) (noting, that the researchers believed contradictions in the interaction between family members predisposes its members to schizophrenia), available online at http://www.goertzel .org/dynapsyc/1998/KoopmansPaper.htm (last visited January 15, 2006).

5. See Koopmans, "Schizophrenia and the Family."

6. See, e.g., Rupesh Shah, "Relational Praxis in Transition toward Sustainability: Business-NGO Collaboration and Participatory Action Research" (Ph.D. diss., University of Bath, 2001), 260.

It is worth noting that this example, though quite useful for its descriptive and illustrative value, reflects certain notions of its time. Commentators might suggest that it reinforces certain stereotypes about women and their contribution to children's poor mental health status. Of course, it fails to invoke a father image, which in turn leaves fathers free from any *blame* or *culpability* in vertical relationships with children.

7. See, e.g., Rupesh Shah, "Relational Praxis."

8. See, e.g., Rupesh Shah, "Relational Praxis."

9. See, e.g., Koopmans, "Schizophrenia and the Family."

10. See Bateson et al., "Towards a Theory of Schizophrenia."

11. Laing, *Self and Others*, 127.

12. Ibid.

13. See, e.g., Marilyn Frye, *Oppression, in Power, Privilege, and Law: A Civil Rights Reader*, ed. Leslie Bender and Dann Braveman (Connecticut: West Group, 1995), 60–61; and John Calmore, "A Call to Context: The Professional Challenges of Cause Lawyering at the Intersection of Race, Space, and Poverty," *Fordham Law Review* 67 (1999): 1927, which reflects upon the role of lawyers and the critical analysis that they can bring to the systemic oppressions that burden marginalized groups. On p. 1938 of the article, Calmore writes:

> Over the years of practicing poverty law from Roxbury to Watts, I was continually struck by the apparently optionless world that most of my clients inhabited. I never associated it with oppression, but rather I saw it as a lack of social and monetary capital. I continued to believe in the myth of Horatio Alger. I simply failed to see the predicament of my clients as oppression—as something that was group-based, structured, and systemic.

14. See, e.g., Kenji Yoshino, "Covering," *Yale Law Journal* 111 (2002): 769, 836–38, which notes that some members of minority groups, such as homosexuals, "tone down" their group characteristics in order to assimilate into mainstream society.

15. See, e.g., Michele Goodwin, "The Economy of Citizenship," *Temple Law Review* 76 (2003): 129, which describes how some groups with immutable characteristics possess fixed status and their external identity cannot be altered by their own group or individual efforts despite achievements, assimilation, and other attempts to belong.

16. *The Greatest Taboo: Homosexuality in Black Communities*, ed. Deloy Constanine-Simms (Los Angeles: Alyson, 2001), 117.

17. See, e.g., Michele Goodwin, "The Black Woman in the Attic: Law, Metaphor, and Madness in Jane Eyre," *Rutgers Law Journal* 30 (1999): 597.

18. Ibid., 633, which describes coverture laws in the United States and England and states that "the doctrine of coverture reinforced the hideous practice of gender subordination and marginalization; it was the legal castration of women."

19. C. Eric Lincoln and Lawrence H. Mamiya, *The Black Church in the African American Experience* (Durham: Duke University Press, 1990), 8.

20. Ibid.

21. See Robert William Fogel and Stanley L. Engerman, *Time on the Cross: The Economics of American Negro Slavery* (New York: Little Brown, 1974), 29–31.

22. See, e.g., W. E. B. Du Bois, *The Souls of Black Folks* (New York: Penguin, 1903).

23. See John H. Franklin, *From Slavery to Freedom* (New York: Knopf, 1967).

24. See E. Franklin Frazier, *The Negro in the United States* (South Bend, Ind.: Notre Dame University Press, 1957).

25. See Winthrop Jordan, *White over Black: American Attitudes toward the Negro, 1550–1812* (Chapel Hill: University of North Carolina Press, 1968).

26. See Thomas Gossett, *Race: The History of an Idea in America* (New York: Oxford University Press, 1965).

27. See Mary E. Goodman, *Race Awareness in Young Children* (New York: Addison-Wesley Press, 1964).

28. See Frantz Fanon, *Black Skin, White Masks* (New York: Grove Press, 1967).

29. Fogel and Engerman, *Time on the Cross*, 30.

30. C. Herton, *Sex and Racism in America* (New York: Grove Press, 1988), cited in *The Greatest Taboo*, 116. The passage notes that African Americans have been viewed as "sexually deviant," "obsessed with sex, [or] sexual predators with uncontrollable desires." These views were often used historically to justify white men's sexual lust for and subsequent rape of black women.

31. Fogel and Engerman, *Time on the Cross*, 160.

32. John W. Blassingame, *The Slave Community: Plantation Life in the Antebellum South* (New York: Oxford University Press, 1972), 85 (passage quotes Alexander Glennie, *Sermons Preached on Plantations to Congregations of Negroes* [Charleston, 1844], 23, 24).

33. See Richard Wade, *Slavery in the Cities: The South 1820–1860* (New York: Oxford University Press, 1964), 82.

34. See, e.g., *State v. Williams,*26 N.C. 400; 1844 N.C. LEXIS 45; 4 Ired. Law 400 (1844).

35. See Wade, *Slavery in the Cities*, 83 (quoting the *True American*, October 15, 1839).

36. See, e.g., *United States v. Brooks,*24 F. Cas. 1244; 1834 U.S. App. LEXIS 284; 4 Cranch C.C. 427(1834).

37. See, e.g., http://www.ame-church.com/aboutus.html (accessed on May 11, 2005).

38. See, e.g., http://www.ame-church.com/aboutus.html (accessed on May 11, 2005).

39. See, e.g., http://www.c-m-e.org/core/CME_Beginnings.htm (accessed on May 11, 2005).

40. See, e.g., www.blackandchristian.com/blackchurch/index.shtml (accessed on May 12, 2005).

41. See, e.g., www.theblackchurchpage.com; www.blackandchristian.com/blackchurch/index.shtml (accessed on May 12, 2005).

42. See Charles Taylor, "The Meaning of Juneteenth—Freedom." Available at http://www.actom.com/njclchistory.htm (accessed May 12, 2005).

43. Lincoln and Mamiya, *Black Church,* 7 (noting that black churches "were one of the few stable and coherent institutions to emerge from slavery").

44. Taylor, "The Meaning of Juneteenth."

45. Taylor, "The Meaning of Juneteenth."

46. See, e.g., "Symposium, 'Each One Pull One': The Inspirational Methodology behind an Impassioned but Somewhat Flawed Protest," *African American Law and Political Representation* 1 (1994): 89, 96.

47. See, e.g., Janet R. Jakobsen and Ann Pellegrini, *Love the Sin: Sexual Regulation and the Limits of Religious Tolerance* (2003), 77.

48. See Michael Paulson, "Black Clergy Rejection Stirs Gay Marriage Backers," *Boston Globe,* February 10, 2004.

49. See, e.g., Office of Minority Health, U.S. Department of Health and Human Services, *HIV Impact,* September/October 2002.

50. Ibid.

51. Ibid.

52. See, e.g., Jacob Levenson, *The Secret Epidemic: The Story of AIDS and Black America* (New York: Pantheon, 2004).

53. See Richard Delgado, "Crossroads and Blind Alleys: A Critical Examination of Recent Writing about Race, Crossroads, Directions, and a New Critical Race Theory," *Texas Law Review* 82 (2003): 121.

54. CDC, "HIV/AIDS Surveillance Report."

55. See, e.g., Johnson, *Secret Gay Encounters.*

56. CDC, "HIV/AIDS Surveillance Report."

57. Ibid. (noting that, of 90 infants reported as having HIV, 62 were African American).

58. See U.S. Department of Health and Human Services, Health Resources and Services Administration, 2005 Fact Sheet: "African Americans and HIV/AIDS in the United States" (January 2005).

59. See, e.g., Jakobsen and Pellegrini, *Love the Sin.*

60. See, e.g., Jakobsen and Pellegrini, *Love the Sin.*

61. See, e.g., Tracie Reddick, "Black, Gay, and Under Fire; In Black Churches throughout the Bay Area, Ministers Are Pounding Their Pulpits against Homosexuality," *Tampa Tribune* (Fla.), July 14, 1996, 1.

62. See, e.g., Tracie Reddick, "Black, Gay, and Under Fire."

63. See UNAIDS, "2004 Report on the Global AIDS Epidemic," July 2004.

64. See CDC, "Fact Sheet-HIV/AIDS," 2004.

65. Ibid.

66. CDC, "HIV/AIDS Surveillance Report." The report notes that, of 59 newly diagnosed AIDS patients under the age of 13, 40 were African American.

67. This term and others have become synonymous with gay sex. For other definitions, see Jonathon Green, *The Big Book of Filth* (New York: Cassell, 1999), 237. Green defines "tossing the salad" as the sex act known as anilingus. The phrase originated in the 1990s and is commonly used among teenagers within African American communities.

68. "The Black Church and AIDS, Religion, and Ethics," PBS broadcast, March 17, 2000. Transcript available at http://www.pbs.org/wnet/religionandethics/week329/cover.html.

18

The Delivery of Controversial Services: Reproductive Health and Ethical and Religious Directives

Maura A. Ryan

In 1995, the city of Austin, Texas, agreed to lease Brackenridge Hospital, a public facility, to the Roman Catholic Seton Healthcare Network. Under the terms of the original agreement, Brackenridge would continue to offer reproductive health services with the exception of abortion. The hospital's lease was subsequently amended, following intervention by the Vatican, to specify that "city employees, rather than hospital staff, would provide [sterilization procedures] and that the city would be financially responsible."[1] This arrangement remained in place until June 2001 when, in the wake of newly revised ethical and religious directives for Catholic Health Care Services issued by the United States Conference of Catholic Bishops, Seton announced that it could no longer manage Brackenridge if sterilization and other contraceptive services were offered, even by city employees. The Austin City Council agreed in February 2002 to create a separate, city-owned and -operated clinic on Brackenridge's fifth floor. This " 'hospital within a hospital' would offer labor and delivery services in addition to tubal ligations, contraception counseling and provision, and emergency contraception for rape victims."[2] Austin-area critics, such as the Ad Hoc Coalition on Women's Reproductive Health, have called the "hospital with a hospital" solution "cumbersome, expensive to implement and ultimately, only temporary."[3]

As Rachel Benson Gold of the Alan Guttmacher Institute observed, "Brackenridge Hospital . . . [can] be seen as a microcosm of the multifaceted debate over the involvement of Catholic hospitals in the provision of reproductive health care."[4] The rapid growth of

Catholic health care over the last decade has been accompanied by considerable controversy over the fate of reproductive health services such as elective sterilization and emergency contraception, particularly where public hospitals and clinics have been absorbed into Catholic-owned or affiliated networks. Although the rate of consolidation has slowed, the questions raised by the trend toward mergers are significant: What are the limits of religious identity in public-private partnerships? To what extent are Catholic-owned or -operated networks obligated to accommodate community interests in preserving reproductive health services within institutional commitments to a distinctive religious and moral mission? What is the moral status of reproductive health services when strategies for accommodation fail or are foreclosed?

Catholic Health Care and the Directives

According to the Catholic Health Association of the United States, Catholic hospitals currently constitute the nation's largest single group of nonprofits. Catholic health care systems are present in all 50 states and include more than 600 hospitals, 600,000 full-time employees, 3,000 social services centers, and more than 1,500 continuing care centers.[5] In 2004, Catholic hospitals accounted for 11 percent of all community hospitals and 15.8 percent of hospital admissions. As described by the association, Catholic health care facilities "serve diverse populations . . . [providing] a wide range of services across the continuum of care to patients of all ages, races, and religious beliefs."[6] Catholic hospitals and clinics lead in offering certain types of public health and other specialty services, among them alcohol and drug abuse treatment, birthing services, well-child care, community outreach, geriatric psychiatry, pain management, and obstetrics.[7]

It is not surprising that Catholic health care centers are more likely to offer "traditionally unprofitable care" than are for-profit centers or that they serve a significant percentage of patients who rely on Medicaid or Medicare.[8] Health care is a valued dimension of the church's social outreach; as such, Catholic health care is understood as a ministry that "exists to carry out the healing mission of Jesus and the church" and that strives to serve the medical, spiritual, and social needs of persons and communities with particular concern for those who are poor, underserved, or otherwise marginalized.[9] Providing health care and advocating for just health care policy are fundamental ways that the church expresses its beliefs about the necessary conditions for promoting human dignity and the meaning of a "good" society. As one medical anthropologist puts it, "operating clinics and hospitals brings Catholic-ness into being; fostering an organization that cares for the sick and the poor makes explicit a particular religious identity."[10]

Increasingly, the expression of Catholic identity in health care has taken on the dimension of cultural critique. Catholic health care has positioned itself as a "point of resistance" against what is viewed as a growing commercialization of medicine in the United States and a deeper instrumentalization of human life manifest in practices such as abortion, physician-assisted suicide, in vitro fertilization, and research on human embryos.

The principal way that the institutional church places its "stamp" on Catholic health care is through a publication called *Ethical and Religious Directives for Catholic Health Care Services*. Issued and periodically updated by the U.S. Conference of Catholic Bishops, the publication is both descriptive and prescriptive. The most recent edition, issued on June 15, 2001, contains a broad theological vision for Catholic health care in the new millennium. The Catholic health care ministry should be seen, it says, as defending human dignity against rapid and potentially threatening technological and social changes, working tirelessly for universal access, and contributing to the common good. Every dimension of health care is cast within "the mystery of Christ": all those involved are enjoined to "see Christian love as the animating principle of health care; to see healing and compassion as a continuation of Christ's mission; to see suffering as a participation in the redemptive power of Christ's passion, death and resurrection; and to see death, transformed by the resurrection, as an opportunity for a final act of communion with Christ."[11] In addition to expressing the spiritual charisma of Catholic health care, the directives provide guidance for applying the church's moral principles to specific issues faced by health care institutions. The 2001 addition contains 72 directives, covering questions such as the role of hospitals within communities, ethical dimensions of the physician-patient relationship, therapeutic options for addressing reproductive problems and the care of the dying. Given Catholicism's strongly hierarchical authority structure, the directives have the status of "requirements" rather than "recommendations."[12]

No Room for Compromise?

Not surprisingly, the directives that have been most controversial have addressed the delivery of reproductive services such as sterilization, assisted reproductive technologies, and emergency contraception; the removal of medical nutrition and hydration and the related issues of assisted suicide and euthanasia; and the requirements for partnerships involving Catholic health care facilities. The 2001 edition contained two significant revisions that bear directly on the Brackenridge case and help to explain what is at stake in mergers involving Catholic health care. The first was the addition of a directive that states: "Catholic health care organizations are not permitted to engage in immediate material cooperation in actions that are intrinsically immoral, such as abortion, euthanasia, assisted suicide, and direct sterilization."[13] The second was the omission of a technical appendix outlining the principles of cooperation. Most readers assumed correctly that the changes were aimed at closing a previously open window of interpretation regarding sterilizations in Catholic health care facilities and networks. Indeed, as Bishop Donald Wuerl, one of the drafters of the 2001 edition, acknowledged, the availability of sterilization under partnership agreements, like the original agreement between Seton and Brackenridge, was the central problem driving the revision process.[14] Earlier editions of *Ethical and Religious Directives* were explicit in directing that under no circumstances could abortion be tolerated in a Catholic health care institution or system, even where the principle of material cooperation could be invoked. The publication was less precise in dealing with sterilization. The newly added Directive 70 does not intend to place direct sterilization as a moral act on the same par with abortion or euthanasia, as some critics argued. What it does intend, as Cathleen Kaveny put it, is to make clear that "the principle of material cooperation with evil can't be used to justify Catholic hospitals performing *any* of these acts."[15]

In linking sterilization with abortion and euthanasia in its invocation of "immediate material cooperation," the bishops weighed in decisively in a lengthy debate over what counts as morally unacceptable cooperation in procedures that are condemned by the church. The principle of immediate material cooperation has been interpreted by Catholic moral theologians as permitting involvement in another's morally evil action under conditions of duress or where a greater evil can be avoided only through these means.[16] As applied in the assessment of hospital mergers, the principle has been used to justify retaining sterilization services when not doing so would result in significant hardship to the community or in the closure of one or more health care centers. Financial duress resulting from the loss of patient revenue was cited, for example, by diocesan officials in explaining the decision to allow St. Louise Regional Hospital (previously South Valley Hospital) in Gilroy, California, to continue to offer tubal ligations following its purchase by Catholic Healthcare West.[17] The earlier appendix to *Ethical and Religious Directives* lent support to this interpretation of the Catholic moral tradition in arguing that "the matter of duress distinguishes immediate material cooperation [usually interpreted as participation in circumstances that are essential to the commission of an act] from implicit formal cooperation [when the cooperating person or organization participates directly in an act or in some sense can be said to share in the intention of the principal agent].[18] Theologians and diocesan officials also relied on a document issued by the National Conference of Catholic Bishops in 1977. The "Commentary on the Reply of the Sacred Congregation for the Doctrine of the Faith on Sterilization in Catholic Hospitals" made it clear that Catholic health institutions cannot *approve* sterilizations. However, it argued that material cooperation in sterilization can be justified in those narrowly defined cases "where the hospital because of duress or pressure cannot reasonably exercise the autonomy that it has."[19]

Two important issues frame the broader theological debate surrounding the revised directives. One concerns what counts as duress. In an initial consultation with the bishops, the Catholic Health Association conveyed a number of concerns expressed by its constituents concerning the proposed revisions, including the danger that Catholic sole-provider hospitals could close. The attractiveness of Catholic health care centers as potential partners could be diminished, and the moral authority of local bishops could be compromised if they were perceived as reneging on earlier agreements or yielding to external pressure from the Vatican. Most important, constituents were concerned that restrictions on the ability to "carve out" sterilization could result in the loss of obstetric and gynecological services, harming services to poor women and children, and seriously weakening the ability of Catholic health care ministries to continue to exert a Catholic presence in the delivery of reproductive care in general.[20] Jesuit moral theologian James Keenan argues that the threatened closure of a needed health care institution or loss of all obstetrics from Catholic health care (the kind of cases the Catholic Health Association's constituents had in mind) constitutes legitimate conditions of duress. Prudential judgments concerning cooperation come into play precisely when one's options are constrained and one seeks to protect a great value that is threatened. Thus, according to Keenan, "if the threat is real and the possibility of offering a real alternative is minimal," immediate material cooperation can be justified.[21]

However, not all Catholic theologians agree that the threatened closure of hospitals or loss of obstetric and gynecological services should be regarded as "duress." One point of contention is the interpretation of duress as one moves from its traditional use (as envisioning the case of an individual forced to participate in a crime at gunpoint) to its application in the conduct of institutions. Debates turn on whether duress is necessarily "episodic" and therefore inappropriately applied to circumstances involving long-term agreements, as well as on what conditions limit the reasonable exercise of moral autonomy. An early draft of the revised ethical and religious directives contained an explicit notation limiting the application of the principle of immediate material cooperation under duress to cases involving individuals. More serious disagreements concern how one should assess the significance of closing Catholic hospitals and clinics.

Seminary professor Germain Grisez argues that the sponsors of Catholic health care institutions should be willing to get out of the hospital business if they can survive only by cooperating, even indirectly, with actions that the church condemns: "The business of a Catholic institution like a hospital is precisely to bear witness to the faith, [to lead] people out of sin, not just leave them there." Echoing Grisez, Christopher Zehnder, editor of the *Los Angeles Mission*, wonders rhetorically: "Is the loss of OB/GYN services more serious than the sacrifice of Catholic principles?" Invoking Catholic teaching concerning the "natural maternal vocation" of women, he asks: "How will women be affected, except positively, by Catholic hospitals treating them according to their true human dignity? And how Catholic are the sponsors who will abandon their Catholicity because they are called to follow Church doctrine?"[22]

However, Keenan argues that the aim of the Catholic health care ministry is not only to avoid wrongdoing but also to contain wrongdoing. Partnership agreements that have preserved sterilization services have also reduced or eliminated abortion and extended the influence of Catholic values in other areas of patient care, for example, in genetic counseling and assisted reproduction. Therefore, he argues, those who sponsor Catholic health care cannot be "satisfied with a self-knowledge that exculpates [them] from getting [their] hands dirty." This does not mean that irresponsible cooperation can be excused. On the contrary, because it is sometimes necessary to cooperate in order to protect threatened values, they should "seek to do it as rightly as possible."[23]

The other issue in the background of the revised directives concerns the boundaries between tolerating and approving an action. The principles of cooperation acknowledge moral ambiguity, the reality that the pursuit of good can sometimes involve undesired involvement in morally questionable actions. Developed within a moral tradition that teaches that one may never do evil so that good may result, the principles of cooperation serve to guide agents in avoiding, limiting, or distancing themselves from the evil which is sometimes to be accepted as a condition of finitude.[24] *Formal* cooperation (i.e., when an agent or organization freely participates in or freely wills a morally prohibited action) and *immediate material* cooperation in the absence of duress (i.e., when an individual or organization freely participates in circumstances that are essential to the commission of an act) are always considered to be morally wrong. *Mediate material* cooperation, which involves participation in circumstances that are not essential to the commission of an act, can be justified for serious reasons and when the danger of scandal can be contained. One factor in the hierarchy's crackdown on "creative solutions" for retaining sterilizations under mergers with Catholic health care was the perception that the principles of cooperation had been incorrectly or disingenuously applied—that some arrangements that were being defended as immediate material cooperation were actually formal cooperation. Deep in the background is a long-standing disagreement between so-called liberal moral theologians and the Vatican over what role circumstances and intentions ought to play in evaluating the morality of an action, and a widespread resistance by the laity to the church's teaching on contraception. But probably most important was the fear that the delivery of sterilization services (or emergency contraception or other forms of controversial reproductive care) in an institution under Catholic sponsorship or within a church-owned system gives the public the impression that the church approves of the services being offered. Though many theologians argue that the danger of misleading patients or the public by tolerating sterilizations under less than optimal merger conditions, the danger of causing scandal, can be averted with good communication and education, the Vatican's concern about diluting Catholicism's "prophetic" or countercultural stance on reproductive ethics loomed large in the revisions. As Bishop Wuerl expressed it: the point of tightening interpretation of the principles of cooperation was to ensure "considerable distance between the Catholic partner and the non-Catholic partner—moral distance—so nobody would get the idea that the Catholic institution was doing anything wrong."[25]

Negotiating "Moral Distance"

What lies ahead for potential partnerships involving Catholic health care? Ron Hamel of the Catholic Health Association observes rightly that the bishops' action in revising the ethical and religious directives does not resolve the deeper theological debates, either over the role of duress in legitimating closer forms of cooperation or over the place of contraception in Catholic health care ministry. But Directive 70 does "resolve the *practice* for Catholic hospitals" in three important ways.[26] Accompanying Directive 70 is the reminder that "Catholic health care providers, as a rule, should avoid partnering with other providers that would involve them in cooperation with the other providers' wrongdoing."[27] Therefore, the presumption is against entering into partnerships in which the issue of "creative solutions" might arise. In addition, Directive 70 limits involvement in sterilization (or other prohibited actions) to mediate material cooperation. According to Hamel, this rules out arrangements which would involve Catholic health care institutions in "ownership, governance or management of the entity that offers prohibited procedures; financial benefit derived from the provision of the procedures; supplying elements essential to the provision of the services such as medical or support staff or supplies; or performing or having an essential role in the procedure."[28] Finally, having replaced the appendix that once contained tools for interpreting morally permissible cooperation with the admonition to seek "reliable theological experts," the bishops make clear that there is unlikely to be much patience with creative or broad interpretations.

Because the final authority to approve merger terms within a diocese resides with the local bishop, it is difficult to say exactly what Directive 70 implies for already existing agreements. However, limiting potential partnerships to mediate material cooperation calls many "creative solutions" into question. Potentially on the block, for example, would be agreements whereby a looser version of the directives, "Common Values for Community Sponsorship" governs some community hospitals within a Catholic health care system, the sort of arrangement that allowed Sierra Nevada Memorial Hospital and Long Beach Community Medical Center in California to continue to offer sterilization as part of Catholic Healthcare West. It is unlikely that "condominium" hospital arrangements—those in which a separate clinic, governed by a separate board of directors, exists within the main institution—would continue to be approved, or that the practice of leasing clinical space within a Catholic hospital to a non-Catholic provider of controversial reproductive services would continue; the latter was done, for example, in the agreement between St. Mary Hospital and Rogers Women's Center in Rogers, Arkansas. According to Frances Kissling of Catholics for a Free Choice, there were 16 cases in 2000 of operating rooms in Catholic hospitals being leased to non-Catholic sterilization providers.

How closely hospitals can merge with partners committed to providing controversial reproductive services will remain a matter of interpretation; however, Kissling is correct that "the deciding point [will be] the degree of financial, administrative and clinical integration between the two players."[29] Very loose affiliations or "virtual mergers" are likely to be safer than more formal mergers from the standpoint of preserving access to controversial reproductive services.

Religion, Conscience, and the Right to Choose

Opponents of mergers in which reproductive services are discontinued argue
that such agreements violate women's fundamental right to make personal
decisions concerning reproduction and compromise access to basic health
care, particularly for low-income women. Often citing extreme cases (e.g., the
Hanover, N.H., woman who traveled 80 miles by taxi for an emergency abortion after her water broke at 14 weeks, and the Medicaid patient suffering from
a pulmonary embolus who waited 10 days for an emergency abortion which
eventually had to be performed in a physician's office), well-known supporters
of reproductive rights, such as the National Women's Law Center, Planned
Parenthood and Catholics for a Free Choice, argue that religious restrictions
have endangered women's lives by limiting access to abortion and contraception. Groups such as the National Women's Law Center have launched intensive public information campaigns, urging communities to block mergers lacking firm commitments to preserve reproductive health services and
encouraging women to seek information concerning their providers' religious
beliefs.[30] Merger Watch, an advocacy group sponsored by the Education Fund
of Family Planning Advocates, has been active in community organizing over
proposed mergers in 21 states, claiming a role in defeating 16 proposed mergers, unraveling 9 existing mergers, and forging compromises in 14 cases that
preserved at least some of the contested services.[31]

At the heart of this debate is the balance between protection for the distinctive religious witness of faith-based health care institutions and protection
for the rights of individuals to seek reproductive services according to their
own needs and particular moral values. Under the Church amendment, passed
by Congress in 1973, and various state laws, sectarian health care providers are
permitted to opt out of providing services they consider to be ethically objec-
tionable. According to the Alan Guttmacher Institute, "conscience clause" legislation is increasingly being broadened, extending beyond providers to encompass health care plans, and extending beyond abortion and sterilization to
encompass " 'any health services about which ethical, religious or moral objection is raised' (including counseling and providing information about those
services)."[32] Indeed, a hastily added rider to the omnibus spending bill for
2005, passed by the House under the sponsorship of Rep. Dave Weldon of
Florida, would extend conscience clause exemptions to permit medical professionals and health care facilities to refuse to provide abortion or abortion re-
ferrals for any reason.[33]

Conscience clauses reflect a deeply entrenched reluctance to force health
care professionals to act against their conscience in the provision of highly
controversial services. As they stand alongside policies that protect access to
reproductive health services, they also express a certain national ambivalence
about reproductive rights, particularly the highly politicized right to abortion.
As a recent publication of Mergerwatch observed:

Policymakers and courts have recognized that access to reproductive services . . . is deserving of legal protection. . . . Court decisions from *Roe vs. Wade* to decisions requiring state funding for abortions for low-income women, and also recent decisions requiring employers to provide contraceptive coverage as part of employee prescription drug benefit, have protected access to reproductive health services. The Medicaid program protects access to family planning services for low-income women and men. [M]any state laws require that insurance companies and managed care organizations cover services such as family planning, sterilization, and fertility services; require employers to provide contraceptive coverage; and require hospital emergency rooms to offer emergency contraceptives to survivors of sexual assault."[34]

Yet legal strategies to assert a positive right to reproductive services, either in the face of conscience-based refusals or other obstacles, have often proven ineffective. One reporter notes: "Although there have been gains in the courts in some states . . . there is no legal precedent for protesting denial of access on the basis of the U.S. Constitution."[35] Admitting that "the law is not on [her] side," Kissling points out that "no hospital—Catholic or non-Catholic—is required to perform an abortion, and most of them don't. They're not required to provide contraception or reproductive healthcare. The only thing a hospital has to do is treat a patient who comes in through the door in a life-threatening situation."[36] Moreover, reproductive health care is notoriously vulnerable to the bottom line. Merger partners are often willing to give up services such as sterilizations and vasectomies without much resistance simply because they are not profitable.

For many people, conscience clauses (which respect free exercise of religious or moral beliefs) are easily reconciled with legally protected reproductive liberty (which recognizes the intimate nature of decisions concerning reproduction as well as a diversity of moral and religious perspectives on reproduction) under two important assumptions: that those patients who choose to seek care within a religiously affiliated facility have sufficient information about what will and will not be offered to make an informed choice; and that patients have alternative sources for services that religiously affiliated institutions choose not to offer. Controversial mergers have called both of these assumptions into question. Several advocacy organizations filed a federal lawsuit in 2000 arguing, among other things, that a partnership between Catholic and public hospitals in St. Petersburg violated Florida statutes mandating open discussion of government affairs. Although it is difficult to find hard data concerning the frequency of public disclosure of proposed mergers, it is a common complaint of advocacy groups, including the plaintiffs in the Florida case, that partnership agreements resulting in the consolidation of secular and religious hospitals are negotiated behind closed doors with little community consultation.[37] The American Public Health Association has urged the development of guidelines for mergers including advance notice to the affected community; the opportunity for public comment; and assurances that services lost through any merger agreement will be available elsewhere in the community.[38]

Making public disclosure of proposed mergers a key strategic tool, opponents charge that patients are frequently uninformed about either the religious commitments of a sponsoring health care institution or what those commitments might imply for the availability of particular services. In a nationwide survey cited in a recent report by the National Women's Law Center, almost half of the 1,000 women surveyed believed that there would be no restrictions on the medical services they could receive upon admission to a Catholic hospital: "Even women who thought services might be limited did not know how broad the restrictions were. While 62 percent identified abortion when asked to name services that are contrary to Catholic teaching, only 43 percent named birth control, and less than seven percent were able to identify any other restricted services, including emergency contraception, sterilization, or infertility treatment."[39] A study conducted in 1997 by the Center for Reproductive Law and Policy raised similar concerns about patients' knowledge of the terms of their insurance coverage. Researchers found that "many Medicaid recipients could not identify the plan in which they were enrolled, whether it covered reproductive services at all, and who their primary provider was."[40] Further, they found that "none of the focus group members enrolled in Fidelis Care (a New York Catholic health plan) knew that the plan did not cover family planning or abortions when they decided to enroll."[41]

Concerns about preserving access to reproductive health services have been particularly acute in cases in which a merger or acquisition results in Catholic health care as the sole provider in an area. Estimates vary, but one frequently cited figure suggests that increased merger activity in the last decade solidified Catholic presence in at least some areas: In 1998 there were 91 Catholic sole-provider hospitals in 27 states, up from 76 in 1997 and 46 in 1994. According to one source, one-quarter of all Wisconsin hospitals are under Catholic sponsorship, and seven Wisconsin counties have only a Catholic hospital.[42] Because low-income women disproportionately rely on hospital care and have a more difficult time obtaining out-of-area or out-of-network care, restrictions on services such as sterilizations and emergency contraception have the most serious implications for them. Moreover, many women access the health care system through reproductive health services. Therefore, women's health advocates worry that the loss of those services within a community has the potential to compromise basic care for an already at risk group.

In a thoughtful article in the Stanford Law Review, Katherine White suggests that breaking the impasse between the legitimate exercise of health care providers' religious beliefs and patients' access to sensitive services depends upon adopting strategies that respect what is valued on each side. "Rather than forcing unwilling providers to make services available [which is the aim of some legal strategies employed by reproductive rights advocates], other strategies, such as subscriber choice and disclosure mandates, disenrollment grace periods, direct and open access laws, and continuity of care guarantees, can help patients get services from other providers." Subscriber choice and disclosure policies would require managed care and insurance plans to notify potential enrollees of any services not covered because of the provider's religious beliefs. Disenrollment grace periods would allow enrollees to transfer to another plan if plan exclusions become known within a reasonable time after the enrollment date. White notes that New York state has adopted both disclosure and disenrollment grace period policies for Medicaid recipients.[43] Direct and open access laws aim at allowing subscribers to bypass a primary caregiver's referral to receive reproductive care services from any caregiver who is willing to provide them. Given ecclesial tensions over the limits of cooperation, continuity of care mandates (which would require providers to refer patients seeking restricted services to a willing provider) are the most problematic strategy in the context of hospital mergers. Yet White shows that if continuity of care mandates respect an upper limit of tolerance for the faith-based provider, on the one hand, and, on the other, encompass the sensitive services of most value to most patients, they can represent an achievable compromise. So, for example, continuity of care policies could exclude abortion, conceding religious refusals to refer in this case, while including the services of most concern for women: tubal ligations, birth control, and emergency contraception for sexual assault victims. Though none of the strategies that White advocates is without limitations, they aim at preserving the sphere of distinctive witness legitimately claimed by the faith-based provider while honoring what women's health advocates most value: the conditions for meaningful exercise of personal autonomy, particularly for those who do not share the faith commitments of the sponsoring community.

One Mission under God?

In response to public outcry in some communities over the anticipated loss of reproductive health services, Catholic health care administrators have countered that restricting services such as sterilization or emergency contraception, even in cases where alternatives to religious providers are not readily available, is not different from choosing not to offer a health care service that is judged to be too costly. Observing that no hospital offers every service, they have argued that decisions to omit services on religious grounds are entitled to at least as much respect as decisions to omit services based on profitability.[44] They have a point. Though the refusal to accommodate access to reproductive health services receives a lot of public attention, the "stealth elimination" of unprofitable care (e.g., mental health services) to boost the bottom line goes unchallenged. Moreover, the past expectation of "everything for everyone everywhere" in the United States has resulted in an overextended and unsustainable health care system.

At the same time, the debate raises crucial questions about the mission of the community hospital. Recent efforts by the National Women's Law Center to use charity laws to block mergers between Catholic and public hospitals highlights continued controversies over the obligations of hospitals to communities. In a variant of the argument that health care institutions that accept public funds are obligated to provide the full range of reproductive health services guaranteed under the law, the National Women's Law Center has successfully argued that a hospital's charitable mission is essentially changed when a secular hospital merges with a Catholic one and consequently discontinues certain reproductive health services. It is a violation of public trust, they assert, for a hospital whose mission in the past has included reproductive health services for women and which has pledged to meet the needs of low-income women, to enter into an agreement that compromises that mission. Recognizing that financial exigencies can limit options for maintaining an institution's historic mission, National Women's Law Center attorneys have pressed state regulators to hold hospital administrators accountable, in adopting strategies for survival, to the diverse and multiple interests of the communities which have supported them.[45] Although as of this writing the approach had not been tested in the courts, it has been successful in derailing or dismantling potential mergers in four states.

It has been rightly argued that challenges resting on the charity laws neglect the considerable charitable contributions of Catholic health care and threaten the continued ability of those institutions to reach out to underserved populations. As Francis Butler put it, "from the perspective of public charity, Catholic hospitals have worked miracles to stay alive. . . . They have capably coped with gross underpayment by insurance companies and managed care; they have dealt with the escalating costs of drugs, nursing shortages and ever greater numbers of poor and uninsured patients who come through their emergency doors."[46] However, underscoring Catholic health care's undeniably long and remarkable record in caring for the most marginalized does not by itself answer the question of what it means for Catholic and secular hospitals to enter into partnerships with communities for the sake of the common good. Allowing for the influence of powerful groups such as the National Women's Law Center, the ability of public controversies over reproductive services to interfere with planned mergers suggests something of value is at issue for community stakeholders that is not settled by invocation of the rights of religious identity. It also reflects resistance by women to the tendency (both within and beyond religious circles) to treat as unimportant the omission or discontinuation of health care having direct implications for women's bodies. The question of what is owed to communities by the health care system—and what, therefore, it would mean to shortchange a community in negotiating a life-saving hospital merger or acquisition—is far from settled. However, the degree of controversy surrounding Catholic health care's growth suggests that even when the alternatives are few, people want some say in what kind of hospital or hospitals will serve their communities.

Beyond "Winner Take All"

Writing in *Mother Jones*, Pam Squyres notes: "If a non-sectarian health care provider like Kaiser Permanente chose not to provide, say, eye exams, the fight to get eye exams back would be a straightforward one, with clear sides and clear motives. But the conflict over reproductive services offered by Catholic hospitals takes place on the uniquely swampy ground where sex and religion intersect, making the struggle particularly complicated."[47]

It is also that uniquely swampy ground which makes the temptation to engage in a "winner takes all" struggle so tempting and so unfortunate. The principal players in the controversy over the provision of reproductive services in Catholic health care institutions, often for sincere reasons, seem to position themselves so that the outcome of the debate can be only a total victory or a total defeat. Thus, in narrowing the window for achieving creative compromises in cases where communities are unwilling to lose sterilization services in a merger, the Roman Catholic hierarchy takes a stand which, at least in the public view, appears to equate abortion and contraception as social ills and identifies "Catholic health care" with the progressive elimination of sensitive reproductive services. Reproductive rights advocates, such as Catholics for a Free Choice and the National Women's Law Center, frequently appear to be engaged, to borrow Kissling's words, in an all-out "crusade to keep Catholic doctrine out of medicine," one in which no outcome is satisfactory short of total institutional support for the broadest interpretation of reproductive choice.

Several things make the "winner take all" posturing in this context unfortunate. First, in the controversies surrounding contested mergers, the mission of Catholic health care becomes almost wholly identified with what it does not do, rather than with the long and rich tradition of spiritual and physical ministry to the sick, particularly to the poor and underserved. Moreover, Catholic identity becomes synonymous with a narrow set of moral positions on reproduction. Such an outcome may advance the church's public witness to respect for human dignity against opposing cultural trends, but it ignores the contested character of those teachings, particularly on the morality of contraception, both within and outside of the church; it also reinforces criticisms of the Catholic hierarchy as indifferent to the moral experience of women. In addition, by feeding residual anti-Catholic prejudices, it threatens to weaken the force of the church's position on other issues of critical concern in health care today, for example, universal access to affordable care.

On the other side, advancing an un-nuanced version of reproductive rights fails to appreciate the religious and sacramental character of Catholic health care and the symbolic function of the fight against legalized abortion and euthanasia for the church. Moreover, it does not discriminate between the broad acceptance of contraception in the United States, on the one hand, and the significant and persistent moral discomfort that surrounds elective abortion, on the other. Finally, such an approach tends to overidentify women's health with access to a particular set of reproductive health services.

The effort to craft creative solutions to conflicts over access to sensitive services reflects a promising alternative to "winner takes all." Agreements which "carve out" sterilization while eliminating abortion (and potentially euthanasia) do not represent a complete victory for any party, nor are they immune from abuse or bad faith. However, they model a way of moving forward in genuine partnerships between faith-based and public institutions which recognizes the complex field of competing forces and competing values in which these new type of institutions will necessarily operate. They also model a way of acknowledging moral ambiguity and the need for careful and wise discernment of the necessary and the possible by local leaders, who are best positioned to weigh the risks and benefits of a suggested compromise and best positioned to educate the community on the reasons for compromise. Clarke Cochran predicts that Catholic health care will lose the public relations battle over services such as contraception, sterilization, and assisted reproduction.[48] Narrowing the range of possibilities for preserving access to sterilization will no doubt hasten the end. Some will surely judge this loss to be a reasonable price to pay for asserting a distinctive and uncompromising moral witness in confusing times. However, as Keenan has argued, loss on this score also results in lost opportunities, not only to realize commitments to social justice, but also to bring a Catholic vision of human dignity to bear in critical and vulnerable areas of medicine.

Conclusion

Cochran has argued that Catholic health care occupies a "unique place on the border of public and private life."[49] Catholic health care is accountable at the same time to its religious and sacramental traditions and to its public responsibilities. It is inevitable that "border skirmishes" will arise. As we have seen, there is no single formula for suggesting what public-private collaboration should comprise or how conflicts between values ought to be resolved. It may be, as Cochran suggests, that increasingly bitter conflicts over widely valued services such as sterilization, combined with market pressures to conform to for-profit trends in health care, will make divestiture of faith-based hospitals in favor of other types of church-community partnerships the best course for the future.

In the meantime, contested mergers between Catholic and public hospitals have raised important questions about the nature of a hospital, the obligations of health care partners to local communities, and the limits of cooperation. For Catholic health care leaders, they raise core questions about the character and vitality of Catholic identity. Internal theological debates over the meaning of "duress" and the conditions for avoiding scandal are unlikely to be settled soon, and the political climate surrounding abortion is unlikely to become undivided, whatever movements toward the center we are now witnessing. Openness to creative solutions which attempt to reconcile conflicting interests in a way that is consistent with the principles of the Catholic moral tradition can steer Catholic health care away from the real but ultimately dangerous temptation to "battle to the death."

NOTES

1. Rachel Benson Gold, "Hierarchy Crackdown Clouds Future of Sterilization, EC Provision at Catholic Hospitals," *Guttmacher Report on Public Policy* 2 (2002): 11–12; 14, at 11.

2. "In the News: Brackenridge Hospital." MergerWatch at www.mergerwatch.org, accessed August 4, 2004. See also Amy Smith, "The City, the New Women's Hospital, and the UTMB," *Austin (Tex.) Chronicle,* November 14, 2003, available at http://www.austinchronicle.com/issues/dispatch/2003-11-14/pols_feature4.html (accessed December 19, 2005).

3. Ibid.

4. Gold, "Hierarchy Crackdown," p. 12.

5. The Catholic Health Care Association of the United States, *Ministry Engaged: Catholic Health Care in the United States* (March 2004), available at www.chausa.org.

6. Ibid. These data are provided by the 2002 American Hospital Association Annual Survey.

7. For example, according to the 2002 American Hospital Association Annual Survey, 25 percent of Catholic hospitals offer alcohol and drug abuse treatment as compared with less than 10 percent of public and for-profit hospitals; 55 percent of Catholic hospitals offer pain management programs as compared with 48 percent of other not-for-profits, 25 percent of for-profits, and 33 percent of public hospitals. See Catholic Health Care Association, *Ministry Engaged.*

8. In 2002, Catholic hospitals accounted for 2.4 million Medicare discharges, as compared with 1.9 million Medicare discharges for for-profit and public hospitals, and 8.1 million for other not-for-profits. Source: 2002 American Hospital Association Annual Survey.

9. Catholic Health Care Association, *Ministry Engaged.*

10. Simon J. Craddock Lee, "Charism and Community: Catholic Women Religious and the Corporate Commitment to Health Care," paper presented at the Independent Sector/ Roundtable on Religion and Social Welfare Policy Spring Research Forum (Washington, D.C.: March 6, 2003).

11. United States Conference of Catholic Bishops, introduction to *Ethical and Religious Directives for Catholic Health Care Services* (Washington, D.C.: United States Catholic Conference, 2001).

12. According to a commentary on an earlier edition by two noted theologians:

If a Catholic healthcare facility were to fail to adhere to the ERD [ethical and religious directives], it might lose its identification as Catholic. That is, if the ERD were not observed, affiliation with the Catholic Church in a particular diocese could be withdrawn by the local bishop. Because some Catholic healthcare facilities are actually owned by a diocese or a religious congregation, the loss of Catholic identification could also result in the closing of the facility." Jean deBlois and Kevin D. O'Rourke, "Introducing the Revised Directives: What Do They Mean for Catholic Healthcare?" *Health Progress* (April 1995): 6

13. United States Conference of Catholic Bishops, *Ethical and Religious Directives*, no. 70.

14. Patrick O'Neill, "Bishops Revise Catholic Health Care Directives," *National Catholic Reporter OnLine* (June 1, 2001), four pages. Available at www.natcath.com/ NCR_Online/archives/060101/060101j.htm.

15. Ibid., p. 2 of 4. Emphasis added.

16. See "Principles of Formal and Material Cooperation," *Ascension Health* (2004), available at www.ascensionhealth.org/ethics/public/key_principles/ cooperation.asp (accessed December 15, 2004). The appendix to the 1994 edition of *Ethical and Religious Directives* read: "Immediate material cooperation is wrong, except in some instances of duress. The matter of duress distinguishes immediate material cooperation from implicit formal cooperation. But immediate material cooperation— without duress—is equivalent to implicit formal cooperation and, therefore, is morally wrong." As cited in Ron Hamel, "Part Six of the *Directives*," *Health Progress* (November/December 2002): 2.

17. Vince Galloro, *Modern Healthcare* 30, 51 (December 11, 2000): 24–26, at 25.

18. See "Principles of Formal and Material Cooperation."

19. United States Catholic Conference, "Sterilization Policy for Catholic Hospitals," *Origins* 7 (December 8, 1977): 399–400. As cited in James F. Keenan, S.J., "Institutional Cooperation and the Ethical and Religious Directives," *Linacre Quarterly* (August 1997): 69.

20. As summarized in Frances Kissling, "Bishops to Revise Directives; Sterilization Loophole to be Closed," *Catholics for a Free Choice News Advisory* (October 23, 2000), available at http://www.catholicsforchoice.org/new/pressrelease/102300CHA _Advisory.htm. See also Christopher Zehnder, "What's Ailing Catholic Hospitals?" *Crisis* (November 2001), five pages, available at www.crisismagazine.com/ november2001/feature8.htm.

21. Keenan, "Institutional Cooperation," 69.

22. Zehnder, "What's Ailing Catholic Hospitals?"

23. Ibid., 66.

24. "Principles of Formal and Material Cooperation."

25. O'Neill, "Bishops Revise Catholic Health Care Directives," p. 3

26. Hamel, "Part Six of the *Directives*," p. 2. Emphasis added.

27. United States Conference of Catholic Bishops, *Ethical and Religious Directives*, introduction to Part 6.

28. Hamel, "Part Six of the *Directives*," p. 4.

29. Kissling, "Bishops to Revise Directives."

30. See *ASK!: Will the Moral or Religious Beliefs of Your Health Care Provider Limit Your Access to Health Care?* Available at http://www.nwlc.org.

31. See Mergerwatch at http://www.mergerwatch.org/mergerwatch/about_mw .html.

32. Alan Guttmacher Institute, "Preserving Consumer Choice in an Era of Religious/Secular Health Industry Mergers," position paper, *American Journal of Public Health* 91, 3 (March 2001): 479.

33. Cynthia L. Cooper, "U.S. Gag Rule Included in Emergency Spending Bill," *Women's Enews* (December 6, 2004), available at http://www.womensenews.org/ article.cfm/dyn/aid/2098/context/archive (accessed December 19, 2005).

34. *Fighting Religious Health Restrictions*, Mergerwatch (2004), pp. 6–7, available at http://www.mergerwatch.org/edfund_docs/fact_sheets/WhPaper_ForProfits_1–12 .pdf.

35. Jennifer Baumgardner, "Immaculate Contraception," *Nation* 268, 3 (January 25, 1999), p. 12.

36. Ibid.

37. See Sandy Oestreich, "DAN Member Active in Hospital Merger Case," at http://www.populationconnection.org/Features/feature78.html.

38. Alan Guttmacher Institute, "Preserving Consumer Choice," p. 479.

39. Elena N. Cohen and Alison Sclater, *Truth or Consequences: Using Consumer Protection Laws to Expose Institutional Restrictions on Reproductive and Other Health Care* (Washington, D.C.: National Women's Law Center: 2003): 6–7. The survey was commissioned by Catholics for a Free Choice in 2000 and conducted by Belden, Russonello, and Stewart.

40. Katherine A. White, "Crisis of Conscience: Reconciling Religious Health Care Providers' Beliefs and Patients' Rights" *Stanford Law Review* 51, 16 (July 1999): 1703ff.

41. Ibid.

42. See "Catholic Health Care State Reports: Wisconsin, Catholics for a Free Choice" (September 2002), 1, available at http://www.catholicsforchoice.org/new/latestpubs/latestpub.htm# (accessed December 19, 2005).

43. White, "Crisis of Conscience," p. 1725.

44. Pam Squyres, "Pro Life, No Choice," *Mother Jones,* June 1, 2000. Available at http://www.motherjones.com/news/feature/2000/06/hospitals.html.

45. See, e.g., "Testimony of Jill Morrison, National Women's Law Center, regarding the Acquisition of West Suburban Hospital by the Resurrection Health System." Testimony before the Illinois Subcommittee on Hospital Closures (December 9, 2003). Available at http://www.nwlc.org/pdf/MorrisonDecember2003Merger Testimony.pdf.

46. Francis J. Butler, "Will Charity Laws Close Catholic Hospitals?" *America* 185, 13 (October 29, 2001): 15.

47. Squyres, "Pro Life, No Choice."

48. See chapter 19.

49. Ibid.

19

Catholic Health Care in the Public Square: Tension on the Frontier

Clarke E. Cochran

Discussions of religion and politics in the United States typically evolve from battles over the relationship between church and state; they depend upon the assumption of conflict between religion and politics. These battles have raged for many, many decades. Although the topics change from time to time, the main adversaries and the positions they defend remain remarkably stable. For example, the Supreme Court in June 2002 approved the constitutionality of educational vouchers available to religious schools in Cleveland, Ohio. Reactions tracked familiar lines—"separationists" perceiving a major breach in the "wall of separation"; "accommodationists" rejoicing in the Court's declaration of government "neutrality" between public and private schools. In another example, during 2001–2002 Congress debated President Bush's "Faith-based and Community Initiative," which would expand the availability of public funds to church-related social service agencies. Opponents predicted a dangerous mixture of religion and politics, the potential for church to corrupt the state and for state support to seduce religious bodies from their proper missions. Supporters saw elemental fairness between secular and religious social service providers.[1]

What is striking about these debates is that no matter what side people take, the metaphors they use and the claims they make aim at harmony and peace. The strict separation position, for example, resembles a mother when her children fight: she sends one child to one room and the other to a different room. It's a way of keeping peace. The early-nineteenth-century American Baptist leader Isaac Backus advocated "sweet harmony" between the separate institutions of church and state.[2]

At the same time, those who seek mutual support between

church and state, the "accommodationists" or "non-preferentialists," use the image of religion having a place at the democratic table. This metaphor too suggests peace. The assumption is that table conversation will be civil. Equal benefits from government will keep religious and civic institutions harmonious.[3]

Other, less prominent participants in the church-state debate seek a "sweet harmony," though on different premises. Theocrats, rare but not unknown in the American political landscape, imagine that civil peace reigns only when the state assumes its rightful place under the authority of God's law. At the same time, those committed to the utility of religion, advocates of "civil religion," imagine religion's power tamed and trained to support the moral order of liberal democracy.

"Sweet harmony" is an impossible goal. In truth, a more accurate characterization of religion-state relations is tension. A better metaphor for religion and politics, for church and state, is the metaphor of borderland or frontier, where many forms of interaction occur, some peaceful and mutually beneficial; others filled with conflict. Life along borders is messy, the very condition that generates their dynamism and their danger. Such messiness is an essential feature of religion and politics, because the relationship is a field of tensions with no final resolution. In fact, tension never should be resolved, because tension is the essence of politics itself. Tension is not a negative or pejorative term. Tension is what makes suspension bridges work. Tension disappears only when politics disappears. Borderlands are discursive sites where multiple cultures, practices, institutions, or authorities meet, not abstractly, but in a fully embodied way. Mestizaje, not purity, characterizes frontiers.[4] Borderlands are sites of robust politics. Indeed, the end of politics is perhaps the unconscious desire of many intellectuals, academics, and religious leaders. What, however, replaces politics? Marx's "administration of things"? A "Strong Man"? Violence? None is a happy alternative.

The dominant trend among academics and intellectuals in the United States, shared by some people of faith, is separationist. The prevailing view is that liberal democracy depends upon drawing a sharp distinction between private life and politics. For such persons, religion belongs firmly on the private side of the line. When religion keeps to its place, it can no longer inspire hatred, intolerance, or wars. This distinction never made sense intellectually or historically. Although private and public spheres of life differ, there is always considerable contact between them, always an important border area where the most interesting political and social action takes place.[5]

Moreover, even if this distinction made sense at one time, it no longer does. One of the chief political struggles of coming decades will be how governments and private organizations manage tensions to address social problems; that is, how they will work together on the frontier, where most social problems exist. The state is a set of structures that distribute and redistribute authority; as such, the borders between public and private authority can never remain fixed.[6] In the United States, examples are public assistance, which now explicitly recognizes the importance of religious social service providers; and criminal justice, where many local police forces work closely with churches and other community institutions.[7] In recent years, cooperation from the other side emerged, albeit reluctantly, as the Catholic priest sexual abuse scandals and some bishops' mishandling of it eroded their legitimacy and required them to bring public authorities into formerly internal church matters at the earliest possible time.

These examples emphasize the "collaborative" side of the public-private relationship; conflict, however, is endemic to any frontier. Civic engagement and civic competence sometimes require churchgoing citizens to challenge government, precisely from religious principles. The Civil Rights movement is the best example. Institutions of civil society also defend citizens against unjust and exploitive government and business practices, for example the various Catholic and Jewish anti-defamation leagues. They advocate for political change as well; witness the long-established Catholic, mainline Protestant, and Jewish lobby offices in Washington.[8] Yet the dominant discourses in political science, the civil society debate, for example, have missed much of this dynamism.

Civil Society

The explosion of theoretical and empirical literature on "civil society" in sociology and political science investigates institutions that link citizen to state, mediate between citizen and state, and defend citizen from state.[9] "State" denotes all institutions of government power and authority: legislatures, courts, executive offices, military, law enforcement, regulatory agencies, and the like. "Civil society" denotes a wide variety of formal and informal associations that are neither state institutions nor individuals nor ad hoc assemblages of individuals. Examples of civil society associations are families, churches and other religious bodies, nonprofit social service agencies, neighborhood associations, fraternal societies (Elks, Rotary Clubs), and sports leagues.

One clear conclusion of this literature is that institutions of civil society are not an alternative to the state; rather, their effectiveness requires a strong and competent state. Civil society is not an alternative to politics and government, but a set of social interactions that have their own dynamics, which impinge upon politics and government. Indeed, civil society institutions live in some tension with the state, economy, and surrounding culture. However, themes of social capital, moral order and disorder, civility and civic virtue dominate this literature.[10] There has been far less attention to institutions and their meanings.[11]

Although the literature sometimes recognizes religious institutions as a vital element of civil society, most often it does so in passing.[12] Political science in particular overlooks the importance of religiously affiliated health care institutions. For example, Catholic health care in the United States exemplifies many styles of cooperation, competition, and conflict in its relationships with government and with other actors in civil society. Yet political scientists and civil society theorists have not studied it. Moreover, political science and policy studies, when they do attend to faith-based organizations, tend to treat them exactly like other institutions; that is, as neutral deliverers of services or as developers of civic competence. Religion, however, differs in important ways from other civil society actors. For example, ecclesial and sacramental qualities, as well as a mission that transcends civil society, make Catholic institutions different from both secular and other religious counterparts.

Religious institutions have a unique place on the border of public and private life. They must attend both to their particular ecclesial traditions and to their public responsibilities. Thus, existence in civil society produces distinctive challenges to their public and private identity. They must defend that identity, but at the same time accept that others with political and social authority may patrol their boundaries.[13] Turning priest sexual abuse cases over to civil authorities and delegating considerable review power to lay dominated boards is a particularly telling example. Even more so will be courts' supervision of diocesan finances where they have declared bankruptcy because of the cost of sex abuse settlements.

Regarding Catholic health care specifically, we must inquire whether alliances with state and medical culture help or hinder Catholic health care's creative articulation of its distinctive mission and identity in situations where these diverge from and indeed challenge state authority and political culture. In the case of Catholic health care the difficulties come primarily from: (1) ideological currents at odds with Catholic theology and culture; (2) medical technology's relentless pressure on Catholic ethics and mission; (3) market forces; and (4) politics and public policy that impinge on Catholic identity. Collaboration and competition are each inseparable features of the fabric of religious and political life.

This chapter considers two interrelated questions, principally from the perspective of Catholic social teaching and the experience of Catholic health care institutions. First, why tension? Why should we think in terms of tensions, and why is it important to recognize them, rather than to seek their elimination? The first purpose of the chapter, therefore, is to specify more fully a theory of tensions that accompany religion in public life, to show how they are irreducible, and to suggest how they contribute to vital politics and vital religion.

Second: How do Catholic health care institutions exist on this border? Does their presence contribute anything special to its dynamics? For example, if all Catholic hospitals do is deliver excellent health care, many others do that as well or better. The second argument of the chapter, in response to this question, is that indeed there is something special in the institutional presence of Catholic health care on the frontier of public and private life. Catholic health care illustrates the potential and the complexity of living with the tensions that characterize this borderland.

Religious Institutions in Civil Society

Separating religion and politics has intellectual appeal—but it is an abstract ideal. When religion is embodied in institutional form, careful observation of the way institutions inevitably interact with their cultural surroundings reveals the fallacy of this ideal and the inevitable presence of tension. For religious institutions in the public square, tension consists of four different dynamics occurring simultaneously and interactively. (See Table 19.1 below.) There is a dynamic of collaboration in which government and religious institutions co-operate to address an issue of mutual concern, for example Catholic Charities administering government grants and implementing public programs. Collaboration applies as well to Catholic hospitals, which receive Medicare and Medicaid funds to do work paid for by government. Second is a dynamic of competition, situations in which different institutions strive to determine who can better implement programs to meet social needs. For example, both government and churches sponsor schools. Third, there is conflict or challenge, a dynamic of confrontation in which, in effect, the religious group says (not necessarily successfully) "thus far and no farther." An example is religious lobbying and public opinion campaigns to restrict abortion. A fourth dynamic is transcendence, the struggle to define and live a mission not confined to the alternatives given by existing political, social, and economic structures. Because these dynamics occur simultaneously and pull in different directions, friction is inevitable.

Moreover, these dynamics occur not only between government and religion, they occur among the institutions of civil society itself as they collaborate, challenge, and compete with each other. These tensions take place within an open public space upon which other forces impinge; most important among those forces are the economy and popular cultural beliefs, attitudes, and behaviors (including particular subcultures—medicine, for example).

One might attempt to simplify these dynamics by imagining a crude ecclesiastical division of labor in which different churches or denominations express different relations to the state. Mennonites or Quakers, for example, challenge government, especially its military adventures. Catholics compete and cooperate with government to meet social needs. Fundamentalists withdraw from interaction with the state in order to pursue evangelization and the salvation of souls. Sociology of religion, of course, has established a modest empirical truth to this division of labor. Different churches in fact relate differently to government and to other political and social entities. However, these differences do not remain fixed over time, and each denomination tends to exhibit some mix of all of the dynamics. Moreover, each of these relationships finds justification in Christian theology; indeed, theologically speaking, every Christian church should, depending upon circumstances and the field of interaction, cooperate with, compete with, challenge, and transcend the institutions of civil society and the state.

Catholic Social Theory, Pluralism, and Political Engagement

However, even though all Christian churches should relate to government in a variety of ways, in principle, there seems to be something about the Catholic Church (its institutional expansiveness, its transpartisan social agenda, and its sacramentality, perhaps) that make it less likely to fall into a one-dimensional strategy.

Nevertheless, despite its many strengths in directing Catholic social and political engagement, Catholic social theory itself falls prey to the fallacy of "sweet harmony." If the relationship between religion and politics is essentially tensional, then Catholicism cannot be fully and effectively engaged in public life if it clings to a nonpluralist, hierarchical, and harmonious social theory. Catholic social theory requires reformulation.

"Subsidiarity," a term first used in an encyclical of Pius XI and elaborated by theologians and subsequent popes, is a good place to begin.[14] It suggests recognition of pluralism. However, elaboration of subsidiarity has been sketchy and largely prudential, seldom going beyond the advice that social tasks be left to the lowest level of society capable of handling them. Catholic social theory still tends, at least in official papal statements, to use hierarchical language (such as "lesser societies") to describe subsidiary relations. The language of pluralism, however, is horizontal. Helpful here is the Dutch Calvinist tradition of social thought, expressed in terms of "sphere sovereignty," and derived from the theology of Abraham Kuyper and Herman Dooyeweerd. This perspective avoids the hierarchical bias of Catholic thought by focusing on discovering the meaning intrinsic to each sphere of life (government, economy, family, religion, and so forth). That intrinsic meaning gives each sphere its identity and mission and a degree of sovereignty vis-à-vis other spheres.[15]

Moreover, Catholic social theory does not fully appreciate the irreducible tensions of public life, but rather sees social relations as essentially harmonious (at least in principle). That is, each natural association has its own purposes, its own job to do in order to realize the common good. The common good happens when all such associations are unimpeded in their essential tasks and when government coordinates their action. Any tension between them would come from deficiency or from sin. Yet this is not so. Yves R. Simon demonstrated that decisions require public authority even in the absence of deficiencies and with only good options before a group.[16] For example, families legitimately pursuing their educational responsibilities may disagree about what new topics to introduce into local school curricula. Moreover, schools, as a form of association with their own purposes, may see their responsibilities differently from families. Politics negotiates such tensions at the boundaries of institutions. Politics confronts ecclesiology.[17]

If groups exist in a hierarchical order, then there is no essential tension between them. Conflict emerges only from human failings. If one conceives of society as essentially pluralist, a notion to which these features of Catholic theology seem to point, then there would be ontological grounds beyond prudential reasons for distributing social responsibilities among associations, state, and economy. Groups then would have rights, immunities, and responsibilities corresponding to their essential purposes.[18] The mere recognition of such rights, in turn, bears within it the recognition of tension. A right is asserted against the possible intervention of another (such as the state). If we expand our view and observe that society contains a plurality of associations addressing a common cause (such as health care) but with different, nonhierarchically ordered purposes, rights, and obligations, then tension and boundary disputes are endemic and built-in. Attention to frontiers between groups becomes essential.

To recognize pluralism is not, however, to assert moral equivalence or to make ethics relative to social institutions in any ultimate sense. The structure of groups in society can have an overarching moral order along with considerable tension over moral questions and orders of moral priority at the practical level. Traditional Catholic social theory places considerable emphasis on prudential judgment and the legitimacy of practical disagreement.

Religion, Civil Society, and State-Economy-Culture: A Schema of Relationships

A full theory of religion and civil society cannot stop with describing relationships between church and state. Tensions exist at other levels. Religious institutions do not interact only with the state and with other institutions of civil society. They operate as well within the economy and the broader culture. "Economy" refers to the ensemble of institutions, beliefs, and practices that determine the exchange of goods and services in society. "Culture" refers to the dominant intellectual and spiritual commitments, artistic expressions, and ethnic, historic, and popular traditions with society. Each of these presents its own set of problems; however, I simplify and provide a schema of relationships. In the final section, I provide detailed illustrations from Catholic health care.

In Catholic theology, the church is both a natural institution (springing from the human need for God) and a supernatural communion founded by Christ to perpetuate his mission. As a public church, historically and theologically engaged with social life in all its manifestations, the church believes itself compelled to cooperate with the state and with other institutions of civil society to further the common good. On the other hand, in addition to cooperating directly, Catholic institutions may operate in parallel and sometimes in competition in order to address a particular need. Historically and theologically convinced of the reality of personal and social evil, the church believes itself compelled to challenge political and civil wrongs. Finally, its transcendent mission of evangelization and salvation place the church above economy and culture, as well as above other institutions of civil society and the state, from which place it pursues a mission they neither define nor limit.

The interactions run both ways. It is not simply a matter of the church defining a set of relationships for the larger society. The shape of public policy, the cultural forces within which church institutions operate, and levels of co-operation affect the ability of religious institutions themselves to embody and transmit distinctive meaning and identity and to reflect them publicly. These interactions affect the internal life of the church and the meanings embodied in Catholic institutions.

Because these relationships are true of all Catholic institutions and because they are highly complex, we can best obtain intellectual and historical purchase if we examine them in particular fields of action. For example, Catholic hospitals must navigate within fields of tension defined by their internal vocation, the external environment, the dynamics of challenge, collaboration, competition, and transcendence, and their particular manifestations in the modern medical, political, and cultural milieu. Catholic Charities organizations must do the same thing within their spheres of action, as must Catholic colleges and universities. All operate within a borderland of tensions, attempting to understand and to remain faithful to their identity and mission as the field of tension changes, as the institutions themselves change, as society changes, and as the political dynamics change.

These examples suggest a schema that ranges from cooperation through competition through challenge to transcendence. (See Table 19.1.) The illustrations are from Catholic health care and other Catholic institutions, particularly social service organizations.

Cooperation/Collaboration

This kind of relationship is so common as to be almost invisible in economy and culture. Indeed, because conflict is minimized, it masks the wide extent of religious involvement in civil society from many who perceive American society as strongly separationist. Churches are economic entities; they purchase, consume, and pay salaries in much the same way as other institutions of civil society. In fact, in most cases, the institutions of civil society, including religious, stand in a cooperative relationship with economy and culture. Just as churches behave in accustomed ways in economic life, they and their members accept the general framework of culture. Catholics and Baptists dress like other people, listen to the same music, tune in the same World Cup matches, and in general act like other citizens. H. Richard Niebuhr, in his famous classification scheme, refers to this as "the Christ of Culture" position.[19] This relationship may become so cozy as to corrupt the church itself.[20]

This position is also quite common with respect to the state and its institutions, although in the United States, a few highly contentious debates obscure the high degree of cooperation and collaboration between government and religious institutions. Cooperation requires a public goal recognized both by government and by a religious entity, along with joint efforts to meet the goal. For example, both government and churches in the United States have an interest in care of children. Government seldom operates its own child-care centers or shelters for orphans; instead, it signs contracts with private-sector

TABLE 19.1. Modes of Interaction—Catholic Examples

Modes of Interaction	State	Economy	Culture	Civil Society Institutions
Collaboration				
General	Catholic child-care providers	Economic activity of the church	Participation in sports, entertainment	Catholic Charity participation in local social service networks
Health Care	Medicare Medicaid	Catholic proportion of hospital beds (15%)	Medical culture's influence on Catholic institutions	Affiliations with non-Catholic health institutions
Competition				
General	Catholic schools	Catholic credit unions & insurance companies	Catholic media	Competition with nonprofits for service grants
Health Care	Competition with public hospitals in some markets	Competition for health market share	Catholic medical & nursing schools	Competition with local hospitals, nursing homes, etc.
Challenge				
General	Abortion Industrial Areas Foundation	Product boycotts Catholic Worker	Catholic social theory v. ideologies	Liberation Theology
Health Care	Advocacy for universal health insurance	Nonprofit status & skepticism re markets in health care	Catholic bioethics v. popular & medical culture	Modeling for others (e.g., "supportive care of dying")
Transcendence				
General	Evangelization Worship	Evangelical poverty	Religious orders	Catholic Worker
Health Care	Conscience clause debates	Invention of new forms of health care delivery renew needs	Spirituality of suffering; healing of whole person	Ministries devoted to health care needs in Third World

institutions, frequently churches. The religious institutions undertake this mission from their own motives; therefore, state and religious structures neither merge nor, in the ideal case, submerge religious identity and motives. Examples abound in the social service sector, especially in health care.[21] Controversy over collaboration seems to occur regularly only in education, which generates much of the American constitutional law of church and state.

Collaboration can be direct (for example, a Catholic child-care agency accepts a federal contract to provide services for a certain population of low-income children). Such collaboration in health care is quite prominent, given the large role that Medicare and Medicaid reimbursements play in Catholic hospitals. The relationship may be (and very often is) indirect and unconscious. For example, churches are agents of socialization and social control for the larger polity, thus reducing the burden on state resources. This, of course, is an example of how churches reinforce culture and the economy as they socialize members.

Competition

There is considerable overlap between competition and challenge (the next category), but they are conceptually distinct. By competition, I mean to designate those situations in which government, or some other institution, and a religious body identify the same need but compete to meet it. A prominent example in the United States is education, where churches (especially the Catholic Church) operate parallel school systems competing to gain students and debating whose education is superior.

In economy and culture, church-sponsored credit unions compete with secular banks; religious novels compete for buyers with secular best-sellers. Catholic health care systems compete for local market share with for-profit and not-for-profit counterparts. This category of relationships has some of the characteristics of Niebuhr's "Christ and Culture in Paradox" and his "Christ above Culture." Examples of this mode may be far less frequent than the cooperation (or even the challenge) relationship.

Challenge

This is the realm of Niebuhr's "Christ against Culture," the realm of St. Paul's admonition to the Roman Christians, "Do not conform yourself to this age, but be transformed by the renewal of your mind" (Romans 12:2).

In the challenge mode, religious institutions, families, and individuals perceive a goal that the state (or the economy or the culture) should be meeting but is not. The state wholly or partly having abandoned its responsibilities, churches challenge it to live up to its obligations. The state wages war unjustly; religious groups challenge its legitimacy. Or, in another variant, religious institutions perceive the state (or the economy or the culture) as positively demonic, as a threat to religious values, principles, and ways of life. Here the church attempts to protect its members (and other citizens) from government, economy, or culture.

Jonathan Chaplin dubs this mode "critical citizenship." Fred C. Harris uses the term "oppositional civic culture" to refer to a mode of African-American political participation in the United States, one most often stirred by distrust of institutions and of politics generally, but a distrust that nonetheless intensifies African-American political action to challenge the political system.[22]

Some religious expressions of the challenge mode are sectarian in the sense often employed by sociologists of religion; that is, churches withdraw from participation in public life and establish cultural and economic institutions separate from the larger society in order to protect and nurture members. Many expressions of the challenge mode, however, reflect a high level of commitment to engage in political participation in order to improve the effectiveness and representativeness of political and social institutions. In health care, Catholic institutions have lobbied regularly for public policy guaranteeing universal health insurance. A particularly good example is the network of Industrial Areas Foundation (IAF) community organizing efforts to improve schools, neighborhoods, and employment opportunities. The IAF frequently employs churches as bases of operation and enjoys particular success among Hispanic Catholic congregations in Texas and California. At the same time, the IAF demonstrates that modes of relationship to government are not mutually exclusive. According to a recent study, IAF organizations "generate effective power by combining confrontation with collaboration."[23]

Another example of the challenge mode is the political theology of radical orthodoxy, a return to "pre-Constantinian" Christian roots to challenge the ready collaboration between Christian churches, liberal democratic regimes, capitalist economies, and liberal culture.[24] Liberation theology is an example from the Latin American context.

Transcendence

There are, of course, transcendence elements in the "challenge mode," particularly in the sectarian rejection of dominant cultural, political, and economic systems in favor of an "original" or more authentic Christian expression. The transcendent mode, however, most often finds expression not so much through rejection of these systems, but through indifference to them. The church has a higher calling, a different calling from politics and economics. These may be fine in their place, or they may be corrupt, but they are not in the same business as the church.

Here the exemplar is Jesus' own reactions to the authorities in his time and place. Confronted with questions about political power and taxation, he simply avoids the questions or dismisses them with a shrug (Lk 13:31–33; Mt 22:15–22; Mk 12:13–17; Lk 20:20–26). He goes about his business of announcing the Kingdom of God in sublime indifference to the political powers around him. His ministry is subversive of them, but only indirectly, by pointing to a new way of life. Faced directly with Roman might in the form of Pilate, the Procurator, Jesus calmly dismisses his claims (Jn 18:28–19:12).

With respect to social services, the transcendent mode identifies and attempts to meet a need (child care, drug addiction, health care) regardless of existing or potential public programs. The church seeks to meet needs in its own way and true to its own traditions, regardless of the intentions and programs of state, economy, or culture. Some faith-based social service agencies, though few Catholic ones, refuse public funds precisely because they fear compromising their divine mandate. With regard to health care, the transcendent dimension spurs Catholic institutions to create new forms of nursing homes, assisted living, or continuous care programs for the elderly that profoundly integrate sacraments, prayer, nursing care, companionship, and medical care.

Religion in Public Life: Life in Tension

Religion (and church as an institutional embodiment of religion) manifests a variety of relationships with the state: competition to meet some needs; cooperation for common purposes; and challenge by mediating between citizens and the state. Religion (and the claim is particularly true for Christian churches) also transcends the state, claiming an eschatological mission beyond the state's competence.

These observations identify tension as the most characteristic feature of religion in public life, a claim both normative and descriptive. Yet, tension is difficult to live with. It is hard for a church to maintain, as it were, four faces to the state and to other associations in civil society. Indeed, the attempt creates intense ecclesiastical politics and a high degree of conflict within the church itself. The stresses and conflicts within Catholicism in the United States and in other parts of the world are at least partly related to divergent views on whether the church should be in competition, cooperation, conflict, or transcendence vis-à-vis state, economy, or culture in particular contexts. Just as the degree of legitimate pluralism within civil society is under debate today, so is the degree of legitimate pluralism within the church, a major issue in contemporary theology, ecclesiology, and Catholic higher education.

This chapter began with the contention that tension produces strong movements to reduce or eliminate it. To reiterate: the first tension-reducing strategy is separation, which comes in various forms of Lockean toleration designed to keep religion private, allowing believers (and unbelievers) to "live and let live," as the American expression goes. Jefferson's comment about theories of one or many gods is characteristic: "They neither pick my pocket, nor break my leg." The strategy is to tame religion's passions and make it fit for liberal culture.

Civil religion, at least in its most popular incarnations, is another way of reducing tension. Religious belief is made to mesh closely with secular culture. "God and country" in the United States. The same is true for the easy identification of Christian faith with the best of art, entertainment, medicine, and business. A recent best-seller bears the title *Jesus CEO*.[25] Here, religious passions are not tamed, but redirected toward regime support.

Just as there are strong pressures to reduce tensions between religion and culture, strong pressures exist to reduce tension within churches. The most typical strategies are sectarianism (placing the church exclusively in the stance of challenge or transcendence to the culture in which it exists) and accommodation (in which the church takes on the main characteristics of its culture).

My argument, however, is that tension is healthy, necessary, and normative, at least for Christian churches, and especially for the Catholic Church, whose theology and ecclesiology do not allow it the civil religious, the separationist, the sectarian, or the accommodationist options. The principal mode of living with tension is politics, especially in the form of debate, judgment, and conversation. Here the Catholic tradition needs development, for its dominant philosophical expressions are apolitical, focused on the common good and the pedagogical role of the state.[26] Politics is not about settling conflicts and tensions, but about living with them. There are other resources and forms of action that facilitate living in tension, as well, and they are equally or more important: art, music, religious rituals, stories, and tolerance.

Catholic Health Care in Tension: Challenges and Responses

Because its collaborative and competitive dynamics are strong, Catholic health care in the United States is a particularly good example of the tensions generated when an institution attempts simultaneously to challenge and to transcend government, economy, and culture. Catholic health care is, in the first place, dependent upon government funding, particularly through the Medicare and Medicaid programs. Economic pressures deeply affect Catholic health care as a major business entity. It is also firmly tied to liberal medical culture through the professionals who staff its hospitals, nursing homes, and clinics. These facts make it difficult to attain the leverage to challenge liberal culture's dedication to scientific rationalism and infinite medical progress.

Markets and Business Ethics

Markets are simultaneously institutions and normative systems. They affect not only cash flow, but the structures and norms of institutions.[27] A good case of institutional change lies no farther away than the nearest Catholic hospital, whose CEO is most likely to be a non-Catholic with an MBA from a state university, instead of a Catholic nun with a Masters of Divinity from Fordham. The same hospital is no longer a free-standing institution, but a member of a major system of Catholic hospitals, long-term care, home health, and other facilities. Of the 10 largest health care systems in the United States as of 2001, 4 are Catholic (Catholic Health Initiatives [70 hospitals], Ascension Health [57], Catholic Healthcare West [47], and Catholic Healthcare Partners [31]). The business practices of Catholic institutions look very much like the business practices of for-profit institutions.[28]

Market forces affect not simply the institutional shell, but the ethical core. Competing "margin/mission" mantras symbolize this effect: "No mission, no margin" versus "no margin, no mission." Labor organizing in Catholic hospitals produces strong three-sided moral conflicts between Catholic social teaching on the rights of labor, the old ideal of the "family" of employees, and new business practices. Headlines like "Christus Shows Market Hunger" (*Modern Healthcare,* August 13, 2001:16) and "Crying Foul: Insurer Takes on Kansas [Catholic] Provider Plan on Antitrust" (*Modern Healthcare,* September 3, 2001:6) would not have appeared two decades ago. Now they are common. When health care centers are no longer profitable, no matter how long they have been part of Catholic mission, the parent Catholic systems look for closure or for buyers, including for-profit ones. Yet many in Catholic health care claim that its primary mission, its distinctive reason for being, is delivery of care to the poor and underserved. Contemporary market conditions make that mission very difficult in present institutional forms, generating considerable tension within Catholic health care itself.

Is health care a mission in the name of Christ or a commodity traded on the health care market? The answer, of course, is both. The tension between them can be resolved only by exiting the health care business altogether or by radical transformation of American medicine. Since neither is on the horizon, living with ethical and mission tension is the future of Catholic health care. Fortunately, it possesses significant resources to negotiate these tensions.

One Catholic advantage is openness to public engagement. As José Casanova effectively demonstrates, Catholicism today is a public church.[29] Catholic institutions possess both the resources of Catholic social thought and a willingness to engage the messiness of life on the frontier between public and private life, between religion and politics. Catholic health care has been ready both to compete in the market and to challenge the market commodification of medical care. It has been a strong advocate for expansion of public programs of health insurance and health care. One essential feature of Catholic identity is advocacy for public programs that provide access to health care for the poor, immigrants, and low-income working people. Yet that advocacy has been tempered by its equally strong advocacy of Medicare payment adjustments to bring more funding into Catholic hospital coffers. There is only so much advocacy energy in any institution. The more resources Catholic hospital leadership devotes to defending institutional viability, the less available for the preferential option for the poor.

While market forces push Catholic health care to adopt strictly secular business models, some resist. Some Catholic institutions have developed new institutions that compete effectively in the market, while delivering high ratios of charity care to the poor and underserved. Others transformed themselves institutionally by getting out of a difficult hospital business and using the resources realized to establish foundations to deliver medical care to the poor in a different institutional form.[30]

"Technological Imperative"

Matters would be relatively simple were the imperatives of the market the only significant challenge. Yet the modern practice of medicine itself creates dilemmas for Catholic health care. American medicine is far more aggressive and curative in focus than medicine in other cultures.[31] Stressing acute care, it neglects chronic conditions and preventive care. Enamored of science and technology, it seeks ever further extensions of life and victory over illness itself, symbolized by the genetic revolution's promise to unlock the secrets of disease, defect, and aging. As William Haseltine, chairman and chief executive officer of Human Genome Sciences, put it, "Death is a series of preventable diseases."[32]

Medicine shaped by this model becomes more impersonal, dominated by machines, pharmaceuticals, and computer-generated images. Human touch and voice withdraw to the margin. Yet healing modeled on Jesus is personal and incarnational. It values care more than cure, regarding death as an enemy, but by no means the most dangerous enemy. Moreover, as the American population ages, and as American culture produces more human wreckage in the form of addictions, mental illness, and serious injuries, need increases for long-term care, mental health care, and recovery programs, all "high touch" healing. The culture of modern medicine and the modern need for healing increasingly are at odds. The ache for transcendence is especially acute in this confrontation.

Dominated institutionally by the acute care hospital, how will Catholic health care negotiate this tension? Can Catholic health care build anew on past tradition, embrace emerging needs, and resist the technological imperative? There are signs of hope, but the challenge is profound. Vital here is the ecclesial character of Catholicism, the ability to create new kinds of institutions, to embody ministry and mission in institutions that have some traction on the ground. The building of hospitals in the late nineteenth and the early twentieth centuries in the United States is one dramatic example. Now the challenge is to use that institutional capacity to build new institutions for the twenty-first century in health care.

What kind of institutions? It is very difficult for a pilgrim community to carry the baggage of multimillion-dollar medical complexes. The very institutions that incarnate the identity of Catholic health care make it extraordinarily difficult to change course nimbly. Like colleges and other Catholic institutions, Catholic health care faces an identity crisis.

The Catholic hospital will and should remain central to the healing mission of the church. However, it has come time for religious sponsors to consider reducing their hospital presence by selling some of these assets and investing the proceeds to found new embodiments of health care. One possibility is community health foundations to fund outreach ministries to the uninsured and to insured persons without ready access to regular primary care services. For example, there is a crying need among the poor for low-cost dental services and among the uninsured for convenient primary care as an alternative to the emergency room. New religious ministries could establish or expand small clinics that combine these services, as well as addiction treatment and counseling, nutrition classes, and so forth. Parishes, congregations, and other religious institutions already operate such clinics, but they could use an infusion of funding from foundations created when Catholic hospitals close. Another possible use of funds from hospital sale is community-based programs that weave together services enabling the frail elderly to remain in their homes. A national model already exists, the Program of All-Inclusive Care for the Elderly (PACE). Such programs combine pooled Medicare and Medicaid funding with private grants and donations to provide adult day care, home-based nursing and nutrition services, transportation, and the like, thus helping low-income and frail elderly persons avoid entering nursing homes for as long as possible. Still another need is spiritually focused mental health care, addiction treatment, and rehabilitative care. High-technology, curatively focused medicine presently neglects these and likely will continue to do so.

Catholic Medical Ethics

The long Catholic tradition of reflection on ethical dilemmas produced in the practice of medicine is and ought to be a strength for the ministry. This tradition is one of the factors that enable Catholic hospitals to be more responsive than the average hospital to the need for palliative and end-of-life care.[33] A deep and comprehensive bioethical theology and practices that embody it are distinctive features of Catholic identity. So is Catholic social teaching's emphasis on service to the poor, the common good, and social justice in health care. These translate into extensive participation in civil society, advocacy for expanding health insurance to all, and commitment to charity care by Catholic providers.

Yet this very ethical strength creates stress. Medical ethicists and most medical practitioners do not share the Catholic view. It is likely that most Catholics do not understand or accept most of the church's bioethical teachings. As market forces push Catholic hospitals toward mergers, Catholic ethical principles create roadblocks. When Catholic hospitals merge with non-Catholic, reproductive rights interest groups, medical societies, and state attorneys general often object that the merger will mean loss of certain women's health services, especially emergency postrape contraception and elective sterilization. Some mergers have faltered, and others have fallen apart over these issues. Catholic ethics is a distinctive identity; yet the focus on what Catholic hospitals refuse to do frames that identity negatively. Negative identity makes institutions reactive, not creative. Defensive struggles obscure positive ethical commitments.

Yet defense sometimes is necessary. There is now a drive in various state legislatures, and within the American Medical Association, to require all hospitals to offer "the full range of reproductive services." Hospitals that do not would lose accreditation or public funding. Existing state "conscience clause" laws that allow religious health centers to opt out of providing these procedures are under attack. Other state laws, notably in California and New York, require employer-based health insurance, including that provided by Catholic employers such as hospitals and Catholic Charities agencies, to cover domestic partners and to pay for birth control prescriptions. Conscience exemptions are so narrowly drawn as to apply only to churches and parish schools. Challenging such requirements in the courts is one way for Catholic institutions to defend religious freedom, but ultimately the case for such exemptions is stronger the more that this "negative" tension is balanced by a "positive" reputation for ethical excellence, represented by generous charity care and community benefit and new health institutions. Moral legitimacy is not won in the courts, but earned by selfless service. Of course, the case for such service is now even more compelling since the moral reputation of all Catholic institutions has been affected by the fallout from the priest sex abuse scandal.

Finally, research condemned by Catholic moral theology (a condemnation not shared by most Catholics or by medicine generally) may well produce treatment modalities whose origin and application will make them difficult for Catholic hospitals to accept: genetic engineering and therapies derived from human embryonic stem cells.

These examples illustrate the challenge relationship in its negative, oppositional form. Challenge also can take the positive form of persuasive modeling, in which new institutional forms or innovations in healing attract secular imitators. An example would be the strong Catholic hospital chaplaincy programs of the 1960s and 1970s; such chaplaincies are now an accreditation requirement for all large hospitals. End-of-life services are a contemporary example of where Catholic institutions could pioneer. It should be possible for Catholic health care to engage the genetic revolution in ways both acceptable to Catholic ethics and to the promise of new treatments. For example, detection of abnormalities in utero through genetic testing can lead to abortion, but it can also be an opportunity for in utero therapies. Catholic ethical concern is well-directed against abortion, but it must equally be directed toward pioneering research and development of treatments as an alternative to abortion. Similarly, although Catholic medical ethics opposes all human cloning and most embryonic stem cell research, Catholic medical research laboratories might lead the way in research on adult stem cells and on morally licit embryo research.

Conclusion

There is a tendency to see the current challenges to Catholic health care ministry as unprecedented, and the particular shape they take certainly is. But it has always been significantly under pressure.[34] The reason is simple: whatever the dominant political, economic, or medical system of a given time and place, Catholic identity must always be at an ethical angle. "Ethical angle" is another way of describing the tensional perspective at the heart of this chapter. Catholics faithful to Jesus' words and deeds are "resident aliens" in every society.

This reflection on social existence in tension began with two interrelated questions. First, how do Catholic institutions exist on the borderland of public and private life, on the frontiers of Catholic identity, marketplace medicine, medical culture, and public policy? One ingredient of a conclusion is that they have been rather successful along a number of dimensions. Most are relatively healthy financially, and they often have a reputation both for excellence of care and for service to the poor and medically underserved of the community. Yet another part of the answer is that mission, identity, and reputation cannot be taken for granted. The multiple tensions of modern politics, culture, medicine, and business call for new institutional creativity and renewed attention to the public manifestations of Catholic healing institutions. The above discussion of Catholic health care's living with these tensions was necessarily suggestive, because there is little social science research on how they collaborate with, compete with, challenge, and transcend other institutions and the state. Moreover, Catholic social theory is deficient with regard to a social ontology of institutions, a theory necessary for the theological foundation of normative pluralism and institutional existence in tension.

The second question was more general: Why tension? Why should political theorists and ethicists think in terms of recognizing and appreciating tension, rather than seeking ways to soften or eliminate it? The chapter argued that civil society (and its relations to government, economy, and culture) is essentially a field of tensions. Therefore, any attempt to eliminate tension is doomed to failure. It just *is* the case that Christian commitment sits uncomfortably with market power, political demands to reduce one's distinctive ethical commitments, and the drive to dominate nature through technology. More important, however, although some tensions are unhealthy, many more are good for religious institutions and for the public arenas in which they act. The tension felt by an athlete before a game, by a teacher prior to class, or by an actor about to step on stage is essential for the excellence of their respective performances.

In short, tension can be constructive. Identity forms in the place of tension and uncertainty (Israel in the desert; Christianity in its first centuries, struggling with heresy and persecution). Neither individuals nor institutions really know who they are or understand the nature of their vocation until confronted with stark choices calling identity and mission into question. Tension's constructive contribution runs both ways: Government challenges keep Catholic institutions on their ethical toes, and politics' tendency toward compromise requires the bracing tonic of prophetic voice. New medical technologies keep Catholic ethical reflection from stale repetition of old teaching and demand new engagement with novel inventions. At the same time, scientific hubris requires the "thus far and no farther" of a distinctive ethical voice.

The value of constructive tension is, therefore, the principal reason to reject theories of religion in public life that seek "sweet harmony." Religious freedom sometimes requires that government leave it alone, but just as often it flourishes when challenged by public authority. Equally, public institutions profit from competition and challenge by religious associations. Keeping the two at arm's length can, for a time, maintain false peace masquerading as harmony. In the long run, however, religious freedom and a vigorous public life profit from the stresses and strains of life on the frontier.

Many of the ideas in this chapter were first formulated for the Conference on Religion and Civil Society in Latin America, August 7–9, 2002, at the Pontifical Catholic University of Peru. I am grateful to Professor Catalina Romero for the invitation, and to the conference participants for critical comments and inspiring conversation about the role of religion in public life. David Guinn and David Yamane made especially helpful suggestions to clarify the argument at critical points. Some of the ideas stem from a stimulating two days (March 22–23, 2002) at Baylor University in Waco, Texas, during a conference, Civil Society and Christian Thought: Three Views, sponsored by the Civitas Program of the Center for Public Justice. The notes record my debt to the participants.

NOTES

1. For example, Joseph Loconte, *God, Government, and the Good Samaritan: The Promise and Peril of the President's Faith-Based Agenda* (Washington: Heritage Foundation, 2001); Jo Renee Formicola, Mary C. Segers, and Paul Weber, *Faith-Based Initiatives and the Bush Administration: The Good, the Bad, and the Ugly* (Lanham, Md.: Rowman & Littlefield, 2003); and Amy E. Black, Douglas L. Koopman, and David K. Ryden, *Of Little Faith: The Politics of George W. Bush's Faith-Based Initiative* (Washington, D.C.: Georgetown University Press, 2004).

2. Barry Hankins, "Avoiding a Scandal: Southern Baptists and Religious Liberty in a Pluralistic Culture." Paper presented at the Civitas Conference, Civil Society and Christian Social Thought: Three Views, Baylor University, Waco, Texas, March 22–23, 2002.

3. Some advocates of "civil" discourse when religion enters public life indeed recognize that considerable disagreement, conflict, and even divisiveness can still occur with a civil conversation. See "Religion and Public Discourse: Principles and Guidelines for Religious Participants" (Chicago: Park Ridge Center for the Study of Health, Faith, and Ethics, 1998).

4. Einar A. Elsner, "Expressions of Mexicanness and the Promise of American Liberal Democracy" (Ph.D. diss., Department of Political Science, Texas Tech University, August 2002), and John Francis Burke, *Mestizo Democracy: The Politics of Crossing Borders* (College Station: Texas A&M University Press, 2002).

5. Clarke E. Cochran, *Religion in Public and Private Life* (New York: Routledge, 1990).

6. For examples in a variety of policy areas, see Donald F. Kettl, "The Transformation of Governance: Globalization, Devolution, and the Role of Government," *Public Administration Review* 60 (November/December, 2000): 488–497. See also Michael Walzer, *Spheres of Justice: A Defense of Pluralism and Equality* (New York: Basic Books, 1983), for examples of how the borders between public and private change over time and for an argument that politics is the chief mechanism for policing boundaries.

7. This is nothing new. American history is replete with examples of government and religious cooperation to achieve policy goals. See, among others, Andrew

Walsh, ed., *Can Charitable Choice Work? Covering Religion's Impact on Urban Affairs and Social Services* (Hartford, Conn.: Leonard E. Greenberg Center for the Study of Religion in Public Life, 2001); Mary Jo Bane, Brent Coffin, and Ronald Thiemann, eds., *Who Will Provide? The Changing Role of Religion in American Social Welfare* (Boulder, Colo.: Westview Press, 2000); and Bob Wineburg, *A Limited Partnership: The Politics of Religion, Welfare, and Social Science* (New York: Columbia University Press, 2001). Mark R. Warren, *Dry Bones Rattling: Community Building to Revitalize American Democracy* (Princeton: Princeton University Press, 2001), describes the vital role of congregations in community organizing and provides a rough count of the thousands of persons and parishes involved (pp. 7–9).

8. The best accounts are Allen D. Hertzke, *Representing God in Washington: The Role of Religious Lobbies in the American Polity* (Knoxville: University of Tennessee Press, 1988), and Daniel J. B. Hofrenning, *In Washington but Not of It: The Prophetic Politics of Religious Lobbyists* (Philadelphia: Temple University Press, 1995).

9. See works cited in following note and John A. Coleman, S.J., "Deprivatizing Religion and Revitalizing Citizenship," in *Religion and Contemporary Liberalism*, ed. Paul J. Weithman (Notre Dame, Ind.: University of Notre Dame Press, 1997); and E. J. Dionne Jr., ed., *Community Works: The Revival of Civil Society in America* (Washington, D.C.: Brookings Institution Press, 1998). Also important are Steven M. Delue, *Political Thinking, Political Theory, and Civil Society* (Boston: Allyn & Bacon, 1997), and Don E. Eberly, ed., *The Essential Civil Society Reader: Classic Essays in the American Civil Society Debate* (Lanham, Md.: Rowman & Littlefield, 2000). On religion and civil society, see José Casanova, *Public Religions in the Modern World* (Chicago: University of Chicago, Press, 1994); and Simone Chambers and Will Kymlicka, eds., *Alternative Conceptions of Civil Society* (Princeton, N.J.: Princeton University Press, 2002).

10. Christopher Beem, *The Necessity of Politics: Reclaiming American Public Life* (Chicago: University of Chicago Press, 1999), especially in chapter 7, tells the story of the emergence of civil society themes in American intellectual life. The debate over Robert Putnam's famous "bowling alone" metaphor is instructive. Although institutions are central to Putnam and his critics in a certain way, they remain secondary to the literature's concern with social trust and social capital and with the decline of character, virtue, civility, and political and social participation. Institutions either do (or don't) generate these. See, for example, "Civil Society and Democratic Citizenship," a special issue of the *Report from the Institute for Philosophy and Public Policy*, University of Maryland, summer 1998. Even Loconte (*God, Government, and the Good Samaritan*), who focuses on faith-based social service institutions, devotes considerable attention to the potential for President Bush's initiatives to restore general public trust. Similarly, the debate in political theory about liberalism, communitarianism, and republicanism involves the moral character of the liberal regimes. Excellent examples are Thomas A. Spragens Jr., *Civic Liberalism: Reflections on our Democratic Ideals* (Lanham, Md.: Rowman & Littlefield, 1999), and Allen D. Hertzke, "The Theory of Moral Ecology," *Review of Politics* 60 (fall 1998): 629–659.

11. See Clarke E. Cochran, "Institutions and Sacraments: The Catholic Tradition and Political Science," in *Religion, Scholarship, and Higher Education: Perspectives, Models, and Future Prospects*, ed. Andrea Sterk (Notre Dame, Ind.: University of Notre Dame Press, 2002), 128–141. See also Mary Douglas, *How Institutions Think* (Syracuse, N.Y.: Syracuse University Press, 1986).

12. Exceptions are E. J. Dionne Jr. and John J. DiIulio Jr., eds., *What's God Got to Do with the American Experiment? Essays on Religion and Politics* (Washington, D.C.: Brookings Institution Press, 2000); Charles L. Glenn, *The Ambiguous Embrace: Gov-*

ernment and Faith-Based Schools and Social Agencies (Princeton, N.J.: Princeton University Press, 2000); E. J. Dionne Jr. and Ming Hsu Chen, eds., *Sacred Places, Civic Purposes: Should Government Help Faith-Based Charity?* (Washington, D.C.: Brookings Institution Press, 2001), and the works cited in note 9.

13. Thanks to Adam Seligman for this formulation.

14. For a general introduction to subsidiarity and its place in Catholic social theory, see Thomas Massaro, S.J., *Living Justice: Catholic Social Teaching in Action* (Franklin, Wis.: Sheed & Ward, 2000); and Rodger Charles, S.J., *An Introduction to Catholic Social Teaching* (San Francisco: Ignatius Press, 1999).

15. For summaries, see Jonathan Chaplin, "Civil Society and the State: A Neo-Calvinist Perspective"; and James Skillen, "The Basis of a Just, Pluralist Society: Herman Dooyeweerd on the Structural Foundations of Human Responsibility in God's Creation." Papers presented at the Civitas Conference on Religion and Civil Society at Baylor University, March 22–23, 2002. Yet it is not entirely clear in this theory how to distinguish one kind of group from another (family, ethnic group, church, labor union, etc.). Moreover, there seems to be an assumption that spheres (at least "given natural communities") are essentially unchangeable. Yet new professions and social relations that emerge over time also demand recognition. In short, like Catholic social theory, sphere sovereignty theology must make room for *politics* (argument, persuasion, judgment) as the preeminent instrument for establishing relations among associations.

16. See Yves R. Simon, *Philosophy of Democratic Government* (Chicago: University of Chicago Press, 1951) and *A General Theory of Authority* (Notre Dame: Notre Dame University Press, 1962). Even in Simon, however, metaphors of coordination and cooperation overpower metaphors of competition, challenge, and transcendence.

17. Clarke E. Cochran, "Taking Ecclesiology Seriously: Religious Institutions and Health Care Policy," in *The Re-Enchantment of Political Science: Christian Scholars Engage Their Discipline*, ed. Thomas W. Heilke and Ashley Woodiwiss (Lanham, Md.: Lexington Books, 2001), 169–192.

18. Kenneth L. Grasso suggests this perspective in "The Subsidiary State: The State and the Principle of Subsidiarity in Catholic Social Thought," paper presented at the Civitas Conference, Religion and Civil Society, at Baylor University, March 22–23, 2002. One possible way of discovering the essential purpose of each would be to explore the idea of *munus* (mission, service, vocation) in recent papal thought, but that would take us too far afield and might simply push the definitional problem back one level. See Russell Hittinger, "The *Munus Regale* in John Paul II's Political Theology," paper presented at the Civitas Conference, Religion and Civil Society at Baylor University, March 22–23, 2002.

19. H. Richard Niebuhr, *Christ and Culture* (New York: Harper & Row, 1951).

20. The all-too-common result according to one school of theologians particularly identified with Stanley Hauerwas. For a Catholic version of the claim, see Michael L. Budde and Robert W. Brimlow, *Christianity Incorporated: How Big Business Is Buying the Church* (Grand Rapids, Mich.: Brazos Press, 2002).

21. Recent studies reveal the extent of government/church cooperation in social service delivery. In addition to the works cited previously, see Stephen V. Monsma, *Putting Faith in Partnerships: Welfare-to-Work in Four Cities* (Ann Arbor: University of Michigan Press, 2004); Paul W. Newachuck, Neal Halforn, Claire D. Brindis, and Dana C. Hughes, "Evaluating Community Efforts to Decategorize and Integrate Financing of Children's Health Services," *Milbank Quarterly* 76 (November 2, 1998); and John McCarthy and Jim Castelli, "Religion-Sponsored Social Service Providers:

The Not-So-Independent Sector" (Washington, D.C.: Aspen Institute Nonprofit Sector Research Fund Working Papers Series, n.d.). A description and bibliography of faith-based human service agencies in collaboration with government is available from the Roundtable on Religion and Social Welfare Policy, "The Use of Public Funds for Delivery of Faith-Based Human Services" (Rockefeller Institute of Government, n.d.).

22. Jonathan Chaplin, oral remarks at the March 22–24, 2002, Civitas Conference, Civil Society and Christian Social Thought: Three Views, Baylor University, Waco, Texas; Frederick C. Harris, "Will the Circle be Unbroken? The Erosion and Transformation of African American Civic Life," *Report from the Institute for Philosophy and Public Policy*, University of Maryland, special issue (summer 1998): 20–26.

23. Warren, *Dry Bones Rattling*, p. 13. See also, Ernesto Cortés Jr., "Reweaving the Social Fabric," *Boston Review* (June–September 1994): 12–14; Timothy Matovino, "Latino Catholics and American Public Life," in *Can Charitable Choice Work? Covering Religion's Impact on Urban Affairs and Social Services*, ed. Andrew Walsh (Hartford, Conn.: Leonard E. Greenberg Center for the Study of Religion in Public Life, 2001), pp. 56–77. Although IAF organizations most frequently engage in challenge tactics, their ultimate goal is collaboration in which the poor and marginalized are full participants.

24. Ashley Woodiwiss, "Deliberation or Agony? Toward a Postliberal Christian Democratic Theory," in *The Re-Enchantment of Political Science: Christian Scholars Engage Their Discipline*, ed. Thomas W. Heilke and Ashley Woodiwiss (Lanham, Md.: Lexington Books, 2001), pp. 149–166. The theologians most often appealed to are Stanley Hauerwas, John Milbank, and Oliver O'Donovan.

25. Laurie Beth Jones, *Jesus CEO: Using Ancient Wisdom for Visionary Leadership* (New York: Hyperion Press, 1995).

26. I owe this formulation to Jeanne Heffernan, who points out that the Calvinist tradition also is deficient with respect to politics, seeing it as corrective or remedial, or as a curb on sin.

27. A convenient summary of the challenges that markets pose to Catholic health care may be found in a special section of the Catholic Health Association's bimonthly journal. Ann Neale, ed., "Negotiating the Health Care Market with Integrity," *Health Progress* 82 (September–October 2001): 23–51. I consider these challenges in "Institutional Identity; Sacramental Potential: Catholic Healthcare at Century's End," *Christian Bioethics* 5 (April 1999): 26–43, and in "Another Identity Crisis: Catholic Hospitals Face Hard Choices," *Commonweal*, February 25, 2000, pp. 12–16.

28. Kenneth R. White and J. W. Begun, "How Does Catholic Hospital Sponsorship Affect Services Provided?" *Inquiry* 35 (winter 1998–99): 398–407.

29. José Casanova, *Public Religions in the Modern World*.

30. For case studies, see Clarke E. Cochran, "Catholic Healthcare and the Challenge of Civic Society," in *American Catholics and Civic Engagement: A Distinctive Voice, Vol. 1: American Catholics in the Public Square*, ed. Margaret O'Brien Steinfels (Lanham, Md.: Rowman & Littlefield, 2004).

31. Lynn Payer, *Medicine and Culture: Varieties of Treatment in the United States, England, West Germany, and France* (New York: Penguin, 1988).

32. Quoted in Daniel Callahan, "Death and the Research Imperative," *New England Journal of Medicine* 342 (March 2, 2000): 654–656.

33. Though the Catholic record itself falls far short of the need. Kenneth R. White, Clarke E. Cochran, and Urvashi B. Patel, "Hospital Provision of End-of-Life Services: Who, What, and Where?" *Medical Care* 40 (January 2002): 17–25.

34. Christopher J. Kauffman, *Ministry and Meaning: A Religious History of Catholic Healthcare in the United States* (New York: Crossroad, 1995); also Kathleen M. Joyce, "Medicine, Markets, and Morals: Catholic Hospitals and the Ethics of Abortion in Early Twentieth-Century America," Cushwa Center for the Study of American Catholicism, University of Notre Dame, Working Paper Series 29, no. 2, fall 1997.

Index